LE BIRTH 9  LONGEST COMA 37 YEA

EC  15,830 LB APPLES PICKED IN 8 HOURS

FLIGHT 2 MIN 59.94 SEC  BALANCING ON ONE

KM  MOST CUSTARD PIES THROWN 3,000  108

EGROOM 103  LONGEST MARRIAGE 86 YEARS

IN 7.3 KM  LONGEST WASHING LINE 5,272.55 M

GINE 5 MM  HIGHEST SCRABBLE SCORE 1,049

SPACE  FASTEST TRANSATLANTIC SOLO 7 DAYS

44 HR 6 MIN  NEW YORK-LONDON 2 HR 54 MIN

SONER 107 YEARS  $31,528 AN HOUR  HIGHEST

ES $85,000  100 BILLION BITS PER SECOND

AY 30 SECONDS  LONGEST SYMPHONY 1 HR 39

TEP PYRAMID 2630 BC  TALLEST MINARET 200 M

EN 35.72 X 29.57 M  LARGEST HOTEL 5,005

.4 M  LONGEST CABLE-STAYED SPAN 856 M

AWN TO 2.4 KM  FASTEST BOMBER MACH 2.2

LANET VENUS 462°  HIGHEST MOON MOUNTAIN

AVALANCHE 400 KM/H  TALLEST LIVING TREE

T GROWING PLANT 0.00003 KM/H  SLOWEST

S LONGEST FEATHER 10.6 M  FASTEST FISH 109

EGG 12 M LONG  OLDEST ALLIGATOR 66 YEARS

62,760 PER MIN  MOST LEGS 375 PAIRS  800

S IN 3:31.18  8,794 ONE ARM PRESS-UPS IN 5

LONGEST BASKETBALL GOAL 27.49 M  5,000

TOP SKATEBOARD SPEED 126.12 KM/H  LONGEST

KM/H  HIGHEST TERMINAL VELOCITY 507 KM/H

# The Guinness Book of Records 1998

British Library cataloguing-in-Publication Data
A catalogue record for this book is available from the British Library
ISBN 0-85112-044-x
Australian edition
ISBN 0-85112-047-4

'Guinness' is a registered trade mark of Guinness Publishing Ltd

**Managing Editor**
Elizabeth Wyse

**Designer**
Karen Wilks

**Editors**
Mark Fletcher
Nic Kynaston
Rhonda Carrier
Gill Moodie

**Page Production**
Juliet MacDonald

**Picture Research**
Richard Philpott

**Fulfilment**
Mary Hill

**Digital Production**
Andrzej Michalski
Steve Tagg

**Proof reading**
Caroline Lucas

**Production Assistant**
Garry Waller

**Index**
Connie Tyler

**Cover Design**
Ron Callow at Design 23
Kevin Baumber at OpSec

**Keeper of the Records**
Clive Carpenter

**Records Editors**
Simon Gold
Della Howes
Stewart Newport

**Production Director**
Chris Lingard

**Colour Origination**
Graphic Facilities

**Correspondence**
Amanda Brooks

**Printing and Binding**
Printer Industria Grafica, S.A.,
Barcelona

**Paper**
Printed on woodfree, chlorine free
and acid free paper

**Cover**
Front cover image produced by
OpSec International Plc

**Joint Publishing Directors**
Ian Castello-Cortes  Michael Feldman

**Managing Director**
Christopher Irwin

**Abbreviations and measurements**

*The Guinness Book of Records* uses both
metric and imperial measurements (imperial
in brackets). The only exception to this rule
is for some scientific data, where metric
measurements only are universally
accepted.

Where possible, the sterling equivalent for
foreign currency values is given in brackets
after the figure. Where a specific date is
given the sterling equivalent is calculated
according to the exchange rates that were
in operation at the time. Where only a year
date is given the exchange rate is
calculated from December of that year.
The billion conversion is one thousand
million.

Guinness Publishing Ltd has a very thorough
accreditation system for records
verification. However, whilst every effort is
made to ensure accuracy, Guinness
Publishing Ltd cannot be held responsible
for any errors contained in this work.
Feedback from our readers on any points of
accuracy is always welcomed.

**General Warning**
Attempting to break records or set new
records can be dangerous. Appropriate
advice should be taken first and all record
attempts are undertaken entirely at the
participant's risk. In no circumstances will
Guinness Publishing Ltd have any liability for
death or injury suffered in any record
attempts. Guinness Publishing Ltd has
complete discretion over whether or not to
include any particular records in the book.

# The Guinness Book
# of Records 1998

THE GUINNESS BOOK OF RECORDS 1998

GUINNESS PUBLISHING

# Contents

352 PAGES; 150 SPREADS; OVER 1,000 NEW RECORDS AND SUPERLATIVES

# 300 PAGES OF RECORDS

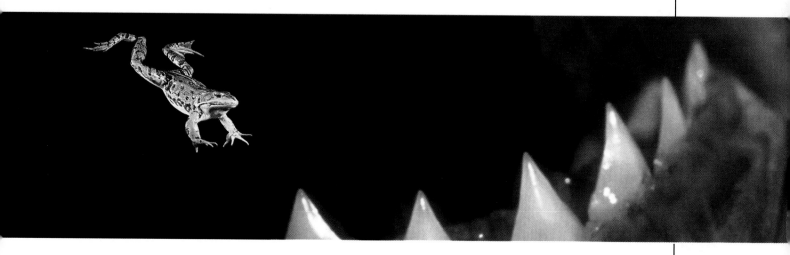

# Introduction

Welcome to the world of Guinness Records 1998.

It has been another amazing year for records with hundreds of new records and new record categories.

Since last year's best-selling edition the Spice Girls have burst onto the scene, breaking almost every pop record in sight. The animal kingdom has revealed more secrets—in the Movile Caves in Romania and the jungles of Vietnam new invertebrates and mammals are still being discovered. In the world of sport, Tiger Woods achieved the lowest score at the US Master's Tournament and Mark Philippoussis broke the record for the world's fastest-ever tennis serve in March and then again in May.

The striking thing about the world of records is how the pace of change is speeding up as we move towards the millennium. You only need to look at the Science and Technology section to discover how much has changed since last year, including the world's largest supercomputer, the fastest chip, the most wired community and the world's biggest internet crash.

New also for this year is the arrangement of the book. At the front you will find the unique, intriguing and wacky Human Achievement records. There are expanded sections on Money, Science and Technology and The Living World. Amongst our totally new spreads, look out for Strange Phenomena, Movies, Animal Discoveries and Endangered Species.

We really enjoyed putting the book together this year—now it's time for you to delve into the amazing *Guinness Book of Records* 1998.

Joint Publishing Directors

# THE WORLD OF GUINNESS

In 1759 Arthur Guinness founded the Guinness Brewery at St James' Gate, Dublin, and by 1833 the brewery was the largest in Ireland. Arthur Guinness Son & Co. Ltd became a limited liability company in London in 1886, and by the 1930s Guinness had two breweries in Britain producing its special porter stout. The slogans 'Guinness is good for you', 'Guinness for strength' and 'My Goodness, My Guinness' appeared everywhere. Guinness was the only beer on sale in every public house, yet Guinness did not actually own any of the pubs—except for the Castle Inn on its hop farms at Bodiam, Sussex. Thus the company was always on the look-out for promotional ideas.

Whilst at a shooting party in Co. Wexford, Ireland, in 1951, Sir Hugh Beaver, the company's managing director, was involved in a dispute as to whether the golden plover was Europe's fastest game bird. Again in 1954, an argument arose as to whether grouse were faster than golden plover. Sir Hugh realized that such questions could arise amongst people in pubs and that a book that answered these questions would be helpful to licensees.

Chris Chataway, the record-breaking athlete, was then an underbrewer at Guinness' Park Royal Brewery. He recommended the ideal people to produce the book—the twins Norris and Ross McWhirter, whom he had met through athletics events, both having won their blues for sprinting at Oxford. The McWhirters were then running a fact-finding agency in Fleet Street.

They were commissioned to compile what became *The Guinness Book of Records* and, after a busy year of research, the first copy of the 198-page book was bound on 27 August 1955. It was an instant success and became Britain's No 1 best-seller before Christmas.

*The Guinness Book of Records* English edition is now published in 40 different countries with another 37 editions in foreign languages. Sales of all editions passed 50 million in 1984, 75 million in 1994 and will reach the 100 million mark early in the next millennium.

Records are constantly changing and few survive from the first edition in 1955. As in 1955, our hope remains that this book can assist in resolving enquiries on facts, and may turn the heat of argument into the light of knowledge.

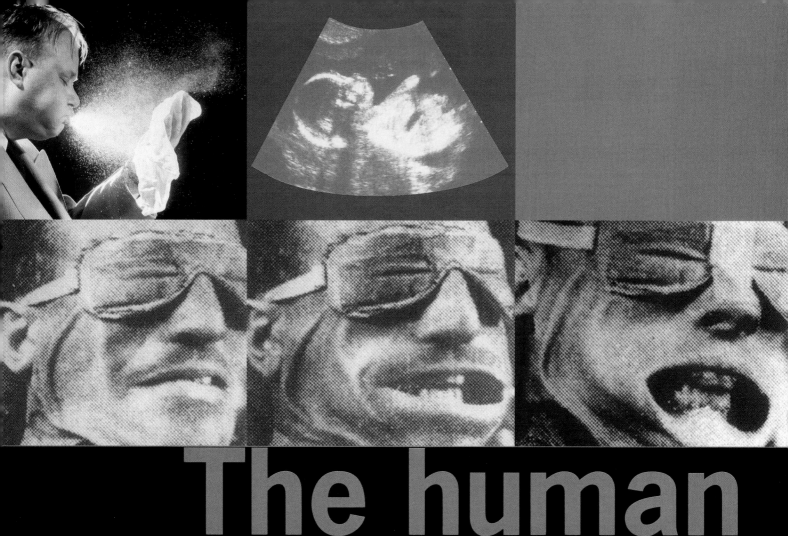

# The human body

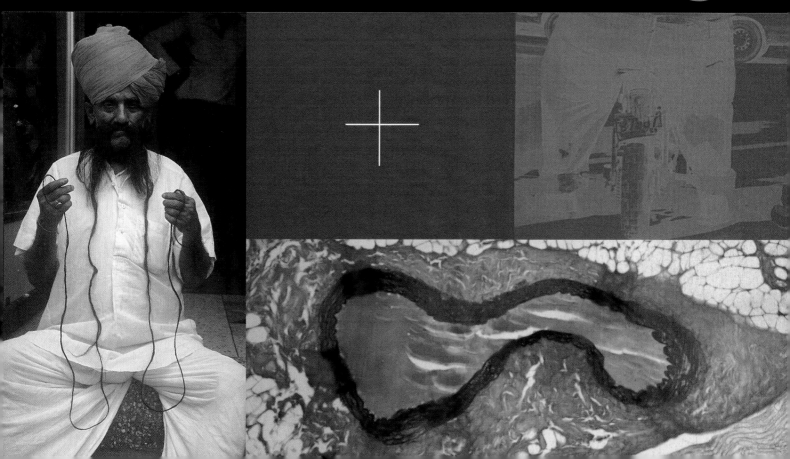

# Anatomical extremes

**Right**
Kalyan Ramji Sain of Sundargarth, India, has been growing his moustache continuously since 1976. The wearing of moustaches is a reflection of such factors as custom, religious belief and personal taste.

01:43:24

02:56:35

John Roy, of Weeley, near Clacton, Essex, UK, boasted the longest moustache grown by a British man. It began to grow in 1939 and attained a peak span of 1.89 m (6ft 2½ in) on 2 April 1976. When he accidentally sat on it in the bath in 1984 he lost 42 cm (16½ in). He took off the same amount from the other side to even out the length of the moustache on both sides.

## Optics
### Highest hyperacuity
In April 1984, Dr Dennis M. Levi of the College of Optometry, University of Houston, Texas, USA, repeatedly identified the relative position of a thin bright green line within 0.85 seconds of arc. This is equivalent to a displacement of some 6 mm (¼ in) at a distance of 1.6 km (1 mile).

### Light sensitivity
Working in Chicago, Illinois, USA, in 1942, Maurice H. Pirenne detected a flash of blue

## Hair
### Longest beard
The beard of Hans N. Langseth of Eidsroll, Norway, was 5.33 m (17 ft 6 in) long at the time of his burial at Kensett, Iowa, USA, in 1927. It was presented to the Smithsonian Institution in Washington DC, USA, in 1967.

### Longest beard on a woman
The 'bearded lady' Janice Deveree of Bracken County, Kentucky, USA, had a 36-cm (14-in) beard in 1884.

### Longest moustaches
Kalyan Ramji Sain of Sundargarth, India, has grown his moustache since 1976. It had a span of 3.39 m (11 ft 11½ in) in July 1993. The right side was 1.72 m (5 ft 7¾ in) long and the left side 1.67 m (5 ft 5¾ in).

Ted Sedman of St Albans, Herts, UK, has grown a 160-cm (5-ft 3-in) handlebar moustache, and is the current record holder in the United Kingdom.

light of 500 nm in total darkness, when as few as five quanta or photons of light were available to be absorbed by the rod photoreceptors of the retina.

## Dentition
### Earliest teeth
There have been many recorded examples of children born with teeth. Sean Keaney of Newbury, Berks, UK, was born on 10 April 1990 with 12 teeth. They were extracted to prevent possible feeding problems.

Molars usually appear at 24 months, but in Pindborg's case (published in Denmark in 1970), a six-week premature baby was documented with eight teeth at birth, four of which were in the molar region.

# LARGEST WAIST 3.02 M

A RECORD 77.8 CM COLD

## Oldest milk tooth

Gladys Turner of Copthorne, W Sussex, UK, has retained a deciduous molar (milk tooth) which her dentists believe dates from 1922, making it 75 years old.

## Most sets of teeth

The growth of a third set of teeth late in life has been recorded several times. A case of a fourth dentition, known as Lison's case, was published in France in 1896.

## Waists

### Largest waist

The waist of Walter Hudson of New York, USA, was 3.02 m (10 ft 11 in) at his peak weight of 545 kg (85 st 7 lb).

### Smallest waist

Ethel Granger of Peterborough, Cambs, UK, had the smallest waist of a person of normal stature. She reduced from a natural 56 cm (22 in) to 33 cm (13 in) from 1929 to 1939.

## Muscles

### Largest chest measurements

Robert Earl Hughes (1926–58) of the USA had the largest chest measurement ever, at 3.15 m (10 ft 4 in).

The largest chest ever recorded in the United Kingdom was William Campbell's which measured 2.44 m (8 ft).

Isaac Nesser of Greensburg, Pennsylvania, USA, had a record muscular chest measurement of 1.88 m (6 ft 2 in).

### Largest biceps

The right biceps of Denis Sester of Bloomington, Minnesota, USA, measures 77.8 cm (30⅝ in) when cold.

## Hands and feet

### Longest fingernails

The combined measurement of the five nails of the left hand of Shridhar Chillal of India was 6.12 m (20 ft 1 in) at the end of March 1997. The thumbnail was 1.40 m (4 ft 7 in), the first fingernail 1.09 m (3 ft 7 in), the second fingernail 1.17 m (3 ft 10 in), the third fingernail 1.25 m (4 ft 1 in) and the fourth fingernail 1.22 m (4 ft) long. Chillal last cut his fingernails in 1952.

### Most fingers and toes (polydactylism)

An inquest which was held on a baby boy at Shoreditch in the East End of London, UK, on 16 Sept 1921, reported that he had 14 fingers and 15 toes.

### Largest feet

If cases of elephantiasis are excluded, then the biggest feet currently known are those of Matthew McGrory of Pennsylvania, USA, who wears US size 26 shoes (UK size 25½).

John Thrupp of Stratford-upon-Avon, Warks, UK, has the largest feet of any person in the United Kingdom. He wears UK size 21 shoes and is 2.11 m (6 ft 11 in) tall.

**Below left**
A life-size footprint equivalent to Matthew McGrory's right foot. He wears US size 26 shoes (42.3 cm).

WAS THAT OF ETHEL GRANGER, WHO REDUCED FROM A NATURAL 56 CM TO 33 CM

A 33-cm (13-in) waist was also claimed for the French actress Mlle Polaire (real name Emile Marie Bouchand) who lived from 1881 to 1939.

## Necks

### Longest neck

The women of the Padaung or Kareni tribe of Myanmar extend their necks by putting coils around them. The maximum recorded length is 40 cm (15¾ in).

100%

# Dimensions

**Right**
As professional tag wrestlers, Billy Leon and Benny Loyd McCrary, alias McGuire, of Hendersonville, North Carolina, USA, were billed at weights up to 349 kg (55 st). They each had waists of 2.13 m (7 ft). Billy died at Niagara Falls, Ontario, Canada, on 13 July 1979.

## Giants

### Tallest men

The tallest man for whom there is irrefutable evidence is Robert Pershing Wadlow, born in 1918 in Alton, Illinois, USA. When he was last measured, on 27 June 1940, he was found to be 2.72 m (8 ft 11¹⁄₁₀ in) tall, with an armspan of 2.89 m (9 ft 5¾ in). His greatest recorded weight was 222.7 kg (35 st 1 lb) on his 21st birthday. When he died on 15 July 1940 he was still growing and could have exceeded 2.74 m (9 ft).

### Tallest true giant

The tallest non-pathological giant was Angus Macaskill (b. 1823), from the Western Isles, UK, who stood at 2.36 m (7 ft 9 in).

### Tallest women

Zeng Jinlian (1964–82) of Hunan Province, China, measured 2.48 m (8 ft 1¾ in) when she died. This figure represented her height with assumed normal spinal curvature because she suffered from severe scoliosis and could not stand up straight. She began to grow abnormally when four months old, stood 1.56 m (5 ft 1½ in) before her fourth birthday and 2.17 m (7 ft 1½ in) when she was 13. Her hands measured 25 cm (10 in).

The tallest British woman was Jane 'Ginny' Bunford (1895–1922) whose skeleton, now preserved in the Anatomical Museum in the Medical School at Birmingham University, measures 2.235 m (7 ft 4 in) in height. Her abnormal growth started at the age of 11 following a head injury, and on her 13th birthday she measured 1.98 m (6 ft 6 in). Shortly before her death she stood 2.31 m (7 ft 7 in) tall, but she would have been at least 2.41 m (7 ft 11 in) if she had been able to stand fully erect.

### Tallest living man

Haji Mohammad Alam Channa (b. 1956) of Pakistan is 2.317 m (7 ft 7¼ in) tall.

The tallest British man alive today is Christopher Paul Greener (b. 1943) of Hayes, Kent, who measures 2.29 m (7 ft 6¼ in) and weighs 165 kg (26 st).

### Tallest woman alive

Sandy Allen (b. 1955) of the USA is currently 2.317 m (7 ft 7¼ in). Her abnormal growth began soon after birth, and she stood 1.905 m (6 ft 3 in) by the age of 10 and 2.16 m (7 ft 1 in) by the age of 16. She now weighs 209.5 kg (33 st) and takes a US size 16 EEE shoe (UK size 14½).

### Tallest married couple

Anna Hanen Swan of Nova Scotia, Canada, was said to be 2.46 m (8 ft 1 in) but actually measured 2.27 m (7 ft 5²⁄₅ in). On 18 June 1871 she married Martin van Buren Bates of Whitesburg, Letcher County, Kentucky, USA, who stood 2.20 m (7 ft 2¾ in).

### Most dissimilar married couple

Fabien Pretou (b. 1968), 1.885 m (6 ft 2 in) tall, married Natalie Lucius (b. 1966), 94 cm (3 ft 1 in) tall, at Seyssinet-Pariset, France on 14 April 1990. They became the married couple with the largest height difference, a total of 94.5 cm (3 ft 1 in).

### Most variable stature

Adam Rainer, born in Graz, Austria, in 1899, measured 1.18 m (3 ft 10½ in) at the age of 21. He then suddenly started growing at a rapid rate and by 1931 he was 2.18 m (7 ft 1⅘ in). He became so weak as a result that he was bedridden for the rest of his life. At the time of his death when aged 51, he measured 2.34 m (7 ft 8 in) and is the only person in history to have been both a dwarf and a giant.

# HEAVIEST MAN 635 KG

SHORTEST LIVING WOMAN

## Dwarves

### Shortest living person
The shortest mature human of whom there is evidence is Gul Mohammed (b. 1957) of New Delhi, India. On 19 July 1990 he was examined at Ram Manohar Hospital, New Delhi, India, and found to measure 57 cm (22½ in) in height (weight 17 kg or 37½ lb).

The shortest living person in the UK is Michael Henbury-Ballan (b. 1958) of Bassett, Southampton, Hants, who is 0.94 m (3 ft 1 in) tall and weighs 35 kg (5½ st).

### Shortest women
Madge Bester (b. 1963) of Johannesburg, South Africa, is only 65 cm (2 ft 1½ in) tall. She suffers from Osteogenesis imperfecta and is confined to a wheelchair.

The shortest female was Pauline Musters, known as 'Princess Pauline'. She was born at Ossendrecht, Netherlands, on 26 Feb 1876 and measured 30 cm (1 ft) at birth. At nine years of age she was 55 cm (21⅔ in) tall and weighed only 1.5 kg (3 lb 5 oz). A post mortem examination showed her to be exactly 61 cm (24 in) tall.

## Weight

### Heaviest man
Jon Brower Minnoch (1941–83) of Bainbridge Island, Washington State, USA, was 1.85 m (6 ft 1 in) tall and weighed 178 kg (28 st) in 1963, 317 kg (50 st) in 1966 and 442 kg (69 st 9 lb) in Sept 1976.

In March 1978, Minnoch was rushed to hospital suffering from heart and respiratory failure. When admitted it was calculated that he must have weighed more than 635 kg (100 st). After nearly two years on a diet of 1,200 calories per day, he was discharged at 216 kg (34 st). In Oct 1981 he had to be readmitted, after putting on over 89 kg (14 st) in a week. When he died on 10 Sept 1983 he weighed more than 362 kg (57 st).

Peter Yarnall of London, UK, weighed 368 kg (58 st) and was 1.78 m (5 ft 10 in) tall. He died on 30 March 1984, aged 34. It took 10 firemen five hours to demolish the wall of his bedroom and winch his body down.

### Heaviest woman
Rosalie Bradford (b. 1943) of the USA is said to have registered a peak weight of 544 kg (85 st) in Jan 1987. After developing a congestive heart failure, she was put on a controlled diet and by Feb 1994 weighed 128 kg (20 st 3 lb).

Muriel Hopkins (1931–79) of Tipton, W Midlands, UK, who was 1.8 m (5 ft 11 in) tall weighed 278 kg (43 st 11 lb) in 1978. Shortly before her death on 22 April 1979 she weighed 301 kg (47 st 7 lb).

### Heaviest twins
Billy Leon and Benny Loyd McCrary, alias McGuire (b. 7 Dec 1946), of Hendersonville, North Carolina, USA, were normal in size until the age of six. In Nov 1978 Billy weighed 337 kg (53 st 1 lb) and Benny 328 kg (51 st 9 lb).

### Greatest weight loss
Jon Brower Minnoch, the world's heaviest man, went from 635 kg (100 st) to 216 kg (34 st) in 16 months to July 1979, a weight loss of at least 419 kg (66 st).

Rosalie Bradford went from 544 kg (85 st) in Jan 1987 to 128 kg (20 st 3 lb) in Feb 1994, a record weight loss for a woman of 416 kg (65 st 7 lb).

Dolly Wager (b. 1933) of Charlton, London, UK, reduced her weight between Sept 1971 and 22 May 1973, from 200 kg (31 st 7 lb) to 70 kg (11 st), losing 130 kg (20 st 7 lb).

Over 24 hours in 1984, Ron Allen sweated off 9.7 kg (21½ lb) in Tennessee, USA. His original weight was 113 kg (17 st 1 lb).

### Greatest weight gain
Jon Brower Minnoch, the heaviest man in medical history, gained 89 kg (14 st) in seven days in Oct 1981, before readmittance to Washington Hospital, Seattle, USA.

Arthur Knorr of the USA gained 133 kg (21 st) in the six months before he died.

Doris James of San Francisco, California, USA, is alleged to have gained 147 kg (23 st 3 lb) in the 12 months before her death.

### Lightest person
Lucia Xarate (1863–89) of San Carlos, Mexico, a dwarf of 67 cm (26½ in), weighed in at 2.13 kg (4.7 lb) at the age of 17. She had 'fattened up' to 5.9 kg (13 lb) by her 20th birthday.

Hopkins Hopkins (1737–54) of Llantrisant, Wales, UK, weighed 8.6 kg (1 st 5 lb) at the age of seven and 6 kg (13 lb) at his death.

**Left**
Rosalie Bradford went from 544 kg (85 st) in Jan 1987 to 128 kg (20 st 3 lb) in Feb 1994. Chubby in her teens, her weight escalated after the birth of her first child. She had to lose 226 kg (500 lbs) before she could lift herself out of bed.

FROM 544 KG IN JAN 1987 TO 128 KG IN FEB 1994, A WEIGHT LOSS OF 416 KG

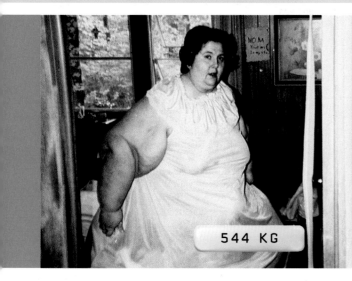
544 KG

128 KG

# Birth and life

**Right**
An ultrasound scanner allows doctors to follow a baby's development in the mother's womb during pregnancy. The most reliably recorded number of babies in a single childbirth is nine, by Geraldine Brodrick in Australia in 1971.

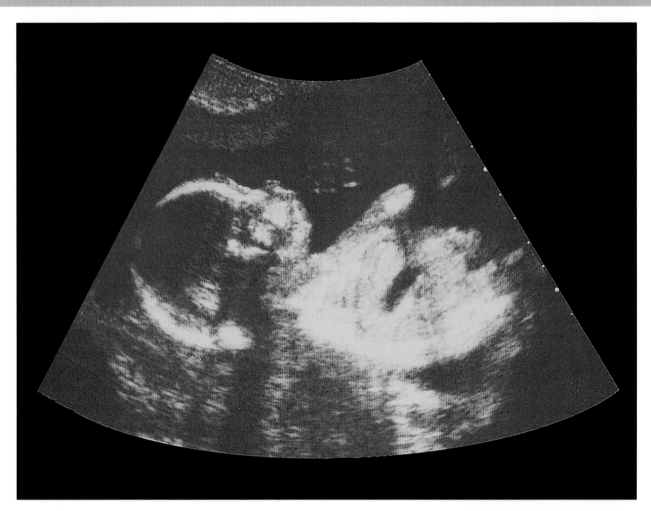

## Motherhood
### Most children
The greatest officially recorded number of children born to one mother is 69. In 1782 it was reported that the wife of a Russian peasant Feodor Vassilyev had given birth to 16 pairs of twins, seven sets of triplets and four sets of quadruplets in 27 confinements between 1725 and 1765. Only two of the children failed to survive beyond infancy.

The most prolific living mother is believed to be Leontina Albina or Alvina of San Antonio, Chile, who had 55 children between 1943 and 1981. Her first five pregnancies produced triplets, all of them boys.

Elizabeth Mott of Monks Kirby, Warks, UK, had 42 children between her marriage in 1676 and her death in 1720.

Mary Speariett of Preston, Lancs, UK, married James Speariett in 1899. She then gave birth every year for the next 26 years and in addition she adopted three children. In 1997 one of her children was still living.

### Most confinements
Elizabeth Greenhille (died 1681) of Abbot's Langley, Herts, UK, is alleged to have had 39 children (32 daughters, seven sons) in a record 38 confinements.

### Oldest mothers
Rosanna Dalla Corta of Viterbo, Italy, gave birth to a baby boy on 18 July 1994 at the age of 63, after fertility treatment. In 1996 Arceli Keh also aged 63, is reported to have given birth at the University of Southern California, USA.

## Babies
### Heaviest single birth
The heaviest surviving baby of which there are records was a 10.2-kg (22-lb 8-oz) boy who was born to Carmelina Fedele of Aversa, Italy, in Sept 1955.

Anna Bates (1846–88) of Canada, gave birth to a boy who weighed 10.8 kg (23 lb 12 oz) at Seville, Ohio, USA, on 19 Jan 1879. However the baby died 11 hours later.

The heaviest British baby this century was Guy Warwick Carr who weighed 7 kg (15 lb 8 oz) when he was born in 1992.

### Lightest single birth
A premature baby girl weighing just 280 g (9⁹⁄₁₀ oz) was reported to have been born on 27 June 1989 at the Loyola University Medical Center, Illinois, USA.

### Most premature baby
James Gill was born 128 days premature to Brenda Gill in Ottawa, Ontario, Canada, on 20 May 1987. He weighed 624 g (1 lb 6 oz).

### Longest interval between multiple births
Peggy Lynn of Huntingdon, Pennsylvania, USA, gave birth to a baby, Hanna, on 11 Nov 1995, but she was not delivered of the other twin, Eric, until 2 Feb 1996, 84 days later.

Jackie Iverson of Saskatoon, Canada, gave birth to quadruplets over 10 days in Nov

# MOST BABIES IN SINGLE BIRTH 9

1993. A boy was born on 21 Nov, a girl on 29 Nov, and a boy and a girl on 30 Nov.

## Multiple births

### 'Siamese' twins

Conjoined twins are termed 'Siamese' after Chang and Eng Bunker, born of Chinese parents at Meklong, Siam (Thailand), on 11 May 1811, and joined by a cartilaginous band at the chest. They married Sarah and Adelaide Yates of North Carolina, USA, who bore them 10 and 12 children respectively. They died within three hours of each other in 1874.

The most extreme form of the 'Siamese' twins syndrome is *dicephales tetrabrachius dipus* (two heads, four arms and two legs). The only reported case is that of Masha and Dasha Krivoshlyapovy, born in the USSR in Jan 1950.

The earliest successful separation of Siamese twins was performed on 14 Dec 1952 on xiphopagic girls (joined at the sternum) at Mount Sinai Hospital, Cleveland, Ohio, USA, by Dr Jac S. Geller.

### Most sets of multiple births in a family

Mrs Vassilyev of Shuya, Russia (b. 1707), bore four sets of quadruplets, seven sets of triplets and 16 sets of twins.

Maddalena Granata (b. 1839) of Italy gave birth to 15 sets of triplets.

Decaplets (in all cases two boys and eight girls) were reported in Spain in 1924, in China in 1936 and in Brazil in April 1946.

Nonuplets were also reported in Philadelphia, Pennsylvania, USA, on 29 May 1971, and at Bagerhat, Bangladesh, in May 1977. In both cases, none of the babies survived.

## Longevity

### Oldest authenticated centenarian

Jeanne Louise Calment was born in France on 21 Feb 1875 and currently lives in Arles, France. She is 122 years old.

### Oldest twins

Eli Shadrack Phipps and John Meshak Phipps were born on 14 Feb 1803 at Affington, Virginia, USA. Eli was the first to die, at the age of 108, on 23 Feb 1911.

Identical twins Mildred Widman Philippi and Mary Widman Franzini of St Louis, Missouri, USA, celebrated their 104th birthday on 17 June 1984. Mildred was the first to die, 44 days short of their 105th birthday.

### Oldest triplets

Faith, Hope and Charity Cardwell were born on 18 May 1899 at Elm Mott, Texas, USA. Faith died first, on 2 Oct 1994, aged 95.

### Oldest quadruplets

Adolf, Anne-Marie, Emma and Elisabeth Ottman were born on 5 May 1912 in Munich,

Germany. Adolf was the first to die, on 17 March 1992, at the age of 79.

## Descendants

### Greatest number of descendants

In countries where the practice of polygamy is lawful, the number of a person's descendants can become incalculable. The emperor of Morocco, Moulay Ismail (1672–1727), was reputed to have had 525 sons and 342 daughters by 1703, and to have fathered a 700th son by the time he was 49 in 1721.

When he died at the age of 96 in Oct 1992, Samuel S. Mast of Fryburg, Pennsylvania, USA, had a total of 824 living descendants: 11 children, 97 grandchildren, 634 great-grandchildren and 82 great-great-grandchildren.

### Descendants spanning most generations

Augusta Bunge of Wisconsin, USA, became a great-great-great-great-grandmother at the age of 110 when her great-great-great-granddaughter gave birth to a son, Christopher John Bollig, on 21 Jan 1989.

### Most living ascendants

Megan Sue Austin (b. 1982) of Bar Harbor, Maine, USA, had 19 direct ascendants when she was born—these consisted of a full set of grandparents and great-grandparents as well as five great-great-grandparents.

Mary Jonas of Chester, UK, (died 1899) gave birth to 15 sets of twins.

Barbara Zulu of Barberton, South Africa, bore six sets of twins between 1967 and 1973. Anna Steynvaait of Johannesburg, South Africa, produced two sets in 10 months in 1960.

### Greatest single pregnancies

Dr Gennaro Montanino of Rome, Italy, claimed to have removed the foetuses of 10 girls and five boys from the womb of a 35-year-old woman who was four months pregnant in July 1971. This unique instance of quindecaplets was due to a fertility drug.

Geraldine Brodrick gave birth to nine babies—the most in a single birth on medical record—at the Royal Hospital for Women, Sydney, Australia, on 13 June 1971. There were five boys and four girls; none of them lived for more than six days.

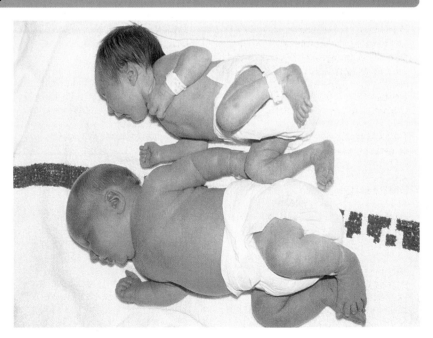

**Left**
Guy Warwick Carr, the heaviest baby born in the United Kingdom this century, next to a baby of the same age. The eighth child of Andrew and Nicola Carr of Kirkby-in-Furness, Cumbria, he weighed 7 kg (15 lb 8 oz) when he was born.

# Disease

**Right**
Cattle being destroyed in 1996 during the beef crisis in the United Kingdom. Scientific studies suggest a link between bovine spongiform encephalitis (BSE), known as mad cow disease, and Creutzfeld Jacob disease (CJD), a rare incurable condition.

## Infectious diseases

### 'Oldest' diseases
Cases of leprosy were described in ancient Egypt as early as 1350 BC.

*Tuberculosis schistosomiasis*, an infectious disease of the liver and kidneys, has also been seen in Egyptian mummies from the twentieth dynasty (1250 to 1000 BC).

The plague and cholera are both referred to in the Old Testament of the Bible.

### 'Newest' disease
The most recently discovered infectious disease found in humanity is a new type of Creutzfeld Jacob disease (CJD) which leads to dementia. It is probably caused by a tiny piece of protein called a prion transmitted from cattle suffering from bovine spongiform encephalitis (BSE).

### Most common disease
The most common infectious disease is the cold. The cold is caused by a group of rhinoviruses of which there are at least 180 types and the condition is almost universal, except for those living in small isolated communities or in the frozen wastes of Antarctica. There are at least 40 different viruses, either airborne or transmitted by direct contact, which cause symptoms such as sneezing, coughing, sore throat, running eyes and nose, headache and mild fever.

### Rarest disease
The rarest disease is smallpox. In May 1978, the World Health Organization registered zero cases in the previous six months worldwide. The last case of smallpox which also resulted in death occurred in Aug 1978 when a medical photographer in Birmingham University, UK, was infected with a sample kept for research purposes. There have been no cases of the disease since then.

### Most dangerous disease
Lassa fever, a condition caused by a rare West African virus, has a mortality rate of over 50%. Marburg fever (Green Monkey disease) and Ebola fever also have very high death rates.

Cholera has killed approximately 20 million people in India since 1900. Death rates can be as high as 50% in untreated outbreaks.

Yellow fever, an increasingly rare mosquito-borne infection, has been reported as killing between 10% and 90% of those infected.

### Most dangerous malarial infection
*Plasmodium falciparum* is the most dangerous malarial infection. It causes malignant tertian malaria, which affects the brain. Fits, coma, or even sudden death, may occur.

### Most virulent re-emerging diseases
Dengue, a viral disease which is carried by mosquitoes, and its more serious variant, dengue haemorrhagic fever, are probably the most widespread re-emerging diseases, with over 275,000 cases in tropical South-east Asia, Central and South America. There were at least 21,000 cases (including over 200 fatalities) in 1995–96.

## Population and disease

### Leading cause of death
In industrialized countries diseases of the heart and of blood vessels account for more than 50% of deaths. The commonest are heart attacks and strokes, usually due to atheroma (degeneration of the arterial walls) obstructing the flow of blood.

In 1995, there were 209,460 deaths in the United Kingdom from diseases of the circulatory system.

### Most common cause of sudden death
Coronary heart disease is the most common cause of sudden death and the most common heart disease in developed countries. An individual is most at risk from cigarette smoking, high blood pressure and high levels of cholesterol in food.

Primary ventricular fibrillation, a condition where the heart beats wildly out of control, is the most common cause of death following a heart attack (up to 80%).

### Highest level of cardiovascular disease
Over 300 men in every 100,000 in Northern Ireland have cardiovascular symptoms.

### Highest level of strokes
Bulgaria's population has the highest level of strokes in the world with over 800 people in every 100,000 suffering fatal strokes.

### Lowest level of heart disease
Heart attacks and strokes are almost unknown to the Inuit peoples of northern Canada, Russia and Greenland.

### Most common cancers in the UK
Lung cancer was the most common cancer among men in the United Kingdom in 1994, the latest year for which data is available, with 24,290 fatalities. In 1994, the most common cancer among women was breast cancer, with 14,443 fatalities.

### Highest cancer death rate
The Channel Island of Guernsey, a British Crown dependency, has 314 deaths per annum per 100,000 from malignant neoplasms (cancers).

# WORST PANDEMIC 75 MILLION DEATHS

## OVER 300 MEN PER 100,000 HAVE THE DISEASE

The country that has the highest death rate from cancers is Hungary with 313 deaths per annum per 100,000.

### Lowest cancer death rate
The former Yugoslav Republic of Macedonia has 6 deaths per annum per 100,000.

### Lowest infectious disease death rate
Austria has 2.8 deaths per annum per 100,000 owing to infectious diseases.

### Respiratory diseases
The Republic of Ireland has the highest death rate from respiratory diseases, at 204 deaths per annum per 100,000.

Qatar and Malaysia have the lowest death rate from respiratory diseases, with 7.5 deaths per annum per 100,000.

### Diseases of the digestive system
The Pacific island-state of Tuvalu has the highest death rate from diseases of the digestive system, at 170 deaths per 100,000 per annum.

Malaysia has the lowest death rate from diseases of the digestive system, at 1.9 deaths per annum.

### Diseases of the circulatory system
The Baltic state of Latvia has the highest death rate for diseases of the circulatory system. Each year 917 people die in every 100,000.

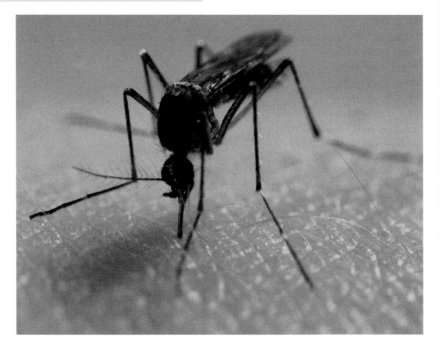

Yemen has the lowest death rate from diseases of the circulatory system with 24 deaths in every 100,000 per annum.

### Most fatal epidemics
AIDS (Acquired Immune Deficiency Syndrome) and rabies encephalitis, a virus infection of the central nervous system, are generally considered to be universally fatal. The disease rabies, however, should not be confused with being bitten by a rabid animal.

### Influenza epidemics
Influenza, or flu, is caused by myxoviruses, (A, B and C, which have three subgroups A0, A1 and A2). They produce similar symptoms but are unconnected, so infection from one confers no immunity to another. Flu epidemics often spread worldwide in waves.

Influenza A tends to reappear in cycles of two to three years and influenza B often reappears in four or five year cycles.

**Left**
Malaria is one of mankind's earliest recorded diseases. Records of the infection date back to the 5th century BC, when the Greek physician Hypocrates described its symptoms. The mosquito which transmits the disease thrives best in the Tropics, passing the infection on to humans when it punctures the skin to feed on blood.

## IS CAUSED BY A RARE WEST AFRICAN VIRUS, HAS A MORTALITY RATE OF 50%

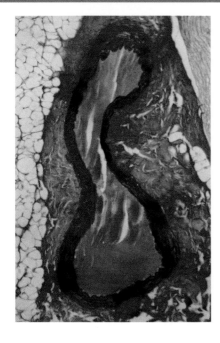

With immediate treatment the virus can be prevented from entering the nervous system and chances of survival are high.

### Worst pandemic
The pneumonic form of plague (bacterial infection), also known as the Black Death (1347–51), killed around a quarter of the population of Europe, and some 75 million worldwide. Estimates based on local archives suggest that between one-eighth and two-thirds of the affected population died of the disease. Contemporary French historian Jean Froissart (1333–1419) believed that about one-third of the population of Europe—some 25 million people—succumbed in the first epidemic, an estimate which is now widely accepted by scientists and historians.

In the United Kingdom it is estimated that 800,000 people died from the Black Death between 1347 and 1351.

Influenza A2, or Asian flu, apparently began in China early in 1957 and by the middle of the year it had circled the globe.

### Worst influenza epidemic in the UK
The worst influenza epidemic in the United Kingdom was from Sept to Nov 1918 and killed around 225,000 people.

### Earliest AIDS case with an HIV diagnosis
The earliest AIDS case for which an HIV diagnosis has been confirmed is that of a youth in the USA who died in 1969.

A Manchester sailor was believed to have died of AIDS in 1959. However, this case is now doubtful, after the discovery that the strain of HIV isolated from stored tissue samples was almost identical to strains prevalent 30 years later. Researchers have argued that such a similarity is implausible as HIV would normally mutate considerably during a 30-year period.

**Left**
A transverse section of an artery. Heart attacks and strokes, the most common forms of fatal diseases in industrialized countries, are usually caused by the degeneration of the arterial walls obstructing the flow of blood.

# Medical extremes

**Right**
The highest recorded speed for expelled particles during a sneeze is 167 km/h (103.6 mph). This sneeze was caught on film by a stroboscope—a machine that allows a series of moving objects to be captured on film.

## Medical oddities

### Highest body temperature
Willie Jones, aged 52, was admitted to Grady Memorial Hospital, Atlanta, Georgia, USA, with heatstroke on 10 July 1980. His temperature was found to be 46.5°C (115.7°F). He was discharged after 24 days.

### Lowest body temperature
The lowest authenticated body temperature on record is a rectal temperature of 14.2°C (57.5°F) for two-year-old Karlee Kosolofski of Regina, Saskatchewan, Canada, on 23 Feb 1994. She had been accidentally locked outside her home for six hours in a temperature of –22°C (–8°F).

### Hiccoughing
Charles Osborne of Anthon, Iowa, USA, began to hiccough in 1922. He led a normal life, marrying twice and fathering eight children, and stopped hiccoughing in 1990.

### Sneezing
Donna Griffiths of Pershore, Hereford and Worcester, UK, began sneezing on 13 Jan 1981. She sneezed an estimated 1 million times in the first 365 days, and stopped after 978 days.

### Snoring
Kåre Walkert of Kumala, Sweden, recorded levels of 93 dBA for his snoring at the Örebro Regional Hospital on 24 May 1993.

### Swallowing
A 42-year-old compulsive swallower who complained of 'slight abdominal pain' in June 1927 was found to have 2,533 objects, including 947 bent pins, in her stomach.

The heaviest object to have been extracted from a human stomach is a ball of hair weighing 2.35 kg (5 lb 3 oz), from a 20-year-old female compulsive swallower in the South Devon and East Cornwall Hospital, UK, on 30 March 1895.

Michel Lotito, or 'Monsieur Mangetout', of Grenoble, France, has eaten 900 g (2 lb) of metal per day since 1959. His diet since 1966 has included a coffin, seven TV sets, 18 bicycles, 15 supermarket trolleys, six chandeliers, two beds, a pair of skis, a Cessna light aircraft and a computer.

### Human cells
Henrietta Lacks' cells are still alive 40 years after her death. A cell was removed which lacked chromosome 11, now known as the tumour suppressor. The result is that the cell replicates and is immortal—a helpful tool in biomedical research.

## Treatment

### Recipient of most blood
A 50-year-old haemophiliac, Warren Jyrich, holds the record for the most blood required during an operation. He was given 2,400 donor units (1,080 litres) of blood during heart surgery at the Michael Reese Hospital in Chicago, Illinois, USA, in Dec 1970.

### Longest operation
The world's longest operation was to remove an ovarian cyst. It lasted 96 hours, and was performed from 4–8 Feb 1951 on Gertrude Levandowski from Chicago, Illinois, USA. After the operation, the patient's weight fell from 280 kg (44 st) to 140 kg (22 st).

### Longest tracheostomy
Winifred Campbell of Wanstead, London, UK, breathed through a silver tube in her throat from the age of four in 1906 until her death 86 years later, in 1992.

### Oldest to undergo an operation
James Henry Brett Jr of Houston, Texas, USA, is the oldest person to have an operation. He had a hip operation on 7 Nov 1960, aged 111 years 105 days.

### Most operations endured
From 1954 to 1994, Charles Jensen of Chester, South Dakota, USA, had 970 operations to remove tumours associated with basal cell naevus syndrome.

### Earliest general anaesthesia
Dr Crawford Williamson Long removed a cyst from the neck of James Venables, using diethyl ether ($C_2H_5)_2O$ as an anaesthetic, in Jefferson, Georgia, USA, in 1842.

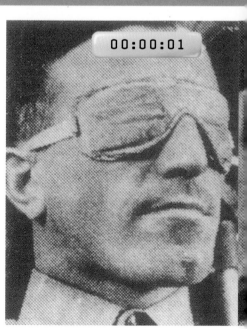

00:00:01

# LONGEST COMA 37 YEARS AND 111 DAYS

## OF 185 TEETH A DAY

### First heart transplant
Prof. Christiaan Neethling Barnard performed the first heart transplant at the Groote Schuur Hospital, Cape Town, South Africa, on 3 Dec 1967. The patient, 55-year-old Louis Washkansky, lived for 18 days.

### Longest kidney transplant survivor
Johanna Leanora Rempel of Red Deer, Alberta, Canada holds the record for being the longest surviving kidney transplant patient. She had a kidney transplant on 28 Dec 1960, at the Peter Bent Brigham Hospital, Boston, Massachusetts, USA.

### Most dedicated dentist
From 1868 to 1903 Brother Giovanni Battista Orsenigo extracted 2,000,744 teeth, indicating an average of 185 teeth, or nearly six total extractions, a day.

### Most operations performed
Dr M.C. Modi of India, has performed as many as 833 cataract operations in one day. He had performed a total of 610,564 operations up to Feb 1993.

## Medical emergencies
### Longest cardiac arrest
When fisherman Jan Egil Refsdahl fell overboard off Bergen, Norway, in Dec 1987, his temperature fell to 24°C (75°F) and his heart stopped beating for four hours. He recovered after being connected to a heart-lung machine at Haukeland Hospital.

### Longest coma
Elaine Esposito of Florida, USA, fell into a coma during an appendectomy on 6 Aug 1941, when she was aged six. She died on 25 Nov 1978 aged 43 years and 357 days, after a coma lasting 37 years 111 days.

### Longest post-mortem birth
The longest gestation interval in a post-mortem birth was 84 days, in the case of a baby girl delivered of a brain-dead woman at Roanoke, Virginia, USA, on 5 July 1983.

## Endurance
### Highest g force
In a crash at Silverstone race circuit, Northants, UK, in July 1977, racing driver David Purley survived a deceleration from 173 km/h (108 mph) to zero in 66 cm (26 in). He endured 179.8 g and suffered a total of 29 fractures, three dislocations and six heart stoppages.

### Highest blood sugar levels
Jonathan Place of Mashpee, Maryland, USA, had a blood sugar level 17 times above average while still conscious on 1 Feb 1997.

### Highest air temperature endurance
The highest recorded dry-air temperature to have been endured by naked men during US Air Force experiments in 1960 was 205°C (400°F). A temperature of 260°C (500°F) was endured by men dressed in heavy clothing.

### Longest in an iron lung
James Firwell of Chichester, Hants, UK, has used a negative pressure respirator since May 1946. John Prestwich of Kings Langley, Herts, UK, has been dependent on a respirator since 24 Nov 1955.

### Most injections
Samuel Davidson (UK) has had at least, 78,900 insulin injections since 1923.

### Most pills taken
The highest recorded number of pills to have been taken by an individual is 565,939 between 9 June 1967 and 19 June 1988 by C. H. A. Kilner of Bindura, Zimbabwe.

### Most artificial joints
Norma Wickwire (USA) who suffers from rheumatoid arthritis has had eight of her ten major joints replaced. Both hips, knees, and shoulders, and her right elbow and left ankle have been replaced between 1976–89.

### Longest without food and water
Andreas Mihavecz of Bregenz, Austria, was put into a holding cell in a local government building in Höchst on 1 April 1979, but was totally forgotten by the police. On 18 April he was discovered close to death

### Longest underwater submergence
In 1986, two-year-old Michelle Funk of Salt Lake City, Utah, USA, made a full recovery after spending 66 minutes underwater having fallen into a swollen creek.

**Left**
Slipstream tests carried out at the Naval Air Material Center, US Naval Base Station, Philadelphia, USA. These test were undertaken to see what a sudden acceleration from 440 km/h (275 mph) to 560 km/h (350 mph) would do to a pilot's face. Pilots would only be subject to acceleration as strong as this in an accident or when forced to parachute.

BY DAVID PURLEY AT SILVERSTONE RACE CIRCUIT, NORTHANTS, UK, IN JULY 1977

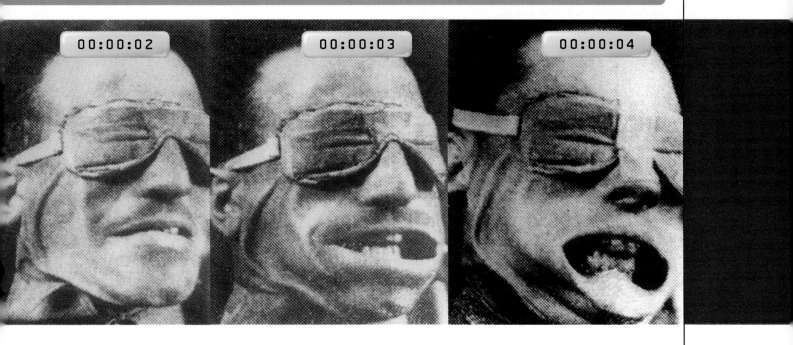

00:00:02   00:00:03   00:00:04

# Human
# achievements

### Bale rolling
Michael Priestley and Marcus Stanley of Heckington Young Farmers' Club rolled a cylindrical bale measuring 1.2 m (3 ft 11 in) wide over a course 50 m (164 ft) long in 18.06 seconds at the Lincolnshire Federation of Young Farmers' Clubs annual sports day, held at Sleaford, Lincs, UK, on 25 June 1989.

### Bed making
The shortest recorded time taken by one person to make a bed is 28.2 seconds, by Wendy Wall of Hebersham, Sydney, Australia, on 30 Nov 1978.

The pair record for making a bed with one blanket, two sheets, an undersheet, an uncased pillow, one counterpane and 'hospital' corners is 14 seconds, by Sister Sharon Stringer and Nurse Michelle Benkel of the Royal Masonic Hospital, London, UK. The record was set at the launch of the 1994 edition of *The Guinness Book of Records*, which was held at Canary Wharf, London, UK, on 26 Nov 1993.

### Beer stein carrying
Duane Osborn covered a distance of 15 m (49 ft 2½ in) in 3.65 seconds with five full steins in each hand in a contest at Cadillac, Michigan, USA, on 10 July 1992.

### Coal shovelling
The world record for filling a 508-kg (1,120-lb) hopper with coal is 26.59 seconds, by Wayne Miller at Wonthaggi, Victoria, Australia, on 17 April 1995.

The record for filling a 508-kg (1,120-lb) hopper with coal by a team of two people is 15.01 seconds, by Brian McArdle and Rodney Spark, both of Middlemount, Queensland, Australia, at the Fingal Valley Festival in Fingal, Tasmania, Australia, on 5 March 1994.

### Drumming
Making a strong claim to be the world's fastest and most manic drummer, Rory Blackwell of Starcross, Devon, UK, played a total of 400 separate drums, one at a time, in 16.2 seconds at Finlake Leisure Park, near Chudleigh, Devon, UK, on 29 May 1995.

He also achieved a total of 3,720 single beats on a single drum, using sticks, in one minute (62 beats per second) at Finlake Leisure Park, near Chudleigh, Devon, UK, on 24 Oct 1991.

### Knitting
The world record for the fastest time for completing a piece of handknitting is held by Gwen Matthewman, of W Yorkshire, UK. She attained a speed of 111 stitches per minute in a test that was carried out at Phildar's Wool Shop, Central Street, Leeds, W Yorkshire, UK, on 29 Sept 1980.

### Knot-tying
The fastest recorded time taken to tie six knots (square knot, sheet bend, sheep shank, clove hitch, round turn and two half hitches, and bowline) on individual ropes is 8.1 seconds, by Clinton R. Bailey Sr of Pacific City, Oregon, USA, on 13 April 1977.

### Railcars
A five-man team that consisted of one pusher and four pumpers, achieved a speed of 33.12 km/h (20.58 mph) while they moved a handpumped railcar over a 300-m (984-ft) course at Rolvenden, Kent, UK, on 21 Aug 1989. They recorded a course time of 32.61 seconds.

### Rapper
Rebel X.D. of Chicago, Illinois, USA, rapped 674 syllables in 54.9 seconds at the Hair Bear Recording Studio, Alsip, Illinois, on 27 Aug 1992. This is the equivalent to 12.2 syllables per second.

### Sailor's Hornpipe
On 26 Oct 1995, Nicholas Hudson, Paul Taylor and Peter Younghusband, from the trombone section of the BNFL band, played the *Sailor's Hornpipe* in 13.99 seconds at the Children's BBC *Big Bash* exhibition at the Birmingham National Exhibition Centre, W Midlands, UK.

### Sheep shearing
The record for shearing a sheep is held by Godfrey Bowen of New Zealand who sheared a Cheviot ewe in 46 seconds at the Royal Highland Show in Dundee, UK, in June 1957.

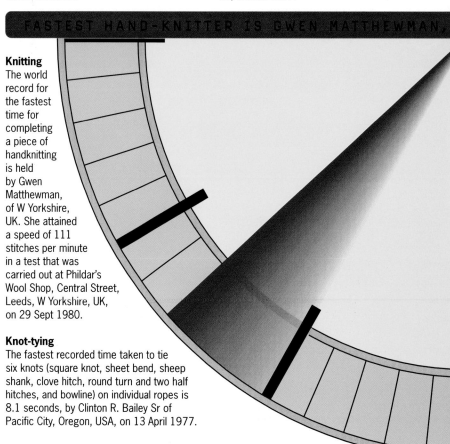

# SIX KNOTS TIED IN 8.1 SECONDS

TOOK 28.2 SECONDS

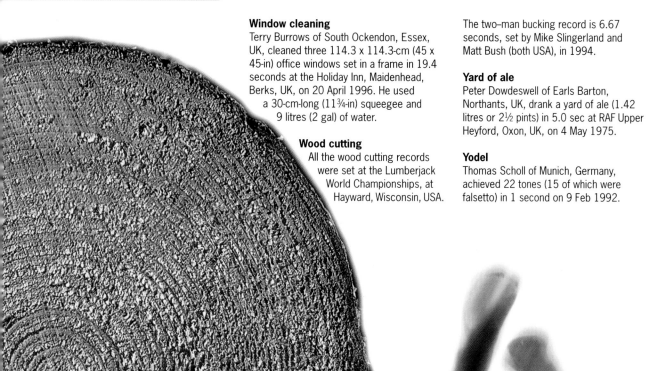

### Window cleaning
Terry Burrows of South Ockendon, Essex, UK, cleaned three 114.3 x 114.3-cm (45 x 45-in) office windows set in a frame in 19.4 seconds at the Holiday Inn, Maidenhead, Berks, UK, on 20 April 1996. He used a 30-cm-long (11¾-in) squeegee and 9 litres (2 gal) of water.

### Wood cutting
All the wood cutting records were set at the Lumberjack World Championships, at Hayward, Wisconsin, USA.

The two-man bucking record is 6.67 seconds, set by Mike Slingerland and Matt Bush (both USA), in 1994.

### Yard of ale
Peter Dowdeswell of Earls Barton, Northants, UK, drank a yard of ale (1.42 litres or 2½ pints) in 5.0 sec at RAF Upper Heyford, Oxon, UK, on 4 May 1975.

### Yodel
Thomas Scholl of Munich, Germany, achieved 22 tones (15 of which were falsetto) in 1 second on 9 Feb 1992.

WHO ATTAINED A SPEED OF 111 STITCHES PER MINUTE

### Somersaults
On 8 Nov 1989, Richard Cobbing of Lightwater, Surrey, UK, completed 75 somersaults on a trampoline in one minute at BBC Television Centre, London, UK.

### Stilt walking
Roy Luiking covered 100 m (328 ft) on 30.5-cm-high (1-ft) stilts in 13.01 seconds at Didam, Netherlands, on 28 May 1992.

### Tree climbing
Guy German of Sitka, Alaska, USA, climbed up and down a 30.5-m (100-ft) fir spar pole in 24.82 seconds on 3 July 1988 at the World Championship Timber Carnival in Albany, Oregon, USA.

### Typewriting
Gregory Arakelian of Herndon, Virginia, USA, set a speed record of 158 wpm, with two errors, on a PC in the Key Tronic World Invitational Type-Off on 24 Sept 1991.

### Walking on hands
Mark Kenny of Norwood, Massachusetts, USA, completed a 50-m (164-ft) inverted sprint in 16.93 seconds on 19 Feb 1994.

The power saw record is 7.45 seconds, by Rick Halvorson (USA) in 1994. It consists of three complete slices of a 51-cm or 20-in diameter white-pine log with a single-engine saw from a dead start.

The one-man bucking record is 16.05 seconds, by Melvin Lentz (USA) in 1994. It consists of one slice of a 51-cm or 20-in diameter white-pine log with a crosscut saw.

**Left**
Trampolining has existed for centuries, but only became popular in the 20th century with circuses. The record for the most somersaults completed on a trampoline in one minute is 75.

# Speed

**Right**
Official bricklaying records have to be achieved in accordance with the rules of the Brick Development Association and the Guild of Bricklayers. On 18 July 1995, Gary Lovegrove achieved the feat of laying 872 bricks, each weighing 2 kg (4 lb 7 oz), in 60 minutes.

872

## An hour and under

### Barrel rolling
The record for rolling a full 1.64-hl (36-gal) metal beer barrel over a measured mile is 8 min 7.2 sec, by Phillip Randle, Steve Hewitt, John Round, Trevor Bradley, Colin Barnes and Ray Glover of Haunchwood Collieries Institute and Social Club, Nuneaton, W Midlands, UK, on 15 Aug 1982.

### Bricklaying
Gary Lovegrove of Wisbech, Cambs, UK, laid 872 2-kg (4-lb 7-oz) bricks in 60 minutes at the East of England Show at Peterborough, Cambs, UK, on 18 July 1995.

### Bridge-building
A team of British soldiers from 21 Engineer Regiment built a bridge across a gap 8 m (26 ft 3 in) wide using a five-bay single-storey MGB (medium girder bridge) in 8 min 44 sec at Hameln, Germany, on 3 Nov 1995.

### Coal carrying
David Jones of Huddersfield, W Yorkshire, UK, set the record for the annual race at Gawthorpe when he carried a 50-kg (110-lb) bag over the 1,012.5-m (1,107.2-yd) course in 4 min 6 sec on 1 April 1991.

### Fastest magician
Eldon D. Wigton, also known as Dr Eldoonic, performed 225 different magic tricks in two minutes at Kilbourne, Ohio, USA, on 21 April 1991.

### Field to loaf
The fastest time for producing 13 loaves (a baker's dozen) from growing wheat is 8 min 13.6 sec, by representatives from Wheat Montana Farms & Bakery at Three Forks,

Montana, USA, on 19 Sept 1995. They used 13 microwaves to bake the loaves.

Using a traditional baker's oven to bake the bread, the record time is 19 min 14 sec, achieved by a team led by John Haynes and Peter Rix at Alpheton, Suffolk, UK, on 22 Aug 1993.

### Kite flying
The most figure-of-eights achieved in an hour is 2,911, by Stu Cohen at Ocean City, Maryland, USA, on 25 Sept 1988.

### Shaving
On 19 June 1988 Denny Rowe shaved 1,994 men in 60 minutes with a retractor safety razor at Herne Bay, Kent, UK, taking an average 1.8 seconds per volunteer, and drawing blood four times.

Tom Rodden of Chatham, Kent, UK, shaved 278 volunteers in 60 minutes with a cut-throat razor on 10 Nov 1993 for *Record Breakers*, averaging 12.9 seconds per face. He drew blood seven times.

### Shorthand
In Dec 1922, Nathan Behrin attained the record speed of 300 words per minute (99.64% accuracy) for five minutes and 350 wpm (99.72% accuracy or two insignificant errors) for two minutes in tests in New York, USA, using the Pitman system.

Arnold Bradley achieved 309 wpm without error using the Sloan-Duployan system, with 1,545 words in five minutes in a test in Walsall, W Midlands, UK, on 9 Nov 1920.

### Somersaults
The most complete somersaults in one minute is 75 by Richard Cobbing of Lightwater, Surrey, UK, at BBC Television Centre, London for *Record Breakers* in 1989.

### Speed march
Paddy Doyle covered 1.609 km (1 mile) with a 18.1-kg (40-lb) rucksack on his back in 5 min 35 sec at Ballycotton, Co. Cork, Republic of Ireland, on 7 March 1993.

### Stair climbing
The speed record for climbing 100 storeys of stairs is 11 min 23.8 sec, set by Dennis W. Martz in the Detroit Plaza Hotel, Detroit, Michigan, USA, on 26 June 1978.

The record for the 1,760 steps (with a vertical height of 342 m or 1,122 ft) in the world's tallest free-standing structure, Toronto's CN Tower, Canada, is 7 min 52 sec, by Brendan Keenoy in Oct 1989.

The record for ascending the 1,336 stairs of the world's tallest hotel, the Westin Stamford Hotel, Singapore, is 6 min 55 sec by Balvinder Singh on 4 June 1989.

### Stamp-licking
Dean Gould of Felixstowe, Suffolk, UK, licked and affixed 450 stamps in 4 minutes outside Tower Ramparts Post Office, Ipswich, Suffolk, UK, on 24 Nov 1995.

### Step-ups
Terry Heidt of British Columbia, Canada, completed 3,967 step-ups in one hour on 18 April 1997.

**Right**
Typing speeds can be assessed over either short or long periods for the net average. Margaret Hamma holds the official record for the most words typed in an hour. On 20 June 1941 she typed 9,316 words (40 errors) in one hour on an IBM electric typewriter, giving a net rate of 149 wpm.

149 wpm

# SHEEP TO SUIT 1 HR 34 MIN 33.42 SEC

## 23.8 SECONDS (OVER 650 WPM) IN AUG 1995

### Stilt-walking
In 1892, M. Garisoain of Bayonne, France, stilt-walked 8 km (4.97 miles) from Bayonne to Biarritz, in 42 minutes.

### 'To be or not to be'
Sean Shannon (Canada) recited Hamlet's soliloquy in 23.8 sec (over 650 words a minute) at Edinburgh, UK, on 30 Aug 1995.

### Typewriting
In 1923, Albert Tangora typed 147 wpm in one hour on a manual machine with a ten-word penalty per error at Dixon, Illinois, USA.

In 1941 in New York, USA, Margaret Hamma typed 9,316 words (40 errors) in one hour on an electric typewriter, a net rate of 149 wpm.

Michael Shestov typed spaced numbers from 1 to 801 on a PC without any errors in five minutes at Baruch College, New York City, USA, on 2 April 1996.

### Walking on hands
A relay team of David Lutterman, Brendan Price, Philip Savage and Danny Scannell covered 1.6 km (1 mile) in 24 min 48 sec in March 1987 at Knoxville, Tennessee, USA.

### Walking on water
On 2 Aug 1989, Rémy Bricka of Paris, France, crossed 1 km (1,094 yd) of a swimming pool in 7 min 7.41 sec. He used ski-floats and a double-headed paddle.

### Woodcutting
The springboard chopping record (scaling a 2.7-m or 9-ft spar pole on springboards

03:58:33

**Left**
The three-legged runners Dale Lyons and David Pettifer cross the finishing line in the 1995 London marathon.

### Coal carrying
On 27 May 1983, Brian Newton of Leicester, UK, covered the marathon distance of 42.195 km (26 miles 385 yd) in a time of 8 hr 26 min while at the same time carrying 50.8 kg (1 cwt) of household coal in an open bag.

### Stair climbing
Brian McCauliff ran a vertical mile (ascending and descending eight times) on the stairs of the Westin Hotel, Detroit, Michigan, USA, in 1 hr 38 min 5 sec on 2 Feb 1992.

Russell Gill climbed the 835 steps of the Rhodes State Office Tower, Columbus, Ohio, USA, 53 times (a vertical height of 8,141.8 m or 26,712 ft) in 9 hr 16 min 24 sec in Feb 1994. He went down by lift each time.

## TRICKS IN JUST TWO MINUTES ON 21 APRIL 1991

and chopping a 35.5-cm or 14-in diameter log) is 1 min 18.45 sec by Bill Youd of Australia in 1985.

## Over an hour
### Bath tub racing
The record for a bath tub race covering 57.9-km (36-mile) is 1 hr 22 min 27 sec. This was achieved by Greg Mutton, who along with other contestants, paddled across water using a bath as a boat at the Grafton Jacaranda Festival, NSW, Australia, on 8 Nov 1987.

### Needle threading
On 21 Feb 1996, Dean Gould of Felixstowe, Suffolk, UK, threaded a strand of cotton 3,471 times through a number 13 needle in two hours.

### Sheep to shoulder
At the International Wool Secretariat Development Centre, Ilkley, W Yorkshire, UK, a team of eight using commercial machinery produced a jumper—from shearing sheep to the finished article—in 2 hr 28 min 32 sec on 3 Sept 1986.

### Speed march
A team of nine representing II Squadron RAF Regiment from RAF Hullavington, Wilts, UK, each with a 18.1-kg (40-lb) pack and a rifle, completed the London marathon in 4 hr 33 min 58 sec on 21 April 1991.

Flt. Sgt. Chris Chandler set an individual record in the RAF Swinderby Marathon at Swinderby, Lincs, UK, on 25 Sept 1992, with a pack weighing 18.1 kg (40 lb). His time was 3 hr 56 min 10 sec.

### Tailoring
On 24 June 1982, 65 members of the Melbourne College of Textiles, Pascoe Vale, Victoria, Australia, manufactured a three-piece suit from catching the sheep to finished article in 1 hr 34 min 33.42 sec.

### Three-legged
Dale Lyons and David Pettifer (GB) ran the London marathon tied together at ankle and wrist and set a record of 3 hr 58 min 33 sec on 2 April 1995.

### Yo-yo
'Fast' Eddy McDonald of Toronto, Canada completed 21,663 loops with a yo-yo in three hours on 14 Oct 1990 at Boston, Massachusetts, USA.

**Right**
The record for harvesting is held by an international team from CWS Agriculture, led by estate manager Ian Hanglin, using a Claas Commandor 228 combine fitter with a Shelbourne Reynolds SR 6000 stripper head.

## A Day's Work

### Apple picking
On 23 Sept 1980, 7,180.3 kg (15,830 lb) of apples were picked in eight hours by George Adrian of Indianapolis, Indiana, USA.

### Baling
On 30 Aug 1989, Svend Erik Klemmensen of Trustrup, Djursland, Denmark, baled 200 tonnes of straw in 9 hr 54 min using a Hesston 4800 baling machine.

### Combine harvesting
Philip Baker of West End Farm, Merton, Bicester, Oxon, UK, harvested 165.6 tonnes

Yogesh Sharma shook hands with 31,118 different people in eight hours during the Gwalior Trade Fair at Gwalior, Madhya Pradesh, India, on 14 Jan 1996.

### Hedge laying
Steven Forsyth and Lewis Stephens of Sennybridge, Powys, UK, hedged 280.7 m (920 ft 11 in) in 11 hours by the 'stake and pleach' method on 23 April 1994.

### Riveting
The world record for riveting is 11,209 in nine hours, by John Moir at the Workman Clark Ltd shipyard, Belfast, UK, in June

1918. His best hour was his seventh, with 1,409 rivets, an average of more than 23 per minute.

### Shearing
The highest speed for sheep-shearing was recorded by Alan MacDonald, who machine-sheared 805 lambs in nine hours (an average of 89.4 per hour) at Waitnaguru, New Zealand, on 20 Dec 1990.

Peter Casserly of Christchurch, New Zealand, achieved a solo-blade (hand-shearing) record of 353 lambs in nine hours on 13 Feb 1976.

## 24 Hours

### Army drill
On 8–9 July 1987, a 90-man squad of the Queen's Colour Squadron performed a total of 2,722,662 drill movements (2,001,384 rifle and 721,278 foot) at RAF Uxbridge, London, UK, from memory and without a word of command in 23 hr 55 min.

### Barrel rolling
On 1–2 Sept 1995, a team of 10 people from Tecza Sports Club, Lódz, Poland, rolled a 63.5-kg (140-lb) barrel 200.11 km (124 miles 560 yd) in 24 hours.

### Bath tub racing
The greatest distance covered by paddling a hand-propelled bath tub on water in 24 hours is 145.6 km (90½ miles), by 13 members of Aldington Prison Officers Social Club, near Ashford, Kent, UK, on 28–29 May 1983.

**Right**
The average milk yield for a cow is 5,570 litres per year, or 15.26 litres per day. Joseph Love of Kilifi Plantations Ltd, Kenya, milked a record 531 litres (117 gal) from 30 cows on 25 Aug 1992.

of wheat in eight hours using a Massey Ferguson MF 38 combine, on 8 Aug 1989.

On 9 Aug 1990, an international team from CWS Agriculture, led by estate manager Ian Hanglin, harvested 358.09 tonnes of wheat in eight hours from 44 ha (108.72 acres) at Cockayne Hatley Estate, Sandy, Beds, UK.

### Hand milking
Joseph Love of Kilifi Plantations Ltd, Kenya, milked 531 litres (117 gal) from 30 cows on 25 Aug 1992.

### Handshaking
President Theodore Roosevelt set a record for a public figure by shaking hands with 8,513 people at an official function at a New Year's Day White House presentation in Washington DC, USA, on 1 Jan 1907.

# 7,180.3 KG APPLES PICKED IN 8 HOURS

## OF HOPSCOTCH IN 24 HOURS ON 2-3 APRIL 1995

### Dribbling
Terry Cole (GB) dribbled a basketball without 'travelling' 144.8 km (90 miles) in 24 hours at Ive Farm Sports Ground, Leyton, Greater London, UK, on 27–28 Jan 1996.

### Hopscotch
The greatest number of games of hopscotch successfully completed in 24 hours is 390, by Ashrita Furman of Jamaica, New York, USA, on 2–3 April 1995.

### Ladder climbing
A team of 10 firefighters from the Pietermaritzburg Msunduzi Fire Services climbed a vertical height of 90.49 km (56 miles 405 yd) up a standard fire-service ladder in 24 hours at Pietermaritzburg, KwaZulu-Natal, South Africa, on 14–15 June 1996.

On 30–31 Aug 1996, a team of 10 firefighters from Worcester Fire Station climbed a vertical height of 87.37 km (54.29 miles) up a standard fire-service ladder in 24 hours at Worcester, UK.

### Ploughing
The greatest area ploughed with a six-furrow plough to a depth of 25 cm (9¾ in) in 24 hours is 91.37 ha (225.7 acres). This was achieved by Matthias Robrahn of Pogeez, Germany, in a John Deere Type 4955 (228 PS) on 23–24 Sept 1992.

### Pram pushing
The greatest distance covered in 24 hours while pushing a pram is 563.62 km

## 89.4 LAMBS PER HOUR

(350.23 miles) by 60 members of the Oost-Vlanderen branch of Amnesty International at Lede, Belgium, on 15 Oct 1988.

A 10-man team from the Royal Marines School of Music, Deal, Kent, UK, with an adult 'baby', covered a distance of 437.3 km (271.7 miles) in 24 hours in Nov 1990.

### Shearing
In a 24-hour shearing marathon, Alan MacDonald and Keith Wilson machine-sheared 2,220 sheep at Warkworth, Auckland Province, New Zealand, on 26 June 1988.

### Tap dancing
Roy Castle achieved one million taps in 23 hr 44 min at the *Guinness World of Records* exhibition, Piccadilly, London, UK, on 31 Oct–1 Nov 1985.

06:48:32

16:23:08

21:35:29

**Left**
Barrel rolling is a traditional event which is popular in many towns that have breweries. A team of 10 people from Tecza Sports Club, Lódz, Poland, rolled a 63.5-kg (140-lb) barrel 200.11 km (124 miles 560 yd) in 24 hours on 1–2 Sept 1995.

# Distance

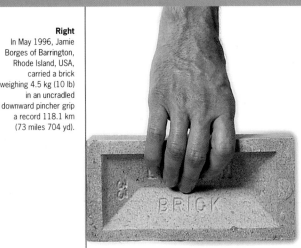

**Right**
In May 1996, Jamie Borges of Barrington, Rhode Island, USA, carried a brick weighing 4.5 kg (10 lb) in an uncradled downward pincher grip a record 118.1 km (73 miles 704 yd).

## Carrying and pushing
### Bed pushing
The record distance for bed pushing is 5,204 km (3,233 miles 1,144 yd), by nine employees of Bruntsfield Bedding Centre, Edinburgh, UK, pushing a wheeled hospital bed. The effort took them from 21 June to 26 July 1979.

### Brick carrying
The greatest distance for carrying a brick weighing 4.5 kg (10 lb) in a nominated ungloved hand in an uncradled downward pincher grip is 118.1 km (73 miles 45 yd), by Jamie Borges of Barrington, Rhode Island, USA, in and around Jupiter, Florida, USA, on 13 and 14 May 1996.

### Lawn mowers
A 12-hour run-behind record of 169.1 km (105 miles 176 yd) was set at Wisborough

Green, W Sussex, UK, on 28 and 29 July 1990 by the 'Doctor's Flyers' team.

The greatest distance covered in the annual 12-hour Lawn Mower Race (under the rules of the British Lawn Mower Racing Association) is 468 km (291 miles) by John Gill, Robert Jones and Steve Richardson of Team Gilliams at Wisborough Green, W Sussex, UK, on 1 and 2 Aug 1992.

### Milk bottle balancing
The greatest distance walked while balancing a milk bottle on the head is 115.87 km (72 miles), by Terry Cole of Walthamstow, London, UK, around the City of London on 4 and 5 June 1996. It took him 25 hours to complete the walk.

### Stretcher bearing
Two teams of four from 1 Field Ambulance Canadian Forces Base Calgary, carried a stretcher with a 63-kg (10-st) 'body' 300.40 km (186 miles 1,160 yd), in 59 hr 19 min from 27 to 30 May 1996. They started from Edmonton, Alberta, Canada, and finished in Calgary, Alberta.

## Eccentric movers
### Backwards unicycling
Ashrita Furman rode 85.56 km (53 miles 300 yd) backwards at Forest Park, Queens, New York, USA, on 16 Sept 1994.

### Crawling
The longest continuous voluntary crawl (progression with one or other knee in unbroken contact with the ground) is

50.6 km (31½ miles), by Peter McKinlay and John Murrie, who covered 115 laps of an athletics track at Falkirk, Scotland, UK, on 28–29 March 1992.

Over 15 months, ending on 9 March 1985, Jagdish Chander crawled 1,400 km (870 miles) from Aligarh to Jamma, India, to appease the revered Hindu goddess, Mata.

### Dancing
David Meenan tap-danced 37.367 km (23 miles 385 yd) for 6 hr 12 min 53 sec at Red Bank, New Jersey, USA, in June 1996.

Rosie Radiator led 12 tap dancers through the streets of San Francisco, California, USA, in a choreographed routine, which covered a distance of 15.47 km (9 miles 1,074 yd) on 11 July 1994.

### ASHRITA FURMAN COVERED

### Escalator riding
The record distance travelled on a pair of 'up' and 'down' escalators is 214.34 km (133 miles 325 yd), by David Beattie and Adrian Simons at Top Shop, Oxford Street, London, UK, from 17 to 21 July 1989. They each completed 7,032 circuits.

### Land rowing
Rob Bryant rowed 5,278.5 km (3,280 miles) across the USA. He left Los Angeles, California, USA, on 2 April 1990, and reached Washington DC on 30 July.

### Leap-frogging
Fourteen students from Stanford University, California, USA, leap-frogged 1,603.2 km (996 miles 352 yd). They started leap-frogging on 16 May 1991 and stopped 244 hr 43 min later on 26 May.

### Pedal-boating
Kenichi Horie of Kobe, Japan, set a pedal-boating distance record of 7,500 km (4,660 miles), leaving Honolulu, Hawaii, USA, on 30 Oct 1992 and arriving at Naha, Okinawa, Japan, on 17 Feb 1993.

### Pogo-stick jumping
Terry Cole set a distance record of 28.96 km (18 miles) in 7 hr 15 min on 5 April 1997 at Leyton, London, UK.

### Riding in armour
Dick Brown left Edinburgh, Scotland, UK, on 10 June 1989 and arrived in Dumfries four days later, after he had covered 334.7 km (208 miles) in a total riding time of 35 hr 25 min.

**Right**
David Meenan tap-dancing his way into the record books after completing a marathon 37.367 km (23 miles 385 yd) on 30 June 1996 at Red Bank, New Jersey, USA. He danced for a total of 6 hr 12 min 53 sec.

12.245 KM

37.367 KM

# PEDAL BOATING RECORD 7,500 KM

### Unicycling
Akira Matsushima (Japan) unicycled 5,248 km (3,261 miles) from Newport, Oregon to Washington DC, USA, from 10 July to 22 Aug 1992.

## Walking
### Catwalk walking
Eddie Warke walked 133.7 km (83 miles 176 yd) on a catwalk at Parke's Hotel, Dublin, Republic of Ireland, in Sept 1983.

The record for female models is 114.4 km (71 miles 176 yd), set by Roberta Brown and Lorraine McCourt on the same occasion.

### Charity fund-raising
The greatest recorded amount raised by a charity walk or run is $Can 24.7 million

3,424 KM

(£9.1 million) by Terry Fox of Canada who, with an artificial leg, ran from St John's, Newfoundland to Thunder Bay, Ontario, Canada, in 143 days from 12 April to 2 Sept 1980. He covered 5,373 km (3,339 miles).

### Stilt-walking
From 20 Feb to 26 July 1980, Joe Bowen stilt-walked 4,804 km (3,008 miles), from Los Angeles, California, USA, to Bowen, Kentucky, USA.

In 1891 Sylvain Dornon stilt-walked from Paris, France, to Moscow, Russia, in 50 stages, covering 2,945 km (1,830 miles). It is said that this took either 50 or 58 days.

### Walking on hands
Johann Hurlinger walked 1,400 km (870 miles) in 55 daily 10-hour stints from Vienna, Austria, to Paris, France, in 1900.

### Walking on water
Rémy Bricka (France) 'walked' across the Atlantic Ocean on skis 4.2 m (13 ft 9 in) long in 1988, covering 5,636 km (3,502 miles).

## Rail Travel
### Calling at all stations
Alan Witton visited 2,362 British Rail stations (every open station) in a continuous tour of 26,703 km (16,593 miles) in 18 days 20 hr 16 min from 13 July to 28 Aug 1980.

Colin Mulvany and Seth Vafiadis visited 2,378 British Rail stations (every open station). They also travelled on the Tyne & Wear, Glasgow and London underground

5,636 KM

systems (333 stations). They travelled over 24,990 km (15,528 miles) in 31 days 5 hr 8 min 58 sec from 4 June to 5 July 1984.

### Four points of the compass
Roger Elliott visited the remotest stations in Great Britain—Thurso, Scotland (northernmost), Lowestoft, Suffolk (easternmost), Penzance, Cornwall (southernmost) and Arisaig, Scotland (westernmost)—in 37 hr 14 min in 1995.

### Most miles in 24 hours
The greatest distance that has been travelled in the United Kingdom in 24 hours is 2,842.5 km (1,766¼ miles) by Norma and Jonathan Carter, aged 15, from 3 to 4 Sept 1992.

### Most countries in 24 hours
The most countries travelled through entirely by train in 24 hours is 11, by Alison Bailey, Ian Bailey, John English and David Kellie on 1 and 2 May 1993. Their journey started in Hungary and continued through Slovakia, the Czech Republic, Austria, Germany, back into Austria, Liechtenstein, Switzerland, France, Luxembourg, Belgium and the Netherlands. The journey lasted 22 hr 10 min.

### Most miles in seven days
Andrew Kingsmell and Sean Andrews of Bromley, Kent, UK, together with Graham Bardouleau of Crawley, W Sussex, UK, travelled 21,090 km (13,105 miles) on the French national railway system in 6 days 22 hr 38 min from 28 Nov to 5 Dec 1992.

## GREATEST DISTANCE FOR THROWING A GRAPE IN THE AIR AND CATCHING IT IN

'Juggled' means that the number of catches made is equal to the number of objects thrown multiplied by the number of hands.

'Flashed' means the number of catches made equals at least the number of objects, but less than a juggle.

## Juggling
*Record historically accepted though not fully substantiated.

### Rings
Eleven rings were juggled by Albert Petrovski* (USSR) in 1963, Eugene Belaur* (USSR) in 1968, and Sergei Ignatov* (USSR) in 1973.

Twelve were flashed by Anthony Gatto (USA) in 1993, and Albert Lucas (USA) in 1995.

### Clubs
Seven clubs were juggled by Albert Petrovski* (USSR) in 1963, Sorin Munteanu*

Seven ping pong balls were flashed with the mouth by Tony Ferko (Czechoslovakia) in 1987, and by Wally Eastwood (USA).

### Plates
Eight plates were juggled by Enrico Rastelli* (Italy) in the 1920s; and eight were flashed by Albert Lucas (USA) in 1993.

### Torches
Seven flaming torches were juggled by Anthony Gatto (USA) in 1989.

### Passing
Eleven clubs were juggled by Owen Morse and John Wee (USA) in 1995.

(1986) and 5,000 m in 16 min 55 sec (1986); Ashrita Furman (USA) over a marathon distance in 3 hr 22 min 32.5 sec (1988) and 50 miles in 8 hr 52 min 7 sec (1989); Michael Hout (USA) over the 110 m hurdles in 18.9 seconds (1993); Albert Lucas (USA) over the 400 m hurdles in 1 min 7 sec (1993); and Owen Morse, Albert Lucas, Tuey Wilson and John Wee (USA) in the 1-mile relay in 3 min 57.38 sec (1990).

The record times for running and juggling five objects are: Owen Morse over 100 m in 13.8 seconds (1988), and Bill Gillen (USA) over 1 mile in 7 min 41.01 sec (1989) and 5,000 m in 28 min 11 sec (1989).

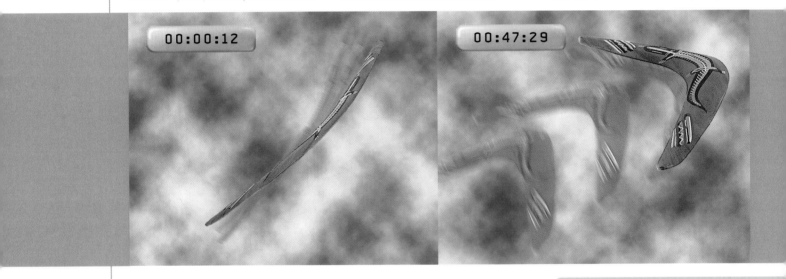

00:00:12          00:47:29

(Romania) in 1975, Jack Bremlov* (Czechoslovakia) in 1985, Anthony Gatto (USA) in 1988, Bruce Tiemann (USA) in 1995 and Albert Lucas in 1996 (1985*).

A total of eight clubs were flashed by Anthony Gatto in 1989, and by Scott Sorensen (USA) in 1995.

### Balls
Ten balls were juggled by Enrico Rastelli* (Italy) in the 1920s and by Bruce Sarafian (USA) in 1996.

Twelve balls were flashed by Bruce Sarafian (USA) in 1995.

Ten balls were bounce juggled by Tim Nolan* (USA) in 1988.

Nine balls were spun on one hand by François Chotard (France) in 1990.

A total of five balls were juggled by Bobby May (USA) while he was standing on his head, in 1953.

Fifteen balls were flashed by Peter Kaseman and Rob Vancko (USA) in 1995.

### Duration (without a drop)
Five clubs were juggled for 45 min 2 sec by Anthony Gatto (USA) in 1989.

Three objects were juggled for 11 hr 4 min 22 sec by Terry Cole (GB) in 1995.

### Most pirouettes with cigar boxes
In 1977, Kris Kremo (Switzerland) did a quadruple turn with three cigar boxes in mid air.

### Most objects kept aloft
In June 1994, 826 people, juggling at least three objects each, kept 2,478 objects aloft at Glastonbury, Somerset, UK.

### 'Joggling'
The record times for running and juggling three objects are held by: Owen Morse (USA) over 100 m in 11.68 seconds (1989) and 400 m in 57.32 seconds (1990); Kirk Swenson (USA) over 1 mile in 4 min 43 sec

## JASON SCHAYOT (USA)

## Projectiles
### Throwing
David Engvall threw a lead weight with a long string tail 385.80 m (1,265 ft 9 in) at El Mirage, California, USA, on 17 Oct 1993.

Scott Zimmerman threw a flying ring 383.13 m (1,257ft) on 8 July 1986 at Fort Funston, California, USA.

### Boomerang throwing
The most consecutive two-handed catches is 817, by Michael Girvin (USA) on 17 July 1994 at Oakland, California, USA.

The longest out-and-return distance is 149.12 m (489 ft 3 in), by Michel Dufayard (France) in 1992 at Shrewsbury, Shrops, UK.

The longest flight duration (with self-catch) is one of 2 min 59.94 sec by Dennis Joyce (USA) at Bethlehem, Pennsylvania, USA, on 25 June 1987.

# BOOMERANG FLIGHT 2 MIN 59.94 SEC

**THE MOUTH IS 99.82 M**

The number of consecutive catches with two boomerangs, keeping at least one boomerang aloft at all times is 555, by Yannick Charles (France) at Strasbourg, France, on 4 Sept 1995.

**Brick throwing**
On 19 July 1978, Geoff Capes threw a 2.27-kg (5-lb) brick 44.54 m (146 ft 1 in) at Orton Goldhay, Cambs, UK.

**Card throwing**
Jim Karol threw a standard playing card a distance of 61.26 m (201 ft) at Mount Ida College, Newton Centre, Massachusetts, USA, on 18 Oct 1992.

Francisco, California, USA; 60.02 m (196 ft 11 in) for women, by Judy Horowitz (USA) on 29 June 1985 at La Mirada, California, USA.

The 24-hour pair distance records are: 592.15 km (367 miles 1,663 yd) for men, by Conrad Damon and Pete Fust on 24–25 April 1993 at San Marino, California, USA; 186.12 km (115 miles 1,143 yd) for women, by Jo Cahow and Amy Berard on 30–31 Dec 1979 at Pasadena, California, USA.

The record times aloft are: 16.72 seconds for men, by Don Cain in May 1984 at Philadelphia, Pennsylvania, USA;

55.11 m (180 ft 10 in) by Alan Pettigrew at Inchmurrin, Argyll, UK, on 24 May 1984.

**Rolling pin throwing**
Lori La Deane Adams threw a 907-g (2-lb) rolling pin a record distance of 53.47 m (175 ft 5 in) at Iowa State Fair, Iowa, USA, on 21 Aug 1979.

**Slinging**
On 13 Sept 1992, David Engvall (USA) hurled a 62-g (2¼-oz) dart a record distance of 477.10 m (1,565 ft 4 in) from a 127-cm (50-in) long sling. The record was achieved at Baldwin Lake, California, USA.

**Below left**
On 25 June 1987 in the USA, Dennis Joyce threw a boomerang so that it stayed in the air for a record 2 min 59.94 sec. The boomerang was first developed by Aborigines in Australia to kill game and as a weapon.

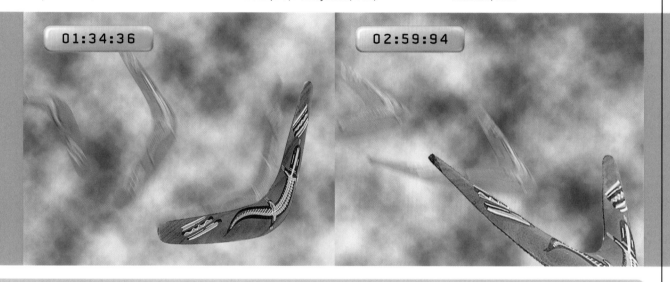

`01:34:36`     `02:59:94`

**SPAT A WATERMELON SEED A RECORD DISTANCE OF 22.91 M IN AUG 1995**

**Cow pat tossing**
The greatest distance achieved under the 'non-sphericalization and 100% organic' rule (established in 1970) is 81.1 m (266 ft), by Steve Urner at the Mountain Festival, Tehachapi, California, USA on 14 Aug 1981.

**Egg throwing**
In Nov 1978, Johnny Dell Foley threw an egg without breaking it 98.51 m (323 ft 2½ in) to Keith Thomas at Jewett, Texas, USA.

**Flying disc (formerly frisbee)**
The distance records are: 200.01 m (656 ft 2 in) for men, by Scott Stokely (USA) on 14 May 1995; 136.31 m (447 ft 3 in) for women, by Anni Kreml (USA) on 21 Aug 1994. Both records were set at Fort Collins, Colorado, USA.

The throw, run and catch records are: 92.64 m (303 ft 11 in) for men, by Hiroshi Oshima (Japan) on 20 July 1988 at San

11.81 seconds for women, by Amy Bekken in Aug 1991 at Santa Cruz, California, USA.

**Grape catching**
The greatest distance at which a grape thrown from level ground has been caught in the mouth is 99.82 m (327 ft 6 in) by Paul J. Tavilla at East Boston, Massachusetts, USA, on 27 May 1991. The grape was thrown by James Deady.

**Gumboot throwing**
The men's record is 56.70 m (186 ft), by Olav Jensen at Fagernes, Norway, on 10 July 1988.

The women's record is 40.70 m (133 ft 6 in) by Mette Bergmann at Fagernes, Norway, on 10 July 1988.

**Haggis hurling**
The longest recorded throw of a haggis (minimum weight 680g or 1 lb 8 oz) is

**Spear throwing**
The record distance achieved for throwing a spear (using an atlatl or hand-held device which fits onto it) is 258.63 m (848 ft 6½ in) by David Engvall at Aurora, Colorado, USA, on 15 July 1995.

**Spitting**
The greatest recorded distance for spitting a cherry stone is 28.98 m (95 ft 1 in), by Horst Ortmann at Langenthal, Germany, on 27 Aug 1994.

The record for spitting a watermelon seed is 22.91 m (75 ft 2 in) by Jason Schayot (USA) at De Leon, Texas, USA, on 12 Aug 1995.

David O'Dell of Apple Valley, California, USA, spat a wad of tobacco a record 15.07 m (49 ft 5½ in) at the 19th World Tobacco Spitting Championships held at Calico Ghost Town, California, USA, on 26 March 1994.

# Strength and balance

**Far right**
Fifteen members of the Aurora Karate Do demolishing a seven-room house in Prince Albert, Saskatchewan, Canada, using only their hands and feet. They took 3 hr 9 min 59 sec. In 1996, they broke their own record by demolishing a 10-room house in 3 hr 6 min 50 sec.

## Balance

### Balancing on one foot
The longest recorded duration for balancing upon one foot is 71 hr 40 min by Amresh Kumar Jha at Bihar, India, from 13–16 Sept 1995. The disengaged foot is not allowed to be rested upon the standing foot nor may any object be used for support or balance.

### Beer mat flipping
Dean Gould from Suffolk, UK, flipped a pile of 111 beer mats (consisting of 1.2 mm-thick 490-gsm of wood pulp board) through an angle of 180° and caught them, at Edinburgh, UK, on 13 Jan 1993.

### Brick balancing
John Evans balanced 100 bricks that weighed a total of 184.6 kg (407 lb) on his head for 14 seconds, on 18 Nov 1996 at London Zoo, UK.

### Cigar box balancing
Terry Cole balanced 220 unmodified cigar boxes on his chin for nine seconds on 24 April 1992.

### Coin balancing
On 15 Nov 1995, Aleksandr Bendikov (Belarus) stacked a pyramid of 880 coins on the edge of a coin free-standing vertically on the base of a coin which was on a table.

The tallest ever single column of coins to be stacked on the edge of a coin was built by Dipak Syal of Yamuna Nagar, India, on 3 May 1991. It consisted of 253 Indian one-rupee pieces on top of a vertical five-rupee coin.

On 1 May 1991, Dipak Syal balanced 10 one-rupee coins and ten 10-paise coins alternately horizontally and vertically in one column.

### Coin snatching
The most 10-pence pieces clean-caught after being flipped from the back of a forearm into the same downward palm is 328, by Dean Gould (UK) on 6 April 1993.

### Domino stacking
Aleksandr Bendikov successfully stacked 522 dominoes on a single supporting domino on 21 Sept 1994.

### House of cards
The most storeys achieved without adhesive in a house of standard playing cards is 100, to a height of 5.85 m (19 ft 2 in). It was completed by Bryan Berg (USA) in Copenhagen, Denmark, on 10 May 1996.

### Egg balancing
On 23 Sept 1990, Kenneth Epperson of Monroe, Georgia, USA, balanced 210 eggs on end simultaneously on a flat surface.

A class at Bayfield School, Bayfield, Colorado, USA simultaneously balanced 467 eggs on 20 March 1986.

### Glass balancing
Ashrita Furman of Jamaica, New York, USA, succeeded in balancing 57 pint glasses on his chin for 11.9 seconds on 18 May 1996.

### Largest bubble
Alan McKay managed to blow a bubble 32m (105 ft) long at Wellington, New Zealand, on 9 Aug 1996.

### Static wall 'sit' (or Samson's Chair)
Rajkumar Chakraborty (India) stayed in an unsupported sitting position against a wall for 11 hr 5 min at Panposh Sports Hostel, Rourkela, India, on 22 April 1994.

### Milk crate balancing
Terry Cole of Walthamstow, London, UK, managed to balance 29 crates on his chin for the minimum specified time of 10 seconds on 16 May 1994.

John Evans of Marlpool, Derbys, UK, balanced 94 crates (each weighing 1.36 kg or 3 lb) on his head for 16 seconds on *The Big Breakfast* television programme on 2 Oct 1996.

### Motionlessness
Radhey Shyam Prajapati (India) stood motionless for 18 hr 5 min 50 sec at Gandhi Bhawan, Bhopal, India, on 25–26 Jan 1996.

## Strength

### Barrow pushing
The heaviest loaded one-wheeled barrow pushed for a minimum 61 level m (200 level ft) weighed a gross 3.75 tonnes (8,275 lb). Loaded with bricks, it was

A 100-STOREY HOUSE OF CARDS, RISING TO 5.85 M,

**Right**
Amresh Kumar Jha balancing on one foot for a record 71 hr 40 min, at Bihar, India, in 1995, He stayed in the same position from 13 to 16 Sept.

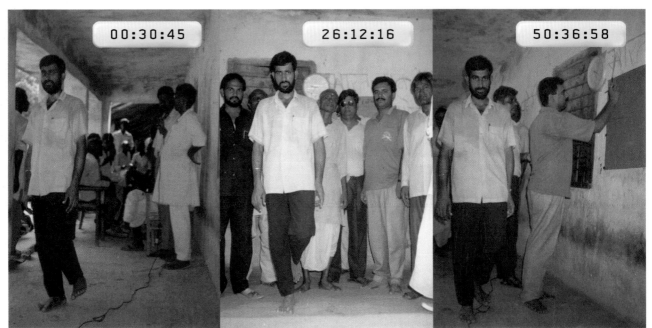

00:30:45    26:12:16    50:36:58

# BALANCING ON ONE FOOT 71 HR 40 MIN

**A DISTANCE OF 54.7 M**

pushed a distance of 74.1 m (243 ft) by John Sarich at London, Ontario, Canada, on 19 Feb 1987.

**Beer keg lifting**
George Olesen raised a keg weighing 62.9 kg (138 lb 11 oz) above his head 737 times in the space of six hours (on average more than twice every minute) at Horsens, Denmark, on 1 May 1994.

**Most bricks lifted**
In June 1992, Russell Bradley lifted 31 bricks—side by side—from a table and then held them at chest height for two seconds.

**Greatest weight of bricks lifted**
The greatest weight of bricks lifted was 96.21 kg (212 lb 11 oz), when Fred Burton of Cheadle, Staffs, UK, held 20 heavier bricks for two seconds on 21 March 1997.

**Demolition work**
Fifteen members of the Aurora Karate Do knocked down a ten-room house in Prince Albert, Saskatchewan, Canada, in 3 hr 6 min 50 sec on 11 May 1996, using only their feet and empty hands.

**Field gun pull**
Three teams of eight from 72 Ordnance Company (V) RAOC pulled a 25-pounder gun over a distance of 177.98 km (110 miles 1,041 yd) in 24 hours at Donnington, Shrops, UK, between 2–3 April 1993.

**Hod carrying**
Russell Bradley of Worcester, UK, carried bricks weighing 164 kg (361 lb 9 oz) up a 3.65-m (12-ft) ladder on 28 Jan 1991 at Worcester City Football Club. As the hod weighed 43 kg (94 lb 13 oz) the total weight was 207 kg (456 lb 6 oz).

On 20 Nov 1993 in Worcester, UK, Russell Bradley carried bricks weighing 264 kg (582 lb) in a hod weighing 48 kg (105 lb 13 oz) a flat distance of 5 m (16 ft 5 in), before ascending a runged ramp to a height of 2.49 m (8 ft 2 in). This gave a total weight of 312 kg (687 lb 13 oz).

**Lifting and pulling with teeth**
Walter Arfeuille of Ieper-Vlamertinge, Belgium, lifted weights of 281.5 kg (620 lb 10 oz) 17 cm (6¾ in) off the ground with his teeth in Paris, France, on 31 March 1990.

On 21 July 1992, Robert Galstyan of Masis, Armenia, pulled two railway wagons coupled together with his teeth, weighing a total of 219,175 kg (483,198 lb) a distance of 7 m (23 ft) along a rail track at Shcherbinka, Moscow, Russia.

**Lung power**
Nicholas Mason of Cheadle, Greater Manchester, UK, inflated a standard 1,000-g (35-oz) meteorological balloon to a diameter of 2.44 m (8 ft) in 45 min 2.5 sec for the BBC *Record Breakers* on 26 Sept 1994.

**WAS BUILT BY BRYAN BERG (USA) ON 10 MAY 1996**

**Plane pulling**
David Huxley pulled a Qantas Boeing 747-400 a distance of 54.7 m (179 ft 6 in) at Sydney Airport, NSW, Australia, on 2 April 1996. The aircraft weighed 187 tonnes.

A team of 60 people pulled a British Airways Boeing 747 weighing 205 tonnes 100 m (328 ft) in 61 seconds at Heathrow airport in the United Kingdom, on 25 May 1995.

**Lifting an elephant**
In 1975 Khalil Oghaby (Iran) lifted an elephant off the ground using a harness and platform at Gerry Cottle's Circus in the United Kingdom. The elephant and lifting gear weighed about two tonnes.

**Rope slide**
The greatest recorded distance for a rope slide is 1,746.5 m (5,730 ft) by L/Cpl Peter Baldwin (UK) and Stu Leggett (Canada) at Mount Gibraltar, Canada, on 31 Aug 1994. They reached up to 160 km/h (100 mph).

# Mass participation

**Right**
On 18 Aug 1996, 6,654 tap dancers danced a single routine outside Macy's department store in New York City, USA, breaking the existing record for this annual event.

**Below**
Boon Lay Community Centre Youth Group, Singapore, constructed a 15.02-km (9-mile 580-yd) long paper clip chain in 20 hours.

## Paper chain
A paper chain 65.44 km (40⅗ miles) long was made by 60 students from the University of Missouri-Rolla on behalf of the Rolla Area Big Brothers/Big Sisters Organization between 1 and 2 March 1997. The chain consisted of over 450,000 links and was made over a period of 24 hours.

## Chain of buckets
A fire service chain of buckets stretched over 3,496.4 m (11,471 ft) with 2,271 people passing 50 buckets along the complete course at the Centennial Parade and Muster held at Hudson, New York, USA, on 11 July 1992.

## Paper clip chain
A paper clip chain which was 15.02 km (9 miles 580 yd) long was made by 40 members of Boon Lay Community Centre Youth Group, Singapore, in 20 hours between 13 and 14 July 1996.

## Large constructions
### Balloon sculpture
The largest balloon sculpture consisted of 41,241 coloured balloons forming the shape of a boat, for an exhibition in Vila Nova de Gaia, Portugal on 30 Oct 1996.

### Longest daisy chain
Villagers of Good Easter, Chelmsford, Essex, UK, made a 2.12-km (6,980-ft 7-in) daisy chain in seven hours on 27 May 1985.

### Sand castle
The tallest sand castle on record, constructed only with hands, buckets and shovels, was 6.56 m (21 ft 6 in) high. It was made by a team led by Joe Maize, George Pennock and Ted Siebert at Harrison Hot Springs, British Columbia, Canada, on 26 Sept 1993.

### Column of coins
The most valuable column of coins was worth $Can 85,618 (£39,898) and was 1.85 m (6 ft 1 in) high. It was built by the British Columbia branch of the Kidney Foundation of Canada at South Surrey on 8 Sept 1996.

### Line of coins
On 6 Aug 1995, representatives of WWF (World Wide Fund for Nature) Malaysia and Dumex Sdn Bhd made a 55.63-km (34-mile 1,000-yd) line of coins in Kuala Lumpur, Malaysia, using 2,367,234 20-sen coins.

### Pile of coins
A pile of 1,000,298 American coins of various denominations with a total value of $126,463.61 (£70,030) was constructed by the YWCA of Seattle-King County, Washington, USA, at Redmond, Washington, on 28 May 1992.

### Domino toppling
Students at Delft, Eindhoven and Twente Technical Universities, Netherlands, set up 1.5 million dominoes. Of these, 1,382,101 were toppled by one push on 2 Jan 1988.

### Origami
A paper crane with a wingspan of 35.7 m (117 ft 2 in) was folded by residents of the district of Gunma at Maebashi, Japan, on 28 Oct 1995. The crane was 16 m (52 ft 6 in) tall and took six hours to make.

## Mass activity
### Kissing
The world's largest simultaneous kiss happened when 1,420 couples kissed at the same time at the University of Maine, Orono, USA, on 14 Feb 1996.

### Litter collection
A record 50,405 volunteers gathered along the Californian coastline, USA, on 2 Oct 1993 in order to collect litter in conjunction with the International Coastal Cleanup.

### Most trees planted
The most trees to be planted in one week by an unlimited number of volunteers was 101,165. The trees were planted at Vanderbijlpark, Pretoria, South Africa between 1 and 2 Nov 1996.

### Most trees planted in shortest time
On 21 Feb 1997, a record 14,000 trees were planted by a maximum of 300 volunteers in 3 hr 45 mins on 6.4 ha (16 acres) of reclaimed farmland at the Charlie Elliott Wildlife Center, Georgia, USA.

### Wine tasting
On 22 Nov 1986, a record 4,000 wine tasters consumed 9,360 bottles of wine at a single wine tasting. The event had been sponsored by KQED, a local television station in San Francisco, California, USA.

# 1,382,101 DOMINOES TOPPLED

## FIRMLY TIED TOGETHER, MOVED 30 M AS A 'HUMAN CENTIPEDE' ON 2 SEPT 1996

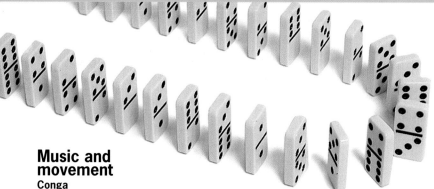

## Music and movement

### Conga
On 13 March 1988, the Miami Super Conga was performed by 119,986 people. It was part of an event held in conjunction with *Calle Ocho*, a Cuban-American group which throws parties for all the people of Miami.

The longest British conga involved 8,659 people from the South-Eastern Region branch of the Camping and Caravanning Club at Brands Hatch, Kent, on 4 Sept 1982.

### Longest chorus line
The world's longest chorus line took place on 28 March 1992, at the Swan Centre, Eastleigh, Hants, UK, when 543 members of the cast of *Showtime News*, a major production by Hampshire West Guides, performed a routine choreographed by professional dancer Sally Horsley.

## WAS CONSTRUCTED BY 60 AMERICAN STUDENTS

### Country dancing
The largest Scottish country dance was a 512-some reel, performed by the Toronto branch of the Royal Scottish Country Dance Society. The dance took place in Toronto, Canada, in 1991.

### Dancing dragon
The longest dancing dragon measured 1,889.76 m (6,200 ft) from the end of its nose to the tip of its tail. A total of 2,431 people brought the dragon to life on 3 Nov 1996, making it dance for more than one minute. The event took place at the Grandstand Forecourt, Shatin Horse Racecourse, Hong Kong, China.

### Hokey-cokey
The most participants in a hokey-cokey was 6,748, at Bangor, Co. Down, UK, as part of the VE day celebrations on 6 May 1995.

### Human centipede
The longest ever 'human centipede' consisted of 1,665 students from the University of Guelph, Canada, who moved 30 m (98 ft 5 in) on 2 Sept 1996. Participants' ankles were firmly tied together and no one fell over during the walk.

### Human logos
The largest logo formed from human beings was the Human US Shield on 10 Nov 1918. It consisted of 30,000 officers and men who were stationed at Camp Custer, Battlecreek, Michigan, USA.

### Largest aerobic/gymnastics display
The largest number of participants for a display is 30,517 at the Great Singapore Workout at The Padang, Singapore, on 27 Aug 1995.

### Largest dance
An estimated 72,000 people took part in a Chicken Dance held during the Canfield Fair, Canfield, Ohio, USA, on 1 Sept 1996.

### Tap dancing
The greatest number of tap dancers to participate in a single routine was 6,654, outside Macy's department store in New York City, USA, on 18 Aug 1996.

### Line dancing
A total of 1,788 dancers took part in a line dance spectacular at Newark Showground, Newark, Notts, UK, on 9 Feb 1997.

### Musical chairs
The largest game on record began with 8,238 participants, and ended with Xu Chong Wei occupying the last chair. It was held at the Anglo-Chinese School, Singapore, on 5 Aug 1989.

### Pass the parcel
The world's largest game of pass the parcel involved 3,464 people who removed 2,000 wrappers in two hours from a parcel measuring 1.5 x 0.9 x 0.9 m (5 x 3 x 3ft) at Alton Towers, Staffs, UK, on 8 Nov 1992. The event was organized by Parcelforce

International. The present that was beneath the wrapping was an electronic keyboard, which was won by Sylvia Wilshaw.

### Unsupported circle
The highest number of people on record to have demonstrated the physical paradox of all being seated without a chair is an unsupported circle of 10,323 employees of the Nissan Motor Co. at Komazawa Stadium, Tokyo, Japan, on 23 Oct 1982.

## Orchestras

### Largest band
The largest band ever to be assembled consisted of 20,100 bandsmen at the Ullevaal Stadium, Oslo, Norway. It was formed from the Norges Musikkorps Forbund bands on 28 June 1964.

### Pipes and drums
The British Telecom Massed Pipes and Drums of the World Event for Marie Curie Cancer Care took place at Edinburgh on 20 Aug 1995 and involved 2,739 registered pipers and drummers.

### Largest choir
A choir of 60,000 singers sang in unison as the finale to a choral contest held among 160,000 participants in Breslau, Germany (now Wroclaw, Poland), on 2 Aug 1937.

### Largest guitar band
On 7 May 1994, a gathering of 1,322 guitarists played *Taking Care of Business* in unison for 68 min 40 sec, in an event that was organized by Music West of Vancouver, Canada.

### Largest marching band
On 27 June 1993, a band of 6,017 players—including 927 majorettes and standard-bearers—marched for 940 m (3,084 ft) at Stafsberg Airport in Hamar, Norway, under the direction of Odd Aspli, chairman of Hamar County Council.

### Largest orchestra
On 17 June 1872, Johann Strauss the Younger conducted an orchestra of 987 pieces supported by a choir of 20,000, at the World Peace Jubilee in Boston, Massachusetts, USA. The orchestra contained 400 first violinists.

On 14 July 1996, an orchestra of 2,023, made up of musicians from various orchestras from around the United Kingdom, gave a concert conducted by Frank Renton at the Molineux Stadium, Wolverhampton, W Midlands, UK.

**Left**
Of the 1.5 million dominoes set up by students at Delft, Eindhoven and Twente Technical Universities, Netherlands, only 117,889 remained standing after the rest had been toppled over.

## Games of skill

### Most marble championships

The British Marbles Championships have been won most often by the Toucan Terribles with 20 consecutive titles (1956–75).

The world record for clearing the ring of 49 marbles is 2 min 56 sec, by the Black Dog Boozers of Crawley, W Sussex, UK, at BBC Television Centre, London, for the *Record Breakers* television programme on 14 Sept 1987.

### Most tiddlywinks world titles

Larry Kahn (USA) has won the tiddlywinks singles title 14 times, 1983–95.

Geoff Myers and Andy Purvis, members of the Cambridge University Tiddlywink Club at Queens' College, Cambridge, UK, on 21 Oct 1989 and 14 Jan 1995.

## Races

### Bog snorkelling

The World Bog Snorkelling Championships are held every year in August at Llanwrtyd Wells, Powys, Wales, UK. About 30 contestants a year put on flippers and a snorkel to swim two lengths of a 60-m (196-ft 11-in) bog. Steve Madeline is the only person to have held the title twice. He won in both 1989 and 1994.

### Pancake race

The record time for completion of the 384-m (420-yd) pancake race course which is held in Melbourne, Victoria, Australia, was 59.5 seconds by Jan Stickland on 19 Feb 1985.

### Plastic duck race

A record 100,000 yellow plastic ducks raced down a 1-km (⅓-mile) stretch of the River Avon, Bath, Somerset, UK, on 26 May 1997 in the world's biggest duck race. At a signal from a cannon, a crane tipped the ducks into the river. It took 2¼ hours for duck No. 24359, owned by Chris Green from Dauntsey, Wilts, UK, to win the race.

### Kenya Rhino Charge

The Kenya Rhino Charge is an off-road driving event in the Kenyan bush, where teams have eight hours to locate 10 points over the shortest possible distance. It is held every year to raise funds for the Rhino Ark charity, which is dedicated to preserving Africa's now rare black rhino species.

The 1997 winning team champions in the Kenya Rhino Charge were Neil McRae, Simon Evans, David Francombe, Michael Carr-Hartley and William Carr-Hartley (GB) who completed the course in the shortest distance of 57.97 km (36 miles), which was just 18% greater than the shortest possible straight-line distance of 48.95 km (30 miles 739 yd).

**Right**
The World Bog Snorkelling Championships held in Llanwrtyd Wells, Powys, UK, started nine years ago when the town needed to raise money for a new community centre—a channel was dug in a bog and people were invited to swim amongst the plankton, weeds, leeches and newts.

MEMBERS OF THE LEGAL PROFESSION AND POLITICIANS ARE BARRED FROM

**Right**
The beginning of the world's biggest ever plastic duck race at Bath, Somerset, UK. At precisely 2 p.m. a cannon was fired and a crane tipped the 100,000 ducks into the River Avon. With almost half of the ducks sponsored at £1 each, the event raised nearly £50,000 for Water Aid.

### Longest tiddlywink jump

The long jump record is 9.52 m (31 ft 3 in) by Ben Soares of St Andrews Tiddlywinks Society, UK, on 14 Jan 1995 .

Geoff Meyers and Andy Purvis have won a record seven pairs titles, 1991–95.

### National tiddlywinks championship

Alan Dean won the singles title six times, 1971–73, 1976, 1978 and 1986, and the pairs title six times. Jonathan Mapley won the pairs title seven times, 1972, 1975, 1977, 1980, 1983–84 and 1987.

### Fastest winks potting

The record for potting 24 winks from 45 cm (18 in) is 21.8 seconds by Stephen Williams of Altrincham Grammar School, Greater Manchester, UK, in May 1966.

The record for potting winks in relay is 41 in three minutes by Patrick Barrie, Nick Inglis,

# 33 CM IN 2 MIN 20 SEC

LONG OBSTACLE COURSE, CARRYING HIS WIFE TIINA, IN 1 MIN 6.2 SEC

## Sedan chair carrying
The National Sedan Chair Carrying Championships have been held every year since 1993 at the Georgian Legacy Festival, Lancaster, Lancs, UK. Teams, consisting of two male chair carriers and a female passenger, cover a course of 73.15 m (80 yds). The reigning champions, who have won the event since 1995, are "The Scholars", comprising two Lancaster University students, Nick Wigmore and Sean Smith and lecturer Dr Deb McVea.

## Snail racing
The World Snail Racing Championships held each year in July at Congham, Norfolk, UK, are conducted on a 33-cm (13-in) circular course outside St Andrew's Church. The snails race from the centre to the perimeter. Some race several times as they are divided into heats to cater for the 150 competitors who enter every year.

The 1996 Champion was a snail called 'Mark' who finished the race in 3 min 2 sec.

The all-time record holder is 'Archie', trained by Carl Banham, who sprinted to the winning post in 2 min 20 sec.

## Championship events
### Biggest liar
Held annually in November at The Bridge Inn, Santon Bridge, Cumbria, UK, the World's Biggest Liar Competition dates back to the

nettles, oatmeal and onion in a jar and then fry it in bacon fat, to make this traditional Yorkshire breakfast. The reigning 1997 champion is Philip Berkley, from the nearby village of Hebden Bridge, who last won the competition in 1994.

### Joke telling
Felipe Carbonell of Lima, Peru, told 345 jokes in one hour on 29 July 1993.

Mike Hessman of Columbus, Ohio, USA, told 12,682 in 24 hours on 16–17 Nov 1992.

and fruit. Florence Ritchie from Carrbridge is the only person to win two years in a row.

### Pram pushing
Craig McGarry pushed his son in a pram for 10 km (6 miles 352 yd) in 38 min 38 sec at the Herald Sun Olympic Dream, Melbourne, Victoria, Australia, on 17 Nov 1996.

### Sheaf tossing
Glen Young of Australia threw a 3.65-kg (8-lb) sheaf 18 m (59 ft) over a crossbar at the Royal Canberra Show on 23 Feb 1997.

**Left**
The custom of pancake races is almost as old as the origin of pancakes themselves. Eating pancakes just before the beginning of the season of Lent began for practical reasons. Lent was a season of abstention when the main ingredients of pancakes—eggs and fat—were banned.

ENTERING IN THE WORLD'S BIGGEST LIAR CHAMPIONSHIP IN CUMBRIA, UK

19th century, when Cumbrian publican Will Ritson was renowned locally for his lies. Members of the legal profession and politicians are barred from entry. The current world champion is John Graham, from Filloth, Cumbria, UK.

## Conkers
About 300 contestants compete at Ashton, Cambs, UK, with the organisers providing the conkers to ensure cheat-free conkering. Contestants are even drug tested. The 1996 World champion was John Bull, from Peterborough, UK; Karen Morgan from Kettering, UK, holds the female title; James Nicol is the intermediate champion and Richard Fuller won the Junior section.

## Dock pudding
This annual event takes place in Mayat Mytholmroyd Community Centre, W Yorkshire, UK. Competitors bring the local delicacy of sweet dock *Polygonum Bistorta*, boiled with

## Mosquito killing
The World Mosquito Killing Championships are held in Pelkosenniemi, Finland. The most mosquitos killed in the 5-minute contest is 21, by Henri Pellonpää in 1995.

## Pea shooting
Held at Wicham, Cambs, UK, since 1969, the skill is to aim at a target the size of a dart-board and smeared with putty, gaining five points for the inner, three for the middle and one for the outer circle from a distance of 3.2 m (10 ft 6 in). The only rule is that the pea shooter should be no longer than 30.48 cm (12 in). The 1996 World Champion was Don Sargent (USA).

## Porridge making
The Porridge Making Championships are held at Carrbridge, Scotland, UK. Three chefs judge the contestants, who must use oatmeal unless they are in the 'freestyle' category in which they can add nuts, whisky

## Toe wrestling
The World Toe Wrestling Championships are held annually at Ye Olde Royal Oak, Wetton, Staffs, UK. Using their toes, contestants have to push an opponent's foot to the other side of a specially constructed ring. The 1996 world champions were Alan Nash and Shirleen Whitehead.

## Wife carrying
The World Wife Carrying Championships are held annually in Sonkajärvi, Finland, over a 235-m (771-ft) long obstacle course. The fastest time is 1 min 6.2 sec by Jouni Jussila, carrying his wife Tiina, in 1996. It was the Jussilas' fourth success, having previously won in 1992, 1993 and 1994.

## Worm charming
The World Worm Charming Championship is held at Willaston, Cheshire, UK. On 5 July 1980, Tom Shufflebotham charmed 511 worms out of the ground in 30 minutes.

# Stunts

01:12:38

01:12:39

## High altitude antics

### Bungee jumping
The longest bungee was 249.9 m (820 ft) long and was used by Gregory Riffi, who made a jump from a helicopter above the Loire Valley, France, in Feb 1992. His cord stretched to 610 m (2,000 ft) during the jump.

### Crate climbing
Philip Bruce stacked 38 beer crates in a single column and climbed up them to a height of 9.65 m (31 ft 8 in) at Sowerby Bridge, W Yorkshire, UK, on 26 Aug 1991.

### High diving
Col. Harry A. Froboess (Switzerland) jumped 120 m (394 ft) into Lake Constance from the airship Hindenburg on 22 June 1936.

The highest regularly performed head-first dives are those of professional divers from La Quebrada ('the break in the rocks') at Acapulco, Mexico, which is 26.7 m (87 ft 6 in) high. The water is 3.65 m (12 ft) deep.

The world record high dive from a diving board is 53.9 m (176 ft 10 in), by Olivier Favre of Switzerland at Villers-le-Lac, France, on 30 Aug 1987.

The women's record high dive from a diving board is 36.8 m (120 ft 9 in), by Lucy Wardle (USA) at Ocean Park, Hong Kong, China, on 6 April 1985.

The greatest height reported for a dive into an air bag is 99.4 m (326 ft), by stuntman Dan Koko, who jumped from the top of Vegas World Hotel and Casino in Las Vegas, Nevada, USA, on to a 6.1 x 12.2 x 4.2 m (20 x 40 x 14 ft) target on 13 Aug 1948. His impact speed was 141 km/h (88 mph).

**Right**
Göran Eliason (Sweden) breaking the world two-wheel speed record over 100 m.

### Largest human mobile
In 1996, 16 performers from *The Circus of Horrors*, based at Addlestone Moor, Surrey, UK, were suspended from a crane to form a human mobile in Munich, Germany.

### Tightrope walking
The greatest ever drop over which anyone has walked on a tightrope is 3,150 m (10,335 ft), above the French countryside, by Michel Menin of Lons-le-Saunier, France, on 4 Aug 1989.

### Tightrope endurance
In 1993, Jorge Ojeda-Guzman of Orlando, Florida, USA, walked, balanced and danced on a 11-m (36-ft) long wire, 10.7 m (35 ft)

above the ground for a record 205 days. His main luxury was a 91 x 91-cm (3 x 3-ft) wooden cabin at the end of the tightrope.

On 1 Nov 1985, Ashley Brophy of Neilborough, Victoria, Australia, took 3½ hours to walk 11.57 km (7 miles 329 yd) on a wire that was 45 m (147 ft 8 in) long and 10 m (32 ft 10 in) above the ground at the Adelaide Grand Prix, Australia.

### Wing walking
Roy Castle, host of the *Record Breakers* TV programme from 1972 to 1993, flew on the wing of a Boeing Stearman biplane for 3 hr 23 min on 2 Aug 1990 from Gatwick, W Sussex, UK, to Le Bourget, France.

# LONGEST 'WHEELIE' 331 KM

## SIGNALS CORPS OF THE INDIAN ARMY IN FEB 1996

`01:12:40`

## Vehicular feats

### Bicycle wheelie
On 2 Dec 1995, Leandro Henrique Basseto did a bicycle wheelie for 10 hr 40 min 8 sec at Madaguari, Paraná, Brazil.

### Two-side wheel driving
Bengt Norberg of Äppelbo, Sweden, drove a Mitsubishi Colt GTi-16V on two side wheels non-stop for 310.391 km (192 miles 1,525 yd) in 7 hr 15 min 50 sec. He also drove 44.808 km (27 miles 1,480 yd) in one hour at Rattvik Horse Track, Sweden. Both records were set on 24 May 1989.

On 20 April 1996, Göran Eliason (Sweden) achieved a speed of 179.29 km/h

established a world record with a pyramid of 140 men on 11 motorcycles at Jabalpur, India. They travelled 200 m (218 yd).

### Motorcycle wheelie
Yasuyuki Kudō rode 331 km (205 7/10 miles) non-stop on the rear wheel of his Honda TLM220R motorcycle at the Japan Automobile Research Institute Proving Ground, Tsukuba, near Tsuchiura, Japan, on 5 May 1991.

The highest speed attained on a back wheel of a motorcycle is 254.07 km/h (157.87 mph) by Jacky Vranken (Belgium) on a Suzuki GSXR 1100 at St Truiden military airfield, Belgium, on 8 Nov 1992.

## Movie stunts

### Earliest stunt professionals
The first stuntman was ex-US cavalryman Frank Hanaway, who won himself a part in Edwin S. Porter's *The Great Train Robbery* (USA, 1903) for his ability to fall off a horse without injuring himself.

The first professional stuntwoman was Helen Gibson, who doubled for Helen Holmes in the first 26 episodes of Kalem's serial *The Hazard's of Helen* (USA, 1914).

### Highest jump without a parachute
The highest jump without a parachute by a movie stuntman was 70.71 m (232 ft), by A.J. Bakunus, doubling for Burt Reynolds in *Hooper* (USA, 1978).

### Greatest free fall
The greatest height a stuntman has leaped from in a free fall was 335 m (1,100 ft), by Dar Robinson from a ledge at the summit of the CN Tower, Toronto, Canada, for a scene in the film *Highpoint*. His parachute opened 91 m (300 ft) from the ground after six seconds of freefall. The $150,000 (£90,000) fee is a record payment for a stunt.

### Longest leap in a car
The longest leap in a car propelled by its own engine was performed by Gary Davis in the film *Smokey and the Bandit II*. Davis raced a stripped-down Plymouth up a ramp at 128 km/h (80 mph) and described a trajectory of 49.6 m (163 ft) before landing safely on the desert floor.

**Left**
The greatest distances in ramp jumping have been achieved by motorcycles rather then cars. Doug Danger managed to ramp jump a distance of 76.5 m (251 ft) on a 1991 Honda CR500 in 1991. This compares with the 70.73 m (232 ft) achieved by Jacqueline De Creed in a 1967 Ford Mustang in 1983.

## IS 53.9 M, BY OLIVIER FAVRE, ON 30 AUG 1987

(111.4 mph) over a 100-m flying start on the two wheels of a Volvo 850 Turbo at the Swedish Air Force airport F7, Lidköping.

Sven-Erik Söderman (Sweden) achieved a record speed for the flying kilometre of 152.96 km/h (95.04 mph) at the Swedish Air Force airport F7, Lidköping, Sweden, on 24 Aug 1990.

On 19 May 1991, Söderman drove a Daf 2800 7.5-ton truck on two wheels for 10.83 km (6 miles 1,284 yd) at Mora Siljan airport.

### Most people on one motorcycle
On 15 Dec 1995, 47 members of the Army Corps of Brasília, Brazil, rode on one 1200-cc Harley Davidson.

### Motorcycle pyramid
On 14 Feb 1996, the 'Dare Devils' team from the Signals Corps of the Indian army

### Ramp jumping in a car
The longest ever ramp jump in a car (with the car landing on its wheels and being driven on) is 70.73 m (232 ft), by Jacqueline De Creed in a 1967 Ford Mustang at Santa Pod Raceway, Beds, UK, on 3 April 1983.

### Ramp jumping on a motorcycle
The longest distance ever achieved for motorcycle long-jumping is 76.5 m (251 ft), by Doug Danger on a 1991 Honda CR500 at Loudon, New Hampshire, USA, on 22 June 1991.

### Wall of death
The greatest endurance feat on a 'wall of death' was 7 hr 0 min 13 sec, by Martin Blume at Berlin, Germany, on 16 April 1983. He rode a Yamaha XS 400 over 12,000 laps on a wall which had a diameter of 10 m (33 ft), averaging 45 km/h (30 mph) for the 292 km (181½ miles).

**Left**
Sixteen performers from *The Circus of Horrors* are suspended from a crane to form the world's largest human mobile. They performed the feat on 6 Dec 1996 over the Bavaria statue in Munich, Germany.

## Dexterity

### Apple peeling
The longest single unbroken apple peel on record is one of 52.51 m (172 ft 4 in), peeled by Kathy Wafler of Wolcott, New York, USA, in 11 hr 30 min at Long Ridge Mall, Rochester, New York, USA, on 16 Oct 1976. The apple weighed 567 g (20 oz).

### Beer stein carrying
Duane Osborn covered 15 m (49 ft 2½ in) in 3.65 seconds with five full steins in each hand at Cadillac, Michigan, USA, in 1992.

### Cucumber slicing
Norman Johnson of Blackpool College, Lancs, UK, set a record of 13.4 seconds for

movements) from a single piece of noodle dough in a record time of 59.29 seconds during the Singapore Food Festival on 31 July 1994. This works out at a rate of more than 138 noodles per second.

### Omelette making
The greatest recorded number of two-egg omelettes made in 30 minutes is 427, by Howard Helmer at the International Poultry Trade Show held at Atlanta, Georgia, USA, on 2 Feb 1990.

### Onion peeling
On 6 July 1980, Alan St Jean peeled 22.67 kg (50 lb) of onions in 3 min 18 sec in Plainfield, Connecticut, USA.

knives is 482.8 kg (1,064 lb 6 oz) net, by Marj Killian, Terry Anderson, Barbara Pearson, Marilyn Small and Janene Utkin at the 64th Annual Idaho Spud Day celebration, held at Shelley, Idaho, USA, on 19 Sept 1992.

### Winkling
The world's fastest winkler is Sheila Bance who picked 50 shells with a straight pin in 1 min 30.55 sec at the European Food and Drink Fair at Rochester, Kent, UK, on 7 May 1993.

## Projectiles

### Champagne cork fight
The longest flight of a cork from an untreated and unheated champagne bottle 1.22 m (4 ft) from level ground is 54.18 m (177 ft 9 in). The feat was achieved by Prof. Emeritus Heinrich Medicus at the Woodbury Vineyards Winery, New York, USA, on 5 June 1988.

### Custard pies
Traditionally, this is the pie used in slapstick comedies. At first the pies used were the real thing, but they tended to disintegrate. A patisserie, Greenberg's in Glendale, California, USA, came up with a solution—a pie with a double pastry thickness filled with flour, water and whipped cream. The filling came in two flavours; blackberry if the recipient was a blonde, lemon for a brunette, to show up better on black and white film.

slicing a 30.5-cm (12-in) long cucumber with a diameter of 3.8 cm (1½ in), at 22 slices to the inch (a total 264 slices) at the studios of Westdeutsche Rundfunk in Cologne, Germany, on 3 April 1983.

### Egg shelling
Two kitchen hands, Harold Witcomb and Gerald Harding, shelled a record 1,050 dozen eggs in a 7¼-hour shift at Bowyers, Trowbridge, Wilts, UK, on 23 April 1971. Both men were blind.

### Egg and spoon racing
Dale Lyons of Meriden, W Midlands, UK, ran the London marathon while carrying a dessert spoon with a fresh egg on it in 3 hours 47 min on 23 April 1990.

### Noodle making
Simon Sang Koon Sung of Singapore holds the world record for noodle making. He made 8,192 noodle strings ($2^{13}$ strings in 13

On 28 Oct 1980, under revised rules stipulating that a minimum of 50 onions have to be peeled, Alfonso Salvo of York, Pennsylvania, USA, peeled 22.67 kg (50 lb) of onions (52 onions) in a record time of 5 min 23 sec.

### Oyster opening
The world record for opening oysters is 100 in a time of 2 min 20.07 sec, by Mike Racz at Invercargill, New Zealand, on 16 July 1990.

### Pancake tossing
The greatest recorded number of times a pancake has been tossed in two minutes is 349, by Dean Gould at Felixstowe, Suffolk, UK, on 14 Jan 1995.

### Potato peeling
The greatest quantity of potatoes peeled by five people in 45 minutes to an institutional cookery standard with standard kitchen

### Biggest custard pie fight
The largest number of pies thrown in a custard pie sequence was 3,000 in the Laurel and Hardy two-reeler *The Battle of the Century* (USA, 1927).

### First filmed ballistic custard pie
Mabel Normand first threw a custard pie at Fatty Arbuckle in the film *A Noise from the Deep* (USA, 1913). In subsequent pictures Mabel was generally the recipient of Arbuckle's pies. Arbuckle had an unerring aim and an extraordinary physical dexterity that enabled him to hurl two pies at once in opposite directions.

## Gluttony
By public demand *The Guinness Book of Records* has reintroduced eating records— not marathon feats of gluttony but short, timed challenges in which the emphasis is on fun. No attempts lasting more than five

# MOST CUSTARD PIES THROWN 3,000

## IN JUST THREE MINUTES

## COLD BAKED BEANS IN FIVE MINUTES USING A COCKTAIL STICK, IN 1996

**Left**
A scene from the 1927 silent film *The Battle of the Century* starring Stan Laurel and Oliver Hardy. The two-reel film had the largest ever sequence of a custard pie fight. In all, 3,000 pies were used.

minutes will be considered, and most food and drink records are less than one minute in duration. These wacky new-style eating records are thus within challenging distance of any healthy adult with a large appetite and a sense of the ridiculous.

The new time restrictions limit the consumption of food or drink to safe quantities, and the categories of food in which challenges will be considered are strictly limited. Would-be record breakers are warned that attempts to break eating and drinking records can only be considered if they adhere to the guidelines which should be obtained in advance from Guinness Publishing Ltd. Challenges should only be made in controlled conditions and in the presence of a doctor.

### HEALTH WARNING
Attempts to break these records or set new records for eating or drinking can be dangerous to health, or even fatal, and medical advice should always be taken before attempting any of these records. In no circumstances will Guinness Publishing Ltd have any liability for death or injury suffered in record attempts. Guinness Publishing Ltd has complete discretion whether or not to include any particular records in the book.

### Baked bean eating
At London Zoo on 18 Nov 1996, Andy Szebini, of London, UK, ate 226 cold baked beans off a plate in five minutes using a cocktail stick, breaking his previous record.

### Tinned pea eating
On 29 Jan 1997, Jago Lee of London, UK, ate 152 cold tinned peas in three minutes, picking them up with a cocktail stick.

There are similar three-minute challenges for the following categories:

The record for eating single grains of boiled rice out of a dish using chopsticks.

The record for eating the most seedless grapes off a plate using a teaspoon.

The record for eating the most sweetcorn off a plate using a cocktail stick.

There is also a challenge for the quickest time taken to eat three cream crackers.

### Barbecue
The record attendance at a barbecue was 44,158, at Warwick Farm Racecourse, Sydney, NSW, Australia, on 10 Oct 1993.

The most meat eaten at a barbecue was at the Lancaster Sertoma Club's Chicken Bar-B-Que at Lancaster, Pennsylvania, USA, on 21 May 1994, when 19.96 tonnes (44,010 lb) of meat and 31,500 chicken halves were eaten in eight hours.

# The circus

**Right**
The world's largest gathering of clowns, at Bognor Regis, W Sussex, UK. This convention has been held annually since 1946 by Clowns International, which is the oldest and largest clown organization in the world.

## Acrobatic feats

### Aerial trapeze
The highest trapeze act was performed by Mike Howard (GB) at an altitude of between 6,000 and 6,200 m (19,600 and 20,300 ft), from a hot-air balloon over Glastonbury and Street, Somerset, UK, on 10 Aug 1995.

### Back somersaults
The back somersault record is a quadruple back, achieved by Miguel Vásquez (Mexico) to Juan Vásquez at Ringling Bros. and Barnum & Bailey Circus, Tucson, Arizona, USA, on 10 July 1982.

The greatest number of consecutive triple back somersaults successfully carried out is 135, achieved by Jamie Ibarra (Mexico) to Alejandro Ibarra, between 23 July and 12 Oct 1989, at various locations in the USA.

### Risley
The first back somersault feet-to-feet was performed by Richard Risley Carlisle and his son, after whom the feat was named at the Theatre Royal, Edinburgh, UK, in Feb 1844.

### Quadruple somersaults
The youngest person to achieve a quadruple somersault was Pak Yong Suk (North Korea) of the Pyongyang Circus troupe, in the Monte Carlo Circus Festival, Monaco, in Feb 1997, when aged 15.

### Flexible pole
The first publicly performed quadruple back somersault on the flexible pole was accomplished by Maxim Dobrovitsky (USSR) and the Egorov Troupe at the

**Right**
Coco the clown was famous for his enormous size 58 boots. His feet are seen here at a Royal Charity Performance of the Bertram Mills Circus, at Olympia, London, UK. Opposite his feet can be seen those of Queen Elizabeth.

International Circus Festival of Monte Carlo in Monaco on 4 Feb 1989. Corina Colonelu Mosoianu (Romania) is the only person to have performed the feat of a triple full twisting somersault, on 17 April 1984, at Madison Square Garden, New York, USA.

### Skipping
Walfer Guerrero (Colombia) achieved 521 consecutive turns skipping on a tightrope at Circus Carré in Haarlem, Netherlands, on 1 June 1995.

## Stunts

### Human cannonball
The first human cannonball was 'Zazel' in 1877. She was shot about 6.1 m (30 ft) at Westminster Aquarium, London, UK.

David Smith (USA) was fired a record distance of 54.94 m (180 ft) at Manville, New Jersey, USA, on 13 Aug 1995.

### Human arrow
Vesta Gueschkova of Bulgaria was fired from a crossbow a distance of 22.9 m (75 ft) at Ringling Bros. and Barnum & Bailey Circus, Tampa, Florida, USA, on 27 Dec 1995.

### Human pyramid
Tahar Douis supported the heaviest ever human pyramid—771 kg (1,700 lb) in weight. This consisted of twelve members of the Hassani Troupe, three levels in height, at the BBC TV studios, Birmingham, W Midlands, UK, on 17 Dec 1979.

The highest human pyramid was 12 m (39 ft), set when Josep-Joan Martínez Lozano of the Colla Vella dels Xiquets mounted a 9-high pyramid at Valls, Spain, on 25 Oct 1981.

### Plate spinning
The greatest number of plates spun simultaneously is 108, achieved by Dave Spathaky of London, UK, for the *Tarm Pai Du* television programme in Thailand on 23 Nov 1992.

### Stilt-walking
The tallest stilts ever mastered were made of aluminium and measured 12.43 m (40 ft 9½ in) from ground to ankle. Eddy Wolf ('Steady Eddy') of Loyal, Wisconsin, USA, used them to walk a distance of 25 steps without touching his safety handrail wires on 3 Aug 1988. The stilts weighed 25.9 kg (57 lb) each and were also the heaviest ever mastered.

### Unicycling
German unicyclist Rudy Horn was the first person to throw six cups and saucers with his feet and balance them on his head while mounted on a unicycle—finally adding a teaspoon and a lump of sugar. He did this at Bertram Mills Circus, London, UK, in 1952.

## Animal acts

### Horseback riding
The record for consecutive somersaults on horseback is 23, achieved by James Robinson (USA) at Spalding & Rogers Circus, Pittsburgh, Pennsylvania, USA, in 1856.

### Horse riding—back somersault
Lucio Cristiani (Italy) did a back somersault from the back of a horse to the back of a

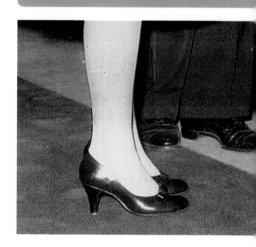

# 108 PLATES SPUN SIMULTANEOUSLY

## FEET AND BALANCED THEM ON HIS HEAD WHILE MOUNTED ON A UNICYCLE

third horse galloping in line at Cirque Medrano, Paris, France, in 1932. With his brothers, Daviso and Oscar, the three riders, using four horses, each simultaneously did a forward somersault to the horse in front.

### Wild animal presentations
Willy Hagenbeck (Germany) worked with 70 polar bears in a presentation at the Paul Busch Circus, Berlin, Germany, in 1904.

Clyde Raymond Beatty (USA) handled 43 lions and tigers simultaneously in 1938.

## Clowns
### Largest gathering of clowns
The largest gathering of clowns in the world was at Bognor Regis, W Sussex, UK, in 1991. There were 850 clowns, including 430 from North America.

### Most clown routines
The most inventive clown was Charlie Cairoli who, with his father, between 1927 and 1937 at the Cirque Medrano, Paris, devised over 700 different routines. He did 40 consecutive seasons at the Blackpool Tower Circus, UK, without repeating a routine in more than one season.

### Largest boots
The circus clown with the largest boots was Coco (Nicolai Poliakoff). He took a size 58.

### Oldest clowns
Many clowns have lived, and performed, to a great age. Grock, Coco and Otto Griebling all worked until aged 74, and Whimsical Walker and Lou Jacobs until they were over 80. But the record is held jointly by Charlie Rivel (Spain) and, still performing, Guggele (Arnold Schmidt, Denmark) at 87.

## Performers and audiences
### Largest circus audience
The largest audience for a circus was 52,385, for Ringling Bros. and Barnum & Bailey, at the Superdome, New Orleans, Louisiana, USA, on 14 Sept 1975.

The largest circus audience in a tent was 16,702 (15,686 paid), also for Ringling Bros. and Barnum & Bailey, at Concordia, Kansas, USA, on 13 Sept 1924.

### Greatest number of performers
The greatest number of performers to take part in a circus act was 263, in the 1890 Barnum & Bailey Circus during its tour of the USA. The circus used a total of around 175 animals.

The record number of performers for an animal-free circus is 61, for Cirque du Soleil on their tour of Japan in 1992.

### Most circus artists
Russia has about 15,000 circus artists, more than any other country.

## Circus edifices
### Oldest circus building
The oldest permanent circus building is Cirque d'Hiver, which opened in Paris, France, on 11 Dec 1852.

### Newest circus building
The newest building used to stage circus shows was constructed in 1993 at the Treasure Island Hotel, Las Vegas, USA.

## BULGARIA WAS FIRED FROM A GIANT CROSSBOW A DISTANCE OF 22.9 M

### Largest big tops
The largest travelling circus tent of all time belonged to Ringling Bros. and Barnum & Bailey and was used on US tours between 1921 and 1924. It covered an area of 8,492 m$^2$ (2.10 acres), consisting of a round top 61 m (200 ft) in diameter with five middle sections each 18 m (60 ft) wide.

The two largest big tops in current use are erected by Carson & Barnes Circus and Clyde Beatty-Cole Brothers in the USA. They are 120.7 m (396 ft) by 37.8 m (124 ft). The Carson & Barnes tent is erected at a new location seven days a week, for 36 continuous weeks every year.

# Oldest record breakers

## Arts and entertainment

### Authors

Sarah Louise Delany's second book, *The Delany Sisters' Book of Everyday Wisdom*, was published in 1994, when she was 105 years old. Her sister and co-author, A. Elizabeth Delany, was 103.

### Ballroom dancing

The oldest competitive ballroom dancer was Albert J. Sylvester (1889–1989) of Corsham, Wilts, UK, who retired at the age of 94. In addition to being a record-breaking ballroom dancer, he was the personal secretary to Prime Minister Lloyd-George.

### Directors

The Dutch director Joris Ivens directed the Franco-Italian co-production, *Une Histoire de Vent*, in 1988 at the age of 89. He had made his directorial debut with the Dutch film *De Brug* in 1928.

### Singers

Ukranian bass Mark Reizen became the oldest opera singer on his 90th birthday on 3 July 1985, when he sang the substantial role of Prince Gremin in Tchaikovsky's *Eugene Onegin* at the Bolshoi Theatre, Moscow, Russia.

Clarissa Lee (b. 1892) has been a chorister at St Mary and St Andrew Church, Pitminster, Somerset, UK, since 1914 and still sings with the choir every week.

### Tightrope walking

The world's oldest ever tightrope walker was 'Professor' William Ivy Baldwin (1866–1953), who crossed the South Boulder Canyon, Colorado, USA, on a 97.5-m (320-ft) wire with a 38.1-m (125-ft) drop on his 82nd birthday on 31 July 1948.

### Hot air balloon flight

On 26 Sept 1996, Florence Laine made a hot air balloon trip near Christchurch, New Zealand, at the age of 102 years 92 days.

### Circumnavigational flights

Fred Lasby completed a solo round-the-world flight at the age of 82 in his single-engined Piper Comanche. Leaving Fort Myers, Florida, USA, on 30 June 1994 he flew 37,366 km (23,218 miles) westwards, stopping 21 times, arriving back at Fort Myers on 20 Aug 1994.

### Pilots

Col. Clarence Cornish (USA) was still flying aircraft at the age of 97. He made his first flight on 6 May 1918 and his first solo flight 21 days later. The last aircraft that he piloted was a Cessna 172, on 4 Dec 1995.

Hilda Wallace of West Vancouver, British Columbia, Canada, became the oldest person to qualify as a pilot when she obtained her licence on 15 March 1989 at the age of 80 years 109 days.

### Oldest passenger

Charlotte Hughes (1877–1993) of Redcar, N Yorkshire, UK, made a flight in Feb 1992 when she was 115 years old.

### Solo transatlantic crossing

The oldest person who ever sailed solo across the Atlantic was Michael Richey (GB) in 1996. He was aged 79 years 36 days, and the crossing took him 55 days.

### Motorcycling

Len Vale-Onslow (b. 1900) of Birmingham, UK, is still riding a motorcycle of his own design, the Super Onslow Special. He has been riding motorcycles for 87 years.

Hollywood's oldest ever director was George Cukor, who was 81 years old when he made his 50th film, *Rich and Famous*, in 1981.

### Screen performers

The oldest screen performer ever to have appeared in a speaking role in a film was Jeanne Louise Calment (b. 1875), who was 114 years old when she portrayed herself in the 1990 Canadian film *Vincent and Me*, a fantasy about a young time-traveller.

British actress Dame Gwen Ffrancon-Davies appeared in the Sherlock Holmes TV movie *The Master Blackmailer* (1991) at the age of 100. She died a month after the screening.

## Travel and exploration

### Parachuting

Edwin C. Townsend is the oldest man ever to make a parachute jump. He parachuted at the age of 89, at Vermillion Bay, Louisiana, USA, on 5 Feb 1986.

Sylvia Brett (GB), was 80 years 166 days when she parachuted at Cranfield, Beds, UK, on 23 Aug 1986.

### Polar exploration

Major Will Lacy went to the North Pole on 9 April 1990 at the age of 82 and the South Pole on 20 Dec 1991 at the age of 84. He went on each occasion by light aircraft.

### Wall of death

Jerry De Roye (b. 1927) still regularly performs on the wall of death riding a 1927 Indian Type 101 'Scout'.

### Driving

Layne Hall (b. 1880 or 1884) of Silver Creek, New York, USA, was issued with a driving licence on 15 June 1989. The licence was valid until his 113th birthday in 1993. However he died on 20 Nov 1990.

Edward Newsom (died 1997) of Brighton, E Sussex, UK, was still driving on his 105th birthday on 22 July 1996. Newsom bought his first car, a Model T Ford, in 1914.

# OLDEST BRIDEGROOM 103

YEARS OLD

**102**

Gerty Edwards Land (b. 1897) passed the Department of Transport driving test on 27 April 1988 in Colne, Lancs, UK, aged 90 years 229 days.

## Marriage and divorce
### Brides
The oldest bride on record is Minnie Munro, who was 102 years old when she married Dudley Reid, aged 83, at Point Clare, NSW, Australia, on 31 May 1991.

Mrs Winifred Clark (b. 1871) married Albert Smith, aged 80, in Cantley, S Yorkshire, UK, on the eve of her 100th birthday.

### Bridegrooms
The oldest bridegroom on record is Harry Stevens, aged 103, who married Thelma

STERN WERE 97 AND 91 YEARS OLD WHEN THEY WERE DIVORCED IN 1984

**105**

**122**

Lucas, 84, at the Caravilla Retirement Home, Wisconsin, USA, on 3 Dec 1984.

British bridegroom George Jameson was 102 when he married Julie Robinson, 53, at Honiton, Devon, UK, on 10 March 1995.

### Divorced couples
The record combined age for a divorced couple is 188, set when a divorce was granted to Simon Stern, 97 years old, and his wife, Ida, aged 91, in Milwaukee, Wisconsin, USA, on 2 Feb 1984.

The British record is 166, set when 101-year-old Harry Bidwell of Brighton, E Sussex, UK, divorced his 65-year-old wife in Nov 1980.

## Public office
### Heads of state
The oldest head of state alive today is Nouhak Phoumsavanh (b. 9 April 1914), who is president of Laos.

The oldest prime minister, El Hadji Muhammad el Mokri, Grand Vizier of Morocco, is said to have been 116 Muslim years (112½ Gregorian years) old when he died in Sept 1957.

Morarji Ranchhodji Desai of India was first appointed as prime minister in 1977 when he was aged 81.

### Ordination
Fr Harold Riley (b. 1903) was ordained a Roman Catholic priest at the age of 91 in 1995 by Cardinal Basil Hume.

**Top**
102-year-old Minnie Munro married Dudley Reid, 19 years her junior, in 1991.

**Middle**
Edward Newsom, of Brighton, E Sussex, UK, who was still driving a car on his 105th birthday.

**Bottom**
Jeanne Louise Calment, the world's oldest living person, was 114 when she played herself in the 1990 Canadian film *Vincent and Me*, a modern-day fantasy about a young girl who travels through time to the 19th century to meet Vincent van Gogh. Ms Calment is the last person alive to have met the artist.

# Youngest record breakers

## Awards and Prizes
### Bravery
In 1989, Kristina Stragauskaitė of Lithuania was awarded a medal 'For Courage in Fire' when she was just four years 252 days old, after saving the lives of her younger brother and sister in a fire at her family home.

The youngest person to have received an official gallantry award is Julius Rosenberg of Winnipeg, Canada, who was given the Medal of Bravery on 30 March 1994. On 20 Sept 1992, the five-year-old saved his three-year-old sister from a black bear by growling at the creature.

### Nobel prize for physics
Prof Sir Lawrence Bragg (GB) won the 1915 physics prize at the age of 25, for work done when he was aged 23.

### Nobel prize for chemistry
The Nobel prize for chemistry was won by Theodore W. Richards of the USA in 1914 when he was 23.

### Victoria Cross
Andrew Fitzgibbon of the Indian Medical Services was 15 years old 100 days when he was awarded a VC for bravery at the Taku Forts in northern China on 21 Aug 1860.

### Chess Grand Masters
On 22 March 1997, Etienne Bacrot (France) became the youngest individual to qualify as an International Grand Master, when he was aged 14 years 59 days.

### Chess World Championships
Gary Kimovich Kasparov (USSR, now Russia) was the youngest to win the men's title on 9 Nov 1985, at 22 years 210 days.

## Education
### Graduate
In June 1994, Michael Kearney (US) became the world's youngest graduate at the age of 10 years 4 months, when he obtained his BA from the University of South Alabama, USA.

In July 1992, Ganesh Sittampalam became Britain's youngest graduate this century, at the age of 13 years 5 months.

### Undergraduate
In the United Kingdom, the record for the youngest undergraduate is 10 years 4 months, by Alexander Hill (1785–1867), who entered St Andrews University, in November 1795, and by William Thomson (1824–1907), later Lord Kelvin, who entered Glasgow University in Oct 1834.

**Right**
Ganesh Sittampalam, Britain's youngest graduate this century, obtained his mathematics degree in July 1992 from the University of Surrey, at the age of 13 years 5 months. He is also the youngest to have passed an A-level—achieving a grade A in Maths and Further Maths aged nine.

In February 1994, Matthew Trout of Upholland, Lancs, UK, became the youngest British undergraduate this century when at the age of 10 years 10 months he began an Open University mathematics course which leads to a degree in mathematics.

### Doctor
On 19 May 1995, Balamurali Ambati of Hollis Hills, New York, USA , became the world's youngest doctor when he graduated from the Mount Sinai School of Medicine in New York at the age of 17.

### Doctorate
On 13 April 1814, the mathematician Carl Witte of Lochau was made a Doctor of Philosophy of the University of Giessen, in Germany—at the time he was 12 years old.

### Professor
Colin Maclaurin was 19 years old when he was elected to Marischal College, Aberdeen, Scotland, as Professor of Mathematics on 30 Sept 1717. In 1725 he was made Professor of Mathematics at Edinburgh University on the recommendation of Sir Isaac Newton, who had become a professor at the University of Cambridge at the age of 26.

Henry Phillpotts became a don at Magdalen College, Oxford, in 1795 at the age of 17.

### A-level pass
Ganesh Sittampalam is the youngest person to have passed an A-level, achieving grade A

in both Mathematics and Further Mathematics in June 1988, at the age of nine years four months.

Michael Kearney of Mobile, Alabama, USA, received his high-school diploma—equivalent to A-levels in the UK—in June 1990, at the age of six years five months.

### GCSE pass
Sonali Pandya obtained a grade E pass in GCSE Computer Studies in June 1993 at the age of eight years two months.

## Politicians and Statesmen
### Youngest Head of State
Mswati III became the current king of Swaziland on 25 April 1986, aged 18.

### Monarchs
King John I of France became sovereign at his birth on 13 or 14 Nov 1316, but died on 19 Nov. King Alfonso XIII of Spain also became king at birth, on 17 May 1886.

King Hussein I of Jordan is the current head of state who ascended to the throne at the youngest age. He became king on 11 August 1952, aged 16 years 254 days.

### Prime Ministers
The youngest prime minister serving currently is Dr Mario Frick, who became Prime Minister of Liechtenstein at the age of 28 on 15 Dec 1993.

# YOUNGEST GRADUATE 10 YEARS 4 MONTHS

## AGED 14 YEARS 59 DAYS

### Male MP
Henry Long (1420–90) was returned for an Old Sarum seat at the age of 15. His precise date of birth is unknown. Minors were debarred from office under the law in 1695.

### Female MP
The youngest-ever woman MP was Josephine Bernadette Devlin, now Mrs McAliskey, who was elected for Mid Ulster (Independent Unity), aged 21 years 359 days on 17 April 1969.

## Artists
### Royal Academy exhibitor
The youngest exhibitor at the Royal Academy of Arts Annual Summer Exhibition was Lewis Melville 'Gino' Lyons. His *Trees and Monkeys*

At South Pole

## $5 MILLION PLUS 5% OF GROSS TAKINGS FOR *HOME ALONE II: LOST IN NEW YORK*

was painted on 4 June 1965, submitted on 17 March 1967 and exhibited on 29 April 1967—the day before his fifth birthday.

### Opera singer
The youngest singer ever to take an adult role in an opera was Ginetta Gloria La Bianca, who sang the part of Gilda in Verdi's *Rigoletto* when she was aged 15 years 316 days at Velletri, Italy, on 24 March 1950.

### Highest earning performer
Child star Macaulay Culkin was paid the sum of $1 million (£550,000) for the film *My Girl* (1991) at the age of 11. This was followed by a contract for $5 million (£3.3 million) plus 5% of gross for *Home Alone II: Lost in New York* (1992). Culkin's fee for *Richie Rich* (1994) was thought to be $8 million (£5 million).

## Adventurers
### Solo transatlantic sailing
In 1976 David Sandeman became the youngest to sail singlehandedly across the Atlantic aged 17 years 176 days.

### Solo transatlantic rowing
Sean Crowley was aged 25 years 306 days when he singlehandedly rowed across the Atlantic in 1988.

### Visits to both poles
Robert Schumann became the youngest person ever to go to the North Pole on 6 April 1992 when he was aged 10 and the youngest to travel to the South Pole on 29 Dec 1993 at the age of 11.

At Basecamp

Morning exercise in Antarctica

**Left**
Robert Schumann is the youngest person to visit both poles. On the North Pole trip (top) he arrived and left by air, but on the South Pole trip (middle and bottom) he arrived by mountain bike (having flown to within a short distance of the pole), leaving by air.

# Durability and persistence

**Right**
In his job as tour guide, Brian Davis has mounted 334 of the 364 steps of the tower in the Houses of Parliament 6,292 times in 13 years to 1 March 1997. This is the equivalent to 38 ascents of Mt Everest.

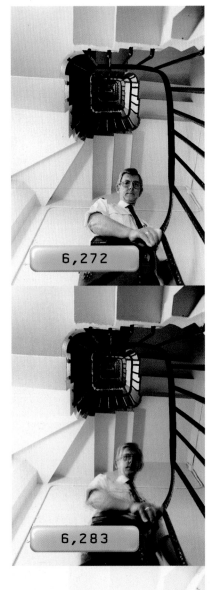

6,272

6,283

6,292

## Professional long service

### Snake milker
Over a 14-year period up to Dec 1965, Bernard Keyter, a supervisor at the South African Institute for Medical Research in Johannesburg, South Africa, personally milked 780,000 venomous snakes and obtained 3,960 litres (870 gallons) of venom. He was never bitten.

### Grave digging
Johann Heinrich Karl Thieme, sexton of Aldenburg, Germany, dug 23,311 graves during a 50-year career. In 1826 his own grave was dug by his understudy.

### Longest serving military pilot
Squadron Leader Norman E. Rose, AFC and bar, AMN (RAF Retd) flew military aircraft without a break in service for 47 years from 1942 to 1989, achieving 11,539 hours of flying in 54 different categories of aircraft. He learnt to fly in a de Havilland Tiger Moth in Southern Rhodesia (now Zimbabwe), and then flew Hawker Hurricanes in WWII.

### Most durable professor
Dr Joel Hildebrand, Professor Emeritus of Physical Chemistry at the University of California, Berkeley, USA, became an assistant professor in 1913. He published his 275th research paper 68 years later.

### Most durable teacher
Medarda de Jesús León de Uzcátegui, alias La Maestra Chucha, has been teaching in Caracas, Venezuela, for 85 years. In 1911, at the age of 12, she and her two sisters set up a school named Modelo de Aplicación. Since marrying in 1942, she has run her own school from her home in Caracas.

### Longest pension
Millicent Barclay was born on 10 July 1872, three months after her father, Col. William Barclay died. She immediately became eligible for a Madras Military Fund pension to continue until her marriage. She died unmarried on 26 Oct 1969, having drawn the pension for every day of her life of 97 years 3 months.

### Stair climbing
Brian Davis, a tour guide at the House of Commons, has climbed 334 of the steps of the tower in the Houses of Parliament 6,292 times in 13 years to 1 March 1997.

## Politicians and leaders

### Members of Parliament
Sir Francis Knollys was elected MP for Oxford in 1575 and died a sitting member for Reading 73 years later in 1648.

### Prime Ministers
The only British prime minister to win four successive general elections was Lord Liverpool, in 1812 (30 Sept–24 Nov), 1818 (11 June–4 Aug), 1820 (1 March–21 April) and 1826 (3 June–23 July).

### Longest term of office
The longest-serving prime minister of a sovereign state is Khalifa bin Sulman al-Khalifa of Bahrain, who had already been in office for 1½ years when Bahrain became independent in Aug 1971.

### Longest all-time reigns
Minhti, King of Arakan, now part of Myanmar (Burma), is reputed to have reigned for a total of 95 years between 1279 and 1374.

### Longest working career
Mr Izumi worked for 98 years. He began work goading draught animals at a sugar mill at Isen, Tokunoshima, Japan, in 1872, and retired as a sugar-cane farmer in 1970 at the age of 105.

### Longest in one job
The longest recorded industrial career in one job was that of Polly Gadsby, who started work with Archibald Turner & Co. of Leicester, UK, at the age of nine. In 1932, after 86 years' service, she was still at her bench wrapping elastic at the age of 95.

Theodore C. Taylor served 86 years with J. T. & J. Taylor of Batley, W Yorkshire, UK, including 56 years as company chairman.

The longest well-documented reign of any monarch is that of Phiops II (also known as Pepi II), or Neferkare, a Sixth-Dynasty pharaoh of ancient Egypt. His reign began c. 2281 BC, when he was six years of age, and is believed to have lasted c. 94 years.

### Longest current reigns
The King of Thailand, Bhumibol Adulyadej (Rama IX), is the longest-reigning monarch, having succeeded to the throne following the death of his older brother on 9 June 1946.

The most durable monarch is the King of Cambodia, Norodom Sihanouk, who first became King on 16 April 1941 but abdicated on 2 March 1955 and then returned to the throne on 24 Sept 1993.

# LONGEST MARRIAGE 86 YEARS

**ALIASES USED BY FRED JIPP OR NIKOLAI PERUSKOV, BETWEEN 1949 AND 1981**

## Performers
### Most durable musicians
The Romanian pianist Cella Delavrancea gave her last public recital at the age of 103. She received six encores.

The career of Yiannis Pipis of Nicosia, Cyprus, a professional folkloric violinist, lasted from 1912 to 1997.

The world's oldest active musician is Jennie Newhouse of High Bentham, N Yorkshire, UK, who has been the organist at the church of St Boniface in Bentham since 1920.

The Singing Webers still perform publicly after forming in 1926—a record span of 70 years. Brothers Ralph (84), Clayton (85), Paul (86) and Jacob (92), who sing in four-part harmony and play instruments, have recently been joined by another brother, Henry (91).

### Longest operatic career
Danshi Toyotake of Hyogo, Japan, sang Musume Gidayu (traditional Japanese narrative) for 91 years from the age of seven. She sang professionally for 81 years.

## Travellers
### Most experienced passenger
Edwin A. Shackleton of Bristol has flown as a passenger in 603 different types of aircraft. His first flight was in March 1943.

### Most flying hours
American John Edward Long logged a total of 62,654 flying hours as a pilot between May 1933 and April 1997—a cumulative total of more than seven years airborne.

## Marriages
### Most marriages
The greatest number of marriages contracted by one person in the monogamous world is 28, by former Baptist minister Glynn 'Scotty' Wolfe of Blythe, California, USA, who first married in 1927. He is currently separated from his 28th wife, but is hoping to marry again. He thinks that he has a total of 41 children.

The most monogamous marriages by a woman is 22, by Linda Essex of Anderson, Indiana, USA, who has had 15 husbands since 1957. Her most recent marriage was in Oct 1991, and ended in a divorce.

The most bigamous marriages is 104, by Giovanni Vigliotto, one of many aliases used by either Fred Jipp (b. New York City, 1936) or Nikolai Peruskov (b. Siracusa, Sicily, 1929) between 1949 and 1981 in 27 US states and 14 other countries.

The only British woman to contract eight legal marriages is Olive Wilson of Marston Green, Birmingham, UK. She has divorced all but one of her husbands.

### Longest engagement
Octavio Guillén and Adriana Martínez were engaged for 67 years. They finally got married in 1969 in Mexico City, Mexico, when they were both aged 82.

### Longest marriages
Sir Temulji Bhicaji Nariman and Lady Nariman were married for 86 years from 1853 to 1940. They were cousins and the marriage took place when both were aged five. Sir Temulji died in Aug 1940 in Bombay, India, aged 91 years 11 months.

**AT THE AGE OF 95, 86 YEARS AFTER SHE STARTED HER WORKING CAREER**

### Most hours as a passenger
Fred Finn has made 709 Atlantic crossings on Concorde. He commutes regularly between London, UK, and New Jersey, USA, and had flown a total distance of 19,247,750 km (11,960,000 miles) up to the end of May 1997.

Up to her retirement in 1988, Maisie Muir of Orkney flew over 8,400 times with Loganair in connection with business duties for the Royal Bank of Scotland.

### Driving test
On 19 June 1987, Git Kaur Randhawa of Hayes, London, UK, triumphed at her 48th attempt at the Department of Transport's driving test, after more than 330 lessons.

Lazarus Rowe and Molly Webber, both born in 1725, were recorded as marrying in 1743. Molly died first, in June 1829 at Limington, Maine, USA, after 86 years of marriage.

The longest marriage in the United Kingdom is 82 years between James Frederick Burgess and his wife Sarah Ann. They were married on 21 June 1883 at St James's, Bermondsey, London, UK. She died first on 22 June 1965.

### Best man
The world champion 'best man' is Ting Ming Siong, from Sibu, Sarawak, Malaysia, who served as best man at 1,089 weddings between Sept 1975 and March 1997.

# Mind and memory

## Mathematical problems

### Most difficult problem

The last theorem of Pierre de Fermat (1601–56) has led to more incorrect proofs than have been published for any other theorem. Andrew J. Wiles of Princeton University, USA, announced he had found a proof of the theorem in June 1993, but in Dec he issued a statement saying he was still working on a 'calculation' that was 'not yet complete'. All doubt was removed when Wiles presented a new proof in 1995.

In 1908, Dr Paul Wolfskehl left DM 100,000 (£34,500) in his will for the first person to solve Fermat's last theorem. As a result of currency fluctuations, it is now worth c. DM 10,000 (£3,450).

### Memorizing π (pi)

Hiroyuki Goto of Tokyo, Japan, recited pi from memory to 42,195 places at NHK Broadcasting Centre, Tokyo, in Feb 1995.

The British record is 20,013 places in 9 hr 10 min, by Creighton Herbert James Carvello at Saltscar Comprehensive School, Redcar, N Yorkshire, UK on 27 June 1980.

### Most accurate version of π (pi)

Pi was calculated to 6,442,450,000 decimal places by Professor Yasumasa Kanada of the University of Tokyo, Japan, who made two independent calculations by different methods and compared the results using a computer programme in 1995.

particularly talented at calculating decimal values and was able to remember the value of pi to 1,000 places.

Dutchman Willem Klein multiplied two 9-digit numbers in 48 seconds, and did six examples of multiplying two 10-digit numbers in an average 65.66 seconds.

### First child calculator

Zerah Colburn (1804–40) of Vermont, USA, was the first child calculating prodigy and

to multiply two 3 digit numbers. An account written when Buxton was still alive stated that he was asked to find the volume of a box of dimension 25,145,789 by 5,642,732 by 54,965 yards in units of cubic eighths of an inch. This took him five hours, during which time he worked in the fields.

### Calculation of square roots

John Wallis, an Oxford professor, was one of the most famous mathematicians of his day. In 1669 he extracted the square root of

## Calculation

### Fastest mental calculators

Johann Dase (1824–61) from Hamburg, Germany, was the fastest of all mental calculators. His feats included calculating pi to 205 places in his head, multiplying two 8-digit numbers in 54 seconds, two 20-digit numbers in six minutes and two 40-digit numbers in 40 minutes. Dase could not manage conventional mathematics and had no intelligence in other fields.

Italian Jacques Inaudi (1867–1950) could multiply two 4-digit numbers in 21 seconds.

In 1927, the blind mental calculator Louis Fleury (1893–1980), from Belfort, France, multiplied a 3-digit number by a 2-digit number in two seconds and a 3-digit number by a 3-digit number in 10 seconds.

Alexander Craig Aitken of New Zealand squared 57,586 in two seconds. Aitken

was the first to do mental calculation professionally. At the age of six he multiplied 12,225 by 1,223. Aged seven he took 10 seconds to calculate how many three-foot steps there are in 65 miles. Colburn became Professor of Latin, Greek, French, Spanish and English classical literature at Norwich University, Vermont, USA.

### Multiplication

George Parker Bidder (1806–78), known as 'The Calculating Boy', did not learn to read or write until he was 10 years old but, at this age he could remember 43 random numbers having read them once, and repeat them an hour later. He could multiply 257,689,435 by 356,875,649 in six minutes. By his late teens Safford had lost his amazing powers.

### Dimensions

Jedediah Buxton (1702–77) of Derbyshire, UK, could work out problems in his head over weeks or months. He took two minutes

3,000,000,000,000,000,000,000,000,000, 000,000,000,000,000,000 on 'a dark night, in bed, without pen, ink or paper, or anything equivalent' and then wrote it down the next day. Once, when asked for a demonstration of mental arithmetic, he took a random 55-digit number and obtained the 27-digit integer approximate square root.

Truman Safford (1836–1901) of Vermont, USA, began to exhibit calculating prowess at the age of six. Aged 10 he calculated the square of 365,365,365,365,365,365 and gave the 36-digit answer in under a minute.

### Integers

Leonhard Euler (1707–83), a Swiss German, was one of the greatest mathematicians of all time. One night he was unable to sleep, so he computed a table of the first six powers of the integers under 20, which he was able to recite days later.

# 257,689,435 X 356,875,649 IN 6 MIN

5 WHEN NO COPY OF THE MUSIC COULD BE FOUND FOR A PERFORMANCE

## Calendar

Thomas Fuller (1710–90), known as the 'Virginian Calculator', was an American slave who had great powers of mental calculation. When aged nearly 80 he calculated in 1½ minutes the number of seconds in the life of a man who had lived 70 years 17 days 12 hours. He replied 2,210,500,800. When challenged, he reminded the questioner of leap years.

## Memory

### Memorizing business records

In 1838, Bartholomew Parker Bidder (1809–49), a younger brother of George Parker Bidder, became an actuary to the Royal Exchange Assurance Company. When the firm's records were destroyed in a fire he was able to reconstruct them from memory in six months.

### Memorizing literature

Both the German mathematicians Gottfried Wilhelm Leibniz (1646–1716) and Leonhard Euler knew the *Aeneid* (Virgil's epic poem in 12 books) by heart.

Andre Marie Ampère (1775–1836), the French physicist, was able to repeat long passages from an encyclopedia on such diverse subjects as heraldry and falconry some 50 years after having read them.

Thomas Macaulay (1800–59), the English historian and essayist, could recite all of

**Left**
Dominic O'Brien set a new record for card-memorizing on 6 June 1996 when he was able to memorize a single pack of shuffled cards in 38.29 seconds at London Zoo, UK.

LIFE OF A MAN WHO HAD LIVED 70 YEARS 17 DAYS 12 HOURS IN 1½ MINUTES

Milton's 10-book epic poem *Paradise Lost* by the time he was 15.

The South African politician Jan Christian Smuts (1870–1950) memorized 5,000 books in his old age.

In May 1974, Bhanddanta Vicittabi Vumsa (1911–93) recited 16,000 pages of Buddhist canonical texts from memory in Rangoon, Myanmar (Burma).

### Memorizing music

After hearing the *Miserere* by Allegri, Wolfgang Amadeus Mozart (1756–91) could write a complete score from memory.

George Enescu (1881–1955), the Romanian violinist and composer, also had an extraordinary ability to remember scores. Once, when he was in rehearsal with Yehudi Menuhin, Maurice Ravel arrived with a new sonata for piano and violin. Enesco and

Ravel played the sonata. Enesco then closed his music and repeated the piece note-perfect from memory.

Arturo Toscanini (1867–1957), the Italian conductor, once wrote down Raff's *Quartet No. 5* from memory for the strings of his orchestra to perform because no copy of the music could be found for a performance in New York, USA.

### Memorizing cards

Dave Farrow (USA) memorized, on a single sighting, a random sequence of 52 separate packs of cards (2,704) (with six errors) all of which had been shuffled together, at the Guinness World of Records Museum, Niagara Falls, Canada, on 24 June 1996.

Dominic O'Brien from the United Kingdom was able to memorize a single pack of shuffled cards in 38.29 sec at London Zoo, UK, on 6 June 1996.

**Left**
Wolfgang Amadeus Mozart had an extraordinary ability to memorize music. After hearing the score of the nine-part *Miserere* by Allegri, kept secret by the Vatican, he returned to his room and wrote a complete score from memory. A second visit revealed a few incorrect notes.

Size

was cooked by representatives of Swatch at Yokohama, Japan, on 19 March 1994.

**Paella**
A 20-m (65-ft 7-in) diameter paella was made by Juan Carlos Galbis and a team of helpers in Valencia, Spain, on 8 March 1992. It was eaten by 100,000 people.

**Pizza**
A pizza 37.4 m (122 ft 8 in) in diameter was made at Norwood Hypermarket, Norwood, South Africa, on 8 Dec 1990.

**Popcorn**
The most popped-corn put in a container occupied a 211.41-m$^3$ (7,466-ft$^3$) box, filled at Pittsville Elementary School, Pittsville, Wisconsin, USA, in March 1996.

**Yorkshire pudding**
A 42-m$^2$ (452-ft$^2$) pudding was made by caterers of Rotherham Council, S Yorkshire, UK, in Aug 1991 to celebrate Yorkshire Day.

## Bread, cheese and garlic
### Loaves
On 6 Jan 1996, a 9,200-m (30,184-ft) *Rosca de Reyes*, a type of twisted loaf, was baked in Acapulco, Mexico.

The largest pan loaf weighed 1.43 tonnes (3,163 lb 10 oz) and measured 3 x 1.25 x 1.1 m (9 ft 10 in x 4 ft 1 in x 3 ft 7 in). It was baked by staff of Sasko in Johannesburg, South Africa, on 18 March 1988.

### Cheese
A 26.09-tonne (57,508-lb 8-oz) cheddar cheese was made on 7 Sept 1995 by Loblaws Supermarkets Limited and Agropur Dairies at Granby, Quebec, Canada.

### Garlic
A 45.7-m (149-ft 11-in) garlic plait was measured by Cheshire County Council Trading Standards officers, UK, on 12 Sept 1996.

## Meat
### Meat pie
The largest meat pie was a chicken pie made by KFC in New York City, USA, in Oct 1995. It weighed 10.06 tonnes (22,178 lb), was 3.66 m (12 ft) in diameter and was used to publicize the Chunky Chicken Pot Pie.

### Haggis
A 303.2-kg (668-lb 7-oz) haggis was made by the Troon Round Table, Burns Country Foods and a team of chefs at the Hilton Hotel, Glasgow, UK, on 24 May 1993.

**Hamburger**
A 2.5-tonne (5,520-lb) hamburger was made at the Outagamie County Fairgrounds, Seymour, Wisconsin, USA, on 5 Aug 1989.

**Kebab**
A 880.6-m (2,889-ft 3-in) kebab was made by the West Yorkshire Family Service Units, the Trade Association of Asian Restaurant Owners and National Power at Bradford, W Yorkshire, UK, on 19 June 1994.

**Salami**
A 20.95-m (68-ft 9-in) long salami weighing 676.9 kg (1,492 lb 5 oz), was made by staff of A/S Svindlands Pølsefabrikk at Flekkefjord, Norway, in July 1992.

**Sausage**
In April 1995, a 46.3-km (28-mile 1,355-yd) sausage was made by M & M Meat Shops in partnership with J.M. Schneider Inc. at Kitchener, Ontario, Canada.

## Dishes and fast food
### Lasagne
A 21.33 x 2.13-m (70 x 7-ft) lasagne was made by the Food Bank for Monterey County at Salinas, California, USA, on 14 Oct 1993. It weighed 3.71 tonnes (8,188 lb 8 oz).

### Omelette
The largest ever omelette covered 128.5 m$^2$ (1,383 ft$^2$) and contained 160,000 eggs. It

## Desserts
### Apple pie
The largest apple pie ever baked was made by ITV chef Glynn Christian in a 12.2 x 7 m (40 x 23 ft) dish at Hewitts Farm, Chelsfield, Kent, UK, in Aug 1982.

### Cherry pie
A cherry pie containing 16.69 tonnes (36,800 lb) of cherry filling and measuring 6.1 m (20 ft) in diameter was baked by Oliver Rotary Club members at Oliver, British Columbia, Canada, on 14 July 1990.

### Jelly
A 35,000-litre (7,700-gal) jelly, made by Paul Squires and Geoff Ross, was set in a tank at Roma Street Forum, Brisbane, Queensland, Australia, in Feb 1981.

### Ice-cream sundae
A sundae made by Palm Dairies Ltd at Alberta, Canada, on 24 July 1988, had 20.27 tonnes (44,689 lb 8 oz) of ice-cream, 4.39 tonnes (9,688 lb 2 oz) of syrup and 243.7 kg (537 lb 3 oz) of topping.

### Strawberry bowl
The world's largest bowl of strawberries, which had a net weight of 2.39 tonnes (5,266 lb), was filled at the Kitchener-Waterloo Hospital, Ontario, Canada, on 29 June 1993. The strawberries had been picked at Joe Moss Farms, Ontario, Canada.

# LONGEST LOAF 9,200 M

**Christmas pudding**
A 3.28-tonne (7,231-lb 1-oz) pudding was made by the villagers of Aughton, Lancs, UK, and unveiled at the Famous Aughton Pudding Festival in July 1992.

**Banana split**
A 7.32-km (4-mile 964-yd) banana split was made by residents of Selinsgrove, Pennsylvania, USA, on 30 April 1988.

**Pancake**
The largest pancake was 15.01 m (49 ft 3 in) in diameter, 2.5 cm (1 in) deep and weighed 3 tonnes (6,614 lb). It was made and flipped in Rochdale, Greater Manchester, UK, in Aug 1994.

**Trifle**
A 3.13-tonne (6,896-lb) sherry trifle which contained 91 litres (20 gal) of sherry was made on 26 Sept 1990 by students of Clarendon College of Further Education, Nottingham, UK.

**Pastry**
In 1992, a 1,037.25-m (3,403-ft) *mille-feuille* (cream puff pastry) was made by employees of Pidy, a company based in Ypres, Belgium.

## Confectionery
**Chocolate model**
In 1991, a 13 x 8.5 x 2.5-m (42-ft 8-in x 27-ft 10½-in x 8-ft 2½-in) model of a ship was made by Gremi Provincial de Pastisseria, Confiteria i Bolleria School, Barcelona, Spain.

**Easter eggs**
A 4.76-tonne (10,482-lb 14-oz) Easter egg was made by staff of Cadbury Red Tulip at their factory at Ringwood, Victoria, Australia. It was completed on 9 April 1992.

**Ice lolly**
The largest ice lolly weighed 8.78 tonnes (19,357 lb) and was made by staff of Augusto Ltd at Kalisz, Poland, in Sept 1994.

**Stick of rock**
The largest stick of rock weighed 413.6 kg (911 lb 13 oz). It was 5.03 m (16 ft 6 in) long and 43.2 cm (17 in) thick, and was made by the Coronation Rock Company of Blackpool, Lancs, UK, on 20 July 1991.

## Drinks
**Milk shake**
The largest milk shake was 16,400 litres (3,607 gal) in volume and strawberry flavoured. It was made by Age Concern, East Cheshire and Lancashire Dairies at Macclesfield, Cheshire, UK on 18 Aug 1996.

**Champagne fountain**
The greatest number of storeys ever to be achieved in a champagne fountain, successfully filled from the top and using traditional long-stem glasses, is 47 (to a height of 7.85 m or 25 ft 9 in). It was constructed from 23,642 glasses

## Biscuits, cakes and pastries
**Biscuit**
The largest biscuit ever made was a chocolate chip cookie with a diameter of 24.9 m (81 ft 8 in) and an area of 486.95 m² (5,241.5 ft²). It was made by Cookie Time at Christchurch, New Zealand, on 2 April 1996 and contained some 2.5 tonnes of chocolate.

**Cakes**
The largest cake weighed 58.08 tonnes (128,238 lb 8 oz), including 7.35 tonnes (16,209 lb) of icing. It was baked in the shape of Alabama to celebrate the 100th birthday of Fort Payne, Alabama, USA.

The tallest cake was 30.85 m (101 ft 2½ in) high, with 100 tiers, and was made by Beth Cornell Trevorrow and helpers at the Shiawassee County Fairgrounds, Michigan, USA, in 1990.

**Doughnut**
A 1.7-tonne (3,739-lb) American-style jelly doughnut was made by representatives from Hemstrought's Bakeries, Donato's Bakery and the radio station WKLL-FM at Utica, New York, USA, on 21 Jan 1993.

**Mince pie**
The largest mince pie was 1.02 tonnes (2,260 lb) and measured 6.1 x 1.5 m (20 x 5 ft). It was baked at Ashby-de-la-Zouch, Leics, UK, on 15 Oct 1932.

**Lollipop**
A lollipop weighing 1.37 tonnes (3,011 lb 5 oz) was made by staff at BonBon, Holme Olstrup, Denmark, on 22 April 1994.

**Sweets**
The largest sweet was a marzipan chocolate weighing 1.85 tonnes (4,078 lb 8 oz), made at Ven International Fresh Market, Diemen, the Netherlands, from 11 to 13 May 1990.

by the Moet & Chandon champagne house at Ceasar's Palace in Las Vegas, Nevada, USA, between 19 and 23 July 1993.

**Cocktail**
The largest cocktail in the world was a Juicy Duce, which was 25,963 litres (5,711 gal) in capacity. It was mixed at the Buderim Tavern, Buderim, Queensland, Australia, on 19 Oct 1966.

**Left**
The world's longest loaf, a *Rosca de Reyes* (a type of twisted loaf) baked in Acapulco, Mexico, in 1996, was 9,200 m (30,184 ft) long. If it were put next to Mt Everest, the world's highest mountain, it would be 352 m (1,155 ft) taller.

## Crafts

### Basket
The world's largest hand-woven basket measures 14.6 x 7.0 x 5.8 m (48 x 23 x 19 ft) and was made by the Longaberger Company of Dresden, Ohio, USA, in 1990.

### Blanket
A blanket measuring 17,289 m² (186,107.8 ft²), hand-knitted, machine-knitted and crocheted by members of the Knitting and Crochet Guild worldwide was assembled at Dishforth Airfield, Thirsk, N Yorkshire, UK, on 30 May 1993.

### Glass blowing
On 26 Sept 1992, a 2.3-m (7-ft 8-in) tall bottle with a 712-litre (157-gal) capacity was blown at Wheaton Village, Millville, New Jersey, USA, by a team led by glass artist Steve Tobin.

### Pencil
Students at Huddersfield Technical College constructed a 2.74-m (9-ft) long pencil for Cliffe Hill School, Lightcliffe, Halifax, W Yorkshire, UK, in 1995.

### Pottery
The world's largest terracotta pot is 1.95 m (6 ft 5 in) tall, with a circumference of 5.23 m (17 ft 1 in). It was hand-built by Peter Start and Albert Robinson at The Plant Pottery, Barby, Northants, UK, in May 1985.

### Quilt
The world's largest quilt was made by The Saskatchewan Seniors' Association of Saskatchewan, Canada. It measured 47.36 x 25.20 m (155 ft 4½ in x 82 ft 8 in), and was constructed on 13 June 1994.

## Manufactured items

### Chandeliers
The largest set of chandeliers, created by the Kookje Lighting Co. Ltd of Seoul, South Korea, is 12 m (39 ft) high and has 700 bulbs. Completed in Nov 1988, it occupies three floors of the Lotte Chamshil Department Store, Seoul.

The largest British chandelier measures 9.1 m (30 ft) and is in the Chinese Room at the Royal Pavilion, Brighton, E Sussex.

### Fireworks
The largest firework ever produced was *Universe I Part II*, exploded for the Lake Toya Festival, Hokkaido, Japan on 15 July 1988. The 700-kg (1,543-lb) shell was 139 cm (54¾ in) in diameter and burst to a diameter of 1.2 km (¾ mile).

A self-propelled vertical firework wheel 19.3 m (63 ft 6 in) in diameter was designed by Tom Archer and built by Essex Pyrotechnics Ltd, of Saffron Walden, Essex, UK. It was fired for eight revolutions at a mean speed in excess of 5 rpm on 9 July 1994.

### Piggy bank
The world's largest piggy bank is 4.7 m (15 ft 5 in) long, 2.64 m (8 ft 8 in) tall and 6.52 m (21 ft 4½ in) in circumference. Called 'Maximillion', it was constructed by The Canadian Imperial Bank of Commerce in Canada in Nov 1995.

### Table cloth
The world's largest table cloth measured 457.81 m (1,502 ft) long and 1.37 m (4 ft 6 in) wide and was made by the Sportex division of Artex International in Highland, Illinois, USA, on 17 Oct 1990.

The largest table cloth made in the United Kingdom is 300.5 m (985 ft 11 in) long and 1.83 m (6 ft) wide made of damask by Tonrose Ltd of Manchester in June 1988.

### Yo-yo
A yo-yo measuring 3.17 m (10 ft 4 in) in diameter and weighing 407 kg (897 lb) was devised by J. N. Nichols (Vimto) Ltd and made by engineering students at Stockport College. It was launched by crane from a height of 57.5 m (187 ft) at Wythenshawe, Greater Manchester, UK, on 1 Aug 1993 and yo-yoed about four times.

## Instruments

### Brass instrument
A contrabass tuba which stands 2.28 m (7 ft 6 in) tall, with 11.8 m (39 ft) of tubing and a bell measuring 1 m (3 ft 4 in) across was constructed for a world tour by the band of American composer John Philip Sousa in c. 1896–98. It is now owned by a circus promoter in South Africa.

### Double bass
A 4.26-m (14-ft) tall double bass was built in 1924 in Ironia, New Jersey, USA, by Arthur K. Ferris. It weighed 590 kg (1,301 lb), with a sound box 2.43 m (8 ft) across, and had leather strings totalling 31.7 m (104 ft). Its low notes could be felt rather than heard.

### Drum
A drum with a diameter of 3.96 m (13 ft) was built by the Supreme Drum Co., London, UK, and was played at the Royal Festival Hall, London, UK, on 31 May 1987.

### Drum set
A drum set consisting of 308 pieces—153 drums, 77 cymbals, 33 cowbells, 12 hi-hats, 8 tambourines, 6 wood blocks, 3 gongs, 3 bell trees, 2 maracas, 2 triangles, 2 rain sticks, 2 bells, 1 ratchet, 1 set of chimes, 1 xylophone, 1 afuche and 1 doorbell was built by Dan McCourt of Pontiac, Michigan, USA, in 1994. A demonstration takes 20 minutes.

### Grand piano
The grandest grand piano weighed 1.25 tonnes and was 3.55 m (11 ft 8 in) long. It was made by Chas H. Challen & Son Ltd of London, UK, in 1935. Its longest bass string measured 3.02 m (9 ft 11 in), and had a tensile strength of 30 tonnes.

### Guitar
The largest playable guitar in the world is 11.63 m (38 ft 2 in) tall and weighs 446 kg (1,865 lbs). Based on a Gibson model, it was made by students of Shakamak High School in Jasonville, Indiana, USA, and unveiled in May 1991.

**Right**
The largest playable guitar in the world was unveiled in May 1991 when it was played simultaneously by six students of Shakamak High School, Jasonville, Indiana, USA. Powered by six amplifiers, it may also be the world's loudest guitar.

# LARGEST PIGGY BANK 4.7 M

## 1.2 KM AT THE LAKE TOYA FESTIVAL, JAPAN, IN 1988

### Organ
The largest and loudest musical instrument ever made is the now only partially functional Auditorium Organ in Atlantic City, New Jersey, USA. Completed in 1930, it had two consoles, 1,477 stop controls and 33,112 pipes. Its volume was equal to 25 brass bands.

### Recorder
A 5-m (16-ft 5-in) long fully-functional recorder made of specially-treated stone pine was made in Iceland by Stefán Geir Karlsson in 1994.

### Stringed instrument
The largest movable stringed instrument ever constructed was a pantaleon, with 270 strings stretched over 4.6 m$^2$ (50 ft$^2$), used by George Noel in 1767.

## Constructions
### Doors
The four doors in the Vehicle Assembly Building which is situated near Cape Canaveral, Florida, USA, have a height of 140 m (460 ft).

**Left**
The world's largest wall hanging on the Takamatsu City Hall, Japan, was designed for the town's Winter Festival in 1996. Made by approximately 3,300 local school children, it depicts Japan's 11th-century Genpei-Gassen battle.

## 1993 IN MANCHESTER, UK, WAS 3.17 M IN DIAMETER AND WEIGHED 407 KG

### Windows
The largest sheets of manufactured glass were two identical pieces 21.64 m (71 ft) long and 2.90 m (9 ft 6 in) wide, made by the Saint Gobain Co. in France, and installed in their Chantereine factory at Thourotte, near Compiègne, France, in 1966.

Three matching windows in the Palace of Industry and Technology at Rondpoint de la Défense, Paris, France, have an extreme width of 218 m (715 ft) and a maximum height of 50 m (164 ft).

### Marquees
A marquee covering an area of 17,500 m$^2$ (188,350 ft$^2$) or 1.75 ha (4.32 acres) was erected by the firm of Deuter from Augsburg, Germany, for the 1958 'Welcome Expo' in Brussels, Belgium.

### Largest wall hanging
A wall hanging measuring 2,025 m$^2$ (21,789 ft$^2$) and made of 400,000 multicoloured plastic chips was hung from the Takamatsu City Hall, Japan, for the 50-day Winter Festival starting on 24 Nov 1996.

### Snow and ice constructions
A snow palace with a volume of 103,591.8 m$^3$ (3,658,310.2 ft$^3$) and

30.29 m (99 ft 5 in) in height was unveiled on 8 Feb 1994 at Asahikawa, Hokkaidō, Japan. It was made to resemble Suwon castle in South Korea.

The world's largest ice construction was the ice palace completed in Jan 1992, using 18,000 blocks of ice, at St Paul, Minnesota, USA, during the Winter Carnival. Built by TMK Construction Specialties Inc., it was 50.8 m (166 ft 8 in) high and contained 4,900 tonnes (10.8 million lb) of ice.

### Wooden buildings
The largest wooden structure in the world is the Woolloomooloo Bay Wharf, Sydney, Australia. Built in 1912, the wharf itself is 400 m (1,310 ft) long and 63 m (206 ft) wide. The building on the wharf is five storeys high, 350.5 m (1,150 ft) long and 43 m (141 ft) wide and is currently being converted to hotel apartments and a marina complex.

Between 1942 and 1943, 16 wooden blimp hangars were built for Navy airships at various locations throughout the USA. Each one is 317 m (1,040 ft) long, 51.91 m (170 ft 4 in) high at the crown and 90.37 m (296 ft 6 in) wide at the base. There are now only eight remaining.

### Camera obscura
The camera obscura at Foredown Tower, Hove, E Sussex, UK, has a 30.48-cm (12-in) lens and a 91-cm (3-ft) diameter display dish.

### Swimming pools
The largest swimming pool in the world is the seawater Orthlieb Pool in Casablanca, Morocco. It is 480 m (1,574 ft) long and 75 m (246 ft) wide, with an area of 3.6 ha (8.9 acres).

The largest land-locked swimming pool with heated water was the Fleishhacker Pool on Sloat Boulevard, near Great Highway, San Francisco, California, USA. It measured 305 x 46 m (1,000 x 150 ft) and was up to 4.26 m (14 ft) deep. It was opened on 2 May 1925 but has now been abandoned.

The largest land-locked pool in current use is Willow Lake at Warren, Ohio, USA. It measures 183 x 46 m (600 x 150 ft).

The pool with the greatest spectator capacity is at Osaka, Japan, which can accommodate 13,614 people.

The largest British swimming pool currently in use is the Royal Commonwealth Pool, Edinburgh, UK, with 2,000 seats.

## Road vehicles

### Largest vehicle
'Big Muskie', built by Bucyrus Erie, is a walking dragline—a machine that removes dirt from coal. It weighs 13,200 tonnes, but is too expensive to run. It is found at Central Ohio Coal Co., Muskingham site, Ohio, USA.

### Longest buses
The 32.2-m-long (105-ft 8-in) articulated DAF Super CityTrain buses have 110 passenger seats and room for 140 'strap-hangers' in the first trailer and 60 seated and 40 'strap-hangers' in the second. Designed by the former president of Zaïre (now called the Democratic Republic of Congo), Mobutu Sese Seko, they weigh 28 tonnes unladen.

The longest rigid single bus is 14.96 m (49 ft) long, carries 69 passengers and is built by Van Hool of Belgium.

### Largest caravan
A two-wheeled five-storey caravan was built in 1990 for Sheik Hamad Bin Hamdan Al Nahyan of Abu Dhabi, United Arab Emirates. It is 20 m (66 ft) long, 12 m (39 ft) wide and weighs 120 tonnes. It has eight bedrooms and bathrooms, four garages and water storage for 24,000 litres (5,275 gal).

### Largest crawler
Two Marion eight-caterpillar crawlers built to convey Saturn V rockets to their launch pads at Cape Canaveral, Florida, USA, each measure 40 x 34.7 m (131 ft 4 in x 114 ft). The loaded train weight is 8,165 tonnes. Now used to take shuttles to their launch pads, they also have the world's largest windscreen wiper blades, measuring 106 cm (42 in).

### Largest dumper truck
The Terex Titan 33–19 manufactured by General Motors Corporation and now in operation at Westar Mine, British Columbia, Canada, has a loaded weight of 548.6 tonnes and a capacity of 317.5 tonnes. It is 17 m (56 ft) high when tipping. The 16-cylinder engine delivers 3,300 hp, and the fuel tank holds 5,910 litres (1,300 gal).

### Largest fork-lift truck
In 1991, Kalmar LMV of Lidhult, Sweden, manufactured three counterbalanced fork-lift trucks capable of lifting loads up to 90 tonnes at a load centre of 2,400 mm

(90 in). They were built to assist in the construction of two pipelines from Sarir to the Gulf of Sirte and from Tazirbu to Benghazi, Libya.

### Largest ambulance
Articulated Alligator Jumbulances (marks VI, VII, VIII and IX), operated by the ACROSS Trust to convey sick and handicapped people on holidays and pilgrimages across Europe, are 18 m (59 ft) long. Built by Van Hool of Belgium at a cost of £200,000, they can carry 44 patients and staff.

### Longest car
A 30.5-m-long (100-ft) 26-wheeled limo was designed by Jay Ohrberg of Burbank, California, USA. Its features include a swimming pool with diving board and a king-sized water bed. It can be driven as a rigid vehicle or modified to bend in the middle.

### Largest car
The Bugatti 'Royale' type 41, also known as the 'Golden Bugatti', was first built in 1927. It is over 6.7 m (22 ft) long and has an eight-cylinder engine with a 12.7 litre capacity.

### Widest lawn mower
The 5-tonne, 18-m-wide (60-ft) 27-unit 'Big Green Machine', used by turf farmer Jay Edgar Frick of Monroe, Ohio, USA, can mow an acre of grass in 60 seconds.

### Longest motorcycle
Douglas and Roger Bell of Perth, Australia, designed and built a 7.6-m (24-ft 11-in) long 250-cc motorbike known as 'Big Ben'.

Les Nash of Coventry, W Midlands, UK, constructed a 'self-made' 3,500-cc machine with a Rover V-8 engine. It measures 3.81 x 1.22 m (12 ft 6 in x 4 ft) and weighs more than 225 kg (500 lb).

### Largest bicycle
The largest bicycle, by the wheel diameter, called the 'Frankencycle', was built by Dave Moore of Rosemead, California, USA, and first ridden by Steve Gordon of Moorpark, California, USA, on 4 June 1989. The wheel diameter is 3.05 m (10 ft) and the bike is 3.40 m (11 ft 2 in) high.

A tricycle with a larger wheel diameter was also constructed by Dave Moore. Designed by Arthur Dillon, the Dillon Colossal has a back wheel diameter of 3.35 m (11 ft), a front wheel diameter of 1.77 m (5 ft 10 in) and was built in 1994.

# LONGEST FREIGHT TRAIN 7.3 KM

## AND CAN MOW AN ACRE OF GRASS IN 60 SECONDS

### Longest bicycle
The longest true bicycle ever built (without a third stabilizing wheel) was designed and built by Terry Thessman of Pahiatua, New Zealand. It measures 22.24 m (72 ft 11½ in) in length and weighs 340 kg (750 lb). It was ridden by four riders a distance of 246 m (807 ft) on 27 Feb 1988.

### Longest tricycle
Philip Koniotes, John Clarke, Peter Openshaw and John Warmerdam built Britain's longest tricycle, with 24 seats, at the Fumair Factory Hertford, UK, in 1996.

### Tallest unicycle
The tallest unicyle ever ridden is one 31.01 m (101 ft 9 in) tall. Steve McPeak rode it for a distance of 114.6 m (376 ft) in Las Vegas, Nevada, USA, in Oct 1980. During the ride he was attached to a safety wire suspended from an overhead crane.

## Trains

### Longest freight train
The longest and heaviest freight train on record, with the largest number of wagons recorded, made a run on the 106.5-cm (3-ft 6-in) gauge Sishen-Saldanha railway in South Africa on 26–27 Aug 1989. The train consisted of 660 wagons (each loaded to 105 tons gross), a tank car and a caboose, moved by nine 50-kV electric and seven diesel-electric locomotives distributed along the train. It was 7.3 km (4½ miles) long and travelled a distance of 861 km (535 miles) in 22 hr 40 min.

### Heaviest freight trains
The heaviest freight train was a BHP Iron Ore train that weighed 72,191.54 tonnes, or 70,381.34 tonnes excluding the locomotives. It comprised 540 ore cars and 10 locomotives and ran from Newman, Western Australia, to Port Hedland, also in Western Australia, covering 408.62 km (253 miles 1,584 yds) on 28 May 1996.

The heaviest freight train in the United Kingdom runs from Merehead Quarry, Somerset, to Acton, Greater London, usually with 5,100 tonnes of limestone in 50 wagons. The train is hauled by a single 'Class 59' Co-Co diesel-electric locomotive.

### Largest steam locomotive
The largest operating steam locomotive in the world is the South African Railways GMA Garratt type 4–8–2+2–8–4. It was built between 1952 and 1954 and weighs a total of 187.4 tonnes.

### Longest passenger train
The longest passenger train measured 1,732.9 m (1,895 yd). Its 70 coaches were pulled by one electric locomotive, and the total weight was 2,786 tonnes. Owned by the National Belgian Railway Company, it took 1 hr 11 min 5 sec to complete the 62.5-km (38¾-mile) journey from Ghent to Ostend, Belgium, on 27 April 1991.

**Left**
The Bugatti 'Royale' type 41, on display at Pebble Beach, California, USA. Known in the United Kingdom as the 'Golden Bugatti', it was the largest car produced for private use. It was assembled at Molsheim, France, by the Italian Ettore Bugatti and first built in 1927. The bonnet alone is over 2.13 m (7 ft) long.

## SUPER CITYTRAINS WERE DESIGNED BY EX-PRESIDENT MOBUTU OF CONGO

**Left**
The longest motor cycle in Britain is a tough-looking 3,500-cc machine built by Lee Nash of Coventry, W Midlands. The bike is powered by a Rover V-8 engine, which would normally power a large luxury car.

# Large air and sea craft

**Right and below right**
The Airbus Super Transporter A300-600ST Beluga is the world's most spacious aircraft. It is shown here being loaded (top) and prepared for take-off (below). It has a main cargo compartment volume of 1,400 m³ (49,441 ft³) and a maximum take-off weight of 150 tonnes. Altogether, four identical aircraft are to be built.

## Aeroplanes
### Largest airliner
The jet airliner with the greatest capacity is the Boeing 747-400, which entered service with Northwest Airlines on 31 Jan 1989. It has a wing span of 64.9 m (213 ft), a range of 13,340 km (8,290 miles) and can carry up to 566 passengers.

### Heaviest aircraft
The aircraft with the highest standard maximum take-off weight is the 600-tonne (1,322,750-lb) Antonov An-225 *Mriya* (Dream). One An-225—flown by Capt. Aleksandr Galunenko and a crew of seven pilots—lifted a payload of 156,300 kg (344,582 lb) to a height of 12,410 m (40,715 ft) on 22 March 1989.

### Most spacious airliner
The Airbus Super Transporter A300-600ST *Beluga* has a main cargo compartment volume of 1,400 m³ (49,441 ft³) and a

maximum take-off weight of 150 tonnes. Its overall length is 56.16 m (184 ft 3 in) and the usable length of its cargo compartment is 37.70 m (123 ft 8 in).

### Largest wingspan
The eight-engined, 193-tonne Hughes H4 Hercules flying-boat, nicknamed the *Spruce Goose*, has a wing span of 97.51 m (319 ft 11 in) and is 66.65 m (218 ft 8 in) long. It ascended 21.3 m (70 ft) into the air in a test run, off Long Beach Harbor, California, USA, on 2 Nov 1947, but never flew again.

## Aircraft
### Largest airship
The 213.9-tonne German *Hindenburg* (LZ 129) and *Graf Zeppelin II* (LZ 130), both had a length of 245 m (803 ft 10 in) and a capacity of 200,000 m³ (7,062,100 ft³). The *Hindenburg* first flew in 1936 and the *Graf Zeppelin II* went into service in 1938.

### Largest working airship
The largest airship that is currently in use is the WDL 1B which has an inflatable volume of 7,200 m³. (9,420 ft³). Built at Mulheim, Germany, it is 60 m (197 ft) long.

### Largest helicopters
The Russian Mil Mi-12 was powered by four 4,847 kW (6,500 hp) turboshaft engines and had a rotor diameter of 67 m (219 ft 10 in), with a length of 37 m (121 ft 4½ in) and a weight of 103.3 tonnes. A prototype was shown at the 1971 Paris Air Show but it was never put into service.

The largest rotorcraft was the Piasecki Heli-Stat, which used four Sikorsky S-58 airframes attached to a surplus Goodyear ZPG-2 airship. It was powered by four 1,525 hp piston engines, and was 104.5 m (343 ft) long, 33.8 m (111 ft) high and 45.4 m (149 ft) wide. It first flew in October 1985 at Lakehurst, New Jersey, USA, but was destroyed in a crash on 1 July 1986.

### Largest helicopter in service
The Russian Mil Mi-26 is the largest helicopter that is currently in active service. It has a take-off weight of 56,000 kg (123,500 lb) and an overall length of 32 m (105 m).

### Largest balloon
The unmanned balloon made by Winzen Research Inc. of South St Paul, Minnesota, USA, had an inflatable volume of 2 million m³ (70 million ft³) and was 300 m (1,000 ft) in height. It did not get off the ground and was destroyed at its launch on 8 July 1975.

## Merchant shipping
### Largest cargo vessel
The world's largest ship is the *Jahre Viking* at 564,763 tonnes deadweight. It is 458.45 m (1,504 ft) long overall, has a beam of 68.8 m (226 ft) and a draught of 24.61 m (80 ft 9 in).

### Largest container ship
The largest container vessel in service is *Regina Maersk*, built at Odense, Denmark, and completed in Jan 1996. It has a gross tonnage of 81,488 and a capacity of 6,000 TEU (Twenty-foot Equivalent Units—the standard container is 6,096 m or 20 ft long).

### Largest liners
Carnival Cruise Line's *Carnival Destiny* has a displacement of 101,353 gross registered tons. It has an overall length of 272 m (893 ft) and is 38 m (125 ft) wide.

# MAX TAKE-OFF WEIGHT 600 TONNES

## WING SPAN OF 97.51 M

The longest passenger liner is the *Norway*, with a grt of 76,049, a length of 315.53 m (1,035 ft 7½ in), and room for 900 crew and 2,032 passengers. She draws 10.5 m (34 ft 6 in), has a beam of 33.5 m (110 ft) and sails at 18 knots for Norwegian Cruise Line.

### Largest barges
The largest RoRo (roll-on, roll-off) ships are four El Rey class barges of 16,432 tonnes and 176.78 m (580 ft) in length. They have lodging for up to 376 truck-trailers and sail between Florida, USA, and Puerto Rico.

### Most powerful tugs
The largest and most powerful tugs are the *Nikolay Chiker* (SB131) and *Fotiy Krylov* (SB135), commissioned in 1989 and built by Hollming Ltd of Finland for the former USSR. With 25,000 bhp and with a bollard pull in excess of 286 tonnes, they are 98.8 m (324 ft) long and 19.45 m (64 ft) wide.

### Largest whale factory
The Russian *Sovietskaya Ukraina* (32,034 gross tons), with a summer deadweight of 46,738 tonnes, was completed in October 1959. It is 217.8 m (714 ft 6 in) in length and 25.8 m (84 ft 7 in) in the beam.

## Ferries
### Largest car and passenger ferry
The *Silja Europa* entered service in 1993 between Stockholm, Sweden, and Helsinki, Finland. Operated by the Silja Line, it has a grt of 59,914, is 201.8 m (662 ft) long and has a beam of 32.6 m (107 ft). It can carry 3,000 passengers, 350 cars and 60 lorries.

carry 250 passengers at 74 km/h (40 knots) across the Öre Sound between Malmö, Sweden, and Copenhagen, Denmark.

### Largest hovercraft
The SRN4 Mk III, a British-built civil hovercraft, weighs 300 tonnes and has space to accommodate 418 passengers and 60 cars. It is 56.38 m (185 ft) in length, and its four Bristol Siddeley Marine Proteus engines give a maximum speed in excess of the scheduled permitted cross-Channel operating speed of 65 knots.

## Sailing vessels
### Largest sailing ship
The largest ship to have been built in the era of the sail was the *France II*, which had a grt of 5,806 and was launched at Bordeaux, France, in 1911. This steel-hulled, five-masted barque had a hull measuring 127.4 m (418 ft). It was wrecked off New Caledonia in the South Pacific in July 1922.

### Largest sailing ship in service
The *Sedov*, which was built in 1921 in Germany and is used for training by the Russians, is 109 m (357 ft) long and 14.6 m (48 ft) wide. It has a displacement of 6,300 tonnes, a grt of 3,556 and a sail area of 4,192 m$^2$ (45,123 ft$^2$).

### Longest sailing ship
The 187-m (613-ft) French-built *Club Med 1*, has five aluminium masts and 2,800 m$^2$ (30,100 ft$^2$) of computer-controlled polyester sails. Operated as a Caribbean cruise vessel for 425 passengers, it has powerful engines

and is really a motor-sailer. A sister-ship, *Club Med II*, has also been commissioned.

### Largest junks
The largest junk on record was the sea-going *Zheng He*, which was the flagship of Admiral Zheng He's fleet of 62 treasure ships which were in service around 1420. It had a displacement of 3,150 tonnes and a length variously estimated at up to 164 m (538 ft). It is believed that the ship had nine masts.

In *c.* AD 280 a 180-m$^2$ (600-ft$^2$) 'floating fortress', built by Wang Jun on the Chang Jiang (Yangtze) River, China, took part in the Jin-Wu river war. Present-day junks do not exceed 52 m (170 ft) in length.

### Largest yachts
The 147-m (482-ft) Saudi Arabian royal yacht *Abdul Aziz* was completed in 1984 at Vospers Yard, Southampton, Hants, UK. In 1987 it was estimated to be worth over $100 million (£61 million).

The largest private (non-Royal) yacht is the 120-m (400-ft) *Alexander* which was converted from a ferry to a yacht in 1986.

### Largest sails
The largest spars carried were those in HM Battleship *Temeraire*, construction of which was completed at Chatham, Kent, UK, on 31 Aug 1877. The fore and main yards measured 35 m (115 ft) in length. The foresail contained 1,555 m (5,100 ft) of canvas weighing 2.03 tonnes and the total sail area was 2,300 m$^2$ (25,000 ft$^2$). The ship was broken up in 1921.

## LARGEST PASSENGER VESSEL EVER BUILT, WITH AN OVERALL LENGTH OF 272 M

### Largest international rail ferries
The German-built *Klaipeda*, *Vilnius*, *Mukran* and *Greifswald*, which operate in the Baltic sea between Klaipeda, Lithuania, and Mukran, Germany, are each 11,513 tonnes deadweight with two decks 190.5 m (625 ft) long and 91.86 m (301 ft 5 in) wide. Each vessel can lift 103 standard 14.83 m (48 ft 8 in), 84-ton railcars and cover 506 km (273 nautical miles) in 17 hours.

### Largest hydrofoils
The 64.6-m (212-ft) long *Plainview* (314 tonnes full load) naval hydrofoil was launched by the Lockheed Shipbuilding and Construction Co. at Seattle, Washington, USA on 28 June 1965.

The largest passenger hydrofoils are three 165-ton Supramar PTS 150 MkIIIs, which

**Left**
The world's largest ship of any kind is the oil tanker *Jahre Viking* (formerly the *Happy Giant* and *Seawise Giant*). Badly damaged in the Iran-Iraq war, it was relaunched in 1991 after a $60-million (£34-million) renovation in Singapore and Dubai, United Arab Emirates.

# Longest...

**Right**
This 7.32-m (24-ft) long red-leather sofa was made by Art Forma (Furniture) Ltd of Castle Donington, near Derby, UK, in May 1995. The sofa, which seats 17 people, was displayed at the Interzum Exhibition in Cologne, Germany from 19 to 23 May 1995.

## Crafts

### Christmas cracker
The longest functional cracker ever made was 45.7 m (150 ft) long. It was made by the rugby league footballer, Ray Price, for Markson Sparks!, NSW, Australia, and pulled at Westfield Shopping Town, Chatswood, Sydney, NSW, Australia on 9 Nov 1991.

### Crochet
On 14 July 1986 Ria van der Honing of the Netherlands completed a 62.50-km (38-mile 1,471-yd) long crochet chain.

### Fan
In Oct 1994, Victor Troyas Oses of Peralta, Spain, made a hand-painted chintz and wood fan that measures 8 m (26 ft 3 in) when it is unfolded.

### French knitting
Ted Hannaford of Sittingbourne, Kent, UK, began work on a piece of French knitting in 1989. It now measures 11.273 km (7 miles 70 yd) in length.

### Kite
On 18 Nov 1990 Michel Trouillet and a team of helpers at Nîmes, France, made and flew a 1,034.45-m (3,394-ft) long kite.

### Rope
A rope 186 m (610 ft) long made out of rice straw was produced for the annual Naha City Festival, Japan, in Oct 1996. It weighs 610 kg (1,345 lbs) and is the largest rope made of natural materials.

### Scarf
The longest scarf ever knitted measured 32.2 km (20 miles). It was made by residents of Abbeyfield Houses for the Abbeyfield Society of Potters Bar, Herts, UK, and was completed on 29 May 1988.

### Stuffed toy
Pupils of Veien School, Hønefoss, Norway, created a stuffed snake 419.7 m (1,377 ft) long in June 1994.

### Washing line
The longest continuous washing line was 5,272.55 m (17,298 ft) and was erected in Bavel, Netherlands, on 2 June 1996.

### Wedding dress train
The longest wedding dress train was 204.1m (670 ft) long and made by Hege Solli for the marriage of Hege Lorence and Rolf Rotset of Norway on 1 June 1996.

The longest in Britain was 29.8 m (97 ft 7¾ in), made by Margaret Riley of Thurnby Lodge, Leics, for the marriage blessing of Diane and Steven Reid on 6 May 1990.

## Manufactured items

### Axe
A steel axe 18.28 m (60 ft) long, weighing 7 tonnes, was designed and built by BID Ltd of Woodstock, New Brunswick, Canada. It was presented to the town of Nackawic on 11 May 1991 to commemorate the town's being made 1991 Forestry Capital of Canada. Calculations suggested it would take a 140-tonne lumberjack to swing the axe, but a crane was used instead to lift it into its concrete 'stump'.

### Banner
On 15 Nov 1995, a banner 7.99 km (4 miles 1,698 yd) long was created by Nestlé's Milo. It was part of an effort between the Ministry of Education, the Thailand Amateur Sports Associations Club and Nestlé to promote the Thai team in the South East Asian Games.

**Right**
The longest continuous washing line in the world was 5,272.55 m (17,298 ft). It was erected at Bavel, the Netherlands, on 2 June 1996 and freshly washed laundry was hung along the entire length of the line.

# LONGEST WASHING LINE 5,272.55 M

Reebok International Ltd of Massachusetts, USA, flew a 30-m (100-ft) long banner from a plane from 13–16 and 20–23 March 1990 for four hours each day. The banner read 'Reebok Totally Beachin'.

### Sofa
The world's largest sofa was made in May 1995, by Art Forma (Furniture) Ltd of Castle Donington, UK. It is 7.32 m (24 ft) long, made of red leather and seats 17 people. It was made for the Swiss company Spühl AG.

### Zip-fastener
The longest zip-fastener was laid around the centre of Sneek, the Netherlands, on 5 Sept 1989. The brass zipper, made by Yoshida (Netherlands) Ltd, is 2,851 m (9,353 ft 8 in) long and consists of 2,565,900 teeth.

## Structures
### Fences
The dingo-proof fence enclosing Australia's main sheep farming areas stretches for 5,531 km (3,437 miles). It is 1.8 m (6 ft) high, and extends 30 cm (1 ft) underground.

### Stairway
The longest stairway is the service staircase for the Niesenbahn funicular railway near Spiez, Switzerland. It climbs a height of 1,669 m (5,476 ft) and has 11,674 steps.

The longest stairs in the United Kingdom are 324 m (1,065 ft), in the Cruachan Power Station, Argyll. There are 1,420 steps.

### Spiral staircase
In May 1981, Systems Control installed a 336-m (1,103-ft) deep spiral staircase with 1,520 steps, in the Mapco-White County Coal Mine, Carmi, Illinois, USA.

## Transport
### Motorable road
The world's longest road is the Pan-American Highway, which stretches from Alaska, USA, to Santiago, Chile, then eastwards to Buenos Aires, Argentina, ending in Brasilia, Brazil. It is over 24,140 km (15,000 miles) long, but has a small incomplete section called the Darién Gap in Panama and Colombia.

### Street
The world's longest street is Yonge Street, Toronto, Canada. Its length, now extended to Rainy River on the Ontario–Minnesota border, is 1,896.3 km (1,178 miles 528 yd).

### Canals
The longest canal in the ancient world was the Grand Canal of China, from Beijing to Hangzhou. It was begun in 540 BC and not completed until 1327, when it extended for 1,781 km (1,107 miles). It was allowed to silt up and had a maximum depth of 1.8 m (6 ft) in 1950, but is now used by vessels weighing up to 2,000 tonnes.

Completed with the use of forced labour in 1933, the Belomorsko-Baltiyskiy Canal from Belomorsk to Povenets, Russia, is 227 km (141 miles) long and has 19 locks. However it is unable to accommodate vessels of more than 5 m (16 ft) in draught.

The longest big-ship canal is the Suez Canal, linking the Red and Mediterranean Seas, opened on 17 Nov 1869. It took 10 years to build, with a workforce of 1.5 million people, 120,000 of whom died during construction. It is 162.2 km (100 miles 1,376 yd) in length from Port Said lighthouse to Suez Roads. It has a minimum width of 300 m (984 ft) and a maximum width of 365 m (1,198 ft).

The largest vessel to navigate the Suez Canal was *Jahre Viking*, on 29 Jan 1995. It has a deadweight tonnage of 564,763 tonnes and is 485.5 m (1,592 ft 10 in) long, with a beam of 68.8 m (225 ft 9 in). The USS *Shreveport* navigated the canal southbound on 15–16 Aug 1984 in a record 7 hr 45 min. There are more than 15,000 transits annually, or some 41 per day.

### Artificial seaway
The St Lawrence Seaway stretches 304 km (189 miles) along the New York State–Ontario border from Montreal to Lake Ontario, Canada. It allows ships up to 222 m (728 ft) long and 8 m (26 ft 3 in) draught to sail 3,769 km (2,342 miles) from the North Atlantic up the St Lawrence estuary and across the Great Lakes to Duluth, Minnesota, USA. The project, begun in 1954, cost $470 million (£167 million) and was opened on 25 April 1959.

### Irrigation canal
The world's longest irrigation canal is the Karakumsky Canal which stretches 1,200 km (745 miles) from Haun-Khan to Ashkhabad, Turkmenistan. Its course length is 800 km (500 miles).

### Rail tracks
The longest rail journey possible without changing trains is 9,297 km (5,777 miles) on the Trans-Siberian line from Moscow to Vladivostok in Russia. There are 70 stops on the fastest regular journey, which is scheduled to take 6 days 12 hr 45 min.

### Straight railway
The Trans-Australian line over the Nullarbor Plain run by Australian National Railways, is dead straight, although not level for 478 km (297 miles) from Mile 496 between Nurina and Loongana, W Australia, to Mile 793 between Ooldea and Watson, S Australia.

**Left**
The dingo-proof wire fence enclosing the main sheep areas of Australia is the longest fence in the world. The Queensland state government discontinued full maintenance in 1982.

# Tallest...

The tallest self-supported tower in the United Kingdom is a 330.5-m (1,084-ft) tall NTL transmitter, at Emley Moor, W Yorkshire, completed in Sept 1971. The structure cost £900,000, has an enclosed room 264 m (865 ft) up, and weighs more than 15,000 tonnes, including its foundations.

## Broadcasting masts
The guyed Warszawa Radio mast at Konstantynow in Poland was the tallest structure ever built. Prior to its fall during renovation work on 10 Aug 1991 it was 646.38 m (2,120 ft 8 in) tall. Designed by Jan Polak, it was completed on 18 July 1974 and weighed 550 tonnes.

The stayed 629-m (2,063-ft) tall television transmitting tower between Fargo and Blanchard, North Dakota, USA, is currently the world's tallest structure. It was built for Channel 11 of KTHI-TV in 30 days (2 Oct–1 Nov 1963) by 11 men of Hamilton Erection Inc. of York, South Carolina, USA. From then until the completion of the mast at Konstantynow it was the tallest structure in the world, and it remained the second tallest between 1974 and 1991.

NTL's Belmont mast, north of Horncastle, Lincs, is the tallest structure in the United Kingdom. It was completed in 1965 to a height of 385.5 m (1,265 ft), with 2.13 m (7 ft) added by meteorological equipment

## Structures
### Buildings demolished by explosives
The largest building ever to be demolished by explosives was the 21-storey Traymore Hotel in Atlantic City, New Jersey, USA, on 26 May, 1972. The demolition was carried out by Controlled Demolition Inc of Townson, Maryland. The 600-room hotel had a total capacity of 181,340 m³ (6,403,926 ft³).

In the United Kingdom Controlled Demolition Group of Leeds demolished eight blocks of flats at Kersal Vale, Salford, Manchester on 14 Oct 1990. The capacity of the tower blocks was 15,000 m³ (5,474,000 ft³).

The tallest chimney to be demolished by explosives was the Matla Power Station chimney, Kriel, South Africa, on 19 July 1981. It stood 275 m (902 ft) tall.

### Chimneys
The tallest chimney in the world is the coal power-plant No. 2 stack at Ekibastuz in Kazakhstan, which was completed in 1987, and is 420 m (1,378 ft) tall. The diameter tapers from 44 m (144 ft) at the base to 14.2 m (46 ft 7 in) at the top.

The tallest chimney in the British Isles is situated at Drax Power Station, N Yorkshire, and is 259 m (850 ft) high. Completed in 1969, it has an untapered diameter of 26 m (85 ft) and the greatest capacity of any British chimney.

### Tallest towers
The tallest building and free-standing tower in the world is the CN Tower in Toronto, Canada, which rises to 553.34 m (1,815 ft 5 in). Excavation began on 12 Feb 1973 for the erection of the 130,000-tonne reinforced, post-tensioned concrete structure, which was 'topped out' on 2 April 1975. The CN Tower's 416-seat restaurant revolves in the 'Sky Pod' at a height of 351 m (1,150 ft) high. On a clear day it is possible to enjoy views of hills that are 120 km (75 miles) away.

# TALLEST TOWER 553.34 M

installed in September 1967. The mast serves Yorkshire TV and weighs 210 tonnes.

## Flagpoles
The tallest flagpole is at Panmunjon, North Korea, near the border with South Korea. It is 160 m (525 ft) high and flies a flag 30 m (98 ft 6 in) long.

The tallest unsupported flagpole in the world is a steel pole 86 m (282 ft) tall and weighing 54,400 kg (120,000 lb), which was erected on 22 Aug 1985 at the Canadian Expo '86 exhibition in Vancouver, British Columbia. This supports a gigantic ice-hockey stick 62.5 m (205 ft) in length.

The tallest British flagpole is a Douglas-fir staff 68 m (225 ft) tall at Kew, Richmond-upon-Thames, London. Cut in Canada, it was shipped across the Atlantic and towed up the river Thames on 7 May 1958, to replace the old staff, 65 m (214 ft) tall, erected in 1919.

## Floodlights
The tallest lighting columns are the six towers of the Melbourne Cricket Ground in Melbourne, Victoria, Australia. They are each 75 m (246 ft) high and weigh 120 tonnes.

## Scaffolding
The scaffolding erected by Regional Scaffolding & Hoisting Co., Inc. of the Bronx, New York, USA, around the New York City

Municipal Building from 1988 to 1992 was 198 m (650 ft) in total height with a volume of 135,900 m³ (4,800,000 ft³). The work required 12,000 scaffold frames and 20,000 aluminium planks.

## Tallest toy bricks structure
A pyramid measuring 25.05 m (82 ft 2 in) high was built in 1996 in Taipei, Taiwan, to commemorate the inauguration of the Taiwanese President Lee Teng-hui.

The tallest British toy brick structure was a Lego tower which measured 20.86 m (68 ft 5 in). It was built by Lego UK Ltd at Earl's Court, London, UK, in March 1993 during the *Daily Mail* Ideal Home Exhibition.

## Totem pole
A totem pole 54.94 m (180 ft 3 in) tall, known as the Spirit of Lekwammen, was raised on 4 Aug 1994 at Victoria, British Columbia, Canada, for the Commonwealth Games which took place there. It took nine months to carve.

## Fences
Security screens, erected by Harrop-Allin of Pretoria, South Africa, in 1981 to protect fuel depots and refineries at Sasolburg, South Africa, from terrorist rocket attacks are 20 m (65 ft) high.

## Snowman
A 29.43-m (96-ft 7-in) high snowman was made by local residents at Ohkura Village, Yamagata, Japan. It took 10 days and nights to build and was finished on 10 March 1995.

# Manufactured items
## Bottles
A 3.11-m (10-ft 2-in) tall plastic bottle was filled with 2,250 litres (495 gal) of Schweppes Lemonade in Melbourne, Victoria, Australia, in March 1994.

A 2.54-m (8-ft 4-in) beer bottle was unveiled at the Shepherd Neame Brewery, Faversham, Kent, UK, on 27 Jan 1993. It took 13 minutes to fill it with 625.5 litres of beer.

## Pottery
The tallest thrown vase on record measured 5.66 m (18 ft 7 in) in height. It was completed on 10 Feb 1996 by Ray Sparks of the Creative Clay Company, Esk, Queensland, Australia.

# Fountains and waterfalls
## Fountain
The fountain at Fountain Hills, Arizona, USA, has a column of water which can reach a height of 171.2 m (562 ft) at full pressure. When all three pumps are on, it can reach 190 m (625 ft), provided conditions are calm and windless. Built at a cost of $1.5 million (£900,000), it is powered by pressure of 26.3 kg/cm² (375 lb/in²).

## Indoor waterfall
The largest indoor waterfall is in the lobby of the International Center Building, Detroit, Michigan, USA. It measures 34.75 m (114 ft) in height and is backed by 840 m² (9,000 ft²) of marble.

**Left**
The tallest toy brick structure in the world was finished on 18 May 1996 in Taipei, Taiwan. The enormous yellow pyramid rose 25.05 m (82 ft 2 in) into the sky.

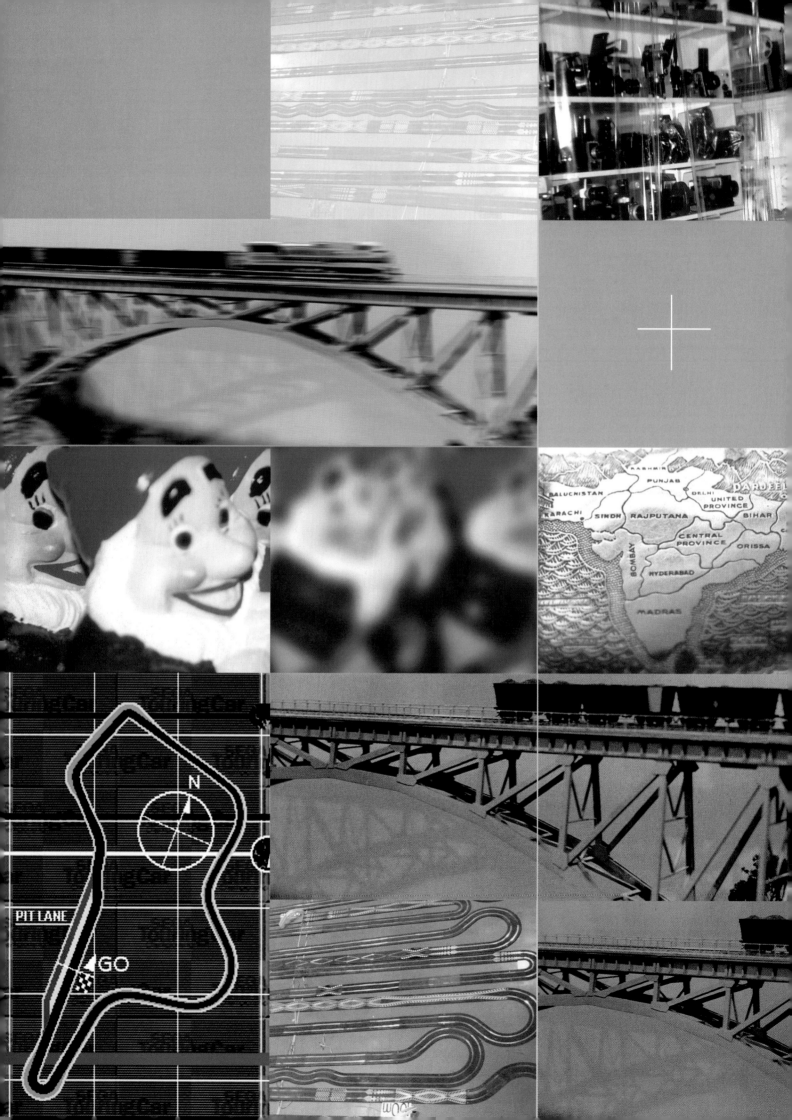

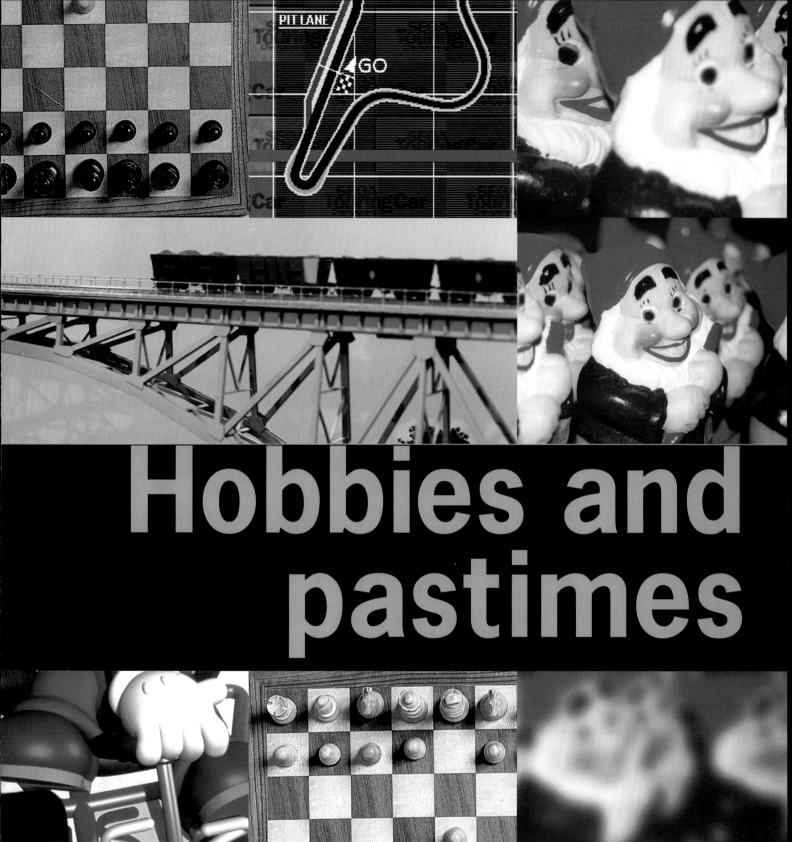

# Hobbies and
# pastimes

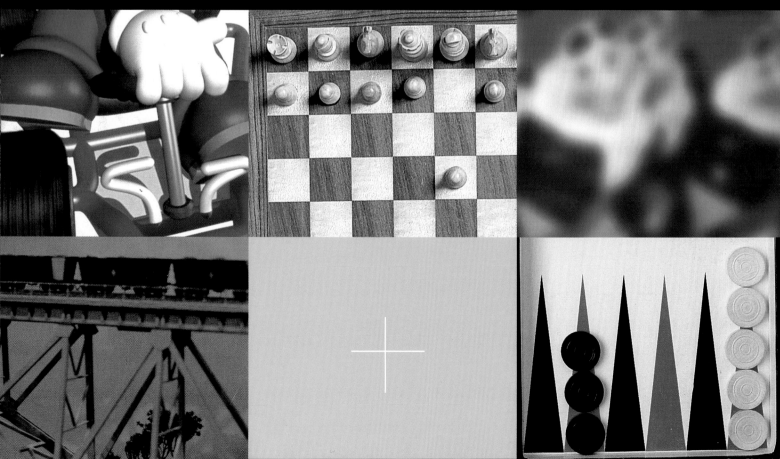

**Right**
Fruit stickers are clearly distinguished by their colourful designs. Antoine Secco, of Bourbon-Lancy, France, has amassed the world's largest collection, totalling 11,000.

## Smoking paraphernalia
### Cigarettes
The largest collection of cigarettes was amassed by Robert E. Kaufman, of New York, USA, and consisted of 8,390 different cigarettes from 173 countries and territories. When he died in March 1992 his wife Naida took over the collection. The oldest brand represented is Lone Jack which dates from around 1885. The collection contains both the world's longest and shortest cigarettes.

### Cigarette cards
The card collection that belonged to Edward Wharton-Tigar of London, UK, consists of over 1 million cigarette and trade cards in 45,000 sets. The collection was bequeathed to the British Museum, London, UK.

### Cigarette cases
Colin Gray of Dover, Kent, UK, has a collection of 1,087 cigarette cases.

### Cigarette lighters
In June 1996, Francis Van Herle of Beringen, Belgium, had 58,259 different lighters.

### Cigarette packets
Since 1962, Claudio Rebecchi of Modena, Italy, has accumulated 130,620 cigarette packets from 268 countries and territories. The most represented country in the collection is Japan, with 14,080 packets.

Alan Barker of Suffolk, UK, has the largest British collection, with 54,803 different cigarette packets.

## Fruit stickers
Antoine Secco of Bourbon-Lancy, France, has collected over 11,000 fruit labels (stickers)—all of the labels are different.

### Matchbook covers
Ed Brassard of Seattle, Washington, USA, had a collection of 3,159,119 matchbook covers by March 1995.

### Matchbox labels
Teiichi Yoshizawa of Chiba-Ken, Japan, has amassed a collection of 743,512 different matchbox labels (including advertising labels) from over 130 countries since 1925.

Phillumenist (someone who collects matchbox labels) Robert Jones of Indianapolis, USA, has a collection of some 280,000 matchbox labels (excluding advertising labels).

### Passports
Guy Van Keer of Brussels, Belgium, has amassed a collection of 3,880 used passports and travel documents which have been used in lieu of passports. They represent 130 countries and passport-issuing authorities (including many countries which are now no longer in existence). The documents range from 1615 to the present day. The most valuable item in the collection is a colourful 1898 Chinese passport, which is estimated to be worth at least $22,500 (£36,000).

## Cards and paper
### Aeroplane sick bags
Niek Vermeulen of Wormerveer in the Netherlands has the world's largest collection of aeroplane sick bags. By May 1997 he had amassed 2,112 different bags representing 470 airlines.

The largest British collection belongs to Dr David Bradford, of Richmond, N Yorkshire, who has 1,112 different plane sick bags.

### Bags
Heinz Schmidt-Bachem of Düren, Germany, has collected 60,000 plastic and paper bags since 1975.

### Bus tickets
Yacov Yosipovv of Tel-Aviv, Israel, collects used bus tickets. In March 1997 he had over 14,000 examples, every one different.

### Robin Christmas cards
Joan Gordon of the Medway Towns, Kent, UK, decorates her home for Christmas each year with Christmas cards which have pictures of robins on them. The collection covers every room in the house and she starts the decorating in November. Her unique collection now numbers 8,001 different cards.

### Tea cards
William 'Bill' Smart from Grimsby, Lincs, UK, began collecting tea cards, which are found in packets of tea and teabags, in the 1960s. In May 1997, his collection stood at over 25,260 picture cards, which included 785 complete sets and examples from 20 countries (although the majority of the cards are British). He possesses almost every card issued by Brooke Bond and nearly every Typhoo card.

# 2,112 AEROPLANE SICK BAGS

## OF ROBINS, COVERS EVERY ROOM IN HER HOUSE

## Writing
### Books
John Q. Benham of Avoca, Indiana, USA, has the world's largest private collection of over 1.5 million books.

### Bookmarks
Ralph Saville of Hull, E Yorkshire, UK, has a collection of 1,416 different bookmarks, made of different materials in a wide variety of shapes and sizes.

### Pens
As of May 1997, Angelika Unverhau, of Dinslaken, Germany, had a collection of 108,500 different ball-point pens.

## Money
### Credit cards
Walter Cavanagh of Santa Clara, California, USA, has 1,397 different credit cards. They are worth more than $1.65 million (£1 million) in credit and are kept in the world's longest wallet which is 76.2 m (250 ft) long and weighs 17.49 kg (38 lb 8 oz).

### Piggy banks
During the past 39 years, Ove Nordström of Spånga, Sweden, has collected a record 3,075 piggy banks.

### Parking meters
Lotta Sjölin of Solna, Sweden, had a collection of 292 different parking meters as of July 1996. She has been collecting since 1989 and has obtained disused meters from local authorities all over the world.

**Left**
Tony Mattia was forced to move out of his bedsit and into a two-bedroom flat in order to have enough space for his collection of Barbie dolls. In March 1997 he had 1,125 dolls (900 Barbies and 225 Sindys) estimated to be worth around £10,000.

## DATES BACK TO THE 1960S AND INCLUDES EXAMPLES FROM 20 COUNTRIES

## Toys
### Barbie dolls
Tony Mattia of Brighton, E Sussex, UK, had collected 900 Barbie dolls as of March 1997. He has about one half of all the Barbie models ever produced since 1959 and many versions of her boyfriend Ken. He changes the costume of every doll once a month and spends hours brushing their hair.

### Star Wars toys
Jason Joiner, of Ealing, London, UK, is a special effects expert who worked on George Lucas' *Star Wars* films, some of which have been produced at studios in Watford, Herts, UK. He has a collection of over 20,000 *Star Wars* toys. In addition, Joiner has the original C3PO robot, the original R2D2 robot and the original Darth Vader costume.

**Left**
Colin Gray's collection of cigarette cases includes a number of highly individual examples, including one which depicts a map of the Indian sub-continent before partition in 1947, another from WWI containing a lady's photograph and a lock of hair and a case made for a snooker player dated 1936.

## Attire and accessories

### Buttons
Students and teacher Ellen Dambach of Rolling Hills Primary School, Vernon, New Jersey, USA, collected 1,000,000 clothing buttons between Jan and June 1995.

### Clothing labels
Leonie Robroek of Heerlen, Netherlands, has 1,729 clothing labels (all different) from a wide variety of garments from different countries.

### Earrings
Carol McFadden of Oil City, Pennsylvania, USA, had collected 24,167 different pairs of earrings to July 1996.

### Ties (grabatology)
The world champion grabatologist is Tom Holmes of Walsall, W Midlands, who has collected over 10,624 different ties. His collection was started 70 years ago and includes yearly birthday ties sent to him by the British prime minister.

The term 'grabatologist' was coined specially for Tom Holmes by the Guild of British Tie Makers.

## Drink

### Beer cans
William B. Christensen of Madison, New Jersey, USA, has a collection of over 75,000 different beer cans from some 125 different countries, colonies and territories.

A collection of 2,502 unopened bottles and cans of beer from 103 countries was bought for $25,000 (£14,000) by the Downer Club of Downer, ACT, Australia, at the Australian Associated Press Financial Markets Annual Charity Golf Tournament on 23 March 1990.

### Beer labels (labology)
Jan Solberg of Oslo, Norway, had amassed 424,868 different beer labels from around the world to June 1995.

### Beer mats (tegestology)
The world's largest collection of beer mats is owned by Leo Pisker of Langenzersdorf, Austria, who has collected 150,125 different mats from 165 countries to date. The largest in his collection is 76 x 76 cm (2 ft 5⅞ in x 2 ft 5⅞ in) ), and the smallest measures just 25 x 25mm (1 x 1 in). Both of these beer mats come from the United Kingdom.

## Bottles
George E. Terren of Southboro, Massachusetts, USA, had a collection of 31,804 bottles (miniatures) of distilled spirits and liquors at 31 May 1993.

Peter Broeker of Geesthacht, Germany, has an unduplicated collection of 8,131 full beer bottles from 110 countries.

David Maund had collected 11,742 miniature Scotch whisky bottles by Nov 1996.

### Bottle caps
Since 1956, Paul Høegh Poulsen of Rødovre, Denmark, has amassed 82,169 different bottle caps from 179 countries.

### Bottle labels
On 4 April 1997, Ian Boasman of Preston, Lancs, UK, had a collection of 4,239 different spirit and liquor labels.

## Kitchen ware

### Bread clips
Ann Muffy, a teacher from a school in New York City, USA, has a specialized collection of plastic bread clips, which are used to

**Right**
Demetrios Pistiola's collection of 305 movie cameras are kept in Greece's smallest museum which measures 3 x 4 m (9 ft 11 in x 13 ft 1 in).

# 424,868 BEER LABELS

MOWERS DATING FROM BETWEEN 1830 AND 1940

fasten the tops of bread wrappers. As part of a recycling project, she and her class collected 5,170 clips (as of April 1997).

## Fridge magnets
Louise J. Greenfarb of Spanaway, Washington, USA, had collected 17,000 refrigerator magnets by May 1996.

## Garden ephemera
### Four leaf clovers
From April 1995, George Kaminski, of Pittsburgh, Pennsylvania, USA, collected 13,382 four-leaf clovers during his recreation time at the State Correctional Institution, Somerset, Pennsylvania, USA. He also found 1,336 five-leaf, 78 six-leaf and six seven-leaf clovers. However prison policy does not allow inmates to collect anything, so the collection was sent to his sister.

### Gnomes
The 10-ha (4-acre) Gnome Reserve, near Bradworthy, Devon, UK, is run by Ann Atkins. She has a collection of 2,010 gnomes and pixies, although there can be up to 800 additional gnomes on sale at any one time. She began her collection in 1978.

IN A PITTSBURGH JAIL

### Lawn mowers
By May 1997, Andrew Hall and Michael Duck had a collection of 680 lawn mowers dating from 1830 to 1940. Their Hall and Duck Trust Collection of Vintage Lawn Mowers at Windsor, Berks, UK, is open to the public.

## Miscellaneous
### Handcuffs
Chris Gower, of Dorset, UK, has a collection of 412 pairs of handcuffs.

### Movie cameras
Demetrios Pistiola has a collection of 305 movie cameras dating from 1901 to the present-day. He has created a small museum for them and it is considered to be the only one of its kind in the world.

### Plasters
Brian Viner of London, UK, has a unique collection of around 3,750 (unused) plasters (medical dressings) of various different colours, styles, shapes and sizes.

### Pliers
LeRoy Bauer, of Shakopee, Minnesota, USA, had 1,834 different types of pliers in his collection in May 1997.

1,064

1,257

2,010

**Left**
Ann Atkins has the largest gnome and pixie collection in the world. Her gnome reserve in north Devon, UK, boasts 2,010 garden gnomes. Visitors are encouraged to wear pixie hats while touring the garden.

# Models and miniatures

## Model cars
### Smallest model car
The world's smallest model car, 0.67 mm (3⁄100 in) long, was built by the Japanese car firm Toyota. Called the Toyota Model AA, it has an electric motor and was built to mark the company's 60th anniversary in 1997.

### Longest running model car
A Scalextric Jaguar XJ8 ran non-stop for 866 hr 44 min 54 sec and covered a distance of 2,850.39 km (1,771.2 miles) from 2 May–7 June 1989.

### Top distance (24 hours) by model cars
In Sept 1994, a 1:64 scale car made by H. O. Racing and Hobbies of San Diego, California, USA, travelled a distance of 603.631 km (375 miles 139 yd).

Under BSCRA rules a 1:64 scale car covered a record 320.238 km (198 miles 1,737 yd) at the Rolls Royce Sports Hall, Derby, UK, on 11 and 12 Nov 1995.

Under BSCRA rules a 1:32 scale car owned by the North London Society of Model Engineers team at the ARRA club, Southport, Merseyside, UK, covered a record-breaking 492.364 km (305 miles 1,670 yd) in 1986.

### Longest slot car track
The world's longest slot car track was constructed by the Oulder Hill Community School, Rochdale, Lancs, UK, and measured 444.8 m (1,459 ft 4 in).

## Model Aircraft
### Altitude
A radio-controlled model aircraft owned by Maynard Hill (USA) climbed to a record-breaking altitude of 8,205 m (26,919 ft) on 6 Sept 1970.

### Distance
In June 1995, Robert Rosenthal and Maynard Hill (USA) set a model aircraft closed-circuit record of 1,250 km (776 miles 1,232 yd).

**100%**

The longest flight in a straight line to a nominated landing point was 737.9 km (458 miles 880 yds), by Maynard Hill and Robert Rosenthal, from Bealeton, Virginia, USA, to Ridgeland, South Carolina, USA, in 8 hr 43 min on 29 Aug 1995.

### Speed
The overall speed record is 395.64 km/h (245.84 mph), by a model flown on control lines by Leonid Lipinski (USSR) in Dec 1971.

The speed record for a radio-controlled model is 390.92 km/h (242.91 mph), by Walter Sitar (Austria) on 10 June 1977.

### Duration records
Maynard Hill (USA) flew a powered model for 33 hr 39 min 15 sec from 1–2 Oct 1992.

An indoor model with a wound rubber motor set a record of 55 min 6 sec in Dec 1993.

Jean-Pierre Schiltknecht flew a solar-driven model airplane for 10 hr 43 min 51 sec at Wetzlar, Germany, on 10 July 1991.

### Smallest model aircraft
The smallest model aircraft weighs 0.1 g (4⁄100 oz). Powered by a horsefly, it was made by Don Emmick of Seattle, USA.

### Largest model aircraft
The largest radio-controlled model aircraft was a glider weighing 163.3 kg (360 lb) with a wingspan of 7.77 m (25 ft 6 in) made by Melton Mowbray and District Model Club, UK.

### Smallest model helicopter
A helicopter 24 mm (15⁄16 in) long, 8 mm (5⁄16 in) high, with a rotor diameter of 13 mm (½ in) was made by the Institut für Mikrotechnik, Mainz, Germany, in 1996.

## Model boats and trains
### Top distances (24 hour) by model boats
Lowestoft Model Boat Club members crewed a radio-controlled model for 178.93 km (111 miles 317 yd) at Dome Leisure Park, Doncaster, UK, from 17–18 Aug 1991.

David and Peter Holland of Doncaster, S Yorkshire, UK, crewed a 71-cm (2 ft 4-in) scale model boat on one battery for 24 hours for 53.83 km (33 miles 742 yds) at the Dome Leisure Complex, Doncaster, in Aug 1992.

### Model railways
Ike Cottingham and Mark Hamrick (both USA) organized a standard 'Life-Like' BL2 HO

**SMALLEST SINGLE-REAR**

scale electric train to pull six eight-wheel coaches for 1,207 hr 30 min from 4 Aug to 23 Sept 1990, c. 1463.65 km (909½ miles).

A model steam locomotive, the 18.4-cm (7¼-in) gauge 'Peggy', covered 269.9 km (167 miles 1,232 yds) in 24 hours at Weston Park Railway, Shrops, UK, in 1994.

Canadian Bob Henderson constructed a miniature model railway to 1:1400 scale. The railway engine measures 5 mm (1⁄5 in).

The longest model train, 70.2-m (228-ft) long, ran in Perth, Australia, on 3 June 1996.

### Largest model railway
A miniature railway in Northlandz, Flemington, New Jersey, USA, has 15,240 m (50,000 ft) of track. There are 125 trains, over 10,000 freight cars and 7,000 buildings.

# MODEL RAILWAY ENGINE 5 MM

## POWERED BY A HORSEFLY

The longest track on which a model train was run was 88.7 m (291 ft) long and was constructed by the Model Railway Club of Union, New Jersey, USA, on 22 July 1978.

## Model sledges
### Chair sledge
A sledge 530 mm (2 in) long, 248 mm (9⁄10 in) high and 380 mm (1½ in) wide was constructed by NORØ Industrier A/S of Tynset, Norway. It was even ridden in 1996.

### Bobsleigh run
The bob run of St Moritz-Celerina, Switzerland, was copied in miniature between 20 Jan–2 Feb 1997 by five members of the Basler Mini-bob Chaote (Switzerland). The course was 55 m (180 ft 5½ in) long, 7 cm (2¾ in) wide, with a 4.5 m (14 ft 9 in) decline. The individual mini-bobs that were used were 17.5 cm (6⁹⁄10 in) long and 5.5 cm (2³⁄20 in) wide.

**Left**
The longest slot car track in the world, built at the Gracie Fields Theatre, Oulder Hill Community School, Rochdale, Lancs, UK, from 31 May to 2 June 1996.

## HELICOPTER HAS EMPTY WEIGHT OF 53 KG AND ROTOR DIAMETER OF 4.5 M

## Smallest things
### Finest paint brush
The 000 in Series 7 by Winsor and Newton is made of 150–200 Kolinsky sable hairs and weighs 15 mg (5⁄10,000 oz).

### Smallest aircraft
The smallest biplane flown was *Bumble Bee Two*, designed and built by Robert Starr (USA). Able to carry one person, it was 2.69 m (8 ft 10 in) long, had a wing span of 1.68 m (5 ft 6 in), weighed 179.6 kg (396 lb) and could reach 306 km/h (190 mph).

The smallest monoplane ever flown is the *Baby Bird*, designed and built by Donald Stits. It is 3.35 m (11 ft) long, has a wing span of 1.91 m (6 ft 3 in) and weighs 114.3 kg (252 lb). Its top speed is 177 km/h (110 mph) and it was first flown on 4 Aug 1984.

The smallest twin-engined aircraft is probably the Colombian MGI5 Cricri, which has a wing span of 4.9 m (16 ft) and measures 3.91 m (12 ft 10 in) in overall length.

### Smallest helicopter
The single-seat Seremet WS-8 ultra-light helicopter built in Denmark in 1976 had a weight when empty of 53 kg (117 lb) and a rotor diameter of 4.5 m (14 ft 9 in).

### Smallest cassette
Sony's NT cassette for dictating machines is 30 x 21 x 5 mm (1³⁄16 x 1³⁄16 x 3⁄16 in).

### Smallest functional record
Six discs 33.3 mm (1⁵⁄16 in) in diameter were made at HMV's studio, Hayes, London, on 26 Jan 1923 for Queen Mary's Dolls' House.

### Smallest TV sets
The Seiko TV-Wrist Watch, launched in 1982, has a black and white screen 30.5-mm (1¼ in) wide. The system, with the receiver unit and headphones, weighs 320 g (11.3 oz).

The smallest single-piece set is the Casio-Keisanki TV-10, weighing 338 g (11.9 oz) with a screen 6.85 cm (2¹¹⁄16 in) wide.

The smallest and lightest colour set, the Casio CV-1, has dimensions of 60 x 24 x 91 mm (2.4 x 0.9 x 3.6 in) and weighs 168.5 g (6 oz) including battery. Launched in July 1992, it has a 35-mm (1³⁄8-in) screen.

### Smallest camera
The smallest camera on the market is the Japanese 'Petal' camera. It has a diameter of 2.9 cm (1⅛ in) and is 1.65 cm (⅝ in) thick.

### Smallest video camera
Oak Ridge National Laboratory, Tennessee, USA, makes video cameras measuring 2.54 x 5.08 x 1.27 cm (1 x 2 x ½ in).

### Smallest watch
The smallest watches, measuring just over 12 mm (⁶⁄127 in) and 476 mm (1⁴⁴⁄50 in) wide, are produced by Jaeger le Coultre of Switzerland. They have a 15-jewelled movement and weigh under 7 g (0.25 oz).

## Paper Aircraft
### Duration
The record for a hand-launched paper plane is 20.9 seconds by Chris Edge and Andy Currey with consecutive throws at Cardington Hangar, Bedford, UK, on 28 July 1996.

### Indoor distance
In 1985 Tony Felch recorded 58.82 m (193 ft) at La Crosse, Wisconsin, USA.

### Largest flying paper aircraft
A paper aircraft with a wingspan of 13.97 m (45 ft 10 in) was constructed by students from Delft University of Technology, the Netherlands, and was flown on 16 May 1995. It flew 34.8 m (114 ft 2 in).

# Games

## Chess

### Longest world champions
The longest undisputed champion was Emanuel Lasker (Germany) who held the title for 26 years 337 days from 1894 to 1921.

The women's world championship title was held by Vera Francevna Stevenson-Menchik (Czechoslovakia, later UK), from 1927 until her death in 1944. She successfully defended the title a record seven times.

### Most World Championship wins
The USSR won the biennial men's team title (Olympiad) a record 18 times between 1952 and 1990, and the women's title 11 times from its introduction in 1957 until 1986.

### Fewest games lost by a world champion
José Raúl Capablanca of Cuba lost only 34 games out of 571 in his adult career, from 1909 to 1939. He was unbeaten from 10 Feb 1916 to 21 March 1924 (63 games) and was world champion 1921–27.

### Most British titles
Jonathan Penrose won 10 British titles between 1958 and 1963 and between 1966 and 1969.

Rowena Mary Bruce won 11 British women's titles between 1937 and 1969.

**Right**
The origins of the game of chess stretch back to the 6th century. Originally an Indian or Chinese game, it was brought to Europe by traders and its rules then refined to those we know today.

**Below right**
Backgammon can be traced back to a game that was played in 3000 BC. The word 'backgammon' is thought to have derived from either the Welsh for 'little battle' or the Saxon for 'back game'.

### Highest ratings
The highest rating ever attained on the officially adopted Elo System is 2,815, by Gary Kasparov (Russia) in 1993.

The highest-rated woman is Judit Polgar (Hungary). Her rating was 2,675 in 1996.

The top British player was Nigel Short who had a peak rating of 2,685 in 1991.

The top British woman is Susan Kathryn Arkell who achieved a rating of 2,355 on 1 July 1988.

### Most consecutive games
The most consecutive games played is 663, by Vlastimil Hort (Czechoslovakia, later Germany) over 32½ hours at Porz, Germany, on 5–6 Oct 1984. He played 60–120 opponents at a time, scoring over 80% wins and averaging 30 moves per game.

### Most games played simultaneously
Ulf Andersson of Sweden played 310 games simultaneously (with just two defeats) at Alvsjö, Sweden, on 6–7 Jan 1996.

### Most active world champion
Champion Anatoliy Karpov (USSR, now Russia) averaged 45.2 competitive games a year in 32 tournaments, from 1975 to 1985. He finished first in 26.

### Slowest moves
The slowest reported move (before time clocks) in an official event is reputed to have been by Louis Paulsen (Germany) against Paul Morphy (USA) at the first American Chess Congress, New York, USA, on 29 Oct 1857. It ended in a draw on move 56 after 15 hours, of which Paulsen used c. 11 hours.

Grand Master Friedrich Sämisch (Germany) ran out of the allotted time (2 hr 30 min for 45 moves) after only 12 moves, in Prague, Czechoslovakia (Czech Republic), in 1938.

The slowest move played since time clocks were introduced was when Francisco Torres Trois took 2 hr 20 min for his seventh move against Luis Santos at Vigo, Spain, in 1980.

The most moves in a Master game was 269 when Ivan Nikolić drew with Goran Arsović in Belgrade, Yugoslavia, on 17 Feb 1989.

## Scrabble

### British Championship winners
Philip Nelkon won the British National Championships a record four times, in 1978, 1981, 1990 and 1992.

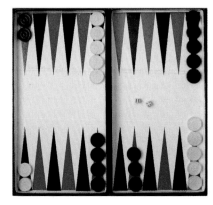

The youngest winner was Allan Saldanha, aged 15 years 239 days in 1993.

### World Championship winners
The first Scrabble World Championship was held in London, UK, in 1991. Peter Morris (USA) won $10,000 (£5,600) as first prize.

The youngest winner was Mark Nyman (GB) who won in 1993 aged 26 years 320 days.

### Highest scores
The highest competitive game score is 1,049 by Phil Appleby in June 1989. His opponent scored 253 and the margin of victory, 796 points, is also a record.

The highest competitive single turn score recorded is 392, by Dr Saladin Karl Khoshnaw at Manchester, UK, in April 1982. He laid down 'CAZIQUES', meaning 'native chiefs of West Indian aborigines'.

THE 1992 EPSON WORLD

The highest score on an opening move is 124, by Sam Kantimathi at Portland, Oregon, USA, in July 1993. He put down the word 'BEZIQUE' which is a type of card game for two or more players.

### Most points in 24 hours
Paul Golder and John Howell scored 111,154 points at BBC Radio Essex, UK, on 4–5 May 1995.

## Monopoly

### Most expensive Monopoly set
A million-dollar gold and precious stones Monopoly set was created in 1988 by jewellery designer Sidney Mobell of San Francisco, USA.

### Monopoly Championships
In the 10 monopoly tournaments held to date, no competitor has won the World Championships more than once.

Only the USA has produced more than one champion: Lee Bayrd of Los Angeles, California, in 1973 and Alvin Aldridge of Dayton, Ohio, in 1974.

The only player to win both the World and UK title was Jason Bunn in 1985.

## Contract Bridge

### Biggest tournament
The Epson World Bridge Championship, held 20–21 June 1992, was contested by more

# HIGHEST SCRABBLE SCORE 1,049

## BRIDGE CHAMPIONSHIP WAS CONTESTED BY MORE THAN 102,000 PLAYERS

than 102,000 players playing the same hands at over 2,000 centres worldwide.

**Most world titles**
The World Championship (Bermuda Bowl) has been won a record 14 times by the USA: 1950–51, 1953–54, 1970–71, 1976–77, 1979, 1981, 1983, 1985, 1987 and 1995.

Italy's Blue Team won 13 world titles and an additional three team Olympiads between 1957 and 1975. Giorgio Belladonna was in all the Italian winning teams.

The USA women's team have won a record six times in the World Championship for the Venice Trophy: 1974, 1976, 1978, 1987, 1989 and 1991, and three wins at the World Team Olympiad: 1976, 1980 and 1984.

**Most hands**
In the 1989 Bermuda Bowl, Perth, Australia, Marcel Branco and Gabriel Chagas of Brazil played 752 out of a possible 784 boards.

**Perfect deals**
The mathematical odds against dealing 13 cards of one suit are 158,753,389,899 to 1, while the odds against a named player receiving a 'perfect hand' consisting of all 13 spades are 635,013,559,599 to 1.

The odds against each of the four players receiving a complete suit (a 'perfect deal') are 2,235,197,406,895,366,368,301, 599,999 to 1.

## Poker
**Two royal flushes in a row**
In May 1994 during a game of seven-card stud in the poker room at The Mirage, Las Vegas, USA, Alex Hemstree was dealt two royal straight flushes in a row.

**World Championship winner**
Johnny Moss of Texas, USA, is the only person to win the World Championship three times, in 1970, 1971 and 1974.

**Largest poker pot**
During the 1996 World Series of Poker at Binion's Horseshoe, Las Vegas, USA, a pot of $2,328,000 (£3,632,000) was recorded.

## Magic the Gathering
**Youngest world champion**
Tom Chanpheng (Australia) became world champion at the age of 19 in 1996.

Each of the three world champions to date has been from a different country: USA, Switzerland and Australia.

**Most team World Championships**
The USA have won the team World Championship twice, in 1995 and 1996.

## Crosswords
**Fastest crossword solution**
On 19 Dec 1970, Roy Dean completed *The Times* crossword in 3 min 45 sec, in the studio of BBC radio's *Today* programme.

Dr John Sykes won *The Times/Collins Dictionaries* championship 10 times between 1972 and 1990. He set a championship time of 4 min 28 sec in 1989.

**Largest published crossword**
In July 1982, Robert Turcot (Canada) compiled a crossword of 82,951 squares. It had 12,489 across clues, 13,125 down and covered 3.55 m² (38¼ ft²).

**Most prolific compiler**
Roger Squires (UK) compiles 38 crossword puzzles each week. His total output up to May 1996 was over 48,000 crosswords.

## Backgammon
**World Champion**
Bill Robertie (USA) is the only person to have ever won the World Backgammon Championship twice, in 1983 and 1987.

**Shortest backgammon game**
In 1982 Alan Beckerson (UK) played the shortest game with just 16 throws.

# Computer challenge

## Games and Competitions

### Largest video game competition
On 24 March 1996, 9,066 people participated at the second annual video game tournament for the game Puyo Puyo held by Compile Corporation of Hiroshima, Japan, at Makuhari Messe, Hiroshima, Japan.

### Earliest video game
The first video game was Pong, invented in 1972 by Nolan Bushell at Atari and released in arcades that year. The home computer version, Home Pong, was introduced in 1974. The game was a simple tennis game, with players hitting a 'ball' back and forth.

### Super Mario Kart
Competing in the Computer Challenge, launched in the 1997 *Guinness Book of Records*, David Burk of Dagenham, London, UK, achieved a time of 1:00.70 on the Time Trial Mode, Mushroom Cup, Mario Circuit 1 of Super Mario Kart for the Super Nintendo Entertainment System in a challenge play-off at the offices of Guinness Publishing Ltd, London, UK, on 30 May 1997.

### Earliest video games system
The first programmable home video games system (via plug-in cartridges) was Channel F, introduced by Fairchild in 1976.

### Guinness Computer Challenge
Would you like to be a **Guinness** record-holder? Once again, the *Guinness Book of Records* has got together with the three leading manufacturers of computer games, Nintendo, Sony and Sega. We have selected from each manufacturer two of the most up-to-date and challenging games.

All that you have to do is record your personal best score, following the individual rules that are set out on this page, and then send a photograph of the screen showing your score to **Guinness Publishing**.

The highest scoring competitors will be required to play the game under **Guinness** supervision, and the top scorers will be invited to attend the final championship play-off.

# BECOME THE NEXT GUINNESS CHAMPION!

## AND THE EVIL EMPIRE

### Nintendo
#### Mario Kart 64
The Mario Kart gang are back, bigger and better in 3-D. The analogue stick gives superb control as you power slide through the turns and straights. The game has 20 different courses filled with valleys, jumps, tunnels and bridges. There are four different game play modes: Grand Prix, Time Attack, VS. Match, and Battle.

#### Rules
Competitors must send photographic evidence of their top time. No game enhancement devices are permitted. The photograph must show both screen and console. The challenge will be on Time Attack mode, three laps on Luigi Raceway, Mushroom Cup. Any character may be used, turbo starts and power slides are allowed, but no other cheats are permitted. A good time will be under 1 min 50 sec.

#### Star Wars: Shadows of the Empire
Shadows of the Empire is set in the time between *The Empire Strikes Back* and *Return of the Jedi*. Take on the role of Dash Rendar, smuggler and mercenary, as you oppose the might of the evil Empire and a new threat from Prince Xisor, leader of the Black Sun organization.

#### Rules
The challenge is to finish The Battle of Hoth, difficulty medium, collecting all challenge

COURSE
**Brick wall town**
1 LAP = 2.277km
**Round:FINAL**
最終戦

SEGA TOURINGCAR CHAMPIONSHIP SINCE 1996

points. Competitors must send photographic evidence of their top time. No game enhancement devices are permitted. A good time will be under 3 min 12 sec.

### Sony
#### Rage Racer by Namco
This sequel to Ridge Racer Revolution provides the fastest and most challenging game released on the PlayStation. As players improve they gain faster vehicles, increasing their speed and ensuring a challenge suited to the player's skill level.

#### Rules
Competitors must send in photographic evidence of their fastest Total Time lap times in Time Attack Mode, Mythical Coast course, with the Gnade Esperanza car with automatic transmission. No cheat modes are allowed.

#### Soul Blade by Namco
Namco have produced the ultimate armed combat simulation, Soul Blade. There are four regular game modes, and for the first time on the PlayStation, a Master Mode which lets advanced players compete for special weapons with new characteristics.

#### Rules
Competitors must send in photographic evidence of Total Time on Time Attack Mode, where all fighters must be fought in the quickest time possible.

### Sega
#### Sega Touring Car
Can you face the challenge of the big boys in the European Touring Car Championship? Choose from a Toyota Supra, an AMG Mercedes C Class, an Opel Calibra V6 or the awesome Alfa Romeo 155 V6 Ti in this race where the pace is hard and fast.

#### Rules
For this challenge, players must send in photographic evidence of their fastest time on the game's first track. You may choose manual or automatic transmission. No cheats are permitted.

#### Worldwide Soccer '98
This game for between one and four players combines stunning graphics, advanced motion capture and fluid movement. Worldwide Soccer '98 has statistics and information on over 1,500 soccer stars from over 100 teams around the world. Players can customize the game with an array of match options, including weather conditions and even the time of day.

#### Rules
Players must send in photographic evidence and full match details of their highest score at full time. There are no restrictions on which of the 100 or more teams on offer are used. The match can be set for any time of day in any weather condition, and must be set to play for 10 minutes.

**Left**
In Sega Touring Car you have a choice of four powerful cars: the Toyota Supra, the AMG Mercedes C Class, the Opel Calibra V61 and the Alfa Romeo 155 V6 Ti.

**Left**
Soul Blade is the enhanced conversion of the smash arcade hit Soul Edge.

**CAN YOU FACE THE CHALLENGE IN THE TOURING CAR CHAMPIONSHIP?**

# Taking it to the limit

# Exploration

**Right**
The record for the longest polar sledge journey is held by the six-member International Trans-Antarctica Expedition. During the expedition they were supported by aircraft and had a team of 40 dogs, some of which were flown out for periods of rest.

## Polar exploration

### North Pole conquest by land
The first people indisputably to have reached the North Pole at ground level were Pavel Afanasyevich Geordiyenko, Pavel Kononovich Sen'ko, Mikhail Mikhailovich Somov and Mikhail Yemel'yanovich Ostrekin (all of the former USSR), on 23 April 1948.

### North Pole conquest by sea
The earliest indisputable journey to the North Pole over the sea-ice took place on 19 April 1968, when Ralph Plaisted (USA), accompanied by Walter Pederson, Gerald Pitzl and Jean Luc Bombardier, reached the pole after a 42-day trek in four skidoos (snowmobiles).

### Solo trek to the North Pole
Naomi Uemura (Japan) became the first person to reach the North Pole in a solo trek across the Arctic sea-ice on 1 May 1978. He had travelled 725 km (450 miles).

Dr Jean-Louis Etienne (France) was the first person to reach the pole solo and without dogs, on 11 May 1986 after 63 days.

### North Pole by skis
The first people to ski to the North Pole were the seven members of a Soviet expedition, led by Dmitry Shparo. They reached the pole on 31 May 1979 after a trek of 1,500 km (900 miles) which took them 77 days.

### Arctic crossing
The British Trans-Arctic Expedition was the first to cross the Arctic sea-ice. Wally Herbert, Ken Hedges, Allan Gill, Dr Roy Koerner and 40 huskies left Point Barrow, Alaska, on 21 Feb 1968 and arrived at the Seven Island archipelago 464 days later, on 29 May 1969. It involved a haul of 4,699 km (2,920 miles) with a drift of 1,100 km (700 miles), compared with the straight-line distance of 2,674 km (1,662 miles).

In 1982 Sir Ranulph Fiennes and Charles Burton crossed the Arctic in a single season in open snowmobiles from Alert, via the North Pole, to the Greenland Sea.

### North Pole conquest
The first British men to reach the North Pole unsupported were Dr Stephen Martin and David Mitchell on 2 June 1997. They had journeyed for more than 1,900 miles.

### South Pole conquest
The South Pole was first reached at 11 a.m. on 14 Dec 1911 by a Norwegian party of five men led by Capt. Roald Engebereth Gravning Amundsen, after a 53-day march with dog sledges from the Bay of Whales.

The first person to reach the South Pole solo and unsupported was Erling Kagge (Norway) on 7 Jan 1993 after a 50-day trek of 1,400 km (870 miles) from Berkner Island.

### First to both poles
Dr Albert Paddock Crary (USA) reached the North Pole in a Dakota aircraft on 3 May 1952. On 12 Feb 1961 he arrived at the South Pole by Sno Cat.

### Pole-to-pole circumnavigation
Sir Ranulph Fiennes and Charles Burton of the British Trans-Globe Expedition travelled south from Greenwich (2 Sept 1979), crossing the South Pole (15 Dec 1980) and the North Pole (10 April 1982), and returned to Greenwich, arriving on 29 Aug 1982 after a 56,000-km (35,000-mile) trek.

### First solo unaided Antarctic crossing
Boerge Ousland (Norway) completed a 64-day trek across Antarctica on 18 Jan 1997, becoming the first person to cross the continent alone and unaided.

### Longest polar sledge journeys
The six-member International Trans-Antarctica Expedition sledged 6,040 km

# 69 DAYS 19 MIN UNDERWATER

(3,750 miles) in 220 days from Seal Nunataks on 27 July 1989 to Mirnyy on 3 March 1990.

### First to walk to both poles
Robert Swan led the three-man Footsteps of Scott expedition, which reached the South Pole on 11 Jan 1986. He also headed the eight-man Icewalk expedition, which arrived at the North Pole on 14 May 1989.

### Antarctic crossing
The first surface crossing of the Antarctic continent was completed on 2 March 1958, after a trek of 3,473 km (2,158 miles) lasting 99 days, from Shackleton Base to Scott Base via the pole. The team of 12 was led by Sir Vivian Ernest Fuchs.

The longest unsupported trek in Antarctica was by Sir Ranulph Fiennes with Dr Michael Stroud, who set off from Gould Bay on 9 Nov 1992, reached the South Pole on 16 Jan 1993 but abandoned their walk on the Ross ice shelf on 11 Feb. They covered 2,170 km (1,350 miles) during their 94-day trek.

### First all-female polar expedition
Five relay teams of four women walked 1,000 km (600 miles) to the North Pole in

(437 ft) by John J. Gruener and R. Neal Watson (US) off Freeport, Grand Bahama, on 14 Oct 1968.

### Simulated dives
The record dive simulated with the use of gas mixtures was achieved in a simulated dive to a depth of 701 m (2,300 ft) of sea-water by Théo Mavrostomos in Marseille, France, on 20 Nov 1992. He was breathing 'hydreliox' (hydrogen, oxygen and helium).

Arnaud de Nechaud de Feral performed a simulated saturation dive of 73 days from 9 Oct–21 Dec 1989 in a hyperbaric chamber, simulating a depth of 300 m (985 ft) at Marseille, France. He was breathing 'hydrox', a hydrogen and oxygen mixture.

Richard Presley spent 69 days 19 min in a module underwater as part of Project Atlantis in Key Largo, Florida, USA, from 6 May–14 July 1992.

### Deepest salvage
The greatest depth where salvage has been done is 5,258 m (17,251 ft). Crew of the USS *Salvor* and personnel from Eastport International managed to raise the wreckage to the surface on 27 Feb 1992.

by the cable ship *John Cabot* after work by *Pisces V*, *Pisces II* and the remote-control recovery vessel *Curv*.

The greatest depth from which an actual escape has been made without the help of any equipment is 68.6 m (225 ft). It was made by Richard Slater from *Nekton Beta* off California, USA, on 28 Sept 1970.

The record for an escape with equipment was by Norman Cooke and Hamish Jones on 22 July 1987. During a naval exercise they escaped from a depth of 183 m (601 ft) from the submarine HMS *Otus* in Bjørnefjorden, off Bergen, Norway.

### Submergence
The continuous duration record for scuba diving is 212 hr 30 min, by Michael Stevens in a Royal Navy tank at the NEC, Birmingham, UK, from 14–23 Feb 1986.

## Survival
### Longest on a raft
The longest survival alone on a raft is 133 days by Poon Lim of the UK Merchant Navy. He was picked up by a fishing boat off Salinópolis, Brazil, on 5 April 1943.

March to May 1997. During the trek, the British teams, which completed a 240-km (150-mile) leg, hauled their own sledges.

### Longest pizza delivery
Eagle Boys Dial-a-Pizza in Christchurch, New Zealand, regularly deliver pizzas to Scott Base, Antarctica, for the NZ Antarctic Programme. After the nine-hour flight, the pizzas arrive complete with re-heating instructions.

## Submarine exploration
### Greatest ocean descent
The US Navy bathyscaphe *Trieste*, manned by Dr Jacques Piccard and USN Lt. Donald Walsh, reached a depth of 10,911 m (35,797 ft) on 23 Jan 1960 in the Challenger Deep of the Marianas Trench, 400 km (250 miles) south-west of Guam.

### Deep-diving records
The record depth for the ill-advised activity of breath-held diving is 130 m (428 ft) by Francisco 'Pipín' Ferreras (Cuba) off Cabo San Lucas, Mexico, on 10 March 1996.

The record dive with scuba (self-contained underwater breathing apparatus) is 133 m

### Deepest underwater escapes
Roger R. Chapman and Roger Mallinson were trapped for 76 hours when the *Pisces III* sank to a depth of 480 m (1,575 ft), at a point 240 km (150 miles) south-east of Cork, Republic of Ireland, on 29 Aug 1973. The vessel was hauled to the surface on 1 Sept

Tabwai Mikaie and Arenta Tebeitabu, from the island of Nikunau in Kiribati, survived 177 days adrift in open seas after their 4-m (13-ft) fishing boat was caught in a cyclone on 17 Nov 1991. They were washed ashore in Western Samoa, 1,800 km (1,100 miles) away.

**Left**
Sir Ranulph Fiennes and Charles Burton who made the first ever pole-to-pole circumnavigation.

# Space exploration

**Below right**
Neil Armstrong climbing down from the lunar module *Eagle* to become the first man to step on the Moon. He was followed by 'Buzz' Aldrin, while Michael Collins remained in the command module *Columbia* which was orbiting above.

## Space flights
### Earliest manned satellite
The earliest manned space flight ratified by the world governing body, the Fédération Aéronautique Internationale (FAI), was by Cosmonaut Flight Major Yuri Alekseyevich Gagarin in *Vostok 1* on 12 April 1961.

During the 40,868.6-km (25,394½-mile) flight the maximum altitude was 327 km (203 miles), and the maximum speed 28,260 km/h (17,560 mph).

### Longest manned space flight
Valeriy Poliyakov was launched to the *Mir* space station aboard *Soyuz TM18* on 8 Jan 1994 and landed in *Soyuz TM20* on 22 March 1995 after a space flight which lasted for 437 days 17 hr 58 min 16 sec.

### Longest space flight by a woman
Shannon Lucid (USA) was launched to the Russian *Mir* space station aboard US Space Shuttle STS 76 *Atlantis* on 22 March 1996 and landed aboard STS 79 *Atlantis* on 26 Sept after a space flight of 188 days 5 hr.

### Longest space shuttle flight
*Colombia* was launched on its 21st mission, STS 80, with a crew of four men and one woman on 19 Nov 1996. The flight lasted 17 days 15 hr 53 min 26 sec.

### Shortest manned flight
The sub-orbital mission by Comdr. Alan Shepard (USA) aboard *Mercury-Redstone 3* on 5 May 1961 lasted 15 min 28 sec.

## Astronauts
### First man in space
The first man in space was Cosmonaut Yuri Gagarin on 12 April 1961 in *Vostok 1*. He landed separately from his spacecraft 118 minutes after the launch, after ejecting 108 minutes into the flight as had been planned.

### First woman in space
Junior Lt Valentina Vladimirovna Tereshkova was launched in *Vostok 6* on 16 June 1963 and landed back on Earth after a flight of 2 days 22 hr 50 min and 48 orbits, a distance of 1,971,000 km (1,225,000 miles).

By 1 April 1997 the total number of women who had flown into space stood at 32. This figure breaks down into 25 Americans, two citizens of the former Soviet Union, one Canadian, one Japanese, one Russian, one French and one Briton. This figure represents 9% of the total of 357 people who have been in space.

### First Briton in space
Helen Sharman became the first Briton in space, in *Soyuz TM12* on 18 May 1991. She was the 15th woman in space, and the first non-Soviet, non-US woman.

### Most experienced space traveller
Valeriy Poliyakov clocked up 678 days 16 hr 33 min 16 sec on two space flights in 1988–89 and 1994–95.

### Most journeys
Capt. John Watts Young (USA) made his six space flights between 1965 and 1983, giving him 34 days flight experience. Story Musgrave (US) completed six space shuttle missions between 1983 and 1996, totalling 53 days.

The most flights by Soviet/Russian cosmonauts is five, by Vladimir Dzhanibekov between 1978 and 1985 and Gennadiy Strekalov between 1980 and 1995.

The most by a woman is five, by Shannon Lucid (flights STS 51G, 34, 43, 58 and 76).

### Largest crew on a space mission
The record for a single space mission is the crew of eight launched on space shuttle STS 61A *Challenger* on 30 Oct 1985. A crew of

**THE LONGEST SPACEWALK EVER UNDERTAKEN LASTED**

`02:56:05`  `02:56:10`

# 357 PEOPLE IN SPACE

## THE FIRST SPACE FUNERAL

eight (six Americans and two Russians) also landed aboard the US Space Shuttle STS 71 *Atlantis* on 7 July 1995.

### Largest crew on a spacecraft
On 29 June 1995 two Russians and one American from *Soyuz TM21* and five Americans and two Russians from STS 71 *Atlantis* were aboard the Russian *Mir* space station, to which STS 71 *Atlantis* docked.

### Most people in space
On 14 March 1995, a record 13 people were in space: seven Americans were aboard the space shuttle STS 67 *Endeavour*, three CIS cosmonauts aboard the *Mir* space station and two cosmonauts and a US astronaut were aboard *Soyuz TM21*.

On 31 July 1992, a record five countries had astronauts or cosmonauts in space at the same time: four CIS cosmonauts and one Frenchman were aboard Mir and five US astronauts, one Swiss and one Italian were on STS 46 *Atlantis*.

On 22 Feb 1996 there were four US, two Italian and one Swiss astronauts on STS 75 *Columbia* and four CIS and one German cosmonauts on the *Mir* space station.

**Left**
A footprint on the Moon's surface left by the Apollo 11 mission commanded by Neil Armstrong and Edwin Aldrin.

*Apollo 10*, carrying Col. Thomas Patten Stafford, USAF, Comdr. Eugene Andrew Cernan and Comdr. John Watts Young, USN, reached this maximum speed on 26 May 1969, when travelling at 11.08 km/sec (6⅞ miles/sec).

### First woman to spacewalk
The first woman to perform a spacewalk was Svetlana Savitskaya from *Soyuz T12/ Salyut 7* on 25 July 1984.

### Most spacewalks
The greatest number of spacewalks is 10, by Russian cosmonaut Aleksandr Serebrov during two missions in 1990 and 1993.

### Longest spacewalks
The longest spacewalk, by Pierre Thuot, Rick Hieb and Tom Akers of STS 49 *Endeavour* on 13 May 1992, lasted 8 hr 29 min.

The longest spacewalk to have been undertaken by Soviet cosmonauts was by Anatoly Solovyov and Aleksandr Balandin of *Soyuz TM9* on 1 July 1990. It lasted 7 hr 16 min outside the *Mir* space station.

The longest spacewalk by a woman, Kathryn Thornton of STS 49 *Endeavour,* lasted 7 hr 49 min on 14 May 1992.

## 8 HR 29 MIN BY THE CREW OF STS 49 *ENDEAVOUR*

### Most isolated human being
The farthest any human has been from another is 3,596.4 km (2,234¾ miles). Alfred M. Worden was the command module pilot on the US *Apollo 15* lunar mission of 30 July–1 Aug 1971, while David Scott and James Irwin were at Hadley Base exploring the surface of the Moon.

## Space achievements
### Greatest altitude attained by a man
The crew of the *Apollo 13*, Capt. James Lovell Jr, Fred Haise and John Swigert, were at apocynthion, or their furthest point, 254 km (158 miles) from the lunar surface, and 400,171 km (248,655 miles) above the Earth's surface, at 1:21 a.m. BST on 15 April 1970.

### Greatest altitude attained by a woman
The greatest altitude by a woman is 600 km (375 miles), by Kathryn Thornton (USA) during the STS 61 *Endeavour* mission.

### Greatest speed
The fastest speed at which humans have ever travelled is 39,897 km/h (24,791 mph). The command module of

### Greatest speed by a woman
The highest speed travelled by a woman is 28,582 km/h (17,864 mph), by Kathryn Sullivan at the end of the STS 31 *Discovery* shuttle mission on 29 April 1990, although Kathryn Thornton may have exceeded this speed at the end of the STS 61 *Endeavour* mission on 13 Dec 1993.

### First space funeral
On 21 April 1997 the ashes of 24 Space enthusiasts and pioneers, including *Star Trek* creator Gene Roddenbery, German rocket scientist Kraffte Ehricke and author Timothy Leary were sent into orbit on the rocket *Pegasus* at a cost of £3,000 each. Held in lipstick-sized capsules, the ashes will stay in orbit for between 18 months to 10 years.

### First spacewalks
Lt-Col. Aleksey Arkhipovich Leonov from *Voskhod 2* was the first person to engage in EVA, or extra-vehicular activity, commonly known as a 'spacewalk', on 18 March 1965.

Capt. Bruce McCandless II, USN, from the shuttle *Challenger*, was the first to engage in untethered EVA, at an altitude of 264 km (164 miles) above Hawaii, on 7 Feb 1984.

## Lunar exploration
### Lunar conquest
Neil Armstrong, the command pilot on the *Apollo 11* mission, was the first man to set foot on the Moon, on 21 July 1969.

### Duration record on the Moon
The longest lunar mission ever undertaken lasted 12 days 13 hr 51 min. It was carried out by Capt. Eugene Cernan and Dr Harrison Hagen 'Jack' Schmitt (USA). They were on the surface of the Moon for a total of 74 hr 59 min between 7–19 Dec 1972.

# Epic sea journeys

**Right**
Steve Fossett in his vessel *Lakota* in which he crossed the Pacific solo in a record time of 20 days 9 hr 52 min 59 sec. The champion yachtsman is also famous for hot air ballooning—just two years after his first balloon ride he attempted to fly across the Pacific Ocean.

**SAILING AND ROWING RECORDS**
Smg=speed made good. All mileages are nautical.

**TRANSATLANTIC**
**First east-west solo sailing**
Vessel: 15-ton gaff sloop
Skipper: Josiah Shackford (USA)
Start: Bordeaux, France, 1786
Finish: Surinam (Guiana)
Duration: 35 days

**First west-east solo sailing**
Vessel: *Centennial*, 6.1 m (20 ft) long
Skipper: Alfred Johnson (USA)
Start: Shag Harbor, Maine, USA, 1876
Finish: Wales, UK
Duration: 46 days

**First west-east solo sailing by a woman**
Vessel: Lugger, 5.5 m (18 ft) long
Skipper: Gladys Gradeley (USA)
Start: Nova Scotia, Canada, 1903
Finish: Hope Cove, Devon, UK
Duration: 60 days

**First east-west solo rowing**
Vessel: *Britannia*, 6.7 m (22 ft) long
Skipper: John Fairfax (GB)
Start: Las Palmas, Canary Islands, 20 Jan 1969
Finish: Fort Lauderdale, Florida, USA, 19 July 1969
Duration: 180 days

**Fastest east-west solo sailing**
Vessel: *Fleury Michon* (IX) 18.3-m (60-ft) trimaran
Skipper: Philippe Poupon (France)
Start: Plymouth, Devon, UK, 5 June 1988
Finish: Newport, Rhode Island, USA, 15 June 1988
Duration: 10 days 9 hr (11.6 knots smg)

**THE FASTEST PACIFIC CROSSING OF 6 DAYS 1 HR 27 MIN WAS MADE BY THE**

## Ocean crossings
**Fastest Atlantic crossing**
The record for the fastest crossing of the Atlantic is 2 days 10 hr 34 min 47 sec (45.7 knots smg), by the 68-m (222-ft) powerboat *Destriero*, from 6–8 Aug 1992.

The boat that makes the fastest regular commercial crossing (and therefore winner of the Hales Trophy or 'Blue Riband') is the liner *United States* (formerly 51,988, now 38,216 gross tons), the former flagship of the United States Lines. From 3–7 July 1952 on her maiden voyage from New York, USA, to Le Havre, France and Southampton, Hants, UK, she averaged 65.95 km/h (35.39 knots) for 3 days 10 hr 40 min (6:36 p.m. GMT, 3 July to 5:16 a.m. 7 July) on a route of 5,465 km (2,949 nautical miles) from the *Ambrose* light vessel to the Bishop Rock lighthouse, Isles of Scilly, Cornwall. From 6–7 July, she steamed the greatest distance ever covered by any ship in 24 hours, at 1,609 km (868 nautical miles),

averaging 67.02 km/h (36.17 knots). The maximum speed attained from her 240,000-shaft horsepower engines was 71.01 km/h (38.32 knots) in trials on 9–10 June 1952.

**Fastest Pacific crossing**
The fastest crossing from Yokohama, Japan to Long Beach, California, USA, (8,960 km or 4,840 nautical miles) took 6 days 1 hr 27 min (30 June–6 July 1973), by the 50,315-ton container ship *Sea-Land Commerce*, at an average speed of 61.65 km/h (33.27 knots).

**Amphibious circumnavigation by car**
The only circumnavigation by an amphibious vehicle was by Ben Carlin (Australia) in the amphibious jeep, *Half-Safe*. He completed the last leg of the Atlantic crossing (the English Channel) on 24 Aug 1951 and arrived back in Montreal, Canada, on 8 May 1958, having completed a circumnavigation of 62,765 km (39,000 miles) over land and 15,450 km (9,600 miles) by sea and river.

**Fastest west-east solo sailing**
Vessel: *Primagaz*, 18.3-m (60-ft) trimaran
Skipper: Laurent Bourgnon (France)
Start: Ambrose Light Tower, USA, 27 June 1994
Finish: Lizard Point, Cornwall, UK, 4 July 1994
Duration: 7 days 2 hr 34 min 42 sec (17.15 knots)

**First west-east solo rowing**
Vessel: *Super Silver*, 6.1 m (20 ft) long
Skipper: Tom McClean (Ireland)
Start: St John's, Newfoundland, Canada, 1969
Finish: Black Sod Bay, Ireland, 27 July 1969
Duration: 70 days 17 hr

**First row in both directions**
Vessel: *QE III*, 6.05 m (19 ft 10 in) long
Skipper: Don Allum (GB)
Start: Canary Islands 1986 and St John's, Canada
Finish: Nevis, West Indies, and Ireland 1987
Duration: 114 days and 77 days

**Fastest east-west crewed sail**
Vessel: *Primagaz*, 18.3-m (60-ft) trimaran
Skipper/crew: Laurent Bourgnon (France) and Cam Lewis (USA)
Start: Plymouth, Devon, UK, 5 June 1994

# FASTEST TRANSATLANTIC SOLO 7 DAYS

Finish: Newport, Rhode Island, USA, 14 June 1994
Duration: 9 days 8 hr 58 min 20 sec (12.49 knots)

**Fastest west-east crewed sail**
Vessel: *Jet Services 5*, 22.9-m (75-ft)
catamaran sloop
Skipper: Serge Madec (France)
Start: Ambrose Light Tower, USA, 2 June 1990
Finish: Lizard Point, Cornwall, UK, 9 June 1990
Duration: 6 days 13 hr 3 min 32 sec
(18.4 knots smg)

## TRANSPACIFIC
**First rowing**
Vessel: *Britannia II*, 10.7 m (35 ft) long
Skippers: John Fairfax (GB) and Sylvia Cook (GB)
Start: San Francisco, USA, 26 April 1971
Finish: Hayman Island, Australia, 22 April 1972
Duration: 362 days

**First east-west solo sailing**
Vessel: *Pacific*, 5.48-m (18-ft) double-ender
Skipper: Bernard Gilboy (US)
Start: 1882
Finish: Australia

**First east-west solo rowing**
Vessel: *Hele-on-Britannia*, 9.75 m (32 ft) long
Skipper: Peter Bird (GB)
Start: San Francisco, USA, 23 Aug 1982
Finish: Great Barrier Reef, Australia, 14 June 1983
Duration: 294 days over 14,480 km (9,000 miles)

**First west-east solo sailings**
Vessel: *Elaine*, 5.48 m (18 ft) long
Skipper: Fred Rebel (Latvia)
Start: Australia, 1932
and:
Vessel: *Sturdy II*, 11.2 m (36 ft) long

## HIP *SEA-LAND COMMERCE*

Skipper: Edward Miles (USA)
Start: Japan, 1932 (via Hawaii)

**First west-east solo rowing**
Vessel: *Sector*, 8 m (26 ft) long
Skipper: Gérard d'Aboville (France)
Start: Choshi, Japan, 11 July 1991
Finish: Ilwaco, Washington, USA, 21 Nov 1991
Duration: 133 days over 10,150 km (6,300 miles)

**Fastest sail**
Vessel: *Lakota*, 18.29 m (60 ft)
Skipper: Steve Fossett (USA), plus four crew
Start: Long Beach, California, USA, 5 July 1995
Finish: Honolulu, Hawaii, 11 July 1995
Duration: 6 days 16 hr 16 min (13.84 knots smg)

**Fastest solo sail**
Vessel: *Lakota*, 18.29 m (60 ft)
Skipper: Steve Fossett (USA)
Start: Yokohama, Japan, 5 Aug 1996
Finish: San Francisco, USA, 24 Aug 1996
Duration: 20 days 9 hr 52 min 59 sec (9.23 knots)

## MARINE CIRCUMNAVIGATION
It is not possible to make a simple circumnavigation
of the world by sea, which would be along the

Equator. The World Sailing Speed Record Council
gives the following rules: the vessel must start and
return to the same point, must cross all meridians of
longitude and must cross the Equator. It may cross
some, but not all, meridians more than once. The
vessel must cover at least 21,600 nautical miles.

A non-stop circumnavigation is self-maintained; no
water supplies, provisions, equipment or
replacements of any sort may be taken aboard on
the journey. Vessels may anchor but no physical help
may be accepted apart from communications.

**First circumnavigation**
Vessel: *Vittoria Expedition of Ferdinand Magellan*
Skipper: Juan Sebastián de Elcano or del Cano
and 17 crew
Start: Seville, Spain, 20 Sept 1519
Finish: San Lucar, Spain, 6 Sept 1522
Distance: 93,573.6 km (30,700 miles)
(Magellan's slave, Enrique, may have been the
first circumnavigator)

**First solo circumnavigation**
Vessel: *Spray*, 11.2-m (36-ft 9-in) gaff yawl
Skipper: Capt. Joshua Slocum (USA) (a non-swimmer)
Start: Newport, Rhode Island, USA, via Magellan
Straits, Chile, 24 April 1895
Finish: 3 July 1898
Distance: 140,028 km (46,000 miles)

**First east-west solo non-stop**
Vessel: *British Steel*, 18-m (59-ft) ketch
Skipper: Chay Blyth, OBE, BEM (GB)
Start: Hamble River, Hants, UK, 18 Oct 1970
Finish: 6 Aug 1971, 292 days (3.08 knots)

**First west-east solo non-stop**
Vessel: *Suhaili*, 9.87-m (32-ft 4-in) Bermudan ketch
Skipper: Sir Robin Knox-Johnston, CBE, RD (GB)
Start: Falmouth, Cornwall, UK, 14 June 1968
Finish: 22 April 1969, 312 days (2.88 knots)

**First solo non-stop by a woman**
Vessel: *First Lady*, 11.24 m (37ft) monohull
Skipper: Kay Cottee (Australia)
Start: Sydney, Australia, 29 Nov 1987
Finish: Sydney, Australia, 5 June 1988
Duration: 189 days 32 min

**Fastest non-stop**
Vessel: *Enza*, 28-m (92-ft) catamaran
Skipper: Sir Peter Blake KBE (NZ), Sir Robin Knox-
Johnston CBE, RD (GB) and six crew
Start: Ushant, France, 16 Jan 1994
Finish: Ushant, 1 April 1994
Duration: 74 days 22 hr 17 min (12.10 knots)

**Fastest east-west solo non-stop**
Vessel: *Group 4*, 20.42-m (67-ft) sloop
Skipper: Mike Golding (GB)
Start: Southampton, UK, 21 Nov 1993
Finish: Southampton, 7 May 1994
Duration: 161 days 16 hr 32 min

**Smallest vessel**
Vessel: *Acrohc Australis*, 3.6-m (11-ft 10-in) sloop
Skipper: Serge Testa (Australia)
Start: Brisbane, Australia, UK, 1984
Finish: Brisbane, 1987
Duration: 500 days

## BRITISH ISLES RECORDS
**Around mainland, fastest**
Vessel: *Drambuie Tantalus*, 15.3-m (50-ft) monohull
Skipper: Dag Pike (GB)
Start: Ramsgate, 9 July 1992
Finish: Ramsgate, 11 July 1992
Duration: 1 day 20 hr 3 min (36.6 knots smg)

**Around mainland, fastest vessel under 50 ft**
Vessel: *Rapier 29*, 8.8-m (29-ft)
Skipper: Steve Brownridge (GB)
Start: Southampton, 25 June 1993
Finish: Southampton, 27 June 1993
Duration: 2 days 15 hr 32 min (24.68 knots)

**Around British Isles, fastest sailing vessel**
Vessel: *Lakota*, 18.29-m (60-ft) trimaran
Skipper: Steve Fossett (USA) and four crew
Start: Ventnor, Isle of Wight, 21 Oct 1994
Finish: Ventnor, 27 Oct 1994
Duration: 5 days 21 hr 5 min (12.67 knots)
Distance: 2875 km (1789 miles)

## ENGLISH CHANNEL
**Both ways, fastest sailing multihull**
Vessel: *Fleury Michon VIII*, 22.9-m (75-ft) trimaran
Skipper: Philippe Poupon (France)
Start: Calais, France, Dec 1986
Finish: Calais via Dover, Kent, UK, Dec 1986
Duration: 2 hr 21 min 57 sec (18.6 knots smg)

## DURATION AND DISTANCE
**Non-stop by sail three times around the world**
Vessel: *Parry Endeavour*, 13.9-m (44-ft)
Bermudan sloop
Skipper: Jon Sanders (Australia)
Start: Fremantle, W Australia, 25 May 1986
Finish: Fremantle, 13 March 1988
Duration: 71,000 miles in 658 days (4.5 knots)

**Best day's run, under sail and solo**
Vessel: *Primagaz*, 18.29-m (60-ft) trimaran
Skipper: Laurent Bourgnon (France)
Start: North Atlantic, 28 June 1994
Finish: North Atlantic, 29 June 1994
Duration: 540 miles in 24 hours (22.5 knots)

**Best day's run, monohull fully crewed**
Vessel: *Intrum Justitia*, 19.51-m (64-ft) monohull
Skipper: Lawrie Smith (GB)
Start: Southern Ocean, 20 Feb 1994
Finish: Southern Ocean, 21 Feb 1994
Duration: 428¹⁄₁₀ miles in 24 hours (17.8 knots)

**Best day's run, sailboard**
Vessel: *Fanatic board*, Gaastra sail
Skipper: Françoise Canetos (France)
Start: Sète, France, 13 July 1988
Finish: Sète, 14 July 1988
Duration: 227 miles in 24 hours (9.46 knots smg)

**Fastest sea passage under sail**
Vessel: *Pierre 1er*, 18.29 m (60 ft) long
Skipper: Florence Arthaud (France)
Start: Marseille, France, 26 Aug 1991
Finish: Carthage, Tunisia, 27 Aug 1991
Duration: 458 miles in 22 hr 9 min 56 sec (20.6 knots)

086

# Epic land journeys

LONGEST MOTORCYCLE JOURNEY, MADE BY EMILIO SCOTTO FROM BUENOS AIRE!

## Travellers
### Most travelled
The world's most travelled man is John D. Clouse from Evansville, Indiana, USA, who has visited all of the sovereign countries and all but six of the non-sovereign or other territories which existed in early 1997.

The most travelled man in the horseback era is believed to have been the Methodist bishop Francis Asbury, who travelled a distance of 425,000 km (264,000 miles) in North America from 1771 to 1815, preaching 16,000 sermons and ordaining almost 3,000 ministers.

### Most travelled couple
Dr Robert and Carmen Becker of Pompano Beach, Florida, USA, have visited all of the sovereign countries and all but seven of the non-sovereign or other territories.

### Most travelled hitch-hiker
Stephan Schlei of Ratingen, Germany, has obtained free rides totalling 807,500 km (501,750 miles) since 1972.

## Walking
### Longest walks round the world
The first person reputed to have walked 'around the world' is George Matthew Schilling (USA), from 3 Aug 1897 to 1904.

The first verified walk was made by David Kunst (USA), who walked 23,250 km (14,450 miles) through four continents from 20 June 1970 to 5 Oct 1974.

'Around the world' walker Arthur Blessitt (USA) has walked 51,500 km (32,002 miles) in more than 26 years since 25 Dec 1969. He has been to 267 countries in all seven continents, carrying a 3.7-m (12-ft) cross and preaching throughout his walk.

Solo walker Steven Newman of Bethel, Ohio, USA, spent four years (from 1 April 1983 to 1 April 1987) walking 24,959 km

LONGEST TAXI RIDE ON RECORD WAS 34,908 KM

(15,509 miles) around the world, at a faster rate than Schilling, Kunst and Blessitt. He visited 20 countries and five continents.

### Trans-Americas
George Meegan from Rainham, Kent, UK, walked 30,431 km (19,019 miles) from Ushuaia, at the southern tip of South America, to Prudhoe Bay in northern Alaska. He left on 26 Jan 1977 and finished on 18 Sept 1983—2,426 days later—having completed the first traverse of the Americas and the western hemisphere.

Sean Eugene McGuire (USA) walked 11,791 km (7,327 miles) from the Yukon River, north of Livengood, Alaska, USA, to Key West, Florida, USA, in 307 days, from 6 June 1978 to 9 April 1979.

The trans-Canada (Halifax to Vancouver) record walk of 6,057 km (3,764 miles) stands at 96 days by Clyde McRae, aged 23, from 1 May–4 Aug 1973.

Briton John Lees walked 4,628 km (2,876 miles) across the USA from City Hall, Los Angeles, California, to City Hall, New York, in 53 days 12 hr 15 min between 11 April and 3 June 1972. He averaged 86.49 km (53 miles 1,314 yd) a day.

### Longest walk around Britain
The longest walk around the coast of the British Isles was one of 15,239 km (9,469 miles) by John Westley (UK) from 5 Aug 1990 to 20 Sept 1991.

Vera Andrews completed the longest walk on mainland Britain, covering a distance of 11,777 km (7,318 miles), visiting every British Gas showroom in the country on her route, between 2 Jan and 24 Dec 1990.

### Wheelchair
Rick Hansen (Canada), who was paralysed from the waist down after a motor accident, wheeled his wheelchair 40,075.16 km (24,901 miles 880 yd) through four continents and 34 countries. He started in Vancouver, Canada, on 21 March 1985 and arrived back on 22 May 1987.

## Cycle touring
### Greatest distances covered on bicycles
Itinerant lecturer Walter Stolle cycled more than 646,960 km (402,000 miles) from 24 Jan 1959 to 12 Dec 1976. He visited 159 countries, starting from Romford, Essex, UK.

From 1922 to 25 Dec 1973, Tommy Chambers of Glasgow, UK, rode a verified total of 1,286,517 km (799,405 miles).

Since leaving his home country of Germany in November 1962, Heinz Stucke has travelled 365,000 km (226,800 miles) and visited 211 countries.

Visiting every continent, John W. Hathaway (b. England) of Vancouver, Canada, covered 81,430 km (50,600 miles) from 10 Nov 1974 to 6 Oct 1976.

### Greatest distances covered on tandems
Laura Geoghegan and Mark Tong travelled a record distance of 32,248 km (20,155 miles) on a tandem from London to Sydney, 21 May 1994–11 Nov 1995.

Veronica and Colin Scargill of Bedford, UK, travelled 29,000 km (18,020 miles) around the world on a tandem, from 25 Feb 1974 to 27 Aug 1975.

# WHEELCHAIR JOURNEY 40,075.16 KM

ARGENTINA, COVERED MORE THAN 735,000 KM

### Most participants in a bike ride
On 19 June 1988, 31,678 people rode in the 90-km (56-mile) London to Brighton Ride.

It is estimated that 45,000 cyclists took part in the 75-km (46-mile) Tour de l'Ile de Montreal, Canada, on 7 June 1992.

In 1988 there were 2,157 starters in the Australian Bicentennial Caltex Bike Ride from Melbourne to Sydney.

### Cycle endurance
In 1939 Thomas Edward Godwin (GB) covered 120,805 km (75,065 miles) in 365 days—an average of 330.96 km (205 miles 1,150 yd) per day. He then completed 160,934 km (100,000 miles) in 500 days to 14 May 1940.

From 2 April to 16 July 1984, Jay Aldous and Matt DeWaal cycled a distance of 22,997 km (14,290 miles) in 106 days on a round-the-world trip from This is the Place Monument, Salt Lake City, Utah, USA.

Tal Burt of Israel circumnavigated the world by bicycle, covering a total distance of 21,329 km (13,253 miles) from Place du Trocadero, Paris, France, in a time of 77 days 14 hr, from 1 June to 17 Aug 1992.

Nick Sanders (GB) cycled 7,728 km (4,802 miles) around Britain in 22 days, between 10 June and 1 July 1984.

## Motorcycling
### Longest motorcycle rides
From 17 Jan 1985 to 2 April 1995, Emilio Scotto from Buenos Aires, Argentina, made the longest ever motorcycle journey, covering more than 735,000 km (457,000 miles) and 214 countries.

Jim Rogers and Tabitha Estabrook of New York, USA, travelled a total of 91,766 km (57,022 miles) across six continents between March 1990 and Nov 1991.

### First woman circumnavigator
The first woman to circumnavigate the world solo was Monika Vega of Rio de Janeiro, Brazil, riding her Honda 125-cc motorcycle. Her journey commenced at Milan, Italy, on 7 March 1990. She returned to Italy on 24 May 1991, having covered a distance of 83,500 km (51,885 miles) and visited 53 countries.

## Other vehicles
### Trans-Americas by car
Garry Sowerby (Canada) and Tim Cahill (USA), co-driver and navigator, drove a 1988 GMC Sierra K3500 23,720 km (14,739 miles) from Ushuaia, Tierra del Fuego, Argentina, to Prudhoe Bay, Alaska, USA, in an elapsed time of 23 days 22 hr 43 min from 29 Sept to 22 Oct 1987.

The vehicle and team were surface freighted from Cartagena, Colombia, to Balboa, Panama, in order to by-pass the Darién Gap.

### Longest journey by motorized vehicle
Emil and Liliana Schmid (Switzerland) have so far travelled a distance of 451,597 km (280,617 miles) from 16 Oct 1984 in a Toyota Landcruiser. Their journey has taken them through 117 countries.

### Horse-drawn caravan
David, Kate, Torcuil, Eilidh and Fionn Grant started their round-the-world journey by horse-drawn caravan from Vierhouten,

in the Netherlands on 25 Oct 1990. The family expedition has so far crossed western Europe, Ukraine, Russia, Kazakhstan, China and Japan—a distance of 27,824 km (17,293 miles). They will return in 1997 via the USA.

### Taxis
Jeremy Levine, Mark Aylett and Carlos Aresse took a taxi from London, UK, to Cape Town, South Africa, and back from 3 June to 17 Oct 1994. Their 34,908-km (21,691-mile) trip cost £40,210.

### Snowmobiles
John Outzen and brothers Andre, Carl and Denis Boucher drove snowmobiles a record distance of 16,499.5 km (10,252 miles 528 yd) in 56 riding days from Anchorage, Alaska, USA, to Dartmouth, Nova Scotia, Canada, from 2 Jan to 3 March 1992.

Tony Lenzini of Duluth, Minnesota, USA, drove his 1986 Arctic Cat Cougar snowmobile a total of 11,604.6 km (7,211 miles) in 60 days of riding, 28 Dec 1985–20 March 1986.

FROM LONDON, UK, TO CAPE TOWN, SOUTH AFRICA

**Below**
Stephan Schlei of Ratingen, Germany, has hitch-hiked a total distance of 807,500 km (501,750 miles).

**Left**
John Outzen and brothers Andre, Carl and Denis Boucher completed the first documented transcontinental drive from the Pacific to the Atlantic on snow. They rode four Arctic Cat Panther Deluxe snowmobiles.

# Epic air journeys

**Right**
Intrepid adventurer
Steve Fossett (USA)
sets off on what was to
become the longest
ever balloon flight.
Fossett is no stranger
to record breaking,
holding a number
of sailing bests in
addition to his
ballooning exploits.

00:00:01

00:00:06

## Circumnavigation
### Round the world

The fastest global circumnavigation under FAI regulations using scheduled flights is 44 hr 6 min by David J. Springbett of Taplow, Bucks, UK. He flew 37,124 km (23,068 miles) from Los Angeles, California, USA, via London, Bahrain, Singapore, Bangkok, Manila, Tokyo and Honolulu from 8 to 10 Jan 1980.

### Round the world—antipodal points

Brother Michael Bartlett of Sandy, Beds, UK, an 'Eccentric Globetrotter', achieved a record time for flying round the world on scheduled flights, taking in only the airports closest to antipodal points, when he flew via Shanghai, China, and Buenos Aires, Argentina, in 58 hr 44 min. He started and finished at Zürich, Switzerland, on 13 Feb 1995 and travelled a total distance of 41,547 km (25,816 miles) before arriving back in Zürich on 16 Feb 1995.

The former Scottish Rugby Union captain, David Sole, travelled round the world on scheduled flights, taking in exact antipodal points, in a time of 64 hr 2 min from 2 to 5 May 1995. He began his journey in London, UK, and flew to Madrid, Spain, then to Napier in New Zealand via Heathrow, Singapore and Auckland. From Napier he travelled by helicopter to Ti Tree Point, on Highway 52 (the point exactly opposite

Madrid airport). He returned via Los Angeles, USA, having covered a total distance of 41,709 km (25,917 miles).

### Fastest helicopter circumnavigation

Ron Bower (USA) and John Williams (USA) flew round the world in a Bell helicopter in a record time of 17 days 6 hr 14 min 25 sec. They left Fair Oaks, London, UK, on 17 Aug 1996 and flew westabout arriving back at Fair Oaks on 3 Sept 1996.

## Fastest flights
### Fastest transatlantic flight

Major James Sullivan (USA) and Major Noel Widdifield (USA) flew a Lockheed SR-71A 'Blackbird' eastwards on 1 Sept 1974 and crossed the Atlantic in 1 hr 54 min 56.4 sec. The average speed, reduced by refuelling from a Boeing KC-135 tanker aircraft, was 2,908.02 km/h (1,806.96 mph) on the 5,570.80-km (3,461½-miles) New York–London journey.

### Fastest solo transatlantic flight

Capt. John J.A. Smith flew a Rockwell Commander 685 twin-turboprop from Gander, Newfoundland, Canada, to Gatwick, W Sussex, UK, on 12 March 1978 in 8 hr 47 min 32 sec.

### London–New York

The shortest time taken to fly from central London, UK, to downtown New York City, USA, is 3 hr 59 min 44 sec by helicopter and Concorde, with a return journey of 3 hr 40 min 40 sec. The record was set by David J. Springbett (GB) and David Boyce (GB) on 8 and 9 Feb 1982.

### Paris–London

The fastest time taken to cover the 344 km (214 miles) from central Paris, France, to central London (BBC TV centre), UK, is 38 min 58 sec by David Boyce of Stewart Wrightson (Aviation) Ltd on 24 Sept 1983. He travelled by motorcycle and helicopter to Le Bourget; Hawker Hunter jet (piloted by Michael Carlton) to Biggin Hill, Kent, UK, and by helicopter to the TV centre car park.

## Longest flights
### Longest non-service flight

The longest non-stop flight by a commercial airliner was 18,545 km (10,008 nautical miles) from Auckland, New Zealand, to Le Bourget, Paris, France, in 21 hr 46 min on 17 and 18 June 1993, by the Airbus Industrie A340-200. The journey was the return leg of a flight which had started at Le Bourget on the previous day.

# AROUND THE WORLD IN 44 HR 6 MIN

## TOOK 264 HR 12 MIN

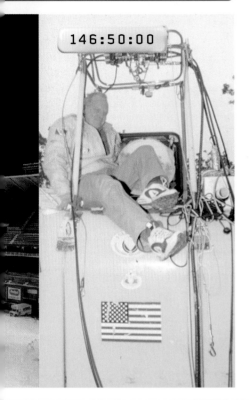

146:50:00

Vijaypat Singhania (India) flew from Biggin Hill, UK, to Delhi, India, a distance of 8,724 km (5,420 miles), in 87 hr 55 min, from 18 Aug to 10 Sept 1988.

## Ballooning

### Longest balloon flight
Though Steve Fosset's attempt to fly around the world in the balloon *Free Spirit* was unsuccessful, he did set the greatest distance record of 16,673.81 km (10,406 miles). Setting off on 13 Jan 1997 from St. Louis, Missouri, USA, he arrived at Sultanpur, India on 20 Jan 1997.

### Pacific crossing by a helium balloon
A Cameron R-150 helium-filled balloon flown by Steve Fossett covered 8,748.11 km (5,435 miles, 1,443 yd) from the Olympic Stadium, Seoul, South Korea, to Mendham, Saskatchewan, Canada, from 17 to 21 Feb 1995. It was the first solo Pacific crossing.

### Atlantic crossing by a helium balloon
Col. Joe Kittinger (USAF) was the first to cross solo in a helium balloon. He lifted off from Caribou, Maine, USA, on 14 Sept 1984

### Balloon endurance
The FAI endurance record for a gas and hot-air balloon is 6 days 2 hr 50 min, set by Steve Fossett in Jan 1997 when he flew from St. Louis, Missouri, USA, to Sultanpur, India, in an attempt to fly around the world.

### First Mt Everest overflight
The first overflight of the summit of Mt Everest was by *Star Flyer 1*, piloted by Chris Dewhirst (Australia) with cameraman Leo Dickinson (GB), and *Star Flyer 2*, piloted by Andy Elson (GB) and cameraman Eric Jones (GB) on 21 Oct 1991. The 6,800 m³ (240,000 ft³) balloons set records for both the highest launch at 4,735 m (15,536 ft) and the highest touch-down at 4,940 m (16,200 ft).

### Greatest number of passengers
*Super Maine* rose to a tethered height of 12.25 m (50ft) on 19 Feb 1988 with 61 passengers on board. Built by Tom Handcock of Portland, Maine, USA, the balloon had a total capacity of 73,600 m³ (2.6 million ft³).

The Dutch balloonist Henk Brink carried 50 passengers and crew in an untethered flight in *Nashua Number One* on 17 Aug 1988. The flight set out from Lelystad airport in the Netherlands, and lasted 25 minutes, reaching an altitude of 100 m (328 ft). The balloon had a capacity of 24,000 m³ (850,000 ft³).

## Airships

### Earliest airship flight
Henri Giffard travelled the 27 km (17 miles) from Paris to Trappes, France, in his 43.8-m (144-ft) long steam-powered coal-gas airship on 24 Sept 1852.

### Greatest passenger loads
The most people carried in an airship was 207, in the US Navy *Akron* in 1931.

The most people on a transatlantic journey is 117, by the German *Hindenberg* in 1937. It exploded at Lakehurst, New Jersey, USA, on 6 May 1937.

## CROSSING BY HELIUM BALLOON, FLYING 8,748 KM

### Longest non-stop flight
The longest unrefuelled non-stop flight was by Robert Ferry, who flew a Hughes YOH-6A a distance of 3,561.6 km (2,213¹⁄₁₀ miles) from Culver City, California, to Ormond Beach, Florida, USA, in April 1966.

### Most scheduled flights in 24 hours
Brother Michael Bartlett of Sandy, Beds, UK, made 42 scheduled passenger flights with Heli Transport of Nice, southern France, between Nice, Monaco and Cannes in 13 hr 33 min on 13 June 1990.

### Most EU countries by scheduled flights
David Beaumont of Wimbledon, London, UK, visited all 15 countries belonging to the European Union on scheduled passenger flights in 35 hr 8 min on 2 and 3 May 1995.

### Endurance
Eve Jackson flew from Biggin Hill, Kent, UK, to Sydney, Australia, from 26 April 1986 to 1 Aug 1987. The flight took 279 hr 55 min and covered 21,950 km (13,639 miles).

From 1 Dec 1987 to 29 Jan 1988, Brian Milton (GB) flew from London, UK, to Sydney, Australia. His flying time was 241 hr 20 min and he covered a total distance of 21,968 km (13,650 miles).

in the 2,850-m³ (101,000-ft³) helium-filled balloon *Rosie O'Grady*, and landed at Montenotte, near Savona, Italy, 86 hours later, having completed a distance of 5,701 km (3,543 miles).

### Trans-Atlantic hot-air crossing
Richard Branson (GB) with his pilot Per Lindstrand (GB) were the first to cross the Atlantic in a hot-air balloon, from 2–3 July 1987. They ascended from Sugarloaf, Maine, USA, and completed the 4,947-km (3,075-mile) journey to Limavady, N Ireland, UK, in 31 hr 41 min.

### Trans-Pacific hot-air crossing
Richard Branson and Per Lindstrand crossed the Pacific in the *Virgin Otsuka Pacific Flyer* from the southern tip of Japan to Lac la Matre, Yukon, north-west Canada, between 15–17 Jan 1991. Their 73,600 m³ (2.6 million ft³) hot-air balloon was the largest ever flown. In making the journey, they set FAI records for both duration (46 hr 15 min) and distance (great-circle distance of 7,671.9 km or 4,768 miles).

### Highest flight
Per Lindstrand reached an altitude of 19,811 m (64,997 ft) in a hot-air balloon over Laredo, Texas, USA, on 6 June 1988.

### Longest flight
The longest recorded flight without refuelling by a non-rigid airship is 264 hr 12 min by a US Navy Goodyear-built ZPG-2 class ship. Cmdr J.R. Hunt, of the USN took off from South Weymouth Naval Air Station, Massachusetts, USA, on 4 March 1957, landing back at Key West, Florida, USA, on 15 March 1957, having flown 15,205 km (9,448 miles).

# Speed: cars and bikes

## Fastest cars

### Highest land speed
The official one-mile land-speed record is 1,019.467 km/h (633.468 mph), set by Richard Noble (GB) on 4 Oct 1983 over the Black Rock Desert, Nevada, USA, in his 17,000-lb thrust Rolls-Royce Avon 302 jet-powered *Thrust2*, designed by John Ackroyd.

### Highest land speed in the UK
The highest speed reached in the United Kingdom is 444 km/h (276 mph), by Poutiaiten Risto (Finland) in a Top Fuel dragster on 27 May 1991, at the Santa Pod County Raceway, Beds.

### Fastest rocket-engined cars
The highest speed ever to have been attained in a rocket-powered car was an average 1,016.086 km/h (631.367 mph) over the first measured kilometre by 'The Blue Flame', a four-wheeled vehicle driven by Gary Gabelich (USA) on the Bonneville Salt Flats, Utah, USA, on 23 Oct 1970. Momentarily Gabelich exceeded 1,046 km/h (650 mph). The liquid natural gas/hydrogen peroxide rocket engine was capable of developing thrust up to 22,000 lb.

The highest reputed land speed figure in one direction is 1,190.377 km/h (739.666 mph), or Mach 1.0106, by Stan Barrett (USA) in the *Budweiser Rocket*, a rocket-engined three-wheeled car, at Edwards Air Force Base, California, USA, on 17 Dec 1979. This published speed of Mach 1.0106 is not officially sanctioned by the USAF as the Digital Instrument Radar was not calibrated or certified. The radar information was not obtained directly from the vehicle but by an operator aiming a dish at the vehicle.

### Highest land speed by a woman
Kitty Hambleton of the United States achieved 843.323 km/h (524.016 mph) in the rocket-powered three-wheeled SM1 Motivator over the Alvard Desert, Oregon, USA, on 6 Dec 1976. Her official two-way record was 825.126 km/h (512.710 mph) and she probably reached 965 km/h (600 mph) momentarily.

### Fastest piston-engined car
The highest recorded speed for a wheel-driven car is 696.331 km/h (432.692 mph) by Al Teague (USA) in *Speed-O-Motive/Spirit of 76* on Bonneville Salt Flats, Utah, USA, on 21 Aug 1991 over the final 132 ft of a mile run. He achieved an average speed of 684.322 km/h (425.230 mph).

### Fastest diesel-engined car
The prototype 3 litre Mercedes C 111/3 attained 327.3 km/h (203.3 mph) in tests on the Nardo Circuit, Italy, from 5 to 15 Oct 1978. In April 1978 the Mercedes averaged 314.5 km/h (195.4 mph) for 12 hours and covered a world record 3,773.5 km (2,344¾ miles).

### Fastest electric car
On 11 March 1994, General Motors' *Impact* driven by Clive Roberts (GB), reached a speed of 295.832 km/h (183.822 mph) over a two-way flying kilometre at Fort Stockton Test Center, Texas, USA.

### Fastest UK electric car
On 22 June 1991, 18-year-old Max Rink of Oundle School, Northants, UK, achieved a speed of 111.37 km/h (69.21 mph) over a 1-km (0.6214-mile) start, at Bruntingthorpe Proving Ground, Leics. Over the two runs the average speed achieved was 106.43 km/h (66.14 mph). The vehicle weighed only 60 kg (132 lb) and was built in 1986 by four 14-year-old pupils from Oundle School.

### Fastest steam car
On 19 Aug 1985, Robert E. Barber broke the 79-year-old record for the fastest time for a steam car when *Steamin' Demon*, built by the Barber-Nichols Engineering Co., reached 234.33 km/h (145.607 mph) at Bonneville Salt Flats, Utah, USA.

### Fastest solar-powered vehicle
Molly Brennan achieved a speed of 78.39 km/h (48.71 mph) in *Sunraycer* at Mesa, Arizona, USA, on 24 June 1988.

### FASTEST SPEED FOR A CAR

### Fastest solar/battery-powered vehicle
Manfred Hermann achieved 135 km/h (83.88 mph) in *Solar Star*, a solar/battery-powered car, on 5 Jan 1991, at Richmond RAAF Base, Richmond, NSW, Australia.

### Fastest car on two wheels
Goran Eliason (Sweden) achieved a speed of 164.71 km/h (102.33 mph) in a car on two wheels over a measured course of 100 m, on 20 April 1996.

**Right**
Black Rock Desert, Nevada, USA, has been the site of many attempts at the world land speed record. The current record was set here by Richard Noble (GB) on 4 Oct 1983. He achieved a speed of 1,019.467 km/h (633.468 mph),

1,019.467 km/h

# 0-60 MPH IN 3.07 SEC

REACHED A SPEED OF 295.832 KM/H IN MARCH 1994

### Fastest road cars
Various de-tuned track cars have been licensed for road use but are not normal production models.

The highest speed ever attained by a standard production car is 349.21 km/h (217.1 mph) for a Jaguar XJ220, driven by Martin Brundle at the Nardo test track, Italy, on 21 June 1992.

### Highest acceleration by a road car
The highest reported road-tested acceleration is 0–60 mph in 3.07 sec by a Ford RS200 Evolution, driven by Graham Hathaway at the Millbrook Proving Ground, Beds, UK, on 25 May 1994.

### Fastest lap by a road car
The fastest lap by a production car on a British circuit was by Colin Goodwin at Millbrook, Beds, on 8 Dec 1995 in a Jaguar 220S. His average speed was

332.98 km/h

**Left**
*Blue Bird* driven by Capt Malcolm Campbell on 19 Feb 1928, breaking the land speed record on Daytona Beach, Florida, USA. Campbell's speed averaged 332.98 km/h (206.95 mph). Today the land speed record is over three times this figure.

ON TWO WHEELS WAS 164.71 KM/H BY GORDON ELIASON ON 20 APRIL 1996

290.4 km/h (180.4 mph), and the peak speed was 294.5 km/h (183 mph).

### Fastest caravan tow
The world speed record for a caravan tow is 204.02 km/h (126.77 mph) for a Roadstar caravan towed by a 1990 Ford EA Falcon saloon and driven by 'Charlie' Kovacs, at Mangalore Airfield, Seymour, Victoria, Australia, on 18 April 1991.

### Largest car engine
The greatest engine capacity of a production car was 13.5 litres, for the US Pierce-Arrow 6-66 Raceabout, 1912–18; the US Peerless 6-60, 1912–14; and the Fageol of 1918.

### Most powerful current production car
The most powerful current production car is the McLaren F1 6.1 which develops in excess of 627 bhp.

295.832 km/h

**Left**
Briton Clive Roberts driving General Motors' *Impact* at Fort Stockton Test Center, Texas, USA, on 11 March 1994. The vehicle broke the record for the fastest electric car with a top speed of 295.832 km/h (183.822 mph) over a two-way flying kilometre.

## Fastest motorcycles

### Highest speed
Official world speed records must be set with two runs over a measured distance made in opposite directions within a time limit of 1 hr for FIM records and of 2 hr for AMA records.

Dave Campos (USA), riding a 7-m (23-ft) long streamliner named *Easyriders*, powered by two 91-in³ Ruxton Harley-Davidson engines, set AMA and FIM absolute records with an overall average of 518.450 km/h (322.150

mph) and completed the faster run at an average of (322.870 mph) 519.609 km/h, at Bonneville Salt Flats, Utah, USA, on 14 July 1990.

### Fastest speed in the UK
Michel Booys riding a streamliner motorcycle built by Alexander Macfadzean and powered by a turbo-charged 588 cc Norton rotary engine, achieved 323.30 km/h (200.9 mph) over two runs, at Bruntingthorpe Proving Ground, Leics, UK, on 24 Aug 1991.

### Fastest single run
The fastest time for a single run over 402 m (440 yd) from a standing start is 6.19 sec—equivalent to 233.79 km/h (145 mph), by Tony Lang of the USA on a supercharged Suzuki at Gainsville, Florida, USA in 1994.

### Highest terminal velocity
The highest terminal velocity at the end of a 402-m (440-yd) run from a standing start is 372.15 km/h (231.24 mph) by Elmer Trett (USA) at Virginia Motorsports Park in 1994.

## Aircraft

### Fastest recorded airspeed
The airspeed record, set on 28 July 1976, is 3,529.56 km/h (2,193.17 mph), by Capt. Eldon W. Joersz and Major George T. Morgan Jr, in a Lockheed SR-71A 'Blackbird' near Beale Air Force Base, California, USA, over a 25-km (15½-mile) course.

### Fastest jet
The USAF Lockheed SR-71, a reconnaissance aircraft, was first flown in its definitive form on 22 Dec 1964. It was reportedly capable of reaching an altitude close to 30,000 m (100,000 ft). It had a wing span of 16.94 m (55 ft 7 in), was 32.73 m (107 ft 5 in) long and weighed 77.1 tonnes (170,000 lb) at take-off. Its reported range at Mach 3 was 4,800 km (3,000 miles) at 24,000 m (79,000 ft).

### Fastest combat jet
The fastest combat jet is the former Soviet Mikoyan MiG-25 fighter (NATO code name 'Foxbat'). The single-seat 'Foxbat-A' has a wing span of 13.95 m (45 ft 9 in), is 23.82 m (78 ft 2 in) long and has an estimated maximum take-off weight of 37.4 tonnes (82,500 lb). The reconnaissance 'Foxbat-B' has been tracked by radar at a speed of about Mach 3.2 or 3,395 km/h (2,110 mph).

### Fastest airliner
The Tupolev Tu-144, first flown on 31 Dec 1968, was reported to have reached Mach 2.4 or 2,587 km/h (1,600 mph), but normal cruising speed was Mach 2.2. It exceeded Mach 2 on 26 May 1970, the first commercial transport to do so.

The BAC/Aérospatiale Concorde, first flown on 2 March 1969, cruises at up to Mach 2.2 or 2,333 km/h (1,450 mph), and became the first supersonic airliner used on passenger services on 21 Jan 1976. The New York–London record is 2 hr 54 min 30 sec, set on 14 April 1990.

### Fastest time to refuel
The record for refuelling an aircraft is 3 min 42 sec, for a 1975 Cessna 310 by the Sky Harbor Air Service line crew at Cheyenne Airport, Wyoming, USA on 5 July 1992. The plane received 388.8 litres (85.5 gal) of fuel.

### Fastest piston-engined aircraft
On 21 Aug 1989, the *Rare Bear*, a modified Grumman F8F Bearcat piloted by Lyle Shelton, set the FAI approved world record for a piston-engined aircraft on a 3-km (1⅞-mile) course at 850.24 km/h (528.33 mph), at Las Vegas, Nevada, USA.

201 km/h

N° 4468

### Fastest propeller-driven aircraft
The Russian Tu-95/142 (code-named by NATO 'Bear') has four 11,033-kW (14,795-hp) engines which drive eight-blade contra-rotating propellers. It has a maximum level speed of Mach 0.82, or 925 km/h (575 mph).

The turboprop-powered Republic XF-84H experimental US fighter, which flew on 22 July 1955, had a top design speed of 1,078 km/h (670 mph), but was abandoned.

### Fastest biplane
The unique Italian Fiat CR42B, that is powered by a 753 kW (1,010 hp) Daimler-Benz DB601A engine, attained 520 km/h (323 mph) in 1941.

### Fastest helicopter
Under FAI rules, the world's speed record for helicopters was set by John Trevor Eggington with co-pilot Derek J. Clews. They averaged 400.87 km/h (249.09 mph) over Glastonbury, Somerset, UK, on 11 Aug 1986 in a Westland Lynx demonstrator.

## Water

### Fastest recorded water speeds
The highest speed achieved on water is an estimated 300 knots (555 km/h), by Kenneth Warby in his unlimited hydroplane *Spirit of Australia* on the Blowering Dam Lake, NSW, Australia, on 20 Nov 1977. The official world water speed record is 275.8 knots (511.11 km/h) set on 8 Oct 1978, by Warby on Blowering Dam Lake.

Mary Rife (USA) set a women's unofficial record of 332.6 km/h (206.72 mph) in her blown fuel hydro *Proud Mary* in Tulsa, Oklahoma, USA, on 23 July 1977. Her official record is 317 km/h (197 mph).

### Fastest car ferry
Built in Finland, Stena Line's HSS *Explorer, Voyager,* and *Discoverer* are powered by quadruple gas turbines, giving a cruising speed of 40 knots (74 km/h) and a top speed of 44 knots (81.4 km/h). They can carry 1,500 passengers and 375 cars. The catamaran hulls have a length of 126.6 m (415 ft) and a beam of 40 m (131 ft).

# NEW YORK–LONDON 2 HR 54 MIN 30 SEC

### Fastest submarine
The Russian Alpha class nuclear-powered submarines had a reported maximum speed of over 40 knots (74 km/h). It is probable that they were able to dive to 760 m (2,500 ft).

## Railed vehicles
### Fastest rail vehicle speed
An unmanned rocket sled became the fastest vehicle ever on a railway track when it reached the speed of Mach 8 or 9,851 km/h (6,121 mph), over the 15.2-km (9½-mile) long rail track at White Sands Missile Range, New Mexico, USA, on 5 Oct 1982.

### Fastest national rail system
The highest speed that has ever been recorded on any national railway system is 515.3 km/h (320.2 mph) by the French SNCF high-speed TGV (Train à Grande Vitesse) Atlantique between Courtalain and Tours on 18 May 1990. TGV Atlantique and Nord services now run at up to 300 km/h (186 mph).

The Eurostar Channel tunnel train reaches 300 km/h (186 mph) on the French side.

The New Series 500 trains on Japan's JR West rail system are also designed to run at 300 km/h (186 mph) in regular service.

### Fastest point-to-point
The fastest point-to-point schedule is between Paris Charles de Gaulle and Lille Europe. The TGV587 covers the 204.2 km (127 miles) in 49 minutes—an average of 250 km/h (155.3 mph).

### Fastest diesel train
British Rail inaugurated their first HST (High Speed Train) daily service between London, Bristol and South Wales, UK, on 4 Oct 1976 using InterCity 125 trains. One of these set the world speed record for diesel trains, at 238 km/h (148 mph), on a test run between Darlington and York, UK, on 1 Nov 1987.

### Fastest trains in service in UK
The 7:30 a.m. London (King's Cross) to Newcastle service is timed to cover the 206.8 km (128½ miles) from Stevenage to Doncaster at a start-to-stop average speed of 174.8 km/h (108⅗ mph). The train is powered by the fastest locomotives in service, the Class 91 25-kV electric type, which hold the record for the fastest train carrying fare-paying passengers, at 247.8 km/h (154 mph), on 2 June 1995.

### Fastest steam locomotive
The highest ever ratified speed for a steam locomotive was 201 km/h (125 mph) over 402 m (440 yd). On 3 July 1938, the LNER 4-6-2 No. 4468 *Mallard* hauled seven coaches that weighed 243 tonnes (gross) down Stoke Bank, near Essendine, UK. The speed recorder showed a brief period when the train reached 203 km/h (126 mph), though it was not sustained long enough to register on the apparatus used for recording the speed.

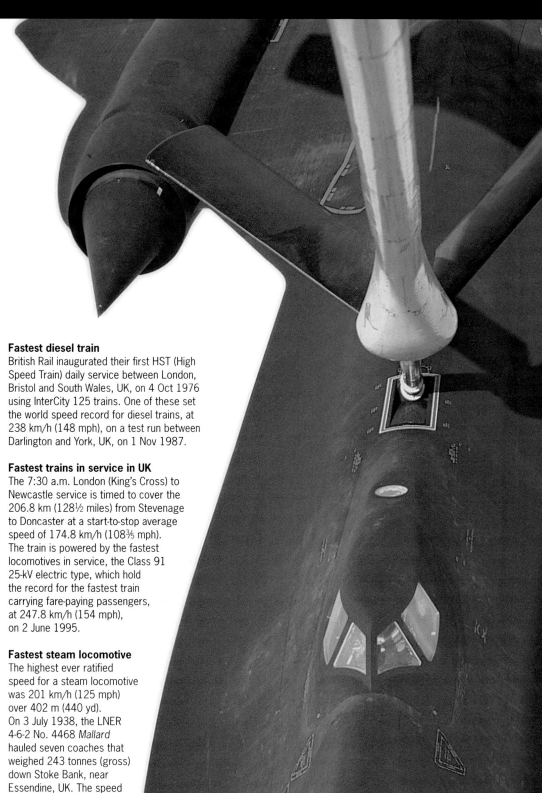

# 'End to end'

## John o' Groats–Land's End
The record for an 'end to end' flight over the United Kingdom, where supersonic overflying is banned, is 46 min 44 sec by a McDonnell F-4K Phantom flown by Wing Cdr. John Brady and Flt. Lt. Mike Pugh on 24 Feb 1988.

### Pedal car
The record for John o' Groats, Highland, to Land's End, Cornwall, is 59 hr 21 min, by a team of five from the Lea Manor High School and Community College, Luton, UK, from 30 May to 1 June 1993.

### Bicycle
Andy Wilkinson cycled from Land's End to John o' Groats in 1 day 21 hr 2 min 18 sec, from 29 Sept to 1 Oct 1990.

Pauline Strong holds the women's cycle record of 2 days 6 hr 49 min 45 sec, from 28 to 30 July 1990.

### Tricycle
Ralph Dadswell rode the distance on a tricycle in a time of 2 days 5 hr 29 min 1 sec, from 10 to 12 Aug 1992.

Andy Wilkinson achieved an unofficial record time of 1 day 17 hr 4 min 22 sec on 20–21 Apr 1996 using a recumbent tricycle with a wheel fully enclosed by a metal guard.

### Unicycle
Mike Day of Southgate, London, UK, and Michel Arets of Brussels, Belgium, rode 1,450 km (901 miles) from Land's End to John o' Groats in 14 days 12 hr 41 min, from 27 Aug to 10 Sept 1986.

### Roller skates
Damian Magee roller skated the distance in 9 days 5 hr 23 min, from 19–28 June 1992.

The fastest time by a woman on roller skates was 12 days 4 hr 15 min by 17-year-old Cheryl Fisher, from 19 Sept to 1 Oct 1987.

### Running
The fastest confirmed run from John o' Groats to Land's End is 10 days 2 hr 25 min, by Richard Brown of the United Kingdom, from 5 to 15 May 1995.

The fastest run by a woman is 13 days 10 hr 1 min, by Sandra Brown, from 5 to 18 May 1995.

A relay team of 10 from Vauxhall Motors A.C. covered the distance in 76 hr 58 min 29 sec from 31 May to 3 June 1990.

### Backwards running
Arvind Pandya of India ran backwards from John o' Groats to Land's End (1,512 km or 940 miles) in 26 days 7 hr, from 6 April to 2 May 1990.

### Walking
The fastest Land's End to John o' Groats walk is 12 days 3 hr 45 min for 1,426.4 km (886 miles 528 yd), by WO2 Malcolm Barnish of the 19th Regiment, Royal Artillery from 9 to 21 June 1986.

The women's record for walking the distance is 13 days 17 hr 42 min, by Ann Sayer from 20 Sept to 3 Oct 1980.

## Irish 'end to end'
The Irish 'end to end' record over the 644 km (400 miles 352 yd) from Malin Head, Donegal, to Mizen Head, Cork, is 5 days 22 hr 30 min, set by John 'Paddy' Dowling from 18 to 24 March 1982.

## Cross Channel
### Earliest air crossing
The earliest air crossing of the English Channel was made on 25 July 1909 when the pioneering French aviator Louis Blériot (1872–1936) flew his Blériot XI monoplane, powered by a 17.25 kW 23-hp Anzani engine, 41.8 km (26 miles) from Les Barraques, France, to Northfall Meadow, near Dover Castle, Kent, UK, in 36 min 30 sec, after taking off at 4:41 a.m.

### Conquests
Merv Sharp of Weymouth, Dorset, UK, has crossed the English Channel in more ways than any other person. He has crossed over it (by plane), on it (by ferry), in it (swum it seven times) and under it (by train).

### Paddleboarding
In Sept 1996, seven members of the Southern California Paddleboard Club paddled on their surfboards from Shakespeare Beach, UK, to Cap Gris Nez, France, in 6 hr 52 min.

## Around Australia
### Driving
The first men to drive round Australia were Nevill Reid Westwood and G.L. Davies in their 5-cv Citroën. They left Perth on 25 Aug 1925 and returned from the opposite direction on 30 Dec, 127 days later.

Mrs Mitchiko Teshima of Osaka, Japan, claimed to have done the same journey solo from 17 June to 10 Sept 1980.

### Motorcycling
In 1924, Arthur Grady of Fremantle, Western Australia, made the first motorcycle circuit of Australia on a Douglas in five and a half months. Neil Bromilow also achieved this on a 1922 678cc Martinsyde, from 2 June to 5 July 1984 over 15,985 km (9,933 miles).

### Walking
On 25 Jan 1976, Tom Hayllar of Sydney, NSW, completed a round-Australia walk of 12,000 km (7,456 miles). He began on 1 March 1975.

# 1,512 KM IN 26 DAYS 7 HR

## CAR IN 59 HR 21 MIN

The first women to walk across Australia, from Steep Point, Western Australia, to Byron Bay, NSW, were Patricia Dysart (USA) and Karen Jeffrey (Australia), from 1 March to 14 Sept 1988.

Sgt. Bob Walters walked from Cape Byron, NSW, to Steep Point, Western Australia, (5,672 km or 3,524 miles), from 3 March to 25 June 1978 and from Wilson's Promontory, Victoria, in the south-east to Kalumburu, Western Australia, in the north-west, 4,324 km (2,687 miles) from 5 May to 5 Sept 1985.

### Cycling across Australia
The record from Perth, Western Australia, to Sydney, NSW (4,502 km or 2,798 miles), is 9 days 23 hr 25 min, by Tomio Uranyu (Japan), from 28 March to 7 April 1992.

08/12/96

OF 12 TOOK 21 DAYS 21 HR 17 MIN TO CYCLE AROUND AUSTRALIA IN 1996

Gabrielle Smith was the first woman to cross Australia, solo and unsupported. She cycled from Avoca Beach, NSW, to Perth, Western Australia, from 4 March to 27 May 1981.

### Cycling around Australia
Hubert Schwarz (Germany) cycled 14,183 km (8,813 miles) around Australia in 42 days 8 hr 25 min, from 23 Aug to 4 Oct 1993.

The first woman to cycle around Australia was Barbara Tipp (Canada), as part of the CYC-RAM 88 team which cycled a distance of 15,687 km (9,747 miles) in 112 days, from 7 May to 8 Oct 1988, starting and finishing in Canberra, ACT.

A relay team of 12 from Charters Towers Wheelers Cycle Club, Queensland, took 21 days 21 hr 17 min in Sept 1996 to travel 14,294 km (8,882 miles).

## Trans-continental
### Motorcycling across Eurasia
Dave Barr went by motorbike from the Breton coast, France, to Vladivostok, Russia, from 8 Dec 1996 to 24 March 1997, a total distance of 15,090 km (9,375 miles).

His epic journey, which was completed in harsh winter conditions, took Barr through only five countries—France, Germany, Poland, Belarus and Russia. Most of his journey was made solo.

### Cycling
The trans-America solo record for the Race Across America (RAMM) is 8 days 3 hr 11 min, by Rob Kish in 1992. The women's

24/03/97

RAMM record is 9 days 4 hr 2 min, by Seana Hogan in 1995.

The trans-Canada record is 13 days 9 hr 6 min, by Bill Narasnek (Canada) in 1991.

Daniel Buettner, Bret Anderson, Martin Engel and Anne Knabe cycled the length of the Americas, from Prudhoe Bay, Alaska, USA, to the Beagle Channel, Ushuaia, Argentina, from 8 Aug 1986 to 13 June 1987.

### Backwards running across the USA
Arvind Pandya of India ran backwards across the USA, from Los Angeles to New York, in 107 days, from 18 Aug to 3 Dec 1984.

### Backwards walking
Plennie L. Wingo, then of Abilene, Texas, USA, completed a 12,875-km (8,000-mile)

trans-continental walk travelling backwards from Santa Monica, California, USA, to Istanbul, Turkey, between 15 April 1931 to 24 Oct 1932.

### Trekking across Antarctica
On 18 Jan 1997, Boerge Ousland of Norway completed a 64-day-long trek across Antarctica, becoming the first person ever to cross the continent alone and unaided.

Ousland set out on 15 Nov 1996 from Berkner Island and ended the journey at Scott Base, a New Zealand Antarctic station.

He used skis and a sail to take advantage of wind currents in Antarctica and had to tow a 180-kg (400-lb) sled which was loaded with his supplies.

**Left**
Dave Barr at the beginning of his epic trek across Europe and Asia at Le Conquet, France and at the journey's end in Vladivostok, Russia. Barr crossed most of Russia at the height of winter, travelling across the frozen Shilka and Arnur Rivers.

# Society

# Nations and politics

## Countries

### Largest country
Russia has a total area of 17,075,400 km$^2$ (6,592,800 miles$^2$)—11.5% of the world's land area. It is 70 times larger than the United Kingdom, but its population is 2.51 times greater, at 148,070,000 in 1996.

### Smallest countries
The smallest independent country is the State of the Vatican City or Holy See (Stato della Città del Vaticano), which was made an enclave within the city of Rome, Italy, on

its legal status is the same as other states. It is thus sometimes called the 'smallest state in the world'.

### Most boundaries
China has 15 land boundaries, more than any other country (with Mongolia, Russia, North Korea, Macau, Vietnam, Laos, Myanmar, India, Bhutan, Nepal, Pakistan, Afghanistan, Tajikistan, Kyrgyzstan and Kazakhstan). They extend for 24,000 km (14,900 miles). Until 1 July 1997 China and Hong Kong also had an international border.

### Shortest boundaries
The 'frontier' between the Vatican City and Rome, Italy, is 4.07 km (2 miles 933 yd).

The land frontier between Gibraltar and Spain at La Línea, which was closed between June 1969 and February 1985, measures 1.53 km (1,672 yd).

## Populations

### World population
The all-time peak annual increase in world population of 2.04% from 1965 to 1970 had declined to 1.57% by the period 1990–95.

The average daily increase in the world's population is approximately 240,000 or an average of some 167 per minute.

### Most populous country
China had an estimated population of 1.22 billion in mid-1996 and has a rate of natural increase of over 12.1 million per year, or more than 33,000 a day. Its current population is more than that of the whole world 150 years ago.

### Least populous country
The Vatican City or the Holy See had just under 1,000 inhabitants in 1996.

### Most densely populated territory
The Portuguese territory of Macau, on the southern coast of China has an estimated

11 Feb 1929. The enclave has an area of 44 ha (108.7 acres).

The world's smallest republic is Nauru, in the Pacific Ocean. It has an area of 2,129 ha (5,261 acres) and had an estimated population of 10,600 in 1996.

The smallest colony in the world is Gibraltar, which has a total area of 5.8 km$^2$ (2¼ miles$^2$).

Pitcairn Island is the only inhabited island of a group of four forming a British colony in Polynesia. The island has an area of 388 ha (960 acres), although the whole colony covers a total area of 48 km$^2$ (18½ miles$^2$). In late 1995 the island's population was 55.

The seat of the Sovereign Military Order of Malta and the official residence of the Grand Master of Rome has an area of 1.2 ha (3 acres). It maintains diplomatic relations with a number of foreign governments and

The country with the largest number of maritime boundaries is Indonesia, with 19.

### Most crossed frontier
The frontier crossed most frequently is between the United States and Mexico. It is 3,110 km (1,933 miles) long, and there are approximately 500 million crossings every year.

### Longest boundaries
Including the Great Lakes boundaries, but excluding the 2,547-km (1,538-mile) frontier with Alaska, the boundary between Canada and the USA extends for a total distance of 6,416 km (3,987 miles).

Excluding the Great Lakes boundary, the longest land boundary is between Argentina and Chile, at 5,255 km (3,265 miles).

The longest maritime boundary is between Greenland and Canada—it is 2,697 km (1,676 miles) long.

population of 433,000 (1996) in an area of 19.3 km$^2$ (7.5 miles$^2$), giving a density of 22,435/km$^2$ (57,733/mile$^2$).

The principality of Monaco, on the south coast of France, has a population of 30,500 (1996) in an area of just 1.95 km$^2$ (0.75 miles$^2$), a density equal to 15,461/km$^2$ (40,667/mile$^2$).

Of countries over 2,500 km$^2$ (1,000 miles$^2$) the most densely populated is Bangladesh, with a population of 123,063,000 (1996) living in 147,570 km$^2$ (56,977 miles$^2$) at a density of 834/km$^2$ (2,160/mile$^2$).

The Indonesian island of Java, which has an area of 132,186 km$^2$ (51,037 miles$^2$), had a population of 118,700,000 in 1997, giving a density of 897/km$^2$ (2,325/mile$^2$).

The United Kingdom had an estimated population of 58,784,000 in early 1997, giving a density of 241/km$^2$ (624/mile$^2$).

# 343,350,000 ELECTORAL VOTES

HAS A DENSITY OF 22,435 PEOPLE PER KM²

### Most sparsely populated country
Antarctica became permanently occupied by relays of scientists from 1943. The population varies seasonally and can sometimes reach 4,000.

The least populated territory, apart from Antarctica, is Greenland, with a population of 56,000 (1996) in an area of 2,175,600 km² (840,000 miles²), giving a density of one person to every 39.0 km² (15.1 miles²).

## World elections

### Largest elections
The elections in April 1996 for the 543 elective seats in the Indian Lok Sabha (Lower House) were the largest elections ever to take place. Over 343,350,000 people voted in the 537 constituencies, out of a total electorate of 592,600,000. There were nearly 565,000 polling stations which were staffed by 3 million people.

### Most decisive elections
In the general election of 8 Oct 1962, North Korea recorded a 100% turnout and a 100% vote for the Workers' Party of Korea.

On 14 Nov 1982, a single voter spoiled national unanimity for the official Communist candidates (the only candidates) in Albania. The Communist party consequently obtained 99.99993% of the poll in a reported 100% turnout of 1,627,968.

### Closest elections
On 18 Jan 1961, the Afro-Shirazi Party won by a single seat in Zanzibar (now part of Tanzania), after the seat of Chake-Chake on Pemba Island had been gained by a single vote.

The narrowest percentage win in an election was for the office of Southern District Highway Commissioner in Mississippi, USA, on 7 Aug 1979. Robert E. Joiner was declared the winner over W. H. Pyron, with 133,587 votes to 133,582. The loser thus obtained more than 49.999% of the votes.

### Most corrupt elections
In the Liberian presidential election of 1927, President Charles D.B. King was returned with a majority over his opponent, Thomas J.R. Faulkner of the People's Party, officially announced as 234,000. President King thereby claimed a 'majority' more than 15½ times as great as the entire electorate.

### Most elections contested
John 'The Engineer' Turmel of Nepean, Ontario, Canada, has contested a record 41 elections at a municipal, provincial and federal level as an Independent candidate since 1979. He founded the federal Abolitionist Party of Canada in 1993.

Screaming Lord Sutch of the Official Monster Raving Loony Party in the United Kingdom has contested 39 elections or by-elections.

THE WORKERS' PARTY RECORDED 100% OF THE VOTE

### Highest personal majority
The highest-ever personal majority for any politician was 4,726,112 in the case of Boris Nikolayevich Yeltsin, the people's deputy candidate for Moscow, in the parliamentary elections held in the Soviet Union on 26 March 1989. Yeltsin received 5,118,745 votes out of the 5,722,937 which were cast in the Moscow constituency. His closest rival obtained 392,633 votes.

Benazir Bhutto achieved 98.48% of the poll in the Larkana-III constituency at the 1990 general election in Pakistan, with 94,462 votes. The next highest candidate obtained just 718 votes.

### Largest ballot paper
For the municipal elections in Prague, Czech Republic, on 18–19 Nov 1994, there were 1,187 candidates for the multi-member all-city constituency. The ballot paper measured 101.5 x 71.5 cm (3 ft 4 in x 2 ft 4 in) and was delivered to all 1,018,527 registered voters, who could nominate up to 55 candidates for the 55 available seats.

### Most candidates for a single seat
The most candidates to stand in a national election for a single constituency was 107, who stood for the Kohat division of the NW Frontier Province, Pakistan, in Feb 1997. Almost all the election candidates were represented on the ballot paper by symbols because of illiteracy.

**Left**
Boris Yeltsin seen waving the Russian flag. He first won the Moscow constituency in the parliamentary elections in 1987 with the largest ever personal majority. On June 12 1991, he won the first ever democratic presidential elections in Russia with more than 57% of the vote.

**Left**
As long ago as 800 BC China had a population of 13,700,000 according to historical records. Today, it is the world's most populous country, although the country's population growth is considered unusually low for a developing country—a result of the one-child policy encouraged by the Chinese government in recent years.

# Societies

## Birth
### Birth rate
The worldwide crude birth rate (the number of births per 1,000) was estimated to be 25 per 1,000 between 1990 and 1995.

The highest crude birth rate estimated by the United Nations for 1995 was 55.2 per 1,000, for Niger.

Excluding the Vatican City, the lowest rate in 1995 was 8.6 per 1,000, for Bulgaria.

### Natural increase
The worldwide rate was estimated to be 15.7 (25 births less 9.3 deaths) per 1,000 in the period 1990–95, compared with a peak 20.4 per 1,000 from 1965 to 1970.

The lowest average life expectancy for 1995–96 is in Rwanda, with 36.4 years for females and 35.9 years for males.

## Demography
### Most and least children per household
The most children (under the age of 15) per household is in Guatemala with an average of 5.4 per household in 1995.

The smallest number of children (under the age of 15) per household is in Monaco with an average of 0.3 per household in 1995.

### Most children
In the Marshall Islands 51% of the population is under the age of 15.

### Secondary schools
India has the most secondary schools, with 231,670 in 1995, while San Marino has the best ratio with 5.8 pupils per teacher.

### Worst teacher-pupil ratios
The Central African Republic has the worst ratio, with 77 pupils per primary teacher.

The Central African Republic has the worst secondary ratio: 55.6 pupils per teacher.

### Higher education
Mexico has the most higher education institutions, with 13,000. The USA has the greatest number of students (14,210,000). Canada has the highest ratio, at 6,980 tertiary-level students per 100,000.

The highest available recorded rate in 1995 is 56.8 per 1,000 for Oman.

The lowest rate in any independent country in 1995 was in Latvia, with a figure of −6.9 per 1,000.

### Gender ratio
The United Arab Emirates has the largest recorded shortage of women—66.4% of the population is male.

Latvia has the largest shortage of males— 53.4% of the population is female.

### Life expectancy
In the decade 1890–1900 life expectancy in India was at a record low of 23.7 years.

The highest average life expectancy is in the Republic of San Marino, with 85.3 years for women and 77.2 years for men in 1995–96.

In the Gaza Strip (under Palestinian Authority) 51.2% of the population is aged under 15.

### Least children
The country with the smallest number of children under 15 is Monaco, with 12.3%.

### Most elderly population
In Monaco 10.8% of the population was aged 75 and over in 1995.

### Least elderly population
In the United Arab Emirates 0.2% of the population was aged 75 and over in 1995.

## Education
### Primary schools
China has the most primary schools— in 1994 there were 857,245. San Marino has the lowest pupil-to-teacher ratio at this level, with 5.2 children per teacher.

### Least university students
Djibouti has only 10 tertiary sector students per 100,000—the worst ratio in the world.

### Lowest literacy rates
Of the adult population in Niger, 13.6% is literate. In Eritrea 20% of the adult male population is literate. In Niger 6.6% of the adult female population is literate.

## Marriage
### Highest marriage rates
The marriage rate for the US Virgin Islands is 35.1 per 1,000 population.

Vanuatu is the sovereign country with the highest marriage rate in the world with 34 per 1,000 population.

# LOWEST LIFE EXPECTANCY 36.4 YEARS

WHERE EACH CITIZEN CONSUMES 153% OF THE BASIC DAILY REQUIREMENT

**Highest divorce rates**
In 1995, the USA had over 1.2 million divorces—4.6 per 1,000 population.

**Youngest bridegrooms**
In 1995, 24% of grooms in the United Kingdom were aged 19 or under.

**Youngest brides**
In 1995, 48% of the brides in Nicaragua were aged 19 or under.

**Oldest bridegrooms and brides**
In 1995, 67% of the grooms in Botswana were aged 30 or over.

In the US Virgin Islands 52% of brides were aged 30 or over in 1995.

**Lowest number of people per doctor**
In Italy there are 193 people to every doctor.

**Most hospitals**
The country with the largest number of hospitals in the world is China, with 63,100 in 1994.

**Most hospital beds**
Monaco has 168 hospital beds for every 10,000 people. Of larger countries, Ukraine has 130 for every 10,000 people.

**Least hospital beds**
Afghanistan, Bangladesh, Ethiopia and Nepal have the world's lowest provision of hospital beds, with only three for every 10,000 people.

## Employment
**Highest unemployment**
In 1996 Bosnia-Herzegovina had the highest rate of unemployment, with 75% of the labour force not in paid employment.

Spain has the highest unemployment figure for developed countries with 23.8% of its total work force out of work in 1994.

**Lowest unemployment**
Luxembourg had the lowest unemployment of any state in 1994 with 98% of its labour force in work.

**Greatest female employment**
Iceland has the greatest female participation in the paid workforce, with 80%.

**Left**
The huge differences in wealth between poor and rich countries are reflected in child mortality rates, education, health, attitudes to disability and life expectancy. The tiny, rich European country of San Marino, for example, has the world's highest life expectancy and the lowest pupil-to-teacher ratio, while Afghanistan, one of the poorest places on Earth, has the highest infant mortality rate, lowest food consumption and least number of hospital beds per head of population.

UNEMPLOYMENT IS BOSNIA-HERZEGOVINA WITH 75% OUT OF WORK IN 1996

St Lucia is the sovereign country with the highest percentage of marriages with brides aged 30 or over at 51% in 1995.

## Health and nutrition
**Infant mortality**
The lowest rate is in Guernsey, Channel Islands, with 1.9 per 1,000 in 1995.

The sovereign country with the lowest rate is Iceland with 3.2 per 1,000 in 1995.

The highest infant mortality rate is 152.8 per 1,000, in Afghanistan in 1995.

**Highest number of people per doctor**
In Niger there is only one doctor for every 54,472 people.

**Highest daily consumption of calories**
The average daily consumption in the Republic of Ireland is 3,952 calories a day.

**Lowest daily consumption of calories**
The average daily consumption in Somalia is just 1,499 calories a day.

**Highest food consumption**
According to the UN's food agency, the Republic of Ireland has the highest food consumption. Each citizen consumes 153% of the basic daily requirement.

**Lowest food consumption**
According to the UN's food agency, the country with the lowest food consumption is Afghanistan, with each citizen consuming only 62% of the basic daily requirement.

## Death
**Death rate**
East Timor had a rate of 45 per 1,000 from 1975–80, although this had subsided to 17.4 per 1,000 in the period 1995–96.

The highest estimated death rate in 1995 was 25.1 per 1,000 for Niger. The lowest estimated rate in 1995 was 1.9 deaths per 1,000 for Kuwait.

**Suicide rate**
The highest suicide rate ever was in 1991 in Sri Lanka, with 47 per 100,000.

The country with the lowest recorded suicide rate ever is Jordan—there was just a single case in 1970 which meant the rate was 0.04 per 100,000.

# War

which ended with the German surrender
on 31 Jan 1943. Only 1,515 civilians from
a pre-war population of more than 500,000
were found alive after the battle.

The final drive on Berlin, Germany, by
the Soviet Army and the ensuing battle for
the city from 16 April to 2 May 1945
involved 3.5 million men, 52,000 guns and
mortars, 7,750 tanks and 11,000 aircraft.

## Greatest civilian evacuation
Following the Iraqi invasion of Kuwait in Aug
1990, Air India evacuated 111,711 Indian
nationals who were working in Kuwait. Over
a two-month period, which began on 13 Aug,
488 flights took the civilians back to India.

## Worst sieges
The worst siege in history was the
880-day siege of Leningrad, USSR
(now St Petersburg, Russia), by the
German Army from 30 Aug 1941
until 27 Jan 1944. It is estimated that
between 1.3 and 1.5 million defenders
and citizens died, including 641,000
people who died of hunger in the city
and 17,000 civilians killed by shelling.
More than 150,000 shells and 100,000
bombs were dropped on the city.

## Land warfare
### Earliest weapon
The oldest known offensive weapon is a
broken wooden spear found in April 1911 at
Clacton-on-Sea, Essex, UK, by S. Hazzledine
Warren. Dating it accurately is beyond the
limit of radiocarbon dating, but it is thought
to have been fashioned before 200,000 BC.

### Longest wars
The longest continuous war was the Thirty
Years' War between various European
countries from 1618 to 1648. The so-called
Hundred Years' War between England and
France was an irregular succession of wars.

The *Reconquista*, a series of campaigns
to recover the Iberian Peninsula from
the Moors, began in 718 and continued
intermittently for 774 years until 1492, when
the last Moorish stronghold was conquered.

### Shortest war
The shortest war was between the United
Kingdom and Zanzibar (now part of
Tanzania), which lasted from 9:00 a.m to
9:45 a.m. on 27 Aug 1896. A Royal Naval
Squadron delivered an ultimatum to the self-
appointed Sultan, Seyyid Khalid bin Bargash,
to evacuate his palace and surrender. The
response demanded was not forthcoming
until after 45 minutes of bombardment.

### Bloodiest wars
By far the most costly war in terms of
human life was WWII (1939–45), in which the
total number of fatalities, including battle
deaths and civilians of all countries, is
estimated to have been 56.4 million. Poland
suffered the most, losing 6,028,000 or
17.2% of its total population of 35,100,000.

In its war of 1864–70 against Brazil,
Argentina and Uruguay, Paraguay's
population was decimated from 407,000
to 221,000 survivors, of whom fewer
than 30,000 were adult males.

### Bloodiest battle
The 142-day long Battle of the Somme in
France in 1916 resulted in an estimated
1.22 million dead and wounded, of whom
398,671 were British (57,470 on the first
day) and more than 600,000 German.

The losses of the German Army Group
Centre on the Eastern Front between 22
June and 8 July 1944 totalled 350,000.

The greatest death toll in a battle has been
an estimated 1,109,000 in the Battle of
Stalingrad, USSR (now Volgograd, Russia),

### Chemical warfare
The most people killed in a single attack
were the estimated 4,000 Kurds who died at
Halabja, Iraq, in March 1988 when President
Saddam Hussein used chemical weapons
against Iraq's Kurds because they had
supported Iran in the Iran-Iraq war.

### Costliest war
The material cost of WWII has been
estimated at $1.5 trillion. The greatest
loss was experienced by the USSR and
was estimated in May 1959 at 2.5 trillion
roubles, a figure that represented 30%
of national wealth.

## Naval warfare
### Greatest naval battles
A total of 282 ships and 1,996 aircraft
were involved in the Battle of Leyte Gulf,
in the Philippines, from 22 to 27 Oct 1944.
Of the 218 Allied and 64 Japanese warships,
26 Japanese and six US ships were sunk.

The greatest purely naval battle of modern
times was the Battle of Jutland on 31 May
1916, in which 151 Royal Navy warships
battled against 101 German warships. The

# COSTLIEST WAR $1.5 TRILLION

## 1896 LASTED 45 MINUTES

Royal Navy lost 14 ships and 6,097 men; the German fleet lost 11 ships and 2,545 men.

### Greatest seaborne invasion
The greatest maritime invasion in history was the Allied land, air and sea operation on the Normandy coast of France on D-Day, 6 June 1944. On the first three days 38 convoys of 745 ships moved in, supported by 4,066 landing craft, with 185,000 men and 20,000 vehicles, and 347 minesweepers. The air assault consisted of 18,000 paratroopers. Within a month, 1,100,000 troops, 200,000 vehicles and 738,000 tonnes of stores had been landed.

### Greatest military evacuation
The greatest military evacuation was at Dunkirk, France: 1,200 Allied naval and civil craft evacuated 338,226 British and French troops from the beachhead between 26 May and 4 June 1940.

### Worst submarine disaster
The worst submarine disaster occured when the American freighter SS *Thompson Lykes* rammed and sank the Free French submarine *Surcouf*, which was carrying 130 officers and men, in the Caribbean on 18 Feb 1942. There were no survivors.

## Air warfare
### Largest airborne invasion
The Anglo-American assault on 17 Sept 1944 near Arnhem, in the Netherlands, consisted of three divisions (34,000 men), 2,800 aircraft and 1,600 gliders.

### Longest-range attacks
The longest range attacks in air history were those undertaken by seven B-52G bombers which took off from Barksdale Air Force Base, Louisiana, USA, on 16 Jan 1991 to deliver air-launched cruise missiles against targets in Iraq shortly after the start of the Gulf War. Each flew a distance of 22,500 km (14,000 miles), refuelling four times in flight, with the round-trip mission lasting some 35 hours.

### Greatest bomb fatalities
The atomic bomb dropped by the USA on Hiroshima, Japan, on 6 Aug 1945, killed more than 100,000 people on that day. A further 55,000 people died from radiation within a year.

On 10 March 1945 during WWII, a bombing raid on the Japanese capital Tokyo killed about 83,000 people and injured 41,000.

## Armies
### Largest armed forces
In 1996, the armed forces of the People's Liberation Army in China had an estimated total personnel of 2,930,000 (comprising land, sea and air forces). Around 1.2 million reserves, plus many more for local militia duty, can be mobilized.

China also has the world's largest army in terms of numbers, with a total of some 2.2 million.

In 1996 the Russian armed forces had an establishment of 1.7 million but their actual strength is estimated at no more than 1.5 million. At their peak strength of 13.2 million in 1944 the Russian armed forces were the most numerous the world has seen.

In 1996, the United Kingdom's total military personnel was 236,900, of which the army had the most, with 116,000. The highest ever strength of the army was 3.8 million, in March 1918.

## AROUND 1,109,000 IN THE BATTLE OF STALINGRAD

# Crime

**Right**
Nine bank robberies
were recorded in the
United Kingdom
in 1996. This
compares with
6,758 that took
place in the United
States in 1995.

15:32:15

Mary Ann Cotton is believed to have killed 14, possibly 20, people. She is thought to have poisoned her victims, including her husbands and children, with arsenic. However she was convicted of only one murder. She was hanged in Durham Jail on 24 March 1873.

Dominic 'Mad Dog' McGlinchey (1955–94) admitted in a press interview in Nov 1983 to at least 30 killings in Northern Ireland. On 11 March 1986 he was jailed for 10 years at Dublin's Special Criminal Court for shooting with intent to resist arrest on 17 March 1984 in Co. Clare, Republic of Ireland. He was released on 5 March 1993 having served just under seven years.

On 7 May 1981, John Thompson was jailed for life for the 'specimen' murder by arson of Archibald Campbell—36 other victims died in the fire at the Spanish Club, Denmark St, London.

15:32:45

The biggest murder in the United Kingdom this century was committed by the unknown person or people who planted the bomb on Pan Am flight PA103. The aircraft crashed over Lockerbie, Dumfries & Galloway, UK, on 21 Dec 1988, killing a total of 270 people (259 in the aeroplane and 11 on the ground).

**Lynching**
The most lynchings to take place during the 20th century in the USA was 130, in 1901. The first year with no cases was 1952.

In the United Kingdom the last lynching case was Alexander Stewart at Dalmarnock Bridge, Glasgow, on 11 Sept 1922. It was falsely thought he had kidnapped a child.

## Assassinations
### Earliest attempt
The earliest recorded assassination attempt was against the Pharaoh of the Middle Kingdom of Egypt, Amonemhat I, in around 2000 BC.

### Most attempts
The target for the most failed assassination attempts in modern times was Charles de Gaulle (1890–1970), President of France from 1958 to 1969. He was reputed to have survived no fewer than 31 plots against his life between 1944, when his shadow government returned to Paris, and 1966 (although some plots were foiled before culminating in actual physical attacks).

## Murderers
### Most prolific murderer
Behram, the Indian Thug, was found guilty of strangling at least 931 victims with his yellow and white cloth strip, or *ruhmal*, in the Oudh district between 1790 and 1840.

### Most prolific 20th-century murderer
Colombian bandit leader, Teófilo 'Sparks' Rojas, is believed to have killed 592 people between 1948 and his death in an ambush near Armenia, Colombia, on 22 Jan 1963.

### Mass killing
Policeman Wou Bom-kon, 27, killed 57 people and wounded 35 on 26–27 April 1982, in a drunken eight-hour rampage in Kyong Sang-namdo province, South Korea.

### Most prolific British murderers
The most prolific British serial killers were William Burke and William Hare who murdered 16 people in Edinburgh, UK, in 1827–28 in order to sell their bodies to the anatomist Dr Robert Knox.

# BIGGEST ROBBERY £2.5 BILLION

RAMPAGE LASTING EIGHT HOURS ON THE NIGHT OF 26—27 APRIL 1982

## Robberies
### Biggest robberies
Between April and May 1945, the Reichsbank was robbed following Germany's collapse after WWII. The book *Nazi Gold* estimated that the total haul would have been worth £2.5 billion at 1984 values.

On 23 April 1986, the government of the Philippines announced that it had succeeded in identifying $860.8 million (£569.5 million) 'salted' away by the former President Marcos and his wife Imelda.

On 2 May 1990 treasury bills and certificates of deposit worth £292 million were stolen from a money-broker's messenger in the City of London. As details of the documents stolen were quickly flashed on the City's market dealing screens and given to central banks worldwide, the chances of the thief benefiting from the theft were considered to be very remote.

## COUNTERFEIT BRITISH NOTES DURING WWII

The robbery in the Knightsbridge Safety Deposit Centre, London, UK, on 12 July 1987, was estimated to be worth £30 million by the Metropolitan Police. However, the robbers themselves claimed that they had stolen around £60 million.

### Biggest bank robbery
In Jan 1976, during extreme civil disorder in Beirut, Lebanon, guerrillas blasted the vaults of the British Bank of the Middle East in Bab Idriss and stole safe-deposit boxes with contents valued at $20–50 million (£9–22 million).

### Biggest train robbery
A mail train from Glasgow was ambushed at Sears Crossing and robbed at Bridego Bridge near Mentmore in Bucks, UK, on 8 Aug 1963. The gang escaped with 120 mailbags containing £2,631,784 in banknotes which were being taken to London for destruction. Only £343,448 was ever recovered.

### Most burglaries
Christine and Vic Kelly, who owned the village shop in Kimberworth, S Yorkshire, UK, are reported to have suffered 72 burglaries at their premises over the 10 years to 1994.

### Biggest jewel theft
On 11 Aug 1994 gems with an estimated value of FF 250 million (£30 million) were stolen from the jewellery shop in the Carlton Hotel in Cannes, France, by three men.

### Largest object stolen by one person
On 5 June 1966, armed only with a sharp axe, N. William Kennedy slashed the mooring lines of the 10,639-dwt *SS Orient Trader* at Wolfe's Cove, St. Lawrence Seaway, Canada. The vessel drifted to a waiting blacked-out tug, thus evading a ban on any shipping movements during a violent wildcat waterfront strike. It then sailed for Spain.

## Kidnapping
### Biggest ever ransom
From 1532 to 1533, a hall full of gold and silver (£1 billion in modern money) was paid to the Spanish conquistador Francisco Pizarro at Cajamarca, Peru, for the release of Atahualpa, the last Inca emperor.

### Biggest modern ransom
On 20 June 1975, the sum of 1,500 million pesos (£26 million) was paid to the left-wing urban guerrilla group *Montoneros* for the release of brothers Jorge and Juan Born of the family firm Bunge and Born in Buenos Aires, Argentina.

## Fraud and forgery
### Biggest bank fraud
On 6 Sept 1989 the Banca Nazionale del Lavoro, Italy, admitted that it had been defrauded of a huge amount of funds, subsequently estimated to be around $5 billion (£3 billion). Its branch in Atlanta, Georgia, USA, had made unauthorized loan commitments to Iraq. Both the bank's chairman, Nerio Nesi, and its director-general, Giacomo Pedde, resigned following the revelation.

### Biggest British tax fraud
Britain's biggest tax fraud was when about £140 million of Nissan UK's profits were siphoned off into a Swiss bank account. It cost the UK Inland Revenue £97 million in lost corporation tax. Michael Hunt, Nissan's deputy chairman, was among those convicted and was jailed for eight years in 1993.

### Greatest banknote forgery
The German Third Reich's forging operation, codenamed 'Operation Bernhard', was run by Major Bernhard Krüger during WWII. It involved more than £130 million in counterfeit British notes in denominations of £5, £10, £20 and £50. The notes had been produced by 140 Jewish prisoners at Sachsenhausen concentration camp.

## Narcotics
### Largest narcotics haul
The most valuable drugs haul was on 28 Sept 1989, when cocaine with a street value of $6–7 billion (£3.7–4.4 billion) was seized in a raid in Los Angeles, California, USA.

The heaviest haul of narcotics was on 23 Oct 1991 when the authorities in Bilo, Pakistan, seized 38.9 tonnes (85,846 lb) of hashish and 3.23 tonnes (7,128 lb) of heroin.

### Largest narcotics operation
In a 14-month-long project codenamed 'Operation Tiburon', carried out by the Drug Enforcement Administration and Colombian authorities, 2,903 tonnes of Colombian marijuana were seized. The arrest of 495 people and the seizure of 95 vessels was announced on 5 Feb 1982.

## Criminal organizations
### Most profitable crime syndicate
In terms of profit, the largest syndicate of organized crime is believed to be the Mafia. Some 3,000 to 5,000 individuals in 25 'families' are federated under 'The Commission', with an annual estimated turnover of $200 billion (£115 billion), and a profit estimated at $75 billion (£51 billion) by Rudolph Giuliani, US Attorney for the Southern District of New York.

### Largest criminal syndicate
The Yamaguchi-gumi gang of the *yakuza* in Japan has 30,000 members. There are some 90,000 *yakuza* or gangsters altogether, in more than 3,000 groups.

**Left**
Alphonse 'Scarface' Capone (1899–1947) dominated the Mafia in Chicago from 1925 to 1931. He ran gambling, prostitution and bootlegging rackets, although the only crime he was punished for was income tax evasion, for which he was sentenced to 11 years in prison, and fines totalling $80,000 (£18,000).

## Litigation and trials

### Most protracted litigation
A dispute started in 1283 between the Prior and Convent of Durham Cathedral with the Archbishop of York over the administering of the spiritualities of the diocese. It flared up again in 1672 and 1890, and in Nov 1975 attempts to settle the 692-year-old issue failed. Neither side admits the legitimacy of writs of appointment issued by the other, although identical persons are named.

### Longest hearings
The longest civil case heard before a jury is *Kemner* v. *Monsanto Co.* at St. Clair County Court House, Belleville, Illinois, USA, from 6 Feb 1984–22 Oct 1987. Testimony that concerned an alleged toxic chemical spill in Sturgeon, Missouri, in 1979, lasted 657 days. The jury then deliberated for two months. Sturgeon residents were awarded $1 million (£609,000) nominal compensatory damages and $16,280,000 (£9,915,000) punitive damages. This was overturned by the Illinois Appellate Court on 11 June 1991 as the jury in the original trial had not found any damage had resulted from the spill.

### Longest criminal trial
The world's longest criminal trial lasted from 30 Nov 1992–29 Nov 1994 in Hong Kong. The High Court sat for 398 days to hear charges against 14 South Vietnamese boat people accused of murdering 24 North Vietnamese adults and children, who died in a blazing hut during a riot at a refugee camp in Hong Kong in Feb 1992. The defendants were acquitted, though some were convicted of lesser charges.

### Best-attended trial
At one point during the 12½-hour trial of 51-year-old Major Jesús Sosa Blanco, 17,000 people were present. The trial, at the Havana Sports Palace, Cuba, was heard between 22–23 Jan 1959. Blanco had allegedly murdered 108 people. He was executed on 18 Feb 1959.

### Most-viewed trial
A daily average of 5.5 million Americans watched live coverage of the O.J. Simpson murder trial between 24 Jan–3 Oct 1995. Simpson, an American footballer and actor, was on trial for the murder, on 12 June 1994, of his ex-wife, Nicole, and a waiter, Ronald Goldman. The jury reached a verdict of not guilty on 3 October.

## British hearings

### Longest civil trial
The Tichborne personation case was the longest British civil trial—lasting 1,025 days. It began on 11 May 1871 and collapsed on 6 March 1872. The criminal trial for the same case had lasted 188 days. Arthur Orton, alias Thomas Castro, claimed to be Roger Tichborne, elder brother of Sir Alfred Tichborne. He was sentenced for two counts of perjury on 28 Feb 1874. The jury reached their verdict in just 30 minutes.

### Longest retirement by a jury
The longest retirement by a British jury was in Jan 1996, at the end of the trial of Kevin and Ian Maxwell on fraud charges. The jury was out for twelve days before acquitting both defendants on 19 January.

### Longest libel trial
The longest libel trial in British legal history lasted two and a half years, from summer 1994 to Dec 1996. The action, brought by fast food firm McDonalds against two environmental campaigners, David Morris and Helen Steel, occupied 314 days at the Royal Courts of Justice, London. The trial heard more than 100 witnesses and examined 40,000 pages of evidence.

### Longest fraud trial
The longest fraud trial was the Britannia Park trial, which began on 10 Sept 1990 and ended on 4 Feb 1992 after 252 working days. The case centred on the collapse of the Britannia theme park near Heanor, Derby, UK, in 1985.

### Longest murder trial
The longest murder trial was 136 trial days from 11 Nov 1976 to 17 June 1977. Reginald Dudley and Robert Maynard were sentenced to life at the Old Bailey, London, for the murder of Billy Moseley and Micky Cornwall.

### Longest civil case
The longest civil case in British history was brought against the contractors of the *Piper*

**Right**
Asil Nadir, the chairman of Polly Peck International, was released on bail of £3.5 million by a British court on 17 Dec 1990. He had developed the company over 20 years from a small clothing concern into an international group, but it collapsed in September 1990 and he subsequently faced 18 charges of theft and false accounting amounting to £25 million. He jumped bail on 4 May 1993 and fled to Cyprus.

*Alpha* oil platform by solicitors acting for Occidental Petroleum (Caledonia) Ltd and the three other members of the consortium that owned the platform. Beginning in the Court of Sessions, Edinburgh, on 3 March 1993, submissions were completed on 31 Oct 1996, after it had proceeded for 391 days.

### Shortest trials
The shortest murder hearings were *R.* v. *Murray* on 28 Feb 1957 and *R.* v. *Cawley* at Winchester assizes on 14 Dec 1959. Both proceedings lasted only 30 seconds.

### Most expensive trial
The Blue Arrow trial, involving illegal support of the company's shares during a rights issue in 1987, is estimated to have cost c. £35 million. The trial at the Old Bailey, London, lasted one year, ending on 14 Feb 1992 with four of the defendants being convicted. They received suspended prison sentences but were later cleared on appeal.

# LARGEST DAMAGES $11.12 BILLION

### Highest bail
The highest bail ever set by a British court was on 24 March 1994, when Leonard Bartlett and Iain Mackintosh were bailed on fraud charges by Bow Street Magistrates' Court, subject to the condition that they should each provide sureties worth £10 million (this was later reduced to £1 million). In Feb 1996, Bartlett was jailed for 5 years and Mackintosh for 3½ years.

The highest bail on which a defendant has been released by a British court was £3.5 million, set on 17 Dec 1990 for Asil Nadir, the chairman of Polly Peck International. He faced 18 charges of theft and false accounting amounting to £25 million after the collapse of the company. He jumped bail and fled to Cyprus.

## Awards and costs
### Greatest damages to a company
The largest civil damages were $11.12 billion (£7.69 billion) to Pennzoil Co. against Texaco Inc. for the latter's allegedly unethical tactics in breaking up a merger in Jan 1984. An out-of-court settlement of $5.5 billion (£3 billion) was reached on 19 Dec 1987.

### Greatest damages to an individual
The largest amount of damages awarded against an individual was set on 10 July 1992 when Charles H.

### Defamation
On 20 March 1997 the *Wall Street Journal* was ordered to pay $222.7 million (£139 million) to a Houston brokerage firm who said an article in the paper contained false information and had contributed to them going out of business. The publisher of the *Wall Street Journal* is contesting the award.

### Sexual harassment
The record damages in a sexual harassment case were $50 million (£32 million), made

## Wills and settlements
### Greatest divorce settlement
The largest publicly declared settlement was in 1982 by the lawyers of Soraya Khashóggi. They secured £500 million plus property from her husband Adnan.

The highest divorce award made by a British court was £9 million to Maya Flick. On 25 Oct 1995 the Court of Appeal rejected an attempt by her former husband to stop her seeking a higher award.

**Left**
On 10 July 1992 Charles H. Keating Jr, the former owner of Lincoln Savings and Loan of Los Angeles, California, USA, was ordered by a federal jury to pay $2.1 billion (£1.1 billion) to 23,000 small investors who were defrauded by his company. These are the largest damages awarded against an individual. The figure was subject to final approval by the judge.

Keating Jr was ordered by a federal jury to pay $2.1 billion (£1.1 billion) to 23,000 investors defrauded by his company, Lincoln Savings and Loan of Los Angeles, California, USA.

### Greatest personal damages
The greatest personal injury damages that have ever been awarded to an individual were $163,882,660 (£109,109,627), ordered by the Supreme Court of the State of New York, USA, on 27 July 1993, to Shiyamala Thirunayagam. She was almost completely paralysed after the car in which she was travelling hit a broken-down truck in the outside lane of the New Jersey Turnpike on 4 Oct 1987. As the defendants would have challenged the jury's verdict in a higher court, Mrs Thirunayagam agreed to accept a sum of $8.23 million (£5.4 million) and a guarantee that the defendants would pay up to $55 million (£36 million) for any future medical costs.

to Peggy Kimzey, a former employee of Wal-Mart, on 28 June 1995. The jury at Jefferson City, Missouri, USA, also awarded her $35,000 (£22,000) for humiliation and mental anguish and $1 (63p) in lost wages. Wal-Mart said it would appeal.

### Individual compensation
Robert McLaughlin was awarded $1,935,000 (£1,225,000) in Oct 1989 for wrongful imprisonment for a murder in New York City, USA, in 1979. Sentenced to 15 years, he had served six when his foster father proved his innocence.

### Group compensation
Compensation for the 1984 Union Carbide Corporation plant disaster in Bhopal, India, was agreed at $470 million (£267 million) in Feb 1989, after settlement between Union Carbide and the Indian government. The government was representing over 500,000 claimants.

### Wills
The shortest valid will is by Bimla Rishi of Delhi, India, dated 9 Feb 1995. It consists of four characters in Hindi meaning 'all to son'.

The longest will was that of Frederica Evelyn Syilwell, proved at Somerset House, London, on 2 Nov 1925. It comprised four volumes containing 95,940 words, mostly concerning around $100,000 (£21,000) of property.

The shortest will in English law was contested in *Thorne* v. *Dickens* in 1906 but subsequently admitted to probate. It consisted of the words 'All for mother', in which 'mother' was his wife.

The smallest will preserved by the Record Keeper is an identity disc 3.8 cm (1½ in) in diameter, engraved with 40 words including the signatures of two witnesses. It belonged to A.B. William Skinner and was proved on 24 June 1922.

# Punishment

## Capital punishment
### Most hangings
The most people hanged from one gallows were 38 Sioux Indians, executed by William J. Duly outside Mankato, Minnesota, USA, on 26 Dec 1862.

A Nazi Feldkommandant hanged 50 Greek resistance men in Athens on 22 July 1944.

### Last public execution in UK
The last public execution in England took place outside Newgate Prison, London, at 8 a.m. on 26 May 1868, when Michael Barrett was hanged for his part in the Fenian bomb outrage on 13 Dec 1867.

The last executions in the United Kingdom were those of Peter Anthony Allen, hanged at Walton Prison, Liverpool, and John Robson Walby (Gwynne Owen Evans), hanged at Strangeways Jail Manchester, both on 13 Aug 1964. They had been found guilty of the murder of John Alan West on 7 April 1964.

### Last burning in UK
The last execution by burning in the United Kingdom was in March 1789, when a woman named Murphy was 'burnt with fire until she was dead' outside Newgate Prison, London.

### First boiling to death in UK
In 1530, John Roose, a cook, became the first person to be executed under a new law of Henry VIII whereby any person convicted of poisoning was to be judged guilty of high treason and executed by being boiled to death. Roose had poisoned two members of the Bishop of Rochester's household.

### Last public beheading
The last person publicly guillotined in France was murderer Eugen Weidmann, who was executed at Versailles on 17 June 1939.

The last person to be guillotined was 28-year-old torturer and murderer Hamida Djandoubi, on 10 Sept 1977 at Baumettes Prison, Marseille, France.

### Last beheading in UK
The last man to be executed by being beheaded in the United Kingdom was Simon Fraser, Lord Lovat, who was beheaded on Tower Hill, London, on 7 April 1747.

### Last execution for witchcraft
The last legal execution of a witch was of Anna Göldi at Glarus, Switzerland, on 18 June 1782. It is estimated that at least 200,000 witches were executed during the witch hunts of the 16th and 17th centuries.

**Right**
Two death row inmates play a game of chess between their cells at the Texas Department of Corrections Ellis Unit 3/11, Texas, USA. The longest stay on death row was 39 years by Sadamichi Hirasawa in Sendai Prison, Japan.

### Youngest people hanged in the UK
The lowest reliably recorded age of a hanging was a seven-year-old girl, hanged at King's Lynn, Norfolk in 1808. In Britain the death penalty for persons under 16 was abolished in the Children Act of 1908.

### Oldest people hanged in the UK
In 1843 Allan Mair was executed at Stirling for murder. He was 82 years old and was hanged sitting in a chair as he was incapable of standing up.

The oldest person hanged in the United Kingdom this century was 71-year-old Charles Frembd (sic), hanged at Chelmsford Jail on 4 Nov 1914 for the murder of his wife at Leytonstone, London.

### Death Row
Sadamichi Hirasawa (1893–1987) spent 39 years in Sendai Prison, Japan, until his death

at the age of 94. He was convicted of poisoning 12 bank employees with potassium cyanide in order to carry out a theft of £100 in 1948.

On 31 Oct 1987 Liong Wie Tong, 52, and Tan Tian Tjoen, 62, were executed by firing squad for robbery and murder in Jakarta, Indonesia, after 25 years on Death Row.

## Prison Sentences
### Longest sentences
Chamoy Thipyaso, a Thai woman known as the queen of underground investing, and seven associates were each sentenced for 141,078 years by the Bangkok Criminal Court, Thailand, on 27 July 1989 for swindling the public through a multi-million dollar deposit-taking business.

A sentence of 384,912 years (9 years for each of the 42,768 letters he failed to deliver) was demanded at the prosecution of Gabriel March Grandos, 22, at Palma de Mallorca, Spain, on 11 March 1972.

The longest sentence imposed on a mass murderer was 21 consecutive life sentences and 12 death sentences. John Gacy killed 33 boys and young men between 1972 and 1978 in Illinois, USA, and was eventually executed on 10 May 1994.

### Longest British sentence
Kevin Mulgrew from Belfast was sentenced on 5 Aug 1983 to life imprisonment for the murder of Sergeant Julian Connolley of the Ulster Defence Regiment. In addition he was given a further 963 years, to be served concurrently for 84 other serious charges, including 13 conspiracies to murder and eight attempted murders.

### Longest time served
Paul Geidel (1894–1987), a 17-year-old hotel porter from New York, USA, was convicted of second-degree murder on 5 Sept 1911. He was released from the Fishkill Correctional Facility, Beacon, New York, aged 85 on 7 May 1980, having served 68 years 245 days.

### Longest time served in the UK
The longest single period spent in prison by a reprieved murderer in the UK in this century is 44 years 10 months up to 31 May 1997, served by John Thomas Straffen, who was convicted at Winchester on 25 July 1952 of the murder of Linda Bowyer, aged five, and sentenced to death. Straffen had escaped from Broadmoor and was reprieved on account of his mental abnormality but was not judged insane. He has been in prison ever since.

### Oldest prisoner
Bill Wallace (1881–1989) was the oldest prisoner on record, spending the last 63 years of his life in Aradale Psychiatric Hospital, at Ararat, Victoria, Australia. He

# OLDEST PRISONER 107 YEARS

had shot and killed a man at a restaurant in Melbourne, Victoria, in Dec 1925 and, having been found unfit to plead, was transferred to the responsibility of the Mental Health Department in February 1926. He remained at Aradale until his death on 17 July 1989, shortly before his 108th birthday.

## Prisons
### Highest prison population
Some human-rights organizations have estimated that there are 20 million prisoners in China, which would be equal to 1,658 people in every 100,000. This figure is not officially acknowledged.

Russia is the country with the highest officially acknowledged prison population per capita. In 1996 there were 570 prisoners per 100,000 people.

**Left**
Spandau Prison, Berlin, Germany, was the world's most expensive prison. Built in 1887 for 600 prisoners, it was used solely for the Nazi war criminal Rudolf Hess for the last twenty years of his life.

### Prison fatalities
The most prison fatalities in a single incident occurred at Fort William, Calcutta, India, on the night of 20 June 1756. Under the order of Surajah Dowlah, Nawab of Bengal, 145 men and one woman were locked in a military prison cell measuring 5.5 x 4.25 m (18 x 14 ft)—the so-called Black Hole of Calcutta. When it was opened at 6 a.m. the next morning 123 men had suffocated or been crushed to death.

### Longest serving prisoner of conscience
Kim Sung-myun served 43 years 10 months in prison in Seoul, South Korea. He was arrested in 1951 for supporting Communist North Korea. Kim was released in Aug 1995, having never read a newspaper or watched TV while in prison.

### Most expensive prison
Spandau Prison, in Berlin, Germany, built in 1887 for 600 prisoners, was used solely for the Nazi war criminal Rudolf Hess (1894–1987) for the last twenty years of his life. The cost of maintaining 105 staff was estimated in 1976 at $415,000 (£230,000) per annum. The prison was demolished in 1987 after Hess strangled himself.

### Most labour-camp escapes
A former Soviet citizen, Tatyana Mikhailovna Russanova, now living in Haifa, Israel, escaped from various Stalinist labour camps in the former Soviet Union on 15 occasions between 1943 and 1954, being recaptured and sentenced 14 times.

### Greatest jailbreak
On 11 Feb 1979 an Iranian employee of the Electronic Data Systems Corporation led a mob into Gasr prison, Tehran, Iran, to rescue two American colleagues (the mob were not looking for the Americans). Some 11,000 other prisoners took advantage of their arrival and the Islamic revolution to escape. The plan to free the Americans was developed by H. Ross Perot, their employer.

### Greatest British jailbreak
On 25 Sept 1983, 38 IRA prisoners escaped from Block H-7 of the Maze Prison, Belfast.

### Longest prison escape
Leonard T. Fristoe, who was jailed in 1920 for killing two sheriff's deputies, escaped from the Nevada State Prison, Carson City, Nevada, USA, on 15 Dec 1923. He was turned in by his son on 15 Nov 1969 at Compton, California, after nearly 46 years of freedom under the name of Claude R. Willis.

### Most arrests
On 9 Sept 1982, Tommy Johns of Brisbane, Queensland, Australia, faced his 2,000th conviction for drunkenness since 1957. He had been arrested almost 3,000 times at the time of his last drink on 30 April 1988.

### Mass arrests
In the greatest mass arrest reported in a democratic country, 15,617 demonstrators were rounded up by South Korean police on 11 July 1988 to ensure security in advance of the 1988 Olympic Games in Seoul.

The largest mass arrest in the United Kingdom was on 17 Sept 1961, when 1,314 demonstrators supporting unilateral nuclear disarmament were arrested for obstructing roads leading to Parliament Square, London.

## Fines
### Heaviest fines
The world's largest fine was imposed on US securities house Drexel Burnham Lambert in December 1988 for insider trading. The total was $650 million (£335 million), of which $300 million (£164 million) was direct fines. The balance was to be placed in an account to pay parties defrauded by Drexel's actions.

### Heaviest fines imposed on an individual
Michael Milken agreed to pay $200 million on 24 April 1990 and settle civil charges filed by the Securities and Exchange Commission. The fine was in settlement of a criminal racketeering and securities fraud suit brought by the US government.

### Heaviest British fines
A £5-million fine was imposed on Gerald Ronson, on 28 Aug 1990 at Southwark Crown Court, London. Ronson was a defendant in the Guinness case concerning the company's takeover bid for Distillers.

The highest fine ever imposed on a British company was 32 million ECUs (equivalent to £24.3 million), levied against British Steel by the European Commission on 16 Feb 1994 for colluding in price-fixing in the 1980s.

# Money

# Private wealth

## World's wealthiest people

The earliest dollar centi-millionaire was Cornelius Vanderbilt, who left $100 million (£20.7 million) on his death in 1877.

The first people to leave $1 billion on their death were John Rockefeller and Andrew Mellon. Rockefeller is believed to be the first to accumulate $1 billion.

### Richest man

Sir Muda Hassanal Bolkiah Mu'izzaddin Waddaulah, Sultan of Brunei, self-appointed prime minister, finance and home affairs minister, has a fortune estimated in 1997 at $30 billion (£19 billion).

### Richest businessman

Bill Gates, the founder of Microsoft, is the richest businessman, with a personal fortune of $28 billion (£18.5 billion) in 1996.

### Richest businessman in the UK

Joseph Lewis has an estimated fortune of £3 billion. In Jan 1997 he took a £40 million stake in Glasgow Rangers, the biggest one-off investment in British football.

### Richest women

HM Queen Elizabeth II is asserted by most to be the world's wealthiest woman, although her exact fortune has always been the subject of controversy. *The Sunday Times* estimated her personal fortune at £250 million in April 1997. This excludes her art collection, worth at least £10 billion, which is now controlled by the Royal Collection Trust, a charitable trust. It also takes into account the fact that she is paying at least £1 million in tax each year.

The sisters Alice and Helen Walton inherited their fortune from the American Wal-Mart Stores retailing giants. Each has a personal wealth of $4.7 billion (£2.9 billion).

The cosmetician Madame C. J. Walker of Delta, Louisiana, USA, is reputed to have become the first self-made millionairess. She was an uneducated black orphan whose fortune was founded on a hair straightener.

### Richest businesswoman in the UK

Chryss Goulandris is probably the richest woman in the United Kingdom, with a fortune of £300 million. A Greek shipping heiress, she married Tony O'Reilly of the Heinz food group in 1991. The couple has a combined fortune of £1 billion.

### Richest family

The Walton retailing family of the USA, has a combined fortune of $24 billion (£14.8 billion), making them the richest family.

### Richest families in the UK

The Sainsbury family, owners of the supermarket chain, has a combined wealth of £2.5 billion. The Weston family, whose fortune comes from food production, also has a fortune estimated at £2.5 billion.

## UK'S HIGHEST PERSONAL

### Wealthiest bachelor

The Earl of Iveagh (b. 1970) had a share of the Guinness fortune estimated by *The Sunday Times* in 1997 to be worth as much as £600 million.

### Shortest period as a millionaire

In 1994, Howard Jenkins of Tampa, Florida, USA, a roofing company employee, discovered that $88 million (£58.6 million) had been transferred mistakenly into his bank account. Initially he withdrew $4 million (£2.7 million), but shortly afterwards he returned the $88 million in full.

### Youngest millionaires

The youngest person ever to accumulate a million dollars was the US child film actor Jackie Coogan, co-star with Charlie Chaplin in the 1921 film *The Kid*. In 1923–24 he was earning $22,000 (£5,000) a week and 60% of his films' profits.

# $31,528 AN HOUR

The youngest millionairess was child film star Shirley Temple, who accumulated wealth exceeding $1 million (£204,500) before she was 10. Her acting career finished in 1939.

### Youngest billionaire
William Henry Gates III (Bill Gates), who founded Microsoft Corporation at the age of 20, became the youngest ever billionaire when he was aged 31.

### Youngest British self-made millionaire
Ruben Singh (b. 1976) has estimated wealth of £27.5 million. This has been made in retailing with the Manchester-based Miss Attitude chain.

## Incomes
### Highest incomes
Lawrence Coss, the chief executive officer of Green Tree Financial, was paid $65.6 million (£41.5 million) in salary and bonuses for the year 1995, which works out at $31,528 (£19,875) an hour.

### Highest salary
Fund manager George Soros earned at least $1.1 billion (£770 million) in 1993 according to *Financial World's* list of the highest-paid individuals on Wall Street.

### Highest personal tax demands
The highest disclosed British personal income tax demand is one for £5,371,220, against merchant banker Nicholas van Hoogstraten.

### Highest fees
The highest paid investment consultant in the world is Harry D. Schultz, based in Monte Carlo, Monaco and Zürich, Switzerland. His consultation fee is $2,400 (£1,500) for 60 minutes on weekdays and $3,400 (£2,125) at weekends. His five-minute phone consultations cost $40 (£25) a minute.

### Highest paid executive in the UK
The United Kingdom's highest earner in 1996 was Carol Galley, who was paid £5.44 million. She is a fund manager at Mercury Asset Management.

## Legacies and bequests
### Greatest bequests
On 12 March 1991, Walter Annenberg announced his intention to leave his $1-billion (£550-million) collection of art works to the Metropolitan Museum of Art in New York City, USA.

The largest ever single cash bequest was $500 million (£180 million), equivalent in 1997 to £2.6 billion, made to 4,157 educational and other institutions and announced on 12 Dec 1955 by the Ford Foundation of New York City, USA.

The greatest benefactions of a millionaire in the United Kingdom were those of car manufacturer Viscount Nuffield, who was born William Richard Morris. His bequests totalled more than £30 million between 1926 and 22 Aug 1963 when he died.

### Largest dowry
The largest ever recorded dowry was of Elena Patiño, who was the daughter of Don Simón Iturbi Patiño, the Bolivian tin millionaire. In 1929 he bestowed £8 million from a fortune once estimated to be worth as much as £125 million.

### Greatest wills in the UK
The largest British will was left by the sixth Marquess of Bute. When he died in 1994 he left an estate which was worth a total of £130,062,015.

On 29 April 1985 the estate of Sir Charles Clore was agreed by a court hearing at £123 million. The Inland Revenue had claimed £84 million in duties but settled for a sum of £67 million.

The largest fortune left by a woman was £92,814,057 net, by Dorothy de Rothschild of the European financial family.

### Greatest miser
If meanness could be measured as a ratio between expendable assets and expenditure then Henrietta Howland ('Hetty') Green, who kept over $31,400,000 (£6.6 million) in one bank alone, was the champion. Her son had to have his leg amputated because of her delays in finding a *free* medical clinic and she herself ate cold porridge because she was too thrifty to heat it. Her estate proved to be worth $95 million (£20 million), equivalent to £816 million in 1996.

**Right**
In 1987, Texaco filed for a record bankruptcy of $35.9 billion (£22.4 billion). This was a result of Judge Solomon Casseb Jr's Dec 1985 ruling that Texaco should make financial reparation to Penzoil for having used unethical practices to break up a proposed merger between Penzoil and Getty Oil.

## Stock exchanges

### Oldest exchanges
The exchange in Amsterdam, Netherlands, was founded in the Oude Zijds Kapel in 1602 for dealings in printed shares of the United East India Company of the Netherlands.

### Largest trading volume
In 1995 the New York Stock Exchange, USA, traded $3.1 trillion (£2 trillion)

### Largest stock exchange
Up to Dec 1996 over 2,900 companies had stock listed on the the New York Stock Exchange. These companies had over 180 billion shares worth $9.2 trillion (£5.75 trillion).

### London Stock Exchange
The highest number of equity bargains in one day on the London Stock Exchange was 114,973 on 22 Oct 1987.

The highest number of equity bargains in one year was 13,557,455 in 1987.

The busiest session on the London market was on 28 Jan 1993, when 1.3 billion shares were traded.

### FT-SE 100 share index
The FT-SE 100 index reached a closing high of 4,964.2 on 16 July 1997.

The lowest closing figure was 986.9 on 23 July 1984.

The greatest rise in a day was 142.2 points to 1,943.8 on 21 Oct 1987.

**Right**
The highest recorded personal paper losses on stock values were incurred by Ray A. Kroc, former chairman of McDonald's Corporation, amounting to $65 million (£27.8 million) on 8 July 1974.

The greatest fall in a day's trading was 250.7 points to 1,801.6 on 20 Oct 1987.

### New York Stock Exchange
The market value of stocks listed on the NYSE reached an all-time high of $6.4 trillion (£4.2 trillion) on 30 April 1996.

The record day's trading was 652,829,000 shares on 15 Dec 1995.

The highest closing figure on the Dow Jones Industrial Average of selected stocks was 8,038.88 on 16 July 1997.

The lowest-ever closing figure was 41.22 on 8 July 1932.

The record daily rise is 186.84 points, to 2,027.85, achieved on 21 Oct 1987.

The largest decline in a day's trading was 508 points on 19 Oct 1987.

### Largest trading losses sustained
In 1996, Japan's fourth largest trading company, Sumimoto Corporation, revealed that they had suffered $2.6 billion (£1.7 billion) copper trading losses through unauthorized dealings over a 10-year period on the London Metal Exchange by one of their top traders, Yasuo Hamanaka.

### Largest flotation
The record number of investors for a single issue is 5.9 million, in the Mastergain '92 equity fund floated by the Unit Trust of India, Bombay, India, in April and May 1992.

### Largest British flotation
The 1997 flotation of the Halifax Building Society was estimated to be worth £11 billion.

### Largest computerized brokerage
The Institutional Network, or Instinet Corp., is now the world's largest computerized brokerage. In 1995, revenues equalled $376 million (£237 million).

### Largest British rights issue
A rights issue of £1.35 billion was announced by Zeneca on 1 June 1993.

# LARGEST FLOTATION £11 BILLION

### Highest share value
A single share in Moeara Enim Petroleum Corporation was worth Dutch fl.165,000 (£50,586) on 22 April 1992.

### Biggest high-yield preferred stock deal
Bear, Sterns & Co. and Morgan Stanley & Co. completed the biggest high-yield preferred stock deal in history in April 1996, with a $1.5 billion (£990 million) offering for Time Warner Inc. in the USA.

### Greatest personal loss in one day
Ray A. Kroc, former chairman of McDonald's Corporation, incurred stock losses of $65 million (£27.8 million) on 8 July 1974.

### Record British fine
In 1997, the British regulator IMRO imposed a £2 million ($3.2 million) fine on Morgan Grenfell Asset Management, for breaching investment rules and not informing it about mounting problems. MGAM has to pay $1 million (£625,000) costs.

### Biggest bankruptcy
The biggest corporate bankruptcy in terms of assets amounted to $35.9 billion (£22.4 billion), filed by Texaco in 1987.

## Financial institutions
### Largest development bank
The International Bank for Reconstruction and Development, generally known as the World Bank, which is based in Washington DC, USA, had assets of $168.7 billion (£107 billion) for the 1994 fiscal year.

### Largest building societies
The biggest lender in the world is the Japanese House Loan Corporation.

The Halifax Building Society of W Yorkshire, UK, had revenues of £8.84 billion in 1996.

## Insurance
### Largest insurance companies
In 1996 Japan's Nippon Life Insurance Company had assets of $364,762.5 million (£240,735.5 million), and profits of $2,426.6 million (£1,601.5 million).

### World's worst insured damage
The worst catastrophe in terms of insured damage was Hurricane Andrew, which hit Homestead, Florida, USA, in Aug 1992. It was the most expensive hurricane ever to hit the world by insured losses, with an estimated cost of $15.5 billion (£8 billion).

### Largest ever marine insurance loss
The largest-ever marine insurance loss was $836 million (£490.5 million) for the Piper Alpha Oil Field in the North Sea. On 6 July 1988 a leak from a gas compression chamber underneath the living quarters

### Largest commercial banks
The Bank of Tokyo–Mitsubishi Ltd had total assets of $692,287 million (£409,907 million) in July 1997.

The State Bank of India had 12,947 outlets on 31 March 1996 and assets of $42 billion (£26.3 billion).

### Largest bank by equity
In 1996 UK-based HSBC Holdings had $26,665 million (£16,665 million) of equity.

### Largest British banks
HSBC Holdings had profits of $3.8 billion (£2.4 billion) in 1996.

The bank with the largest network of branches in the United Kingdom is Barclays plc, with consolidated total assets of £186,002 million in 1996.

The Prudential Insurance Company of USA has almost 93,000 employees.

### Largest policy
A life-assurance policy for $100 million (£55.5 million) was bought by a major US entertainment corporation on the life of a leading US entertainment-industry figure. It was sold in 1990 by Peter Rosengard of London and placed by Shel Bachrach of Albert G. Ruben & Co. Inc. of California, USA, and Richard Feldman of the Feldman Agency, East Liverpool, Ohio, USA, with nine companies spreading the risk.

### Biggest payout on a single life
On 14 Nov 1970, $18 million (£7.5 million) was paid to Linda Mullendore, widow of a rancher from Oklahoma, USA. Her murdered husband had paid $300,000 (£126,000) in premiums in 1969.

ignited and triggered a series of explosions which blew Piper Alpha apart. Of the 232 people on board, only 65 survived.

### Earthquakes
The Jan 1994 earthquake that struck Northridge, California, USA, cost around $12,500,000,000 (£7,500,000,000) in terms of damaged property.

### Floods
The floods that swept through Louisiana, USA, in May 1995 caused the world's worst flood disaster by insured losses, costing $570,388,405 (£359,571,580).

### Fire
The fire following the 18 April 1906 San Francisco earthquake in the USA cost around $5,748,000,000 (£1,185,888,178), making it the most costly fire ever.

## Profit and loss

### Greatest sales
The *Fortune 500* list of leading industrial corporations of April 1996 is headed by General Motors Corporation of Detroit, Michigan, USA, with sales of $168.8 billion (£141 billion) for 1995.

The first company to surpass the $1 billion mark in annual sales was the United States Steel (now USX) Corporation of Pittsburgh, Pennsylvania, USA, in 1917.

### Greatest profit
The greatest net profit made by a corporation in 12 months is the $7.6 billion (£4.1 billion), made by American Telephone and Telegraph Company (now AT&T Corp) from 1 Oct 1981 to 30 Sept 1982.

### Greatest loss
The worst annual net trading loss is $23.5 billion (£15.5 billion), in 1992 by General Motors. The bulk of this figure was due to a charge of some $21 billion (£14 billion) for employees' health costs and pensions.

The greatest annual loss for a company in the United Kingdom is £3.91 billion, made by the National Coal Board in the year ending 31 March 1984.

## Businesses

### Largest company by profits
The largest company in the world measured by its profits is the jointly-owned Anglo-Dutch Royal Dutch Shell Group, a petroleum refining company, which had profits of $6,904.6 million (£4,556.9 million) in 1996.

### Largest companies by employees
The largest company employer in the world is the US Postal Service which has over 870,000 employees as of 1996.

The world's largest commercial or utility employer is Indian Railways, with a total of 1,645,000 staff in 1995.

### Largest company by assets
The American multi-national motor manufacturer Ford Motor Company is the largest company in the world in terms of assets. In 1996 its assets were worth a total of $243,283 million (£160,561.6 million).

### Largest company revenues
Japan's Mitsubishi Corporation, a trading company, was the company with the largest revenue in the world. In 1996 it had revenues of $184,365.2 million (£121,677.1 million).

### Company directorships
The all-time record for directorships was set by Hugh T. Nicholson (1914–85), formerly senior partner of Harmood Banner & Sons of London, UK, who, as a liquidating chartered accountant, became director of all 451 companies of the Jasper group in 1961 and had seven other directorships.

### Smallest company equity
The smallest-ever British company was Frank Davies Ltd, incorporated on 22 Aug 1924 with a ½d share capital divided into two ¼d shares (£0.002 divided into two shares of £0.001 in decimal coinage). The company was finally dissolved in 1978 without ever having increased its share capital.

## Takeovers

### Highest takeover bid
The highest bid in a corporate take-over was $21 billion (£12 billion) for RJR Nabisco Inc, the tobacco, food and beverage company, made by Kohlberg Kravis Roberts, which offered $90 (£50) a share on 24 Oct 1988. By 1 Dec 1988 the bid, led by Henry Kravis, had reached $109 (£60) per share to aggregate $25 billion (£14 billion).

A proposed bid of $22.8 billion (£14.1 billion) for Chrysler by Tracinda Corporation was announced on 12 April 1995. It was withdrawn on 1 June 1995.

### Highest British takeover bid
The largest successful takeover bid in British history was the offer of almost £9 billion by Glaxo plc for Wellcome, the rival drugs company, on 23 Jan 1995.

The largest bid for a British company is £13 billion for BAT Industries on 11 July 1989, made by Hoylake, led by James Goldsmith, Jacob Rothschild and Kerry Packer.

## Corporate records

### Largest aerospace group
The largest aerospace group is Lockheed Martin Corporation founded in Hollywood, California, USA, in 1926. In 1996 its revenue was $22,853 million (£15,100 million).

### Largest airline
The largest airline in the world is AMR Corporation, based in Fort Worth, Texas, USA, which had a total annual revenue of $17,753 million (£11,096 million) in 1996.

### Largest beverage company
The Coca-Cola Company had revenues of $18,018 million (£11,900 million) in 1996.

### Largest brokerage
The largest brokerage firm is Merrill Lynch & Company, founded in 1914, which had an annual revenue of $21,513 million (£14,198 million) in 1996.

### Largest chemicals firm
The chemicals firm E.I. Du Pont de Nemours and Company Inc had revenues of $37,607 million (£24,819 million) in 1996.

### Largest department stores
The largest department store in the United Kingdom is Harrods Ltd of Knightsbridge, London, named after Henry Charles Harrod

# 1996 REVENUE $184,365.2 MILLION

## MAKING A PROFIT OF $6,904.6 MILLION IN 1996

(1800–85), who opened a grocery in Knightsbridge in 1849. It now has a total selling floor space of 10.5 ha (25 acres), with 50 lifts and 36 flights of stairs and escalators. It employs between 3,500 and 4,000 people depending on the time of year, and achieved record sales of over £459 million in the year ending 27 Jan 1996.

### Largest electric and gas company
The Japanese Tokyo Electric Power Company Inc. had a total revenue of $52,361.5 million (£34,500 million) in 1996.

### Largest food company
The largest food company is Unilever N.V./Unilever plc, which had revenues of $49,738 million (£32,826 million) in 1996.

### Largest delivery company
The largest mail, package and freight delivery firm is the United States Postal Service. In 1996 its total revenues reached $54,293.5 million (£35,832.5 million).

### Largest market research company (UK)
The United Kingdom's top market research company is Taylor Nelson AGB, which had a total turnover of £84.2 million in 1996.

### Largest petroleum company
The largest petroleum refining company is the Exxon Corporation. In 1996 its revenue was $110,009 million (£72,604 million).

### Largest pharmaceuticals company
The American-based pharmaceuticals firm Johnson & Johnson had revenues of $18,842 million (£12,435 million) in 1996.

### Largest PR company
The largest public relations company in the world is Burson-Marsteller, founded over 40 years ago by Harold Burson and Bill Marsteller from a single office in New York, USA. It had net fees of more than $211 million (£127.7 million) in 1995.

### Largest PR company (UK)
The largest PR company in the United Kingdom is Shandwick, a group of 11 consultancies, with a total fee income of $36 million (£24 million) in 1994.

### Largest publishing company
The largest publishing and printing company is Bertelsmann AG. In 1996 its revenue was $13,746.7 million (£9,072.5 million).

### Largest media corporation
The world's largest media corporation is Viacom Inc. It had assets which totalled $29,026 million (£19,156.5 million) in 1996 and operates in 100 countries.

### Largest building society (UK)
Following the changing of their mutual status, several British building societies are now banks: this includes the Halifax, which

he called 'The Great Five Cent Store', in Utica New York, USA, on 22 Feb 1879.

### Largest restaurateurs
The McDonald's Corporation of the USA is the world's largest global food service retailer. Brothers Dick and Mac McDonald pioneered the fast food industry concept and

## LARGEST MEDIA CORPORATION, WITH ASSETS IN 1996 OF $29,026 MILLION

used to be the largest building society in the United Kingdom. Consequently, the Nationwide Building Society, whose operating profits were £584.1 million in 1996, is now the largest.

### Largest retailers
The largest retailing firm in the world is Wal-Mart Inc. of Bentonville, Arkansas, USA, which was founded by Sam Walton in 1962. It had sales of $93.6 billion (£56.1 billion) and an unaudited net income of $2.74 billion (£1.8 billion) at 31 Jan 1996. At 1 May 1996, Wal-Mart Inc. had 3,032 retail locations and employed as many as 658,200 people.

As of 28 Jan 1996, the Woolworth Corporation of New York City, USA, had more retailing outlets than any other company in the world. The company has as many as 8,178 retail stores operating throughout the world. The company's founder, Frank Winfield Woolworth, opened his first shop, which

later sold their business to their national franchising agent, Ray A. Kroc (1902–1984), creating McDonald's Corporation. In 1955, Kroc opened his first restaurant in Des Plaines, Illinois, USA. By the end of 1996, McDonald's operated 21,000 restaurants in 101 countries. Worldwide sales in 1996 exceeded $30 billion (£19 billion).

### Largest soaps and cosmetics company
The largest soaps and cosmetics firm in the world is the Proctor & Gamble Company. It had total annual revenues of $33,434 million (£22,065.7 million) in 1996.

### Largest telecommunications company
The largest telecommunications company in the world is Nippon Telegraph and Telephone Corporation with revenues of $81,973.2 million (£54,100.5 million) in 1996.

### Largest railway company
In 1996 the East Japan Railway Company had total revenues of $25,623.7 million (£16,911 million).

**Right**
The gold bullion depository at Fort Knox, Kentucky, USA, stores 147 million fine oz of gold and has been the principal federal depository of US gold since Dec 1936. Gold's peak price was on 21 Jan 1980 when it cost $850 (£365) per fine oz.

**Most rapidly expanding economy**
The gross national product of Thailand grew by an average 9.8% per annum in the decade ending 1995.

**Most rapidly decreasing economy**
The GNP of Armenia decreased by an average of 12.9% per annum in the decade ending 1995.

**Largest national debt**
The USA has the largest national debt of any country in the world. During fiscal year 1996 it was $5.129 trillion (£3.385 trillion), and the gross interest paid on the debt was $332.414 billion (£199.4 billion). The net interest was $202.957 billion (£122 billion).

**Largest net foreign debt**
The largest net foreign debt, calculated as a percentage of GDP, for a developed country is in New Zealand where the debt stood at 80% of GDP in 1996. There is disagreement concerning which developing country has the greatest indebtedness as a percentage of gross domestic product.

The British national debt was less than £1 million during the reign of James II in 1687; at the end of March 1995 it amounted to some £349,163 million, of which around £18,500 million was in currency other than sterling.

**Most overseas debt**
The country most heavily in overseas debt at fiscal year-end 1994 was the USA, with over $654 billion (£419 billion).

Among developing countries, Mexico has the highest foreign debt, with $147.5 billion (£94.6 billion) at the end of 1994.

## Wealth debt and aid
### Richest countries
According to the World Bank the highest gross domestic product (GDP) per head in 1995 was in Luxembourg, with $39,850 (£25,253), Switzerland came second with $37,180 (£23,560) and Japan was third with $34,360 (£21,774). The GDP per capita in the United Kingdom was $18,410 (£11,666).

### Poorest countries
Mozambique and Rwanda have the lowest GDP per capita in the world, according to the World Bank. In 1995 GDP per capita in both Mozambique and Rwanda was $80 (£60), which represented a decrease on the previous year.

**Largest GNP**
The country with the largest gross national product (GNP) is the USA, with a record $7,238,000 million (£4,700,000 million) for the year ending 31 Dec 1995.

The GNP of the United Kingdom in 1995 amounted to £1,069,000 million.

**Largest gold reserves**
The world's greatest monetary gold reserves belong to the US Treasury. They amounted to around 262 million fine oz during 1996, which was equivalent to $100 billion (£87 billion) at the June 1996 gold price of $382 (£252) per fine oz. The principal depository is at Fort Knox, Kentucky, USA.

**Balance of payments**
The record deficit for any country for a calendar year was $167.1 billion (£100.2 billion), reported by the USA in 1987. Japan holds the surplus record with $131.5 billion (£88.8 billion) for 1993.

The most favourable current yearly balance-of-payments figure for the United Kingdom was a surplus of £6,748 million in 1981. The worst figure was a total deficit of £21,726 million in 1989.

**Largest foreign aid donors**
The largest foreign aid donor by expenditure was Japan in 1995, with aid which amounted to $14.5 billion (£9.4 billion).

# US NATIONAL DEBT $5.129 TRILLION

## TAX OF OVER 100% ON INCOME CAN BE IMPOSED IN EXTREME SITUATIONS

In 1995 Norway had the highest ratio of official development assistance to gross national product, with 1.05%.

In 1996 France and Germany overtook the USA for the first time as aid donors.

## Budgets and inflation

### Largest budget
The greatest governmental expenditure for any country was $1.519 trillion (£950 billion), spent by the US government for the fiscal year 1995. The highest-ever revenue figure was $1.355 trillion (£847 billion), made by the USA in the same year.

### Greatest fiscal surplus
The country with the greatest fiscal surplus ever was the USA in 1947/8 with $11.796 billion (£3.063 billion).

### Greatest fiscal deficit
The highest deficit amounted to $290 billion (£160 billion), by the USA in the fiscal year 1992.

### Highest budget for education
Canada, Finland and Norway have the largest expenditure for education, each spending 7.3% of their GDP on primary, secondary and tertiary education.

### Lowest spending on education
The country that spends least on education is Turkey, which allocates just 3.3% of its GDP.

### Highest health budget
The USA is the country with the highest health expenditure as a percentage of GDP. The US health budget was 14.2% of GDP in

### Most industrial country
Slovakia is the most industrial country with 53% of GDP from manufacturing industry.

### Highest inflation
The worst inflation occurred in Hungary in June 1946, when the 1931 gold pengó was valued at 130 million trillion ($1.3 \times 10^{20}$) paper pengós. Notes were issued for 'Egymillárd billió' (1,000 trillion or $10^{21}$) pengós on 3 June and withdrawn on 11 July 1946. Vouchers for 1 billion trillion ($10^{27}$) pengós were issued for taxation use only.

In 1923, the circulation of the Reichsbank mark in Germany reached a record 400,338,326,350,700,000,000; inflation was 755,700 millionfold on 1913 levels.

## Taxation

### Highest taxation
In Denmark the top income tax is 68%, but a net wealth tax of 1% can result in tax of over 100% on income in extreme situations.

### Highest British taxation
The former top earned and unearned rates were 83% and 98% until 1979 in the United Kingdom. The standard rate of tax was reduced to 25% and the higher rate to 40% in the 1988 Budget.

The all-time British record was set in 1967/8, when a 'special charge' of up to 9s (45p) in the pound additional to surtax brought the top rate to 27s 3d (£1.36½p) in the pound (or 136%) on investment income.

## IN THE WORLD IN 1995 WAS IN MOZAMBIQUE AND RWANDA AT JUST $80

1994, the last year for which comparable figures are available.

### Highest defence budget
The USA has the highest government budget for defence research and development (R&D); defence R&D alone accounts for 55.3% of all government R&D expenditure.

### Largest financial sector
Singapore and the United Kingdom have the largest financial sectors, representing 27% of their gross domestic product.

### Most rural country
Somalia is the most rural country with 65% of GDP coming from agriculture.

Belarus experienced the highest inflation rate in 1995, at 243.96%

The highest recorded annual rate of inflation for the United Kingdom was 36.5% in 1800. The highest rate of deflation was 23% in 1902. The worst rate in a year was for Aug 1974 to Aug 1975, when inflation ran at a rate of 26.9%.

### Lowest inflation
The Seychelles had deflation in 1995, when the consumer price index (CPI) fell by 1.28%.

### Most worthless currency
In June 1997, there were 196,919 Angolan Kwanza to the pound sterling.

From April 1941 until 1946 during WWII the record peak of 10s (50p) in the pound was maintained to assist in the financing of the war effort.

### Lowest taxation
The countries with the lowest income tax are Bahrain and Qatar, where the rate is nil.

### Lowest British taxation
Income tax was first introduced in the United Kingdom in 1799 on incomes above £60 per annum. It was discontinued in 1815, only to be reintroduced in 1842 at the rate of 7d (2.92p) in the pound. It was at its lowest at 2d (0.83p) in the pound in 1875, gradually climbing to 1s 3d (6.25p) by 1913.

The shortest-priced Derby winner was *Ladas* (1894) at 2 to 9. The hottest losing favourite was *Surefoot*, fourth at 40 to 95 in 1890.

### Greatest payout
A payout of $1,627,084.40 (£988,211)—after income tax $406,768.00 (£249,550)—was paid to Britons Anthony Speelman and Nicholas Cowan on a $64 (£39.25) nine-horse accumulator at Santa Anita racecourse, California, USA, on 19 April 1987. Their first seven selections won and the payout was for a jackpot, accumulated over 24 days.

The largest payout by a bookmaker in the United Kingdom is £567,066.25, by Ladbrokes to Dick Mussell of Havant, Hants, for a combination of an accumulator, trebles, doubles and singles on five horses at Cheltenham on 12 March 1992.

### Biggest tote win
The biggest recorded tote win was £341 2s 6d (£341.12½p) to 2s (10p), representing

## Bingo
### Largest 'house'
The largest 'house' in bingo sessions was 15,756 at the Canadian National Exhibition, Toronto, on 19 Aug 1983. There was a record one-game payout of $Can100,000 (£58,000) at the same event.

### Earliest and latest 'Full House'
The earliest 'Full House' calls were on the 15th number, by: Norman A. Wilson at Guide Post Working Men's Club, Bedlington, Northumberland, UK, on 22 June 1978; Anne Wintle of Bryncethin, South Wales, UK, on a coach trip to Bath on 17 Aug 1982; and by Shirley Lord at Kahibah Bowling Club, NSW, Australia, on 24 Oct 1983.

'House' was not called until the 86th number at the Hillsborough Working Men's Club, Sheffield, S Yorkshire, UK, on 11 Jan 1982. There were 32 winners.

### Most bingo numbers called in one hour
On 16 Feb 1997, 2,668 numbers were called in one hour at the Riva Club, Brighton, E Sussex, UK.

## Football pools
### Biggest win
The record individual payout in the United Kingdom is £2,924,622.60, paid by Littlewoods Pools to a syndicate at the Yew

Tree Inn, Worsley, Greater Manchester, for matches played on 19 Nov 1994. The one week record is £4,457,671, by Littlewoods for matches on 12 March 1994.

## Horse racing
### Highest odds
The highest secured odds were 3,072,887 to 1, by a unnamed woman from Nottingham, UK. On 2 May 1995, she won £153,644.40 for a five-pence accumulator, and £208,098.79 in total, with bets on five horses that won at odds of 66 to 1, 20 to 1, 20 to 1, 12 to 1 and 7 to 1.

Edward Hodson of Wolverhampton, W Midlands, UK, landed a 3,956,748 to 1 bet for a 55p stake on 11 Feb 1984, but his bookmaker had a £3,000 payout limit.

The record odds on a 'double', 31,793 to 1, were paid by the New Zealand Totalisator Agency Board on a five-shilling tote ticket on *Red Emperor* and *Maida Dillon* at Addington, Christchurch, New Zealand, in 1951.

### Longest winning odds in British racing
The longest odds were 250 to 1, when *Equinoctial* won at Kelso in Nov 1990.

Three winners have been returned at 100–1 in the Derby: *Jeddah* (1898), *Signorinetta* (1908) and *Aboyeur* (1913).

odds of 3,410¼ to 1, by Catharine Unsworth of Blundellsands, Liverpool, Merseyside, UK, at Haydock Park on a race won by *Coole* on 30 Nov 1929.

The highest return in Irish tote history was £289.64 for a 10-pence unit on *Gene's Rogue* at Limerick on 28 Dec 1981.

### Largest bookmaker
The largest bookmaker is Ladbrokes with a peak turnover from gambling in 1988 of £2,107 million. In 1993 it had over 1,900 betting shops in the United Kingdom and the Republic of Ireland.

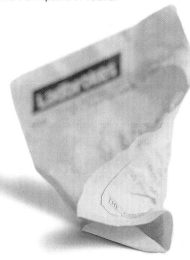

# HIGHEST ODDS 3,072,887 TO 1

IN LAS VEGAS, NEVADA, USA, ON 14 APRIL 1997

### Topmost tipsters
The only recorded instance of a racing correspondent forecasting 10 out of 10 winners on a race card was at Delaware Park, Wilmington, Delaware, USA, on 28 July 1974, by Charles Lamb who was working for the *Baltimore News American.*

The record in the United Kingdom is seven out of seven winners for a meeting at Wolverhampton on 22 March 1982, by Bob Butchers of the *Daily Mirror.* This British record was equalled by Fred Shawcross of *Today* newspaper at York on 12 May 1988.

In greyhound racing the best performance is 12 out of 12 by Mark Sullivan of the *Sporting Life* for a meeting at Wimbledon, London, UK, on 21 Dec 1990.

## Lotteries
### Biggest individual win
The world's biggest ever individual gambling win was $111,240,463.10 (£74,353,689),

**HEY SHARED £16,293,830**

by Leslie Robbins and Colleen DeVries of Fond du Lac, Wisconsin, USA, for the Powerball lottery drawn on 7 July 1993.

### Largest lottery jackpot
The largest lottery jackpot, $118.8 million (£71.28 million), in California, USA, on 17 April 1991, was divided among 10 winners.

### UK national lottery
The largest jackpot (and the largest prize won in a competition in the United Kingdom) is £22,590,829, won by Mark Gardiner and Paul Maddison of Hastings, E Sussex, UK, for the draw made on 10 June 1995.

The largest single winner is Terry Benson of Hessle, E Yorkshire, UK, who won £20,088,838 on 8 July 1995.

The largest number of winners of a single jackpot is 133, who shared £16,293,830 for the draw on 14 Jan 1995.

The highest ticket sales were for the draw on 6 Jan 1996 which reached a total of £127.8 million. The jackpot had 'rolled over' three times amassing £42,008,610.

### Slot machines
The biggest win was $12,510,559.90 (£7.2 million), by Suzanne Henley at the New York New York Hotel and Casino, Las Vegas, Nevada, USA, on 14 April 1997.

## Poker
### Biggest pot at poker
In poker, players try to collect combinations of two or more cards of a kind, sequences of five cards or five cards in the same suit.

The biggest pot ever was during a private poker match in 1889 at Bowen's Saloon, Santa Fe, New Mexico, USA. The two players were Ike Jackson, one of the richest ranchers in the West, and the legendary gambler Johnny Dougherty. Jackson and Dougherty were playing five-card draw, no-limit according to Western rules. A couple of hours into the match, which was being watched by over 100 people including

L. Bradford Prince, who was the governor of the then-territory of New Mexico, there was more than $100,000 in the pot. Jackson then wrote out a deed to his ranch which comprised 10,000 head of cattle, and put it into the pot. Dougherty in reply scribbled a few lines on a piece of paper, rose from his chair, pressed the paper into the hands of L. Bradford Prince and pulled his Colt and held it to the governor's head. 'Sign or I'll pull the trigger,' he said. Prince signed without hesitation and Dougherty returned to the table and put the paper in the pot. 'I'll raise you the territory of New Mexico,' he said defiantly. 'Here's the deed.' Jackson swore, and threw away his cards.

**Left**
A punter prays for good fortune before a race. Betting on horse racing is the principle form of gambling in English-speaking countries and France. Every year tens of millions of pounds are bet on classic races such as the Derby in the UK, the Kentucky Derby in the USA and the Prix de l'Arc de Triomphe in France.

# Sport: prizes and earnings

**Right**
Martin Offiah moved from Widnes to Wigan for a Rugby League cash-only transfer record of £440,000 on 3 Jan 1992.

**Centre**
'Frankie' Dettori earned £2,924,854 in prize-money in 1995.

£440,000

£2,924,854

British golfer Nick Faldo won a record £1,558,978 worldwide in 1992.

The record for tour career earnings is £5,364,718 earned by Bernhard Langer of Germany, from 1976 to 1997.

The record for the US LPGA tour is $1,002,000 (£642,181) by Karrie Webb (Australia) in 1996.

Annika Sorenstam (Sweden) earned a season record of £130,324.50 in 1995.

## Racing horse (career)
*Cigar* earned a career record for a racing horse of $9,999,815 (£6,410,000) from 1993 to the end of 1996.

*Hokuto Vega* is the leading money-winning filly or mare, making $8.3 million (£4.02 million) in Japan from 1993 to 1997.

## Racing horse (year)
The most prize money ever earned in a year by a horse is $4,910,000 (£3,146,820) by *Cigar* in 1996.

## British racing horse (season)
The British racing horse record for the greatest amount of prize money to have been won in a season is £1,731,168, by *Singspiel* in 1996.

## Transfer fees
### Highest soccer transfer fee
The highest transfer fee quoted for a soccer player is a reported £15 million for Alan Shearer, who moved from Blackburn Rovers to Newcastle United, UK, on 29 July 1996.

### Highest Rugby League transfer fees
Paul Newlove moved from Bradford Bulls to St Helens for a deal which was valued at £500,000 on 29 Nov 1995.

Va'aiga Tuiagamala moved from Wigan to Newcastle Rugby Union club for a reported fee of £750,000 on 20 Feb 1997.

The costliest cash-only transfer was £440,000 for Martin Offiah who moved from Widnes to Wigan on 3 Jan 1992.

## Highest earnings
### Tennis players (season)
Pete Sampras (USA) won a men's season's record–$5,415,066 (£3,430,949) in 1995.

Arantxa Sánchez Vicario (Spain) won a women's season's record of $2,943,665 (£1,920,325) in 1994.

### Tennis players (career)
Pete Sampras (USA) won $25,562,347 (£16,382,900) from 1988 to 1996.

Martina Navrátilová (Czechoslovakia, later USA) won $20,334,061 (£13,282,630) from 1974 to the end of 1996.

### Golf players (career)
Greg Norman (Australia) holds the all-time career earnings record on the US PGA circuit with $10,605,907 (£6,792,000) from 1976 to May 1997.

Betsy King earned record US LPGA tour career earnings of $5,730,407 (£3,300,000) from 1977 to March 1997.

### Golf players (season)
Tom Lehman of the USA holds the season's record on the US PGA circuit of $1,780,159 (£1,128,000) in 1996.

Colin Stuart Montgomerie won a season's record £875,146.36 in European Order of Merit tournaments in 1996.

### British racing horse (career)
The British-trained horse *Singspiel* has won £3,332,892 in his career from 1994 up to May 1997.

### British jumper (career)
*Desert Orchid* earned £652,802 during his career from 1983 to 1991.

### Jockey worldwide (career)
Christopher McCarron (USA) earned $192 million (£127 million) from 1974 to May 1996.

### Jockey worldwide (year)
Yutaka Take earned ¥3,133,742,000 (£18,795,310) in Japan in 1993.

### Jockey in the UK (year)
Lanfranco 'Frankie' Dettori made a record £2,924,854 in the UK in 1995.

### British jump jockey (season)
Norman Williamson holds the record for the most money made by a British jump jockey in one season, earning a record £1,235,170 in 1994/5.

# RECORD TRANSFER FEE £15 MILLION
## OF $25,562,347 BY 1996

**Owner worldwide (year)**
Allen Paulson won record prize money in a year of $9,086,629 (£5,823,620) in North America and Dubai in 1996.

**Owner in the UK (season)**
In 1994 Sheikh Mohammed bin Rashid al Maktoum of Dubai won record prize money in a season of £2,666,730.

**Trainer worldwide (career)**
Darrell Wayne Lukas also won over $155 million (£93 million) in his career from 1977 to 1997.

**Trainer worldwide (year)**
Darrell Wayne Lukas (USA) was the most successful trainer in the world in one year. He won $17,842,358 (£10,026,050) in 1988.

**Trainer in UK (season)**
John Leeper Dunlop (UK) earned a record £2,018,748 in one season in 1995.

Michael Ronald Stoute (UK) set a record for worldwide earnings of £2,778,405 in 1986.

**Greyhound (career)**
*Homespun Rowdy* earned a record $297,000 (£162,535) in prize money in the USA, from 1984 to 1987.

## Greatest prizes
**Greatest tennis prize**
Pete Sampras (US) won the most first-place prize money of $2 million (£1,038,583) when he won the Grand Slam Cup at Munich, Germany, on 16 Dec 1990.

**Highest total tennis prize money**
A total of $10,893,890 (£7,200,000) was awarded for the 1996 US Open Championships.

**Greatest golf prize**
In 1987 Ian Woosnam (Wales) was the first winner of the highest golf prize of $1,000,000 (£660,000), which was awarded annually from 1987 to 1991 to the winners of the Sun City Challenge in Bophuthatswana, South Africa.

**Highest total golf prize money**
The greatest total prize money that has ever been paid out in golf was $2.7 million (£1.8 million) for the Johnnie Walker World Championship which was held at Tryall Golf Club, Montego Bay, Jamaica, in 1992, 1993 and 1994. This total included a first prize of $550,000 (£359,000).

**Greatest darts prize**
John Lowe won £102,000 for achieving the first 501 scored with the minimum nine darts in a major event on 13 Oct 1984 at

£6,792,000

## WON BY *BEN G SPEEDBOAT* IN THE USA IN AUG 1986

**Harness horse (career)**
The trotter *Peace Corps* won $4,907,307 (£3,158,668) in prize money, from 1988 to 1993.

**Harness horse (year)**
The pacer *Nihilator* won $3,225,653 (£2,230,588), and 35 out of 38 races, from 1984 to 1985.

**Harness horse (season)**
The pacer *Cam's Card Shark* won $2,264,714 (£1,907,449) in 1994 and the trotter *Mack Lobell* won $1,878,798 (£1,028,183) in 1987.

**Rodeo rider (career)**
Roy Cooper is the world's most financially successful rodeo rider. He earned $1,742,278 (£1,116,620) between 1975 and June 1996.

**Rodeo rider (season)**
The record figure for prize money in a single rodeo season is $297,896 (£199,877), by Ty Murray in 1993.

Slough, Berks, UK, in the quarter-finals of the World Match-play Championships. His darts were six successive treble 20s, treble 17, treble 18 and double 18.

**Greatest greyhound race prize**
The largest first prize for a greyhound race was $125,000 (£84,079) won by *Ben G Speedboat* in the Great Greyhound Race of Champions at Seabrook, New Hampshire, USA, on 23 Aug 1986.

**Greatest prize for a single horse race**
The one-race record is $2.6 million (£1.56 million) by *Spend A Buck* for the Jersey Derby, Garden State Park, New Jersey, USA, on 27 May 1985. A bonus of $2 million (£1.6 million) was awarded for already having won the Kentucky Derby, USA, and two preparatory races at Garden State Park.

**Highest prize money for a day's racing**
The highest prize money for a day's racing is $11 million (£7.4 million) for the Breeders' Cup series of seven races, staged annually in the USA since 1984.

**Highest single race purse**
The largest purse for a single race was $4 million (£2.6 million) which included a record first prize of $2.4 million (£1.6 million) won by *Cigar* on 27 March 1996 and *Singspiel* on 3 April 1997 for the Dubai World Cup.

**Greatest prize over jumps in UK**
The richest prize over jumps in the United Kingdom is £178,146 for the Grand National, held at Aintree, Liverpool, Merseyside. On 7 April 1997 it was won by *Lord Gyllene*.

**Greatest harness horse prize**
The largest ever harness horse purse was $2,161,000 (£1,644,597) awarded for the Woodrow Wilson two-year-old race over one mile at the Meadowlands, New Jersey, USA, on 16 Aug 1984. Of this sum, a record $1,080,500 (£822,298) went to the winner *Nihilator*, which was ridden by William O'Donnell.

**Indianapolis 500 motor racing prize**
The highest prize fund ever awarded in the Indianapolis 500 was $8,028,247 (£5,086,642), in 1995.

### Furniture
Barbara Piasecka Johnson paid £8.58 million at Christie's, London, UK, on 5 July 1990 for the 18th-century Italian 'Badminton Cabinet' owned by the Duke of Beaufort.

### Gun
A Colt single action .45 calibre army revolver, Serial No. 1, made in 1873, sold at Christie's, New York, USA, for $242,000 (£145,232) on 14 May 1987.

### Helmet
A native North American Tlingit Kiksadi frog helmet made c. 1600 was sold for $66,000 (£34,667) in New York, USA, in Nov 1981.

### Jewellery
The Duchess of Windsor's jewellery collection was sold for £31,380,197 at Sotheby's, Geneva, Switzerland, on 3 April 1987.

### Surgical instrument
A 19th-century German mechanical chain saw used in surgery sold for £23,368 at Christie's, London, UK, on 19 Aug 1993.

### Tapestry
A fragment of a Swiss tapestry woven near Basle in the 1430s was sold to Swiss dealer Peter Kleiner for £638,000 at Christie's, London, UK, on 3 July 1990.

### Teddy bear
A Steiff bear named 'Teddy Girl' was sold for £110,000, more than 18 times the estimate, by Christie's, London, UK, on 5 Dec 1994 to Japanese businessman Yoshihiro Sekiguchi.

### Toys
The highest price paid for a toy was for a hand-painted tin-plate replica of the 'Charles' hose reel (a piece of fire-fighting equipment) made in c. 1870. It was sold to a telephone bidder for $231,000 (£128,330) at Christie's, New York, USA, on 14 Dec 1991.

The most paid for a single toy soldier is £3,375 for a uniformed scale figure of Hitler's deputy, Rudolf Hess, made by the Lineol company of Brandenburg, Germany.

**Above**
The figure being lifted up is a uniformed scale model of Hitler's deputy, Rudolf Hess. One of a series of Nazi leaders, it became the most expensive single toy soldier when it was sold for £3,375.

IN 1991, $748,000 WAS PAID FOR A LETTER WRITTEN BY PRESIDENT ABRAHAM

## Antiques
### Art nouveau
An art nouveau standard lamp in the form of three lotus blossoms, by the Daum Brothers and Louis Majorelle of France, sold for $1.78 million (£1.11 million) at Sotheby's, New York, USA, on 2 Dec 1989.

### Bronze statue
An Italian statuette of Hercules by Antico, dated towards the end of the 1400s, was sold for £3,081,500 at Bonhams, London, UK, on 25 May 1996.

### Camera
An Enjalbert Revolver de Poche camera c. 1882 sold for £55,750 at Christie's, London, UK, on 31 August 1995.

### Carpets
On 9 June 1994, a Louis XV Savonnerie carpet 5.4 m x 5.8 m (18 ft x 19 ft), made in the 1740s, fetched £1,321,000 at Christie's, London, UK.

### Clock
An 'Egyptian Revival' Cartier clock made in 1927 sold for $1,585,475 (£905,882) at Christie's, New York, USA, on 24 April 1991.

Two pear-shaped diamond drop earrings of 58.6 and 61 carats, were sold for £3.1 million at Sotheby's, Geneva, Switzerland, on 14 Nov 1980.

### Music box
A Swiss music box which was made for a Persian prince in 1901 sold for £20,900 at Sotheby's, London, UK, on 23 Jan 1985.

### Paperweight
A mid-1840s Clichy Millefiori basket without a handle sold for $258,500 (£151,220) on 26 June 1990 at Sotheby's, New York, USA.

### Playing cards
The Metropolitan Museum of Art, New York, USA, paid $143,352 (then equivalent to £99,000) for the oldest known complete hand-painted set of cards, dating from c. 1470–85, at Sotheby's, London, UK, on 6 Dec 1983.

### Roman glass
A Roman glass cage-cup which was made in c. AD 300, sold at Sotheby's, London, UK, on 4 June 1979, for £520,000.

It was sold by the Danish auction house Boyes in London, UK, on 23 April 1991.

### Vanity case
A Cartier jewelled vanity case was sold at Christie's, New York, USA, for $189,000 (£127,651) on Nov 17 1993.

## Books and writing
### Books
The Hermann Abs consortium paid £8.14 million for the 226-leaf manuscript *The Gospel Book of Henry the Lion, Duke of Saxony* at Sotheby's, London, UK on 6 Dec 1983. The book is 34.3 x 25.4 cm (13½ in x 10 in) and was illuminated c. 1170 by Herimann, a monk at Helmarshausen Abbey, Germany, with 41 full-page illustrations.

### Broadsheet
The highest price ever paid for a printed page was $2,420,000 (£1,466,755) for one of the 24 known copies of *The Declaration of Independence*, printed by John Dunlap in Philadelphia, Pennsylvania, USA, in 1776. It was sold by Samuel T. Freeman & Co. to Donald Scheer of Atlanta, Georgia, USA, on 13 June 1991.

# 18TH-CENTURY CABINET, £8.58 MILLION

## COINS, SOLD IN APRIL 1997 FOR $1.815 MILLION

### Manuscripts
The 'Codex Hammer', an illustrated manuscript by Leonardo da Vinci in which he predicted the invention of the submarine and the steam engine, was sold for a record $30.8 million (£19,388,141) at Christie's, New York, USA, on 11 Nov 1994. The buyer was computer tycoon Bill Gates. It is the only Leonardo manuscript in private hands.

### Violoncello
The highest ever auction price for a violoncello is £682,000 paid at Sotheby's, London, UK, on 22 June 1988 for a Stradivarius known as the 'Cholmondeley', which was made in Cremona, Italy, c. 1698.

## Stamps
### Most expensive stamps
The Swedish 'Treskilling Yellow' set a world record for a single stamp when it was sold for £1.42 million at Zürich, Switzerland, on 11 Nov 1996. The 1855 stamp is the only one of the issue known to exist.

The Mauritius 'Bordeaux Cover', a letter sent to wine merchants in Bordeaux, France, in 1847 franked with the one-penny and 2d first issues of Mauritius, was bought for Sw.Fr.5.75 million (£2.59 million), by an anonymous buyer in less than a minute, at a sale at the Hotel International in Zürich, Switzerland, on 3 Nov 1993.

### Most expensive stamp collection
A stamp collection comprising 183 pages of the classic issues of Mauritius was bought by the Japanese engineer-industrialist Hiroyuki Kanai for Sw.Fr.15,000,000

(£6,756,756) at the Mauritius auction of 3 Nov 1993, conducted by the Geneva-based auctioneer David Feldman.

### Largest purchase
The Marc Haas collection of 3,000 US postal and pre-postal covers to 1869, was bought by Stanley Gibbons Ltd, London, UK, in Aug 1979 for £24.6 million.

## Coins
### Record price for a collection
The Garrett family collection of US and colonial coins collected from 1860–1942, was sold for $25,235,360 (£11,560,000).

### Most expensive coins
A silver dollar made in 1804, one of only 15 known to exist, fetched $1.815 million (£1.1 million) at an auction at Bowers and Morena, New York, USA, on 8 April 1997. The coin was part of a collection of Louis Eliasberg, Sr, the only person ever to have had a complete collection of US coins.

The most expensive coin in the United Kingdom was a gold penny from the reign of Henry III. It was sold at Spink's, London, UK, on 9 July 1996 for £159,500.

LINCOLN ON 8 JAN 1863 WHICH DEFENDED THE EMANCIPATION PROCLAMATION

### Atlas
A version of Ptolemy's *Cosmographia* dating from 1492 was sold for a record $1,925,000 (£1,666,660) at Sotheby's, New York, USA, on 31 Jan 1990.

### Letters
The highest price on the open market for a single signed letter was $748,000 (£409,680) paid for one written by President Lincoln on 8 Jan 1863 defending the Emancipation Proclamation against criticism. It was sold at Christie's, New York, USA, to Profiles in History of Beverly Hills, California, USA, on 5 Dec 1991.

## Music
### Piano
A Steinway grand piano made in c. 1888 was sold by the Martin Beck Theater for $390,000 (£177,272) at Sotheby's, New York, USA, on 26 March 1980.

### Violin
The highest price paid for a violin at auction was for a 1720 'Mendelssohn' Stradivarius. It was sold for £902,000 at Christie's, London, UK on 21 Nov 1990.

## TOOTH BELONGING TO SIR ISAAC NEWTON WAS PURCHASED FOR £730 IN 181[

### Prince clothing
A complete stage costume worn by the singer Prince was sold at Christie's, London, UK, for £12,100 in Dec 1991.

### Watches
A Patek Philippe 'Calibre '89' pocket watch with 1,728 parts sold for Sw.Fr.4.95 million (£1,864,300) at Habsburg Feldman, Geneva, Switzerland, on 9 April 1989.

A Patek Philippe 'Calatrava' 1939 wristwatch sold for Sw.Fr.2.09 million (£1,140,000) at Antiquorum, Geneva, Switzerland, in 1996.

### Pen
In May 1997 the 5079 Caran d'Ache solid gold fountain pen with 4,147 diamonds and 108 rubies sold for £128,448.

### Wallet
A platinum-cornered, diamond-studded crocodile wallet made by Louis Quatorze of Paris, France, and Mikimoto of Tokyo, Japan, sold in Sept 1984 for £56,000.

## Memorabilia
### Most expensive wine
A bottle of 1787 Château Lafite claret was sold for £105,000 (USA) at Christie's, London, UK, in 1985. It was engraved with the initials 'Th J' for Thomas Jefferson, third US president.

### Most valuable tooth
In 1816 a tooth that had belonged to Sir Isaac Newton was sold in London, UK, for

## ONE OF THE OLDEST SURVIVING PAIRS OF LEVI JEANS MADE C. 1886–1902 WA[

## Clothes and accessories
### Shoes
Emperor Jean-Bédel Bokassa of the Central African Empire (now the Central African Republic) commissioned pearl-studded shoes costing $85,000 (£48,571) from the House of Berluti, Paris, France, for his self-coronation at Bangui, on 4 Dec 1977.

The red slippers that were worn by Judy Garland in the film *The Wizard of Oz* sold at Christie's, New York, USA, on 2 June 1988 for $165,000 (£90,000).

### Dress
A wedding outfit created by Hélène Gainville with jewels by Alexander Reza is estimated to be worth over $7.3 million (£4.2 million). The dress is embroidered with diamonds mounted on platinum and was unveiled in Paris, France, in 1989.

The most valuable dress sold at auction was a blue silk and velvet gown owned by Diana, Princess of Wales. It sold for $200,000 (£134,000) at Christie's, New York, USA, on 26 June 1997.

### Pair of jeans
In 1997 Levi Strauss & Co. paid $25,000 (£15,616) for some Levi 501 jeans believed to have been made between 1886 and 1902.

### John Lennon clothing
An afghan coat worn by John Lennon on the cover of the Beatles' *Magical Mystery Tour* album in 1967 was bought for £34,999 on behalf of Julian Lennon on 22 March 1997.

### Madonna clothing
A corset designed by Jean Paul Gaultier for Madonna sold for £12,100 at Christie's, London, UK, in May 1994.

the sum of £730. The purchaser had it set in a ring.

### Most valuable hair
In 1988 a bookseller from Cirencester, Glos, UK, paid £5,575 for a lock of Vice Admiral Lord Nelson's hair at an auction held at Crewkerne, Somerset, UK.

## Cars
### Most expensive car
The most expensive list-price for a British standard car is the McLaren F1, quoted at £634,500 including tax.

The greatest confirmed price that has ever been paid for a used car is $15 million (£9 million), for the 1931 Bugatti Type 41 Royale Sports Coupé by Kellner, which was sold on 12 April 1990.

# MOST EXPENSIVE SHOES $85,000

### AND SET INTO A RING

### Vehicle registrations
Licence plate 'No. 9' was sold at a Hong Kong government auction for HK$13 million (£1.07 million) on 19 March 1994 to Albert Yeung Sau-shing. The word 'nine' sounds like the word 'dog' in Chinese and was considered lucky because 1994 was the Year of the Dog.

## Ephemera
### Acetate
A double-sided acetate of the Beatles performing at The Cavern Club, Liverpool, UK sold for £16,500 at Christie's, London, UK, in Aug 1993.

### Jazz instrument
A saxophone owned by jazz musician Charlie Parker sold for £93,500 at Christie's, London, UK, in Sept 1994.

### Jigsaw puzzle
A dissected map of Europe by John Spilsbury and dated 1767 was bought at Sotheby's, London, UK, in July 1984 by Anne Williams of Maine, USA, for £1,650.

### Guitar
A Fender Stratocaster which belonged to the rock star Jimi Hendrix was sold by his former drummer 'Mitch' Mitchell for £198,000 at Sotheby's, London, UK, on 25 April 1990.

### Kiss memorabilia
Four costumes owned by the glam rock band Kiss sold for £20,900 at Christie's, London, UK, in May 1993.

### Loaf of bread
A burnt loaf of bread from the Great Fire of London of 1666 was bought for £322.

### Magic lantern
A Newton & Co. Triunial lantern made in around 1880 realised £33,000 on 17 Jan 1996 at Christie's, London, UK.

### Money order
An 1842 money order sold for a record £120 in Exeter, Devon, UK, in 1989.

### Postal order
The highest price that has ever paid for a postal order was £385, for a George VI 6d order at the Postal Order Society Auction, UK, in 1995.

### Plastic pen
The highest sum ever to have been paid for a plastic pen is £6,325, for a Parker prototype Mandarin Yellow Lucky Curve Duofold Senior sold at Bonhams, London, UK, on 24 May 1996.

### Radio
The highest price paid for a piece of wireless receiver equipment is £15,997, for a Marconi Multiple Tuner at Phillip's, London, UK, on 11 May 1993.

### Radio related equipment
The most expensive piece of wireless related equipment is a German Enigma coding (ciphering/enciphering) machine which sold for £24,172.50 at Phillip's, London, UK, in April 1993.

### Song lyrics
Paul McCartney's hand-written lyrics for the Beatles' song *Getting Better* sold for £161,000 in Sept 1995.

### Spy camera
The highest price paid for a spy camera is £18,700 for a Lucky Strike Cigarette carton camera which was sold at Christie's, London, UK, on 9 Dec 1991.

### Tracksuit
In 1997, 20 limited edition silver-coloured fabric tracksuits with solid silver details were made to celebrate the sale of 100,000 running jackets by Olympic bronze medalist Brendan Foster's company View From. Each tracksuit is valued at £2,000.

### Most expensive racehorse
The most paid for a yearling is $13.1 million (£9.5 million) on 23 July 1985 at Keeneland, Kentucky, USA, by Robert Sangster and partners for *Seattle Dancer*.

**Left**
John Lennon wearing the afghan coat bought for a record £34,999 on behalf of his son Julian in 1997.

**Left**
Charlie 'Bird' Parker (1920–55) was one of the most influential figures in jazz. His skill in improvisation has probably never been surpassed. His saxophone was the most expensive jazz instrument, selling for £93,500 in 1994.

### SOLD BACK TO LEVI STRAUSS & CO. FOR $25,000

# Gems and precious stones

**Right**
This 100.10-carat pear-shaped 'D' Flawless diamond is the most expensive diamond in the world. It was sold at auction in Switzerland for a record $16,548,750 (£10,507,143) in 1995.

## Diamonds
### Highest-priced diamonds
The world's most expensive diamond was a 100.10-carat pear-shaped 'D' Flawless diamond. It was sold at Sotheby's, Geneva, Switzerland, on 17 May 1995 for $16,548,750 (£10,507,143) to Sheikh Ahmed Fitaihi, who obtained it for his chain of jewellery shops in Saudi Arabia.

The highest price known to be paid for a rough diamond was £5.8 million, for a

The largest known single piece of rough diamond still in existence weighs 1,462 carats and is retained by De Beers in London, UK.

### Largest cut diamond
The *Golden Jubilee Diamond*, purchased from De Beers by a syndicate of Thai businessmen and presented to the King of Thailand to commemorate his golden jubilee, weighs 545.67-carats and is now mounted in the Thai royal sceptre.

## Largest star ruby
The 6,465-carat *Eminent Star* ruby, believed to be of Indian origin, is owned by Kailash Rawat of Eminent Gems Inc. of New York, USA. It is an oval cabochon with a six-ray star and measures 109 x 90.5 x 58 mm (4¼ x 3⅝ x 2¼ in).

## Emeralds
### Highest-priced emeralds
An emerald and diamond necklace (a total of 12 stones weighing 108.74 carats) made by Cartier, London, UK, in 1937 was sold at Sotheby's, New York, USA, on 26 Oct 1989 for $3,080,000 (£1,951,219).

The highest price for a single emerald is $2,126,646 (£1,320,488), for a 19.77-carat emerald and diamond ring made by Cartier in 1958, which was sold at Sotheby's, Geneva, Switzerland, on 2 April 1987. This is also the record price per carat for an emerald, at $107,569 per carat.

### Largest cut emeralds
A natural beryl weighing 86,136 carats was found in Carnaiba, Brazil, in Aug 1974. It was carved by Richard Chan in Hong Kong and was valued at £718,000 in 1982.

### Largest single crystal
The largest emerald crystal of gem quality was a 7,025-carat example found in 1969 at the Cruces Mine, near Gachala, Colombia. It is owned by a private mining concern.

255.10-carat stone from Guinea, paid by the William Goldberg Diamond Corporation in partnership with the Chow Tai Fook Jewellery Co. Ltd of Hong Kong, in March 1989.

The record price per carat is $926,315.79 (£574,700), for a 0.95-carat fancy purplish-red stone sold at Christie's, New York, USA, on 28 April 1987.

### Largest diamonds
The largest diamond was the *Cullinan*, which weighed 3,106 carats and was discovered on 26 Jan 1905 at the Premier Diamond Mine, near Pretoria, South Africa. It was cut into 106 polished diamonds and produced the largest cut fine-quality colourless diamond, which weighs 530.2 carats.

Several large pieces of lower-quality diamonds have been found, including a carbonado of 3,167 carats discovered in Brazil in 1905.

### Smallest brilliant cut diamond
A 57-facet stone weighing 0.0000743 carats was fashioned by hand by Pauline Willemse at Coster Diamonds B.V. in Amsterdam, Netherlands, between 1991 and 1994. At 0.16–0.17 mm (0.0062–0.0067 in) in diameter and 0.11 mm in height, it is smaller than the average grain of sand.

## Rubies
### Highest-priced ruby
The most expensive ruby was in a ruby and diamond ring made by Chaumet in Paris, France, weighing 32.08 carats. It was sold for $4,620,000 (£2,926,829) at Sotheby's, New York, USA, on 26 Oct 1989.

The record price per carat for a ruby is $227,300 (£130,767), for a ruby ring with a stone weighing 15.97 carats which was sold at Sotheby's, New York, USA, on 18 Oct 1988.

## Sapphires
### Highest-priced sapphire
A step-cut stone of 62.02 carats was sold as part of a sapphire and diamond ring at Sotheby's, St Moritz, Switzerland, on 20 Feb 1988 for $2,791,723 (£1,581,713).

### Largest star sapphire
A 9,719.50-carat stone was cut in London, UK, in Nov 1989. It has been named *The Lone Star* and is owned by Harold Roper.

## Opals
### Largest opal
A white opal of gem quality weighing 26,350 carats was found in July 1989 at the Jupiter Field at Coober Pedy in South Australia. It is called *Jupiter-Five* and is in private hands.

### Largest black opal
A piece of black opal discovered on 4 Feb 1972 at Lightning Ridge, NSW, Australia,

# RUBY AND DIAMOND RING $4,620,000

## A 255.10-CARAT STONE

produced a finished gem called the *Empress of Glengarry*, which weighs 1,520 carats and is 121 x 80 x 15 mm (4¾ x 3⅛ x ⅝ in).

### Largest rough black opal
The largest uncut black opal of gem quality weighed 1,982.5 carats and was found at Lightning Ridge, NSW, Australia, on 3 Nov 1986. It measured 100 x 66 x 63 mm (4 x 2⅝ x 2½ in) after cleaning.

## Jade and amber
### Largest piece of jade
A single lens of nephrite jade weighing 577 tonnes was found in the Yukon Territory of Canada by Max Rosequist in July 1992. It is owned by Yukon Jade Ltd.

### Largest amber
The *Burma Amber* which weighs 15.25 kg (33 lb 10 oz) is kept in the Natural History Museum, London, UK.

## Pearls
### Highest-priced pearl
*La Régente*, an egg-shaped pearl weighing 15.13 g (302.68 grains) was sold at Christie's, Geneva, Switzerland, on 12 May 1988 for $864,280 (£457,533).

### Largest pearl
The *Pearl of Lao-tze* (also known as the *Pearl of Allah*) was found at Palawan, Philippines, on 7 May 1934 in the shell of a giant clam.

It weighs 6.37 kg (14 lb 1 oz) and is 24 cm (9½ in) long and 14 cm (5½ in) in diameter.

### Largest abalone pearl
A 469.13-carat baroque abalone pearl measuring 7 x 5 x 2.8 cm (2¾ x 2 x 1⅛ in), called the *Big Pink*, was found at Salt Point State Park, California, USA, in May 1990.

### Largest cultured pearl
A 138.25-carat cultured pearl with a diameter of 4 cm (1½ in) and weighing

27.65 g (1 oz) was found near Samui Island, off Thailand, in Jan 1988. The pearl is owned by the Mikimoto Pearl Island Company, Japan.

## Gold
### Largest single mass of gold
The *Holtermann Nugget*, a slab of slate weighing 235.14-kg (7,560-troy oz), was found on 19 Oct 1872 in the Beyers & Holtermann Star of Hope mine, Hill End,

## SOLD FOR $3,080,000 BY SOTHEBY'S, NEW YORK, USA, ON 26 OCT 1989

NSW, Australia. It contained some 82.11 kg (2,640 troy oz) of pure gold.

### Largest pure nugget
The *Welcome Stranger*, found at Moliagul, Victoria, Australia, in 1869, yielded 69.92 kg (2,248 troy oz) of pure gold from a 70.92-kg (2,280¼-troy oz) nugget.

## Platinum
### Largest platinum nugget
The largest platinum nugget ever was discovered in the Ural Mountains in Russia in 1843. It weighed 9,635 g (340 oz), but was melted down shortly afterwards.

### Largest existing nugget
The largest surviving platinum nugget weighs 7,860.5 g (277¼ oz) and is known as the *Ural Giant*. It is currently in the custody of the Diamond Foundation in the Kremlin, Moscow, Russia.

Left
Pearls are found inside oysters, especially those species found in the Persian Gulf. They are formed by foreign matter inside the oyster shell, which is surrounded by nacre, the material that lines the oyster shell, to form a round pearl. Those found inside edible oysters are dull and have no value.

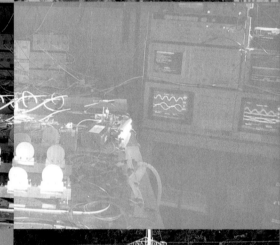

Media

# Television

**Right**
Granada TV's
*Coronation Street* is
the UK's longest
running domestic
drama, averaging
20 million viewers per
episode. In 1971, a
record 1,144 episodes
were sold by Granada
Television to the
Canadian station
CBKST Saskatoon.

The most durable British current affairs programme is BBC's *Panorama*, which was first transmitted on 11 Nov 1953 and from then on broadcast weekly but with breaks in the summer.

**Longest-running religious programme**
*Songs of Praise,* a programme where people are filmed singing in their local church, was introduced by the BBC on 1 Oct 1961.

**Longest-running domestic drama**
Granada's *Coronation Street* ran twice weekly in the United Kingdom from 9 Dec 1960 until 20 Oct 1989, after which viewers were treated to a third weekly episode.

**Longest-running comedy**
The British comedy series *Last of the Summer Wine* started in 1973 and starred Bill Owen as Compo, Peter Sallis as Clegg and Michael Bates as Blamire.

## Networks
### Most expensive TV rights
In Nov 1991, it was reported that a group of US and European investors, led by CBS, had paid $8 million (£4.5 million) for the television rights to *Scarlett*, the sequel to Margaret Mitchell's *Gone With the Wind*, written by Alexandra Ripley. The eight-hour mini-series was screened in Nov 1994.

### Most expensive TV production
The mini-series *War and Remembrance* cost $110 million (£61 million), and took three years to shoot. It lasted for 14 episodes and was aired on US television by ABC in two parts in Nov 1988 and March 1989.

### Largest TV contracts
Oprah Winfrey reportedly earned $146 million (£94 million) between 1994 and 1995. She is said to have signed a contract in March 1994 which will earn her company Harpo $300 million (£193 million) by 31 Dec 2000, or $46.150 million (£29.7 million) per annum for 6½ years.

The largest British TV contract was reported to be worth £9 million, inclusive of production expenses. It was signed in 1968 by Tom Jones with ABC-TV of the USA and ATV in London, UK, for 17 one-hour shows a year from Jan 1969 to Jan 1974.

### Biggest TV sale
A record 1,144 episodes of *Coronation Street* were sold by Granada Television to CBKST Saskatoon, Saskatchewan, Canada, on 31 May 1971. This constituted 20 days 15 hr 44 min of continuous viewing.

### Shortest-lived monopoly
The BBC's *Breakfast Time,* launched on 17 Jan 1983 on BBC1, was operating for 15 days before ITV introduced TV-AM on 1 Feb 1983 as a rival breakfast programme.

## Programmes
### Most durable TV shows
NBC's *Meet the Press* was first transmitted on 6 Nov 1947 and was shown weekly from 12 Sept 1948. It was originally conceived by Lawrence E. Spivak, who appeared on each show as either moderator or panel member until 1975. By 17 April 1995, 2,391 shows had been aired.

The most durable surviving British television programme is the seasonal ballroom dancing show *Come Dancing*, first transmitted on 29 Sept 1950.

### Longest-running children's programme
*Sooty* was first presented on the BBC by its deviser Harry Corbett in 1952. In 1968, *Sooty* moved to Thames Television, and when Harry retired in 1975 the show was continued by his son Matthew.

### Longest-running news programmes
The BBC *News and Newsreel* was inaugurated on 5 July 1954—Richard Baker read the news for a record 28 years from 1954 to Christmas 1982.

### Longest-running pop show
The longest-running British pop music show is *Top of the Pops*. The first edition was shown on 1 Jan 1964. Artists appearing were Dusty Springfield, the Rolling Stones, the Dave Clark Five, the Swinging Blue Jeans and the Hollies. The Beatles and Cliff Richard and the Shadows were shown on film. The programme celebrated its 1,000th edition on 5 May 1983.

### Longest-running talent show
The British talent show *Opportunity Knocks* ran from 1956 to 1977 and was hosted by Hughie Green. Contestants were judged by a 'clappometer', which was activated by the audience's level of applause. Out of the thousands of acts that were featured over the years, only a few achieved significant careers, including singer Mary Hopkins and comedian Les Dawson.

### Longest-serving presenter
The monthly British astronomy programme *Sky at Night* has been presented by Patrick Moore CBE without any breaks or interruptions since it started on 24 April 1957. By July 1997, 529 editions of the show had been broadcast.

### Longest uninterrupted live broadcast
The French-language state-owned Swiss television station Suisse 4, broadcast the 1996 Olympic Games held in Atlanta, USA, around the clock for 16 days, 22 hr and 45 min. The transmission began on 19 July and ended on 5 Aug 1996.

# TV RIGHTS $8 MILLION

PATRICK MOORE WITHOUT A BREAK SINCE APRIL 1957—A TOTAL OF 529 SHOWS

### Most quiz show contestants
Japan's *Ultra Quiz*, produced by Nippon Television, had 5,000 contestants taking part—the greatest number that have ever taken part in a TV quiz. The contestants first congregated in a stadium to answer 'Yes' or 'No' to general knowledge questions. Survivors then boarded a jumbo-jet to face another 'Yes' or 'No' question round—those who got it wrong were immediately unloaded. Those still aboard faced an 800-question two-hour examination paper. Finally two remaining finalists faced a play-off on top of the Pan Am skyscraper in New York, USA. Prizes included a racehorse, a helicopter and some land in Nevada.

### Greatest TV audiences
The highest ever audience for a single TV programme was 138.5 million viewers, for the NBC transmission of *Super Bowl XXX* on 28 Jan 1996.

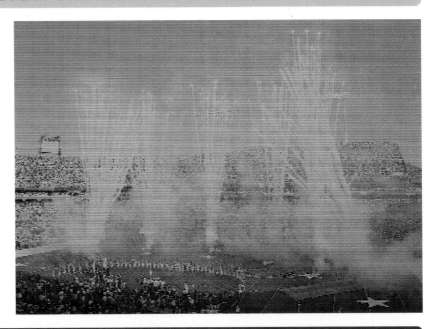

REMEMBRANCE WHICH COST $110 MILLION AND TOOK THREE YEARS TO SHOOT

*Baywatch* is the most widely viewed programme in the world, with an estimated weekly audience of more than 1.1 billion in more than 103 countries and every continent (except Antarctica), as of June 1997.

The biggest audience for a single broadcast on British television was 30.15 million for the 1986 Christmas edition of the BBC soap opera *EastEnders*.

### Fastest video production
Live filming of the Royal Wedding of Prince Andrew and Sarah Ferguson ended on 23 July 1986 at 4:42 p.m., with the honeymoon couple's departure from Chelsea Hospital. The first fully edited and packaged tapes were purchased at 10.23 p.m., 5 hr 41 min later, from the Virgin Megastore in Oxford Street, London, UK.

## Television advertising
### Fastest advertisement
An advertisement for Reebok's InstaPUMP shoes was created, filmed, and aired during Super Bowl XXVII at the Atlanta Georgia Dome, USA, on 31 Jan 1993. Filming continued up until the beginning of the fourth quarter of play, editing began in the middle of the third quarter and the finished product was aired during the advertisement break at the two-minute warning of the fourth quarter.

### Longest advertisement
The longest advertisement broadcast on British television was a 7-min 10-sec slot by Great Universal Stores on TV-AM's *Good Morning Britain* on 20 Jan 1985. The broadcast cost £100,000.

### Shortest advertisement
An advertisement lasting only four frames (there are 30 frames in a second) was aired on KING-TV's *Evening Magazine* on 29 Nov 1993. It was for Bon Marche's Frango candies, and cost $3,780 (£2,500).

The shortest advertisement on British TV was for the 1993 edition of *The Guinness Book of Records*; it lasted just three seconds.

### Highest advertising rates
The highest TV advertising rate was $2.2 million (£1.43 million) per minute, for NBC network prime time during the transmission of *Super Bowl XXIX* and *XXX*, on 29 Jan 1995 and 28 Jan 1996.

### Only advertising obituary
In 1971, *The Times* wrote an obituary when Captain Birdseye (played by actor John Hewer) was dropped from the fish-fingers advertising campaign he had been promoting since 1967. In 1974 he was back—in full colour.

# Publishing

**Right**
The US horror writer
Stephen King, who
was reported to have
received the greatest
advance in publishing
history—£26 million
for four books.

The entire Buddhist scriptures are inscribed on 729 marble slabs measuring 1.5 x 1 m (5 ft x 3 ft 6 in) housed in 729 stupas in the Kuthodaw Pagoda, Myanmar (Burma). They were incised in 1860–68.

The 1,112-volume set of *British Parliamentary Papers* was published by the Irish University Press in 1968–72. A set weighs 3.3 tonnes and would take six years to read at 10 hours per day. The production involved 34,000 Indian goat skins and the use of £15,000 worth of gold ingots.

The standard German dictionary, *Deutsches Wörterbuch*, started by Jacob and Wilhelm Grimm in 1854, was completed in 1971 and consists of 34,519 pages and 33 volumes.

The largest dictionary of the English language is the *Oxford English Dictionary*. The printed version of the second edition (1989), now also available on CD-ROM, contains 21,543 pages in 20 volumes, with over 231,000 main entries. In 1993 a series of Additions Volumes, containing entries for additional vocabulary, began to appear: approximately 4,000 new entries are produced annually. The longest entry is for the verb 'set', with over 60,000 words of text. The greatest outside contributor was Marghanita Laski, who supplied a reputed 250,000 quotations.

Brazilian author Jorge Amado has had his 32 novels published in 48 different languages in 60 countries. His first book *O País do Carnaval* was published in 1931, and the most recent, *A Descoberta da América pelos Turcos*, in 1994.

### Highest paid author

In 1958 Deborah Schneider of Minneapolis, Minnesota, USA, wrote 25 words to complete a sentence in a competition for the best blurb for Plymouth cars. She beat about 1.4 million entrants to claim a prize of $500 (£179) every month for life. On normal life expectations she should collect $12,000 (£4,270) per word. The winning phrase is in a deed box at her bank 'Only to be opened after death'.

### Most prolific author

A lifetime output of 72–75 million words has been calculated for Charles Harold St John Hamilton, alias Frank Richards, the creator of Billy Bunter. In his peak years, 1915–26, he wrote up to 80,000 words a week for the boys' school weeklies *Gem*, *Magnet* and *Boys' Friend*.

### Most prolific novelist

Brazilian novelist José Carlos Ryoki de Alpoim Inoue has had 1,046 of his novels printed from 1 June 1986 to Aug 1996. He writes science fiction, westerns and thrillers.

**Right**
Agatha Christie, the
world's top-selling
fiction writer. Her
estate is estimated to
receive £2.5 million in
royalties per year.

## Books and writing

### Oldest book

The oldest handwritten book still intact is a Coptic Psalter made about 1,600 years ago, and found in 1984 at Beni Suef, Egypt.

### First mechanically printed book

It is accepted that the earliest mechanically printed full-length book was the Gutenberg Bible, printed in Mainz, Germany, *c.* 1454, by Johannes Henne zum Gensfleisch zur Laden, known as Johann zu Gutenberg.

### Oldest Koran

The Mushaf Koran, owned by Uzbekistan's Office for Islamic Affairs, belonged to Caliph Usman, third successor to the Prophet. Of the 706 pages, barely one half remains.

### Largest publications

The largest publication ever compiled was the *Yongle Dadian* (the great thesaurus of the Yongle reign), consisting of 22,937 manuscript chapters (370 still survive) in 11,095 volumes, and written by 2,000 Chinese scholars between 1403 and 1408.

The largest encyclopedia in current use is *La Enciclopedia Universal Ilustrada Europeo-Americana*, printed by J. Espasa & Sons, Madrid and Barcelona, Spain, with 105,000 pages and an annual supplement of 1.652 million words.

### Longest novel

The original edition of Marcel Proust's novel *À la Recherche du Temps Perdu* (Remembrance of Things Past) had 9,609,000 characters.

## Authors

### Top selling authors

The world's top-selling fiction writer is Agatha Christie, whose 78 crime novels have sold around 2 billion copies in 44 languages. Agatha Christie also wrote 19 plays and six romantic novels under the pseudonym Mary Westmacott.

The top-selling living author is Dame Barbara Cartland, who has achieved global sales of over 650 million for her 635 published titles.

# LIFETIME OUTPUT 75 MILLION WORDS

WIND (1936); *TO KILL A MOCKINGBIRD* (1960); *VALLEY OF THE DOLLS* (1966)

### Most pseudonyms

The writer with the greatest number of pseudonyms is the minor Russian humourist Konstantin Arsenievich Mikhailov, whose 325 pen names are listed in the *Dictionary of Pseudonyms* by I. F. Masanov, published in Moscow in 1960. The names, ranging from Ab. to Z, were nearly all abbreviations of his real name.

### Greatest publisher's advance

It was reported in Aug 1992 that Berkeley Putnam had paid $14 million (£7.3 million) for the North American rights to *Without Remorse* by Tom Clancy, representing the greatest advance for a single book.

On 9 Feb 1989, Stephen King was reported to have scooped an advance of £26 million for his next four books.

On 6 May 1992, Barbara Taylor Bradford concluded a deal with HarperCollins for £17 million over five years for three novels.

### Greatest unreturned advance

In Feb 1996, the New York State Supreme Court ruled that Joan Collins could retain a $1.2 million (£750,000) advance for her unpublished novel *A Ruling Passion*. Her publisher, Random House, had found her first draft unsatisfactory and sued her unsuccessfully for the return of the money.

### 117 YEARS TO COMPLETE

### Most translated author

The most translated novelist in the world is Sidney Sheldon, whose books have been distributed in over 180 countries to date. His novels which include *Rage of Angels*, have been translated into 51 languages.

## Sales

### Best selling non-fiction

The best-selling and most widely distributed book is the Bible, with an estimated 2.5 billion copies sold between 1815 and 1975. By the end of 1996, combined global sales of *Today's English Version* (*Good News*) New Testament and Bible approached 18 million copies, and the whole Bible had been translated into over 350 languages; at least one book of the Bible has been translated into 2,123 languages. The oldest publisher of Bibles is Cambridge University Press, which published the Geneva version in 1591.

Excluding non-copyright works such as the Bible and the Koran, the world's all-time best-selling copyright book is *The Guinness Book*

*of Records*, first published in Oct 1955 by Guinness Superlatives, and edited by Norris McWhirter and his twin brother Alan Ross McWhirter. Global sales in 37 languages had passed 80 million to July 1997.

### Best-selling fiction

Due to a lack of audited figures, it is impossible to state which single work of fiction has had the highest sales. Three novels have been credited with sales of around 30 million: *Valley of the Dolls* (1966) by Jacqueline Susann, which sold 6.8 million copies in the first six months, although it is now out of print; *To Kill a Mockingbird* (1960) by Harper Lee; and *Gone With the Wind* (1936) by Margaret Mitchell.

The British author Alistair MacLean wrote a total of 30 books, 28 of which sold over 1 million copies each in the United Kingdom alone. His books have been translated into as many as 28 languages, and 13 of them have been made into films. It has been estimated that an Alistair MacLean novel is purchased every 18 seconds.

### Most weeks on a bestseller list

The longest duration on the *New York Times* bestseller list is for *The Road Less Travelled* by M. Scott Peck, which had its 598th week on the lists on 14 April 1995. Over 5 million copies of the book, published by Touchstone, are currently in print.

### Most weeks on a UK bestseller list

In the United Kingdom, the hardback edition of *A Brief History of Time* by Prof. Stephen Hawking, published by Transworld/Bantam Press, had appeared in *The Sunday Times* bestseller list (which excludes books published annually) for a record 237 weeks as of May 1995. The paperback, which was released on 6 April 1995, reached the list's number one position within three days.

### Most weeks as UK No. 1 best-seller

The recipe book, *Summer Collection*, by Delia Smith, which was published in 1993, has spent 68 weeks at No. 1 in *The Sunday Times* bestseller listings. The book accompanied the author's BBC television cookery programme.

## Newspapers

### Oldest newspapers

There is a surviving copy of a news pamphlet published in Cologne, Germany, in 1470.

The oldest existing newspaper in the world is the Swedish official journal *Post och Inrikes Tidningar*, founded in 1645 and published by the Royal Swedish Academy of Letters.

The Austrian morning newspaper *Wiener Zeitung*, which is the official government paper, has been published every weekday, virtually without a break, since 1703.

### Oldest British newspaper

The *London Gazette* (originally the *Oxford Gazette*) was first published in Nov 1665.

The oldest British newspaper still published is *Berrow's Worcester Journal* (originally *Worcester Post Man*), published in Worcester. According to tradition it was founded in 1690 and has appeared weekly since June 1709, but no complete file exists.

The oldest British newspaper still published under the same title is the *Stamford Mercury*, founded in 1712.

The oldest Sunday newspaper in the United Kingdom is *The Observer*, which was first issued on 4 Dec 1791.

### Largest newspaper

The 14 June 1993 edition of the daily newspaper *Het Volk*, published in Ghent, Belgium, had a 142 x 99.5-cm (4-ft 7⅞-in x 3-ft 3³⁄₁₆-in) page size. It sold 50,000 copies.

The *Worcestershire Chronicle* was the largest British newspaper, and a surviving issue of 16 Feb 1859 measures 82 x 57 cm (32³⁄₁₀ x 22½ in).

### Heaviest newspaper

The 14 Sept 1987 edition of *The Sunday New York Times* weighed more than 5.4 kg (12 lb) and contained 1,612 pages.

### Smallest newspaper

A Bengali newspaper entitled *Bireswar-Smriti*, measures just 5 x 4 cm (1¹⁵⁄₁₆ x 1⁹⁄₁₆ in). The periodical has appeared monthly since 1991 and is published by Kuntal Saha of Habra, India.

### Highest circulation

*Komsomolskaya Pravda*, the youth paper of the former Communist Party of the Soviet Union, reached a peak daily circulation of 21,975,000 copies in May 1990.

The eight-page weekly newspaper *Argumenty i Fakty*, of Moscow, Russia, attained a figure of 33,431,100 copies in May 1990, when it had an estimated readership of over 100 million.

The highest circulation for any currently published newspaper is that of *Yomiuri Shimbun*, founded 1874. Published in Tokyo, Japan, its daily circulation in 1997 was 14,500,000, of which the morning edition accounts for 10,141,458 and the evening edition 4,424,016.

In the United Kingdom the *News of the World*, which was founded on 1 Oct 1843, attained peak sales of 8,480,878 in April 1951 and had an estimated readership of over 19 million. Average sales from Dec 1996 to May 1997 were 4,487,282, with an estimated readership of 11.78 million.

The highest net sale of any British daily newspaper was that for *The Sun* on 18 Nov 1995, with a sale of 4,889,118, at a reduced cover price for that day only of 10p.

### Most misprints

The record for misprints was set by *The Times* of London, UK. On page 19 of the 22 Aug 1978 edition there were 97 misprints in 5½ single column inches. The passage concerned 'Pop' (Pope) Paul VI.

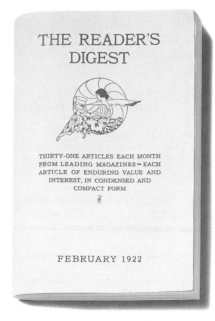

THE READER'S DIGEST

THIRTY-ONE ARTICLES EACH MONTH
FROM LEADING MAGAZINES ~ EACH
ARTICLE OF ENDURING VALUE AND
INTEREST, IN CONDENSED AND
COMPACT FORM

FEBRUARY 1922

## Editors and contributors

### Longest editorship

Sir Etienne Dupuch of Nassau, Bahamas, was editor-in-chief of the *Tribune* from 1 April 1919 to 1972 and continued as a contributing editor until his death on 23 Aug 1991, a total of 72 years.

The longest editorship of any British national newspaper was 57 years, by C. P. Scott of the *Manchester Guardian* (*The Guardian* from 1959), who occupied the post from the age of 26 in 1872 until his retirement in 1929.

### Longest-running feature

Mary MacArthur of Port Appin, Argyll and Bute, UK, has contributed regular features to *The Oban Times* and *West Highland Times* since 1926.

### Most syndicated columnist

Ann Landers (*née* Esther Pauline Friedman) appears in over 1,200 newspapers with an estimated readership of 90 million. Her only rival is Abigail Van Buren, known as 'Dear Abby' (*née* Pauline Esther Friedman), Landers' identical twin sister, based in Beverly Hills, California, USA.

## Cartoons

### Longest running comic strip

The longest-lived newspaper comic strip is the 'Katzenjammer Kids' (Hans and Fritz), which was created by Rudolph Dirks and first published in the *New York Journal* on 12 Dec 1897. The strip is now drawn by cartoonist Hy Eisman and is syndicated to 50 newspapers by King Features Syndicate.

### Most syndicated strip

The most syndicated strip is 'Peanuts' by Charles M. Schulz of Santa Rosa, California, USA. First published in Oct 1950, it currently appears in 2,620 newspapers in 75 countries and 26 languages.

## Periodicals

### Oldest periodicals

The *Philosophical Transactions* of the Royal Society, published in London, UK, first appeared on 6 March 1665.

The oldest British weekly periodical is *The Lancet*, which was first published in 1823.

### Oldest British periodicals

The longest-running annual is *Old Moore's Almanack*, which has been published since

# WEEKLY CIRCULATION 37.166 MILLION

1697, when it appeared as a broadsheet produced by Dr Francis Moore of Southwark, London, UK, to advertise his 'physiks'. Published by W. Foulsham & Co. Ltd of Chippenham, Berks, UK, total sales to date are more than 113 million.

## Largest periodical

The bulkiest consumer magazine ever published was the 10 Jan 1990 issue of *Shukan Jutaku Joho* (*Weekly Housing Information*), which ran to 1,940 pages. Published in Japan by the Recruit Company Ltd, it retailed for ¥350 (£1.50).

## Largest circulations

By May 1996, total sales of *The Truth that Leads to Eternal Life*, which is sold by Jehovah's Witnesses through non-commercial channels, were 107,686,489.

In 1974 the *US TV Guide* became the first weekly magazine to sell a billion copies in a year. It has the highest paid circulation of any weekly magazine, at 13,175,549 to 31 Dec 1995.

In its 47 basic international editions, the *Reader's Digest* circulates more than 27 million copies monthly in 18 languages.

*Parade*, the US syndicated colour magazine, is distributed with 340 newspapers every Sunday. As of April 1996 it had a circulation of 37.166 million, the highest in the world for any magazine. At $629,600 (£409,000) for a four-colour page, it is also the most expensive magazine in which to advertise.

Before deregulation of the listings market in March 1991, the highest circulation of any periodical in the United Kingdom was that of the *Radio Times*. Average weekly sales for July to Dec 1989 were 3,037,129 copies, with a readership of 9,031,000. The highest sales figure for any issue was 11,037,139 copies for the 1989 Christmas edition.

## Largest free circulation magazine

A quarterly free magazine, *Idé-nyt*, about homes and gardens, is published in Denmark and has a circulation of 2.49 million.

# Letters to editor

## Longest letter to an editor

The *Upper Dauphin Sentinel* of Pennsylvania, USA, published a 25,513-word letter by John Sultzbaugh of Lykens, Pennsylvania, USA, over eight issues from Aug to Nov 1979.

## Most letters to an editor

David Green, an author and solicitor from Castle Morris, Pembrokeshire, UK, had his 140th letter published in the main correspondence columns of *The Times* on 17 April 1997. Green's most prolific year was 1972, when 12 of his letters were published. His shortest letter was "Sir, 'Yes'.", on 31 May 1993.

## Shortest letter to *The Times*

The shortest letter to *The Times* comprised the single abbreviated symbol "Dr2?". The letter was written by R. S. Cookson of north London, UK, on 30 July 1984 concerning the correct form of recording a plurality of academic doctorates.

On 8 Jan 1986, a letter was sent to *The Times* by a seven-year-old girl from the Isle of Man, UK. The brief epistle read "Sir, Yours faithfully Caroline Sophia Kerenhappuch Parkes". It was intended to inform readers of her unusual name, Kerenhappuch, which had been mentioned in a letter the previous week from Rev. John Ticehurst on the subject of unusual 19th-century names.

# Advertising

**Right**
The Marlboro Man, created by Philip Morris Inc. in the 1960s. Today Marlboro is the most valuable brand name in the world.

**Largest radio advertiser**
The largest commercial radio expenditure world-wide was $9.7 million (£5.8 million), spent by the US telecommunications giant AT&T in 1996 on network and national spot radio advertising.

**Largest British radio advertiser**
The largest radio advertiser in the United Kingdom is McDonald's—in 1994 it had a total spend in excess of £3.7 million.

**Largest press advertiser**
In 1995 the world's top consumer magazine advertiser, by total spend, was the General Motors Corporation, who spent $142 million (£85 million).

**Largest press advertiser in the UK**
The biggest press advertiser in newspapers and magazines in the United Kingdom over the period 1990–95 was Gallaher Tobacco, with a total press spend of £140 million.

## Campaigns
**Largest advertising campaign**
The largest campaign, in terms of expenditure, was the 1996 campaign for AT&T telephone services during which the parent company, AT&T Corporation, spent $474 million (£284 million).

**Most expensive advertising campaigns**
The most expensive advertising campaigns were in the pharmaceutical industry. Both Johnson & Johnson/Merck Consumer Pharmaceutical Co. and SmithKline Beecham unleashed $100 million (£63 million) plus marketing campaigns in 1994 for Johnson & Johnson's Pepcid AC and SmithKline Beecham's Tagamet HB, both of which act as acid blockers. The heartburn, acid

## Advertisers
**Largest advertiser in the world**
The largest advertiser in the world is Proctor & Gamble, the detergents company, who was the leading national advertiser in the USA in 1995 with a total expenditure of $2,777 million (£1,666 million).

**Largest advertising nation**
The USA has the world's largest advertising and promotional expenditure. In 1996 it was more than $63,811 million (£38,286 million).

**Largest advertiser in the UK**
The largest British advertiser, in terms of total expenditure in 1995, was Unilever, whose portfolio of products range from soaps and cosmetics to food. Unilever spent £210 million on advertising.

**Largest advertising agency**
The largest advertising agency in the world is McCann-Erickson Worldwide, who spent $2,605.1 million (£1,563 million) in 1995.

**Largest television advertiser**
The largest television advertiser in the world is AT&T Corporation, who spent $174 million (£105 million) on cable, network, spot and syndicated TV advertising in 1994.

**Largest television advertiser in the UK**
Unilever is the largest television advertiser in the United Kingdom with an annual expenditure greater than that of the largest advertiser in any other European country.

indigestion and sour stomach remedy advertising category is worth as much as $1.12 billion (£672 million).

**Longest advertising campaign**
The Jos Neel Co., a clothing store in Macon, Georgia, USA, ran an advertisement in the upper left corner of page 2A of *The Macon Telegraph* every day from 22 Feb 1889 to 16 Aug 1987. This amounted to a total of 35,291 advertisements.

**Most valuable brand name in the world**
Marlboro cigarettes hold the most valuable brand name in the world, with an estimated value of $40 billion (£25 billion) in 1997.

# MOST EXPENSIVE TV AD $1,600,000

HE INDIGESTION REMEDY SECTOR IS WORTH AS MUCH AS $1.12 BILLION

**World's strongest advertising image**
According to various world, US and UK surveys, the world's strongest advertising image is the Coca-Cola brand name and its various symbols.

## Television advertising

**Most expensive television advertisement**
The most expensive television advertisement ever produced was one made for the computer manufacturer Apple Macintosh.

of the same commercial were made for the campaign—nine executions were shown throughout the film (three in each of the advertising breaks) and an embargo was placed on all other alcohol advertisers. The cost of obtaining this media airtime was £1 million. This, according to Zenith Media (the UK's largest media buying agency) and Saatchi & Saatchi Advertising, is the most that has ever been spent in one night by one advertiser in one cinema programme in the United Kingdom.

carried book advertisements from Nov 1646 for 6 pence (2½ p) per insertion.

**Largest newspaper volume**
The New York Times has an average advertising volume of 4.5 million column inches per annum.

**Largest newspaper revenue in the UK**
The Financial Times has the largest advertising revenue for a British newspaper: over £165 million per annum since 1994.

**Left**
Coca-Cola was launched in 1886 as a tonic by Dr John Pemberton, an Atlanta pharmacist. Asa Chandler, another druggist, acquired control of the product and formed the Coca-Cola company in 1891. Today, Coca-Cola has the world's strongest advertising image and more than 900 million Coca-Cola products are consumed each day in almost 200 countries.

& GAMBLE, WITH AN EXPENDITURE IN THE USA IN 1995 OF $2,777 MILLION

The commercial was produced by Ridley Scott, the director of Blade Runner and Thelma and Louise. It was based on the novel by George Orwell, Nineteen Eighty-Four. However, its impact was so great, and the recall so high, that it is considered to be one of the most cost-effective commercials ever made. The advertisement cost $600,000 (£360,000) to produce and $1,000,000 (£600,000) to show. It was shown only once—in 1984.

**Most spent in one night in the UK**
Castlemaine XXXX 'hi-jacked' the movie premier showing of Demolition Man on 17 Aug 1996. Seventeen different versions

**Most ads for one product in one evening**
All 17 versions of the Castlemaine XXXX commercial were shown on the first night of Granada Sky Broadcasting on 1 Oct 1996.

**Most television awards**
The Levi 'Drugstore' 501 jeans television advertisement won 33 awards in 1995.

## Press advertising

**Earliest newspaper advertising**
The earliest advertising carried by a paper devoted primarily to news in the United Kingdom was in Samuel Peck's Perfect Diurnall, published in London, UK, which

**Most advertising pages**
The most pages of advertisements that have ever been sold in a single issue of a periodical is 829.54, in the Oct 1989 edition of Business Week.

**Most magazine advertising revenue**
The American magazine TV Guide had an advertising revenue of $1,068.8 million (£641 million) in 1995.

**Most display advertisements**
The Radio Times, a radio and television listings magazine, is the largest consumer magazine in the United Kingdom in terms of its display advertising.

### First stored-programme computers
The first stored-programme computer was the Manchester University Mark I Prototype in Manchester, UK, which incorporated the Williams storage cathode ray tube. The first programme was run by Prof. Tom Kilburn for 52 minutes on 21 June 1948.

The first usable full-scale stored programme computer was, despite its name, the Electronic Delay Storage Automatic Calculator (EDSAC), developed at Cambridge University, UK, by a team led by Maurice Wilks. The computer first ran in 1949.

### First commercially produced computer
The first commercially manufactured computer was the Ferranti Mk 1, developed in conjunction with Manchester University, UK. It was first run in Feb 1951.

### First business computing machine
The first machine designed specifically for commercial purposes was LEO (Lyons Electronic Office). The computer was unveiled in Britain in 1951.

### First microcomputer
The invention of the microcomputer was formerly attributed to a team led by M. E. Hoff Jr of Intel Corporation with the production of the microprocessor chip '4004' in 1969–71. On 17 July 1990, however, with the award of US Patent No. 4942516, priority was accorded to Gilbert Hyatt, who had devised a single-chip microcomputer at Micro Computer Inc. of Van Nuys, Los Angeles, USA, from 1968–71.

### First personal computer
The MITS Altair 8800 featured on the cover of the Jan 1975 issue of US magazine *Popular Electronics* as the "World's First

FASTEST GENERAL-PURPOSE VECTOR-PARALLEL COMPUTER IS THE CRAY Y-MI

## Computer firsts
### First electronic computer
The earliest programmable electronic computer was the 1,500-valve Colossus devised by Prof. Max Newman and built by T. H. Flowers. It was run in Dec 1943 at Bletchley Park, UK, to break the German Lorenz Schlussel-zusat 40 coding machine.

The credit for being the world's first electronic computer is often given to ENIAC (Electronic Numerical Integrator Analyzer and Computer), developed at the University of Pennsylvania, USA, by J. Presper Eckert and John W. Mauchly. However ENIAC is now regarded as a calculator, not a computer.

It was based on about 18,000 vacuum tubes or valves, and ran its first programme in Nov 1945, though it was not officially unveiled until early the following year.

In 1946, Eckert and Mauchly set up the USA's first computer company, which led eventually to the development of the first popular commercial system, the Univac.

The Atanasoff-Berry, developed in 1942 at the University of Iowa, USA, by John Atanasoff and Clifford Berry, was credited as the first electronic computer when a US court invalidated ENIAC patents. Like ENIAC, it is now classed as a calculator, not a computer.

Minicomputer Kit to Rival Commercial Models". For $395 (£180) it offered an Intel 8800 processor and 256 bytes of memory, toggle switches for data input and LEDs (light-emitting diodes) for output, but no keyboard or screen. It prompted Microsoft co-founders Bill Gates and Paul Allen to write a version of Basic, the simple, powerful computer language.

### First biological computer
On 11 Nov 1994, Prof Leonard Adleman reported in *Science* that he had used molecules of DNA in a test tube to solve a complex mathematical problem. The experiment, which took place at the Institute

# MICROPROCESSOR SPEED 600 MHZ

## HAS A PEAK PERFORMANCE OF 1.8 TERAFLOPS

for Molecular Medicine and Technology, which is associated with the University of Southern California, USA, lasted four hours and the strands of genetic material interacted to give an answer to the notorious "travelling salesman" problem: plotting the shortest route between several locations. The Institute has now started research into biological computers because they use far less energy and are far more compact than silicon processors.

### First computer virus
The first computer programme that was able to replicate itself surreptitiously was demonstrated by Fred Cohen, a student at the Massachusetts Institute of Technology, USA, on 11 Nov 1983.

## Fastest computers
### Fastest general-purpose computer
The fastest general-purpose vector-parallel computer is the Cray Y-MP C90 supercomputer, with two gigabytes (one gigabyte equals one billion bytes) of central memory and with 16 CPUs (central processing units), giving a combined peak performance of 16 gigaflops (one gigaflop equals 1 billion flops, or floating point operations per second).

Intel installed the world's fastest supercomputer at Sandia, Texas, USA, in 1996. It uses 9072 Intel Pentium Pro processors, each running at about 200 MHz, and 608 gigabytes of memory. It has a peak performance of about 1.8 teraflops (trillions of flops per second).

Several suppliers now market 'massively parallel' computers which, with enough processors, have a theoretical aggregate

### World supercomputing speed record
In Dec 1994, a team of scientists from Sandia National Laboratories and Intel Corporation, USA, linked together two of the largest Intel Paragon parallel-processing machines. The system achieved 281 gigaflops on the Linpack benchmark and achieved 328 gigaflops running a programme used for radar signature calculations. The two-Paragon system used 6,768 processors working in parallel.

### Best chess computer
IBM's Deep Blue supercomputer was the first computer to beat a human chess grandmaster in a regulation game when it played Gary Kasparov in Philadelphia, USA, in 1995. On 11 May 1997, it beat grandmaster Kasparov again for the first time in a series. It won the six-match series by 3½ points to 2½.

600 Mflops per PE, 969 PEs, with an additional 48 in support, and 800 Gbytes of disk storage capacity.

### Largest number ever crunched
Computer scientists at Purdue University, Indiana, USA, co-ordinated researchers worldwide to find the two largest numbers that, multiplied together, equal a known 167-digit number, $(3^{349}-1)/2$. The breakthrough was in April 1997, after 100,000 hours computing time. The two factors had 80 digits and 87 digits. The previous factorization record was 162 digits long.

### Smallest keyboard
The smallest computer keyboard with a full complement of alphanumeric, symbol and command keys was patented on 18 March 1997 by David Levy, of the Massachusetts Institute of Technology, USA. It has 65 keys,

**Left**
The chess grandmaster Gary Kasparov in the process of being beaten in a chess series by IBM's Deep Blue supercomputer on 11 May 1997. The computer won the six-match series by 3½ points to 2½. Deep Blue, which can look at an average of 200 million positions per second, is the fastest chess computer to date.

**Below**
The world's smallest keyboard is 40% smaller than a credit card and yet the keys have been designed using technology that makes each of the keys large enough to be operated by an adult's thumb.

## C90 SUPERCOMPUTER, WITH A COMBINED PERFORMANCE OF 16 GIGAFLOPS

performance exceeding that of a C90, though the performance on real-life applications may be less. This is because it may be harder to harness effectively the power of a large number of small processors than a small number of large ones.

### Fastest chip
The Alpha 21164, developed by Digital Equipment Corporation of Maynard, Massachusetts, USA, was first unveiled on 31 March 1997. It is used in workstation computers and can run at speeds of 600 MHz (this compares to 266 MHz for a modern personal computer).

## Largest and smallest
### Largest supercomputer
The Intel in Sandia, Texas, USA, is the world's largest supercomputer. It has a top performance of about 1.8 teraflops.

### The largest supercomputer in the UK
The new T3E Cray supercomputer used by the main Met Office and for Hadley Centre for Climate Change at Bracknell, Berks, UK, has hundreds of Processor Elements (PEs) which consist of fast CPUs, each having their own local memories. All the PEs have 128 Mbytes of local memory except for eight which have a total of 512 Mbytes. The system has a peak performance of

each large enough to be operated by the thumb of a large person, yet the whole device is 60% the size of a credit card. The device uses passive chording™ technology which allows groups of keys to act as one. For example, to hit the 'G' key a finger has to press all the keys touching the G. The keyboard is 7.62 x 3.048 cm (3 x 1.2 in).

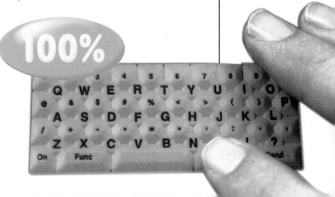

**Right**
In Sweden there are 229 cellular telephone subscribers for every 1,000 people—the highest concentration in the world. This compares to the United Kingdom where there are 93 cellular subscribers for every 1,000 people.

## Telephones and facsimiles
### Telephones
The country with the most telephones in 1996 was the USA, with 165 million, or 66 for every hundred people.

The United Kingdom has 29 million telephones, or 50 for every 100 people.

Liechtenstein has most subscribers per head of population, with 1.5 for each receiver.

The most calls made in any country is in the USA, with just over 550 billion in 1994.

The United Kingdom's busiest telephone route is with the USA—1.6 billion minutes of two-way traffic in 1995.

### Busiest telephone exchange
On 27 June 1989, GPT (GEC Plessey Telecommunications Ltd) demonstrated the ability of the 'System X' telephone exchange to handle 1,558,000 calls in an hour through one exchange at Beeston, Nottingham, UK.

### Largest switchboard
The Pentagon, Arlington, Virginia, USA, has 34,500 lines handling almost one million calls per day through 322,000 km (200,000 miles) of telephone cable. Its busiest day was the 50th anniversary of D-Day (6 June 1994) when there were 1,502,415 calls.

### Largest and smallest fax machines
The largest facsimile machine was manufactured by WideCom Group Inc. of Mississauga, Ontario, Canada. 'WIDEfax 36' is able to transmit, print and copy 91-cm (3-ft) wide documents.

The Real Time Strategies Inc. hand-held device, 'Pagentry', is 7.6 x 12.7 x 1.9 cm (3 x 5 x ¾ in) and weighs 141.75 g (5 oz).

### Longest telephone submarine cable
The FLAG (Fibre-optic Link Around the Globe), runs for 27,000 km (16,800 miles) from Japan to the United Kingdom and links the continents of Europe, Africa and Asia and 11 countries. It can support 600,000 simultaneous telephone calls.

### Optical fibre
The highest rate of transmission is 1.1 terabits per second, which is equivalent to 17 million simultaneous telephone calls. This was achieved by Fujitsu Laboratories at Kawasaki, Japan, in March 1996.

The longest transmission distance at a data rate of 20 gigabits/sec over a fibre path containing repeaters is 125,000 km (78,000 miles), achieved by using a recirculating fibre loop at BT laboratories at Martlesham, Suffolk, UK, and reported in Sept 1994.

**Right**
On 27 June 1989, at BT laboratories at Martlesham, Suffolk, UK, data was transmitted at a rate of 20 gigabits per second over a record distance of 125,000 km (78,000 miles).

### Mobile phones
The USA has the most cellular telephone subscribers—35 million at the start of 1996.

There were 5.7 million mobile phones in the United Kingdom at the start of 1996.

Sweden has the greatest penetration of mobile phones, where there are 229 subscribers for every 1,000 people.

### Busiest telecommunications exchange
During the Olympic Games, from 19 July to 4 Aug 1996, the Bellsouth network used at the International Broadcast Center, Atlanta, Georgia, USA, could transmit 100 billion bits of information per second.

### Busiest international telephone routes
In 1995 there were a total of 6.1 billion minutes of two-way telephone traffic between the USA and Canada.

# 100 BILLION BITS PER SECOND

### Morse code
The highest recorded speed at which anyone has been able to receive Morse code is 78 words per minute, by Henrique Bulcão de Oliveira Redig in Rio de Janeiro, Brazil, on 16 Dec 1961.

The highest speed recorded for hand key transmitting is 175 symbols per minute (equivalent to 35 wpm) by Harry A. Turner of the US Army Signal Corps at Camp Crowder, Missouri, USA, on 9 Nov 1942.

Thomas Morris, an operator with the British GPO, was reputed to have been able to send messages at 39–40 wpm c. 1919, but this has never been verified.

## Radio
Radio waves from the Milky Way were first detected by Karl Jansky of Bell Telephone Laboratories, Holmdel, New Jersey, USA, in 1931, while he was investigating 'static' with an improvised 30.5-m (100-ft) aerial.

The only purpose-built radio telescope, built before the outbreak of WWII in 1939, was made by an amateur, Grote Reber, who detected radio emissions from the sun. The diameter of the dish was 9.5 m (31 ft 2 in).

### Largest radio dishes
The first large 'dish' was the 76-m (250-ft) telescope at Jodrell Bank, Cheshire, UK, now known as the Lovell Telescope, which was completed in 1957. The dish is part

and Culgoora, NSW. It also has links with tracking stations at Usuada and Kashima, Japan, and with the TDRS (Tracking and Data Relay Satellite), which is in a geosynchronous orbit. This is equivalent to a radio telescope with an effective diameter of 2.16 earth diameters, or 27,523 km (17,102 miles).

The VLA (Very Large Array) of the US National Science Foundation is Y-shaped, with a total of 27 mobile antennae, each of which has a diameter of 25 m (82 ft). Each arm is 20.9 km (13 miles) long. The installation is situated 80 km (50 miles) west

equipment failure led a network in Florida to claim 'ownership' of 30,000 of the Internet's 45,000 routes. There was widespread disruption, data packets were routed incorrectly and connections failed across the Internet. Although some service providers took action within 15 minutes the problem persisted until 19.00 EST.

### Most wired community
Blacksburg, Montgomery County, Virginia, USA, claims to be the community that has the highest number of electronic mail and Internet users relative to its size. According

**Left**
The world's largest single-unit radio telescope is situated 16 km (10 miles) south of the city of Arecibo, Puerto Rico. It was built in the early 1960s and has a 305-m (1,000-ft) spherical reflector that focuses incoming radio waves.

of the MERLIN network, which includes other dishes in various parts of the United Kingdom.

The world's largest dish radio telescope is the partially-steerable ionospheric assembly built over a natural bowl at Arecibo, Puerto Rico. Completed in Nov 1963, the dish has a diameter of 305 m (1,000 ft) and covers an area of 7.48 ha (18½ acres).

The world's largest fully-steerable dish is the 100-m (328-ft) diameter assembly at the Max Planck Institute for Radio Astronomy of Bonn in the Effelsberger Valley, Germany. It was completed in 1971 and weighs 3,048 tonnes.

### Largest radio installations
The Australia Telescope includes a 64-m (210-ft) diameter dish at Parkes, NSW, and 22-m (72-ft) diameter dishes at Siding Spring

of Socorro in the Plains of San Augustin, New Mexico, USA, and was completed on 10 Oct 1980.

## The Internet
### Largest computer network
The number of computers using the 'Net' has been doubling ever year since 1987 and in Jan 1996 there were at least 9,472,000 computers on the 'Net'. There may, however, be many more computers attached than this figure suggests, since many 'host', or server, computers are behind corporate 'firewalls' which are designed to exclude electronic visitors, including hackers.

### Biggest Internet crash
On Friday 25 April 1997, at approximately 11.30 EST, the global computer network ran into major problems and much of the system became unusable. A human error and

to a 1995 survey, there were approximately 30,000 regular users of wired data communications in a county with a 70,000 population. Around 20,000 users were connected through their local university, Virginia Tech.

### First Internet shopping mall
The Branch Mall was launched in Dec 1993 by Jon Zeeff, with two virtual shops, Grant's Flowers and Calling Cards. It registered 400 hits in its first month. Today it registers 3 million at http://www.branchmall.com/

### First Internet arrest
On 19 May 1996, Leslie Ibsen Rogge became the first man to be arrested as a result of his picture being posted on the FBI's web-site. Rogge, a convicted bankrobber and one of America's 10 Most Wanted, had escaped from federal custody in 1985.

# The arts

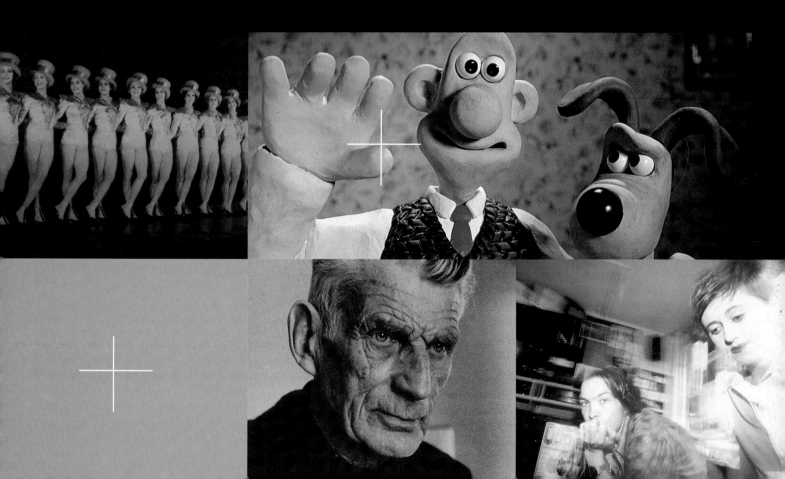

# Stars of stage and screen

**Right**
Jack Nicholson starred
as the 'The Joker' in
the film *Batman*. He
stood to make a record
$60 million (£40
million) through a
percentage of the
film's receipts.

## Film

### Highest earnings
Through a percentage of the film's receipts
in lieu of salary, Jack Nicholson stood to
receive up to $60 million (£40 million) for
playing 'The Joker' in Warner Brothers'
$50 million *Batman* (USA, 1989).

### Most leading roles
John Wayne appeared in 153 movies from
*The Drop Kick* (USA, 1927) to *The Shootist*
(USA, 1976). In all but 11 he played the lead.

### Most honoured entertainer
Bob Hope is the only entertainer to have
been awarded the USA's highest civilian
honours: the Congressional Gold Medal
(1963), the Medal of Merit (1966), the
Medal of Freedom (1969), the Distinguished
Service Gold Medal (1971) and the
Distinguished Public Service Medal (1973).

### Youngest to receive star billing
Leroy Overacker, known on screen as Baby
Leroy, was chosen at the age of six months
to play opposite Maurice Chevalier in
*Bedtime Story* (USA, 1933).

### Youngest number one box-office star
Shirley Temple was seven years old when
she became number one at the box-office
in 1935, retaining the title to 1938.
She made her last film in 1949 and later
became a diplomat.

### Oldest number one box-office star
Canadian Marie Dressler was 64 when she
became number one box-office star in 1933.

### Most durable performers
The German actor Curt Bois had the longest
screen career, spanning 80 years. He made
his debut in *Der Fidele Bauer* (1908) at the
age of eight and his final appearance in
*Wings of Desire* (1988) at the age of 88.

The most enduring Hollywood star was
Lillian Gish, who first appeared in *An
Unseen Enemy* in 1912 and ended her
career with *The Whales of August* in
1987, 75 years later.

## Most generations of stars in a family
There are four generations of screen actors
in the Redgrave family. Roy Redgrave made
his screen debut in 1911. His son Sir
Michael Redgrave married actress Rachel
Kempson and their two daughters Vanessa
and Lynn and son Corin are all actors.
Vanessa's daughters Joely and Natasha
and Corin's daughter Jemma are now all
successful actresses.

## Theatre
### Most acting roles
Jan Leighton has played 3,395 theatrical,
film and television roles since 1951.

### Most theatrical roles
Kanzaburo Nakamura has performed in 806
*Kabuki* titles from 1926 to 1987. As each
title in this Japanese theatrical form lasts 25
days, he has played 20,150 performances.

### Most durable theatre performers
Kanmi Fujiyama played the lead in 10,288
performances by the comedy company
Sochiku Shikigeki from 1966 to 1983.

David Raven played Major Metcalfe in *The
Mousetrap* on 4,575 occasions between
22 July 1957 and 23 Nov 1968.

Dame Anna Neagle played the lead role in
*Charlie Girl* at the Adelphi Theatre, London,
UK, for 2,062 of 2,202 performances
between 15 Dec 1965 and 27 March 1971,
and in all 327 performances in Australasia.

**Right**
Bob Hope is the world's
most honoured
entertainer. He has
been awarded the
USA's highest civilian
honours, the CBE and
appointed Hon.
Brigadier of the US
Marine Corps.
He also has 44
honorary degrees.

**Far right**
Bob Hope receiving a
*Guinness Book of
Records* certificate
from publishing
director Michael
Feldman to
commemorate the
longest contract in
radio and TV. Hope
completed the 60th
year of his NBC
contract on
23 Nov 1996.

# LONGEST APPLAUSE 1 HR 20 MIN

**Longest consecutive performance**
James O'Neill, father of dramatist Eugene, played *The Count of Monte Cristo* over 6,000 times from 1883 to 1891.

**Most durable understudy**
On 12 March 1994, Nancy Seabrooke aged 79, retired from the Company of *The Mousetrap* after understudying the part of Mrs Boyle for 15 years and 6,240 performances, and performing it 72 times.

**Largest theatrical family ensemble**
At Ellen Terry's Jubilee Matinée, Drury Lane, London, UK, on 12 June 1906, 22 members of the Terry Family (including Sir John Gielgud's mother, Kate) appeared in the Masked Dance in *Much Ado About Nothing*.

**Earliest actor to be ennobled**
Laurence Olivier was created a Baron in 1970. He made his debut as Lennox in *Macbeth* in 1924, received nine Oscar nominations and was knighted in 1947.

**Earliest actor to be knighted**
Henry Irving made his London stage debut in 1866 in *The Belle's Stratagem*, and achieved his greatest triumph as a guilt-stricken Alsatian burgomaster in *The Bells* at the Lyceum, London, UK, in 1871. He was knighted in May 1895.

**Earliest professional English actress**
Margaret Hughes appeared as Desdemona in Thomas Killigrew's version of *Othello, The Moor of Venice* on 3 Dec 1660, at a converted tennis court called the Vere Street Theatre, London, UK.

**Longest time in bed together on stage**
Jessica Tandy and Hume Cronyn were married in 1942 and spent more time in bed together on stage than any other couple. In Oct 1951, they opened at the Ethel Barrymore Theatre, USA, in Jan de Hartog's *The Fourposter* and played the bed-bound characters on Broadway and on tour for the next two years.

## Opera and Ballet
**Longest applause**
On 30 July 1991, the Spanish tenor Placido Domingo was applauded through 101 curtain calls for 1 hr 20 min after a performance of *Otello* at the Vienna Staatsoper, Austria.

**Most curtain calls**
On 24 Feb 1988, the Italian tenor Luciano Pavarotti received 165 curtain calls and was applauded for 1 hr 7 min after singing the part of Nemorino in Gaetano Donizetti's *L'Elisir d'amore* at the Deutsche Oper in Berlin, Germany.

The most curtain calls ever received at a ballet is 89, by Dame Margot Fonteyn de Arias and Rudolf Hametovich Nureyev after a performance of *Swan Lake* at the Vienna Staatsoper, Austria, in Oct 1964.

**Longest operatic encore**
The only opera to have been encored in its entirety is *Il Matrimonio Segreto* by Domenico Cimarosa. The Austrian Emperor Leopold II is reputed to have so enjoyed the work in 1792 that he invited all the participants to supper, and then had them perform it all again.

**Most revered singer**
In 1850, up to $653 (£392) was paid for a single seat at the US concerts of Johanna Maria ('Jenny') Lind, the 'Swedish Nightingale'. She had a vocal range from g to $e^{111}$, the middle register of which is still regarded as unrivalled.

**Left**
Dame Margot Fonteyn and Rudolf Nureyev received a record 89 curtain calls after a performance of *Swan Lake*. Fonteyn's celebrated partnership with Nureyev began in the early 1960s and helped both enrich and lengthen her career, which lasted 45 years.

## Sets, props and extras
### Largest film set
The Roman Forum for *The Fall of the Roman Empire* (USA, 1964) was built by 1,100 workmen on a 22.25-ha (55-acre) site outside Madrid, Spain. It measured 400 m x 230 m (1,312 ft x 754 ft).

### Smallest film set
The set built for *Bill and Coo* (USA, 1947) was filmed entirely in a model village mounted on a 9.14 x 4.57 m (30 x 15 ft) table. The performers were love birds.

### Largest land-based prop
A 18.29-m (60-ft) long, 12.19-m (40-ft) high horse was constructed for the film *Wooden Horse of Troy* (USA, 1954).

### Most expensive single prop
A full scale replica of a Spanish galleon, which was built for Roman Polanski's *Pirates* (USA/Tunisia, 1986), cost £7 million.

### Greatest destruction of crockery
In the film *Little Nightingale* (USSR, 1936), the story of a revolt of women workers in a porcelain factory on the Volga, 150,000 plates were shattered.

### Largest production crew
Producer Suketaru Taguchi employed 556 craftsmen and technicians on Kon Ichikawa's documentary *Tokyo Olympiad* (Japan, 1965).

### Largest assemblage of animals
*Around the World in Eighty Days* (USA, 1956) featured a total of 8,552 animals.

### Most film extras
It is believed that over 300,000 extras appeared in the funeral scene of the 1982 epic *Gandhi*.

## Movie subjects
### Most portrayed story
There have been 95 productions of *Cinderella*, including cartoon, modern ballet, and pornographic, from *Fairy Godmother* (GB, 1898) to *The Magic Riddle* (Aus, 1991).

### Most portrayed character
Sherlock Holmes has been portrayed by 75 actors in over 211 films since 1900.

Count Dracula or his descendants have been portrayed 161 times in horror films.

### Most portrayed historical character
Napoleon Bonaparte has been portrayed in 177 films between 1897 and 1986.

### Most portrayed cartoon character
Zorro was the first comic strip character to be made into a feature film in *The Mark of Zorro* (USA, 1920). The film appeared one year after the cartoon, making it the fastest cartoon character to make it to the screen.

### Most filmed author
There have been 309 straight adaptations or relatively straight film versions of the plays of William Shakespeare—*Hamlet* has been filmed 75 times, *Romeo and Juliet* 51 times and *Macbeth* 33 times. There have also been 41 more unconventional interpretations such as *West Side Story*.

### Most filmed novelist
Edgar Wallace has had his books and short stories made into at least 179 films. In addition there have been other films based on his plays, scripts and unidentified sources, making him the most filmed 20th-century writer.

## Directors
### Most successful director
Steven Spielberg has seven of his movies in the all-time top 10. Collectively they have grossed over $2.17 billion (£1.35 billion).

### Longest directorial career
The directorial career of King Vidor lasted for 67 years, beginning with *Hurricane in Galveston* (1913) and culminating in a documentary called *The Metaphor* (1980).

### Youngest director of a feature film
*Lex the Wonderdog* (1972), a canine thriller, was written, produced and directed by Sydney Ling when he was 13 years old.

MOST FILMED AUTHOR IS SHAKESPEARE; WITH 75 VERSIONS OF *HAMLET* AND

**Right**
The enormous wooden horse designed for the film *Wooden Horse of Troy* was the largest land-based prop. It weighed 81,280 kg (80 tons) and 30 trees and over 453.6 kg (1,000 lbs) of nails were needed to build it. A modern air conditioning system was installed to save the 25 occupants from heat exhaustion.

## Film length and durability
### Longest film
The longest film commercially released in its entirety was Edgar Reitz's *Die Zweite Heimat* (Germany, 1992), which lasted 25 hr 32 min. It was premiered in Munich, Germany, from 5 to 9 Sept 1992.

### Longest first-run of a film in one cinema
*Emmanuelle* (France, 1974) was seen by 3,268,874 patrons during the 10 years and 32 weeks it ran at the Paramount City Cinema in Paris, France, between 1974 and 1985.

### Most durable film series
In Hong Kong, 103 features have been made about the 19th-century martial-arts hero Huang Fei-Hong, starting with *The True Story of Huang Fei-Hong* (1949).

### Most films watched
Gwilym Hughes saw his first film in 1953. On 28 Feb 1997, he had logged a total of 22,990 films in his diary. Most of the films he watched were on video.

# LARGEST SET 400 M X 230 M

## Box office and budget

### Most profitable film series
The 18 James Bond movies, from *Dr No* (GB, 1962) to *GoldenEye* (GB/USA, 1995) have grossed over $1 billion worldwide.

### Record budget/box office ratio
The $350,000 Australian production *Mad Max* (1980) had a record budget/box office ratio of 1:285. It grossed $100 million in its first two years of international distribution.

### Smaller audience than cast
The Nazi epic *Kolberg* (Germany 1945) was released in Jan 1945 when few Berlin cinemas were still operating. The audience was rather less than the cast of 187,000.

### Least expensive full-length feature film
The 1927 Australian film *The Shattered Illusion*, by Victorian Film Productions, cost £300. It took 12 months to complete.

### Largest simultaneous movie premiere
On the 11 Dec 1992, *A Few Good Men* was simultaneously released in the USA and 50 other countries by Columbia Pictures.

## Industries and archives

### Largest output
India produces more feature-length films than any other country. A record 948 films were produced in 1990.

### Smallest film-producing country
The smallest country with an established film industry is Iceland, whose population of 251,000 are amongst the most frequent filmgoers in the world with an average of 9.4 visits a year.

### Largest collection of film stills
The National Film Archive Stills Collection in London, UK, has 6.5 million black and white stills and over 1 million colour transparencies from over 80,000 films.

### World's largest film archive
Britain's National Film Archive has a total of 135,000 films. This is compared to the Centre Nationale de la Cinématographie in Paris, France, which holds 95,000 and the Gosfiolmofund in Russia which has 45,000 films.

### Biggest single loss of archive film
In March 1982, 6,506 films were destroyed by fire and explosions at the Cineteca Nacional in Mexico City, Mexico.

4

800

17

**Left**
*Around the World in Eighty Days* featured the largest number of animals ever in a film. In all, there were 3,800 sheep, 2,448 buffalo, 950 donkeys, 800 horses, 512 monkeys, 17 bulls, 15 elephants, 6 skunks and 4 ostriches

# Hollywood

**Right**
In July 1996, *Independence Day* passed the $100 million (£62 million) mark in six and a half days, beating the previous record held by *Jurassic Park* which took nine and a half days. The record was beaten again in May 1997 when *The Lost World: Jurassic Park* passed the $100 million mark in five and a half days, the fastest box office gross.

HIGHEST LOSS IN HOLLYWOOD HISTORY WAS MGM'S *CUTTHROAT ISLAND* WHICH

## Box office and budget
**Most expensive silent film ever made**
MGM's *Ben Hur* (USA, 1925) cost $3.9 million (£2.34 million). Filming started in Italy in 1923 but after $2 million had been spent it was continued in Hollywood.

**Top grossing silent film**
King Vidor's *The Big Parade* (USA, 1925) grossed $22 million (£13.2 million) globally.

**Most expensive film ever released**
Universal's *Waterworld* (USA, 1995) cost an estimated $160 million (£104 million).

Problems with Paramount's *Titanic* mean it will not be released until December 1997—a delay that may add $20 million (£12 million) to its cost, making it the most expensive film ever made, at $250 million (£150 million).

**Most expensive film rights**
In 1978, Columbia paid a record sum of $9.5 million (£5 million) for the film rights to the Broadway musical *Annie*, by Charles Strouse starring Andrea McCardle, Dorothy Loudon and Reid Shelton.

A contract worth $4 million (£2.75 million) plus profit-sharing was signed by New Line on 20 July 1993 for the US psycho-thriller *The Long Kiss Goodnight* by Shane Black.

**Largest publicity budget**
Universal and licensed merchandisers spent $68 million (£45.5 million) on promoting Steven Spielberg's *Jurassic Park* (USA, 1993) in the USA alone. This was $8 million (£5.3 million) more than the cost of the film.

**Most licences for merchandising**
Warner Bros. issued 160 licences at the time of the premier of *Batman* (USA, 1989). It was also the most successful merchandising operation in terms of licence fees, adding an estimated $50 million (£31.3 million) to the movie's box office gross of $250 million (£156.7 million).

**Highest box office gross**
If figures are inflation-adjusted *Gone with the Wind* (USA, 1939) earned $863 million (£518 million), rather than its actual total gross of $193.5 million (£116 million).

**Fastest box office gross**
From May 1997 *The Lost World: Jurassic Park* (Universal) passed the $100 million (£62 million) mark in five and a half days, faster than any other movie.

**Highest opening day box office gross**
*The Lost World: Jurassic Park* brought in $22 million (£14 million) on 23 May 1997.

**Largest loss**
MGM's *Cutthroat Island* (USA, 1995), directed by Renny Harlin, cost over $100 million (£65 million) to produce, promote and distribute, and in its first weekend grossed a mere $2.3 million (£1.5 million). By May 1996, it had reportedly earned back just $11 million (£7.3 million).

# $100 MILLION IN 5.5 DAYS

*EAGLES,* INCLUDING WORKS BY DE KOONING, LICHTENSTEIN AND PICASSO

## Studios and stars

### Largest studio
The largest film complex in the world is at Universal City, Los Angeles, California, USA. It measures 170 ha (420 acres), and comprises 561 buildings and 34 stages.

### Largest studio stage
The 007 stage at Pinewood Studios, UK, built in 1976 for the film *The Spy Who Loved Me*, measures 102 x 42 x 12 m (336 x 139 x 41 ft) and accommodated 4.54 million litres (1.2 million gal) of water, a full-scale section of a 600,000-ton supertanker and three scaled-down nuclear submarines.

### Busiest Hollywood star
Comedienne Joan Blondell starred in 32 feature films in 27 months between 1930 and 1933.

### Longest contract to a single studio
Lewes Stone became an MGM contract artist at the studio's inception in 1924 and remained with them until his death in 1953—29 years in all.

### Lowest paid contract player
Robert Taylor signed with MGM for $35 (£7) a week in 1934. He stayed with them for 25 years, longer than any other major star.

### Youngest film producer
Steven Paul was 20 when he produced and directed *Falling In Love Again* (USA, 1980).

### Most changes of costume
Madonna changed costume 85 times in *Evita* (USA, 1996) in her role as Eva Perón.

### Most expensive costumes
Constance Bennett's sable coat in *Madam X* (1965) was valued at $50,000 (£17,880).

The mink and sequins dance costume worn by Ginger Rogers in *Lady in the Dark* (1944) and designed by Edith Head cost Paramount $35,000 (£8,690).

### Lowest fee for a feature film script
Preston Sturges was paid the sum of $10 (£2.50) for writing the script to *The Great McGinty* (USA, 1940). He was a scriptwriter who wanted to direct, so Paramount allowed him to direct the film in return for writing the script for a nominal fee.

### Most co-writers credited
The film *Forever and a Day* (USA, 1943) is credited with 21 writers.

COST OVER $100 MILLION AND REPORTEDLY EARNED BACK JUST $11 MILLION

### Most valuable assemblage of props
Paintings and sculptures worth $10 million (£7 million) were used for the art gallery scenes in Universal's *Legal Eagles* (USA, 1986). They included works by Willem de Kooning, Roy Lichtenstein and Pablo Picasso.

### Greatest number of costumes
The most costumes used for any one film was 32,000, for the 1951 film *Quo Vadis*.

## Scripts and screenwriters

### Highest fee for a speculative script
Carolco Pictures paid $3 million (£1.8 million) to Joe Eszterhas for *Basic Instinct*.

### Highest fee for a commissioned script
Carolco Pictures paid $2 million (£1.2 million) to Oscar-winning *Rain Man* (USA, 1988) scriptwriter Ronald Bass for an adaptation of T. R. Wright's supernatural thriller *Manhattan Ghost Story* in 1990.

## Oscar awards ceremony

### Most people thanked
The longest roster of people thanked by an Oscar winner was the 27 named by Olivia de Havilland when she won Best Actress for *To Each His Own* (USA, 1946).

### Longest speech
Greer Garson's speech on receiving Best Actress award for *Mrs Miniver* (USA, 1942) lasted 5 min 30 sec.

# Shows

**Right**
The Edinburgh Fringe started in 1947 as an alternative to the Edinburgh Festival. Its aim was to allow the public a chance to see more alternative arts than had been performed up till then at the Edinburgh Festival. Between 1958 and 1996 the Fringe grew from 19 companies to become the world's largest arts event, surpassing the Edinburgh Festival itself.

## Theatrical runs

### Longest theatrical runs
The longest continuous run of any show in the world is *The Mousetrap*, by Agatha Christie, which opened on 25 Nov 1952 at the Ambassadors Theatre, London, UK, (capacity 453) and moved next door after 8,862 performances to the St Martin's Theatre on 25 March 1974. The 18,503rd performance was on 9 May 1997, and the box office has grossed £20 million from more than nine million visitors.

The greatest number of performances of any theatrical presentation is 47,250 (to April

*White Minstrel Show*, later *Magic of the Minstrels*. The aggregate, but non-consecutive, number of performances was 6,464, with a total attendance of 7,794,552 people. The show opened at the Victoria Palace, London, UK, on 25 May 1962 and closed on 4 Nov 1972. It reopened for a season in June 1973 at the New Victoria and finally closed on 8 Dec 1973.

### Longest-running British comedy
The longest-running comedy was *No Sex Please We're British*, by Anthony Marriott and Alistair Foot. It opened at the Strand Theatre, London, UK, on 3 June 1971,

### Longest-running revue
The longest-running annual revues were *The Ziegfeld Follies* (1907–57), which went through 25 editions.

### Shortest runs
The shortest run was of *The Intimate Revue* at the Duchess Theatre, London, UK, on 11 March 1930. Anything which could go wrong did—with scene changes taking up to 20 minutes apiece, the management scrapped seven scenes to get the finale on before midnight. The show was then cancelled.

## Sales and attendance

### Greatest advance sales
The musical *Miss Saigon*, produced by Cameron Mackintosh and starring Jonathan Pryce, opened on Broadway in April 1991 after generating record advance sales of $36 million (£20 million).

### Greatest theatrical losses
The largest loss by a theatrical show was borne by the US producers of the Royal Shakespeare Company's musical *Carrie*, which closed after five performances on Broadway, New York, USA, on 17 May 1988 at a cost of $7 million (£4.2 million).

*King*, the musical about Martin Luther King, lost £3 million in a 6-week run in London, UK, ending on 2 June 1990, equalling the losses of *Ziegfeld*, also in London, in 1988.

### Lowest theatre attendance
The ultimate low attendance was achieved on 24 Nov 1983, when the comedy *Bag,*

1986) for *The Golden Horseshoe Revue*, a show staged at Disneyland Park, Anaheim, California, USA, from 16 July 1955 to 12 Oct 1986. It was seen by 16 million people.

### Longest-running musicals
*Cats* is the longest-running musical in the history of the West End (London, UK) and Broadway (New York, USA). It opened on 12 May 1981 at the New London Theatre, Drury Lane, London, UK, where the 6,935th show was performed on 3 July 1997.

On 19 June 1997, *Cats* became the longest-running musical on Broadway with 6,138 performances. It opened on 7 Oct 1982 at the Winter Gardens Theatre, New York, USA.

The longest-running musical show performed in the United Kingdom was *The Black and*

transferred to the Duchess Theatre on 2 Aug 1986 and finally ended on 5 Sept 1987, after 16¼ years and 6,761 performances.

### Longest-running one-man shows
The longest run for a one-man show is 849, by Victor Borge in *Comedy in Music* from 2 Oct 1953 to 21 Jan 1956 at the Golden Theater, Broadway, New York, USA.

The world aggregate record for one-man shows is 1,700 performances of *Brief Lives* by Roy Dotrice, at the Mayfair Theatre, London, UK, ending on 20 July 1974. Dotrice was on stage for more than 2½ hours per performance for this 17th-century monologue and required three hours for make-up and one hour for its removal. He thus spent an aggregate 40 weeks in the make-up chair during the run.

written by Bryony Lavery and directed by Michele Frankel, opened to an audience of nil at Grantham Leisure Centre, Lincs, UK.

### Largest arts festival
The world's largest arts festival is the annual Edinburgh Festival Fringe. In 1993, a record 582 groups gave 14,108 performances of 1,643 shows between 15 Aug and 4 Sept.

Nigel Tantrum of East Kilbride, Lanarkshire, UK, attended a record 169 separate performances at the 1994 Edinburgh Festival between 13 Aug and 4 Sept.

### Most ardent theatre-goers
Dr H. Howard Hughes, Prof. Emeritus of Texas Wesleyan College, Fort Worth, Texas, USA, attended 6,136 shows in the period from 1956 to 1987.

# SHORTEST PLAY 30 SECONDS

Britain's leading 'first nighter', Edward Sutro, saw 3,000 first-night productions from 1916 to 1956 and possibly more than 5,000 shows in his 60 years of theatre-going. The highest precisely recorded number of theatre attendances in the United Kingdom is 3,687 shows in 33 years from 28 March 1953 until his death on 10 Sept 1986 by John Iles of Salisbury, Wilts, UK.

Queen Victoria was the most assiduous royal patron of the British stage. Between the ages of 12 and 42, she attended the theatre as many as three times a week. For the last 40 years of her life, after the death of Prince Albert, she never entered a theatre again.

## Plays

### Longest play on record
John Arden wrote *The Non-Stop Connolly Show* in 1975, which took a full 26½ hours to perform in Dublin.

### Shortest play in world drama
Samuel Beckett, author of the most influential play in post-war drama, *Waiting For Godot* (1953), also wrote the shortest play, the 30-second *Breath* (1969).

### Most frequently adapted play
*A Day Well Spent*, written by John Oxenford in 1835, has been adapted as follows: *Einen Jux Will Er Sich Machen* by Johann Nestroy in 1842; *The Merchant of Yonkers* by Thornton Wilder in 1938; *The Matchmaker* by Thornton Wilder in 1954; *Hello Dolly* by Jerry Herman and Michael Stewart in 1963; *On The Razzle* by Tom Stoppard in 1981.

### Oldest practising playwright
George Bernard Shaw started as a dramatist at the age of 36 and wrote 57 plays. His last play, *Buoyant Billions*, was written in 1949 at the age of 93. There is an annual festival devoted to him at Niagara-on-the-Lake, Ontario, Canada.

### Most West End shows by one playwright
In 1908, Somerset Maugham had four plays running simultaneously at theatres in the West End of London. They were *Lady Fredrick* at the Court, *Mrs Dot* at the Comedy, *Jack Straw* at the Vaudeville and *The Explorer* at the Lyric.

### Most dramatic death on stage
In 1913 American conjuror Chung Ling Soo (William Elsworth Robinson) was shot on stage at the Wood Green Empire, London, UK, during his act, which included catching bullets, fired by his assistant, in a plate. It was never clear whether it was suicide or an accident.

## Musicals

### Highest insured show
When the musical *Barnum* opened at the London Palladium, UK, on 11 June 1981, it became the highest insured show in British theatre history. Producers put the total cover at £5 million, with £3 million of that covering Michael Crawford who walked the high-wire and slid down a rope extending from the topmost box to the stage. For the first time in the theatre's history, the boxes were out of commission as they were used during the performance.

### Longest chorus line
The longest chorus line in performing history numbered up to 120 in some of the early *Ziegfeld Follies*. In the finale of *A Chorus Line* on the night of 29 Sept 1983, 332 top-hatted 'strutters' performed on stage, though the stage was not long enough for them all to perform in one long chorus line.

On 28 March 1992, 543 members of the cast of *Showtime News*, a major production by Hampshire West Guides, performed a routine choreographed by professional dancer Sally Horsley at the Swan Centre, Eastleigh, Hants, UK.

**Left**
Samuel Beckett was born in Ireland and spent most of his life in Paris, France. As well as holding the record for the shortest play, he is the only Nobel Prize winner to appear in the cricketer's almanac, *Wisden*.

**Left**
The musical *A Chorus Line* holds the record for the most dancers on stage simultaneously in a musical, with 332 in one performance in the finale.

# Pop music

## Record sales

### Biggest-selling single
The biggest-selling single of all time is *White Christmas,* written by Irving Berlin and recorded by Bing Crosby on 29 May 1942. It is estimated that global sales exceed 30 million.

### Biggest-selling pop record
The highest claim for any pop record is an unaudited 25 million for *Rock Around the Clock,* which was copyrighted in 1953 by James E. Myers under the name Jimmy DeKnight and the late Max C. Freedman. It was recorded on 12 April 1954 by Bill Haley and the Comets.

### Biggest-selling single in the UK
The single *Do They Know It's Christmas?* which was written and produced by Bob Geldof and Midge Ure and recorded by Band Aid in 1984, had sales of 3.6 million. All profits from the record's sales went to the Live Aid Ethiopian Famine Relief Fund.

### Best-selling non-charity single in the UK
*Bohemian Rhapsody* by Queen has sold more than 2.5 million copies. It is the only single to top the UK chart on two separate occasions: in 1975, and after singer Freddie Mercury's death in 1991.

### Biggest-selling UK single worldwide
The single *I Want to Hold Your Hand* by The Beatles, which was released in 1963, has sold over 13 million copies worldwide.

### Biggest-selling album
The biggest-selling album of all time is *Thriller* by Michael Jackson with global sales of over 47 million copies to date.

### Biggest-selling album by a group
The album *Their Greatest Hits 1971–75* by The Eagles has sold more than an estimated 25 million copies worldwide.

### Biggest-selling debut album
*Jagged Little Pill* by Canadian vocalist Alanis Morissette has sold more than 27 million copies worldwide, making it the best-selling debut album of all time.

### Biggest-selling British albums
The best-selling album by a British act is *Dark Side of the Moon* by Pink Floyd with sales estimated at 23 million worldwide.

The album to have sold the greatest number of copies in the United Kingdom is *Sgt Pepper's Lonely Hearts Club Band* by The Beatles, with a reported 4.25 million sales since its release in June 1967.

The best-selling debut album in the United Kingdom is *Robson & Jerome* by Robson Green and Jerome Flynn, with sales of nearly 2.5 million by 1996.

### Best-selling film soundtrack
The best-selling movie soundtrack of all time is *Saturday Night Fever* (USA, 1978) with sales of over 30 million.

### Fastest-selling record
The fastest-selling record of all time is *John Fitzgerald Kennedy A Memorial Album,* which was recorded on 22 Nov 1963, the day of President Kennedy's assassination. Four million copies were sold at 99 cents in six days from 7–12 Dec 1963.

### Fastest selling album in the UK
The album *Robson & Jerome* by Robson Greene and Jerome Flynn sold 483,000 copies from 18 to 23 Dec 1995.

### Fastest selling charity singles
The single *We Are The World* by USA For Africa, the American version of Band Aid, reportedly sold 800,000 in just three days in March 1985.

The UK Band Aid's *Do They Know It's Christmas?* single sold 1.6 million copies in its first week in Dec 1984.

### Fastest selling non-charity UK single
The fastest-selling non-charity single in the UK is Babylon Zoo's *Spaceman.* Released on 15 Jan 1996, it entered the chart at No. 1, after selling 400,000 copies in six days, 28.8% of all singles sold that week.

### Most successful US debut
Mariah Carey was the first act to top the US chart with her first five singles, breaking the record of four established by the Jackson Five in 1970.

### Most successful solo artists
Elvis Presley holds the record for the most No.1 hits by a solo artist since the beginning of the rock era in 1955, with 18 in the US and 17 in the UK.

Bing Crosby started his solo recording career in 1931 and had accumulated 156 hits by 1940. He recorded an estimated 2,600 songs in his lifetime and had 317 hits in America before the rock era.

### Most successful solo British artist
Elton John is the most successful British solo artist worldwide. Since his debut in 1970, he has had six UK and seven US No. 1 albums. On the US singles chart he has scored at least one hit every year since 1970 and in the United Kingdom he has had at least one hit a year since 1971.

### Most successful group
The Beatles have achieved more sales than any other group. The band from Liverpool, UK, consisted of George Harrison, John Lennon, Paul McCartney and Richard Starkey, alias Ringo Starr. All-time sales have been estimated by EMI at over 1 billion discs and tapes.

### Most hit albums
Elvis Presley holds the record for having had more hit albums than anyone else, with 97.

### Advance sales
The greatest worldwide advance sale for a single is 2.1 million for *Can't Buy Me Love* by The Beatles, released on 21 March 1964.

The UK record for advance sales of an album is 1.1 million for *Welcome to the Pleasure Dome,* the debut album by Frankie Goes To Hollywood, released in 1984.

## Artists

### Most successful UK debuts
Kylie Minogue's first 11 singles reached the top five of the the UK chart and her debut album *Kylie* topped the chart in July 1988.

In Sept 1994, *Saturday Night* by Whigfield, entered the UK chart at No. 1 making her the first new artist to debut in that position.

### Most hit singles
The Bee Gees have had 35 hits, the most achieved by any family act, in a career which has spanned more than 30 years—the longest time span for any artist producing new material. The brothers have had five No. 1s in the UK chart and another four of their songs have reached No. 1 recorded by other artists.

### Youngest artist to reach No. 1 in USA
Stevie Wonder was only 13 years old when his debut album *Little Stevie Wonder— The Twelve Year Old Genius* went to the top of the US chart.

### Oldest artist to reach No. 1 in USA
Jazz musician and singer Louis Armstrong was almost 63 years old when *Hello Dolly!* reached No. 1 in the USA.

# MOST HIT ALBUMS 97

**ENTERED THE CHARTS AT NO. 1, SELLING 400,000 IN THE FIRST SIX DAYS**

**Left**
The Spice Girls relax
during their 1997
Japanese tour. Mel B,
or Scary Spice,
shows off her most
distinguished mark:
her pierced tongue.

**WAS THE FIRST EVER BRITISH DEBUT ALBUM THAT REACHED NO. 1 IN THE USA**

## The Spice Girls

The Spice Girls—Melanie Janine Brown
(Scary Spice), Melanie Jayne Chisholm
(Sporty Spice), Emma Lee Bunton (Baby
Spice), Geraldine Estelle Halliwell (Ginger
Spice) and Victoria Adams (Posh Spice)—
have enjoyed levels of popularity not seen
since the days of The Beatles. They had their
first big break with the single *Wannabe* after
having worked together for three years, and
since then have achieved a string of hits
both in the United Kingdom and abroad.

**Biggest selling single by a female group**
*Wannabe*, released in July 1996, spent
seven weeks at No. 1 in the UK in July and
Aug 1996, selling 1.2 million copies. It went
on to top the US chart for four weeks, selling
more than 2 million copies and was No. 1 in
a further 30 countries around the world.

**First three singles over 1 million**
The Spice Girls are the only group to have
had each of their first three singles pass
the 1 million sales mark.

**Most successful run of No. 1 hits**
The Spice Girls are the only group to have
their first four releases hit the No. 1 spot:
*Wannabe* spent seven weeks at No. 1
from July 1996, *Say You'll Be There* spent
two weeks in the top slot from Oct 1996,
*2 Become 1* was No. 1 for three weeks as
was their double A side hit *Mama/Who Do
You Think You Are* in Dec 1996.

**Most successful US debut by UK act**
Their single *Say You'll Be There* entered
the US chart at No. 5 in May 1997,
becoming the highest new entry in the
US chart ever by a UK act.

**Longest No. 1 album in the 1990s**
*Spice* topped the album chart in the UK in
Nov 1996 and has spent 15 weeks at No. 1
to May 1997, the longest running No. 1 of
the 1990s in the UK.

**Fastest selling album**
The album *Spice* reached No. 1 in the
charts of 14 countries and sold 12 million
copies worldwide in six months, making
it the fastest-selling album ever by a
British act.

**Most successful debut album by UK act**
The most successful debut album by
a UK act in the USA was *Spice*. It topped
the US charts for four weeks (as of June
1997) and became the only debut album
by a wholly British group which has
gone to No. 1.

# Pop charts

**From left to right**
In May 1997, Meat Loaf's album *Bat Out of Hell* had spent a record total of 472 weeks on the UK album chart.

The Beatles' album *Sgt Pepper's Lonely Hearts Club Band* is the biggest selling album ever in the UK. The Beatles also hold the record for the most No. 1 hit singles in the UK, with 17.

Nigel Kennedy's recording of Vivaldi's *Four Seasons* has been in the UK album charts for 81 weeks, a record for a classical album.

Everything But The Girl released a dance re-mix of their single *Missing* in 1995 which went on to become a massive hit both in the UK and the USA. It was on the US singles chart for a record-breaking 55 consecutive weeks.

## UK charts; singles

The UK singles chart was introduced by the *New Musical Express* (*NME*) on 14 Nov 1952 as a Top 12. Since then, the chart has become a Top 75 and is now compiled by CIN, with 21,000 singles charting for more than 5,000 artists.

### Most weeks on singles chart

Elvis Presley's 111 hits have spent a total of 1,149 weeks on the UK singles chart since *Heartbreak Hotel* débuted on 11 May 1956.

The group Oasis had nine singles that spent 134 weeks on the singles chart in 1996, a record total for a calendar year.

The longest time that a single has spent on the chart is 124 weeks, for *My Way* by Frank Sinatra, which entered and re-entered the chart no fewer than 10 times between 1969 and 1994.

### Most consecutive weeks on the chart

The most consecutive weeks on the singles chart is 56, for Engelbert Humperdinck's *Release Me*, from 26 Jan 1967.

Elvis Presley is the artist with the most consecutive weeks on chart. His 13 hit singles from *A Mess of Blues* in 1960 to *One More Broken Heart for Sale* in 1963 spent an unbroken 144 weeks on the chart.

### Most hit singles

Cliff Richard holds the record for the most hit singles, with 119 to May 1996.

The Jam hold the record for the most hits in one calendar year, with 14 in 1983. However, all of these were old hits, re-issued after the band's demise.

The Wedding Present are the only act to chart as many as 12 new hits in one year, a feat they achieved in 1992.

### Most Top Ten hit singles

Cliff Richard has scored an unprecedented 63 Top Ten hits between 1958 and 1993.

Madonna is the artist who has achieved the most consecutive Top Ten hits in the chart. All 32 of her single releases between *Like A Virgin* in 1984 to *Secret* in 1994 went into the Top Ten.

### Most No. 1 singles

The Beatles and Elvis Presley hold the record for the most No. 1 hit singles, with 17 each.

The record for the most consecutive No. 1s is held by The Beatles, who had 11 in a row between 1963 and 1966 (from *From Me to You* through to *Yellow Submarine*).

### Most weeks at No. 1

*I Believe* by Frankie Laine held the No. 1 position for 18 weeks (non-consecutive) from April 1953.

### Most consecutive weeks at No. 1

Bryan Adams spent 16 consecutive weeks at No. 1 from July to Oct 1991 with *(Everything I Do) I Do It For You*, taken from the film *Robin Hood: Prince of Thieves* (USA, 1991).

### Most charted song

*Unchained Melody*, written by Alex North and Hy Zaret, has been a hit in a total of eight

different versions, five of which have made the Top Ten. It has been a No. 1 hit by three separate acts: Jimmy Young in 1955, the Righteous Brothers in 1990 and Robson Green and Jerome Flynn in 1995.

The only other song to reach No. 1 in three versions is *You'll Never Walk Alone*, from the Rogers and Hammerstein musical *Carousel*. Gerry and the Pacemakers took it to No. 1 in 1963, as did the Crowd in 1985 and Robson Green and Jerome Flynn in 1996.

### Longest gap between chart hits

On the basis that re-issues and re-entries do not count as a hit, Perez Prado and his Orchestra waited 36 years 27 days between their hit *Patricia*, which topped the UK charts on the 7 Nov 1958, and their next hit *Guaglione*, which entered the charts on the 4 Dec 1994 after it had been used in an advertising campaign for Guinness stout.

## UK charts; albums

The UK album chart began on 8 Nov 1958 and has featured more than 14,000 albums by some 3,500 performers.

### Most weeks on album chart

The album with the most weeks on the chart is *Bat Out of Hell* by Meat Loaf, with 472 weeks to May 1997.

The most weeks on the chart for a classical album is 81, for Vivaldi's *Four Seasons* by Nigel Kennedy and the English Chamber Orchestra to Dec 1993.

The act with the most weeks on the album chart is The Beatles whose 29 hit albums have spent a total of 1,200 weeks on chart as of May 1997.

### Most No. 1 albums

The Beatles have had the most No. 1 albums in the UK with 14.

### Most weeks at No. 1 on album chart

The film soundtrack to *South Pacific* (USA, 1958), was the first No. 1 album in the UK and held the position for a record 70 consecutive weeks, eventually spending 115 weeks at No. 1.

## US charts; singles

Charts showing the relative popularity of records and songs can be traced back to the early 1890s, but it was not until 20 July 1940 that *Billboard* magazine published the first 'official' record sales chart. The listing was headed by the single *I'll Never Smile Again* by Tommy Dorsey (featuring Frank Sinatra) and contained 10 songs. Gradually the number of positions increased until the

# 111 HITS ON CHARTS FOR 1,149 WEEKS

chart became a Top 100 in Aug 1958, the length it remains to this day.

### Most weeks on singles chart
*White Christmas* by Bing Crosby spent a total of 86 weeks on the chart between 1942 and 1962.

### Most consecutive weeks on chart
The remix by record producer Todd Terry of *Missing* by the British group Everything But The Girl accumulated a record-breaking 55 consecutive weeks on the US singles chart from Aug 1995.

### Most hit singles
Elvis Presley has had a record 149 hit singles on the Billboard Hot 100 from 1956 to 1997.

### Most No. 1 singles
The Beatles have had the most No.1 hits ever, with 20.

### Most weeks at No. 1
*Near You* by Francis Craig topped the chart for 17 weeks in 1947.

Since 1955, the longest chart-topper has been *I Will Always Love You* by Whitney Houston—No. 1 for 14 weeks in 1992.

Elvis Presley's 18 No. 1 records have been in the top of the charts for 80 weeks.

### Longest chart span
Louis Armstrong first appeared on a Billboard chart on 6 April 1946. His most recent entry to the listings came in 1988, 17 years after his death, with the single *What A Wonderful World*. Armstrong had appeared on an even earlier chart in 1926

with *Muskrat Ramble*, thus taking his span of hits to more than 61 years.

### Most complete domination of the chart
On 4 April 1964, The Beatles held the Top 5 positions on the Top 100 and placed a further seven titles elsewhere on the chart. In descending order the Top 5 were: *Can't Buy Me Love, Twist and Shout, I Want To Hold Your Hand, Please Please Me*.

## US charts; albums
### Most weeks on album chart
*Dark Side of the Moon* by Pink Floyd has been on the Billboard chart for over 1,000 weeks, 741 of which were in the Top 200, after which it was placed in the separate catalogue chart where it remains.

### Most No. 1 albums
The most No. 1 albums by a group is 18, by The Beatles.

Elvis Presley has had a record nine solo albums at No. 1.

The best-selling female singer of all time, with the most No. 1 albums (6), and most hit albums (43 between 1963 and Oct 1994), is Barbra Streisand.

The only act to have four No. 1 albums in a calendar year is the Monkees who topped the chart with each of their first four albums in 1967.

### Most weeks at No.1 on album chart
The soundtrack album of Rogers and Hammerstein's stage musical *South Pacific* spent 69 weeks (un-consecutive) at No. 1 in the USA, from May 1949.

## Best-selling US albums

1   *Thriller* (1982)
    Michael Jackson
2   *Their Greatest Hits 1971–75* (1976)
    The Eagles
3   *Rumours* (1977)
    Fleetwood Mac
4   *Led Zeppelin IV* (1971)
    Led Zeppelin
5   *Jagged Little Pill* (1995)
    Alanis Morissette
6   *Boston* (1970)
    Boston
7   *Cracked Rear View* (1995)
    Hootie and the Blowfish
8   *Born in The USA* (1984)
    Bruce Springsteen
9   *Hotel California* (1976)
    The Eagles
10   *The Bodyguard* (1992)
    Original Soundtrack

Michael Jackson's *Thriller* rapidly established itself as the best-selling album of all-time, both in America and worldwide. Over 24 million copies have been sold in the USA, including a million in Los Angeles alone.

The Eagles are the only act to have two albums in the top ten and the only one represented by a 'best of' package. Their *Greatest Hits 1971–75*, released in 1976 has sold over 22 million copies and may ultimately overtake *Thriller*.

The best selling album of the 1990s is Canadian singer-songwriter Alanis Morissette's *Jagged Little Pill*, which has sold 16 million copies in little over two years.

## Best-selling UK albums

1   *Sgt. Pepper's Lonely Hearts Club Band* (1967)
    The Beatles
2   *(What's The Story) Morning Glory* (1995)
    Oasis
3   *Bad* (1987)
    Michael Jackson
4   *Greatest Hits* (1981)
    Queen
5   *Brothers In Arms* (1985)
    Dire Straits
6   *Stars* (1991)
    Simply Red
7   *Thriller* (1982)
    Michael Jackson
8   *Bridge Over Troubled Water* (1970)
    Simon and Garfunkel
9   *Spice* (1996)
    The Spice Girls
10   *Jagged Little Pill* (1996)
    Alanis Morissette

*Sgt. Pepper's Lonely Hearts Club Band* is the UK's biggest-selling album. It makes regular appearances in the Top 200 album chart and adds to its four million sales at the rate of 50,000 a year. If it is ever to be overtaken, it is likely to be by Oasis' *(What's The Story) Morning Glory*, which has topped 3.9 million in under two years.

Queen's *Greatest Hits* is the only album on the list to spend fewer than ten weeks at No. 1.

Dire Strait's *Brothers In Arms* was the first album to sell a million copies on CD.

*Jagged Little Pill* by Alanis Morissette is the biggest selling album ever by a female soloist.

## Booker Prize for Fiction

### Most nominations to one person
Most nominations to be awarded to one person are six to Iris Murdoch over 18 years for her novels *The Nice and the Good* (1969), *Bruno's Dream* (1970), *The Black Prince* (1973), *The Good Apprentice* (1985) and *The Book and the Brotherhood* (1987). She won in 1978 with *The Sea, the Sea*.

### Most nominations without winning
The most nominations without winning are three, held jointly by Timothy Mo with *Sour Sweet* (1982), *An Insular Possession* (1986) and *The Redundancy of Courage* (1991), and Brian Moore with *The Doctor's Wife* (1976), *The Colour of Blood* (1987) and *Lies of Silence* (1990).

### Oldest winner
The oldest winner is William Golding, who was 69 when he was awarded the prize in 1980 for his book *Rites of Passage*.

### Youngest winner
Ben Okri was 32 when he won in 1991 with *The Famished Road*.

## Grammy awards

### Most Grammy awards
The Hungarian-born British conductor Sir Georg Solti has won an all-time record 31 individual awards since 1958, including a special Trustees' award presented in 1967.

The most Grammy Awards won by a solo pop performer is 17, by Stevie Wonder.

The most Grammy Awards won by a pop group is eight, by the 5th Dimension.

The Grammy Award shared by the largest number of people was the one presented to the 46 members of the Chicago Symphony Orchestra, USA.

The greatest number won in one year is eight, by Michael Jackson, in 1984.

### First Grammy won by a US First Lady
Hillary Rodham Clinton won the 1997 Grammy for Best Spoken Word or Non-Musical Album, for a three-hour reading of her book on child rearing, *It Takes A Village*, which at the time of the award had spent five months on the US best-sellers list.

### Most RIAA certificates
Since the Recording Industry Association of America (RIAA) introduced its awards in 1958, Elvis Presley holds the record for the most platinum certificates, with 54.

The group with the most platinum certificates are The Beatles who have 33. They also hold the record for the most multiplatinum albums, with 13.

The recording artist with the most certified titles ever is Elvis Presley with 182: 111 gold, 54 platinum, 17 multiplatinum.

## Oscars

### Most Oscar nominations
*All About Eve* (USA, 1950) had 14 nominations, beating the previous holder *Gone With the Wind* (USA, 1939) which had 13. *All About Eve* eventually won six Oscars, including Best Film, Best Director (Joseph L. Mankiewicz) and Best Supporting Actor (George Sanders).

### Most consecutive Oscar nominations
The most consecutive Oscar nominations have gone to Aardman Animation from Bristol, UK, who received six from 1991 to 1997 for Best Short Animated Film.

### Most nominations with no awards
Most nominations for a film that did not win any awards were for *Turning Point* (USA, 1977) and *The Colour Purple* (USA, 1986). Each received 11 nominations.

### Most nominated star never to have won
Richard Burton never won an Oscar but had six nominations for the films *My Cousin Rachel* (USA, 1952); *The Robe* (USA, 1953); *The Spy Who Came in from the Cold* (GB, 1965); *Who's Afraid of Virginia Woolf* (USA, 1966); *Anne of the Thousand Days* (GB, 1970) and *Equus* (GB, 1977).

### Most Oscar awards
Walt Disney has won more Oscars than any other individual. His total consists of 20 statuettes and 12 other plaques and certificates, which includes awards given posthumously.

In 1953, Walt Disney won four Oscars—the most at a single presentation—for Best Cartoon *Toot, Whistle, Plunk and Boom*; Best Documentary Short *The Alaskan Eskimo*; Best Documentary Feature *The Living Desert* and Best Two-Reel Short *Bear Country*.

### Most Best Actress awards
Katharine Hepburn won four Oscars in a starring role, for *Morning Glory* (USA, 1933), *Guess Who's Coming to Dinner* (USA, 1967), *The Lion in Winter* (1968) and *On Golden Pond* (USA, 1981). She has been nominated

# MOST GRAMMY AWARDS 31

12 times. She also holds the record for the longest award-winning career of 48 years.

## Most Oscar-winning film
The film that has won the most awards is *Ben Hur* (1959) with 11: Best Picture; Best Director; Best Actor; Best Supporting Actor; Cinematography; Art Direction; Sound; Music Score; Film Editing; Special Effects; Costume.

The most awards won by a British film went to *Ghandi* (1982) with eight. It received awards for Best Picture, Best Actor, Best Director, Best Original Screenplay, Cinematography, Film Editing, Costume Design and Art Direction.

## Most Best Actor awards
Six actors have won two Oscars for Best Actor. Spencer Tracy won for *Captains Courageous* (USA, 1937) and *Boys Town* (USA, 1938); Fredric March for *Dr Jekyll and Mr Hyde* (USA, 1932) and *The Best Years of Our Lives* (USA, 1946); Gary Cooper for *Sergeant York* (USA, 1941) and *High Noon* (USA, 1952); Marlon Brando for *On the*

*Waterfront* (USA, 1954) and *The Godfather* (USA, 1972); Dustin Hoffman for *Kramer Vs. Kramer* (USA, 1979) and *Rain Man* (USA, 1988); and Tom Hanks for *Philadelphia* (USA, 1993) and *Forrest Gump* (USA, 1994). Tracy received nine nominations during his career, as opposed to seven for Brando, six for Hoffman and five each for Cooper and March.

## Individual creative achievement awards
Cedric Gibbons of MGM film studios won 11 awards for Art Direction.

The most won by a woman are eight, by costume designer Edith Head.

## Only non-professional winners
Only two non-professionals have won acting Oscars. Canadian war veteran Harold Russell received an Oscar for Best Supporting Actor for his role as the handless ex-soldier in *The Best Years of Our Lives* (USA, 1946) (Russell had both his arms blown off in combat). Cambodian refugee Dr Haing S. Nigor won an Oscar for Best Supporting Actor for his role as a victim of the Cambodian Pol Pot regime in *The Killing Fields* (GB, 1984).

## Three generations of Oscar winners
The Hustons are the only family to have three generations of Oscar winners. Walter Huston won Best Supporting Actor for *The Treasure of the Sierra Madre* (USA, 1948). His son John won Best Director for the same film and John's daughter Angelica won best Supporting Actress for *Prizzi's Honour* (USA, 1985).

## Only Oscar-winner disqualification
The only Oscar winner disqualification was in 1968 when it was revealed that Best Documentary *The Young Americans* had been shown theatrically the preceding calendar year. The Oscar was recalled.

## Most versatile personalities
Only three performers have won Oscar, Emmy, Tony and Grammy awards: the actress Helen Hayes, the composer Richard Rodgers, and the actress/singer/dancer Rita Moreno.

Barbra Streisand has received Oscar, Grammy and Emmy awards in addition to a special 'Star of the Decade' Tony award.

**Left**
The British creators of the animated characters of Wallace and Gromit have won a record six consecutive Oscar nominations for their films.

## Largest works
### Largest painting
A 8,586-m² (92,419-ft²) painting of the sea was made by ID Cultur at The ArenA, Amsterdam, Netherlands, to mark the venue's opening on 14 Aug 1996.

The largest British painting, the *Triumph of Peace and Liberty* by Sir James Thornhill at the Royal Naval College, Greenwich, London, UK, is 32.3 x 15.4 m (106 x 51 ft).

### Largest mural
The Pueblo Levee Project in Colorado, USA, made the largest mural in the world, at 16,554.8 m² (178,200 ft²).

The largest British mural was 1,709 m² (18,396 ft²). It was painted on the Stage V wall, BBC Television Centre, London, in Sept 1991 and designed by Vicky Askew.

### Largest poster
A 21,936-m² (236,119-ft²) poster was made by the Community Youth Club, Hong Kong, on 26 Oct 1993. It was put on display at Victoria Park, Hong Kong.

### Largest inflatable castle installation
A 12-m (39-ft) tall and 19-m (62-ft) wide inflatable castle, entitled *Tight Roaring Circle,* designed by Dana Caspersen and William Forsythe, was erected in the Roundhouse, London, UK, in 1997.

## Sculptures and carvings
### Largest sculpture
The mounted figures of Jefferson Davis, Gen. Robert Edward Lee and Gen. Thomas (Stonewall) Jackson on the face of Stone

Mountain, near Atlanta, Georgia, USA, are 27.4 m (90 ft) high and cover 0.5 ha (1.33 acres). Sculptor Walker Kirtland Hancock was with assistant Roy Faulkner and others carving the sculpture with a thermo-jet torch for 8 years 174 days from 1963 to 1972.

The largest scrap-metal sculpture was built by Sudhir Deshpande of Nashik, India, and unveiled in Feb 1990. Entitled *Powerful,* it is 17 m (55 ft 9 in) tall and weighs 27 tonnes.

### Longest sand sculpture
The longest sand sculpture was entitled the *GTE Directories Ultimate Sand Castle.* It was built by over 10,000 volunteers at Myrtle Beach, South Carolina, USA, on 31 May 1991 and was 26,375.9 m (86,535 ft) long.

### Tallest sand sculpture
The *Invitation to Fairyland* was 17.12 m (56 ft 2 in) high and was built by 2,000 local volunteers at Kaseda, Japan, on 26 July 1989 under the supervision of Sand Sculptors International, San Diego, USA.

### Hill carvings
In Aug 1968, a 100-m (330-ft) tall figure was discovered on a hill above Tarapacá, Chile.

The 'Long Man' at Wilmington, E Sussex, UK, is 68 m (226 ft) long.

### Highest price paid for a sculpture
*Petite Danseuse de Quatorze Ans* by Edgar Degas was sold for $10,800,000 (£6,506,024) on 12 Nov 1996 at Sotheby's, New York, USA.

*The Dancing Faun* by Adriaen de Vries sold for £6,200,000 on 7 Dec 1989 at Sotheby's, London, UK.

## Most valuable works
### Most valuable painting
Leonardo da Vinci's *Mona Lisa (La Gioconda)* was painted *c.* 1503–07. Now in the Louvre, Paris, France, it was assessed for insurance purposes at $100 million (£36 million) in 1962. King Francis I of France first bought the painting in 1517 for 4,000 gold florins (about £124,000).

### Highest price paid for a painting
*Portrait du Dr Gachet* by Vincent Van Gogh sold for $75,000,000 (£44,378,696) on 15 May 1990 at Christie's, New York, USA.

### Highest price in a UK auction house
*Dans la Prairie* by Claude Monet sold for £13 million on 28 June 1988 at Sotheby's, London, UK.

### Highest price for a landscape
*Au Moulin de la Galette* by Pierre Auguste Renoir sold at auction for $71,000,000 (£42,011,832) on 17 May 1990 at Sotheby's, New York, USA.

### Highest price for an abstract
*Los Noces de Pierrette,* 1905, by Pablo Picasso sold for F.Fr.315,000,000 (£33,123,028) on 30 Nov 1989 at Binoche et Godeau, Paris, France.

### Highest price for a still-life
*Nature Morte—les Grosses Pommes* by Paul Cézanne sold for $26,000,000 (£16,993,464) on 11 May 1993 at Sotheby's, New York, USA.

### Highest price for a watercolour
*Acrobate et Jeune Arlequin* by Pablo Picasso sold for £19 million on 28 Nov 1988 at Christie's, London, UK.

# Architecture
# and design

# New building projects

**Right**
The Pudong New Area, Shanghai, China, is the world's largest urban complex currently under construction. The building programme includes the Nanpu and Yangpu bridges, ring roads, an international airport and residential areas. By 2010 the multi-functional urban area will include suburban farming projects.

JIN MAO BUILDING

金茂大厦
JIN MAO BUILDING

金茂大厦基地面积 23260 平方米，建筑总面积
230208 平方米，地面 88 层，建筑高度 360 米，顶
高 420.5 米，地下三层，面积 57151 平方米。
金茂大厦主楼 1-52 层为办公用房 51-85 层为五星
级宾馆，86-88 层为俱乐部和观光层，裙楼为金融、
商业、会议、服务、餐饮、展览和康乐等多功能设施。
金茂大厦体现了中国传统文化与现代高新科技融
合的特点，既是中国古老塔式建筑的延伸和发展，又
是海派建筑风格在浦东的再现，既与浦西外滩建筑群
又与东方明珠电视塔南北相对。

范围

The city will have state-of-the-art communications and transport and will be completed by 2005. The new seat of Malaysia's government is named after the nation's first prime minister, Tunku Abdul Rahman Putra Al-Haq.

**Fastest growing city**

In 1980 Shenzhen, Guangdong province, China, had about 30,000 inhabitants. In the same year, the town, which is on the border with Hong Kong, was designated a Special Economic Zone and began its development.

Shenzhen has now been transformed into a modern city dominated by skyscrapers and has the highest standard of living in China.

Major building projects have included developing the entire infrastructure to the standard of a major city within 15 years, the construction of a business district, 300 major hotels, an international airport, highways, residential quarters and 35 million m$^2$ (377 million ft$^2$) of commercial buildings.

At the end of 1995, Shenzhen had 3,450,000 inhabitants, including 2,450,000 non-permanent residents. This represents an annual increase of 43% since 1980.

**Tallest office building**

The Universal Financial Centre, in the new Pudong business district of Shanghai, China, will overtop Petronas Towers, Kuala Lumpur, on completion in 2001.

Work on the foundations of the Centre began in Aug 1997 and it is planned that the

## Urban architecture

### Largest urban complex

Pudong New Area, which faces the Chinese city of Shanghai across the Huangpu River, covers an area of 520 km$^2$ (201 miles$^2$) and in 1995 had a population of 1.4 million.

The site has a strategic position—sited where China's principal waterway, the Chang Jiang (Yangtze), meets the coast. The New Area comprises the Lujiazui finance and trade zone, the Jinqiao export-processing zone, the Waigaoqiao free trade zone and the Zhangjiang hi-tech zone.

Construction began in April 1990 and by June 1997, 2,660 foreign enterprises were established. In the finance and trade zone over 80 structures are in progress including what will be the world's tallest building.

By 2010 an open multi-functional modern urban area will offer China's most advanced infrastructure which will include suburban farming projects.

A vital part of the scheme is the new port at Gaoqiao, which, by 2020, will have 6.2 km (nearly 4 miles) of quays and will be Shanghai's main port.

### World's first 'intelligent' capital

The world's first 'intelligent' capital city is being developed at Putrajaya, 32 km (20 miles) south of Kuala Lumpur, Malaysia.

The entire 4,400-hectare (10,870-acre) site lies in a 15 x 50 km (9 x 31 mile) corridor, largely through virgin jungle, from Kuala Lumpur to the city's new international airport at Sepang.

building will be the new record-holder for the millennium. The Centre will be 454 m (1,489 ft 6 in) high and have 95 storeys of offices and hotel accommodation above ground level and three storeys below. It will contain a total area of 325,718 m$^2$ (3,506 million ft$^2$) of floorspace.

### World's largest city-centre building site

Federal investment in a new Chancellery, embassies and government buildings is transforming the derelict city centre of Berlin, Germany, into a showcase new capital. The city will also acquire two new mainline rail stations, while a new airport will be built to the south. In June 1997, there were 320 major building projects under construction involving a massive total investment of as much as DM 50 billion (£17.3 billion).

# CONSTRUCTION PROJECT £12.78 BILLION

CHANG JIANG, AND WILL INVOLVE THE RESETTLEMENT OF 1,131,800 PEOPLE

## Transportation
### Largest transport project
The largest single construction project in the world is the new Hong Kong Airport at Chek Lap Kok. It is built on a 1,670-ha (4,127-acre) artificial island with 1,326 ha (3,277 acres) of its area constituting reclaimed land.

The total value of the project, including new road and rail links, is £12.78 billion (excluding the cost of the second runway). The airport is due to open in 1998. The airport is linked to the centre of Hong Kong by the £550 million Tsing Ma Bridge, the world's largest combined road/rail bridge, which opened in April 1997.

### UK's largest construction project
The largest single construction project in the United Kingdom is the £2.6 billion Jubilee Line Extension on the London Underground system which will connect the West End at Green Park to the regenerated commercial district of London Docklands, to the east of the city, via the South Bank of the River Thames.

It is due to open in the autumn of 1998. The extension runs for 12.4 km (7 miles 1,232 yd) of its 16-km (9-mile 1,584-yd) length in twin tube tunnels running up to 30 m (98 ft) below ground level. Construction has involved shifting 3 million tonnes of spoil.

The length of the automatic platform-edge doors on the below-ground stations, used for the first time on the London Underground, totals 2.25 km (1 mile 704 yd).

The 118 escalators will double the number on the Underground, while 34 lifts will make the extension the world's most accessible underground line for the disabled.

## Infrastructure
### Largest urban sewerage scheme
The £2-billion Cairo Wastewater Scheme in Egypt is due for completion in 2010 after 26 years of construction. The first phase involves a 12-km (7½-mile) main on the east bank of the River Nile and 3 km (2 miles) of branch sewers. Design and construction is by a consortium of British and US firms.

### Largest civil engineering project
The Three Gorges—Qutang, Wuxia and Xiling—is an area of scenic beauty on China's largest river, the Chang Jiang (Yangtze). This civil engineering project will prevent flood disasters and harness the river for Hydro Electric Power (HEP). A diversion dam (185 m or 607 ft high) will have storage of 39,300 million m$^3$ (1,388 billion ft$^3$). The HEP station will be the largest in the world. There are 153 new towns under construction for resettlement.

The scheme will involve the most people ever relocated for a single engineering

RUN FOR 12.4 KM AND HAS INVOLVED SHIFTING 3 MILLION TONNES OF SPOIL

project. According to official Chinese figures, 1,131,800 people will be relocated from inundated areas. In all, 13 cities, 13 county towns, 140 other towns and 4,500 villages will be inundated.

The entire project now beginning will take 17 years. Some 1,084 km$^2$ (418 miles$^2$) will be inundated. Hundreds of historic sites will be moved to museums or relocated higher up the gorge.

The Three Gorges Hydroelectric Station will beat the existing record-holder, the Itaipu HEP station in Brazil. The Three Gorges project will have installed 26 water turbogenerators with 700,000 kW capacity each and a total of 18.2 million kW in one single station—40% more than the capacity of Itaipu.

# Commercial architecture

## Largest spaces

### Largest commercial buildings

In terms of floor area, the largest commercial building under one roof is the flower-auction building, Bloemenveiling Aalsmeer (VBA), in Aalsmeer, Netherlands, which covers 710,000 m² (7.6 million ft²).

The most capacious building is the Boeing Company's main assembly plant in Everett, Washington, USA, which was 5,564,200 m³ (196,476,000 ft³) when it was completed in 1968. Subsequent expansion schemes have increased the volume of the building to 13.4 million m³ (472 million ft³).

In the United Kingdom, the Ford Parts Centre at Daventry, Northants, covers an area of 142,674 m² (1.5 million ft²). It was opened on 6 Sept 1972 at a cost of c. £8 million, and 1,300 people are employed there.

### Largest industrial building

The largest multi-level industrial building forming one discrete structure is the container freight station of Asia Terminals Ltd at Hong Kong's Kwai Chung container port. The 15-level building was completed in 1994 and has a total area of 865,937 m² (9,320,867 ft²). It measures 276 x 292 m (906 x 958 ft) and is 109.5 m (359 ft 3 in) tall. The entire area of each floor of the building is directly accessible by 14-m (46-ft) container trucks, and there are 26.84 km (16 miles 1,179 yd) of roadway and 2,609 container-truck parking spaces.

### Largest exhibition centre

The Hanover Fair Exhibition Complex in Lower Saxony, Germany, has 478,000 m² (5,154,830 ft²) of covered space in 26 halls.

### Largest British exhibition centre

The National Exhibition Centre, Birmingham, W Midlands, which opened in 1976, has 16 halls covering 158,000 m² (1.7 million ft²), a 12,300-seat arena, parking for 21,000 cars, two hotels, numerous restaurants and a lake on a 250-ha (618-acre) site. A further four halls, containing an additional 30,000 m² (344,450 ft²), are under construction and are due to open in 1998.

### Largest urban development

The London Docklands Canary Wharf project is part of the world's largest regeneration project. More than 2.35 million m² (25.32 million ft²) of commercial-development space and over 24,300 new homes have been completed or are under construction over an area of 22 km² (8½ miles²). Over £12.6 billion will have been invested from the private and public sector, including £4.5 billion in new public transport links such as the Jubilee Line Underground extension.

### Largest building project

The largest public-works project of modern times is the Madinat Al-Jubail Al-Sinaiyah project in Saudi Arabia. The construction of the new industrial city was begun in 1976, and the site covers 1,014,600,000 m² (250,705 acres). At the peak of its construction, nearly 52,000 workers were employed, representing 62 nationalities. A total of 270 million m³ (9,535 million ft³) of earth has been dredged and moved—enough to construct a 1-m (3-ft 3-in) high belt around the Earth's Equator seven times over.

**Right**
The main assembly plant at Boeing in Everett, Washington, USA, is the building with the greatest capacity. The indoor floor area is 39.8 ha (98.3 acres) and the entire site covers some 410 ha (1,025 acres).

# TALLEST OFFICE BLOCK 451.9 M

## IN GERMANY WITH 478,000 M² OF COVERED SPACE

## PROJECT, WHICH COVERS OVER 2.35 MILLION M²

## Largest offices

### Largest administrative building
The Pentagon, in Arlington, Virginia, USA, covers the largest ground area of any office building. Built to house the US Defence Department's offices, it was completed on 15 Jan 1943 and cost an estimated $83 million (£29.7 million). Its five storeys enclose a floor area of 604,000 m² (149.2 acres).

### Largest office buildings
The largest rentable office complex is the World Trade Center in New York City, USA, with a total of 1,115,000 m² (12 million ft²) of rentable space available in the seven buildings, including 406,000 m² (4.37 million ft²) in each of the twin towers. There are 99 lifts in each tower and 43,600 windows containing 183,000 m² (600,000 ft²) of glass.

The largest single open-plan office in the United Kingdom is owned by British Gas West Midlands at Solihull, W Midlands, and was built by Spooners (Hull) Ltd in 1962. It currently measures 230 x 49 m (753 x 160 ft) and can accommodate 2,125 staff.

### Tallest office
In March 1996, the Petronas Towers in Malaysia overtook the Sears Tower's 22-year-old record as the world's tallest office building. The 73.5-m (241-ft) stainless steel pinnacles placed atop the 88-storey towers brought their height to 451.9 m (1,483 ft).

The Canary Wharf tower in London Docklands is the tallest British building, at 243.8 m (800 ft). The tallest of three towers at the development, a 50-storey building, resembling an obelisk, was designed by US architect Cesar Pelli and consists of nearly 16,000 pieces of steel. It overtook the National Westminster tower block by 61 m (200 ft) when it was finished in Nov 1990.

## Real estate
### Most expensive office locations
The world's most expensive office location is Bombay (Mumbai), India. Quoted rents for prime space in the central business district (CBD) in Jan 1997 were £831 per m² (£86.50 per ft²), while total occupational costs (TOCs), including property taxes and service charges, were £1,017 per m² (£94.50 per ft²) for a typical three-year lease. These TOCs are 31% higher than in Hong Kong and 39% higher than in the inner central area of Tokyo, the world's second and third most expensive locations.

The most expensive office location in Europe, and the fourth in the world, is the West End of London, with rents of £484 per m² (£45 per ft²) and TOCs of £683 per m² (£63.50 per ft²). These TOCs are slightly ahead of Moscow, at £644 per m² (£60 per ft²). Moscow rents alone are higher at £566 per m² (£53 per ft²), as are those of the City of London at £606 per m² (£56 per ft²).

### Highest rent in the UK
In the West One Shopping Centre, above Bond Street Underground station, London, UK, a 6.5-m² (70-ft²) kiosk was let to Mercury Communications Ltd in 1996 for £45,000 a year, or £6,923 per m² (£643 per ft²), making it the most expensive single British property to rent.

**Left**
The flower-auction building Bloemenveiling Aalsmeer (VBA) in Aalsmeer, Netherlands, is the largest commercial building in the world. Every year the flower auction sells more than 1 billion guilders (£317,500,000) worth of flowers and plants.

**Left**
The Pentagon in the USA is the world's largest administrative building. Each of its outermost sides is 281 m (921 ft) long, and the perimeter of the building is about 1,405 m (4,610 ft). The total length of the corridors is 28 km (17½ miles), and there are 7,754 windows to be cleaned. A total of 23,000 military and civilian employees work in the building.

# Monumental architecture

**Right**
Life-size soldiers stand ready for battle in the largest tomb in the world. The Mount Li tomb in China is the burial place of Qin Shi Huangdi, first Emperor of Qin, and was built during his reign from 221 to 210 BC.

## Monuments
### Tallest monument
The stainless steel Gateway to the West arch in St Louis, Missouri, USA, was completed on 28 Oct 1965 to commemorate the westward expansion after the 1803 Louisiana Purchase. It is a sweeping arch spanning 192 m (630 ft) and rising to the same height. It cost $29 million and was designed in 1947 by Eero Saarinen.

### Tallest monumental column
The tapering monumental column on the bank of the San Jacinto River near Houston, Texas, USA, was constructed from 1936–39 to commemorate the battle of San Jacinto in 1836. It is 173 m (570 ft) tall, 14 m (47 ft) square at the base and 9 m (30 ft) square at the observation tower. It is topped by a star weighing 199.6 tonnes.

### Largest monolithic obelisks
The obelisk of Tuthmosis III, brought from Aswan, Egypt, by Emperor Constantius in AD 357 and repositioned in the Piazza San Giovanni in Rome, Italy, on 3 Aug 1588, was 36 m (118 ft 1 in) tall, but is now 32.81 m (107 ft 7 in) tall and weighs 455 tonnes.

The unfinished obelisk which stands in situ at Aswan, Egypt, is 41.75 m (136 ft 10 in) long and weighs 1,168 tonnes. It was probably commissioned by Queen Hatshepsut around 1490 BC.

### Largest obelisk in the UK
Cleopatra's Needle, London, is 20.88 m (68 ft 5 in) and weighs 189.35 tonnes. It was put in position on 13 Sept 1878.

### Largest British trilithons
Stonehenge, Wilts, UK, has single sarsen blocks weighing over 45 tonnes. The earliest part of the henge is dated to 2950 BC.

### Largest British henge
The largest British megalithic prehistoric monument and the largest henge is the 11.5-ha (28½-acre) earthworks and stone circles of Avebury, Wilts, 'rediscovered' in 1646. The earliest calibrated date in the area of this Neolithic site is c. 4200 BC. The work is 365 m (1,200 ft) in diameter with a ditch 12 m (40 ft) wide around the perimeter.

**Right**
The stainless steel Gateway arch in St Louis, Missouri, USA, designed by Finnish architect Eero Saarinen to commemorate the city's historic role as the 'Gateway to the West'.

### Oldest British scheduled monument
Kent's Cavern, near Torquay, Devon, UK, is a cave site containing deposits more than 300,000 years old, which date from the Lower Palaeolithic period.

### Newest British scheduled monument
A hexagonal pillbox and 48 concrete tank-traps built in WWII near Christchurch, Dorset, UK, have been protected since 1973.

## Earthworks and mounds
### Largest earthworks
The longest, most extensive pre-mechanical earthworks were the Linear Earth Boundaries (c. 1300) of the Benin Empire and earlier in the Edo state, Nigeria. It is estimated their length was about 16,000 km (10,000 miles), and the volume of earth moved was 75 million m³ (100 million yd³).

# OLDEST STEP PYRAMID 2630 BC

UK—ONE OF THE FEW MAN-MADE STRUCTURES THAT CAN BE SEEN FROM SPACE

The greatest British prehistoric earthwork is Wansdyke (originally Wodensdic), which ran 138 km (86 miles) from Portishead, Somerset to Inkpen Beacon and Ludgershall, south of Hungerford, Berks. It was built by the Belgae tribe around 150 BC.

## Largest man-made mounds
The gravel mound built as a memorial to the Seleucid king Antiochus I that stands on the summit of Nemrud Dağı, Turkey, is 59.8 m (197 ft) tall and covers 3 ha (7.5 acres).

The largest British mound is Silbury Hill, a 39-m (130-ft) high cone with a base of 2 ha (5½ acres) near Marlborough, Wilts. Its construction, dated at 2745±185 BC, involved the moving of 680,000 tonnes of chalk and took over 18 million hours.

# Walls and columns
### Tallest columns
The world's tallest columns are the 36 27.5-m (90-ft) tall fluted pillars of Vermont marble in the colonnade of the Education Building, Albany, New York State, USA.

The tallest load-bearing stone columns are 21 m (69 ft), built in c. 1270 BC in the Hall of Columns of the Temple of Amun at Karnak, the ancient capital of Upper Egypt.

### Longest walls
The Great Wall of China is the world's longest with a main-line length of 3,460 km (2,150 miles), nearly three times the length of the United Kingdom. Built around 221–210 BC,

### Largest ziggurat
A ziggurat is a type of rectangular tower, built by the Sumerians, Akkadians and Babylonians. The largest was the Ziggurat of Choga Zambil of the Elamite king Untas (c. 1250 BC), situated near Haft Tepe, Iran. It had an outer base of 105 x 105 m (344 x 344 ft), and a fifth 'box' above it which measured 28 x 28 m (92 x 92 ft).

The largest partially surviving ziggurat is the Ziggurat of Ur (now Muqayyar, Iraq), built in the reign of Ur-nammu (c. 2250–2232 BC). It has a base of 61 x 45.7 m (200 x 150 ft).

### Oldest crematorium
The oldest crematorium in the United Kingdom was built in 1879 at Woking, Surrey. The first cremation took place there on 26 March 1885.

### Largest pyramid
The Quetzalcóatl Pyramid at Cholula de Rivadabia in Mexico, is the largest monument ever constructed. Its total volume is estimated at some 3.3 million m$^3$ (4.3 million yd$^3$), compared with the Pyramid of Khufu at Giza, Egypt, at 2.4 million m$^3$ (3.1 million yd$^3$).

**Left**
The Grand Mosque rises above the weekly open market in Djenne, Mali. The present structure was built in 1905, based on an 11th-century mosque and is the largest mud-brick building in the world.

CREMATORIUM WITH SEVEN TWIN CREMATORS, COVERING AN AREA OF 210 HA

it is one of the few man-made structures on Earth that can be seen from space.

Britain's longest Roman wall was Hadrian's Wall, built from AD 122–126. It ran 118 km (73½ miles) from Bowness-on-Solway, Cumbria, to Wallsend-on-Tyne, Tyne & Wear.

### Thickest walls
Ur-nammu's mud brick city walls at Ur (now Muqayyar, Iraq) were 27 m (88 ft) thick. They were destroyed by the Elamites in 2006 BC.

# Temples
### Largest mud-brick building
The largest mud-brick building in the world is the Grand Mosque in Djenne, Mali, which is based on the design of an 11th-century mosque. It was built in 1905 and is 100 m (328 ft) long and 40 m (131 ft) wide.

# Burial places
### Largest cemetery
Ohlsdorf Cemetery in Hamburg, Germany, built in 1877, covers an area of 400 ha (990 acres). There had been 982,117 burials and 413,589 cremations up to 31 Dec 1996.

### Largest crematorium
The Nikolo-Arkhangelskiy Crematorium in Moscow, Russia, has seven twin cremators. Completed in March 1972, it covers an area of 210 ha (519 acres) and has six Halls of Farewell which are used for funerals.

### Tallest cemetery
Built in 1983, the Memorial Necrópole Ecumênica in Santos, Brazil, has tombs that are stacked to 10 storeys high. The cemetery occupies an area of 1.8 ha (4.4 acres).

### Oldest pyramid
The 62-m (204-ft) high Djoser Step Pyramid at Saqqâra, Egypt, was built by Imhotep (Djoser's royal architect) in c. 2630 BC.

### Largest tomb
The Mount Li tomb, the burial place of the first Emperor of Qin, Qin Shi Huangdi, is the world's largest tomb. Built between 221–210 BC, it is 40.2 km (25 miles) east of Xianyang, China. The two walls surrounding the grave measure 2,173 x 974 m (7,129 x 3,195 ft) and 685 x 578 m (2,247 x 1,896 ft). Several pits in the tomb contained a vast army of terracotta soldiers and horses which are life-sized and larger.

A tomb housing 180,000 WWII dead in Okinawa, Japan, was enlarged in 1985 to accommodate another 9,000 bodies that were thought to be buried on the island.

## Cathedrals and churches

### Largest cathedrals
The largest cathedral is St John the Divine, cathedral church of the Diocese of New York, USA, with a floor area of 11,240 m² (121,000 ft²). The cornerstone was laid on 27 Dec 1892, but work on the building was stopped in 1941 and only restarted in earnest in July 1979. The nave is the longest in the world at 183.2 m (601 ft) in length, with a vaulted ceiling 37.8 m (124 ft) high.

The cathedral covering the largest area is Santa María de la Sede in Seville, Spain. It was built in Spanish Gothic style between 1402 and 1519 and is 126.2 m (414 ft) long, 82.6 m (271 ft) wide and 30.5 m (100 ft) high to the vault of the nave.

The largest cathedral in the United Kingdom is the Cathedral Church of Christ in Liverpool. Finally consecrated on 25 Oct 1978 after 74 years, the building encloses 9,687 m² (104,275 ft²) and has an overall length of 193.9 m (636 ft).

### Smallest cathedrals
The smallest church designated as a cathedral is the Christ Catholic Church, Highlandville, Missouri, USA, consecrated in July 1983. It measures 4.3 x 5.2 m (14 x 17 ft) and can seat only 18 people.

The smallest cathedral in use in the United Kingdom is Cumbrae Cathedral at Millport on the isle of Cumbrae, North Ayrshire. However it is not the mother church of a diocese. The nave measures 12.2 x 6.1 m (40 x 20 ft), and the total floor area is 197.3 m² (2,124 ft²).

### Largest churches
The largest church in the world is the Basilica of Our Lady of Peace (Notre Dame de la Paix) at Yamoussoukro, Ivory Coast. Completed in 1989, it has a total area of 30,000 m² (323,000 ft²) with seating for 7,000 people. Including its golden cross, it is 158 m (518 ft) high.

The elliptical basilica of St Pius X (Saint-Pie X) at Lourdes, France, was completed in 1957. It can hold 20,000 under its giant span arches and is 200 m (660 ft) long.

The largest parish church is the Parish Church of the Most Holy and Undivided Trinity at Kingston-upon-Hull, E Yorkshire. It covers an area of 2,530 m² (27,235 ft²), with an external length and width of 87.7 x 37.7 m (288 x 124 ft).

### Smallest church
The chapel of Santa Isabel de Hungría in Colomares—a monument to Christopher Columbus—at Benalmádena, Málaga, Spain, is irregular in shape and has a total floor area of only 1.96 m² (21⅛ ft²).

### Longest crypt
The crypt of the underground Civil War Memorial Church in the Guadarrama Mountains, 45 km (28 miles) from Madrid, Spain, is 260 m (853 ft) in length.

### Tallest spires
The tallest cathedral spire in the world is that of the Protestant Cathedral of Ulm in Germany. The tower, which was only finished in 1890, is 160.9 m (528 ft) high.

The world's tallest church spire is that of the Chicago Temple/First United Methodist Church on Clark Street, Chicago, Illinois, USA. The building consists of a 22-storey skyscraper (erected in 1924) surmounted by a parsonage at 100.5 m (330 ft), a 'Sky Chapel' at 121.9 m (400 ft) and a steeple cross at 173.1 m (568 ft) above street level.

### Largest stained-glass window
The largest stained-glass window covers 2,079 m² (22,381 ft²) in 2,448 panels. It is in the Resurrection Mausoleum in Justice, Illinois, USA, which was completed in 1971.

Although its stained glass is not one continuous window, the Basilica of Our Lady of Peace (Notre Dame de la Paix) at Yamoussoukro, Ivory Coast, contains a number of stained-glass windows covering a total area of 7,430 m² (80,000 ft²).

### Oldest stained glass
Pieces of stained glass excavated by Prof. Rosemary Cramp at Monkwearmouth and Jarrow, and dated before AD 850 were set into a window of that date in St Paul's Church, Jarrow, Tyne & Wear, UK.

The oldest complete stained glass in the world shows the Prophets in a window at the Cathedral of Augsburg, Germany. It dates from the second half of the 11th century.

## Temples and stupas

### Largest temple
The largest religious structure ever built is Angkor Wat ('City Temple'), enclosing 162.6 ha (402 acres) in Cambodia. Built to the Hindu god Vishnu by the Khmer king Suryavarman II between 1113 and 1150, its curtain wall measures 1,280 x 1,280 m (4,200 x 4,200 ft), and its population, before it was abandoned in 1432, was 80,000. The whole complex of 72 major monuments extends over an area of 24 x 8 km (15 x 5 miles).

### Largest Hindu temple outside India
The largest Hindu temple to be built outside Asia using traditional stone construction and according to the Hindu scriptures is the Shri Swaminarayan Mandir, which was opened in London, UK, in 1995. The whole complex covers 1.56 ha (3.85 acres), and the main prayer hall can hold 4,000 worshippers.

# TALLEST MINARET 200 M

MONUMENTS, AND HAD A POPULATION OF 80,000

DE HUNGRÍA IN COLOMARES AT MÁLAGA, SPAIN—ITS AREA IS ONLY 1.96 M²

**Far left**
The tallest minaret in the world is that of the Great Hassan II Mosque in Casablanca, Morocco. The mosque features a 9-ha (22-acre) prayer hall, sculptured marble and *zellige* (tile mosaics).

**Left**
The spire on Ulm Cathedral in Germany is 160.9 m (528 ft) tall. The cathedral, begun in 1377, was not finished until 1890. Unlike the ancient city of Ulm, the cathedral and its soaring spire escaped damage in WWII.

### Largest Buddhist temple
Borobudur, near Jogjakarta, Indonesia, built in the 8th century, is 31.4 m (103 ft) tall and measures 123 m² (403 ft²).

### Largest Mormon temple
The largest Mormon temple is the Salt Lake City Temple, Utah, USA, which was dedicated on 6 April 1893, with a floor area of 23,505 m² (253,015 ft²) or 5.8 acres.

### Highest temple
The Rongbu temple, between Tingri and Shigatse in Tibet, is at an altitude of c. 5,100 m (16,750 ft), 40 km (25 miles) from Mt Everest. It contains nine chapels, and is home to a number of lamas and nuns.

### Tallest stupa
The now largely ruined Jetavanarama dagoba in the ancient city of Anuradhapura, Sri Lanka, is some 120 m (400 ft) in height.

### Oldest stupa
The Shwedagon pagoda in Rangoon, Myanmar (Burma), is built on the site of a pagoda dating from 585 BC. It is 99.3 m (326 ft) tall.

## Mosques and synagogues
### Largest mosque
The Shah Faisal Mosque, near Islamabad, Pakistan, can accommodate 100,000 worshippers in the prayer hall and the courtyard and a further 200,000 people in the adjacent grounds. The complex area is 18.97 ha (46.87 acres) and the covered area of the prayer hall 0.48 ha (1.19 acres).

### Tallest minaret
The minaret of the Great Hassan II Mosque, Casablanca, Morocco, is 200 m (656 ft) high. The mosque was completed in 1984 and can accommodate 25,000 worshippers.

The tallest from earlier centuries is the Qutb Minar, south of New Delhi, India, built in 1194 to a height of 72.54 m (238 ft).

### Largest synagogues
The largest synagogue in the world is Temple Emanu-El on Fifth Avenue at 65th Street, New York City, USA. The temple was finished in Sept 1929 and the main sanctuary can accommodate 2,500 people, with the adjoining Beth-El Chapel seating 350. When these and the Temple's other three sanctuaries are in use, 5,500 people can be accommodated.

The largest British synagogue is Edgware Synagogue, London, which was completed in 1959, with seating for 1,630.

The British synagogue with the highest membership is Stanmore and Canons Park Synagogue, London, with 3,405 members.

## Remote dwellings

### Highest altitude
The highest inhabited buildings in the world are those in the Indo-Tibetan border fort of Bāsisi by the Māna Pass (31°04'N, 79°24'E) at *c.* 5,990 m (19,700 ft).

In April 1961, a three-room dwelling believed to date from the late pre-Columbian period (*c.* 1480) was discovered at 6,600 m (21,650 ft) on the mountain of Cerro Llullaillaco between Argentina and Chile.

### Northernmost habitation
The Danish scientific station set up in 1952 in Pearyland, northern Greenland, is over 1,450 km (900 miles) north of the Arctic Circle and is manned every summer.

The former USSR's drifting research station 'North Pole 15' passed within 2.8 km (1¼ miles) of the North Pole in Dec 1967.

The most northerly continuously inhabited place is the Canadian Department of National Defence outpost at Alert on Ellesmere Island, Northwest Territories (82°30'N, 62°W), which was set up in 1950.

### Southernmost habitation
The most southerly permanent human habitation is the United States' Amundsen-Scott South Polar Station. It was completed in 1957 and replaced in 1975.

## Palaces

### Largest palace
The Imperial Palace in the centre of Beijing, China, covers a rectangle measuring 960 x 750 m (3,150 x 2,460 ft) over an area of 72 ha (178 acres). The outline survives from the construction of the third Ming Emperor, Yongle (1402–24), but owing to constant reconstruction work, most of the intra-mural buildings (five halls and 17 palaces) date from the 18th century.

The Palace of Versailles, near Paris, France, is 580 m (1,902 ft) long and has a façade with 375 windows. The building was completed in 1682 for Louis XIV, and more than 30,000 people worked on it.

### Residential palaces
Istana Nurul Iman, the palace of the Sultan of Brunei, in the capital Bandar Seri Begawan, was completed in Jan 1984 at a reported cost of £300 million. With 1,788 rooms and 257 lavatories, it is the largest residence in the world. The underground garage houses the Sultan's 153 cars.

The largest royal palace in the United Kingdom is Hampton Court, London. Acquired by Henry VIII from Cardinal Wolsey in 1525 and greatly enlarged by him and later by William III, Queen Anne and George I, it covers 1.6 ha (4 acres) on a site extending over 271 ha (669 acres).

The largest palace in royal use in the United Kingdom is Buckingham Palace, London, which stands in 15.8 ha (39 acres) of garden and has 600 rooms, including a 34-m (111-ft) long ballroom used for investitures.

## Castles and forts

### Earliest castle
The castle at Gomdan, Yemen, dates from before AD 100 and originally had 20 storeys.

### Oldest castle
The oldest stone castle in the United Kingdom is Chepstow Castle, Monmouthshire, built *c.* 1067 on the west bank of the River Wye by William fitz Osbern.

### Largest castle
The largest castle in the world is Hradčany Castle in Prague, Czech Republic, which was built in the 9th century. The building is an

LARGEST MODERN UNDERGROUND HOUSE COVERS

# 1,788 ROOMS, 257 LAVATORIES

oblong irregular polygon with an axis of 570 m (1,870 ft) and an average transverse diameter of 128 m (420 ft), giving a surface area of 7.28 ha (18 acres).

### Largest inhabited castle
The royal residence of Windsor Castle at Windsor, Berks, UK, was originally constructed in the 12th century. It is in the form of a parallelogram measuring 576 x 164 m (1,890 x 540 ft).

### Largest moat
The moats surrounding the Imperial Palace in Beijing, China, are 49 m (54 yd) wide and have a total length of 3,290 m (3,600 yd). In all, the city's moats total 38 km (23½ miles).

### Largest residence
The largest non-palatial residence in the world is St Emmeram Castle in Regensburg, Germany. It has 517 rooms and a floor area of 21,460 m² (231,000 ft²). The castle is valued at over 336 million DM (£122 million).

### Largest fort
Fort George in Ardersier, Highland, UK, built in 1748–69, is 640 m (2,100 ft) long and has an average width of 189 m (620 ft) on a site covering a total of 17.2 ha (42½ acres).

## Housing
### Earliest housing
Eastry Court near Sandwich, Kent, UK, includes part of a Saxon building said to have been built in AD 603 by King Ethelbert I of Kent, possibly as a palace.

**Left**
Residential tower blocks rise beyond the Arts Centre at the Barbican in the City of London, UK. The complex was designed by architects Chamberlin, Bon & Powell and finished on 24 March 1969.

AN AREA OF 325 M²; ITS GRASS ROOF IS MAINTAINED BY GRAZING SHEEP

### Oldest inhabited house
Barton Manor in Pagham, W Sussex, UK, has features dating from Saxon times c. AD 800.

### Most rooms
The British house with the most rooms is Knole, near Sevenoaks, Kent, believed to have had 365 rooms, one for each day of the year. Built around seven courtyards, its depth from front to back is c. 120 m (400 ft).

### Largest modern underground house
Underhill in Holme, W Yorkshire, UK, has an internal area of 325 m² (3,500 ft²). Invisible from outside, its roof is covered with grass, kept short by grazing sheep.

### Smallest house
The 19th-century fisherman's cottage at The Quay, Conwy, Wales, UK, consists of two tiny rooms and a staircase. It has only 182 cm

(72 in) of frontage, is 309 cm (122 in) high and 254 cm (100 in) from front to back.

### Narrowest house
The house frontage of 50 Stuart Street, Millport, on the island of Great Cumbrae, North Ayrshire, UK, is 119 cm (47 in).

### Largest housing estate
The United Kingdom's largest housing estate is the 675-ha (1,667-acre) Becontree Estate on a site covering 1,214 ha (3,000 acres) in Barking and Redbridge, London, UK. Built between 1921 and 1929, it contains a total of 26,822 homes, with an estimated 90,000 residents.

### Most rock houses
The largest collection of rock houses in the United Kingdom is around the sandstone cliffs of Kinver Edge, Staffs.

## Flats
### Tallest block of flats
The John Hancock Center in Chicago, Illinois, USA, is 343.5 m (1,127 ft) high and has 100 storeys—floors 44–92 are residential.

The tallest purely residential block of flats is the 70-storey Lake Point Tower in Chicago, Illinois, USA, which is 195 m (639 ft) high and has 879 apartments.

The tallest residential block in the United Kingdom is Shakespeare Tower, Barbican, City of London. The 44-storey block has 116 flats and is 127.77 m (419 ft 2½ in) high.

### Largest complex
The largest aggregation of private blocks is the Barbican Estate, London, UK. The site occupies 16 ha (40 acres) and includes 2,014 flats and parking for 1,710 cars.

# Leisure architecture

## Cinemas

### Largest
Radio City Music Hall, New York City, USA, opened on 27 Dec 1932 with 5,945 seats. It now has 5,910 seats.

Kinepolis in Brussels, Belgium, is the world's largest cinema complex. It has 26 theatres with seating for between 160 and 700, and an IMAX theatre that has a 20 x 30 m (65 ft 7 in x 98 ft 5 in) screen and seats 450 people. The total seating capacity of the complex is around 6,000.

### Biggest screens
The world's largest permanently installed cinema screen is in the Panasonic IMAX Theatre at Darling Harbour, Sydney, Australia. The screen measures 35.72 x 29.57 m (117 ft x 97 ft).

A temporary screen measuring 90.5 x 10 m (297 x 33 ft) was used at the 1937 Paris Exposition, France.

### First circular cinema
The European Park of the Moving Image at Fururoscope, near Poitiers, France, has a circular cinema with nine projectors and nine screens covering a total surface area of 272 m$^2$ (2,928 ft$^2$).

### Largest image wall
The European Park of the Moving Image contains a wall of 850 video screens that covers a surface area of 162 m$^2$ (1,744 ft$^2$).

## Stadia

### Largest stadium
The open Strahov Stadium in Prague, Czech Republic, completed in 1934, can hold 240,000 spectators. It was used for mass displays of up to 40,000 Sokol gymnasts.

### Largest football stadium
The Maracanã Municipal Stadium in Rio de Janeiro, Brazil, has a normal capacity of 205,000, of whom 155,000 can be seated.

### Largest covered stadium
The Aztec Stadium in Mexico City, Mexico, which was opened in 1968, has a capacity of 107,000 for football. Almost all the seats are under cover.

### Largest indoor stadium
The Superdome in New Orleans, Louisiana, USA, is 83.2 m (273 ft) tall, covers 5.26 ha (13 acres), and has a maximum seating capacity of 97,365.

### Largest roof
The transparent acrylic glass 'tent' roof over the Munich Olympic Stadium, Germany, measures 85,000 m$^2$ (915,000 ft$^2$) in area.

### Longest roof span
The longest roof span in the world is the major axis of the elliptical Texas Stadium, Irving, Texas, USA. It is 240 m (787 ft 4 in).

### LARGEST EXTENDABLE ROOF

**Right**
The largest indoor waterpark is the Ocean Dome at Miyazaki, Japan. Miyazaki is a coastal resort on the island of Kyushu, and is traditionally a favoured location for honeymoon couples.

# CINEMA SCREEN 35.72 X 29.57 M

AROUND 6,000 PEOPLE

## Largest retractable roof
The roof of the SkyDome, Toronto, Canada is the world's largest retractable roof. It covers 3.2 ha (8 acres), spans 209 m (674 ft) at its widest point and rises to 86 m (282 ft). It takes 20 minutes to retract the roof fully.

## Largest air supported building
The octagonal Pontiac Silverdome Stadium in Detroit, Michigan, USA, is 235 m (770 ft) long and 183 m (600 ft) wide and has a capacity for 80,311. The air pressure supporting the 4-ha (10-acre) 'Fiberglas' roofing is 34.4 kPa (5 lb/ft$^2$). The main floor covers 123 x 71 m (402 x 232 ft).

The largest standard-size airhall is 262 m (860 ft) long, 42.6 m (140 ft) wide and 19.8 m (65 ft) high. First sited at Lima, Ohio, USA, it was manufactured by Irvin Industries of Stamford, Connecticut, USA.

**Left**
The European Park of the Moving Image at Futuroscope near Poitiers, France, contains the largest image wall in the world, consisting of 850 video screens.

AT THE SKYDOME IN TORONTO, CANADA, TAKES 20 MINUTES TO RETRACT FULLY

# Resorts
## Largest amusement resort
Disney World, Florida, USA, covers an area of 12,140 ha (30,000 acres).

## Largest pleasure beach
Virginia Beach, Virginia, USA, has 45 km (28 miles) of beach front on the Atlantic and 16 km (10 miles) of estuary frontage on Chesapeake Bay. The city of Virginia Beach has 147 hotels and 2,323 campsites.

## Largest indoor waterpark
The Ocean Dome at Miyazaki, Japan, is 300 m (985 ft) long, 100 m (328 ft) wide and 38 m (124 ft) high and contains a beach 140 m (459 ft) long.

# Fun fairs
## Largest fair
The site of the Louisiana Purchase Exposition in St Louis, Missouri, USA, in 1904 covered 514.66 ha (1,271.76 acres). It was attended by 19,694,855 people.

## Largest big wheels
In 1897 a Ferris wheel with a diameter of 86.5 m (284 ft) was erected for the Earl's Court Exhibition, London, UK. It had ten 1st-class and 30 2nd-class cars each carrying 30 people.

The largest-diameter wheel currently in operation is the *Cosmoclock 21* at Yokohama City, Japan. It is 105 m (344 ft 6 in) high and 100 m (328 ft) in diameter, with 60 gondolas each with eight seats.

**Left**
The world's first circular cinema at the European Park of the Moving Image at Futuroscope. The projection of nine electronically synchronised films offers a 360° field of vision.

## Largest swing
A 9.1-m (30-ft) high swing was constructed in 1986 in Saskatchewan, Canada, for Uncle Herb's Amusements. It takes four riders to a height of 7.6 m (25 ft) off the ground.

## Longest roller coaster
*The Ultimate* at Lightwater Valley Theme Park, Ripon, N Yorkshire, UK, has a tubular steel track of 2.29 km (1 mile 740 yards).

## Greatest number of loops or inversions
On *Dragon Khan* at Port Aventura, Salou, Spain, riders are turned upside-down eight times over the steel track, which extends for 1,269.8 m (4,166 ft 1 in).

## Tallest and fastest roller coaster
*Superman the Escape* at Six Flags Magic Mountain, Valencia, California, USA, has a steel support structure of 126.5 m (415 ft) and a design speed of 160 km/h (100 mph).

## Tallest complete-circuit roller coaster
*Fujiyama*, at the Fujikyu Highland Amusement Park, Japan, measures 79 m (259 ft) at its highest point and has a lift height of 71.5 m (235 ft), a vertical drop of 70 m (230 ft) and a design speed of 130 km/h (81 mph).

## Greatest number of roller coasters
Cedar Point Amusement Park/Resort, Sandusky, Ohio, USA, has 12 roller coasters.

# Buildings for recreation

## Restaurants

### Oldest restaurant
The Casa Botín was opened in Calle de Cuchilleros 17, Madrid, Spain, in 1725.

### Largest restaurant
The Royal Dragon (Mang Gorn Luang) restaurant in Bangkok, Thailand, opened in Oct 1991 and can seat 5,000 customers. Because of the vast 3.37-ha (8.35-acre) service area the staff wear roller skates in order to give prompt service.

### Highest restaurants
The restaurant at the Chacaltaya ski resort, Bolivia, is at 5,340 m (17,519 ft).

The Ptarmigan Observation Restaurant near Aviemore, Highland, UK, is at 1,112 m (3,650 ft) above sea level on Cairngorm.

### Fish and chip restaurant
The world's largest fish-and-chip shop is Harry Ramsden's at White Cross, Guiseley, W Yorkshire, UK. It has 140 staff serving 1 million customers annually. Each year 213 tonnes of fish and 356 tonnes of potatoes are eaten. On 5 April 1996 the branch in Melbourne, Victoria, Australia, sold a record 12,105 portions of fish and chips.

## Bars and Public Houses

### Largest pub
The largest beer-selling establishment in the world is the 'Mathäser', Bayerstrasse 5, Munich, Germany, where they sell up to 48,000 litres (84,470 pints) per day. The bar was established in 1829, demolished in WWII and rebuilt by 1955. It now seats 5,500 people.

The largest British public house is the 'Moon Under Water', Deansgate, Manchester.

### Tallest bar
The bar at Humperdink's Seafood and Steakhouse in the Las Colinas business development in Irving, Texas, USA, is 7.69 m (25 ft 3 in) high with two levels of shelving containing over 1,000 bottles. If an order has to be met from the upper level, the drinks are reached by climbing a ladder.

### Longest bars
The longest permanent continuous bar is the 123.7-m-long (405-ft 10-in) counter in the Beer Barrel Saloon, which opened at Put-in-Bay, South Bass Island, Ohio, USA, in 1989. The bar is fitted with 56 beer taps and surrounded by 160 bar stools.

The longest British bar with beer pumps is the Long Bar at the Cornwall Coliseum Auditorium at Carlyon Bay, St Austell, Cornwall. It measures 31.8 m (104 ft 3 in) and has 34 dispensers.

The Grandstand Bar at Galway Racecourse, Republic of Ireland, which was completed in 1955, is 64 m (210 ft) long.

The longest pub bar is the 31.7-m (104-ft 4-in) long counter at 'The Horse Shoe', Drury Street, Glasgow, UK.

### Smallest pubs
The smallest bar room measures 1.27 x 2.39 m (4 ft 2 in x 7 ft 10 in). It is in the 'Dove Inn', Chiswick, London, UK.

The ground floor of 'The Nutshell' in Bury St. Edmunds, Suffolk, UK, is 4.82 x 2.28 m (15 ft 10 in x 7 ft 6 in). It was personally granted a licence by a thirsty King Charles II.

The 'Lakeside Inn', The Promenade, Southport, Merseyside, UK, has a floor area of 6.7 x 4.87 m (22 x 16 ft) and is 4.57 m (15 ft) in height.

'The Smiths Arms' in Godmanstone, Dorset, UK, has external dimensions of 12.04 x 3.5 m (39 ft 6 in x 11 ft 6 in) and is 3.65 m (12 ft) in height.

The smallest commercial brewery is at the Tynllidiart Arms, Capel Bangor, Ceredigion, UK. Its capacity is 327 litres (9 gallons) per brew.

## Hotels and Casinos

### Oldest hotel
The Hōshi Ryokan at the village of Awazu in Japan, dates back to AD 717, when

Garyo Hōshi built an inn near a hot-water spring which was said to have healing powers. The hotel now has 100 bedrooms.

### Largest hotel
The MGM Grand Hotel/Casino in Las Vegas, Nevada, USA, consists of four 30-storey towers on a site covering 45.3 ha (112 acres). The hotel has 5,005 rooms, with suites of up to 560 m² (6,000 ft²), a 15,200-seat arena, and a 13.3-ha (33-acre) theme park.

The largest hotel in the United Kingdom is the Grosvenor House Hotel in Park Lane, London, which opened in 1929. It is eight storeys high, covers 1 ha (2½ acres) and caters for over 100,000 visitors per year in its 470 rooms and 140 fully-serviced apartments. The Great Room is the largest single hotel room measuring 55 x 40 m (181 x 131 ft), with a ceiling height of 7 m (23 ft).

The London Forum Hotel in Cromwell Road, London, has the greatest capacity of any hotel in the United Kingdom. It provides accommodation for up to 1,856 guests in a total of 910 bedrooms. Opened in 1973, the hotel employs 330 staff.

### Tallest hotel
Measured from the street level of its main entrance, the 73-storey Westin Stamford in Raffles City, Singapore, was completed in March 1985 at 226.1 m (742 ft).

# LARGEST HOTEL 5,005 ROOMS

## WITH 2,580 SHOWROOMS

If measured from its rear entrance level, the Westin Stamford Detroit Plaza, USA, is 227.9 m (748 ft) tall.

The Ryujyong Hotel, North Korea, which has been under construction for 20 years, is reported to be 105 storeys high.

The tallest British hotel, the London Forum, has 27 storeys and is 132 m (380 ft) tall.

### Most expensive hotel room
The Galactic Fantasy Suite in the Crystal Tower of the Crystal Palace Resort and Casino in Nassau, Bahamas, is the world's most expensive hotel room. It costs $25,000 (£17,360) per night, but the casino's big spenders are likely to be accommodated on a complimentary basis.

The Presidential Suite of the Hotel Hyatt Carlton Tower, London, UK, costs £2,350 per night (inc VAT).

**Left and below left**
The Galactic Fantasy Suite in the Crystal Tower of the Crystal Palace Resort and Casino in Nassau, Bahamas. Its facilities include 'Ursula', the personal robot servant, a rotating sofa and bed, a thunder-and-lightning sound-and-light show and pulsating light columns activated by body heat.

## LARGEST CASINO, WITH 3,854 SLOT MACHINES AND 3,500 BINGO SEATS

### Largest hotel lobby
The lobby at the Hyatt Regency in San Francisco, California, USA, is 107 m (350 ft) long, 49 m (160 ft) wide, and 52 m (170 ft) high—the height of a 17-storey building.

### Largest casino
Foxwoods Resort Casino in Ledyard, Connecticut, USA, includes a total gaming area of 17,900 m$^2$ (193,000 ft$^2$). There are 3,854 slot machines, 234 gaming tables and 3,500 bingo seats.

## Shopping Centres
### Largest shopping centre
The world's largest shopping centre is the $1.1-billion West Edmonton Mall in Alberta, Canada, which was opened on 15 Sept 1981 and was completed four years later. It covers 483,000 m$^2$ (5.2 million ft$^2$) on a 49-ha (121-acre) site and encompasses over 800 stores and services, as well as 11 major department stores. Parking is provided for 20,000 vehicles. In 1995 over 20 million shoppers visited the centre.

The largest shopping complex in Europe is the MetroCentre in Gateshead, Tyne & Wear, UK, which consists of a 54.63-ha-site (135-acre) covering an area housing 350 retail units. It includes the largest single-storey branch of Marks & Spencer. In total the area devoted to sales is 145,000 m$^2$ (1.56 million ft$^2$). The complex also includes a leisure centre, an 11-screen cinema, a 28-lane

bowling centre, parking for 12,000 cars, a coach park and its own purpose-built rail and bus station.

### Largest wholesalers
The world's largest wholesale merchandise mart is the Dallas Market Center on Stemmons Freeway, Dallas, Texas, USA. The floor has an area of nearly 641,000 m$^2$ (6.9 million ft$^2$) and is spread over five buildings. The whole complex covers a 70-ha (175-acre) site and houses

some 2,580 permanent showrooms which display the merchandise of more than 50,000 manufacturers. The Center holds 50 annual markets and trade shows every year, which attract more than 800,000 buyers.

### Longest mall
The longest mall in the world is at the £40-million shopping centre in Milton Keynes, Bucks, UK. Its total length is 720 m (2,360 ft).

# Garden design

## Parks and gardens

### Largest garden
The magnificent formal gardens and parkland created for Louis XIV by André Le Nôtre at Versailles, France, in the late 17th century are arguably the largest gardens. They cover over 6,070 ha (15,000 acres), of which the famous formal garden covers 100 ha (247 acres).

### Most visited British garden
The most visited British garden charging admission is Kew Gardens, London.

### Largest sunken garden
The garden created for Béatrice de Rothschild at Villa Ephrussi de Rothschild, St Jean-Cap Ferrat, France, is carved out of solid rock. Most of the 17-ha (10-acre) garden is, therefore, sunken.

### Smallest park
The smallest park in the United Kingdom is Prince's Park, a small triangular piece of ground on the main road at the east end of the churchyard in Burntwood, Staffs. It was planted with six trees to commemorate the

## Fountains and mazes

### Largest fountain
The world's largest fountain is the Suntec Fountain in Singapore, with a base volume of 1,683.07 m² (18,117 ft²).

The largest British fountain is Whitley Court Fountain, Worcs. Its total volume of water at the base is 1,334.9 m² (14,369 ft²).

### Largest maze
The K.I.D.S. maze in Shaw Park, Clayton, Missouri, USA, was made of PVC posts, with fencing and clear plastic stretched between the posts, and covered an area of 16,281 m² (175,250 ft²) with a total path length of 3.98 km (2 miles 827 yd). The construction was dismantled after three weeks in June 1996.

### Largest permanent mazes
The beech hedge maze at Ruurlo in the Netherlands is 8,740 m² (94,080 ft²). It was created in 1891.

The maze with the greatest path length is at Longleat, near Warminster, Wilts, UK. It has 2.72 km (1.69 miles) of paths flanked by 16,180 yew trees and was opened in 1978.

## Floral specialities

### Largest rose garden
The largest rose garden in the world is at Cavriglia, Italy. In the garden there are over 7,500 different varieties of roses.

Hampton Court, London, is the most visited British garden without an admission fee. In 1996 it had 2 million visitors.

### Oldest botanic gardens
The Pisa Botanic Garden, Pisa, Italy, was founded in 1543.

The Oxford Botanic Garden, Oxford, UK, was established in 1621.

### Largest scented garden for the blind
The Kirstenbosch National Botanical Gardens on the eastern slopes of Table Mountain, Cape Town, South Africa, includes a 'Braille Trail' and allows blind and visually handicapped visitors to touch the plants.

### Largest community garden
The City Beautiful Council and the Benjamin Wegerzyn Garden Center at Dayton, Ohio, USA, comprise 1,173 allotments, each measuring 74.5 m² (812 ft²).

marriage of the future Edward VII to Princess Alexandra of Denmark in 1863. With its own park railings and gate, this miniature park is 9.1 x 4.6 m (30 x 15 ft). It is maintained by Lichfield District Council.

### Longest border
The longest continuous herbaceous border in the British Isles is in Strokestown Park Gardens, Co. Roscommon, Republic of Ireland. It is 152.4 m (500 ft) long.

### Biggest seed collection
Wakehurst Place (a 'country branch' of Kew Gardens), near East Grinstead, W Sussex, UK, has the greatest number of plant specimens held as seeds, with over 4,000 in all.

### Biggest garden centre
Bridgemere Garden World, Cheshire, UK, covers 10.1 ha (25 acres) with over one third of the total area being a display garden.

# LONGEST HERBACEOUS BORDER 152.4 M

NATIONAL BOTANICAL GARDENS ON TABLE MOUNTAIN, CAPE TOWN, SOUTH AFRICA

The largest British rose garden is The Royal National Rose Society's Gardens, at St Albans, Herts. It has 30,000 roses and over 1,700 different varieties.

## Largest collection of rhododendrons
Savill and Valley Gardens at Windsor, Berks, UK, has the largest single collection of rhododendrons.

## Largest area of bulbs
Each year from mid-March to the end of April the bulb fields between Leyden and Haarlem, Netherlands, an area over 12,370 ha (over 30,600 acres), are covered with tulips, narcissi, hyacinths and other bulbs.

## Largest bulb garden
The Keukenhof Gardens, near Haarlem, Netherlands, cover 32 ha (80 acres) and contain 6 million bulbs.

## Largest hanging basket
A giant 8.05-m (26-ft 5-in) diameter hanging basket containing about 2,000 fuchsias was created by Fuchsiavrienden de Kempen VZW of Neerpelt, Belgium, in 1996. It was 4.25 m (13 ft 11 in) deep and weighed an estimated 20 tonnes when filled.

## Trees and arboreta
### Longest avenue of trees
The Nikko Cryptomeria Avenue comprises three parts which converge on Imaichi City in the Tochigi Prefecture of Japan. It is

**Left**
The Nikko Cryptomeria Avenue, Japan, in the late 19th century. It remains the world's longest tree-lined avenue to this day. Over 13,500 of its original 200,000 Japanese cedar (*Cryptomeria japonica*) trees survive, at an average height of 27 m (88 ft 6 in).

COVERS 32 HA AND CONTAINS AS MANY AS 6 MILLION DIFFERENT BULBS

35.41 km (22 miles) in total length. The trees were planted between 1628 and 1648.

The longest avenue of trees in the United Kingdom is the privately-owned stretch of 1,750 beeches measuring 5.8 km (3 miles 1,056 yd) in Savernake Forest, near Marlborough, Wilts.

## Largest British arboretum
Westonbirt Arboretum, near Tetbury, Gloucestershire, is both the largest and oldest arboretum in the United Kingdom. It covers an area of 243 ha (600 acres).

## Biggest collection of trees in a pinetum
The world's biggest collection of conifers is at Bedgebury Pinetum, Kent, UK, with 402 species and 1,950 classifications of plants.

Bedgebury is the United Kingdom's biggest pinetum in terms of area, covering 121.4 ha (300 acres).

## Most trees planted in a public park
Central Park, New York City, USA, one of the largest parks in the world, was begun in 1856. In the course of laying out the park a total of 5 million trees were planted.

## Garden with the tallest trees
In Kew Gardens, London, UK, there is the tallest known specimen of as many as 138 species, a world record.

## Biggest fruit collection
Brogdale, near Faversham, Kent, UK, has over 4,500 fruit trees, including 2,300 apple trees and 400 pears, making it the biggest fruit collection in the world.

## Hedges
### Tallest and longest hedges
The world's tallest and longest hedge is the Meikleour beech hedge in Perth & Kinross, UK, which was planted in 1746 by Jean

Mercer and her husband Robert Murray Nairne. Its tapered height when trimmed now varies from 24.4 m (80 ft) to 36.6 m (120 ft) along its length of 550 m (1,804 ft). The trimming of the hedge takes place every 10 years or so and was last completed in six weeks in 1988.

## Largest yew hedge
A yew hedge planted in 1720 in Earl Bathurst's Park, Cirencester, Glos, UK, runs for 155.5 m (510 ft), reaches 11 m (36 ft) in height and is 4.5 m (15 ft) thick at its base. Every year in August the hedge is trimmed by two men for 12 days. The hedge trimmings are used in research work in the fight against cancer.

## Tallest box hedge
The tallest box hedge in the world is 11 m (36 ft) high, and grows at Birr Castle, Co. Offaly, Republic of Ireland. It is at least 300 years old.

# Transport terminals

**Right**
A cargo ship being loaded at Hong Kong, the world's busiest container port. About 42,000 ocean-going vessels entered the port in 1996 and on an average day there are more than 200 ocean-going ships working there.

## Ports

### Largest port
The Port of New York and New Jersey, USA, has a navigable waterfront of 1,215 km (755 miles) and covers over 238 km$^2$ (92 miles$^2$). A total of 261 general cargo berths and 130 other piers can take 391 ships at a time.

The largest British port by tonnage is London (including Tilbury), which handles some 55 million tonnes each year.

The largest container port in the United Kingdom is Felixstowe, Suffolk, which handled 2,064,947 TEUs (Twenty-foot Equivalent Units) in 1996.

### Busiest ports
The world's busiest port is Rotterdam, Netherlands, which covers 100 km$^2$ (38 miles$^2$), with 122.3 km (76 miles) of quays. It handled 292 million tonnes of sea-going cargo in 1996.

Hong Kong handles less tonnage but is the world's leading container port, handling 13.5 million TEUs in 1996.

The busiest British port is Dover, Kent, which in 1996 handled 27,959 movements, including those of hovercraft. It also handled 18,979,719 passengers, 3,054,781 accompanied vehicles, 153,647 coaches and 1,071,602 road haulage vehicles.

### Largest dry dock
The Daewoo Okpo No. 1 Dry Dock, Koje Island, South Korea, is 530 m (1,740 ft) long and 131 m (430 ft) wide with a maximum shipbuilding capacity of 1,200,000 tons dwt. The dock gates are the world's biggest—standing 14 m (46 ft) high and 10 m (33 ft) thick at the base.

The largest British dry dock is the Harland & Wolff building dock, Queen's Island, Belfast, N Ireland. At 556 m (1,825 ft) in length and 93 m (305 ft) wide it can accommodate tankers of 1 million ton dwt.

### Largest breakwaters
The South Breakwater at Galveston, Texas, USA, is 10.85 km (6 miles 1,300 yd) long.

The longest British breakwater is the North Breakwater at Holyhead, Anglesey, Wales, which is 2.39 km (1 mile 862 yd) long.

### Longest deep-water jetty
The 1,520-m-long (5,000-ft) Quai Hermann du Pasquier at Le Havre, France, is part of an enclosed basin and has a constant depth of water of 9.8 m (32 ft) on both sides.

### Deepest underwater facility
The deep basin (Wet Test facility No. 3) at Euro-Seas, Blyth, Northumberland, UK, is 140 m (495 ft) long and has a maximum water depth of 9 m (29 ft).

## Stations

### Largest railway stations
Grand Central Terminal, New York City, USA, covers 19 ha (48 acres) on two levels with 41 tracks on the upper level and 26 on the lower. On average more than 550 trains and 210,000 commuters use it every day.

### THE WORLD'S LONGEST

The largest British railway station is Waterloo, London, covering 12.3 ha (30½ acres). In 1993 five new platforms were added for trains using the Channel Tunnel. Its 24 platforms have a total length of 6,194 m (3 miles 1,496 yd).

### Oldest station
Liverpool Road Station, Manchester, UK, is the world's oldest station. It was first used on 15 Sept 1830 and was finally closed on 30 Sept 1975. Part of the original station is now a museum.

### Highest stations
Condor station in Bolivia is at an altitude of 4,786 m (15,705 ft) on the metre-gauge Rio Mulato to Potosi line.

### Largest waiting room
The four waiting rooms in Beijing Station, Chang'an Boulevard, Beijing, China, have a total standing capacity of 14,000.

# HIGHEST STATION 4,786 M

VEHICLES AND 18,979,719 PASSENGERS IN 1996

### Largest platforms
The longest railway platform in the world is the Kharagpur platform, West Bengal, India, which measures 833 m (2,733 ft) in length.

The State Street Center subway platform on 'The Loop' in Chicago, Illinois, USA, measures 1,066 m (3,500 ft) in length.

### Largest goods yard
The Bailey Yard at North Platte, Nebraska, USA, covers 1,153 ha (2,850 acres), has 418 km (260 miles) of track and handles an average of 108 trains and some 8,500 wagons every day.

## Airports
### Largest airports
The £2.1-billion King Khalid international airport outside Riyadh, Saudi Arabia, covers an area of 225 km² (55,040 acres).

The largest airport terminal is at Hartsfield International Airport, Atlanta, Georgia, USA. Opened in Sept 1980, it has a floor area covering 53 ha (131 acres) and is still expanding. The terminal handled 57,734,755 passengers in 1995, but it has a capacity for 70 million.

The Hajj Terminal at the £2.8-billion King Abdul-Aziz airport near Jeddah, Saudi Arabia, designed to cater for the annual influx of pilgrims, is the world's largest roofed structure, covering 1.5 km² (370 acres).

### Busiest landing area
The busiest landing area ever was Bien Hoa Air Base, South Vietnam, which handled 1,019,437 take-offs and landings in 1970.

### Largest heliport
The largest heliport was An Khe, South Vietnam. During the Vietnam War, it covered an area of 2 x 3 km (1¼ x 1¾ miles) and could accommodate 434 helicopters.

The heliport at Morgan City, Louisiana, USA, has pads for 48 helicopters. It is owned and operated by Petroleum Helicopter, Inc. for energy-related offshore operations into the Gulf of Mexico.

### Largest baggage handling unit
Denver International Airport, Colorado, USA, has the world's largest airport conveyor system. There are 35 km (22 miles) of track and 9 km (6 miles) of conveyor belts. The entire system is controlled via 4 million m (14 million ft) of wiring.

### Highest landing fields
La Sa (Lhasa) airport, Tibet, China, is at an altitude of 4,363 m (14,315 ft).

The heliport at Sonam, on the Siachen Glacier in Kashmir, is situated at an altitude of 5,950 m (19,500 ft).

### Lowest landing fields
El Lisan on the east shore of the Dead Sea is 360 m (1,180 ft) below sea level, making it

the world's lowest landing field. During WWII BOAC Short C-class flying boats operated there from the surface of the Dead Sea at 394 m (1,292 ft) below sea level.

### Longest runway
The runway at Edwards Air Force Base on the west side of Rogers dry lake bed at Muroc, California, USA, is the world's longest, at 11.92 km (7 miles 715 yd). The Voyager aircraft, taking off for its round-the-world unrefuelled flight, used 4.3 km (14,200 ft) of the 4.6 km (15,000 ft) long main base concrete runway.

### Longest civil runways
The world's longest civil runway, at Pierre van Ryneveld Airport, Upington, South Africa, is 4.89 km (3 miles 79 yd) long. It was built between Aug 1975 and Jan 1976.

A paved runway 6.24 km (3 miles 1,548 yd) long is on maps of Jordan at Abu Husayn.

### Longest UK runway
The longest British runway which is normally available to civil aircraft is the 3.90-km (2-mile 739-yd) long Northern Runway (09L/27R) at Heathrow Airport, London.

### Tallest control tower
The tallest control tower in the world is at Denver International Airport, Colorado, USA. It is 99.7 m (327 ft) tall and made of 5,000 tonnes of concrete and 650 tonnes of steel.

RUNWAY AT EDWARDS AIR FORCE BASE, CALIFORNIA, USA, IS 11.92 KM

The largest British airport is Heathrow, London, at 1,197 ha (2,958 acres). Some 92 airline companies from 83 countries operate scheduled services into the airport, and in 1995 a staff of 56,700 handled 419,000 air transport movements and 54,450,000 passengers (including transit).

### Busiest airports
O'Hare International Airport, near Chicago, Illinois, USA, had 69,153,528 passengers and 909,593 aircraft movements in 1996, making it the busiest airport in the world.

Heathrow, London, UK, handles more international traffic than any other airport, with an estimated 55 million international passengers per annum, but is only the fourth busiest including domestic flights. On 30 June 1995, a record 193,678 passengers passed through. The busiest hour ever was on 14 July 1995 when 14,695 passengers passed through the four terminals.

**Left**
The opulent £2.1-billion King Khalid international airport outside Riyadh in Saudi Arabia is the world's largest airport.

# Bridges and tunnels

## Bridges

### Longest bridge
The Second Lake Pontchartrain Causeway, which joins Mandeville and Metairie, Louisiana, USA, is 38.42 km (23 miles 1,538 yd) long. It was completed in 1969.

### Longest bridge continuously over sea
The Confederation Bridge, which joins Prince Edward Island to New Brunswick on the Canadian mainland, is 11 km (6 miles 1,478 yd) long including approaches. It was opened in June 1997.

### Longest cable-suspension bridge
The 1,991-m (6,532-ft) main span of the Akashi-Kaikyo bridge, joining the Japanese island of Awaji to the main island Honshū, was completed in 1997. The bridge, which is part of a scheme to link Honshū to Shikoku, will be open to traffic early in 1998.

### Longest cable-suspension bridge in UK
The longest British bridge span is the main span of the Humber Estuary Bridge, linking East Yorkshire and Lincolnshire, at 1,410 m (4,626 ft). It was completed in 1980. Including the Hessle and Barton side spans, the bridge is 2,220 m (1 mile 670 yd) long.

### Longest covered bridge
The bridge at Hartland, New Brunswick, Canada, measures 390.8 m (1,282 ft) overall and was completed in 1899.

### Busiest bridge
The San Francisco Oakland Bay Bridge was used by an average 274,000 vehicles a day in 1996—over 100 million vehicles a year.

### Longest plastic bridge
The longest span reinforced-plastic bridge is at the Aberfeldy Golf Club at Aberfeldy, Perth and Kinross, UK. The main span is 63 m (206 ft 8 in) and the overall bridge is 113 m (370 ft 9 in) long.

### Longest span for road and rail bridge
The Tsing Ma Bridge, Hong Kong, China, was opened in April 1997. The road and rail suspension bridge has the world's largest single span, at 297 m (974 ft 5 in).

### Longest steel arch bridge
The New River Gorge bridge, built near Fayetteville, West Virginia, USA, has a span measuring 518 m (1,700 ft).

### Longest cantilever bridge
The Pont de Québec over the St Lawrence River, Canada, has the longest cantilever truss. It measures 549 m (1,800 ft) between piers, 987 m (3,239 ft) overall and carries a railway track and two carriageways.

### Longest cable-stayed bridges
The Pont de Normandie, in Le Havre, France, has a cable-stayed main span of 856 m (2,808 ft). It was opened to traffic in 1995.

The longest span cable-stayed bridge in the United Kingdom is the second Severn Bridge, with a main span of 456 m (1,496 ft). The length of the crossing structure is 5.168 km (3 miles 370 yd).

### Longest stone arch bridges
Rockville Bridge north of Harrisburg, Pennsylvania, USA, was completed in 1901. It is 1,161 m (3,810 ft) long, and its 48 spans contain 196,000 tonnes of stone.

## WORLD'S LONGEST TUNNE

The longest stone arch span is the Wuchaohe Bridge at Fenghuang, Hunan Province, China, at 120 m (394 ft).

### Longest bridge for road and rail traffic
The Seto-Ohashi double-deck bridge linking Kojima, Honshū, with Sakaide, Shikoku, Japan, is the longest road and rail bridge, at 12.3 km (7 miles 1,132 yd). Built at a cost of £4.9 billion, it was opened in 1988.

### Longest bicycle/pedestrian bridge
The Old Chain of Rocks Bridge, Madison, Illinois, USA, is 1,631 m (5,350 ft) long.

# LONGEST CABLE-STAYED SPAN 856 M

BRIDGE, WHICH LINKS AWAJI AND HONSHŪ, JAPAN

**Left**
The Confederation Bridge, which joins Prince Edward Island to New Brunswick on the Canadian mainland, has 44 spans, each approximately 250 m (825 ft), totalling 11 km (6 miles 1,478 yd). The bridge, which has been designed to last for 100 years, was designed with curves in order to maintain the concentration of drivers.

IS THE NEW YORK CITY WEST DELAWARE WATER-SUPPLY TUNNEL, AT 169 KM

### Longest pedestrian bridge
Walnut Street Bridge, Chattanooga, Tennessee, USA, was built in 1891 and reopened to the public in 1992. The 722-m (2,370-ft) truss bridge spans the Tennessee River from Frazier Ave in the north to Walnut Street in the south. A 780-ft viaduct forms the northern approach to the bridge.

### Longest concrete girder bridge
The 298-m (978-ft) main span of the Raftsundet Bridge, linking the main islands in the Lofoten group, Norway, was completed in 1997. The bridge will open in 1998.

### Longest steel box bridge
The steel box Ponte Costa e Silva, Rio de Janeiro, Brazil, is 300 m (984 ft) long. It opened in 1974.

### Longest concrete arch bridge
The east span of Krk-1 Bridge, linking Krk island to the Croatian mainland, is 390 m (1,279 ft) long. It opened to traffic in 1980.

### Longest bascule bridge
The Erasmus Bridge, in Rotterdam, Netherlands, was opened in Sept 1996. It has two components: an unusual single-pylon suspension bridge and the world's longest bascule (drawbridge), which is 82 m (269 ft) long.

### Widest bridge
The Sydney Harbour Bridge, NSW, Australia, is 48.8 m (160 ft) wide. It carries two electric overhead railway tracks, eight lanes of roadway, a cycle track and a footway.

### Tallest bridge
The towers of the Akashi-Kaikyo Bridge, between Honshū and Awaji islands, Japan, rise to a height of 297 m (974 ft 5 in). The bridge is scheduled to open to traffic in March 1998.

### Highest road bridge
The suspension bridge over the Royal Gorge of the Arkansas River in Colorado, USA, is 321 m (1,053 ft) above the water level. It has a main span of 268 m (880 ft) and was constructed in six months in 1929.

### Highest rail bridge
The world's highest railway bridge is the Yugoslav Railways Mala Reka viaduct at Kolasin on the Belgrade-Bar line. It is 198 m (650 ft) high and was opened in 1976.

## Tunnels
### Longest undersea tunnel
Each twin rail tunnel of the Channel Tunnel, which runs under the English Channel between Folkestone, Kent, UK, and Calais, France, is 49.94 km (31 miles 32 yd) long. Although the overall length of the Channel Tunnel is less than the Seikan tunnel, the section under the sea is 14.7 km (9 miles 17 yd) longer than that of the Seikan rail tunnel. It was officially opened in 1994.

### Longest water-supply tunnel
The longest tunnel of any kind is the New York City West Delaware water-supply tunnel, begun in 1937 and completed in 1944. It has a diameter of 4.1 m (13 ft 6 in) and runs for 169 km (105 miles) from the Rondout reservoir into the Hillview reservoir, in Yonkers, New York, USA.

### Longest rail tunnel
The Seikan rail tunnel is 53.85 km (33 miles 809 yd) long and was bored to 240 m (787 ft) beneath sea level and 100 m (328 ft) below the seabed of the Tsugaru Strait between Tappi Saki, Honshū, and Fukushima, Hokkaidō, Japan. It was bored through on 27 Jan 1983 and the first test run took place on 13 March 1988.

### Longest road tunnel
The two-lane St Gotthard road tunnel from Göschenen to Airolo, Switzerland, is 16.32 km (10 miles 246 yd) long and was opened to traffic in Sept 1980. Construction began in 1969, and cost Sw.Fr 690 million (then £175 million) and 19 workers' lives.

### Largest road tunnel
The road tunnel which has the largest diameter was blasted through Yerba Buena Island, San Francisco, California, USA. It is 24 m (77 ft 10 in) wide, 17 m (56 ft) high and 165 m (540 ft) long. Around 250,000 vehicles pass through on its two decks every day.

# Road and rail

## Roads

### Highest road

The highest road in the world is above the Changlung Valley in Aksai, China, (administered by China, but claimed by India) at an altitude of about 5,889 m (19,320 ft). This military road is closed to foreign traffic.

The highest trail in the world is a 13-km (8-mile) stretch of the Gangdise, Tibet, between Khaleb and Xinjifu, Tibet, which in two places exceeds 6,080 m (20,000 ft).

The highest motor road in Europe is the Pico de Veleta in the Sierra Nevada, Spain. The climb of 36 km (22.4 miles) brings the motorist to 3,469 m (11,384 ft) above sea level and became, on completion of a road on the southern side of the range in 1974, arguably Europe's highest mountain pass.

The highest unclassified road in the United Kingdom is a lane leading to the summit of Great Dun Fell, Cumbria, at an altitude of 847 m (2,780 ft). The road leads to a Ministry of Defence and Air Traffic Control installation, and a permit is needed to use it.

The highest classified road in the United Kingdom is the A93 over the Grampians, which reaches an altitude of 665 m (2,182 ft) at the Cairnwell Pass.

### Lowest road

A road along the shores of the Dead Sea in Israel is 393 m (1,290 ft) below sea level.

### Widest road

The widest road in the world is the Monumental Axis, running for 2.4 km (1½ miles) from the Municipal Plaza to the Plaza of the Three Powers in Brasilia, Brazil. The six-lane boulevard was opened in April 1960 and is 250 m (820.2 ft) wide.

The San Francisco–Oakland Bay Bridge Toll Plaza has 23 lanes (17 westbound) serving the bridge in Oakland, California, USA.

The only 17 carriageway lanes side by side in the United Kingdom are on the M61 at Linnyshaw Moss, Worsley, Manchester.

### Traffic volume

The most heavily travelled stretch of road is Interstate 405 (San Diego Freeway) in Orange County, California, USA. Its peak-hour volume is 25,500 vehicles on a 1.45 km (0.9 mile) stretch between Garden Grove Freeway and Seal Beach Boulevard.

The greatest traffic volume on a British motorway is 168,000 vehicles a day on the M25/M4 to M25/A3313 (Airport Way).

The United Kingdom's busiest non-motorway road is the A3 Broadway/Kingston bypass/Kingston Road to Malden Road/Kingston bypass, with 125,000 vehicles per day.

### Most complex interchange

The junction known officially as 5/22/57 Interchange, and nicknamed Orange Crush Junction, Orange County, California, USA, is on two levels and comprises 34 routes with 66 lanes. The total average daily traffic volume on these lanes is 629,000 vehicles.

The most complex interchange on the British road system is at Gravelly Hill, north of Birmingham, on the Midland Link Motorway section of the M6. Popularly known as 'Spaghetti Junction', it includes 18 routes on six levels (together with a diverted canal and river). Its construction consumed 26,000 tonnes of steel, 250,000 tonnes of concrete and 300,000 tonnes of earth, and cost £8.2 million.

### Longest ring-road

The M25 London Orbital Motorway is 195.5 km (121½ miles) long. Constructed from 1972 to 1986, it cost an estimated £909 million, or £7.5 million per mile.

### Longest viaduct

The longest elevated viaduct on the British road system is the 4.78 km (2 miles 1,702 yd) Gravelly Hill to Castle Bromwich section of the M6 in the West Midlands.

## Streets

### Largest square

Tiananmen 'Gate of Heavenly Peace' Square in Beijing, China, covers 39.6 ha (98 acres).

### Longest street name

The longest street name in Britain is the 34-letter Bolderwood Arboretum Ornamental Drive in the New Forest, Hants.

### Shortest street

The world's shortest street is Elgin Street in Bacup, Lancs, UK, which has a total length of only 5.2 m (17 ft).

Trianglen, a designated road with buildings on only one side, at Store Heddinge, Denmark, is 1.85 m (6 ft 1 in) long. It forms one side of a road junction.

### Narrowest street

Vicolo della Virilita (which translates as Virility Alley) in Ripatransone in Italy's Marche region

### MOROCOCHA BRANCH OF

averages 43 cm (1 ft 5 in) in width but is just 38 cm (1ft 3 in) wide at the narrowest point.

### Steepest street

The steepest street in the world is Baldwin Street, Dunedin, New Zealand, which has a maximum gradient of 1 in 1.266.

The steepest motorable road in the British Isles is the unclassified Chimney Bank at Rosedale Abbey, N Yorkshire, marked '1 in 3'.

An unclassified road at Ffordd Penllech, Harlech, Gwynedd, UK, officially described as not suitable for motor vehicles, is 1 in 2.91 at its steepest point.

## Railways

### Widest and narrowest gauge

The widest gauge in standard use is 1.676 m (5 ft 6 in), as used in Spain, Portugal, India, Pakistan, Bangladesh, Sri Lanka, Argentina and Chile.

The narrowest gauge on which public services are operated is 260 mm (10¼ in) on the Wells Harbour and the Wells Walsingham Railways in Norfolk, UK.

### Deepest railway line

The Seikan Tunnel, which crosses the Tsugaro Strait between Honshū and Hokkaidō, Japan, descends to 240 m (786 ft) below sea level. The tunnel was opened on 13 March 1988 and is 53.85 km

**Right**
The Katoomba Scenic Railway in the Blue Mountains of NSW, Australia, is the world's steepest railway. It was originally part of the Katoomba mining tramways, constructed between 1880 and 1900. It descends through sandstone cliffs, taking advantage of a natural rock tunnel.

KATOOMBA
SCENIC RAILWAY
BLUE MOUNTAINS AUSTRALIA

# STEEPEST STREET 1 IN 1.266

## 240 M BELOW SEA LEVEL

(33 miles 810 yds) long. Trains stop in the middle for two minutes so that passengers can take pictures through the windows of panels on the walls of the tunnel.

The deepest European line is the Channel Tunnel between England and France. The rails are 127 m (417 ft) below mean sea level.

The Severn Tunnel is the deepest in the UK, descending 43.8 m (144 ft) below sea level.

### Highest line
The standard gauge 1,435 mm (4 ft 8½ in) track on the Morococha branch of the Peruvian State Railways at La Cima is 4,818 m (15,806 ft) above sea level.

The Snowdon Mountain Railway, which rises from Llanberis, Gwynedd to 1,064 m (3,493 ft) above sea level, just below the summit of Snowdon (Yr Wyddfa), is the highest railway in the United Kingdom.

**Left**
The country with the greatest length of graded roads is the United States with 6,244,497 km (3,880,151 miles).

## PERUVIAN STATE RAILWAYS AT LA CIMA IS WORLD'S HIGHEST AT 4,818 M

### Steepest railway
The Katoomba Scenic Railway in the Blue Mountains, NSW, Australia, is 311 m (1,020 ft) long with a gradient of 1 in 0.82. A 220-hp electric winding machine hauls the car by 2.2-cm (⅞-in) diameter steel cables. The ride takes about 1 min 40 sec and carries around 420,000 passengers a year.

### Steepest gradient
The steepest gradient worked by adhesion rather than being hauled by winding, is 1 in 11, between Chedde and Servoz on the metre-gauge SNCF Chamonix line, France.

### Busiest rail system
The railway that carries the most passengers is the East Japan Railway Co. In 1995/6, a total of 6.067 million journeys were made.

### Greatest length of railway
The country that has the greatest length of railway is the United States with 223,155 km (138,666 miles) of track.

**Left**
A house in Baldwin Street, Dunedin, New Zealand, the world's steepest street. The camera has been tilted to the same gradient as the hill, making the hill's incline 'disappear'. The angle of the front door to the ground shows how far the shot has been turned to make the street appear level.

## Underground railways
### Longest system
The most extensive underground or rapid transit railway system is the London Underground, UK. Its total length is 408 km (253 miles), of which 154 km (95 miles) are bored tunnels and 32 km (20 miles) use the 'cut and cover' method. It has 16,865 staff and serves 267 stations. The 3,985 cars form a fleet of 547 trains. From 1995–96 a total of 784 million journeys were made.

### Shortest system
Opened in 1875, the Istanbul Metro, Turkey, is just 650 m (2,133 ft) long.

### System with most stations
The underground system that has the greatest number of stations is MTA New York City Transit, in New York, USA. Its first section was opened on 27 Oct 1904. There are now 469 stations in the system, (277 of which are underground) and the network covers 370 km (230 miles). The MTA New York Transit serves an estimated 7.1 million passengers daily.

### Busiest system
The Greater Moscow Metro, Russia, opened in 1935. It serves between 3.2 and 3.3 billion passengers a year. Its rolling stock consists of 3,925 railcars, and it has 158 stations and 244 km (152 miles) of track.

# Science and technology

# Strange phenomena

**Right**
In the 1970s, a cat was found in a builder's yard at Trafford Park, Manchester, UK with a pair of fluffy wings projecting from its back, which according to workers at the yard, could be raised above its body. Winged cats have been recorded all over the world, but until recently there was no explanation for their 'wings'. The phenomenon is now known to be due to a condition called feline cutaneous asthenia (FCA).

**Far right**
On 20 Oct 1967, Roger Patterson and fellow rancher Bob Grimlin allegedly encountered Big Foot at Bluff Creek, northern California, USA. Anthropologist Prof. Grover Krantz, from Washington State University, believes that a human wearing a Big-Foot suit could not achieve the muscle movements and precise striding gait performed by the filmed creature.

**Right**
A photograph of an alleged autopsy on one of the 'bodies' found in 1947 at Roswell, New Mexico, USA. The bodies, found next to the wreckage of a 'huge disc', were described as having round heads, small eyes and hairless bodies, with yellow or orange skin. A report published by the US military in June 1997 stated that the 'bodies' were dummies from a test aircraft.

## The paranormal

### Most hauntings by a royal ghost?
Anne Boleyn's ghost has been seen in Hampton Court, London, UK; on Tower Hill close to where she was imprisoned in the Tower of London; at Rochford Hall, Essex, and at Blickling Hall, Norfolk.

### Most haunted village in the UK?
Pluckley, Kent, UK, is said to be home to at least 14 ghosts, including a screaming man, a red lady and a monk, all of which have been seen and heard by residents.

### Most haunted mountain?
In 1891, Prof. Norman Collie claimed to have been followed by someone taking steps three or four times the length of his own when descending the summit of the 1,309-m (4,296-ft) high Ben MacDhui in the Cairngorms, Aberdeenshire, UK. Since then, many mountaineers claim to have experienced similar sensations of uncontrollable yet inexplicable fear and panic. The malign humanoid entity is referred to locally as 'Am Fear Liath Mor', the Big Grey Man.

### Most paranormal world leader?
President Abraham Lincoln of the USA is said to have had a vision of his own death 10 days before his assassination. He was woken by the sound of sobbing and went downstairs to the East Room, where there was a corpse. When he asked who had died, a soldier guarding the body replied, "The President. He was killed by an assassin".

### Most mysterious footprints?
On 8 Feb 1895, residents of the towns of Topsham, Lympstone, Exmouth, Teignmouth and Dawlish, in Devon, UK, awoke to find footmarks in the snow belonging to a mysterious animal. The footprints, thought to be made by a biped, had a spread of 20 cm (8 in) and resembled a donkey shoe 38–68 mm (1½–2½ in) across. The prints were found on narrow walls, on roofs and in gardens enclosed by high walls. No known meteorological effect can create these 'hoofprints' or 'devil's footprints'.

### Most dangerous ghostly creature?
British reports of phantom-like creatures or hounds all share certain characteristics; they are said to be the size of labradors, have black shaggy coats, exude a sulphurous odour and have eyes that glow like fire. They also appear solid, but vanish, sometimes into a fiery explosion.

The most terrifying case is said to have occurred in Aug 1577, during a morning service at Bungay church in Suffolk, UK. A ferocious black dog materialised in the aisle and attacked the congregation, killing two people and burning another very severely. It was then seen in nearby Blythburgh church where it left behind scorched claw marks on the church door, which are still visible today.

### First reported flying saucer?
On 24 June 1947, Idaho businessman Kenneth Arnold saw nine flying disc-shaped objects near Mount Rainier, Washington, USA, while piloting a Callair aeroplane. The term 'flying saucer' was later coined by a reporter documenting the case.

### Most controversial alien encounter?
In New Mexico, USA, on 3 July 1947, rancher Mac Brazel heard a strange explosion, and on investigating found his fields covered by small wooden beams engraved with hieroglyphics, and thin sheets of extremely durable metal. He also found wreckage believed to be from a huge disc. Brazel alerted nearby Roswell Army Air Field.

When service personnel located the 'disc' there appeared to be non-humans lying beside it, some still alive. The burned bodies and the wreckage were taken to Roswell. On 8 July the base's public information officer, Walter Haut, issued an unauthorized press release stating that the army had gained possession of a flying disc. This was denied by a senior Air Force officer, who claimed that the object was the remains of a weather balloon.

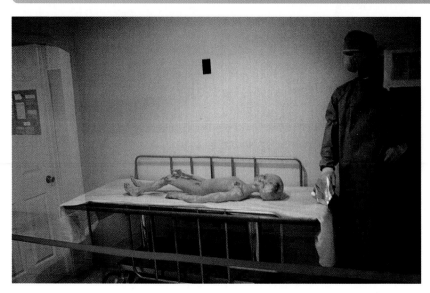

# 14 GHOSTS IN ONE VILLAGE

ITS WAY INTO THE BLOODSTREAM OF ITS VICTIM

## Natural phenomena

**Earliest ball lightning?**
In the 6th century, St Gregory of Tours wrote about a fire ball incident during a ceremony marking the dedication of a chapel.

**Earliest crop circles?**
A pamphlet of 1678 showing an illustration of a crop circle, blamed a 'mowing devil' for a configuration in an oat field in Herts, UK. Explanations for their appearance range from animals, over fertilization, bickering flocks of birds and landing marks left behind by UFOs. Some of the more elaborate circles are thought to be hoaxes.

**Most elusive islands?**
The three Aurora Islands reputedly lay midway between the Falkland Islands and South Georgia in the Atlantic Ocean. They were first reported in 1762 by the whaler *Aurora* and in the late 18th century the captain of the *Atrevida* charted, sketched and named them. During the 1820s, several vessels visited their documented location, but the islands had vanished without trace.

The island of Brasil reputedly makes rare appearances off the west coast of Ireland.

Sarah Ann Island was recorded to have been sited far to the west of Ecuador, but has now vanished without trace.

The St Vincent Islands were discovered off Panama's west coast by Antonio Martinus in 1789 and were said to be inhabited for a time by Father Santa Clara, a priest, but no trace of them can now be found.

**Most dangerous mystery animal?**
The Mongolian death worm is reputed to live in the southern Gobi desert and resemble a large fat worm, up to 1 m (4 ft) long and dark red in colour, with spike-like projections at both ends. It is said to squirt corrosive poison which kills by burning its way through the flesh and into the victim's bloodstream.

**Earliest rat kings?**
On 13 July 1748, German miller Johann Heinrich Jager found 18 rats linked to one another by their tails, intertwined in a large, intricate knot. This is the earliest record of this type of gathering of rats, called a rat king or *roi de rats*.

In May 1828, a rat king with 32 rats was found in a chimney at Buchheim, Germany.

**Largest winged cats?**
The phenomenon of 'winged cats' is now known to be due to a condition known as FCA (feline cutaneous asthenia), which causes the cat's skin to be abnormally elastic, especially on their shoulders, back and haunches, stretching it into long, fur covered, wing-like projections. In 1949 a Swedish specimen was on record as having a wing span of 58.42 cm (23 in).

**First Loch Ness monster picture?**
On 8 Aug 1972, Dr Robert Rhine and his Academy of Applied Science team detected on sonar a very large solid object, 6–9 m (20–30 ft) long, pursuing a shoal of fish in Urquhart Bay, Loch Ness, Highland, UK. After underwater photos were developed, they showed a flipper-like structure,

13:35:42

13:35:43

OWN ASSASSINATION, 10 DAYS BEFORE HE DIED

## Mystery creatures

**Most controversial photos?**
North America's Big Foot, a giant ape-like creature that walks on its hind legs and is reputed to live in dense forested regions, is said to be 1.8–3 m (6–10 ft) tall and weigh 320–1,135 kg (700–2,500 lb). On 20 Oct 1967, Roger Patterson shot a film that purportedly portrays a Big Foot seen at Bluff Creek, northern California, USA.

In July 1917, 15-year-old Elsie Wright took photographs in woodland near Cottingley, W Yorkshire, UK, of her cousin Frances with a group of fairies dancing in front of her. Photographic experts could not explain how such images had been taken by the girls. Only on 17 March 1983 did Frances confess that the fairies had been cut out and painted by Frances, then held in place by hatpins.

1.25–2 m (4–6 ft) long and rhomboidal in shape, attached to a much larger body, similar to a plesiosaur (extinct marine reptiles of Jurassic and Cretaceous times).

**Closest encounter with a water monster?**
One morning in July 1974, Mrs B. Clark was swimming near Lake Okanagan's southern shore in Canada when she reported that she felt something heavy make contact with her legs. She claimed she saw a hump 2.5 m (8 ft) long, 1.2 m (4 ft) above the water, travelling away from her. Through the clear water she saw a dark grey striped body with a forked horizontal tail 1.5–3 m (5–10 ft) behind the hump. She estimated the creature to be 7.6–9 m (25–30 ft) long, but only 0.9–1.2 m (3–4 ft) across. This description corresponds closely to zeuglodonts (officially 'extinct' serpentine whales).

13:35:44

TUNGSTEN IS THE METAL WITH BOTH THE HIGHEST MELTING POINT, AT 3,414°C

## Isotopes

### Most and fewest isotopes
There are at least 2,670 isotopes—tin (Sn) and barium (Ba) have the most with 38. Hydrogen (H) has the least number of accepted isotopes, with just three.

### Lightest and heaviest isotopes
The lightest nuclide is hydrogen 1 (H 1) or protium, whilst the heaviest is ununbium 277 (Uub 277), discovered in Feb 1996.

### Most and least stable isotopes
The most stable radioactive isotope is tellurium 128 with a half-life of $1.5 \times 10^{24}$ years. The least stable isotope is lithium 5 which decays in $4.4 \times 10^{-22}$ seconds.

### Least stable hadron
The least stable hadron is the N (2600) baryon (discovered 1978–79), of lifetime $1.0 \times 10^{-24}$ sec.

### Lightest and heaviest leptons
The three neutrino leptons are predicted as having zero mass, while the heaviest lepton is the tau with a mass of 1.777 GeV.

## The 112 elements

### Most common elements
Hydrogen is the most common element in both the Universe (over 90%) and the Solar System (70.68%). Iron is the most common element found on Earth, (36% of the mass), while molecular nitrogen ($N_2$) is the most common element in the atmosphere (78.08% by volume or 75.52% by mass).

### Rarest elements
Only 0.16 g (0.0056 oz) of astatine (At) is present in the Earth's crust, of which the isotope astatine 215 (At 215) accounts for only 4.5 nanograms ($1.6 \times 10^{-10}$ oz).

Radon (Rn) is the rarest element in the atmosphere at only $6 \times 10^{-18}$ parts by volume, equivalent to only 2.4 kg (5 lb 5oz).

### Newest element
The heaviest and newest element is 112, which was produced in Feb 1996 at the Gesellschaft für Schwerionenforschung,

Darmstadt, Germany. It has a mass of 277 and decays in a lifetime of 240 millionths of a second.

### Hardest element
The diamond allotrope of carbon (C) has a Knoop value of 8,400. The Knoop value of one of the softest minerals, gypsum, is 40.

### Most ductile element
One gram of gold (Au) can be drawn to a length of 2.4 km (or 1 oz to 43 miles).

### Highest tensile strength
Boron (B), has a tensile strength of 5.7 GPa ($5.7 \times 10^9$ Pa or $8.3 \times 10^5$ lbf/in²).

### Lightest and densest gases
At NTP (normal temperature and pressure, 0°C and one atmosphere), the lightest gas is hydrogen (H) at 0.00008989 g/cm³

(0.005612 lb/ft³). The densest is radon (Rn) at 0.01005 g/cm³ (0.6274 lb/ft³).

### Highest melting and boiling points
Among metals, tungsten or wolfram (W) has the highest melting point at 3,414°C (6,177°F), and the highest boiling point at 5,847°C (10,557°F). The graphite form of carbon sublimes directly to vapour at 3,704°C (6,699°F) and can be obtained as a liquid only from above a temperature of 4,730°C (8,546°F) and a pressure of 10 MPa (100 atmospheres).

### Lowest melting and boiling points
Helium (He) cannot be obtained as a solid at atmospheric pressure, the minimum being 2.532 MPa (24.985 atmospheres) at a temperature of −272.375°C (−458.275°F). Helium also has the lowest boiling point at −268.928°C (−452.070°F).

For metallic elements, mercury (Hg) has the lowest melting and boiling points, at −38.829°C (−37.892°F) and 356.62°C (673.92°F) respectively.

## Chemical extremes

### Strongest acid
The strongest known acid is an 80% solution of antimony pentafluoride in hydrofluoric acid. A weaker 50% solution is $10^{18}$ times stronger than concentrated sulphuric acid.

### Bitterest substance
The substances that have the bitterest taste are based on the denatonium cation

SMALLEST HOLES IN THE WORLD WERE MADE ON

and have been produced commercially as benzoate and saccharide.

### Sweetest substance
Talin, obtained from arils (appendages found on certain seeds) of the katemfe plant (*Thaumatococcus daniellii*) which was discovered in West Africa, is 6,150 times sweeter than a 1% sucrose solution.

### Smelliest substance
The most evil of the 17,000 smells so far classified are considered to be ethyl mercaptan ($C_2H_5SH$) and butyl seleno-mercaptan ($C_4H_9SeH$).

### Most powerful nerve gas
Ethyl S-2-diisopropylaminoethylmethyl phosphonothiolate, or VX, developed at the Chemical Defence Experimental Establishment, Porton Down, Wilts, UK,

# 1 G GOLD DRAWN TO 2.4 KM

## AND THE HIGHEST BOILING POINT, AT 5,847°C

in 1952, is 300 times more powerful than the phosgene ($COCl_2$) used in WWI.

### Most lethal man-made chemical
The compound 2, 3, 7, 8-tetrachlorodibenzo-p-dioxin), or TCDD, is the most deadly of the 75 known dioxins. It is 150,000 times more deadly than cyanide.

### Most absorbent substance
'H-span', or Super Slurper, composed of one half starch derivative and one quarter each of acrylamide and acrylic acid can, when treated with iron, retain water at 1,300 times its own weight.

### Least dense solid
Silica aerogels are the least dense solids. They consist of tiny spheres of bonded silicon and oxygen atoms joined into long strands separated by pockets of air. Aerogels, with a density of only 0.005 $g/cm^3$ (5 $oz/ft^3$), were produced at the Lawrence Livermore Laboratory, California, USA.

### Most heat-resistant substance
The existence of a complex material known as NFAAR, or Ultra Hightech Starlite, was announced in April 1993. It is apparent that it can temporarily resist plasma temperatures (10,000°C or 18,032°F).

### Coldest atoms
The lowest kinetic energy, or coldest atoms, was set at 10 nanoKelvins, 10 thousand millionths of 1°C above absolute zero, at the JILA Research Institute, University of Colorado, USA.

## Physical extremes

### Highest temperature
In 1994 a temperature of 510 million°C (920 million°F) was attained at the Princeton Plasma Physics Laboratory, New Jersey, USA, using a deuterium-tritium plasma mix.

### Lowest temperature
A temperature of 280 picoKelvin (2.8 x $10^{-10}$ K or 280 trillionths of a degree) was achieved in a nuclear demagnetization device at the Helsinki University of Technology, Finland.

### Highest superconducting temperature
The highest critical temperature yet attained is –140.7°C (–221.3°F), achieved at the Laboratorium für Festkörperphysik, Zürich, Switzerland, for a mixture of oxides of mercury, barium, calcium and copper.

### Highest critical current in a tube
Scientists at Hoechst, Germany, found that a 11-cm-diameter (4⅓-in) superconducting ceramic tube could bear a current of 12,500 amperes at a temperature of 77 K.

### Highest pressure
A sustained laboratory pressure of 170 GPa (1.7 million atmospheres) was reported from the giant hydraulic diamond-faced press at the Carnegie Institution's Geophysical Laboratory, Washington, DC, USA, in 1978.

### Most powerful electric current
In 1996, scientists at Oak Ridge National Laboratory, USA, sent a current of 2 million amperes/$cm^2$ down a superconducting wire.

### Lowest friction
The lowest coefficient of static and dynamic friction of any solid is 0.03. This result was achieved by sliding Hi-T-Lube on itself.

### Hottest flame
Carbon subnitride ($C_4N_2$) is capable, at one atmosphere pressure, of generating a flame calculated to reach 4,988°C (9,010°F).

### Smallest hole
In July 1992, at the University of Munich, Germany, holes corresponding to a diameter of 3.16 x $10^{-10}$ m (3.16 Å) were produced on the surface of molybdenum disulphide using a mercury drill.

### Brightest light
Scientists at the University of Michigan, USA, achieved 10–20 watts/$cm^2$ with a pulse in an argon laser. The pressure in the laser's plasma was 1,000 million atmospheres.

### Highest velocity
A plastic disc was projected at 150 km/sec (93 miles/sec) in Aug 1980 at the Naval Research Laboratory, Washington, DC, USA.

### Magnetic fields
The strongest continuous field strength was 38.7±0.3 teslas, at Massachusetts Institute of Technology, USA, in 1994. The weakest was 8 x $10^{-15}$ teslas in the same laboratory.

### Highest voltage
The highest obtained was 32±1.5 MV by the National Electrostatics Corporation at Oak Ridge, Tennessee, USA, in 1979.

## THE SURFACE OF MOLYBDENUM DISULPHIDE USING A MERCURY DRILL

**Left**
Gears and sprockets can be protected against friction wear by General Magnaplate's solid dry lubricant Hi-T-Lube, which produces the lowest coefficient of static and dynamic friction of any solid at 0.03.

# Energy

**Right**
The most powerful installed power station in the world is the Itaipu hydro-electric plant on the Paraná River near the border between Brazil and Paraguay. The reservoir behind the dam has drowned the world's second and sixth greatest waterfalls by volume.

## Oil

### Oil production
The world's largest oil producer is Saudi Arabia, with production in 1995 estimated at 7.867 million barrels per day.

### Oil consumption
The USA is the largest with 17.7 million barrels a day in 1994, 26% of the world total.

### Largest oil field
The world's largest oil field is the Ghawar field in Saudi Arabia, developed by Aramco, and measuring 240 x 35 km (150 x 22 miles), with EUR (estimated ultimate recovery) of 82 billion barrels of oil.

### Largest oil refinery
Amoco's refinery in Texas City, Texas, USA, has a crude capacity of 433,000 barrels per day as of 1 Jan 1996.

### Heaviest oil platform
The Pampo platform in the Campos Basin off Rio de Janeiro, Brazil, built and operated by the Petrobrás company, weighs 24,000 tonnes, covers 3,900 m$^2$ (42,000 ft$^2$) and produces 33,000 barrels per day.

### Tallest oil platform
In May 1997 the Ram-Powell tension leg platform was installed in the Gulf of Mexico. Designed and engineered by Shell Oil Company, it sets a new water-depth record for a production platform, extending 980 m (3,214 ft) from seabed to surface.

### Largest oil tanks
The five Aramco 1½-million-barrel storage tanks at Ju'aymah, Saudi Arabia, are 21.9 m (72 ft) tall with an 117.6-m (386-ft) diameter. They were completed in March 1980.

### Longest oil pipeline
The Interprovincial Pipe Line Inc. installation, which spans the North American continent from Edmonton, Alberta, Canada, through Chicago to Montreal, is 3,787.2 km (2,353 miles) long.

### Oil gusher
The Alborz No. 5 well, near Qum, Iran, blew on 26 Aug 1956. The uncontrolled oil gushed to a height of 52 m (170 ft), an amount of 120,000 barrels per day at a pressure of 62,100 kPa (9,000 lb/in$^2$). It was closed after 90 days' work by B. Mostofi and Myron Kinley of Texas, USA.

## Natural Gas

### Largest natural gas producer
Russia produced 643 billion m$^3$ (22,707 billion ft$^3$) of natural gas in 1996.

### Largest natural gas deposits
The gas deposit at Urengoi, Russia, has an EUR of 8 trillion m$^3$ (285 trillion ft$^3$).

### Greatest gas fire
A gas fire burnt at Gassi Touil in the Algerian Sahara from noon on 13 Nov 1961 to 9:30 a.m. on 28 April 1962. A pillar of flame

**Right**
The record-breaking Ram-Powell oil and gas production platform in the Gulf of Mexico is Shell's third tension leg platform. It extends to a depth of 980 m (3,214 ft). Shell also holds the world record for a fixed leg platform: the Bullwinkle, also in the Gulf of Mexico, stands in 413 m (1,353 ft) of water.

rose 137 m (450 ft) and smoke rose to 180 m (600 ft). Paul Neal ('Red') Adair of Houston, Texas, USA, extinguished it using 245 kg (540 lb) of dynamite.

### Largest gasholder
The largest gasholder ever was one at Oberhausen, Germany, with a height of 102 m (335 ft), a diameter of 66 m (217 ft) and a working gas volume of 630,000 m$^3$ (22,500,000 ft$^3$) under standard conditions.

Currently the largest is at the Prosper coking plant of Ruhrkohle AG at Essen, Germany. It has a working gas volume of 325,000 m$^3$ (11,480,000 ft$^3$) under standard conditions.

### Longest gas pipeline
The longest natural gas pipeline in the world is the TransCanada pipeline, which transported a record 66.6 billion m$^3$ (2,351.5 billion ft$^3$) of gas over 13,955 km (8,671 miles) of pipe in 1995.

# 643 BILLION M³ OF NATURAL GAS

TRANSPORTING 66.6 BILLION M³ OF GAS OVER 13,955 KM OF PIPE IN 1995

## Wind power

### Tallest windmill
The tallest windmill is St Patrick's Distillery Mill, Dublin, Ireland. It is 45.7 m (150 ft) tall.

### Largest wind generator
The $55-million Boeing Mod-5B wind generator in Oahu, Hawaii, USA, has 97.5-m (320-ft) rotors, and produces 3,200 kW when the wind reaches 51 km/h (32 mph).

### Largest British wind farms
In the United Kingdom the largest wind farm by number of machines is Llandinam Wind Farm, Powys, with 103 machines. The largest by capacity is Carno Wind Farm, Powys, with a 33.6 megawatt capacity.

## Power plants

### Largest power plant
The Itaipu hydro-electric plant on the Paraná River near the Brazil-Paraguay border was opened in 1984. It has now attained its ultimate rated capacity of 13,320 MW.

### Largest operational generator
The turbo-generator at the Ignalina atomic power station in Lithuania has a rated capacity of 1,450 MW (net).

### Largest transformers
Of the eight single-phase transformers rated 1,500,000 kVA in service with the American Electric Power Service Corporation, five step down from 765 to 345 kV.

Electric for use in nuclear fusion tests. Installed in the Japan Atomic Energy Research Institute in May 1995, it is 16.5 m (54 ft) long and weighs 353 tonnes.

### Biggest black out
The greatest power failure on record took place in seven north-eastern US states and Ontario, Canada, on 9–10 Nov 1965. About 30 million people over an area of 207,200 km² (80,000 miles²) were plunged into darkness, but only two were killed.

The highest voltages on a 3-phase AC line is the 1,200 kV line in Russia and Kazakhstan which runs over 1,610 km (1,000 miles). The first section takes the current from Siberia to North Kazakhstan, and the second section goes from Siberia to the Urals.

### Largest hydraulic turbines
Turbines at the Grand Coulee Third Powerplant, Washington, USA, are 9.7 m (32 ft) in diameter with a 407-tonne runner and a 317.5-tonne shaft.

**Left**
Solar panels in the Mojave Desert, California, USA. The facility is the largest solar electric power station in the world with a site covering 519 ha (1,280 acres).

ARABIA, WITH AN ESTIMATED ULTIMATE RECOVERY OF 82 BILLION BARRELS

### Largest solar electric power facility
In terms of nominal capacity, the largest solar electric power facility in the world is the Harper Lake Site (LSP 8 & 9) in the Mojave Desert, California, USA, operated by UC Operating Services. These two solar electric generating stations (SEGS) have a nominal capacity of 160 MW (80 MW each).

### Largest nuclear power station
The 6-reactor Zaporizhzhya power station in Ukraine gives a gross output of 6,000 MW.

### Highest level of fusion power
The highest level of controlled fusion power is 10.7 million watts in the Tokamak Fusion Test Reactor (TFTR), achieved at the Princeton Plasma Physics Laboratory, New Jersey, USA, on 2 Nov 1994.

### Largest DC generator
A DC generator with an overall capacity of 51,300 kW was developed by Mitsubishi

## Power lines

### Longest transmission lines
The longest span of any power line between pylons is 5,376 m (17,638 ft) across the Ameralik Fjord near Nuuk, Greenland. Built and erected by A.S. Betonmast of Oslo, Norway, in 1991/2 as part of the 132-kV line serving the 45-MW Buksefjorden Hydro Power Station, each of the four conductors weighs 38 tonnes.

### Highest transmission lines
The power lines across the 3,630-m (11,900-ft) Straits of Messina, Italy, are 205 m (675 ft) high on the Sicily side and 224 m (735 ft) high on the Calabria side.

### Highest voltages
The DC Pacific Inter-Tie in the USA, which stretches from east of Portland, Oregon, to a location east of Los Angeles, California, carries a voltage of 1,330 kV over a distance of 1,970 km (1,224 miles).

### Smallest turbines
A gas turbine with compressor and turbine wheels measuring just 4.0 cm (1⅗ in) and a maximum operating speed of 100,000 rpm was developed at the University of New South Wales, Sydney, Australia. Its first successful test run was on 4 Feb 1989.

## Batteries

### Largest battery
The 10 MW lead-acid battery at Chino, California, USA, has a design capacity of 40 MWh. It is currently used at an electrical sub-station for levelling peak demand loads. The project cost $13 million (£7.8 million).

### Most durable battery
The zinc foil and sulphur dry-pile batteries made by Watlin and Hill of London, UK, have powered ceaseless tintinnabulation inside a bell jar at the Clarendon Laboratory, Oxford, UK, since 1840.

# Heavy engineering

**Right**
The highest concrete dam in the world is the Grande Dixence in Switzerland. A total of 5,960,000 m³ (7,800,000 yd³) of concrete was used in its construction.

168 m (550 ft) high. The volume of concrete poured was 8,092,000 m³ (10,585,000 yd³) to a weight of 19,595,000 tonnes.

### Highest concrete dam
Grande Dixence, on the River Dixence in Switzerland, is the highest concrete dam. It was built between 1953 and 1961 to a height of 285 m (935 ft), with a crest length of 700 m (2,297 ft).

### Shortest-lived major dam
The Kara-Boguz Dam was built across the narrow strait between two sandy spits that separate the Kara-Bogaz-Gol Gulf, Turkmenistan, from the Caspian Sea, the largest inland salt lake, in 1982. The project proved to be ill-conceived, reducing the gulf to salt flats and causing the waters of the Caspian Sea to rise, thereby flooding coastal areas of the lake not only in Turkmenistan but also in Kazakhstan, Russia, Azerbaijan and Iran. In 1992 the dam was demolished restoring the 12,000-km² (4,600-mile²) gulf, which is only 10 m (33 ft) deep but, being lower than the Caspian itself, draws water in from the lake at a rate of 200–300 m³ (7,000–11,000 ft³) a second.

### Longest irrigation dam
Preliminary work on the Sardar Sadovar Dam, India, the world's largest irrigation dam, began in 1995–96 and was scheduled

for completion in 2000. The dam on the Narmada River, together with its network of canals, will provide drinking water for 5,614 villages and 130 towns in the Saurashtra and Kutch regions of Gujarat. The Narmada project, which will link all these settlements by pipeline, has been the subject of considerable controversy, with objections being raised by environmentalists.

## Waterworks
### Water tower
The Waterspheroid at Edmond, Oklahoma, USA, built in 1986 by Chicago Bridge and Iron Na-Con, Inc., rises to a height of 66.5 m (218 ft) and has a capacity of 1,893,000 litres (416,000 gal).

### Largest reservoir
The most voluminous fully human-made reservoir is the Bratskoye Reservoir, on the River Angara in Russia, with a volume of 169.3 km³ (40.6 miles³) and an area of 5,470 km² (2,112 miles²). It was completed in 1967.

## Dams
### Biggest dam
Measured by volume, the largest dam is New Cornelia Tailings on Ten Mile Wash, Arizona, USA, with a volume of 209.5 million m³ (274.5 million yd³). When completed, the Syncrude Tailings Dam near Fort McMurray, in Alberta, Canada, will be the largest, with a planned volume of 540 million m³ (706.3 million yd³). Both are earth-fill dams.

The largest dam in the United Kingdom is National Power's Gale Common Tailings Dam at Cridling Stubbs, N Yorkshire. It is an ash disposal scheme and to date c. 15 million m³ (20 million yd³) of compacted fill has been put in place.

### Highest dam
The Nurek Dam, 300 m (984 ft) high, on the River Vakhsh, Tajikistan, is currently the highest dam, but this should be surpassed by the Rogunskaya Dam, at 335 m (1,098 ft), also across the river Vakhsh. However, the break-up of the former Soviet Union has delayed its completion.

The rock-fill Llyn Brianne Dam, Ceredigion, is the United Kingdom's highest dam, reaching 91 m (298 ft 7 in) in Nov 1971. It became operational on 20 July 1972.

### Longest dam
The Yacyretá Dam across the River Paraná on the Argentina/Paraguay border, due for completion in 1998, is designed to be 69.6 km (43 miles 352 yd) long.

### Strongest dam
The Sayano-Shushenskaya Dam on the River Yenisey, Russia, is designed to bear a record load of 18 million tonnes from a fully-filled reservoir of 31,300 million m³ (41,000 million yd³) capacity. The dam, which was completed in 1987, is 245 m (803 ft) high.

### Largest concrete dam
The Grand Coulee Dam on the Columbia River, Washington State, USA, was begun in 1933 and became operational on 22 March 1941. It was finally completed in 1942 at a cost of $56 million (£14 million). It has a crest length of 1,272 m (4,173 ft) and is

# WATER VOLUME 209.5 MILLION M³

BY 1969 HAD FILLED TO AN AREA OF 8,482 KM²

The largest artificial lake in the world, measured by surface area, is Lake Volta, Ghana, formed by the Akosombo Dam, completed in 1965. By 1969 the lake had filled to an area of 8,482 km² (3,275 miles²), with a shoreline 7,250 km (4,500 miles) in length.

The completion in 1954 of the Owen Falls Dam near Jinja, Uganda, marginally raised the level of the natural lake by adding 204.8 km³ (49.1 miles³), and technically turned it into a reservoir with a surface area of 69,484 km² (26,828 miles²) and a capacity of $2.7 \times 10^{12}$ m³ ($3.5 \times 10^{12}$ yd³).

## Reclamation
### Largest polder
Of the five great polders in the old Zuider Zee, Netherlands, the largest is the East (Oostelijk) Flevoland Polder, at 528.4 km² (204 miles²). The largest would have been the Markerwaard, at 603 km² (231 miles²). However, although its dykes are complete, the project has been abandoned following national debate concerning environmental issues. The water area remaining after the erection of the dam (32 km or 20 miles in length), built between 1927 and 1932, is called IJsselmeer, which has an area of 1,262.6 km² (487½ miles²).

### Largest artificial island
The two Flevoland polders, the East (Oostelijk) Polder and the South (Zuidelijk) Polder, form a continuous land area and are linked to the rest of the Netherlands by dykes, bridges and causeways. Together these two polders could be considered a single artificial island, and they form the new Dutch province of Flevoland, with an area of 1,426 km² (551 miles²). Based on the new town of Lelystad, Flevoland includes two other sizeable new towns, Dronten and Almere, and had a population of 262,000 in 1995. The 'artificial island' has important industrial

S THE 69.6-KM YACYRETÁ DAM THAT STRETCHES OVER THE RIVER PARANÁ

### Largest British reservoir
The largest reservoir in the United Kingdom is Loch Quoich, Highland, Scotland, which was filled with 382 billion litres (84 billion gal) of water between Feb 1954 and Jan 1957. The reservoir has a surface area which covers 1,922 ha (4,750 acres) and its perimeter is 44.1 km (27 miles 700 yd) long.

About one half of the Netherlands is comprised of polders, either former fen or marsh, or land reclaimed from the sea. The area of reclaimed land exceeds 16,900 km² (6,540 miles²).

Since 1958 Monaco has increased in land area by 20% with the reclamation of 0.4 km² (³⁄₂₀ mile²) of land from the sea.

and recreational interests rather than being used solely for agricultural production, which was the original intention.

### Largest tidal river barrier
The largest tidal river barrier is the Oosterscheldedam, a storm-surge barrier in the south-west of the Netherlands. It has 65 concrete piers and 62 steel gates and covers a total length of 9 km (5½ miles).

### Largest levees
A levee is an embankment which is constructed in order to prevent flooding. The Mississippi levees, USA, were the largest ever built. They extended for 2,787 km (1,732 miles) along the main branch of the Mississippi River from Cape Girardeau, Missouri, USA, to the Gulf of Mexico and comprised more than 765 million m³ (1,000 million yd³) of earthworks. Levees on tributaries made up another 3,200 km (2,000 miles). Extensive flooding in the summer of 1993 has resulted in widespread damage to the levees.

## Scientific instruments

### Largest scientific instrument
The largest scientific instrument (and arguably the world's largest machine) is the Large Electron Positron (LEP) storage ring at CERN, Geneva, Switzerland, which is 3.8 m (12 ft 6 in) in diameter and 27 km (17 miles) in circumference. Over 60,000 tonnes of technical equipment have been installed in the tunnel and its eight working zones.

### Most powerful particle accelerator
In 1987 the 2-km (1.25-mile) diameter proton synchroton 'Tevatron' at the Fermi National Accelerator Laboratory (Fermilab) near Batavia, Illinois, USA, achieved a centre of mass energy of 1.8 TeV ($1.8 \times 10^{12}$ eV) by colliding beams of protons and antiprotons.

through the aluminium coil. The magnet is taller than a four-storey building, has a volume of about 1,728 m$^3$ (59,320 ft$^3$) and weighs 7,685 tonnes.

### Heaviest magnet
The 10-GeV synchrophasotron in the Joint Institute for Nuclear Research at Dubna, near Moscow, Russia, weighs 36,000 tonnes and is 60 m (196 ft) in diameter.

### Most powerful laser
In 1996, the 'Petawatt' at the Lawrence Livermore National Laboratory, California, USA, produced laser pulses capable of generating $1.3 \times 10^{15}$ W of power, much of which was delivered to a target the size of a grain of sand, in $1 \times 10^{-12}$ seconds. For this

### Smallest prism
In 1989, a glass prism with 0.01-mm (0.005-in) sides was created at the National Institute of Standards and Technology in Colorado, USA.

### Finest cut
In June 1983, it was reported that the $13-million Large Optics Diamond turning Machine at the Lawrence Livermore National Laboratory in California, USA, could sever a human hair 3,000 times lengthways.

### Finest balance
The Sartorius Microbalance Model 4108, made in Göttingen, Germany, can weigh objects of up to 0.5 g (⁹⁄₅₀₀ oz) to an accuracy of 0.01 µg, or $1 \times 10^{-8}$ g

### Fastest centrifuge
The highest man-made rotary speed ever achieved is 7,250 km/h (4,500 mph) by a tapered 15.2-cm (6-in) carbon fibre rod rotating in a vacuum at Birmingham University, UK, on 24 Jan 1975.

### Slowest machine
A nuclear environmental machine for testing stress corrosion, developed by Nene Instruments of Wellingborough, Northants, UK, can be controlled at one million millionth of a millimetre per minute, or 1 m (3 ft 4 in) in 2,000 million years.

### Largest electromagnet
An octagonal magnet forming part of the L3 detector experiment at the LEP storage ring at CERN, has 6,400 tonnes of low carbon steel yoke and 1,082 tonnes of aluminium coil. A uniform magnet field of 5 kilogauss is created by 300 amperes of current flowing

brief instant, that power was 1,300 times greater than the combined output of all US electrical generating plants. The laser is used to explore the fundamental properties of matter.

### Largest one-piece glass mirror
The Steward Observatory Mirror Laboratory at the University of Arizona, USA, has cast an 8.4-m (27-ft 9-in) mirror for a telescope made of borosilicate glass.

### Thinnest glass
Type D263 glass, made by Deutsche Spezialglas AG of Grünenplan, Germany, for use in electronic and medical equipment, has a minimum thickness of 0.025 mm (0.00098 in) and a maximum thickness of 0.035 mm (0.00137 in).

($3.5 \times 10^{-10}$ oz)—little more than one sixtieth of the weight of the ink on this full stop.

### Smallest test tube
In 1996 test tubes 1 micron (1 millionth of a metre) long with an internal diameter of less than ten nanometres (10 billionths of a metre) for containing a chemical reaction were made at the Ecole Polytechnique Fédérale de Lausanne, Switzerland.

### Sharpest objects
The sharpest manufactured objects are glass micro-pipette tubes whose bevelled tips have outer and inner diameters of 0.02 µm and 0.01 µm respectively, the latter being 6,500 times thinner than a human hair. They are used in intracellular work on living cells in techniques developed in 1977.

# HIGHEST ROTARY SPEED 7,250 KM/H

BILLION FRAMES/SECOND

### Thinnest metal wire
In Feb 1995, nanotechnologists at Glasgow University, Scotland, UK, made nickel wires just 3 nanometres (3 billionths of a metre) wide. The creation of the wires was a by-product—the main reason for the research was to investigate the resolution limits of electron beam lithography.

### Smallest ruler
In 1994 a ruler used for measuring lengths in an electron microscope was developed by John McCaffrey and Jean-Marc Baribeau of the Institute for Microstructural Sciences at the National Research Council, Canada. The ruler's smallest division is 18 atoms thick and five of the rulers stacked end to end would equal the diameter of a human hair.

### Smallest microphone
The world's smallest microphone measures 1.5 x 0.76 mm ($\frac{3}{50}$ x $\frac{3}{100}$ in), and has a frequency response of 10 Hz–10 kHz. It was developed in 1967 by Prof. Ibrahim Kavrak of Bogazici University, Istanbul, Turkey, to measure pressure in fluid flow.

### Smallest radar system
Tom McEwan invented a radar device on a silicon chip, 4 cm$^2$ (1½ in$^2$), with the key component costing less than $15 (£9) to manufacture. It can detect moving objects at up to 50 m (164 ft) away, and is being used as a virtual dipstick in industrial liquid tanks as well as an electronic stethoscope.

### Smallest thermometer
Dr Frederich Sachs of the State University of New York at Buffalo, USA, has developed an

## Timepieces
### Most accurate timekeeping device
A commercially available atomic clock accurate to one second in 1.6 million years, manufactured by Hewlett-Packard of Palo Alto, California, USA, was unveiled in Dec 1991. Designated the HP 5071A primary frequency standard with caesium-2 technology, it costs $54,000 (£32,400). It is about the size of a desktop computer.

### Oldest working clock
The world's oldest surviving clock is the faceless clock at Salisbury Cathedral in the United Kingdom, which dates from c. 1386. It was restored in 1956, having struck the hours for 498 years and ticked more than 500 million times.

It is 2.69 m (8 ft 10 in) high, 2.51 m (8 ft 3 in) wide and 14.02 m (46 ft) long. The f16 Cooke Apochromatic lens measures 160 cm (63 in).

A pinhole camera was created from a Portakabin unit measuring 10.4 x 2.9 x 2.64 m (34 ft x 9 ft 6 in x 9 ft) by photographers John Kippen and Chris Wainwright at the National Museum of Photography, Film and Television in Bradford, W Yorkshire, UK, on 25 March 1990. The unit produced a direct positive measuring 10.2 x 1.8 m (33 x 6 ft).

### Largest lens
The National Museum of Photography, Film and Television in Bradford, W Yorkshire, UK,

**Left**
Electronic engineer Tom McEwan has invented a radar device on a silicon chip, 4 cm$^2$ (1½ in$^2$), with the key component costing less than $15 (£9) to manufacture.

WIRES JUST 3 NANOMETRES (3 BILLIONTHS OF A METRE) WIDE IN FEB 1995

ultra-microthermometer for measuring the temperature of single living cells. Its tip is one micrometre in diameter—about $\frac{1}{50}$th the diameter of a human hair.

### Smallest man-made object
The tips of probes scanning tunnelling microscopes (STMs) have been shaped to end in a single atom—the last three layers constituting the world's smallest man-made pyramid of 7, 3 and 1 atoms. In Jan 1990, it was announced that D. M. Eigler and E. K. Schweizer of the IBM Almaden Research Center, San Jose, California, USA, had used an STM to move and reposition single atoms of xenon on a nickel surface in order to spell out the initials 'IBM'. Other laboratories have used similar techniques on single atoms of other elements.

### Largest clock
The astronomical clock in the Cathedral of St Pierre, Beauvais, France, was constructed between 1865–68. It has 90,000 parts and is 12.1 m (40 ft) high, 6.09 m (20 ft) wide and 2.7 m (9 ft) deep.

### Heaviest watch
The 24.3-m (80-ft) Eta 'watch' on the Swiss pavilion at Expo '86 in Vancouver, British Columbia, Canada, weighed 35 tonnes.

## Cameras
### Largest camera
The largest and most expensive industrial camera is the 27-tonne Rolls-Royce camera commissioned in 1956 and owned by Brian Coxon of BDC Holdings Ltd in Derby, UK.

currently displays the largest lens, made by Pilkington Special Glass Ltd of St Asaph, Denbighshire, UK. It has a focal length of 8.45 m (27 ft 9 in), a diameter of 1.37 m (4 ft 6 in) and weighs 215 kg (474 lb). The lens allows for writing on the museum's walls to be read from a distance of 12.2 m (40 ft).

### Fastest cameras
A camera built for research into high-power lasers by the Blackett Laboratory of Imperial College of Science and Technology, London, UK, registers images at a rate of 33 billion frames per second.

The fastest production camera is currently the Imacon 675, made by Hadland Photonics Ltd of Bovingdon, Herts, UK, operating at up to 600 million frames per second.

# Defence technology

## Ships and submarines
### Largest battleships
The Japanese vessels *Yamato* and *Musashi* had a full load displacement of 67,884 tonnes, an overall length of 263 m (863 ft), a beam of 38.7 m (127 ft) and a full load draught of 10.8 m (35 ft 5 in). They were armed with nine 460-mm (18⅛ in) guns in three triple turrets. Each gun weighed 164.6 tonnes, was 22.8 m (75 ft) long and fired 1,450-kg (3,200-lb) projectiles.

### Largest aircraft carriers
The warships with the largest full-load displacement are the Nimitz class US Navy aircraft carriers USS *Nimitz, Dwight D. Eisenhower, Carl Vinson, Theodore Roosevelt, Abraham Lincoln, George Washington* and *John C. Stennis*. The last three displace 100,368 tonnes. The ships are 332.9 m (1,092 ft) long, have 1.82 ha (4½ acres) of flight deck and can reach speeds of well over 56 km/h (30 knots).

### Fastest warship
On 25 Jan 1980, a US Navy hovercraft, the 23.7-m (78-ft) long, 98.4-tonne test vehicle SES-100B, achieved a speed of 170 km/h (91.9 knots).

### Fastest destroyer
The highest speed attained by a destroyer was 83.42 km/h (45.25 knots) by the 3,148-tonne French ship *Le Terrible* in 1935. She was built in Blainville, France, and decommissioned at the end of 1957.

### Largest submarine
The largest submarines are of the Russian Typhoon class and are believed to have a dived displacement of 26,500 tonnes, to be 171.5 m (562 ft 8 in) long, and be armed with 20 multiple warhead SS-N-20 missiles with a range of 8,300 km (4,500 nautical miles). Six are now in service.

### Fastest submarine
The Russian Alpha class nuclear-powered submarines had a reported maximum speed of over 74 km/h (40 knots). Only one is thought to be still in service as a trials boat.

## Tanks
### Heaviest tanks
The German Panzer Kampfwagen Maus II weighed 192 tonnes. It was abandoned in 1945 while still at the experimental stage.

The heaviest operational tank was the 75.2-tonne 13-man French Char de Rupture 2C bis of 1922. It carried a 15.5-cm (6⅛-in) howitzer and had a top speed of 12 km/h (7.5 mph).

The most heavily armed tanks in recent times have been the Russian T-64, T-72, T-80 and T-90, all of which have a 12.5-cm (4⅞-in) gun-missile system.

The American Sheridan light tank mounts a 15.2-cm (6-in) weapon which is a combined gun and missile launcher.

### Fastest tanks
The fastest tracked armoured reconnaissance vehicle is the British *Scorpion*, which can touch 80 km/h (50 mph) with a 75% payload.

The British Warrior's top speed is officially given as 75 km/h (46.6 mph). However this is when it has a full payload.

The US experimental tank M1936 was clocked at 103.4 km/h (64.3 mph) during official trials in the United Kingdom in 1938.

### Most prolific tank
More than 50,000 of the Soviet T-54/55 series were built between 1954 and 1980 in the USSR, with further production in the one-time Warsaw Pact countries and China.

## Bombs
### Heaviest bombs
The Royal Air Force's Grand Slam weighed 9,980 kg (22,000 lb) and was 7.74 m (25 ft 5 in) long. It was first dropped on Bielefeld railway viaduct, Germany, on 14 March 1945. In all, 41 Grand Slam bombs were dropped by 617 Sqn RAF in 1945.

In 1949 the United States Air Force tested a bomb weighing 19,050 kg (42,000 lb) at Muroc Dry Lake, California, USA.

The heaviest known nuclear bomb was the MK 17, carried by US B-36 bombers in

**Right**
An Iraqi Soviet-made T-55 tank strewn with ammunition belts stands abandoned following the advance of Allied Forces in the Gulf War.

the mid-1950s. It weighed 19,050 kg (42,000 lb) and was 7.47 m (24 ft 6 in) long.

### First atomic bomb
The first atom bomb was dropped on Hiroshima, Japan, by the USA at 8:16 a.m. on 6 Aug 1945. It had an explosive power equivalent to that of 15 kilotons of trinitrotoluene ($C_7H_5O_6N_3$), called TNT. Code-named *Little Boy*, it was 3.05 m (10 ft) long and weighed 4,080 kg (9,000 lb). It burst 565 m (1,850 ft) above the city centre.

### Most powerful atomic bomb
The most powerful thermonuclear device so far tested is one with a power equivalent to that of *c.* 57 megatons of TNT, detonated by the former USSR in the Novaya Zemlya area at 8:33 a.m. GMT on 30 Oct 1961. The shockwave circled the world three times, taking 36 hr 27 min for the first circuit. Some estimates put the power of this device at between 62 and 90 megatons.

# FASTEST BOMBER MACH 2.5

CAN ACHIEVE UP TO 80 KM/H WITH A 75% PAYLOAD

### Largest nuclear weapons
The most powerful ICBM (intercontinental ballistic missile) is the former USSR's SS-18 (Model 5), officially called the RS-20, which is believed to be armed with 10 MIRVs (multiple independently targetable re-entry vehicles), each of 750 kilotons. SS-18 ICBMs are still in the territories of both Russia and Kazakhstan, although the dismantlement of those in Kazakhstan has begun.

The 1.2-megaton W-56 is the most powerful of all the USA's weapons.

### Heaviest bombers
The former Soviet four-jet Tupolev Tu-160 bomber has a maximum take-off weight of 275 tonnes (606,270 lb).

The ten-engined Convair B-36J, weighing 185 tonnes, had the greatest wing span at 70.1 m (230 ft). It is no longer in service.

### Fastest bombers
The world's fastest operational bombers include the French Dassault Mirage IV, which can fly at Mach 2.2 (2,333 km/h or 1,450 mph) at 11,000 m (36,000 ft), and the American variable-geometry or 'swing-wing' General Dynamics FB-111A, which has a maximum speed of Mach 2.5.

The former Soviet swing-wing Tupolev Tu-22M, known to NATO as 'Backfire', has an estimated over-target speed of Mach 2.0 but could be as fast as Mach 2.5.

WHICH ARE 332.9 M IN LENGTH, AND HAVE A FLIGHT DECK AREA OF 1.82 HA

## Guns

### Largest gun
In July 1942, during the siege of Sevastopol, USSR (now Ukraine), the Germans used an 80-cm (31½-in) calibre gun with a 28.87-m (94-ft 8½-in) long barrel. The gun weighed 1,344 tonnes and had a crew of 1,500. The range for an 8.1-tonne projectile was 20.9 km (13 miles) and for a 4.8-tonne projectile 46.7 km (29 miles).

### Greatest altitude and range
On 19 Nov 1966, an 84-kg (185-lb) projectile was fired to an altitude of 180 km (112 miles) by the 150-tonne HARP (High Altitude Research Project) gun at Yuma, Arizona, USA.

The V3 underground firing tubes built in 50° shafts during WWII near Mimoyècques, near Calais, France, to bombard London, UK, were never operative, but they would have had a distance of 150 km (95 miles).

The famous Paris-Geschütz (Paris Gun) long-range gun was designed to have a range of 127.9 km (79½ miles). In 1918, during WWI the 21-cm (8¼-in) calibre gun achieved a range of 122 km (76 miles) from the Forest of Crépy, France.

### Largest mortars
The largest mortars ever constructed were Mallet's mortar made in London, UK, and the Little David, made in the USA, used in WWII. Each had a calibre of 91.4 cm (36 in), but neither was used in action.

### Heaviest mortars
The heaviest mortar employed was the tracked German 60-cm (23½-in) siege piece Karl, seven specimens of which were built. Only six of these were actually used in action, although never all at the same time: at Sevastopol, USSR (now Ukraine), in 1942; at Warsaw, Poland, in 1944; at Budapest, Hungary, in 1944.

### Largest cannon
The highest-calibre cannon ever constructed is the Tsar Pushka (Emperor of Cannons), now in the Kremlin, Moscow, Russia. It was built in the 16th century with a bore of 89 cm (35 in) and a barrel that is 5.34 m (17 ft 6 in) long. It weighs 39.3 tonnes.

The Turks fired up to seven shots a day from a 7.92-m (26-ft) bombard, with an internal calibre of 106.6 cm (42 in), against the walls of Constantinople (now Istanbul, Turkey), from 12 April to 29 May 1453. The cannon was dragged by 60 oxen and 200 men and fired a 540-kg (1,200-lb) stone ball.

### Heaviest cannon
The heaviest cannon was built in 1868 at Perm, Russia, and weighs 144.1 tonnes, although it has a bore of only 50.8 cm (20 in) and a barrel 4.6 m (15 ft 1 in) long. It fired 300 shots in tests, using iron balls weighing nearly half a tonne.

# Environmental disasters

**Right**
Oil wells burning in the Kuwaiti desert during the Gulf War in 1991. The Iraqi forces deliberately set fire to the wells causing one of the world's worst ecological disasters.

## Industrial waste
### Worst marine pollution
Between 1953 and 1960 a plastics factory on Minimata Bay, Kyushu, Japan, deposited mercury waste into the sea. A total of 43 people died from the poisoning and 111 others suffered permanent damage.

### Worst river pollution
On 1 Nov 1986, firemen fighting a blaze at the Sandoz chemical works in Basel, Switzerland, flushed 30 tonnes of agricultural chemicals into the River Rhine. Half a million fish died as a result.

On 24 Aug 1995, President Jagan of Guyana declared a 88-km (50-mile) stretch of the Essquibo river a disaster zone after the banks of a pond holding cyanide used in gold extraction leaked and the chemicals polluted the water.

### Most devastating air pollution
On 3 Dec 1984, a poisonous cloud of methyl isocyanate escaped from Union Carbide's pesticide plant near Bhopal, India, killing over 6,300 people. The company made a settlement of £293 million to compensate the victims and their relatives.

On 10 July 1976, a cloud of dioxin escaped from the Icmesa chemical factory at Seveso, near Milan, Italy—780 people were evacuated. It is not known how many were directly affected by the poison but, within 20 days, 250 cases of poisoning were officially

recognized. A year later, 417 children were diagnosed as suffering from chloracne, a dioxin-related eruption of boils and pimples.

### Most lethal smog
From 4 to 9 Dec 1952, between 3,500 and 4,000 people, mainly the elderly and children, died in London, UK, from acute bronchitis caused by thick smog.

### Industrial explosion
On 1 June 1974, an explosion at a chemical plant in Flixborough, near Scunthorpe,

Lincs, UK, killed 55 people and injured 75. The factory manufactured caprolactam—a chemical used for making nylon.

## Oil pollution
### Worst oil spills
On 3 June 1979, an oil spill occurred after a blow-out beneath the drilling rig *Ixtoc I* in the Gulf of Campeche, Gulf of Mexico. The slick reached 640 km (400 miles) by 5 Aug 1979. It was capped on 24 March 1980 after an estimated loss of up to 500,000 tonnes.

**Right**
Firemen fighting a blaze at the Sandoz chemical works in Basel, Switzerland, in Nov 1986. Around 30 tonnes of agricultural chemicals, mainly pesticides, were flushed into the Rhine as the firemen tried to control the fire. It took more than 10 years for the river to recover.

The worst spill in British waters was from the 118,285-dwt *Torrey Canyon* which struck the Pollard Rock off Land's End, Cornwall, on 18 March 1967, resulting in the loss of up to 120,000 tonnes of oil.

### Worst coastal damage
On 25 March 1989, the *Exxon Valdez* oil tanker ran aground in Prince William Sound, Alaska, USA, and spilled more than 30,000 tonnes of oil. Over 2,400 km (1,500 miles) of coast were polluted and the company was fined $5 billion (£3.2 billion), on top of a clean-up bill of $3 billion (£1.9 billion). The captain, Joseph Hazelwood, admitted drinking three double vodkas before setting sail with the 274.3-m (300-yd) long ship.

### Worst oil tanker accidents
On 19 July 1979, the *Atlantic Empress* collided with the *Aegean Captain* off the coast of Tobago in the Caribbean Sea and 280,000 tonnes of oil were lost.

# CLEAN-UP BILL $3 BILLION

COLLIDED WITH THE *AEGEAN CAPTAIN*—280,000 TONNES OF OIL WERE LOST

In March 1978, the *Amoco Cadiz* broke up 96.6 km (60 miles) off the Brittany coast, France, and spilled 220,000 tonnes of oil.

### Largest offshore disaster
The largest offshore oil disaster occurred when there was a fire on the Piper Alpha oil production platform in the North Sea on 6 July 1988. As a result 167 people died.

### Worst land pollution
From Feb to Oct 1994, following a burst pipeline, thousands of tonnes of crude oil flowed across the pristine Arctic tundra of the Komi region, Russia. Estimates of the amount of oil lost range from 60,000 to 280,000 tonnes, in a slick 18 km (11 miles 352 yd) long.

## Water
### Water extraction
The level of the Aral Sea has fallen by 14 m over 30 years due to water being extracted from the rivers that flow into it.

Land in the San Joaquin Valley, California, USA, subsided by 9 m (29 ft 6 in) because from 1920 to 1960 water was extracted from the ground to irrigate the fields. The subsidence still continues in some locations.

### Reservoir-induced earthquakes
In 1962 water filled the new Koyna reservoir in India that had been built to supply Bombay. The weight of the water was so

the clean-up operation died in the five-year period following the disaster, since no systematic records were kept.

On 10 Oct 1957, there was a fire at Windscale (now Sellafield), Cumbria, UK. Nobody died as a direct result, but the number of cancer deaths was estimated by the National Radiological Protection Board in 1989 to be 100.

### Worst nuclear waste accident
In 1957, the overheating of a nuclear waste container caused an explosion at a complex at Kyshtym, Russia, that released radioactive compounds that dispersed over an area of 23,000 km$^2$ (8,900 miles$^2$). More than 30 small communities within a 1,200-km$^2$ (460-mile$^2$) radius were eliminated from maps of the USSR in the three years following the accident, and about 17,000 people were evacuated. A 1992 report indicated that 8,015 people died over a 32-year period as a direct result of discharges.

## Mining accidents
### Worst mining disaster
On 26 April 1942, a total of 1,549 people were killed by a coal dust explosion at Honkeiko (Benxihu) Colliery, China.

On 14 Oct 1913, a methane explosion that was caused by a spark on faulty signalling equipment caused the deaths of 440 people at the Universal Colliery, Senghenydd,

Caerphilly, UK. A total of 439 people died in the initial explosion and one rescue worker died the following day.

## The ecosystem
### Deforestation
It is estimated that tropical forests are being cut down at a rate equivalent to 200 football pitches every minute.

### Most devastating animal introduction
In 1859, a farmer introduced 24 wild rabbits to Australia. Their natural predators were few and the population exploded. Today there are up to 300 million rabbits in Australia. They eat crops, chew the bark and buds of young trees, destroy seedlings and their burrows damage the soil.

### Biggest assault on the ecosystem
On 19 Jan 1991 during Gulf War hostilities, the Iraqi president, Saddam Hussein, gave the order for crude Gulf oil to be pumped from the Sea Island terminal, Kuwait, and from seven large oil tankers. Provisional estimates put the loss at 816,000 tonnes.

During the same campaign, Iraqi forces set fire to 600 oil wells, creating massive clouds of black smoke and turning day into night. The smoke rose up to 2,133.6 m (7,000 ft) high, enveloped warships 80.5 km (50 miles) offshore and deposited soot on the Himalaya in Kashmir, India. The last blazing well was extinguished on 6 Nov 1991.

COAL DUST EXPLOSION AT HONKEIKO COLLIERY, CHINA, ON 26 APRIL 1942

great that it set up stresses in the rock formations below and, on 10 Dec 1967, there was an earthquake measuring 6.3 on the Richter scale. As a result 177 people were killed and 2,300 injured.

### Reservoir-induced landslips
On 9 Oct 1963, 240 million m$^3$ of rock slipped from the side of Mt Toc in the Italian Alps into a reservoir behind the Vaiont Dam. The 266.7-m (875-ft) high dam held firm but a wave of water 100 m (328 ft) high flowed over the top, wiping out the community of Longarone and killing up to 2,500 people.

## Nuclear accidents
### Worst nuclear reactor disaster
The worst nuclear reactor disaster took place at Chernobyl No. 4 in the USSR (now the Ukraine). Although the official Soviet total of immediate deaths was 31, it is not known how many of the 200,000 people involved in

**Left**
It is predicted that unless extraction of water from rivers that flow into the Aral Sea slows down, the lake will disappear in the 21st century. It was once the fourth largest lake in the world.

# Space technology

## Telescopes

### Largest telescope
The Keck telescope on Mauna Kea, Hawaii, USA, has a 10-m (32-ft 8-in) mirror, made up of 36 segments fitted together to produce the correct curve. The first image of the spiral galaxy NGC1232 was obtained on 24 Nov 1990, when nine of the segments were in place. A twin Keck telescope is to be set up close to the first. When completed, Keck I and Keck II will be able to work together as an interferometer.

### Largest reflectors
The largest single-mirror telescope now in use is the 6-m (19-ft 8-in) reflector on Mt Semirodriki, near Zelenchukskaya in the Caucasus Mts, Russia, at an altitude of 2,080 m (6,830 ft). Completed in 1976, it has not fulfilled expectations, partly because it is not on a suitable site for observation.

The largest satisfactory single-mirror telescope is the 5.08 m (16-ft 8-in) Hale reflector at Mount Palomar, California, USA.

The largest British reflector is the 4.2-m (13-ft 9-in) William Herschel, completed in 1987, and set up at the Los Muchachos Observatory on Las Palmas, Canary Islands.

### Largest refractors
A 1.16-m (3-ft 4-in) refractor was completed in 1897. Situated at the Yerkes Observatory, Williams Bay, Wisconsin, USA, it is 18.9 m (62 ft) long and belongs to the University of Chicago, Illinois. Although the refractor is almost 100 years old, it is still fully operational on clear nights.

Britain's largest refractor is the 71.1-cm (28-in) Great Equatorial Telescope of 1893, in the Old Royal Observatory, London.

### Largest planned telescope
The VLT (Very Large Telescope), which is being planned by the European Southern Observatory, should be the largest telescope built this century. It will be situated at Cerro Paranal, Chile, and will comprise four 8.2-m (26-ft 8-in) telescopes, providing the light-grasp of a 16-m (52-ft 6-in) mirror. The first units should be working in 1998.

### Largest infra-red telescope
The UKIRT (United Kingdom Infra Red Telescope), which is situated on Mauna Kea, Hawaii, USA, has a 3.74-m (12-ft 3-in) mirror and is good enough to be used for visual as well as infra-red work.

### Largest sub-millimetre telescope
The James Clerk Maxwell telescope, Mauna Kea, Hawaii, USA, has a 15-m (49-ft 3-in) paraboloid primary. It is used for study of the sub-millimetre part of the electromagnetic spectrum, 0.3–1.0 mm (0.01–0.03 in), but does not produce a visual image.

### Largest solar telescope
The McMath solar telescope at Kitt Peak, Arizona, USA, has a 2.1-m (6-ft 11-in) primary mirror. The light is sent to it via a 32° inclined tunnel from a coelostat (rotatable mirror) at the top end. Extensive modifications to it are now being planned.

### Largest Schmidt telescope
A Schmidt telescope uses a spherical mirror with a correcting plate and can cover a very wide field with a single exposure—this makes it invaluable in astronomy. The largest is the 2-m (6-ft 6¾-in) instrument at the Karl Schwarzschild Observatory at Tautenberg, Germany. It has a clear aperture of 1.34 m (4 ft 4¾ in) with a 2 m (6 ft 6¾-in) mirror and a focal length of 4 m (13 ft). It was first used in 1960.

### Largest space telescope
The $2.1 billion (£1.4 billion) NASA Edwin P. Hubble Space Telescope weighs 11 tonnes and is 13.1 m (43 ft) in overall length, with a 240-cm (7-ft 10½-in) reflector. It was placed in orbit at 613 km (381 miles) altitude aboard a US space shuttle on 24 April 1990.

### Highest observatory
The observatory on Chacaltaya, Bolivia, is at 5,200 m (17,060 ft) and was opened in 1962. It is equipped with gamma ray sensors, but has no telescopes.

### Lowest observatory
The 'observatory' at Homestake Mine, South Dakota, USA, is 1.7 km (1.1 miles) below ground level, in the shaft of a gold mine. The 'Telescope' is a tank of cleaning fluid (perchloroethylene), which contains chlorine, and can trap neutrinos from the Sun.

### Largest planetarium
The Ehime Prefectural Science Museum, Niihama City, Japan, has a dome with a diameter of 30 m (98 ft 5 in). Up to 25,000 stars can be displayed, and viewers can observe space as seen from other planets.

## Rockets

### Earliest rockets
The first launch of a liquid-fuelled rocket was by Dr Robert Goddard (1882–1945) of the USA, at Auburn, Massachusetts, USA, on 16 March 1926. It reached an altitude of 12.5 m (41 ft) and travelled 56 m (184 ft).

The earliest Soviet rocket was the semi-liquid-fuelled GIRD-R1 (object 09), begun in 1931 and tested on 17 Aug 1933. The Soviet Union's first fully liquid-fuelled rocket, GIRD-X, was launched on 25 Nov 1933.

# LARGEST TELESCOPE MIRROR 10 M

CARRY OUT 22 MILLION INSTRUCTIONS PER SECOND

### Highest velocity
The first space vehicle to achieve the Third Cosmic velocity sufficient to break out of the Solar System was *Pioneer 10*. The Atlas SLV–3C launcher with a modified Centaur D second stage and a Thiokol TE–364–4 third stage left the Earth at 51,682 km/h (32,114 mph) on 2 March 1972.

The fastest escape velocity from Earth was 54,614 km/h (34,134 mph), by the ESA *Ulysses* spacecraft, powered by an IUS-PAM upper stage after deployment from the Space Shuttle *Discovery* on 7 Oct 1990. It was en route to an orbit around the poles of the Sun via a fly-by of Jupiter.

*Mariner 10* reached a recorded speed of 211,126 km/h (131,954 mph) as it passed Mercury in September 1974.

The speed of 252,800 km/h (158,000 mph) is recorded by the NASA–German *Helios A* and *B* solar probes each time they reach the nearest point to the Sun of their solar orbits.

### Most powerful rocket
The NI booster of the former USSR (also known as the G–1 in the West), had a thrust of 4,620 tonnes when first launched from the Baikonur Cosmodrome at Tyuratam, Kazakhstan, on 21 Feb 1969. It exploded at take-off +70 seconds and three other launch attempts also failed.

### Rocket engine
The most powerful rocket engine was built by the Scientific Industrial Corporation of Power Engineering in the former USSR in 1980. The RD–170 had a thrust of 806 tonnes in open space and 740 tonnes at the Earth's surface. It also had a turbopump rated at 190 MW, burned liquid oxygen and kerosene, and powered the four strap-on boosters of the *Energiya* booster, launched in 1987 but now grounded by budget cuts.

### Lunar records
The first direct hit on the Moon was achieved at 2 min 24 sec after midnight (Moscow time) on 14 Sept 1959, by the Soviet space probe *Luna II* near Mare Serenitatis.

The first photographic images taken of the hidden side of the Moon were collected by the Soviet *Luna III* from 6:30 a.m. on 7 Oct 1959 from a range of up to 70,400 km (43,750 miles), and transmitted to the Earth from a distance of 470,000 km (292,000 miles).

AND COST $2.1 BILLION

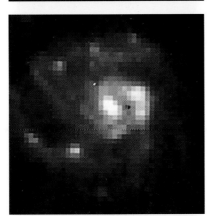

### Remotest man-made object
*Pioneer 10*, which was launched from Cape Canaveral, Florida, USA, crossed the mean orbit of Pluto on 17 Oct 1986, when it was 5.91 billion km (3.67 billion miles) away from the Earth. It is now more than 9.6 billion km (6 billion miles) away.

*Voyager 1*, travelling faster, will have surpassed *Pioneer 10* in remoteness from the Earth by the end of the century. *Pioneer 11* has left the Solar System and *Voyager 1* and *Voyager 2* are also leaving it.

### Most powerful computer in space
The lander of the *Mars Pathfinder* is controlled by an IBM RAD6000 computer. Its 32-bit architecture can carry out 22 million instructions per second and has 128 million bytes of memory. *Pathfinder* landed on Mars on 4 July 1997.

## Satellites
### Satellite with the longest life
The *International Ultraviolet Explorer* was shut down after 18 years 8 months 4 days 1 hr 6 min of elapsed mission time, on 30 Sept 1996. It had been designed to work for just three years.

### Most reliable launch system
US Space Shuttles have placed 108 out of 110 satellites in to orbit between 12 April 1981 and 6 May 1997, making them 98.18% reliable.

The Soviet/Russian *Soyuz* system has put 1,040 satellites into orbit out of 1,068 from 16 Nov 1981 to 6 May 1997, making them 97.38% reliable.

### Least reliable launch system
The US *Pegasus* solid rocket is launched from under an aeroplane. In 26 attempts between 5 April 1990 and 6 May 1997 it has failed to launch 12 times, making it 53.85% reliable.

### Greatest payload
The US Space Shuttle is capable of placing a satellite weighing 23,500 kg (51,800 lb) into low Earth orbit or of placing a satellite weighing 5,900 kg (13,010 lb) into a higher geosynchronous orbit.

The *Titan iVB* system launch, which was situated at Cape Canaveral, Florida, USA, on 23 Feb 1997, is capable of placing a satellite weighing 2,640 kg (47,710 lb) into low Earth orbit or of placing a satellite weighing 8,620 kg (19,000 lb) into a higher geosynchronous orbit.

**Left**
The NASA Edwin P. Hubble Space Telescope can photograph galaxies many light years away. Images taken by the telescope show the development of spiral galaxies like our own, the Milky Way. The first photograph shows a galaxy that is two billion years old, the second a six-billion-year-old galaxy, the third a nine-billion-year-old galaxy, and the bottom image is a galaxy that is 14 million years old—the same age as our own galaxy.

# Transport disasters

## Maritime
### Most massive collision
On 16 Dec 1977, 35 km (22 miles) off the coast of southern Africa, the tanker *Venoil* (330,954 dwt) struck her sister ship *Venpet* (330,869 dwt).

### Largest shipwreck
The 321,186-tonne deadweight VLCC (very large crude carrier) *Energy Determination* blew up and broke in two in the Strait of Hormuz, Persian Gulf, on 12 Dec 1979.

The largest wreck removal was carried out in 1979 by Smit Tak International, which took 20 months to remove the remains of the 118,000-tonne French tanker *Betelgeuse* from Bantry Bay, Republic of Ireland.

### Greatest number of deaths on one ship
There were 7,700 fatalities when the German liner *Wilhelm Gustloff* (25,076 tonnes) was torpedoed off Danzig (now Gdansk, Poland), by a Soviet S-13 submarine on 30 Jan 1945.

A total of 1,513 perished when the cruise liner *Titanic* sank after hitting an iceberg off Newfoundland in April 1912.

### Worst British single-ship disaster
In Aug 1782, about 800 people died on the HMS *Royal George* off Spithead, Hants, UK.

On 17 June 1940, 4,000 men were lost on the HM *Lancastria* off St Nazaire, France.

### Worst ferry disasters
In the early hours of 21 Dec 1987, the *Dona Paz*, sailing from Tacloban to Manila, Philippines, collided with a tanker, the *Victor*. After being engulfed in flames both vessels sank in minutes. The *Dona Paz* officially had

1,550 passengers on board but it may have had as many as 4,000. They all died.

The worst European ferry disaster was when the 15,318-tonne *Estonia* sank in 91 m (300 ft) of water off Finland in the Baltic Sea on 28 Sept 1994. A total of 912 people died.

On 6 March 1987, the *Herald of Free Enterprise* capsized off Zeebrugge, Belgium, with the loss of 193 lives, all British.

### Worst yacht racing disaster
In Aug 1979, 19 people died during the 28th Fastnet Race (run in waters off south-west Britain and Ireland), when 23 boats sank or were abandoned in force 11 gales.

# WORST SHIPWRECK 7,700 CASUALTIES

*CHALLENGER* EXPLODED 73 SECONDS AFTER TAKE-OFF ON 28 JAN 1986

**Worst British submarine disaster**
On 1 June 1939, 99 people were killed during trials of HMS *Thetis*, in Liverpool Bay.

**Worst accidental explosion**
On 17 Dec 1917, the freighter *Mont Blanc*, packed with 5,000 tonnes of explosives and combustibles, collided with another ship in Halifax harbour, Nova Scotia, Canada, creating a blast felt more than 95 km (60 miles) away and killing 1,635 people.

## Road and rail
**Worst road accident**
At least 176 people died when a petrol tanker exploded inside the Salang Tunnel, Afghanistan, on 3 Nov 1982.

**Worst British road accident**
On 27 May 1975, 33 people died in a coach crash near Grassington, N Yorkshire.

**Worst train disaster**
On 6 June 1981, more than 800 passengers died when their train plunged off a bridge into the Bagmati River in Bihar, India.

**Worst British train disaster**
On 22 May 1915, 227 people died in a triple collision at Qunitinshill, Dumfries & Galloway, Scotland, UK.

**Worst underground train disaster**
On 28 Oct 1995, approximately 300 people were killed in a fire in an underground train at Baku, Azerbaijan.

**Worst British underground disaster**
On 28 Feb 1975, 43 people died when a train ran unbraked through Moorgate station, crashing into the end of a blind tunnel.

INSIDE THE SALANG TUNNEL, AFGHANISTAN, KILLING AT LEAST 176 PEOPLE

## Air
**Most fatalities in a terrorist attack**
A bomb exploded aboard an Air India Boeing 747 on 23 June 1985 killing 329 passengers. It crashed into the Atlantic Ocean off the south-west coast of Ireland.

**Worst air accident**
The worst ever air disaster took place on 27 March 1977, when two Boeing 747s (Pan-Am and KLM) collided on the runway at Tenerife, Canary Islands, killing 583 people.

**Worst single air accident**
The single worst air accident was on 12 Aug 1985, when a JAL Boeing 747 crashed near Tokyo killing 520 passengers and crew.

**Worst mid-air collision**
A total of 351 people died in a crash 80 km (50 miles) south-west of New Delhi, India, on 12 November 1996, when a Saudi Boeing-747 scheduled flight collided with a Kazakh Ilyushin-76 charter flight.

**Worst helicopter disaster**
A Russian military helicopter carrying 61 refugees was shot down near Lata, Georgia, on 14 Dec 1992.

**Worst British helicopter disaster**
A total of 45 passengers travelling in a Chinook helicopter were killed when it crashed off Sumburgh, Shetland, UK, on 6 Nov 1986.

## Space
**Worst disaster in space**
Excluding ground accidents, the most deaths in a space accident is seven, when US space shuttle *Challenger 51L* exploded 73 seconds after take-off from the Kennedy Space Center in Florida, USA, on 28 Jan 1986.

On 29 June 1971, Soviet cosmonauts Georgi Dobrovolsky, Viktor Patsayev and Vladislav Volkov died when their *Soyuz 11* spacecraft depressurized during the re-entry.

**Worst spacecraft disasters**
On 24 Oct 1960, 91 people died when an R-16 rocket exploded at the Baikonur Space Center, USSR (now Kazakhstan).

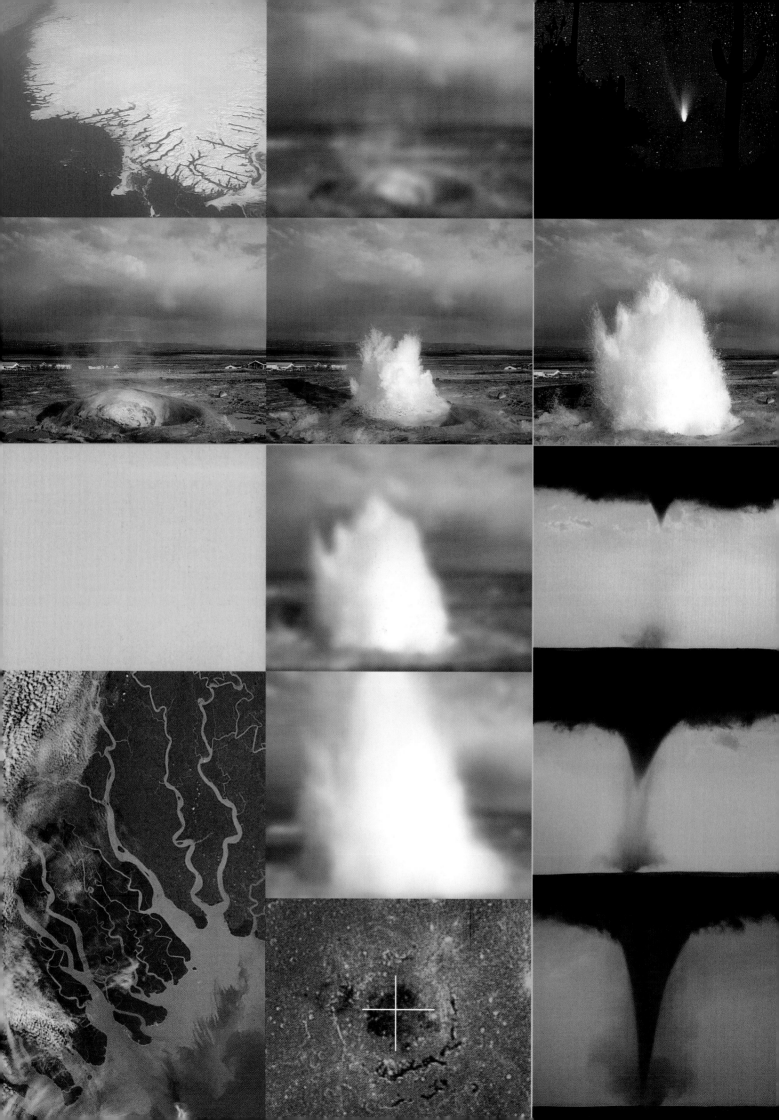

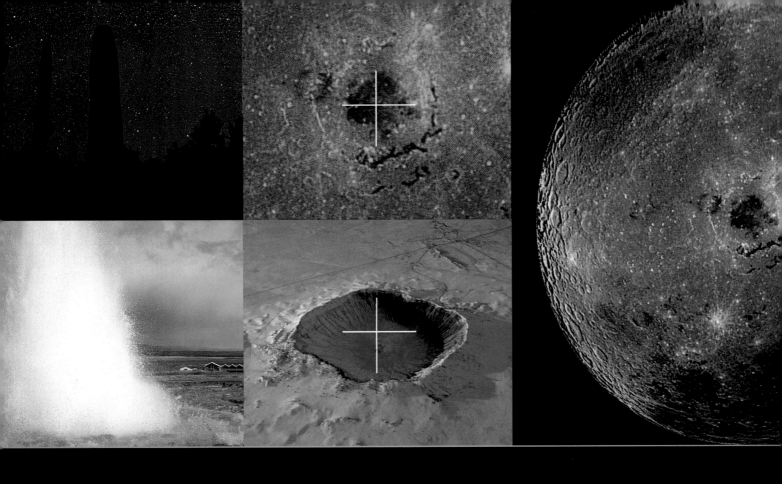

# Earth

# The Universe

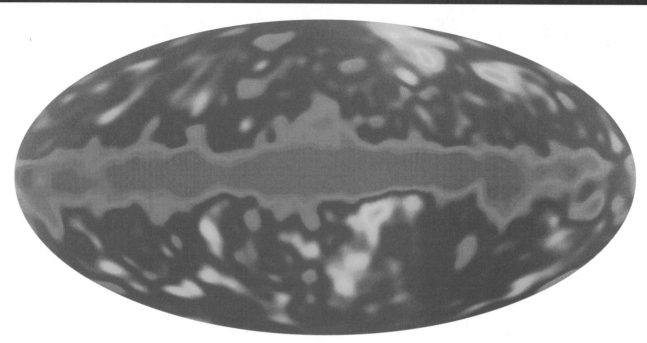

**Right**
False-colour microwave map of the whole sky, showing variations or 'ripples' in the cosmic microwave background gathered by the Cosmic Background Explorer (COBE) satellite. The mean temperature of the background radiation is shown as deep blue; pink and red areas are warmer, while white masses are cooler. The red band across the centre is radiation from our own galaxy.

## The Cosmos

### Largest structure in the Universe
A cocoon-shaped shell of galaxies that surrounds the Local Supercluster was discovered by a team of French astronomers led by Georges Paturel in June 1994. It measures c. 650 million light years across.

### Largest galaxy
The discovery was announced in July 1990 of the central galaxy of the Abell 2029 galaxy cluster, 1,070 million light years distant in Virgo. It has a major diameter of 5.6 million light years—80 times the diameter of the Milky Way—and light output equivalent to 2 trillion ($2 \times 10^{12}$) Suns.

### Most luminous galaxy
The highest luminosity reported for a galaxy is $4.7 \times 10^{14}$ times that of the Sun for the hyperluminous IRAS (Infra Red Astronomy Satellite) galaxy FSC 10214 + 4724 (discovered in 1990). However this value may be 10 to 100 times too large due to gravitational lensing by at least one and probably two intervening galaxies. In this case the brightest galaxy would be the hyperluminous IRAS F15307 + 3252 (discovered in 1990) with luminosity $1.0 \times 10^{13}$ times that of the Sun.

### Most remote galaxy
In March 1996, Esther Hu (USA) and Richard McMahon (UK) reported the detection of two star-forming galaxies both of which had red shifts of 4.55— this is equal to the distance of 13,100 million light years.

In July 1995, a UK team reported the discovery of the remotest radio galaxy, 6C0140 + 326, with a red shift of 4.41.

### Most remote object
Quasi-stellar radio sources (quasars or QSOs) are believed to be the active centres of distant galaxies. The record red shift is 4.897 for the quasar PC1247 + 3406, announced in May 1991. If it is assumed that there is an 'observable horizon', where the speed of recession equals the speed of light, i.e. at 14,000 million light years or $1.32 \times 10^{23}$ km ($8.23 \times 10^{22}$ miles), then an interpretation would put the quasar at 94.4% of this value, or 13,200 million light years.

## Stars

### Nearest star
Except for the Sun, the nearest star is the faint Proxima Centauri, 4.225 light years away or $4.00 \times 10^{13}$ km ($2.48 \times 10^{13}$ miles).

The nearest 'star' visible to the naked eye is the southern-hemisphere binary alpha Centauri at 4.35 light years distant.

### Largest star
The M-class supergiant Betelgeuse (alpha Orionis), which is 310 light years distant, has a diameter of 700 million km (400 million miles)—this is about 500 times that of the Sun.

### Most massive star
The variable eta Carinae, 9,100 light years away in the Carina Nebula, is thought to have a mass 150–200 times greater than the Sun.

### Most luminous stars
If all the stars could be viewed at the same distance, eta Carinae would be the most luminous star, with a total luminosity 6.5 million times greater than the Sun. However the visually brightest star is the hypergiant

Cygnus OB2 No. 12 which has an absolute visual magnitude of –9.9 (visually 810,000 times brighter than the Sun). This may be matched by the supergiant IV b 59 in the nearby galaxy Messier 101.

### Smallest stars
Neutron stars, which may have a mass up to three times that of the Sun, have diameters of only 10–30 km (6–19 miles).

### Youngest stars
Two protostars, known as IRAS-4, in the nebula NGC1333 (1,100 light years distant), seem to be the youngest stars. They will not be properly developed for 100,000 years.

### Oldest stars
The oldest stars are in the halo above the disc of the Milky Way—70 were discovered by Jan 1991, but 500 are expected to be found. They were probably formed around 1 billion years after Big Bang.

# HOTTEST PLANET VENUS 462°C

**Largest constellations**
Of the 88 constellations, Hydra (the Sea Serpent), is the largest. It covers 1302.844 deg$^2$ or 3.16% of the whole sky and contains at least 68 stars visible to the naked eye.

**Smallest constellation**
Crux Australis (Southern Cross) is the smallest constellation, covering only 0.16% of the whole sky.

## The solar system
**Largest planet**
Jupiter has an equatorial diameter of 142,984 km (88,846 miles) and a polar diameter of 133,708 km (83,082 miles). Its mass is 317.828 greater than the Earth's and its volume 1,323.3 times greater. It also has the shortest period of rotation, resulting in a day on Jupiter being only 9 hr 50 min 30.003 sec in the equatorial zone.

**Smallest and coldest planet**
Pluto has a diameter of 2,320 km (1,442 miles) and has a mass 0.0021 times that of the Earth. Its surface composition suggests that its temperature is similar to –235°C (–391°F) recorded on Neptune's moon Triton, which is the lowest temperature recorded for any natural body within the Solar System.

**Hottest planet**
The surface temperature on the planet Venus has been estimated at 462°C (864°F), making it the hottest planet.

miles) from the Sun for 248.54 years, but due to orbital eccentricity it has been closer to the Sun than Neptune from 23 Jan 1979, and will be until 15 March 1999.

**Fastest planet**
Mercury orbits the Sun at a mean distance of 57,909,200 km (35,983,100 miles) and has an orbital period of 87.9686 days, giving the highest average speed in orbit of 172,248 km/h (107,030 mph).

**Most dense and least dense planet**
Earth is the most dense planet of all, with an average density that is 5.515 greater than that of water. Saturn has an average density of one-eighth this value or 0.685 times that of water.

**Largest satellite**
Ganymede (Jupiter III) is the largest of Jupiter's 16 moons and is the largest and heaviest satellite in the solar system.

## Asteroids
**Largest asteroid**
Ceres is the largest asteroid, or minor planet, with an average diameter (for an irregular shape) of 941 km (585 miles).

**Smallest asteroid**
The smallest known asteroid, 1993KA2, has a diameter of only 5 m (16 ft). It was discovered in May 1993, when it approached Earth to within 150,000 km (93,000 miles).

**First 'little planet'**
The object 1996TL66, which was discovered in 1996, is 320 km (20 miles) across. It is believed to be one of the many 'little planets' (that is, objects in-between planets and asteroids in size) that orbit around the Sun.

**Closest asteroid approach**
The asteroid 1994XM$_1$ was discovered by James Scotti of the USA on 9 Dec 1994 only 14 hours before its record close approach to the Earth at 100,000 km (62,000 miles). It is 10 m (33 ft) in diameter.

## Comets
**Earliest recorded comet**
Apppearances of Halley's Comet can be traced back as far as 240 BC. The comet's return was first predicted by Edmund Halley (1656–1742).

**Largest comets**
The object 2060 Chiron has a diameter of 182 km (113 miles).

**Shortest orbital period**
Encke's Comet has a recordbreaking orbital period of just 1,198 days (3 years 108 days) and the closest approach to the Sun, at 49.5 million km (30.8 million miles).

**Longest orbital period**
The comet with the longest confirmed orbital period is Herschel-Rigollet, at 156 years.

**Nearest planet**
Venus can come to within 38 million km (24 million miles) of the Earth, but its average distance is 41.4 million km (25.7 million miles) inside the Earth's orbit.

**Faintest planet**
Uranus, which has a magnitude of 5.5, can only be seen with the naked eye under certain conditions. The faintest of the nine planets seen from Earth is Pluto. It can only be viewed through a telescope.

**Brightest planet**
Viewed from the Earth, the brightest of the five planets (Jupiter, Mars, Mercury, Saturn and Venus) that are normally visible to the naked eye is Venus, with a maximum magnitude of –4.4.

**Outermost planets**
The Pluto–Charon system orbits at a mean distance of 5,914 million km (3,675 million

**Left**
An optical image taken on 9 March 1997 of Comet Hale-Bopp above cacti in the Superstition Mts, Arizona, USA. Hale-Bopp was the brightest comet visible from Earth this century. A comet is a ball of ice and dust. As it approaches the Sun its surface evaporates, creating a tail that can be millions of kilometres in length. Comet Hale-Bopp was first discovered on 23 June 1995.

## The Moon

### Closest lunar approach
The Moon orbits the Earth at a mean distance of 384,399.1 km (238,854½ miles) centre-to-centre. In this century, the closest approach (smallest perigee) was 356,375 km (221,441 miles) centre-to-centre on 4 Jan 1912. The farthest distance between the two was 406,711 km (252,718 miles) on 2 March 1984.

### Largest crater
Only 59% of the Moon's surface is directly visible from the Earth because it is in 'captured rotation': the period of rotation equal to the period of orbit. The largest wholly visible crater is the walled plain Bailly, near to the Moon's South Pole—it is 295 km (183 miles) across, with walls rising to 4,250 m (14,000 ft). The largest crater on the Moon is the far-side South Pole-Aitken, which is 2,500 km (1,550 miles) in diameter and has an average depth of 12,000 m (39,000 ft). This is the largest and deepest crater that is known in the Solar System.

### Largest sea
The largest regular 'sea', or mare, on the Moon is the Mare Imbrium, which has a diameter of 1,300 km (800 miles).

### Highest mountains
In the absence of a sea level, lunar altitudes are measured relative to an adopted radius of 1,738 km (1,079 miles 1,660 yd). On this basis the highest elevation is 8,000 m (26,000 ft) for the highlands north of the Korolev Basin on the lunar far side.

### Hottest and coldest temperatures
When the Sun is overhead, the temperature on the lunar equator reaches 117°C (243°F), 17°C (31°F) above the boiling point of water. By sunset the temperature is 14°C (58°F), but after nightfall it sinks down to –163°C (–261°F).

## The Sun

### Largest sunspots
The largest sunspot ever recorded was in the Sun's southern hemisphere on 8 April 1947. It had an area of about 18 billion km$^2$ (7 billion miles$^2$), with an extreme longitude of 300,000 km (187,000 miles) and an extreme latitude of 145,000 km (90,000 miles). Sunspots appear darker because they are more than 1,500°C (2,700°F) cooler than the rest of the Sun's surface temperature of 5,504°C (9,939°F).

### Longest solar eclipse
The maximum possible duration of an eclipse of the Sun is 7 min 31 sec. The longest of recent date took place on 20 June 1955, west of the Philippines, and lasted 7 min 8 sec, although it was clouded out along most of its track. An eclipse of 7 min 29 sec should occur in the mid-Atlantic Ocean on 16 July 2186.

Durations can be 'extended' when observers are airborne. For example, the total eclipse of the Sun on 30 June

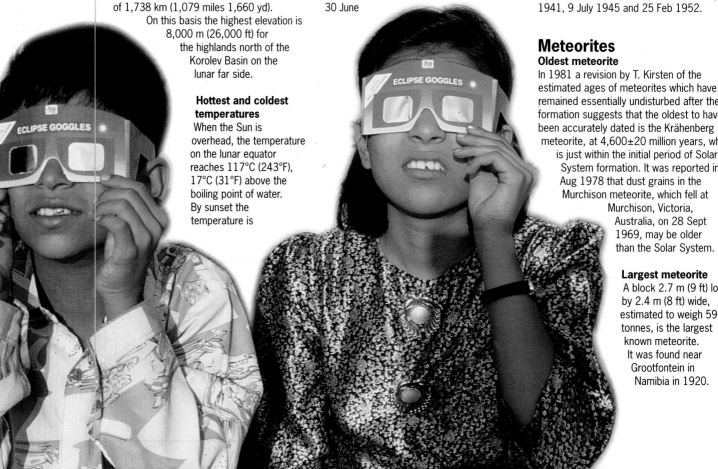

1973 was extended to 1 hr 14 min for observers on a Concorde airliner which took off from Toulouse in France, and stayed in the Moon's shadow from 10:51 a.m. to 12:05 a.m. GMT over the Atlantic before landing in Chad.

The longest possible eclipse in the British Isles is 5 min 30 sec. In recent times that of 3 May 1715 was 4 min 4 sec, but that of 22 July 2381, which will be observed in the Scottish Borders, will last 5 min 10 sec.

The longest totality of any lunar eclipse is 1 hr 47 min. It will occur on 16 July 2000.

### Most eclipses
The highest number of eclipses that are possible in a year is seven, as in 1935, when there were five solar and two lunar eclipses. In 1982 there were four solar and three lunar eclipses. The least number of eclipses that are possible in one year

is two, both of which must be solar, as in 1944, 1969 and 1984.

The only recent example of three total solar eclipses occurring at a single location was at a point 44°N, 67°E in Kazakhstan, east of the Aral Sea. These took place on 21 Sept 1941, 9 July 1945 and 25 Feb 1952.

## Meteorites

### Oldest meteorite
In 1981 a revision by T. Kirsten of the estimated ages of meteorites which have remained essentially undisturbed after their formation suggests that the oldest to have been accurately dated is the Krähenberg meteorite, at 4,600±20 million years, which is just within the initial period of Solar System formation. It was reported in Aug 1978 that dust grains in the Murchison meteorite, which fell at Murchison, Victoria, Australia, on 28 Sept 1969, may be older than the Solar System.

### Largest meteorite
A block 2.7 m (9 ft) long by 2.4 m (8 ft) wide, estimated to weigh 59 tonnes, is the largest known meteorite. It was found near Grootfontein in Namibia in 1920.

# HIGHEST MOON MOUNTAIN 8,000 M

PLACE ON 16 JULY 2000

The largest meteorite ever to have been exhibited by any museum is the Cape York meteorite, which weighs 30,883 kg (68,085 lb), and was found in 1897 near Cape York on the west coast of Greenland by the expedition led by Commander Robert Edwin Peary (1856–1920). It is known to the Inuit as the Abnighito and is now on display at the Hayden Planetarium in New York City, USA.

The largest piece of stony meteorite ever recovered is a piece weighing 1,770 kg (3,902 lb). It was part of a 4-tonne shower that struck Jilin (formerly Kirin), China, on 8 March 1976.

The heaviest of the 23 meteorites known to have fallen on the British Isles since 1623 fell at around 4:15 p.m. on 24 Dec 1965 at Barwell, Leics. It weighed at least 46 kg (102 lb). The largest fragment was 7.88 kg or 17 lb 6 oz.

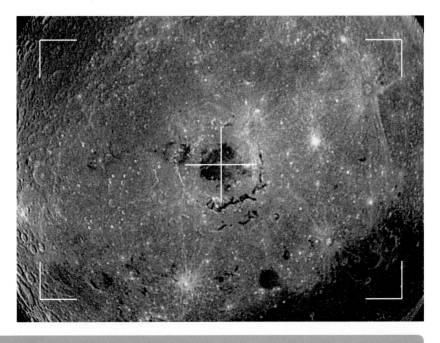

**Left**
The largest impact basin on the Moon is the far-side South Pole-Aitken. It is both the largest and deepest found in the Solar System.

TO MOON'S SOUTH POLE, IS 295 KM ACROSS WITH 4,250-M-HIGH WALLS

### Greatest explosion

The explosion over the basin of the Podkamennaya Tunguska River, Russia, on 30 June 1908 was equivalent to 10–15 megatons of high-explosive and resulted in the devastation of a total area of 3,900 km² (1,500 miles²). The shock wave was felt up to 1,000 km (620 miles) away. The cause is thought to be the energy released when a stony meteoroid 30 m (98 ft) in diameter travelling at hypersonic velocity at an incoming angle of 45° totally disintegrated at an altitude of 10 km (6 miles).

### Greatest meteor shower

The greatest shower on record occurred on the night of 16–17 Nov 1966, when the Leonid meteors (which recur every 33¼ years) were visible between western North America and eastern Russia (then the USSR). It was calculated that meteors passed over Arizona, USA, at a rate of 2,300 per min for 20 min from 5 a.m. on 17 Nov 1966.

### Largest meteorite craters

In 1962, a crater 240 km (150 miles) in diameter and 800 m (½ mile) deep was attributed to a meteorite in Wilkes Land, Antarctica. To create a crater of this size the meteorite would have had to weigh approximately 13 billion tonnes and strike the Earth at a speed of 70,800 km/h (44,000 mph).

In Dec 1970, Soviet scientists reported an astrobleme (a large meteorite crater) with a

diameter of 95 km (60 miles) and a maximum depth of 400 m (1,300 ft) in the basin of the River Popigai in Siberia.

There is a crater-like formation 442 km (275 miles) in diameter on the eastern shore of Hudson Bay, Canada.

The largest and best-preserved crater which was definitely formed by a meteorite is Coon Butte (or Barringer Crater), discovered in 1891, near Winslow, Arizona, USA. It is

1,265 m (4,150 ft) in diameter and now about 175 m (575 ft) deep, with a parapet rising 40–48 m (130–155 ft) above the surrounding plain.

### Fireball

The brightest fireball ever photographically recorded was over Sumava, Czechoslovakia (now Czech Republic) and was photographed by Dr Zdenek Ceplecha in Dec 1974. It had a momentary magnitude of –22, or 10,000 times brighter than a full Moon.

**Below left**
Coon Butte (or Barringer Crater), near Winslow, Arizona, USA, is the largest and best preserved crater definitely formed by a meteorite. It has been estimated that an iron-nickel mass of some 2 million tonnes and a diameter of 61–79 m (200–260 ft) gouged this crater in about 25,000 BC.

**Below right**
The Landscape Arch
in Arches National
Park, Utah, USA. The
National Park, a desert
area of rock pinnacles
and arches, is one of
Utah's major tourist
attractions. The red
limestone has been
eroded into a variety of
unusual shapes with
descriptive names
including the Devil's
Garden and the
Landscape Arch.

## Mountains

### Highest mountain
Peak XV on the Tibet–Nepal border in the eastern Himalayas was found to be the world's highest mountain by the Survey Department of the Government of India in 1856, from theodolite readings taken in 1849 and 1850. Its height was calculated to be 8,840 m (29,002 ft) and it was named Mt Everest after Col. Sir George Everest. There have been a number of surveys since then, with 8,848 m (29,029 ft) now being the most widely accepted height.

At 1,343 m (4,406 ft) Ben Nevis near Fort William is the United Kingdom's highest peak.

### Furthest summit from the Earth's centre
The Andean peak of Chimborazo is 6,267 m (20,561 ft) high, and lies 158 km (98 miles) south of the equator in Ecuador. The summit is 2,150 m (7,054 ft) further from the Earth's centre than the summit of Mt Everest, because the Earth's radius in Ecuador is longer than the radius at the latitude of Everest.

### Tallest mountain
When measured from its submarine base at 6,000 m (3,280 fathoms) in the Hawaiian Trough to its peak, Mauna Kea ('White Mountain') on the island of Hawaii, USA, is 10,205 m (33,480 ft) high. Of this, 4,205 m (13,796 ft) are above sea level.

### Greatest mountain ranges
The submarine Mid-Ocean Ridge, extends 65,000 km (40,000 miles) from the Arctic Ocean to the Atlantic Ocean, around Africa, Asia and Australia, and under the Pacific Ocean to the west coast of North America. Its greatest height is 4,200 m (13,800 ft) above the base ocean depth.

The greatest land mountain range in the world is the Himalaya-Karakoram, which contains all of the 14 peaks that are over 8,000 m (26,247 ft).

The longest range of mountains is the Andes of South America, which is approximately 7,600 km (4,700 miles) in length.

### Greatest plateau
The most extensive high plateau is the Tibetan Plateau in Central Asia. Its average altitude is 4,900 m (16,000 ft) and it covers an area of 1,850,000 km² (715,000 miles²).

### Longest lines of sight
Vatnajökull in Iceland is 2,119 m (6,952 ft) high and has been seen from the Faeroes 550 km (340 miles) away by refracted light.

In Alaska, Mt McKinley, 6,194 m (20,320 ft) tall, has been sighted from Mt Sanford, which is 4,949 m (16,237 ft) tall and situated 370 km (230 miles) away.

The longest line of sight in the British Isles is 144.08 km (89½ miles). Under exceptional circumstances it is possible to see Merrick, Dumfries and Galloway, Scotland, from the summit of Snowdon, Gwynedd, Wales.

## Rock formations

### Highest rock pinnacle
Ball's Pyramid near Lord Howe Island in the Pacific Ocean is 561 m (1,843 ft) high but it has a base axis that measures only 200 m (220 yd).

SUBTERRANEAN SALT MOUNTAINS, OR HALITES, RIS

### Natural arches
Landscape Arch, in Arches National Park, and Kolob Arch, in Zion National Park, both in Utah, USA, are the longest arches in the world. They stand over openings 94.5 m (310 ft) wide. Rainbow Bridge in Lake Powell National Monument, also in Utah, is larger than both. It is only 82.3 m (270 ft) long, but is a massive feature rising to a height of 88.4 m (290 ft).

### Cliffs
The sea cliffs on the north coast of east Moloka'i, Hawaii, near Umilehi Point, descend 1,010 m (3,300 ft) to the sea at an average angle of inclination of more than 55° and an average gradient of more than 1.428.

The Conachair cliffs on St Kilda, Western Isles, UK, are 400 m (1,300 ft) high. The highest sheer sea cliffs on the British mainland are at Clo Mor, 5 km (3 miles) south-east of Cape Wrath, Sutherland, which drop 281 m (921 ft).

### Tallest halite
A halite is a crystal structure which is formed out of rock salt. Along the northern shores of the Gulf of Mexico there are 330 of these subterranean 'mountains' of salt which extend for 1,160 km (725 miles). The tallest halites rise to more than 18,300 m (60,000 ft) from the bedrock and appear as low salt domes. These mineral structures were first discovered in 1862.

## Caves

### Longest cave
The most extensive cave system is beneath Mammoth Cave National Park, Kentucky, USA. Interconnected passages under the Flint, Mammoth Cave and Toohey Ridges have a mapped length of 565 km (351 miles).

### Largest cave
The world's largest cave chamber is the Sarawak Chamber, Lubang Nasib Bagus, in the Gunung Mulu National Park, Sarawak, discovered and surveyed in 1980 by the British-Malaysian Mulu Expedition. It is 700 m (2,300 ft) long, with an average width of 300 m (980 ft) and a minimum height of 70 m (230 ft).

# TALLEST MOUNTAIN MAUNA KEA 10,205 M

DEEP OF WHICH 1,181 M IS BELOW SEA LEVEL

### Underwater cave
The longest explored underwater cave is the Sistema Ejido Jacinto Pat cave system in Quintana Roo, Mexico, which has 56.9 km (35 miles) of mapped passages. It was first explored in 1987 by the CEDAM Cave Diving Team from the USA.

### Longest stalactite
The longest free-hanging stalactite in the world is believed to be one that is more than 28 m (92 ft) long in the Gruta do Janelão, in Minas Gerais, Brazil.

### Tallest stalagmite
The tallest indisputable stalagmite, at 32 m (105 ft) in height, is located in Krásnohorská cave, near Rožňava, Slovakia.

Burog Co, the world's highest named lake, lies just to the north of the highest lake, at an altitude of about 5,600 m (18,400 ft).

### Deepest valley
The Yarlung Zangbo valley is 5,075 m (16,650 ft) deep where it turns through the Himalayas, Tibet. The peaks of Namche Barwa and Jala Peri which are 7,753 m (25,436 ft) and 7,282 m (23,891 ft) high, are 21 km (13 miles) apart on either side of the River Yarlung Zangbo, which is at an elevation of 2,440 m (8,000 ft) at that point.

### Largest gorge
The largest land gorge is the Grand Canyon on the Colorado River in north-central Arizona, USA. It extends over 446 km

## Depressions
### Deepest depression
The bedrock of the Bentley sub-glacial trench, Antarctica, at 2,538 m (8,326 ft) below sea level, is the deepest depression so far discovered.

The greatest submarine depression is an area of the north-west Pacific floor which has an average depth of 4,600 m (15,000 ft).

The deepest exposed depression on land is the shore surrounding the Dead Sea, now 400 m (1,310 ft) below sea level. The deepest point on the bed is 728 m (2,388 ft) below sea level. The rate of fall in the lake surface since 1948 has been 35 cm (13¾ in). per annum.

TO MORE THAN 18,300 M ABOVE THE BEDROCK ALONG THE GULF OF MEXICO

## Gorges, canyons and lakes
### Deepest lake
Lake Baikal in the southern part of eastern Siberia, Russia, is the deepest lake in the world. It is 620 km (385 miles) long and 32–74 km (20–46 miles) wide. In 1974 the lake's Olkhon Crevice was measured by the Hydrographic Service of the Soviet Pacific Navy and it was discovered to be 1,637 m (5,371 ft) deep, of which 1,181 m (3,875 ft) is below sea level.

### Highest lakes
The highest lake in the world is one that is as yet unnamed in Tibet at 34°16′N, 85°43′E, located at an altitude that is c. 5,800 m (19,000 ft) above sea level.

(277 miles) from Marble Gorge to the Grand Wash Cliffs, and is an average 16 km (10 miles) wide and 1.6 km (1 mile) deep.

The submarine Labrador Basin canyon, between Greenland and Labrador, Canada, is 3,440 km (2,140 miles) long.

### Deepest canyon
The Vicos Gorge in the Pindus mountains in Greece is 900 m (2,950 ft) deep and only 1,100 m (3,600 ft) between its rims.

The deepest submarine canyon discovered is 40 km (25 miles) south of Esperance, Western Australia, and is 1,800 m (6,000 ft) deep and 32 km (20 miles) wide.

The deepest part of the bed of Lake Baikal in Russia is 1,181 m (3,875 ft) below sea level.

### Largest depression
The Caspian Sea basin in Azerbaijan, Russia, Kazakhstan, Turkmenistan and Iran is over 518,000 km² (200,000 miles²), of which 371,800 km² (143,550 miles²) is lake.

## Fulgurites
### Longest fulgurite excavated
In 1996, a fulgurite (a tube of glassy mineral matter found in rock formed by lightning) was excavated in Florida, USA, with two branches extending down from the strike point, 5.2 m (17 ft) and 4.9 m (16 ft) deep.

# Fresh water

**Right**
The Pantanal swamp in the states of Mato Grosso and Mato Grosso do Sul, Brazil, is the largest swamp in the world. The Pantanal is frequently flooded, but its fertile grazing lands make it ideal for raising cattle.

**Below**
The Ganges River Delta is the largest inter-tidal delta in the world. As this aerial photograph shows, the tributaries and distributaries of the Ganges and Brahmaputra Rivers (collectively known as the Padma) deposit huge amounts of silt and clay, creating a shifting maze of waterways and islands in the Bay of Bengal.

## Rivers

### Longest river
The world's longest rivers are the Nile, in Africa, and the Amazon, in South America. Which of the two is longer is a question of how their total length is defined.

The Amazon begins in Peru with a number of lakes and streams that converge to form the Apurimac. This joins other streams to become the Ene, the Tambo and then the Ucayali. For the final 3,700 km (2,300 miles), from the confluence of the Ucayali and the Marañón, the river is called the Amazon. It has several mouths so it is not clear precisely where it ends. If the most distant mouth is counted, the river is approximately 6,750 km (4,195 miles) long.

The River Nile—which stretches from Burundi to the Mediterranean Sea—was 6,670 km (4,145 miles) long before the loss of a few kilometres of meanders when Lake Nasser formed behind the Aswan High Dam.

### Longest river in the United Kingdom
The River Severn is 354 km (220 miles) long and its basin covers an area of 11,419 km$^2$ (4,409 miles$^2$). It has 17 tributaries—the most of any British river.

### Shortest river
The two shortest rivers in the world are the Roe River, near Great Falls, Montana, USA, and the D River, at Lincoln City, Oregon, USA. The Roe River flows into the larger Missouri River and one of its two forks, the

North Fork River, measures just 17.7 m (58 ft). The D River connects Devil's Lake to the Pacific Ocean and has a total length of 37±1.5 m (120±5 ft).

### Submarine river
In 1952, a submarine river 300 km (190 miles) wide, known as the Cromwell Current, was discovered flowing eastward below the surface of the Pacific for 6,500 km (4,000 miles) along the equator. In places it flows at depths of up to 400 m (1,300 ft).

### Subterranean river
In Aug 1958 a concealed river, tracked by radioisotopes, was discovered flowing under the Nile, with six times its mean annual flow, or 500 billion m$^3$ (20 trillion ft$^3$).

### Largest basin
The Amazon river basin covers about 7,045,000 km$^2$ (2,720,000 miles$^2$).

### Longest tributary
Of the Amazon's tributaries, the Madeira, at 3,380 km (2,100 miles) is the longest in the world. Only 17 other rivers are larger.

### Longest estuary
The longest estuary is the Ob', in the north of Russia, which is 885 km (550 miles) long and up to 80 km (50 miles) wide. It is also the widest river which freezes solid.

### Largest delta
The Ganges and Brahmaputra delta in Bangladesh and West Bengal, India, covers an area of 75,000 km$^2$ (30,000 miles$^2$).

### Greatest flow
The Amazon discharges an average of 200,000 m$^3$/sec (7.1 million cusec) of water into the Atlantic Ocean. This increases to more than 340,000 m$^3$/sec (12 million cusec) in full flood.

### Greatest bore
The bore (abrupt rise of tidal water) on the Qiantong Jiang (Hangzhou He) in eastern China is the most remarkable of the 60 river bores in the world. At spring tides the wave reaches a height of 7.5 m (25 ft) and a speed of 24–27 km/h (13–15 knots) and is heard from as far away as 22 km (14 miles).

### Highest waterfall
The Salto Angel in Venezuela, on a branch of the Carrao River, an upper tributary of the Caroní, has a total drop of 979 m (3,212 ft). The longest single drop is 807 m (2,648 ft). They were named after the US pilot Jimmie Angel, who recorded them in his log book on 16 Nov 1933, but they are known to the Indians as Churun-Meru.

### Greatest waterfall
Boyoma Falls, Congo (ex-Zaïre), has an average annual flow of 17,000 m$^3$/sec (600,000 cusec).

### Greatest submerged waterfall
Before the closing of the Itaipú dam submerged the falls in 1982, the flow of the Guaíra (Salto das Sete Quedas) on the Alto Paraná River between Brazil and Paraguay had sometimes attained a rate of 50,000 m$^3$/sec (1.75 million cusec).

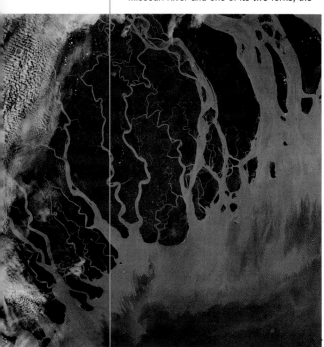

# GREATEST FLOW 200,000 M³/SEC

**HAS A WIDTH OF 300 KM**

### Widest waterfall
The Khône Falls in Laos are 10.8 km (6¾ miles) wide and have a flood flow of 42,500 m³/sec (1,500,000 cusec).

## Lakes and glaciers
### Largest freshwater lake
Lake Superior, one of the North American Great Lakes, has the greatest total surface area of any freshwater lake, at 82,350 km² (31,800 miles²). Of this, 53,600 km² (20,700 miles²) are in Minnesota, Wisconsin and Michigan, USA, and 27,750 km² (11,100 miles²) in Ontario, Canada. It is 180 m (600 ft) above sea level.

The freshwater lake with the greatest volume of water is Lake Baikal in Siberia, Russia, which has an estimated volume of 23,000 km³ (5,500 miles³).

### Largest lake within a lake
Covering 106.42 km² (41¹/₁₀ miles²), Lake Manitou is found on the world's largest lake island, Manitoulin Island 2,766 km² (1,068 miles²), in the Canadian part of Lake Huron. The lake itself contains a number of islands.

### Largest underground lake
The largest known underground lake is located within the Drachenhauchloch cave near Grootfontein, Namibia, and was discovered in 1986. A survey in 1991 revealed the surface area to be 2.61 ha (6⁴⁵/₁₀₀ acres). It is 66 m (217 ft) underground at its surface.

### Largest lagoon
Lagoa dos Patos in Rio Grande do Sul, Brazil, is 280 km (174 miles) long, extends over 9,850 km² (3,803 miles²) and has a maximum width of 70 km (44 miles).

**RUSSIA, 885 KM LONG AND UP TO 80 KM WIDE**

### Largest swamp
The Pantanal in the states of Mato Grosso and Mato Grosso do Sul, Brazil, is about 109,000 km² (42,000 miles²) in area.

### Longest glacier
The Lambert Glacier was discovered in Australian Antarctic Territory in 1956–57. Draining about a fifth of the East Antarctic ice sheet, it is up to 64 km (40 miles) wide and, including its seaward extension (the Amery Ice Shelf), as much as 700 km (440 miles) long.

### Greatest melting of a modern glacier
Meltwater flowed from Lake Grimsvotn, at an estimated 45,000 m³ per sec (1.6 million ft³) following a volcanic eruption under Vatnajokul ice cap, Iceland, in Oct 1996.

### Fastest moving glacier
The Columbia Glacier, between Anchorage and Valdez, in Alaska, USA, flows at an average of 20 m (65 ft) per day.

**Left**
Glaciers, extensive sheets of ice formed when permanent deposits of firm snow compress over hundreds of years, take up approximately 15 million km² (6 million miles²) of the Earth's surface.

# Oceans and seas

## Oceans

### Largest ocean
Excluding adjacent seas, the Pacific Ocean represents 45.9% of the world's oceans and has an area which is 166,241,700 km² (64,186,300 miles²).

### Smallest ocean
The Arctic Ocean has an an area of 13,223,700 km² (5,105,700 miles²).

### Deepest ocean
In 1995, the Japanese probe *Kaiko* reached the bottom of the Marianas Trench in the Pacific Ocean, and recorded a depth of 10,911 m (35,797 ft).

### Largest gulf
The Gulf of Mexico is 1,544,000 km² (596,000 miles²) with a shoreline of 5,000 km (3,100 miles) from Cape Sable, Florida, USA, to Cabo Catoche, Mexico.

### Most southerly ocean
The most southerly part of the oceans is the snout of the Scott Glacier, 320 km (200 miles) from the South Pole at 87°S, 151°W.

### Clearest sea
A 30-cm-diameter (1-ft) white 'Secchi' disc was visible to a depth of 80 m (262 ft) in the Weddell Sea off Antarctica (71°S, 15°W) when measured by Dutch researchers at the German Alfred Wegener Institute in 1986.

### Remotest spot from land
A point in the South Pacific, at 47°30'S, 120°W, is about 2,575 km (1,600 miles) from the nearest land masses—Pitcairn Island, Ducie Island and Peter 1 Island.

## Sea temperature
Water temperature at the sea's surface can be as low as –2°C (28°F) in the White Sea and as high as 36°C (96°F) in the shallow areas of the Persian Gulf in summer.

The highest temperature ever recorded in the ocean is 404°C (759°F), measured in 1985 at a hot spring 480 km (300 miles) off the west coast of the USA.

### Largest sea
The South China Sea has an area of 2,974,600 km² (1,148,500 miles²).

### Thickest ice
The thickest ice on record is 4.78 km (2.97 miles). It was measured by radio echo soundings at 69°56'17"S, 135°12'9"E, 440 km (270 miles) from the coast in Wilkes Land, Antarctica, on 4 Jan 1975.

### Most recently discovered sea
In April 1997, photographs of Jupiter's moon Europa from the satellite *Galileo* indicated a cold sea beneath an icy crust.

## Waves

### Highest waves
During a hurricane on 6–7 Feb 1933, a 34-m (112-ft) sea wave was measured between Manila, Philippines, and California, USA.

The highest instrumentally measured wave was 26 m (86 ft) high, recorded at 59°N, 19°W, by the British ship *Weather Reporter* in the North Atlantic on 30 Dec 1972.

### Highest tsunami
On 9 July 1958, a landslip on land caused a wave moving at 160 km/h (100 mph) to wash a record 524 m (1,720 ft) high along the fjord-like Lituya Bay in Alaska, USA.

## Currents

### Greatest current
In 1982, the Antarctic Circumpolar Current, or West Wind Drift, was found to be flowing at 130 million m³ (4.3 billion ft³) per second. Results from computer modelling in 1990 estimate a higher figure of 195 million m³ (6.9 billion ft³) per second.

### Fastest ocean current
The Somali current flows at 12.8 km/h (9 mph) in the northern Indian Ocean.

### Strongest current
The flow of the Nakwakto Rapids, Slingsby Channel, British Columbia, Canada, may reach a rate of 30 km/h (16 knots).

### Largest area of calm water
The Sargasso Sea in the north Atlantic Ocean covers about 6 million km² (2.33 million ft²) of relatively still water. Its surface is largely covered by sargassum seaweed.

## Islands and reefs

### Greatest archipelago
The East Indian or Malay Archipelago is made up of more than 17,000 islands. It is 5,600 km (3,500 miles) long and forms the Republic of Indonesia.

### Largest islands
The island of Greenland has an area of about 2. 17 million km² (840,000 miles²).

The largest sand island in the world is Fraser Island, Queensland, Australia, with a sand dune 120 km (75 miles) long.

The largest island surrounded mostly by fresh water is the 48,000-km² (18,500-mile²) Ilha de Marajó at the mouth of the Amazon River, Brazil.

The largest inland island is the 20,000-km² (7,700-miles²) Ilha do Bananal in Brazil.

### Largest atoll
Kwajalein in the Marshall Islands in the central Pacific Ocean is 283 km (176 miles) long, and encloses a 2,850-km² (1,100-mile²) lagoon.

# PACIFIC OCEAN 45.9%

A RECORD 524 M HIGH ALONG THE FJORD-LIKE LITUYA BAY IN ALASKA, USA

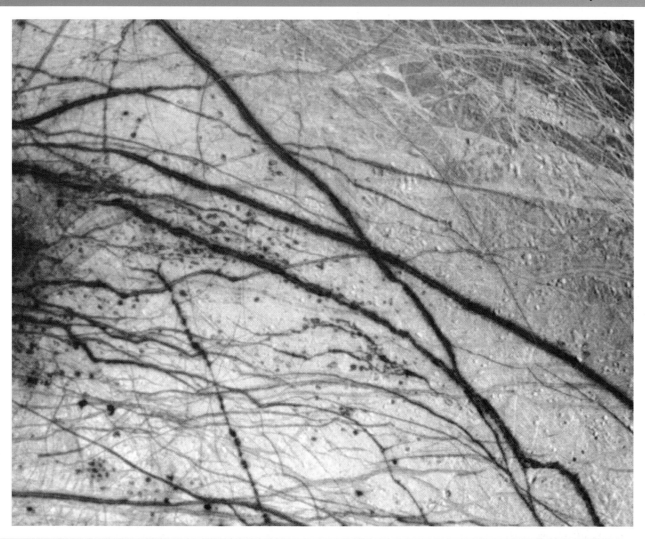

RAPIDS, BRITISH COLUMBIA, WHERE THE FLOW RATE CAN REACH 30 KM/H

**Left**
The sea on Jupiter's moon Europa was first photographed by the satellite *Galileo* in April 1997. The photographs show a surface composed of icy 'rafts' comparable to icebergs on Earth and impact craters. These craters are not as large as would be expected on a rock-solid surface; it has been deduced, therefore, that Europa must have a thin ice crust covering either liquid water or slush.

The atoll with the largest land area is Christmas Atoll, Line Islands, in the Pacific. It has an area of 649 km² (251 miles²) of which 321 km² (124 miles²) is land.

## Longest reef
The Great Barrier Reef off Queensland, Australia, is 2,027 km (1,260 miles) long and consists of thousands of individual reefs. Between 1962 and 1971, and again between 1979 and 1991, corals on large areas of the central section of the reef were devastated by the crown-of-thorns starfish (*Acanthaster planci*). In 1995, the devastation of the reef started again.

## Inland water
### Largest lake
The Caspian Sea (in Azerbaijan, Russia, Kazakhstan, Turkmenistan and Iran) is

1,225 km (760 miles) long with an area of 371,800 km² (143,550 miles²). Its estimated volume is 89,600 km³ (21,500 miles³) of saline water.

### Longest fjord
The world's longest fjord is the Nordvest Fjord arm of Scoresby Sund in eastern Greenland, which extends inland 313 km (195 miles) from the sea.

## Straits and bays
### Broadest strait
The broadest named strait in the world is Davis Strait between Greenland and Baffin Island, Canada, with a minimum width of 338 km (210 miles).

The Drake Passage between the Diego Ramirez Islands, Chile, and the South

Shetland Islands off the coast of Antarctica is 1,140 km (710 miles) across.

### Narrowest strait
The narrowest navigable strait is the Strait of Dofuchi, between Shodoshima Island and Mae Island, Japan. At the bridge linking the two islands the strait is just 9.93 m (32 ft 7 in) wide.

### Longest straits
The Tatarskiy Proliv, or Tartar Strait, between Sakhalin Island and Russia runs 800 km (500 miles) from the Sea of Japan to Sakhalinsky Zaliv.

### Largest bays
The largest bay in the world measured by shoreline length is Hudson Bay, Canada, with a shoreline of 12,268 km (7,623 miles) and an area of 1,233,000 km² (476,000 miles²).

# Weather

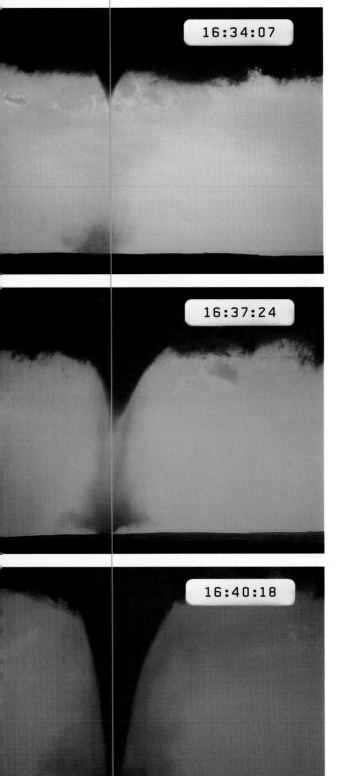

16:34:07

16:37:24

16:40:18

## Temperature

### Smallest temperature range
From 1927–35, the lowest temperature recorded at Garapan on Saipan in the North Mariana Islands, was 19.6°C (67.3°F). The highest was 31.4°C (88.5°F), giving an extreme range of 11.8°C (21.2°F).

### Greatest temperature range
Temperatures in Verkhoyansk, Siberia (67°33′N, 133°23′E), have ranged 105°C (188°F), from –68°C (–90°F) to 37°C (98°F).

The greatest temperature variation recorded in 24 hours is 56°C (100°F), in a fall from 7°C (44°F) to –49°C (–56°F) at Browning, Montana, USA, on 23–24 Jan 1916.

### Highest shade temperature
At Al'Azíziyah, Libya, a temperature of 58°C (136°F) was recorded on 13 Sept 1922.

In the United Kingdom, a temperature of 37.1°C (98.8°F) was recorded at Cheltenham, Glos, on 3 Aug 1990.

### Hottest place
In 1960–66, the average mean temperature at Dallol, Ethiopia, was 34°C (94°F).

In Death Valley, California, USA, maximum temperatures in excess of 49°C (120°F) were recorded on 43 consecutive days between 6 July and 17 Aug 1917.

Marble Bar, Western Australia, has had a maximum temperature of 49.2°C (120.5°F).

The lowest temperature recorded in the United Kingdom was –27°C (–17°F), on 11 Feb 1895 and on 10 Jan 1982, both at Braemar, Aberdeenshire, and on 30 Dec 1995, at Altnaharra, Highland. The –31°C (–23°F) that was recorded at Blackadder, Scottish Borders, on 4 Dec 1879, and the –29°C (–20°F) recorded at Grantown-on-Spey, Highland, on 24 Feb 1955, were not recorded to official standards.

Polyus Nedostupnosti or 'Pole of Inaccessibility' (78°S, 96°E) in Antarctica is the coldest location in the world, with an extrapolated annual mean of –58°C (–72°F).

The coldest measured mean is –57°C (–70°F), at Plateau Station, Antarctica.

The coldest mean temperature recorded in the United Kingdom is 6.3°C (43.4°F), at Braemar, Aberdeenshire (based on readings taken between 1952 and 1981).

## Sunshine and rain

### Most sunshine
The annual average at Yuma, Arizona, USA, is 4,055 out of 4,456 possible hours of sun.

St Petersburg, Florida, USA, recorded 768 consecutive sunny days from 9 Feb 1967 to 17 March 1969.

### Highest rainfall
A record 1,870 mm (73⅔ in) of rain fell within a 24-hour period at Cilaos, Réunion

Temperatures of 37.8°C (100°F) or higher were recorded there on a total of 160 consecutive days between 31 Oct 1923 and 7 April 1924.

At Wyndham in Western Australia, the temperature reached 32.2°C (90°F) or more on 333 days in 1946.

### Lowest temperature
On 21 July 1983, a record low temperature of –89.2°C (–128.6°F) was registered in Vostok, Antarctica, at an altitude of 3,420 m (11,220 ft).

The coldest permanently inhabited place in the world is the Siberian village of Oymyakon (63°16′N, 143°15′E) in Russia, at an altitude of 700 m (2,300 ft). The temperature reached –68°C (–90°F) in 1933. More recently, an unofficial report cited a new low of –72°C (–98°F).

Island, on 15 and 16 March 1952. The altitude was 1,200 m (3, 940 ft). This figure is equivalent to 3,057 tonnes of rain per ha (7,554 tons per acre).

The greatest rainfall within a 12-month period was at Cherrapunji, Meghalaya, India, where 26,461 mm (1,041¾ in) fell between 1 Aug 1860 and 31 July 1861.

By average annual rainfall, the wettest place is Mawsynram, Meghalaya, India, with 11,873 mm (467½ in) of rain per annum.

### Most rainy days
Mt Wai-'ale-'ale on Kauai, Hawaii, has had as many as 350 rainy days per annum.

### Least rainfall
The annual mean rainfall on the Pacific coast of Chile between Arica and Antofagasta is less than 0.1 mm (1/250 in).

# HEAVIEST HAILSTONE 1 KG

AND MID-WESTERN STATES OF THE USA ON 3-4 APRIL 1974

### Longest drought
The Atacama Desert in northern Chile experiences virtually no rain, although on several occasions during a century a squall will strike a small area.

### Longest-lasting rainbow
A rainbow was visible for six hours over Sheffield, S Yorkshire, UK, on 14 March 1994, from 9 a.m. to 3 p.m.

## Wind
### Windiest place
Gales in Commonwealth Bay, Antarctica, can reach a speed of 320 km/h (200 mph).

## Storms
### Thunder
In Tororo, Uganda, an average of 251 days of thunder per year was recorded between 1967 and 1976.

The record number of days of thunder in a specific place in a calendar year in the United Kingdom is 38. The first time was in 1912, at Stonyhurst, Lancs; the second was in 1967, at Huddersfield, W Yorkshire.

### Lightning
Ex-park-ranger Roy C. Sullivan of Virginia, USA, was struck by lightning a total of seven times. In 1942 he lost a big toe nail, in July

1969 he lost his eyebrows, in July 1970 he seared his left shoulder, in April 1972 his hair was set on fire, in Aug 1973 his hair was set alight again and his legs seared, and in June 1976 he injured his ankle. On 25 June 1977, Sullivan was sent to Waynesboro Hospital with chest and stomach burns after being struck while fishing. In Sept 1983 he killed himself, reportedly rejected in love.

## Snow and hail
### Greatest snowfall
Between 19 Feb 1971 and 18 Feb 1972, 31,102 mm (1,224½ in) of snow fell at Paradise, Mt Rainier, Washington State, USA.

The record snowfall in a single snowstorm is the 4,800 mm (189 in) which fell at Mt Shasta Ski Bowl, California, USA, between 13 and 19 Feb 1959.

The greatest snowfall within 24 hours is 1,930 mm (76 in) at Silver Lake, Colorado, USA, on 14–15 April 1921.

The greatest depth of snow ever recorded was 1,146 cm (37 ft 7 in) at Tamarac, California, USA, in March 1911.

The UK's 12-month snowfall record is 1,524 mm (60 in) which fell in both Upper Teesdale and the Denbighshire Hills in 1947.

### Heaviest hailstones
Hailstones weighing up to 1 kg (2 lb 3 oz) fell in Gopalganj district, Bangladesh, in 1986.

LIGHTNING SEVEN TIMES BUT DIED BY HIS OWN HAND, REJECTED IN LOVE

### Highest surface wind speed
A record surface wind speed of 371 km/h (231 mph) was recorded at Mt Washington, New Hampshire, USA, on 12 April 1934.

The highest wind speed at a low altitude was registered on 8 March 1972 at the USAF base at Thule in Greenland. A peak speed of 333 km/h (207 mph) was recorded.

### Tornadoes
The most tornadoes in a 24-hour period is 148 in the southern and mid-western states of the USA on 3–4 April 1974.

The highest speed measured in a tornado is 450 km/h (280 mph) at Wichita Falls, Texas, USA, on 2 April 1958.

The UK's strongest tornadoes were in London in 1091 and at Portsmouth, Hants, on 14 Dec 1810. Both registered Force 8.

# Dynamic Earth

**Below left to right**
The Strokkur ('The butter churn') geyser, in the Geysir Hot Springs area in Iceland, erupts approximately every three minutes.

## Volcanoes
### Greatest explosion
The greatest explosion in historic times happened on 27 Aug 1883 when Krakatoa, an island in the Sunda Strait between Sumatra and Java, Indonesia, erupted. The tidal wave it caused wiped out 163 villages and killed 36,380 people. Pumice was thrown 55 km (34 miles) high, and dust fell 5,330 km (3,313 miles) away 10 days later. The noise of the explosion is estimated to have been heard over 8% of the Earth's surface. This explosion is estimated to have had about 26 times the power of the largest ever H-bomb test.

### Longest lava flow
The longest lava flow in historic times is a mixture of *pahoehoe* 'ropey' lava (twisted cord-like solidifications) and *aa* 'blocky' lava, resulting from the eruption of Laki in south-east Iceland in 1783. It flowed a distance of 65–70 km (40½–43½ miles).

The largest prehistoric flow is the Roza basalt flow in North America c. 15 million years ago. It was 300 km (190 miles) long, with an area of 40,000 km² (15,400 miles²).

### Most active volcano
Lava is discharged at a rate of 5 m³ (7 yd³) per second from Kilauea, on Hawaii, USA.

### Northernmost volcano
Mt Beerenberg on the island of Jan Mayen at 71°05'N in the Greenland Sea, is the world's most northerly volcano. When it erupted on 20 Sept 1970, the island's 39 inhabitants had to be evacuated.

The Ostenso seamount 556 km (346 miles) from the North Pole at 85°10'N, 133°W, was once volcanic.

### Southernmost volcano
The most southerly known active volcano is Mt Erebus, 3,794 m (12,447 ft) high, situated on Ross Island (77°35'S) in the Antarctic Ocean's Ross Sea.

12:55:06

12:55:07

Volcanologists believe that the greatest volcanic explosion that occurred in prehistoric times was around 1628 BC on the island of Santorini in the Aegean Sea, 95 km (60 miles) north of Crete.

### Greatest eruption
The total volume of matter discharged during the eruption of Tambora, a volcano on the Indonesian island of Sumbawa, from 5–10 April 1815, was 150–180 km³ (36–43 miles³). Around 20 km³ (5 miles³) is thought to have been ejected by Krakatoa, and 60–65 km³ (14–16 miles³) by Santorini. The energy of the Tambora eruption, which lowered the height of the island by 1,250 m (4,100 ft) from 4,100 m (13,450 ft) to 2,850 m (9,350 ft), was 8.4 x 10¹⁹ joules.

The most violent of all documented volcanic events is the Taupo eruption which occurred in New Zealand around AD 130. It is estimated to have ejected 30,000 million tonnes of pumice at 700 km/h (400 mph). It flattened 16,000 km² (6,200 miles²). Less than 20% of the 14 x 10⁹ tonnes of pumice carried up into the air fell within 200 km (125 miles) of the vent.

### Largest active volcano
Mauna Loa, on Hawaii, USA, is 4,170 m (13,680 ft) high, 120 km (75 miles) long and 50 km (31 miles) wide. It has a total volume of 42,500 km³ (10,200 miles³), 84.2% of which is below sea level. Mokuaweoweo, its volcanic crater, covers 10.5 km² (4 miles²) and descends to a depth of 150–180 m (500–600 ft). It averaged one eruption every 4½ years between 1843–1984. However it now seems to be dormant.

### Highest volcano
Cerro Aconcagua, a snow-clad peak 6,690 m (22,834 ft) high in the Andes of Argentina, is the highest volcano but it is no longer active.

### Highest active volcano
The Ojos del Salado on the border between Chile and Argentina is the world's highest active volcano. It is 6,887 m (22,595 ft) high.

### Highest temperature in a fumarole
A temperature of 645°C (1,193°F) was measured in a fumarole (or smoke vent) in the Valley of Ten Thousand Smokes, which was formed by the Katmai volcano in Alaska, USA, in 1912.

### Largest crater
Toba in north-central Sumatra, Indonesia, is the world's largest caldera (volcanic crater). It covers an area of 1,775 km² (685 miles²).

### Newest volcanic island
An island in Tonga's Ha'apai group, as yet unnamed, is the world's newest island. Located halfway between the islands of Kao and Late, it was formed as a result of submarine volcanic activities, first observed on 6 June 1995, the earliest date that the presence of the island is known to exist. The island covers an area of 5 ha (12 acres) and has a maximum height of 40 m (131 ft).

## Earthquakes
The Richter Scale, or $M_s$ scale, is most commonly used to measure the size of earthquakes. However, the Kanamori Scale, or $M_w$ scale, was developed to measure earthquake vibrations that exceed the maximum reading of the Richter Scale.

# FASTEST AVALANCHE 400 KM/H

OF LAVA PER SECOND

### Deepest recorded hypocentres
The deepest hypocentres (the point beneath the earth's surface where an earthquake originates) of 720 km (450 miles) were recorded in Indonesia in 1933, 1934, 1943.

### Strongest earthquake on the $M_w$ scale
The Chilean shock of 22 May 1960 measured $M_w$=9.5.

### Most violent recorded earthquake
The most violent earthquake ever recorded was in Assam, India, in 1950. It was so severe that it sent needles skidding off seismographs and it was later assigned a reading of at least 9 on the Richter Scale.

four years. There were periods in the 1960s when it erupted as frequently as every 4–10 days. Its maximum height ranges from 60–115 m (195–380 ft).

### Greatest measured water discharge
The greatest measured water discharge was an estimated 28,000–38,000 hl (616,000–836,000 gal). It was made by the Giant Geyser in Yellowstone National Park in the 1950s.

### Largest 'boiling river'
Cascades of boiling water issue from hot springs at Deildartunguhver, Iceland, at a rate of 245 litres (65 gallons) per second.

The highest tsunami caused by an offshore earthquake appeared off Ishigaki Island in the Ryukyu island chain, Japan, on 24 April 1771. The wave, which may have reached a height of 85 m (279 ft), tossed a 750-tonne block of coral more than 2.5 km (1½ miles).

## Avalanches
### Greatest avalanches
The greatest natural avalanches, though rarely seen, occur in the Himalayas, but estimates of their volume have never been published. It was estimated 3.5 million m³ (120 million ft³) of snow fell during an avalanche in the Italian Alps in 1885.

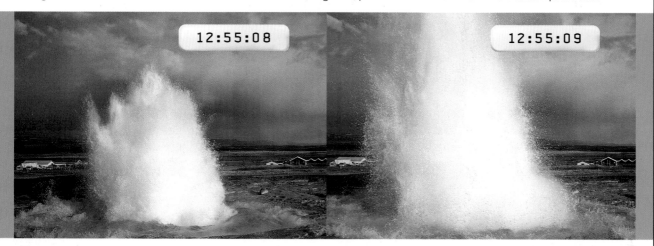

IN 1815 LOWERED THE HEIGHT OF THE ISLAND OF SUMBAWA BY 1,250 M

### Most violent British earthquake
The Dogger Bank event of 7 June 1931 measured 5.5 on the Richter scale.

The Swansea earthquake which occurred on 27 June 1906 in South Wales and the Lleyn earthquake of 19 July 1984 in Gwynedd both measured 4.8 on the Richter Scale, the highest figure measured on land in Britain.

## Geysers
### Tallest geysers
The world's tallest recorded geyser is the Waimangu geyser in New Zealand, which erupted every 30–36 hours to a height in excess of 460 m (1,500 ft) in 1903. In Aug 1903, four people were killed during an eruption. However in 1904 the geyser fell inactive and has remained so ever since.

The world's tallest active geyser is Steamboat Geyser in Yellowstone National Park, Wyoming, USA. During the 1980s it erupted at intervals of between 19 days and

The temperature at the place of issue from vents and fissures in a steep rock wall is 99°C (210°F). Downstream at the confluence with the Reykjadalsá the water temperature is 82°C (180°F).

## Tsunamis
### Highest tsunamis
A tsunami is a large destructive wave which is produced by a submarine earthquake, a volcanic eruption or subsidence; it is sometimes incorrectly called a tidal wave. On 9 July 1958, a landslip on land caused a wave to move at a speed of 160 km/h (100 mph). It washed a record 524 m (1,720 ft) high along the fjord-like Lituya Bay in Alaska, USA.

The highest tsunami that has ever been triggered by a submarine landslide struck the island of Lanai in the Hawaiian island chain approximately 105,000 years ago. It deposited sediment up to an altitude of about 375 m (1,230 ft).

**Left**
Avalanches are most frequent in spring, or during winter when there is a sudden change in the milder air. An avalanche can reach speeds of up to 80 km/h (50 mph) along the ground.

# Natural disasters

**Right**
On 4 Feb 1976,
a giant earthquake
ripped along the
Montagua Fault
on the boundary
between the
Caribbean and North
American plates.

when a series of avalanches, caused by a combination of hurricane force winds and wet snow overlaying powder snow, thundered through the Swiss, Austrian and Italian Alps.

**Highest death toll in landslides**
On 31 May 1970, approximately 18,000 people were killed by a landslide in Yungay, Huascaran, Peru.

On 16 Dec 1920, a series of landslides triggered off by an earthquake in Gansu Province, China, claimed the lives of 180,000 people.

**Worst material damage by a landslide**
From 18 to 26 Jan 1969, a series of mudslides in southern California, USA, caused a record $138-million (£58-million) worth of damage. The mudslides occurred during nine days of torrential rain and subtropical storms.

## Earthquakes
**Worst death toll**
There were an estimated 830,000 fatalities in an earthquake in the Shaanxi, Shanxi and Henan provinces of China on 2 Feb 1556.

The highest death toll in modern times was the result of the Tangshan earthquake (Mag. $M_s$=7.9) in eastern China on 28 July 1976. On 4 Jan 1977, the official death toll stood at 655,237, but this figure was later adjusted to 750,000. On 22 Nov 1979, the New China News Agency inexplicably reduced the death toll to 242,000.

**Worst material damage**
The greatest physical devastation caused by an earthquake was on 1 Sept 1923 on the Kanto plain, Japan (Mag. $M_s$=8.2). In Tokyo and Yokohama 575,000 dwellings were destroyed. The official total of people killed and missing in this earthquake and its resultant fires was 142,807.

**Highest homeless toll**
Over 1 million residents in a 1,310-km² (3,400-mile²) area of Guatemala were made homeless on 4 Feb 1976 at 3:02 a.m. when a giant earthquake ripped along the Montagua Fault which is the boundary between the Caribbean and North American plates.

**Highest British death toll**
The record undisputed death toll for an earthquake in the United Kingdom is two. Apprentice Thomas Grey was struck by

falling masonry from Christ's Hospital Church, near Newgate, London, at 6 p.m. on 6 April 1580. A young woman, Mabel Everet, died of injuries four days later.

## Volcanoes
**Highest death toll from a volcano**
The eruption of Tambora on Sumbawa, Indonesia, from 5 to 10 April 1815, lowered the height of the island by 1,250 m (4,100 ft) from 4,100 m (13,450 ft) to 2,850 m (9,350 ft). Some 92,000 people were killed or died as a result of the subsequent famine.

## Avalanches and landslides
**Highest death toll in avalanches**
An estimated 40,000–80,000 men died during WWI in the Tyrolean Alps, not from enemy gunfire, but from avalanches that were caused by the sound of gunfire.

**Worst mass burial**
In terms of devastation of the local population, the worst avalanche burial was when two avalanches fell on the small Austrian village of Blons near the Arlberg Pass on 11 Jan 1954. Of the village's 376 residents, 111 were killed, 29 out of 90 homes were destroyed and 300 out of around 600 miners were buried alive.

**Highest number of people trapped**
On 20 Jan 1951, a total of 240 people were killed and more than 45,000 were trapped

## Geysers
**Most people killed by a geyser**
Four people were killed in Aug 1903 during a violent eruption from the Waimangu geyser, New Zealand. They were standing 27 m (90 ft) from it, but their bodies were found up to 800 m (½ mile) away; one body was jammed between two rocks, one was in a hole in the ground, one was suspended in a tree and the fourth was on flat ground.

## Floods and tsunami
**Most fatalities in a flood**
The most disastrous flood occured when the Huang He River, China, flooded in Oct 1887, causing 900,000 deaths.

**Worst property damage**
In Aug 1950, 489 people drowned and 10 million were made homeless by flooding from the Hwai and Chang Jiang Rivers in China. About 890,000 dwellings were destroyed and 5 million acres of cultivated land was under water, leaving about 3.5 million acres of land unworkable for the entire planting season.

**Highest homeless toll**
In Sept 1978, monsoon rains caused river flooding in India's Bengal state. Around 1,300 people drowned and 1.3 million dwellings were destroyed, rendering 15 million people homeless. The financial loss was put at £6.7 million but unofficial estimates were three times that amount.

# MOST EARTHQUAKE FATALITIES 830,000

## 1978 DESTROYED 1.3 MILLION DWELLINGS AND MADE 15 MILLION HOMELESS

### Worst British flash flood
A flash flood totally destroyed the town of Lynmouth, UK, on 15 Aug 1952. There were 34 deaths and the remaining 1,200 residents were made homeless.

### Highest death toll caused by a tsunami
A tsunami that inundated the Japanese coast in 1896 caused 27,000 people to drown.

## Storms
### Worst cyclone
The worst cyclone in recorded history was on 12 Nov 1970 in East Pakistan (now called Bangladesh). Between 300,000 and 500,000 people were killed by a combination of wind and water. Winds of up to 240 km/h (150 mph) and a tidal wave 15 m (50 ft) high lashed the East Pakistan coast, the Ganges Delta, and the offshore islands of Bhola, Hatia, Kukri Mukri, Manpura and Rangabali.

Left
In Sept 1988, Hurricane 'Gilbert' hit the Caribbean, Mexico and Texas, USA, killing over 350 people and causing extensive damage. However, early warning technology greatly helped reduce the death toll.

### OUT OF THE 1278 RESIDENTS AS WELL AS BURYING ALIVE 300 MINERS

### Worst British cyclone
Around 8,000 people were killed as a result of a circular storm in the English Channel on 26 Nov 1703.

### Most damaging hurricane
Hurricane 'Gilbert' killed over 350 people, rendered 750,000 homeless and caused at least $10 billion (£5.5 billion) worth of damage between 12 and 19 Sept 1988 in the Caribbean, Mexico and Texas, USA.

### Most fatalities caused by a tornado
On 26 April 1989, the town of Shaturia in Bangladesh was wiped out. The death toll was put at 1,300 and as many as 50,000 people were made homeless.

### Worst British tornado
On 28 Dec 1879, 75 people were killed in the worst tornado disaster in the United Kingdom. The two tornadic vortices caused Tay Bridge, Fife, to collapse.

### Worst monsoon
In 1983, monsoons raged in Thailand killing 10,000 people. As many as 100,000 people contracted water-borne diseases, 15,000 were evacuated and over £264 million worth of damage was caused.

### Highest death toll in a typhoon
Some 10,000 people died when a typhoon with winds of up to 161 km/h (100 mph) struck Hong Kong on 18 Sept 1906.

### Highest homeless toll in a typhoon
On 2 Sept 1984, Typhoon 'Ike', with winds of 220 km/h (137 mph), hit the Philippines. It killed 1,363 people, 300 were injured and 1,120,000 were made homeless.

### Most damage caused by a snowstorm
Five hundred people died in a monumental winter storm that traversed the entire east coast of the USA from 12 to 13 March 1993. A meteorologist called it "a storm with the heart of a blizzard and the soul of a hurricane" and $1.2 billion (£800 million) worth of damage was caused.

### Most fatalities caused by hail
The worst hailstorm on record claimed the lives of 246 people in Moradabad, Uttar Pradesh, India, on 20 April 1888.

### Most fatalities caused by lightning
A lightning strike downed a Boeing 707 jet liner near Elkton, Maryland, USA, on 8 Dec 1963, killing 81 passengers.

Left
In March 1993, a devastating winter storm crossed the entire east coast of the USA.

# The living world

# Trees

The oldest recorded tree in the United Kingdom, the Fortingall yew (*Taxus baccata*) near Aberfeldy, Perth & Kinross, is estimated to be 4,200 years old. In 1777 it had a 15-m (50-ft) girth and part of the tree still grows.

## Size and spread

### Most massive tree

'General Sherman' a giant sequoia (*Sequoiadendron giganteum*) growing in the Sequoia National Park, California, USA, stands 83.82 m (275 ft) tall, has a diameter of 11.1 m (36 ft 5 in) and a girth of 31.3 m (102 ft 8 in). It is estimated to contain the equivalent of 606,100 board feet of timber, enough to make 5 billion matches, and its bark is 61 cm (2 ft) thick in parts.

### Greatest spread

The great banyan (*Ficus benghalensis*) in the Indian Botanical Garden, Calcutta, India, has the largest tree canopy with 1,775 prop or supporting roots and a circumference of 412 m (1,350 ft). It covers some 1.2 ha (3 acres) and dates from before 1787.

### Most massive organism

In Dec 1992, a network of quaking aspen trees (*Populus tremuloides*) grown from a single root system was reported in the Wasatch Mountains, Utah, USA. It covered 43 ha (106 acres) and weighed an estimated 6,000 tonnes.

### Greatest girth

A pollarded (trimmed to encourage a more bushy growth) European chestnut (*Castanea sativa*) known as the 'Tree of the Hundred Horses' (*Castagno di Cento Cavalli*) on Mt Etna, Sicily, Italy, had a recorded circumference of 57.9 m (190 ft) in 1770 and 1780. It is now split into three parts.

'El Arbol del Tule' in Oaxaca state, Mexico, a 41-m (135-ft) tall Montezuma cypress (*Taxodium mucronatum*), had a girth in 1982 of 35.8 m (117 ft 6 in) and measured 1.52 m (5 ft) above the ground.

Generally speaking, the largest girths are attributed to African baobab trees (*Adansonia digitata*), with measurements of 43 m (141 ft) having been recorded.

## Oldest trees

### Earliest tree

The oldest surviving species of tree is the maidenhair (*Ginkgo biloba*) of Zhejiang, China, which first appeared about 160 million years ago during the Jurassic era. The species was 'rediscovered' by Engelbert Kaempfer, a German physician, in 1690 and reached England *c.* 1754. It has been grown in Japan since *c.* 1100, where it was known as *ginkyo* ('silver apricot'); it is today known as *icho*.

### Longest-lived trees

Dendrochronologists estimate the potential life-span of a bristlecone pine (*Pinus longaeva*) to be nearly 5,500 years, and that of a giant sequoia (*Sequoiadendron giganteum*) at perhaps 6,000 years.

The oldest living tree is a redwood called 'Eternal God' that is 12,000 years old. It has a diameter of 5.974 m (19.6 ft) and a height of 72.542 m (238 ft), and is at the Prairie Creek Redwoods State Park, California, USA.

### Tallest trees

The tallest tree currently standing is the 'Mendocio Tree', a coast redwood (*Sequoia sempervivens*) at Montgomery State Reserve, near Ukiah, California, USA. Its

# TALLEST LIVING TREE 112.014 M

IN CALIFORNIA, USA, NAMED 'ETERNAL GOD', WHICH IS 12,000 YEARS OLD

height was measured as 112.014 m (367 ft 6 in) in December 1996 and its diameter was 3.139 m (10 ft 4 in). The tree is still growing and is estimated to be 1,000 years old.

The tallest tree ever measured was an Australian eucalyptus at Watts River, Victoria, Australia, reported in 1872. It was 132.6 m (435 ft) tall and must have been over 150 m (500 ft) originally.

The 'Dyerville Giant', which grew in Humboldt Redwoods State Park, California, USA, and fell in March 1991 was the tallest tree of modern times. It was 113.4 m (372 ft) high, not including the 1.5-m (5-ft) buried base.

The two tallest known trees in the United Kingdom are two Douglas firs (*Pseudotsuga menziesii*), one at the Forestry Commission property at The Hermitage, Perthshire, and the other at Dunans, Argyll and Butem. Both were 64.5 m (212 ft) high in 1993.

### Tallest Christmas tree
A 67.4-m (221-ft) Douglas fir (*Pseudotsuga menziesii*) was erected at Northgate Shopping Center, Seattle, Washington, USA, in Dec 1950.

### Fastest growing tree
The fastest recorded growth rate is 10.74 m (35 ft 3 in) in 13 months, or *c.* 28 mm (1 1/10 in) per day, by an *Albizzia falcata* planted in June 1974 in Sabah, Malaysia.

### Slowest growing tree
The slowest growing tree is a white cedar (*Thuja occidentalis*) located on a cliffside in the Canadian Great Lakes area. After 155 years, it was less than 10.2 cm (4 in) high and weighed only 17 g (3/5 oz), averaging an annual wood growth of 0.11 g (1/250 oz).

### Largest forests
The largest forested areas are the coniferous forests found in northern Russia, lying between 55°N and the Arctic Circle. The forest covers a total area of 1.1 billion ha (2.7 billion acres).

The largest area of tropical forest in the world is the Amazon rainforest that stretches from Peru to Brazil, covering a total of some 330 million ha (815 million acres).

### Largest British forest
The largest British forest is the Kielder Forest District in Northumberland, which covers 39,380 ha (97,309 acres).

### Largest tree transplant
On 27 March 1997, a 100-year-old horse chestnut (*Aesculus hippocastanum*) weighing 180 kg (396 lbs) and measuring 16 m (52 ft) high was transplanted 60 m (197 ft) by Bomen BSI Service of the Netherlands. The tree was moved because it stood in the way of a planned road tunnel entrance.

## Roots and leaves
### Most leaves
A large oak has perhaps 250,000 leaves, but a cypress may have as many as 45–50 million leaf scales.

### Largest leaves
The raffia palm (*Raffia farinifera=R. ruffia*) of the Mascarene Islands in the Indian Ocean, and the Amazonian bamboo palm (*R. taedigera*) of South America and Africa, have leaf blades of up to 20 m (65 ft 6 in) long, with petioles measuring 4 m (13 ft).

### Deepest roots
A wild fig tree at Echo Caves, near Ohrigstad, Mpumalanga, South Africa, is reported to have roots which have penetrated to 120 m (400 ft) in depth.

An elm root at least 110 m (360 ft) long was reported from Auchencraig, Largs, N Ayrshire, UK, in about 1950.

**Left**
The scale of the notch cut into the trunk of a huge redwood tree in California, USA, can be seen from the size of the people in this photograph. Coast redwoods can live for many thousands of years.

**Left**
Members of a safari stand against an enormous African baobab tree (*Adansonia digitata*). The baobab has the largest girth of all trees.

# Plants and flowers

## Plants

### Oldest plant
King's holly (*Lomatia tasmania*), found in
south west Tasmania, Australia, is thought
to be 40,000 years old—the world's oldest
plant. The shrub was dated using a fossil
of an identical specimen found nearby.

### Most northerly plants
The yellow poppy (*Papaver radicatum*) and
the Arctic willow (*Salix arctica*) survive at a
latitude of 83°N and are the world's most
northerly plants, although the Arctic willow
exists there in an extremely stunted form.

### Most southerly plants
Lichens resembling *Rhinodina frigida*
were found in Moraine Canyon, Antartica,
86°09'S, 157°30'W, in 1971 and in
the Horlick Mountain area of Antarctica,
86°09'S, 131°14'W, in 1965.

In 1981 the flowering plant, Antarctic hair
grass (*Deschampsia antarctica*), was found
on Refuge Island, Antarctica, at 68°21'S.

### Smallest seed
Epiphytic orchid seeds are the smallest
seeds in the world—992.25 million seeds

are required to make up one gramme
(28,129.81 million seeds per oz).

### Largest seed
The largest seed in the world is from the
giant fan palm (*L.callipyge, L.sechellarum*),
often called the double coconut or *coco de
mer*. Found in the Seychelles, a single-
seeded fruit weighs up to 20 kg (44 lb)
and can take 10 years to develop.

### Fastest growing plant
Some species of bamboo are known to
grow at up to 91 cm (3 ft) per day,
or 0.00003 km/h (0.00002 mph).

### Highest plant
In 1955, the flowering plants *Ermania
himalayensis* and *Ranunculus lobatus* were
found at 6,400 m (21,000 ft) on Mount
Kamet in the Himalayas by N.D. Jayal.

### Deepest underwater plant
Mark and Diane Littler discovered algae at
a depth of 269 m (884 ft) off San Salvador
Island, Bahamas, in Oct 1984. Although
99.9995% of sunlight is filtered out at
these depths, the plants still survived.

### Largest undivided leaf
A specimen of *Alocasia macrorrhiza*, found
in 1966 in Sabah, Malaysia, was 3.02 m
(9 ft 11 in) long, 1.92 m (6 ft 3½ in) wide,
with a surface area of 3.17 m$^2$ (34.12 ft$^2$).

The largest leaf in the UK was a specimen of
the Longwood hybrid water lily (*Victoria
amazonica*), cultivated at the Royal Botanical
Gardens, Kew, London. It measured 2.6 m
(8 ft 6½ in) in diameter in July 1995.

## Weeds

### Largest weed
Giant hogweed (*Heracleum mantegazzianum*)
is the world's largest weed. It can be 3.65 m
(12 ft) tall with leaves 91 cm (3 ft) long.

### Most damaging weed
The world's most destructive weed is purple
nutgrass or nutsedge (*Cyperus rotundus*), a
weed native to India. It can kill more than 52
types of crop and is found in 92 countries.

The most damaging cereal weeds in the
United Kingdom are the wild oats *Avena
fatua* and *A. ludoviciana*. Crops affected by
them can lose up to 50% of their yield.

### Largest weed colony
On 18 July 1920, a single clonal growth
of wild box huckleberry (*Gaylussacia
brachycera*) near the Juniata River,

# FASTEST GROWING PLANT 0.00003 KM/H

## IN 14 DAYS, A RATE OF ABOUT 25.4 CM PER DAY

Pennsylvania, USA, covered about 40 ha (100 acres) of land. The colony had first been recorded in 1796. It is estimated that it first started to grow about 13,000 years ago.

### Most destructive aquatic weeds
The most damaging tropical and subtropical aquatic weed is the water hyacinth (*Eichhornia crassipes*), native to the Amazon Basin, but now found from 40°N to 45°S.

## Flowers
### Oldest flower
A flower that is believed to be 120 million years old was identified in 1989 from a fossil found near Melbourne, Victoria, Australia, by Drs Leo Hickey and David Taylor. The flowering angiosperm, which resembles the black pepper plant, had two leaves and one flower and is known as the Koonwarra plant.

## GRAMMATOPHYLLUM SPECIOSUM ORCHID CAN GROW UP TO 7.6 M TALL

### Smallest flowering and fruiting plant
The floating, flowering aquatic duckweed (*Wolffia angusta*) of Australia is 0.6 mm (1/42 in) long and 0.33 mm (1/77 in) wide. It weighs about 0.00015 g (5.2 x 10⁻⁶ oz) and its fruit weighs 0.00007 g (2.4 x 10⁻⁶ oz).

### Fastest growing flowering plant
In July 1978, a *Hesperoyucca whipplei* of the Liliaceae family from Tresco Abbey, Isles of Scilly, UK, grew 3.65 m (12 ft) in 14 days, a rate of about 25.4 cm (10 in) per day.

### Slowest flowering plant
A specimen of the rare *Puya raimondii*, the largest herb, was discovered in Bolivia in 1870 at a height of 3,960 m (13,000 ft). It has a panicle which emerges after 80–150 years, after which it dies.

### Largest bloom
The blooms of the parasite *Rafflesia arnoldi*, found in the jungles of Southeast Asia, can measure up to 91 cm (3 ft) across, with 1.9-cm (3/4-in) thick petals weighing up to 11 kg (36 lb).

### Largest orchids
The tallest orchid in the world is the *Grammatophyllum speciosum*, native to Malaysia. Some specimens have been recorded up to 7.6 m (25 ft) tall.

The largest orchid flower is *Paphiopedilum sanderianum*, whose petals can grow up to 90 cm (3 ft) long in the wild.

### Largest cactus
The largest cactus is the saguaro (*Cereus giganteus* or *Carnegiea gigantea*) found in Arizona, USA and Mexico. The green fluted column is surmounted by candelabra-like branches. A height of 17.67 m (57 ft 11¾ in) was recorded for one discovered in the Maricopa Mts, near Gila Bend, Arizona, USA, on 17 Jan 1988. An armless 24 m (78 ft) tall cactus was measured in April 1978 by Hube Yates in Cave Creek, Arizona, USA. It was toppled in a windstorm in July 1986 at an estimated age of 150 years.

### Largest rhododendron
An example of the scarlet *Rhododendron arboreum* found on Mount Japfu, Nagaland, India, reportedly grew 20 m (65 ft) tall.

### Largest rose bush
A Lady Banksia rose bush (*Rosa banksiae*) in Tombstone, Arizona, USA, known as 'Banks' rose bush has a trunk 409 cm (13 ft 9 in) in circumference, stands approximately 2.75 m (9 ft) high, and covers an area of 740 m² (8,000 ft²). It is supported by 77 posts and several thousand feet of piping, and as many as 250 people can sit under its branches.

### Largest inflorescence
The largest known inflorescence, the flower bearing stalks as distinct from one bloom, is that of *Puya raimondii*. Its erect 2.4-m (8-ft) diameter panicle grows to a height of 10.7 m (35 ft) and each of these bears up to 8,000 white blooms.

# Vegetables

**Right**
Growing giant-sized marrows has become a popular competitive activity for many gardeners. The record-holder is a 49.04-kg specimen grown by Bernard Lavery in South Wales in 1990.

**Corn cob**
92 cm (36¼ in), Bernard Lavery, Llanharry, S Wales, UK, 1994.

**Courgette**
29.25 kg (64 lb 8 oz), Bernard Lavery, Llanharry, S Wales, UK, 1990.

**Cucumber**
9.65 kg (21 lb 4½ oz) P. Glazebrook, Newark, Notts, UK, 1996.

A Vietnamese variety of cucumber 1.83 m (6 ft) long was reported by L. Szabó of Debrecen, Hungary, in September 1976.

**Garlic**
1.19 kg (2 lb 10 oz), Robert Kirkpatrick, Eureka, California, USA, 1985.

**Grapefruit**
3.065 kg (6 lb 12 oz), Debbie Hazleton, Queensland, Australia, 1995.

**Grapes (bunch)**
9.4 kg (20 lb 11½ oz), Bozzolo y Perut Ltda, Santiago, Chile, 1984.

**Green beans**
121.9 cm (48¾ in), H. Hurley, Fuguay-Varina, North Carolina, USA, 1996.

**Leek (pot)**
5.5 kg (12 lb 2 oz), Paul Harrigan, Linton, Northumberland, UK, 1987.

**Lemon**
3.88 kg (8 lb 8 oz), Charlotte and Donald Knutzen, Whittier, California, USA, 1983.

**Largest Fruits and Vegetables**
In the interests of fairness and to minimize the risk of mistakes, all plants should, where possible, be entered in official international, national or local garden contests. Only produce grown primarily for human consumption will be considered. The help of *Garden News* and the World Pumpkin Confederation is gratefully acknowledged.

## World's largest specimens
**Apple**
1.47 kg (3 lb 4 oz), Hanners family, Hood Rivers, Oregon, USA, 1994.

**Beetroot**
18.37 kg (40 lb 8 oz), Ian Neale, Newport, S Wales, UK, 1994.

**Broccoli**
15.87 kg (35 lb), John and Mary Evans, Palmer, Alaska, USA, 1993.

**Cabbage**
56.24 kg (124 lb), Bernard Lavery, Llanharry, S Wales, UK, 1989.

**Cantaloupe melon**
28.12 kg (62 lb), Gene Daughtridge, Rocky Mount, North Carolina, USA, 1991.

**Carrot**
7.13 kg (15 lb 11½ oz), Bernard Lavery, Llanharry, S Wales, UK, 1996.

**Celery**
21.80 kg (48 lb 1 oz) Ian Neale, Newport, S Wales, UK, 1996.

**Marrow**
49.04 kg (108 lb 2 oz), Bernard Lavery, Llanharry, S Wales, UK, 1990.

**Onion**
7.24 kg (15 lb 15½ oz), Mel Ednie, Anstruther, Fife, UK, 1994.

**Parsnip**
4.36 m (171¾ in), Bernard Lavery, Llanharry, S Wales, UK, 1990.

**Pepper**
34.29 cm (13½ in), J. Rutherford, Hatch, New Mexico, 1975.

**Pineapple**
8.06 kg (17 lb 12 oz), Ermand Kamuk, Ais Village, WNBP, Papua New Guinea, 1994.

# LONGEST BEAN 121.9 CM

**Potato**
A 12.93-kg (28-lb 8-oz) potato is reported to have been dug up by Joseph Johnson in his garden in Sedgley, UK, on 1 Oct 1905.

Three specimens of 3.5 kg (7 lb 13 oz), Ken Sloane, Patrick, Isle of Man, 1994.

**Pumpkin**
481 kg (1,061 lb) Nathan and Paula Zehr, Lowville, New York, USA, 1996.

**Radish**
17.2 kg (37 lb 15 oz), Litterini family, Tanunda, South Australia, 1992.

**Rhubarb**
2.67 kg (5 lb 14 oz), Eric Stone, E Woodyates, Wilts, UK, 1985.

**Squash**
408.5 kg (900 lb 8 oz), John and Chris Lyons, Baltimore, Ontario, Canada, 1994.

**Strawberry**
231 g (8.17 oz), George Andersen, Folkestone, Kent, UK, 1983.

**Swede**
28.27 kg (62 lb 3 oz), Norman Craven, Stouffville, Ontario, Canada, 1996.

**Tomato**
3.51 kg (7 lb 12 oz), Gordon Graham, Edmond, Oklahoma, USA, 1986.

**Tomato plant**
16.3 m (53 ft 6 in), Gordon Graham, Edmond, Oklahoma, USA, 1985.

**Gooseberry**
61.04 g (2.18 oz), Kelvin Archer, Scholar Green, Cheshire, 1993.

**Grapefruit**
1.67 kg (3 lb 11 oz), Willington Garden Centre Club, Bedford, 1986.

**Lemon**
2.13 kg (4 lb 11 oz), Pershore College, Pershore, Hereford and Worcester, 1986.

**Peach**
411 g (14½ oz), Jean Bird, London, 1984.

**Squash**
252.4 kg (556 lb 7 oz), Richard Hope, Shevington, near Wigan, Lancs, 1995.

**Tomato**
2.54 kg (5 lb 9½ oz), R. Burrows, Huddersfield, W Yorkshire, 1985.

**Tomato plant**
13.96 m (45 ft 9½ in), Chosen Hill School, Glos, 1981.

**Watermelon**
52.98 kg (116 lb 13 oz), Bernard Lavery, Llanharry, S Wales, 1995.

**Left**
The longest green bean in the world (121.9 cm or 48¾ in long) and other giant green beans grown by H. Hurley of Fuguay-Varina, North Carolina, USA, in 1996.

WORLD'S HEAVIEST CELERY, PRODUCING A SPECIMEN WEIGHING 21.80 KG

**Watermelon**
118.84 kg (262 lb), Bill Carson, Arrington, Tennessee, USA, 1990.

## Largest British specimens
**Cantaloupe melon**
9.91 kg (21 lb 13½ oz), Bernard Lavery, Llanharry, S Wales, 1995.

**Carrot**
A 5.14-m (16-ft 10½-in) long carrot was grown by Bernard Lavery of Llanharry, S Wales, in 1991.

**Cucumber**
Rayment of Chelmsford, Essex, grew a cucumber measuring 1.10 m (43½ in) in 1984–86.

# Mammals

## Mammal size

### Largest mammal on earth
The blue whale (*Balaenoptera musculus*) is the largest mammal. Adult females have an average weight of 120 tonnes and a length of 26.2 m (86 ft). Newborn calves are 6–8 m (20–26 ft) long and weigh up to 3 tonnes.

### Largest land mammal
An average-sized African bush elephant bull (*Loxodonta africana africana*) stands 3–3.7 m (9 ft 10 in–12 ft 2 in) at the shoulder and weighs between 4–7 tonnes. The largest specimen ever recorded is a bull shot in Mucusso, Angola, on 7 Nov 1974—its weight was calculated at 12.24 tonnes.

### Largest carnivorous land mammal
Adult male polar bears (*Ursus maritimus*) often weigh 400–600 kg (880–1,320 lb), and have a nose-to-tail length of 2.4–2.6 m (7 ft 11 in–8 ft 6 in).

The male Kodiak bear (*Ursus arctos middendorffi*) is usually shorter than the polar bear but more robustly built.

### Heaviest mammal
A female blue whale weighing 190 tonnes and measuring 27.6 m (90 ft 6 in) in length was caught in the Southern Ocean on 20 March 1947.

### Heaviest land mammal
In 1960, a polar bear estimated to weigh 900 kg (2,000 lb) was shot in the Chukchi Sea, Alaska, USA. It was said to measure 3.5 m (11 ft 3 in) from nose to tail over its body contours, 1.5 m (4 ft 10 in) round the body and 43 cm (1 ft 5 in) around the paws.

A Kodiak bear named 'Goliath' from the Space Farms Zoo, Sussex, New Jersey, USA, reportedly weighed more than 900 kg (2,000 lb) in the early 1980s.

### Longest mammal
A female blue whale measuring 33.58 m (110 ft 2½ in) landed in 1909 at Grytviken, South Georgia, in the South Atlantic.

### Tallest mammal
The giraffe (*Giraffa camelopardalis*) is found in the dry savannah and open woodland areas of Africa, south of the Sahara. The tallest recorded specimen was a Masai bull (*G. c. tippelskirchi*) which was named 'George', brought to Chester Zoo, Cheshire, UK, from Kenya on 8 Jan 1959. His 'horns' almost grazed the roof of the 6.1-m (20-ft) high Giraffe House when he was nine years old.

### Largest toothed mammal
The lower jaw of a sperm whale or cachelot (*Physeter macrocephalus*) measuring 5 m (16 ft 5 in) in length, exhibited in the British Museum, belonged to a bull reputedly measuring nearly 25.6 m (84 ft) long.

The longest officially measured specimen was a sperm whale measuring 20.7 m (67 ft 11 in), captured in the summer of 1950 off the Kurile Islands in the north-west Pacific.

### Smallest mammal
The smallest mammal in the world is the bumblebee or Kitti's hog-nosed bat (*Craseonycteris thonglongyai*), which lives in about 21 limestone caves on the Kwae Roi River, Kanchanaburi Province, south-west Thailand. Its body is no bigger than a large bumblebee—its head–body length measures just 29–33 mm (1¹⁄₇–1³⁄₁₀ in). Its wingspan is approximately 130–145 mm (5¹⁄₁₀–5⁷⁄₁₀ in), and its weight 1.7–2.0 g (³⁄₅₀–⁷⁄₁₀₀ oz).

### Smallest non-flying mammal
The smallest non-flying mammal in the world is Savi's white-toothed pygmy shrew, or the Etruscan shrew (*Suncus etruscus*). It has a head–body length of 35–48 mm (1¹⁄₅–1⁴⁄₅ in), a tail length of 25–30 mm (⁹⁄₁₀–1⁷⁄₁₀ in) and specimens normally weigh between 1.5–2.5 g (¹⁄₂₀–⁹⁄₁₀₀ oz). It lives along the coast of the Mediterranean Sea and is found as far south as Western Cape, South Africa.

## Mammal speed

### Fastest land mammal
Up to a distance of 550 m (600 yd), the cheetah (*Acinonyx jubatus*) of the open plains of east Africa, Iran, Turkmenistan and Afghanistan, has a probable maximum speed of 100 km/h (60 mph) on level ground.

The pronghorn antelope (*Antilocapra americana*), of the western USA, south-western Canada and parts of northern Mexico, is the fastest land animal over long distances. It has been observed to travel at 56 km/h (35 mph) for 6 km (4 miles), at 67 km/h (42 mph) for 1.6 km (1 mile) and 88.5 km/h (55 mph) for 0.8 km (½ mile).

### Fastest marine mammal
In 1958, a bull killer whale (*Orcinus orca*) was timed at 55.5 km/h (34.5 mph) in the eastern North Pacific. Similar speeds have also been reported for Dall's porpoise (*Phocoenoides dalli*) in short bursts.

### Slowest mammal
The three-toed sloth of tropical South America (*Bradypus tridactylus*) has an average ground speed of 1.8–2.4 m (6–8 ft) per minute or 0.1–0.16 km/h (0.07–0.1 mph), but in trees it can accelerate to 4.6 m (15 ft) per minute or 0.27 km/h (0.17 mph).

## Felines

### Largest feline
The male Siberian tiger (*Panthera tigris altaica*), averages 3.15 m (10 ft 4 in) in length from the nose to the tip of the tail,

**Right**
The highest swimming speeds for the pinniped order of mammals have been recorded for the California sea-lion (*Zalophus californianus*). In a short spurt it can achieve speeds of 40 km/h (25 mph).

# SLOWEST MAMMAL 0.1–0.16 KM/H

## 25.6 M IN LENGTH AND WITH A LOWER JAW OF 5 M

stands 99–107 cm (3 ft 3 in–3 ft 6 in) at the shoulder and weighs about 265 kg (585 lb).

An Indian tiger (*P. t. tigris*) which was shot in northern Uttar Pradesh, India, in 1967 weighed 389 kg (857 lb). An average male Indian tiger weighs approximately 190 kg (420 lb).

### Heaviest lion
The heaviest wild African lion (*Panthera leo leo*) on record was shot in South Africa in 1936. It weighed 313 kg (690 lb).

### Smallest feline
The rusty-spotted cat (*Prionailurus rubiginosus*) which is found in southern India and Sri Lanka has a head–body length of 350–480 mm (13⅘–18⁹⁄₁₀ in). An average female weighs 1.1 kg (2 lb 7oz), while a male is 1.5–1.6 kg (3 lb 5 oz–3 lb 8 oz).

56 KM/H

**Left**
A pronghorn antelope (*Antilocapra americana*), running at top speed through the prairie grasslands of Montana. It is the world's fastest land animal over long distances—over 6 km (4 miles) it can travel at 56 km/h (35 mph), while over 0.8 km (½ mile) it can reach speeds of 88.5 km/h (55 mph).

## REACHING SPEEDS OF 100 KM/H ON LEVEL GROUND OVER SHORT DISTANCES

## Primates
### Largest primate
The male eastern lowland gorilla (*Gorilla gorilla graueri*) of eastern Congo (ex-Zaïre) has a bipedal standing height of up to 1.7 m (5 ft 9 in) and weighs up to 163.4 kg (360 lb).

### Tallest primate
The greatest height (top of crest to heel) recorded for a gorilla in the wild is 1.95 m (6 ft 5 in) for a mountain bull shot in the eastern Belgian Congo (now the Democratic Republic of Congo) in 1938.

### Heaviest primate
The heaviest gorilla in captivity was a male of the mountain race called 'N'gagia'. At his heaviest he was 310 kg (683 lb). He died in San Diego Zoo, California, USA, in 1944.

### Smallest primate
The smallest true primate (excluding tree shrews which are usually classified separately) is the pygmy mouse lemur (*Microcebus myoxinus*), recently discovered in Madagascar. Its head–body length is about 62 mm (2⅕ in), its tail is 13.6 cm (5⅕ in) long and it weighs around 30.6 g (1¹⁄₁₀ oz).

## Pinnipeds
### Largest pinniped
The pinniped order includes seals, sea-lions and walruses. Largest of the 34 species is the southern elephant seal (*Mirounga leonina*) of the sub-Antarctic islands. Bulls have a maximum girth of 3.7 m (12 ft) and weigh 2,000–3,500 kg (4,400–7,720 lb).

88.5 KM/H

### Smallest pinniped
The smallest pinniped is the Galapagos fur seal (*Arctocephalus galapagoensis*). Adult females average 1.2 m (3 ft 11 in) in length and weigh about 27 kg (60 lb). Males are usually larger, averaging 1.5 m (4 ft 11 in) in length and weighing around 64 kg (141 lb).

### Fastest pinniped
The highest swimming speed for a pinniped is a short spurt of 40 km/h (25 mph) by a California sea-lion (*Zalophus californianus*).

The fastest pinniped on land is the crabeater seal (*Lobodon carcinophagus*), which has been timed at 25 km/h (15½ mph).

## Rodents
### Largest rodent
The capybara (*Hydrochoerus hydrochaeris*), of northern South America, has a head-and-body length of 1.0–1.3 m (3 ft 3 in–4 ft 6 in) and can weigh up to 79 kg (174 lb), although one animal that became obese in captivity weighed as much as 113 kg (250 lb).

### Smallest rodent
The northern pygmy mouse (*Baiomys taylori*) found in Mexico and Arizona and Texas, USA, and the Baluchistan pygmy jerboa (*Salpingotulus michaelis*) from Pakistan, both have a head–body length of 3.6 cm (1⁷⁄₁₆ in) and a tail length of 7.2 cm (2¹³⁄₁₆ in).

# Mammal lifestyle

**Right**
Prairie dogs form the largest colonies of mammals. The animals are not in fact dogs but members of the rodent family. Their name comes from their characteristic alarm call which sounds similar to a dog's bark.

## Birth and life
### Shortest gestation period
The shortest mammalian gestation period is 12–13 days, which is common in a number of species. These include the Virginia opossum (*Didelphis marsupialis*) of North America and the rare water opossum, or yapok, (*Chironectes minimus*) of central and northern South America. On rare occasions,

### Largest nest-building mammal
The European wild boar (*Sus scrofa*) is the largest mammal to construct a nest. It does this in order to protect its young from predators and keep them warm. Even though the boar is the largest of all the wild pigs, the piglets it produces are surprisingly small and helpless when they are first born.

The fin whale (*Balaenoptera physalus*) is probably the longest lived mammal, with a maximum lifespan of around 90–100 years.

## Sound and motion
### Loudest animal sound
The low-frequency pulses made by blue whales (*Balaenoptera musculus*) and fin

gestation periods of eight days have been recorded for some of these species.

### Longest gestation period
The Asiatic elephant (*Elephas maximus*) has an average gestation period of 609 days and a maximum of 760 days—more than two and a half times that of humans.

### Largest litter
The greatest number of young born to a wild mammal at a single birth is 31 (30 of which survived) in the case of a tailless tenrec (*Tenrec ecaudatus*), found on Madagascar and in the Comoro Islands.

### Earliest pregnancy
The female true lemming (*Lemmus lemmus*) of Scandinavia can become pregnant aged 14 days. Their gestation period is 16 to 23 days, and litter size varies from one to 13.

### Most rampant animal
The male brown antechinus (*Antechinus stuartii*), a marsupial mouse from eastern Australia, has an insatiable sexual appetite. Every year the entire adult male population goes on a rampage for two weeks in a desperate bid to mate with as many females as possible. They are so busy chasing females and fighting off rival males that they do not eat, and all die within a matter of days due to starvation, ulcers or infection.

### Mammal longevity
No land mammals live longer than human beings (*Homo sapiens*), but the Asiatic elephant (*Elephas maximus*) probably comes closest. There are some claims for animals living to over 80, but the greatest verified age was 78 years for an elephant cow called 'Modoc', who died in Santa Clara, California, USA, on 17 July 1975.

whales (*B. physalus*) when communicating with each other have registered at up to 188 decibels, making them the loudest sounds emitted by any living source. They have been detected 850 km (530 miles) away.

### Sleepiest mammal
Some armadillos (*Dasypodidae*), opossums (*Didelphidae*) and sloths (*Bradypodidae* and *Megalonychidae*) spend up to 80% of their lives sleeping or dozing. The least active of all mammals are probably the three species of three-toed sloths in the genus *Bradypus*.

### Slowest awakening from hibernation
Marmots (*Marmota*) are rodents native to the mountains of North America and Eurasia, which hibernate in winter. The hoary marmot (*Marmota caligata*) of North America and Siberia may hibernate for up to nine months and takes many hours to wake up.

# LONGEST GESTATION 760 DAYS

WHO ARE SUCCESSFUL IN 50–70% OF THEIR HUNTS

## Habitat and distribution

### Highest altitude
The highest-living mammal in the world is the large-eared pika (*Ochtona macrotis*), which has been recorded at 6,130 m (20,106 ft) in mountain ranges in Asia.

The yaks (*Bos mutus*) of Tibet and the Sichuanese Alps, China, climb to an altitude of 6,100 m (20,000 ft) when foraging.

### Lowest altitude
The little brown bat (*Myotis lucifugus*) has been recorded at a depth of 1,160 m (3,805 ft) in a zinc mine in New York, USA. The mine serves as winter quarters for 1,000 members of this species.

### Largest colony of mammals
The black-tailed prairie dog (*Cynomys ludovicianus*), a rodent of the family Sciuridae, found in the western USA and northern Mexico, builds large colonies. One single 'town' discovered in 1901 contained about 400 million individuals and was estimated to cover 61,400 km² (24,000 miles²), an area almost the size of the Republic of Ireland, making it the largest colony of mammals ever recorded.

### Largest herd of mammals
The largest herds on record were of the springboks (*Antidorcas marsupialis*) which migrated across the plains of south-western Africa in the 19th century. In 1849, John Fraser observed a herd of springboks that took three days to pass through the settlement of Beaufort West, South Africa.

## Diet

### Most fatty diet
In spring and early summer the diet of the polar bear (*Ursus maritimus*) consists of recently weaned ringed seal pups (*Pusa hispida*), which can be up to 50% fat. From April to July the seals are in such plentiful supply that the bears sometimes feed only on the fat below the skin and leave the rest of the carcasses untouched.

### Fussiest eater
The koala (*Phascolarctos cinereus*) of eastern Australia feeds almost exclusively on eucalyptus leaves. It feeds regularly on only half a dozen of the 500 species and prefers certain individual trees above others. It is even choosy when it comes to specific leaves, sometimes sifting through up to 9 kg (20 lb) of leaves every day to find the 0.5 kg (1¼ lb) that it consumes.

## Survival

### Most successful predator
African hunting dogs, also known as Cape hunting dogs or Dog hyenas (*Lycaon pictus*), are successful in 50–70% of their hunts, consistently the highest figure for any hunting mammal.

FEMALES AS POSSIBLE THAT IT DIES OF STARVATION WITHIN A FEW DAYS

### Most fearless mammal
The ratel or honey badger (*Mellivora capensis*) will defend itself against animals of any size, especially if they dare to wander too close to its breeding burrow. Its skin is so tough that it is impervious to the stings of bees, the quills of porcupines and the bites of most snakes. The honey badger also has such loose skin that if the creature is held by the scruff of the neck, for example by a hyena or a leopard, it can turn inside its skin and bite the attacker until it lets go.

### Most dominant females
Female hyenas (family Hyaenidae), and females of the South and Central American common squirrel monkeys (*Saimiri sciureus*), are both larger and more aggressive than the males of the same species, which they usually dominate.

**Left**
The lemming has the earliest pregnancy of all mammals. They are also prolific breeders—one pair of lemmings was reported to have produced eight litters in 167 days, after which the male died.

## Horses and Ponies
### Largest horse
The tallest and heaviest documented horse was the shire gelding 'Sampson' (later renamed 'Mammoth'), bred by Thomas Cleaver of Toddington Mills, Beds, UK. The horse was 21.2½ hands (2.19 m or 7 ft 2½ in) in 1850. He was later said to have weighed 1,524 kg (3,360 lb).

### Smallest horse
The smallest known horse in the world is the miniature horse 'Tara Stables' Hope for Tomorrow', owned by Kenneth and Elizabeth Garnett of Vinton, Virginia, USA. In June 1997 it measured 53.34 cm (21 in) from the ground to the highest point of the withers.

The smallest British horse is 'Toyhorse Countess Natushka', owned by Tikki Adorian of Billingshurst, W Sussex, UK. It measured 68.9 cm (27 ⅛ in) in Sept 1996.

HEAVIEST PIG, A POLAND-CHINA HOG CALLED 'BIG BILL', WAS 1,157.5 K

### Oldest horse
The greatest reliably recorded age for a horse is 62, for 'Old Billy' (died 1822), bred by Edward Robinson of Woolston, Lancs, UK.

The oldest recorded age for a thoroughbred racehorse was 42 for the chestnut gelding 'Tango Duke', owned by Carmen J. Koper of Barongarook, Victoria, Australia. The horse died on 25 Jan 1978.

### Oldest pony
A pony owned by a farmer in central France died in 1919 at the age of 54.

A moorland pony called 'Joey', owned by June and Rosie Osborne of the Glebe Equestrian Centre, Wickham Bishop, Essex, UK, died in May 1988 at the age of 44.

### Largest mules
Apollo and Anak, owned by Herbert L. Mueller of Columbia, Illinois, USA, are the largest mules. Apollo stands 19.1 hands (1.96 m or 6 ft 5 in) tall and weighs 998 kg (2,200 lb), with Anak at 18.3 hands (1.91 m or 6 ft 3 in) and 952.2 kg (2,100 lb).

## Cattle
### Heaviest cow
A Holstein–Durham cross named 'Mount Katahdin', frequently weighed 2,270 kg (5,000 lb) from 1906 to 1910. She stood 1.88 m (6 ft 2 in) at the shoulder and had a girth measuring 3.96 m (13 ft). The cow died in a barn fire c. 1923.

The British record is 2,032 kg (4,480 lb) for the Bradwell Ox, owned by William Spurgin of Orpland Farm, Bradwell-on-Sea, Essex. In 1830, when he was six years old, this bull measured 4.6 m (15 ft) from nose to tail with a maximum girth of 3.35 m (11 ft).

The largest breed of cattle in the United Kingdom is the South Devon. Bulls can measure up to 1.55 m (5 ft 1 in) at the shoulder and weigh about 1,250 kg (2,755 lb). The heaviest example on record weighed 1,680 kg (3,700 lb).

### Smallest cows
The smallest breed of domestic cattle is the Ovambo of Namibia, with bulls and cows averaging 225 kg (496 lb) and 160 kg (353 lb) respectively.

In May 1984, a height of 86.3 cm (34 in) was reported for an adult Dexter cow named 'Mayberry', owned by R. Hillier of Church Farm, South Littleton, Evesham, Worcs, UK.

### Highest milk yields
The highest lifetime yield of milk is 211,025 kg (465,224 lb) to 1 May 1984 from cow No. 289, owned by M. G. Maciel & Son of Hanford, California, USA.

The greatest recorded yield for one lactation (maximum 365 days) is 26,963 kg (59,443 lb) in 1995 from a Friesian cow, 'Acme Goldy 2', owned by Bryce Miller of Woodford Grange Farm, Islip, Northants, UK.

## Pigs
### Largest pigs
The heaviest pig ever recorded was a Poland–China hog named 'Big Bill', who weighed 1,157.5 kg (2,552 lb) just before being put down after accidentally breaking a leg on the way to the Chicago World's Fair for exhibition in 1933.

A British Gloucester Old Spot boar bred by Joseph Lawton of Astbury, Cheshire, UK, weighed 639.5 kg (1,410 lb), stood 1.43 m (4 ft 8¼ in) at the shoulder and was 2.94 m (9 ft 8 in) long.

### Smallest pigs
The smallest breed of pig is the Mini Maialino, developed after 10 years' experimentation with Vietnamese pot-bellied pigs, by Stefano Morini of St Polo d'Enza, Italy. The piglets weigh 400 g (14 oz) at birth and 9 kg (20 lb) at maturity.

## Sheep
### Largest sheep
A Suffolk ram named 'Stratford Whisper', owned by Joseph and Susan Schallberger of Boring, Oregon, USA, weighed 247.2 kg (545 lb) and was 1.09 m (43 in) tall in 1991.

### Smallest sheep
The smallest breed of sheep is the Ouessant, from the Ile d'Ouessant, Brittany, France, which weighs 13–16 kg (29–35 lb) and stands 45–50 cm (1 ft 6 in–1 ft 8 in) at the withers.

# 371 EGGS IN 364 DAYS

### Oldest sheep
A crossbred sheep owned by Griffiths & Davies of Dolclettwr Hall, Taliesin, near Aberystwyth, Ceredigion, UK, gave birth to a healthy lamb in 1988 at the age of 28, after lambing successfully more than 40 times. She died a week before her 29th birthday.

## Goats
### Largest goat
A British Saanen named 'Mostyn Moorcock', owned by Pat Robinson of Ewyas Harold, Hereford & Worcester, UK, weighed 181.4 kg (400 lb), was 111.7 cm (44 in) high at the shoulder and had an overall length of 167.6 cm (66 in). He died in 1977 when he was four years old.

### Smallest goats
Some pygmy goats weigh as little as 15–20 kg (33–44 lb).

## Largest litters
### Most prolific cows
On 25 April 1964, it was reported that a cow named 'Lyubik' had given birth to seven calves in Mogilev, Belarus (then part of the USSR).

Five live calves at one birth were reported in 1928 by T.G. Yarwood of Manchester, UK.

'Big Bertha', a Dremon owned by Jerome O'Leary of Co. Kerry, Republic of Ireland, gave birth to a record 39 calves in her lifetime. She was also the oldest ever cow, having died just short of her 49th birthday in 1993.

'Nordjydens Hubert', a Danish Holstein-Friesian bull which died at the age of 12 in Jan 1996, left 250,002 surviving progeny that were the result of artificial insemination.

### Most prolific pigs
A world record litter of 37 piglets was born to Sow 570, a Meishan cross Large White-Durum on 21 Sept 1993, at Mr & Mrs M. P. Ford's Eastfield House Farm in Melbourne, York. Of the 36 piglets that were born alive, 33 survived.

A Large White which was owned by H. S. Pedlingham farrowed 385 pigs in 22 litters from December 1923 to September 1934.

Between 1940 and 1952 a Large Black sow belonging to A. M. Harris of Lapworth, Warks, UK, farrowed 26 litters.

A Newsham Large White Landrace sow from Meeting House Farm, Staintondale, near Scarborough, N Yorkshire, UK, gave birth to 70 piglets in a 12-month period beginning 6 May 1987.

## Poultry
### Largest chickens
The heaviest breed of chicken is the White Sully, a hybrid of large Rhode Island Reds and other varieties. The largest, a rooster named 'Weirdo', reportedly weighed 10 kg (22 lb) in Jan 1973.

A rooster named 'Big Snow', owned and bred by Ronald Alldridge of Deuchar, Queensland, Australia, weighed 10.51 kg (23 lb 3oz) on 12 June 1992, with a chest girth of 84 cm (2 ft 9 in) and stood 43.2 cm (1 ft 5 in) at the shoulder. He died on 6 Sept 1992.

### Egg-laying
A White Leghorn (No. 2,988) laid 371 eggs in 364 days in an official test conducted by Prof. Harold V. Biellier ending on 29 Aug 1979 at the College of Agriculture, University of Missouri, USA.

### Most yolks
The claim for the greatest number of yolks in a hen's egg is nine, reported by Diane Hainsworth of Hainsworth Poultry Farms, Mount Morris, New York, USA, in 1971, and also from a hen in Kyrgyztan (then USSR) in Aug 1977.

### Heaviest turkey
The greatest dressed weight recorded for a turkey is 39.09 kg (86 lb) for a stag named 'Tyson' reared by Philip Cook of Leacroft Turkeys Ltd, Peterborough, Cambs, UK.

### Most prolific ewe
On 4 Sept 1991, a Finnish Landrace ewe owned by the D.M.C. Partnership (comprising Trevor and Diane Cooke, Stephen and Mary Moss and Ken and Carole Mihaere) of Feilding, Manawatu, New Zealand, gave birth to eight lambs.
On 19 April 1994, the record was equalled by a six-year-old ewe '835 Ylva', owned by Birgitta and Kent Mossby of Halsarp Farm, Falkoping, Sweden.

**Below left**
The largest sheep ever was this Suffolk ram named 'Stratford Whisper'.

# Dogs

## Size and age

### Largest dog
The heaviest breeds of domestic dog (*Canis familiaris*) are the Old English mastiff and the St Bernard, with males of both species regularly weighing 77–91 kg (170–200 lb).

The heaviest and longest dog on record is *Aicama Zorba of La-Susa*, an Old English mastiff owned by Chris Eraclides of London, UK. 'Zorba' stood 94 cm (3 ft 1 in) at the shoulder and weighed a peak 155.58 kg (343 lb) in Nov 1989.

The tallest dog on record was *Shamgret Danzas,* a great Dane owned by Wendy and Keith Comley of Milton Keynes, Bucks, UK. This dog stood 105.4 cm (41½ in) tall and weighed up to 108 kg (238 lb).

### Smallest dog
A matchbox-sized Yorkshire terrier owned by Arthur Marples of Blackburn, Lancs, UK, stood 6.3 cm (2½ in) at the shoulder and was 9.5 cm (3¾ in) from the tip of its nose to the root of its tail. It weighed 113 g (4 oz) and died in 1945, at almost two years old.

The smallest living dog is 'Big Boss', a Yorkie owned by Dr Chai Khanchanakom of Bangkok, Thailand. On his first birthday on 7 Dec 1995 he measured 11.94 cm (4⁷⁄₁₀ in) tall and 12.95 cm (5¹⁄₁₀ in) long, and weighed 481 g (1 lb 1 oz).

### Oldest dog
The greatest age reliably recorded for a dog is 29 years 5 months, for an Australian cattle-dog named 'Bluey', owned by Les Hall of Rochester, Victoria, Australia.

A Welsh collie named 'Taffy', owned by Evelyn Brown of Forge Farm, West Bromwich, W Midlands, UK, lived for 27 years and 313 days.

## Canine achievements

### Highest jump by a dog
The canine high jump record for a leap and scramble over a smooth wooden wall (without ribs or other aids) is 3.72 m (12 ft 2½ in), by an 18-month-old lurcher named 'Stag', at the annual Cotswold Country Fair in Cirencester, Glos, UK, on 27 Sept 1993. The dog is owned by Mr and Mrs Matthews of Redruth, Cornwall, UK.

'Duke', a three-year-old German shepherd dog handled by Corporal Graham Urry of RAF Newton, Notts, UK, scaled a ribbed wall with regulation shallow slats to a height of 3.58 m (11 ft 9 in) on BBC TV's *Record Breakers* programme on 11 Nov 1986.

The highest freestyle jump is 1.5 m (4 ft 11 in), by 'Olive Oyl' at the Chicagoland Family Pet Show at Arlington Heights, Illinois, USA, on 22 March, 1996.

### Longest dog jump
A greyhound named 'Bang' jumped 9.14 m (30 ft) while hare coursing at Brecon Lodge, Glos, UK, in 1849. He cleared a 1.4-m (4-ft 6-in) gate and landed on a road, damaging his pastern bone.

## Top show dogs
The greatest number of Challenge Certificates won by a single dog in all-breed shows is 275, by the German shepherd bitch *Altana's Mystique*, formerly owned by Jane Firestone and now owned by James A. Moses of Alpharetta, Georgia, USA.

The most 'Best-in-Show' awards won by any dog in all-breed shows is 203, by the Scottish terrier bitch *Ch. Braeburn's Close Encounter*, owned by Sonnie Novick of Plantation Acres, Florida, USA.

### Guide dogs
The longest period of active service reported for a guide dog is 14 years 8 months, by a Labrador-retriever bitch named 'Cindi-Cleo', owned by Aron Barr of Tel Aviv, Israel. The dog died on 10 April 1987.

'Donna', a hearing guide dog owned by John Hogan of Pyrmont Point, Australia, completed 10 years of service in Australia and eight years of service before that in New Zealand. 'Donna' was also the first hearing dog to be licensed under Australian law in 1985.

### Largest dog walk
The three-mile 'Pooches on Parade' held on 5 Oct 1996 at Wickham Park, Manchester, Connecticut, USA, involved 1,086 dogs.

### Tracking
In 1925, a Dobermann pinscher named 'Sauer', trained by Detective Sergeant Herbert Kruger, tracked a stock-thief

**Right**
On 5 Oct 1996, a total of 1,086 dogs took part in the world's largest dog walk in Wickham Park, Manchester, Connecticut, USA. The event raised money for guide dog charities.

160 km (100 miles) across the Great Karroo, South Africa, by scent alone.

### Drug sniffing
'Snag', a US customs labrador retriever trained and partnered by Jeff Weitzmann, has made 118 drug seizures worth a record $810 million (£580 million).

In Oct 1988 a German shepherd owned by the Essex police force sniffed out 2 tonnes of cannabis worth £6 million when it was sent into a cottage near Harlow, Essex, UK.

### Most effective sniffer dog
Florida Police Department Golden retriever 'Trepp' is credited with over 100 arrests and recovering *c.* $63 million (£28.6 million) worth of narcotics. 'Trepp' was once set to detect 10 hidden packets of drugs at a police academy demonstration—and found 11.

# CANINE HIGH JUMP 3.72 M

14:34:16          14:47:57          14:52:12

**Left**
'Olive Oyl', the freestyle jumping record-holder, at the Chicagoland Family Pet Show, Arlington Heights, Illinois, USA, in 1996. Though jumping looks like fun it also serves a serious purpose. Specialist training such as this helps dogs perform a variety of duties—from police work to assisting firefighters.

**Most ineffective sniffer dogs**
In 1967 a dog handler was questioning two suspects during a drugs raid in the English Midlands, when his sniffer dogs 'Laddie' and 'Boy' lay down in front of the suspects. The dogs then dozed off in front of the fire and woke only to bite their handler on the leg as he tried to handcuff one of the suspects.

**Ratting**
Sometime between 1820 and 1824, an 11.8-kg (26-lb) 'bull and terrier' dog named 'Billy' killed 4,000 rats in 17 hours. On 23

in 1942 with the ship's crew and interned at a PoW camp at Medan, Indonesia.

**World's earliest canine film star**
The dog 'Rover' featured in the 1905 film *Rescued by Rover,* which was directed by Cecil Hepworth.

**Most celebrated canine rescuer**
The most famous canine rescuer of all time is 'Barry', a St Bernard. 'Barry' rescued more than 40 people during his 12-year career on the Swiss Alps. His rescues

**Most valuable showbusiness animal**
The original *Lassie* star, 'Pal', was the first of a total of nine male dogs to play the canine heroine. His great-great-great-great-great grandson 'Lassie IX', also known as 'Howard', is now the most valuable animal in showbusiness history.

**Top earning literary dog**
In 1991 springer spaniel *Mildred Kerr,* known as 'Millie', brought in a salary more than four times that of her master US President George Bush, when her 'autobiography' sold 400,000 copies. 'Dictated' to First Lady Barbara Bush, *Millie's Book* was described as an "under the table look at life in the Bush family". The book was estimated to have earned $900,000 (£510,000).

April 1825, he killed 100 rats in 5 min 30 sec at the Cockpit in Tufton Street, Westminster, London, UK.

James Searle's famous 'bull and terrier' bitch 'Jenny Lind' was another outstanding ratter. On 12 July 1853, she was backed to kill 500 rats in under three hours at the Beehive in Old Crosshall Street, Liverpool. She completed the job in 1 hr 36 min.

**Only dog to become a saint**
Healing miracles were recorded at the tomb of 'St Guinefort,' a French greyhound who died saving a child from a snake in the 13th century and was popularly acclaimed as a saint. The Church never recognized the cult.

**Only pet recognized as PoW**
Pointer bitch, 'Judy', a mascot of the HMS *Grasshopper,* was captured by the Japanese

included that of a boy who lay half frozen under an avalanche in which his mother had died. 'Barry' spread himself across the boy's body to warm him and licked his face until he woke him up. He then carried the boy back to the nearest dwelling.

## Canine finances
**Most valuable dog**
The largest legacy ever left to a dog was £15 million which was bequeathed by Ella Wendel of New York, USA, to her standard poodle 'Toby' in 1931.

**First dog with share trading account**
The owner of a sheepdog named 'William' set up a share trading account in the dog's name. He then traded shares on the stock exchange and amassed a fortune of over £100,000 on his dog's behalf.

**Richest dog**
German shepherd 'Gunther' was left $65 million (£40 million) by his owner, German Countess Carlotta Liebenstein, and became, probably, the richest dog in the world in the 1990s. 'Gunther' lives in Tuscany, Italy, and enjoys taking trips round the Tuscan countryside in his chauffeur-driven convertible BMW, despite being fined when police caught him sitting on the front seat while the car was moving during the filming of a documentary for the German television channel ZDF. His hobbies include swimming in Livorno's Bastia pool, of which he is honorary chairman. He also became the chairman of a football club after receiving begging letters from cash-strapped clubs.

## Cats

### Fattest cat
The heaviest reliably recorded cat was called 'Himmy' and owned by Thomas Vyse of Cairns, Queensland, Australia. It weighed 21.3 kg (46 lb 15¼ oz) when it died on 12 March 1986 aged 10 years 4 months.

### Smallest cat
'Tinker Toy', a male blue point Himalayan-Persian cat owned by Katrina and Scott Forbes of Taylorville, Illinois, USA, is just 7 cm (2¾ in) tall and 19 cm (7½ in) long.

### Oldest cat
The oldest reliably recorded cat was the female tabby 'Ma', who was put down on 5 Nov 1957 aged 34. Her owner was Alice St George Moore of Drewsteignton, Devon, UK.

### Most prolific cat
A tabby named 'Dusty' from Bonham, Texas, USA, produced 420 kittens. She gave birth to her last litter on 12 June 1952.

### Oldest feline mother
In May 1987, a 30-year-old cat named 'Kitty', owned by George Johnstone of Croxton, Staffs, UK, had two kittens.

### Best climber
A four-month-old kitten owned by Josephine Aufdenblatten of Geneva, Switzerland, followed climbers to the summit of the Matterhorn (4,478 m or 14,691 ft) on 6 Sept 1950.

### Mousing champion
A female tortoiseshell cat named 'Towser', that was owned by Glenturret Distillery Ltd near Crieff, Perth and Kinross, UK, killed 28,899 mice in her lifetime. She died on 20 March 1987.

### Earliest cat to have a name
The first cat which is recorded as having a name was 'Nedjem' (meaning 'sweet' or 'pleasant'). The cat lived during the reign of the Egyptian pharaoh Thutmose III (1479 BC to 1425 BC).

### Most travelled cats
'Hamlet', escaped from his cage on a flight from Toronto, Canada, and travelled 965,600 km (600,000 miles) in just over seven weeks until he was caught in Feb 1984.

'Tabitha' also escaped in flight and travelled 48,280 km (30,000 miles) in 12 days.

### Richest cat
'Blackie', the last in a household of 15 cats, was left £15 million in the will of his millionaire owner Ben Rea.

### Most expensive cat
A Californian Spangled Cat was bought for the record sum of $24,000 (£15,925) in January 1987 and was the display cat for the *Neiman Marcus Christmas Book* of 1986.

### Most famous feline fall
'Patricia', a pregnant cat, was hurled from the top of a bridge in Portland, Oregon, USA, by a vicious motorist in 1981. Two fishermen hauled 'Patricia' out of the freezing waters of the Williamett River. The unfortunate cat lost her kittens, but made a full recovery. She went on to make guest appearances at cat shows all over the USA.

### Most influential cat
'Socks', a stray that was rescued by a neighbour of Bill and Hilary Clinton when they lived at the governor's house in Little Rock, Arkansas, was adopted by the future First Family of the USA in 1991. He is now said to receive 75,000 letters and parcels a week.

TORTOISE WHO ESCAPED

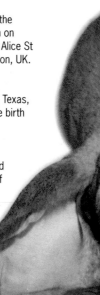

## Rabbits

### Largest rabbit
In April 1980 a five-month-old French lop doe weighing 12 kg (26 lb 7 oz) was exhibited at the Reus Fair in north-east Spain.

### Smallest rabbit
Both the Netherland dwarf and the Polish dwarf rabbit have a weight range of 0.9–1.13 kg (2–2½ lb). However, in 1975 Jacques Bouloc of Coulommière, France, announced the creation of a new hybrid of these two breeds which weighed only 396 g (14 oz).

# BUDGERIGAR VOCABULARY 1,728 WORDS

ANADA, IN 1994, ACCIDENTALLY TRAVELLED 965,600 KM IN OVER SEVEN WEEKS

### Longest ears
'Toby II', a sooty-fawn English lop owned and bred by Phil Wheeler of Barnsley, S Yorkshire, UK, has ears measuring 74.3 cm (2 ft 5¼ in) long and 18.7 cm (7⁷⁄₁₀ in) wide.

## Birds
### Best 'talking' birds
A female African grey parrot (*Psittacus erythacus*) 'Prudle', originally owned by Lyn Logue and then in the care of Iris Frost of Seaford, E Sussex, UK, won the 'Best talking parrot-like bird' title in London, UK, for 12 consecutive years (1965–76).

'Puck', a budgerigar owned by Camille Jordan of Petaluma, California, USA, had an estimated vocabulary of 1,728 words at its death in 1994.

'Alex', an African Grey, has learned labels for over 35 objects and seven colours, a functional use of phrases, and a distinction between three-, four-, five- and six-sided shapes. His accuracy averages 80%.

### Most expensive parrots
The Leah's Macaw are virtually priceless on the black market, as is the Spix Macaw. The Hiyacinth's Macaw can be reliably valued at around £35,000 for a breeding pair.

### World's richest budgie
'Sparkie' became the world's richest budgerigar after mastering 531 words, 383 sentences and eight nursery rhymes and winning a BBC talking budgie contest in 1958. 'Sparkie' died at the age of eight

**Left**
'Wil Cwac Cwac' with his owner, Gryfudd Hughes of Pwllheli, Gwynedd, Wales, and a huge cake complete with candles, on the duck's 25th birthday.

IN 1960 WAS FOUND 35 YEARS LATER, AFTER TRAVELLING ONLY 686 M

and was then stuffed and displayed in a museum in Newcastle-upon-Tyne, UK.

### Most expensive pigeon
On 23 July 1992, Louella Pigeon World of Markfield, Leics, UK, paid £110,800 for a four-year-old cock bird called *Invincible Spirit*. The bird was the winner of the 1992 Barcelona International race.

### Oldest duck
'Wil Cwac Cwac', who belongs to Gryfudd Hughes of Pwllheli, Gwynedd, Wales, UK, celebrated its 25th birthday in 1991.

## Other animals
### Slowest travelled pet
'Chester' the tortoise, painted with a white streak for identification, escaped in 1960,

and was found in 1995 by a neighbour after travelling only 686 m (750 yards).

### First chimp to use a computer language
'Lana' the chimpanzee was trained at the Yerkes Primate Research Centre in Atlanta, USA, in 1972, to write and read Yerkish, a language of words represented by abstract symbols on a PC keyboard. After three years she had a vocabulary of 120 words and could ask for a cup of coffee 23 ways.

### First chimp to communicate in words
'Washoe' the chimpanzee was taught Ameslan (American Sign Language for the Deaf) in an experiment at the University of Nevada at Reno, USA, in 1966. After three years of training, she could make 132 signs and 245 combinations of three or more words.

### Most famous TV animal
In 1953, J. Fred Muggs, a 10-month-old chimpanzee in a nappy became TV's first famous animal when he joined NBC's *Today Show*, causing ratings to soar and saving the ailing show.

### First pig to win a bravery award
The first pig to win the William O. Stillman Award for bravery was 'Snort', who alerted her owners, Deborah and Collin Stolpe, to a gas leak in 1995 by oinking and running around frantically.

### Most courageous cow
Bruno Cipriano's pet cow 'Carletta' saved him from being gored by a boar at his farm in Tuscany, Italy, in 1986 when she rushed at the boar and butted it with her horns.

# Birds

## Largest and smallest

### Tallest flightless bird
Male North African ostriches (*Struthio c. camelus*) have been recorded at heights of up to 2.74 m (9 ft) tall.

### Tallest flying bird
The tallest of the flying birds are cranes, tall waders of the family *Gruidae*—some stand almost 2 m (6 ft 6 in) high.

### Smallest birds
Males of the bee hummingbirds (*Mellisuga helenae*) of Cuba and the Isle of Pines are 5.7 cm (2¼ in) long and weigh 1.6 g (¹⁄₁₈ oz). Half of this length is the bill and tail. Females are slightly larger.

The smallest birds of prey are the black-legged falconet (*Microhierax fringillarius*) of South-east Asia and the white-fronted or Bornean falconet (*M. latifrons*) of north-western Borneo. Both species are on average 14–15 cm (5½–6 in) long, including a 5-cm (2-in) tail, and weigh about 35 g (1¼ oz).

### Largest prehistoric birds
Fossil leg bones found near Alice Springs in 1974 indicate that the flightless *Dromornis stirtoni*, a huge emu-like creature which lived in central Australia between 15 million and 25,000 years ago, must have been 3 m (10 ft) tall and weighed about 500 kg (1,100 lb).

The giant moa (*Dinornis maximus*) of New Zealand may have been even taller, possibly attaining a height of 3.7 m (12 ft). It weighed about 230 kg (500 lb).

The largest known flying bird was the giant teratorn, *Argentavis magnificens,* which lived in Argentina c. 6–8 million years ago. Fossil remains discovered in 1979 indicate that this gigantic vulture-like bird had a wing span of over 6 m (19 ft 8 in), possibly even up to 7.6 m (25 ft). It weighed about 80 kg (176 lb).

### Longest feathers
A tail covert measuring 10.6 m (34 ft 9½ in) was reported for a rooster Phoenix fowl or Yokohama chicken. This strain of red junglefowl (*Gallus gallus*) has been bred in Japan since the mid-17th century for ornamental purposes. The rooster was owned by Masasha Kubota of Kochi, Shikoku, Japan.

## Motion

### Most airborne bird
The common swift (*Apus apus*) remains airborne for 2–4 years, during which time it sleeps, drinks, eats and even mates on the wing. A young swift probably completes a non-stop 500,000 km (310,000 miles) flight between fledging and its first landing two years later.

### Longest bird flight
A common tern (*Sterna hirundo*), ringed on 30 June 1996 in central Finland, was recaptured in Jan 1997 at Rotamah Island, Victoria, Australia, having covered 26,000 km (16,250 miles).

### Slowest flying bird
The American woodcock (*Scolopax minor*) and the Eurasian woodcock (*S. rusticola*) have been timed during their courtship displays at 8 km/h (5 mph) without stalling.

### Heaviest flying bird
Weights of 19 kg (42 lb) have been reported for the Kori bustard or paauw (*Ardeotis kori*) of north-east and southern Africa. The heaviest reliably recorded great bustard (*Otis tarda*) of Europe and Asia weighed 18 kg (39 lb 11 oz), although there is an unconfirmed record of 21 kg (46 lb 4 oz) for a male great bustard that was shot in Manchuria and was too heavy to fly.

The heaviest bird of prey is the Andean condor (*Vultur gryphus*). Males average 9–12 kg (20–27 lb) and have a wingspan of 3 m (10 ft) or more. A male California condor (*Gymnogyps californianus*) now preserved in the California Academy of Sciences at Los Angeles, USA, was claimed to weigh 14.1 kg (31 lb).

### Largest wingspan
The wandering albatross (*Diomedea exulans*) has the largest wingspan. A very old male with a wingspan of 3.63 m (11 ft 11 in) was caught by members of the Antarctic research ship USNS *Eltanin* in the Tasman Sea on 18 Sept 1965.

00:00:00

### Highest flying birds
A Ruppell's vulture (*Gyps rueppellii*) collided with a commercial aircraft at 11,277 m (37,000 ft) over Abidjan, Ivory Coast, on 29 Nov 1973. Enough of the bird's feathers were recovered to allow the US Museum of Natural History to make a positive identification.

On 9 Dec 1967 about 30 whooper swans (*Cygnus cygnus*) were recorded at an altitude of just over 8,230 m (27,000 ft), as they flew in from Iceland to winter at Loch Foyle on the Northern Ireland–Republic of Ireland border. They were spotted by an airline pilot over the Outer Hebrides, and the height was also confirmed by radar.

### Fastest bird
The fastest bird on land is the ostrich which, despite its bulk, can run at up to 72 km/h (45 mph) when necessary.

# LONGEST FEATHER 10.6 M

### Fastest flying bird
Experiments indicate that the peregrine falcon (*Falco peregrinus*) is able to reach a maximum speed of at least 200 km/h (124 mph) when swooping from great heights during territorial displays or when catching prey birds in mid-air.

### Fastest wing-beat
The wing-beat of the horned sungem (*Heliactin cornuta*), a hummingbird living in tropical South America, is 90 beats/sec.

### Fastest swimmer
The gentoo penguin (*Pygoscelis papua*) has a top speed of about 27 km/h (17 mph).

International Crane Foundation, Baraboo, Wisconsin, USA, was reported to have lived to the age of 82. The bird died in late 1988, after breaking its bill while repelling a visitor.

The greatest irrefutable age for any bird is over 80 years for a male sulphur-crested cockatoo (*Cacatua galerita*) named 'Cocky', who died at London Zoo, UK, in 1982.

Excluding the ostrich, which has been known to live for up to 68 years, the longest-lived domesticated bird is the goose (*Anser a. domesticus*), which has a normal life-span of about 25 years. In 1976 a gander named 'George' died aged 49 years 8 months.

The deeper but narrower bee hummingbird (*M. helenae*) nest is thimble-sized.

### Smallest egg
The smallest egg laid by any bird is that of the vervain hummingbird (*Mellisuga minima*) which inhabits Jamaica and two nearby islets. The tiniest specimens are less than 10 mm (²⁄₅ in) long and can weigh as little as 0.365 g (¹⁶⁄₁₂₅ oz).

The smallest egg laid by a bird in the United Kingdom is that of the goldcrest (*Regulus regulus*), 12.2–14.5 mm (¹²⁄₂₅–¹⁹⁄₃₃ in) in length and 9.4–9.9 mm (³⁄₈–¹³⁄₃₃ in) in diameter, weighing 0.6 g (¹⁄₅₀ oz).

00:46:30    00:46:32

## A BIRD IS 483 M, BY AN EMPEROR PENGUIN IN ROSS SEA, ANTARTICA

**Left**
When in the water the gentoo penguin (*Pygoscelis papua*) has a maximum burst speed of about 27 km/h (17 mph).

### Deepest dive
The deepest dive measured for any bird is 483 m (1,584 ft) by an emperor penguin (*Aptenodytes forsteri*) in the Ross Sea, Antarctica, in 1990.

### Most birds ringed
Óskar Sigurósson, a lighthouse keeper on Heimay, Westmann Islands, Iceland, has ringed 65,243 birds from 1953 to 1997.

## Birth and life
### Oldest wild bird
The oldest confirmed age for a bird in the wild is 45 years. A fulmar was ringed on the Eynhallow Island in the Orkneys, UK, in 1951 and has been sighted every year since.

### Oldest bird
A Siberian white crane (*Crus leucogeranus*) named 'Wolf', which was kept at the

### Largest bird's nest
The incubation mounds built by the mallee fowl (*Leipoa ocellata*) of Australia measure up to 4.57 m (15 ft) in height and 10.6 m (35 ft) across. It has been calculated that a nest may involve the mounding of 249 m³ (8,800 ft³) of material weighing 300 tonnes.

A nest measuring 2.9 m (9 ft 6 in) wide and 6 m (20 ft) deep was built by a pair of bald eagles (*Haliaeetus leucocephalus*), and possibly their successors, near St Petersburg, Florida, USA. It was examined in 1963 and was estimated to weigh more than 2 tonnes. The golden eagle (*Aquila chrysaetos*) also constructs huge nests, and one 4.57 m (15 ft) deep was reported in Scotland, UK, in 1954.

### Smallest bird's nest
The vervain hummingbird (*Mellisuga minima*) nest is about half the size of a walnut shell.

### Largest bird's egg
The egg of an ostrich (*Struthio camelus*) normally measures 150–200 mm (6–8 in) long, 100–150 mm (4–6 in) in diameter and weighs 1.0–1.78 kg (2 lb 3 oz–3 lb 14 oz), about two dozen hens' eggs in volume. The shell, although only 1.5 mm (³⁄₅₀ in) thick, can support the weight of a person.

The largest egg on record weighed 2.3 kg (5 lb 2 oz) and was laid on 28 June 1988 by a two-year-old northern/southern ostrich hybrid (*Struthio c. camelus* x *S. c. australis*) at the Kibbutz Ha'on collective farm, Israel.

The extinct elephant bird (*Aepyornis maximus*) laid eggs which measured 330 mm (1 ft) in length and had a liquid capacity of 8.5 litres (2¼ gallons). This capacity is equivalent to seven ostrich eggs, 183 chicken eggs, or more that 12,000 hummingbird eggs.

# Marine life

**Right**
The largest single
concentration of
crustaceans, a swarm
of krill (*Euphausia
superba*) estimated to
weigh 10 million
tonnes. Krill, a rich
source of vitamin A,
forms the staple diet of
whales, and has been
suggested as
a possible food
source for humans.

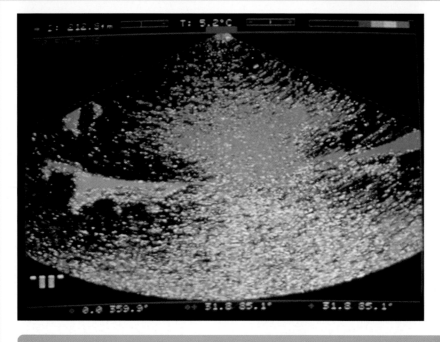

## Starfish
### Largest starfish
The largest of the 1,600 known species of starfish is the fragile brisingid (*Midgardia xandaros*). A specimen collected by the Texas A&M University research vessel *Alaminos* in the Gulf of Mexico in 1968 was 1.38 m (4 ft 6 in) from tip to tip, but its disc was only 26 mm (1 1/50 in) in diameter.

### Smallest starfish
The smallest known starfish is the asterinid sea star *Patiriella parvivipara*, discovered on the west coast of the Eyre peninsula, South Australia, by Wolfgang Zeidler in 1975. It has a maximum radius of only 4.7 mm (9/50 in) and a diameter of less than 9 mm (7/20 in).

## Jellyfish
### Largest jellyfish
An Arctic giant (*Cyanea capillata arctica*) of the north-eastern Atlantic that washed up in

**Far right**
The heaviest marine
crustacean is the
American, or North
Atlantic, lobster
(*Homarus americanus*).
The species is found in
deep waters from
Labrador (Canada) to
the Carolinas (USA).

## Fish
### Largest prehistoric fish
No prehistoric fish larger than any living species has yet been discovered. Modern estimates suggest that the largest in prehistoric times was the *Carcharodon megalodon* shark, which abounded in middle and late Tertiary seas 50–4.5 million years ago. Recent studies suggest that it had a maximum length of 13.7 m (45 ft).

### Largest fish
The world's largest fish is the rare plankton-feeding whale shark (*Rhincodon typus*), which is found in the warmer areas of the Atlantic, Pacific and Indian oceans. The largest scientifically recorded example was 12.65 m (41 ft 6 in) long, measured 7 m (23 ft) round the thickest part of the body and weighed an estimated 15–21 tonnes. It was captured off Baba Island, near Karachi, Pakistan, on 11 Nov 1949.

The largest fish recorded in British waters was a basking shark (*Cetorhinus maximus*) measuring 11.12 m (36 ft 6 in) and weighing an estimated 8 tonnes, washed ashore at Brighton, E Sussex, in 1806.

The largest predatory fish is the great white shark (*Carcharodon carcharias*). Adult specimens average 4.3–4.6 m (14–15 ft) in length, and generally weigh 520–770 kg (1,150–1,700 lb). There are claims of 10-m (33-ft) long specimens and, although few have been authenticated, there is plenty of

circumstantial evidence to suggest that they can grow to more than 6 m (20 ft) in length.

### Smallest fish
The dwarf goby of the Indo-Pacific (*Trimmatom nanus*) is the shortest marine fish. Average lengths recorded in 1978–79 for a series of specimens were 8.9 mm (17/50 in) for males and 9 mm (7/20 in) for females.

### Lightest fish
The lightest of all vertebrates and the smallest catch possible is the dwarf goby of Samoa (*Schindleria praematurus*), which weighs only 2 mg (just under 1/14,000 oz) and is 12–19 mm (1/2–3/4 in) long.

### Fastest fish
In speed trials carried out at the Long Key Fishing Camp, Florida, USA, a cosmopolitan sailfish (*Istiophorus platypterus*) took out 91 m (300 ft) of line in 3 seconds, equivalent to a velocity of 109 km/h (68 mph).

### Deepest-living fish
Brotulids of the genus *Bassogigas* are often regarded as the deepest-living vertebrates. The greatest depth from which a specimen has been taken is 8,300 m (27,230 ft) in the Puerto Rico Trench in the Atlantic Ocean by the US research vessel *John Elliott*.

### Most fish eggs
The ocean sunfish (*Mola mola*) produces up to 30 million eggs, each about 1.3 mm (1/20 in) in diameter at a single spawning.

Massachusetts Bay, USA, in 1870, had a bell diameter of 2.28 m (7 ft 6 in) and tentacles measuring 36.5 m (120 ft).

The largest ever cnidarian found in British waters is the rare lion's mane jellyfish (*Cyanea capillata*). A specimen which was measured at St Andrew's Marine Laboratory, Fife, Scotland, had a bell diameter of 91 cm (3 ft) and tentacles over 13.7 m (45 ft).

## Molluscs
### Oldest mollusc
The mollusc which lives the longest is the ocean quahog (*Arctica islandica*), a thick-shelled clam found on both sides of the Atlantic and in the North Sea. A specimen with 220 annual growth rings was collected in 1982, but not all biologists accept these growth rings as an accurate measure of age.

### Slowest growth
The North Atlantic deep-sea clam *Tindaria callistiformis* has the slowest growth rate in the animal kingdom. It takes c. 100 years to grow 8 mm (1/3 in).

### Largest clam
The largest bivalve shell is from the marine giant clam (*Tridacna gigas*). A specimen 115 cm (3 ft 9 1/4 in) long, weighing 333 kg (734 lb) was found off Ishigaki Island, Okinawa, Japan, in 1956, but was not scientifically examined until Aug 1984. It probably weighed just over 340 kg (750 lb) alive.

# FASTEST FISH 109 KM/H

## TAKING 100 YEARS TO REACH A LENGTH OF 8 MM

### Largest gastropod
A trumpet or baler conch (*Syrinx aruanus*) found off the coast of Western Australia in 1979 had a shell 77.2 cm (30⅖ in) long, with a maximum girth of 101 cm (39¾ in). It weighed nearly 18 kg (40 lb) when alive.

## Sponges
### Largest sponge
The largest sponge is the barrel shaped loggerhead sponge (Spheciospongia vesparium), measuring up to 105 cm (3 ft 6 in) in height and with

a diameter of up to 91 cm (3 ft). It is found in the Caribbean and off the coast of Florida, USA.

6 oz) and measuring 1.06 m (3 ft 6 in) from the end of the tail-fan to the tip of the largest claw was caught off Nova Scotia, Canada, and sold to a New York restaurant.

### Largest concentration
A swarm of krill (*Euphausia superba*) with an estimated weight of 10 million tonnes was tracked by US scientists off Antarctica in March 1981.

## LONG, WITH ONE TENTACLE THAT MEASURED 10.7 M

### Smallest sponge
The world's most widely distributed sponge is *Leucosolenia blanca*. It is just 3 mm (1¹⁄₁₀₀ in) in height when it reaches full maturity.

## Cephalopods
### Largest invertebrate
On 2 Nov 1878, an Atlantic giant squid (*Architeuthis dux*) ran aground in Newfoundland, Canada. Its body was 6.1 m (20 ft) long and one of its tentacles measured 10.7 m (35 ft).

## Marine crustaceans
### Largest marine crustacean
The largest of all crustaceans is the taka-ashi-gani or giant spider crab (*Macrocheira kaempferi*). A specimen with a claw-span of 3.7 m (12 ft 1½ in) weighed 18.6 kg (41 lb).

The heaviest is the American, or North Atlantic, lobster (*Homarus americanus*). In 1977 a specimen weighing 20.14 kg (44 lb

# Freshwater life

**THE ANABAS OF SOUTHERN ASIA IS THE ONLY FISH THAT CAN WALK ON LAND**

**Below and right**
On 21 May 1977, a South African sharp-nosed frog (*Ptychadena oxyrhynchus*) named 'Santjie' achieved 10.3 m (33 ft 5½ in) in a triple jump at a frog Derby at Lurula Natal Spa, Pietersburg, KwaZulu-Natal, South Africa.

## Fish and crustaceans

### Largest freshwater fish
In the 19th century a Russian specimen of the European catfish or wels (*Silurus glanis*) was reported as being 4.6 m (15 ft) long and weighing 336 kg (720 lb). Today any freshwater fish that is over 1.83 m (6 ft) and weighs more than 90 kg (200 lb) is considered to be large.

*Pangasius gigas*, which lives principally in the Mekong river basin of southern Asia, and *Pangasius sanitwongse*, found mostly in the Chas Phraya River basin of Thailand, are both reputed to attain 3 m (9 ft 10 in) in length and 300 kg (661⅓ lb) in weight.

The *Arapaima gigas* of South America is reported to grow to 4.5 m (14 ft 9 in) in length but weighs only about 200 kg (440 lb).

### Largest British freshwater fish
The largest fish that was ever caught in a British river was a common sturgeon (*Acipenser sturio*) weighing 230 kg (507½ lb) and measuring 2.7 m (9 ft). It was netted accidentally in the River Severn at Lydney, Glos, UK, on 1 June 1937.

### Smallest freshwater fish
The shortest and lightest freshwater fish is the dwarf pygmy goby (*Pandaka pygmaea*). This colourless and almost transparent species is found in the streams and lakes of Luzon in the Philippines. Male specimens are only 7.5–9.9 mm (¹⁴⁄₅₀–¹⁹⁄₅₀ in) in length and weigh just 4–5 mg (⁷⁄₅₀,₀₀₀–⁹⁄₅₀,₀₀₀ oz).

The world's smallest commercially exploited fish is the now endangered sinarapan (*Mistichthys luzonensis*), a goby found only in Lake Buhi on Luzon island, Philippines. Males are only 10–13 mm (⅖–½ in) long, and a dried 454-g (1-lb) fish cake would need to contain approximately 70,000 of them.

### Oldest fish
In 1948, the death of an 88-year-old female European eel (*Anguilla anguilla*) called 'Putte' was reported at the aquarium in Hälsingborg Museum, Sweden. The eel was allegedly born in 1860 in the Sargasso Sea, North Atlantic, and was caught in a river as a three-year-old elver.

### Oldest goldfish
In China, goldfish (*Carassius auratus*) have been reported to live for over 50 years, although there are few records which have been authenticated.

A goldfish named 'Fred', owned by A. R. Wilson of Worthing, W Sussex, UK, died on 1 Aug 1980, at the age of 41 years.

### Most electric fish
The world's most powerful electric fish is the electric eel (*Electrophorus electricus*) which is found in the rivers of Brazil, Colombia, Venezuela and Peru. An average-sized specimen can discharge 1 amp at 400 volts, but measurements up to 650 volts have been recorded.

### Fewest fish eggs
The mouth-brooding cichlid (*Tropheus moorii*) of Lake Tanganyika, east Africa, produces the fewest fish eggs—seven eggs or fewer during normal reproduction.

### Most valuable fish
The world's most valuable fish is the Russian sturgeon (*Huso huso*). A 1,227-kg (2,706-lb) female caught in the Tikhaya Sosna River in 1924 yielded 245 kg (540 lb) of best-quality caviar, which would be worth almost £200,000 in today's market.

The 76-cm (2-ft 6-in) long ginrin showa koi, which won the supreme championship in nationwide Japanese koi shows in 1976, 1977, 1979 and 1980, was sold two years later for 17 million yen (about £50,000). In March 1986 this ornamental carp (*Cyprinus carpio*) was acquired by Derry Evans, owner of the Kent Koi Centre near Sevenoaks, Kent, UK, for an undisclosed sum, but the 15-year-old fish died five months later. It has since been stuffed and mounted.

### Longest journey made by a fish
The European eel (*Anguilla anguilla*) spends between seven and 15 years in freshwater. It then changes colour to become silver and grows a longer snout and larger eyes. Once it has changed, it begins a marathon journey to the Atlantic Ocean. The entire journey is between 4,800 and 6,400 km (3,000 and 4,000 miles) and takes about six months.

**RECORD-BREAKING GIANT SALAMANDER SPECIMEN**

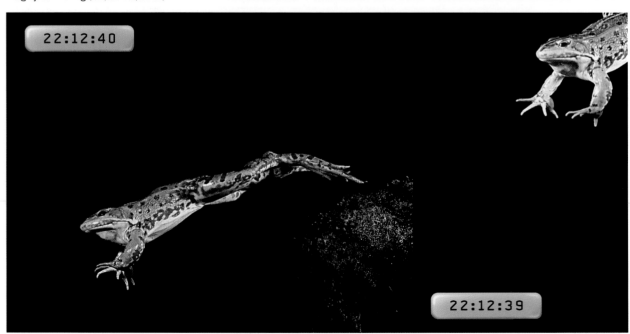

22:12:40

22:12:39

# LONGEST FROG JUMP 10.3 M

**Only shooting fish**
The archer fish (*Toxotes*), a yellow and black banded fish from Thailand, is the only animal that hunts its prey by shooting pellets of water. The fish lurks near river banks and waits for a suitable insect to come within range. The archer's pellets are accurate—direct hits on cockroaches at a distance of 1.5 m (5 ft) have been recorded in controlled aquarium conditions.

**Smallest frog**
The smallest frog, and the smallest known amphibian, is *Eleutherodactylus limbatus* of Cuba, which is 0.85–1.2 cm (¹⁷⁄₅₀–½ in) long from snout to vent when fully grown.

**Largest toad**
The largest known toad is the cane or marine toad (*Bufo marinus*) of tropical South America and Queensland, Australia.

South African sharp-nosed frog (*Ptychadena oxyrhynchus*) named 'Santjie' at a frog Derby held at Lurula Natal Spa, Pietersburg, KwaZulu-Natal, South Africa, on 21 May 1977.

**Most paternal amphibian**
The midwife toad (*Alytes obstetricans*), found in western Europe, has a unique method of looking after its eggs. After the female has laid her eggs, the male fertilizes them and

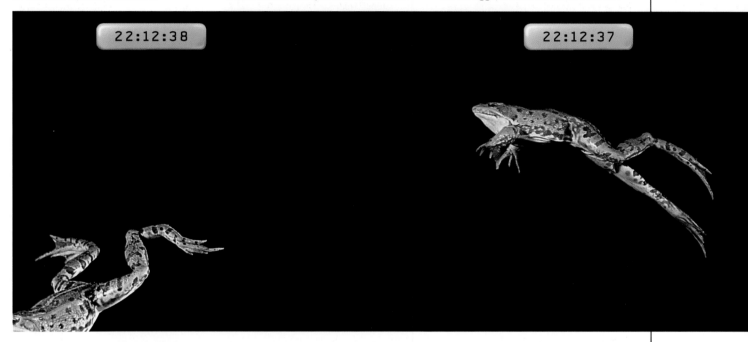

22:12:38

22:12:37

**COLLECTED IN CHINA MEASURED 1.8 M IN LENGTH**

**Only tree climbing fish**
The anabas, or climbing perch, found in southern Asia is the only fish that comes out on to the land and even climbs trees. It will 'walk' across country to find better habitats. The species' gills are specially adapted to allow the absorption of oxygen.

**Largest freshwater crustacean**
The crayfish or crawfish (*Astacopsis gouldi*), found in the streams of Tasmania, Australia, has been measured at up to 61 cm (2 ft) in length and may weigh as much as 4.1 kg (9 lb). In 1934 an unconfirmed weight of 6.35 kg (14 lb) and total length of 73.6 cm (2 ft 5 in) were reported for one caught at Bridport, Dorset, UK.

## Frogs and toads
**Smallest toad**
The smallest toad is the sub-species *Bufo taitanus beiranus* of Africa, the largest specimen of which was 24 mm (1 in).

An average specimen weighs 450 g (1 lb). In 1991, a male named 'Prinsen' ('The Prince'), owned by Håkan Forsberg of Åkers Styckebruk, Sweden, was found to weigh 2.65 kg (5 lb 13½ oz) and measured 38 cm (15 in) from snout to vent, or 53.9 cm (1 ft 9¼ in) when fully extended.

**Largest British toad**
The United Kingdom's largest toad and heaviest amphibian is the common toad.

**Largest frog**
A goliath frog (*Conraua goliath*) found in April 1989 on the Sanaga River, Cameroon, by Andy Koffman of Seattle, Washington State, USA, had a snout-to-vent length of 36.83 cm (14½ in), and an overall length of 87.63 cm (34½ in) with legs extended. It weighed 3.66 kg (8 lb 1 oz) on 30 Oct 1989.

**Longest jump by a frog**
The greatest distance covered by a frog in a triple jump is 10.3 m (33 ft 5½ in) by a

wraps the strings of spawn around its legs. The eggs are carried around in this manner for four weeks. When the spawn is ready to hatch, the toad swims to suitable water for the release of the tadpoles.

## Newts and salamanders
**Largest amphibians**
Giant salamanders (family Cryptobranchidae), are the world's largest amphibians. There are three species of giant salamander, and the record-holder for greatest size is the Chinese giant salamander (*Andrias davidianus*), which lives in mountain streams in north-eastern, central and southern China. One record-breaking specimen which was found in Hunan Province was 1.8 m (5 ft 11 in) long and weighed 65 kg (143 lb).

**Smallest newt**
The world's smallest newt or salamander is the lungless salamander (*Bolitoglossa mexicana*) which is found in Mexico. When fully grown, specimens can reach a maximum length of approximately 2.54 cm (1 in) including the tail.

# Dinosaurs

**Right**
Although the *Stegosaurus* ('plated lizard') was as long as 9 m (30 ft), it had a brain the size of a walnut weighing only 70 g (2½ oz). This represented 0.002 of 1% of its computed bodyweight of 3.3 tonnes (compared with 0.06 of 1% for an elephant and 1.88% for a human).

New Mexico, USA, *Seismosaurus halli*, was estimated to be 39–52 m (128–170 ft) long, based on comparisons of bones.

The longest dinosaur from a complete skeleton is the diplodocid *Diplodocus carnegii* ('double beam'), assembled from remains found in Wyoming, USA, in 1899. It was 26.6 m (87 ft 6 in) long, and probably weighed 5.8–18.5 tonnes.

## Largest footprints
In 1932 the footprints of a large bipedal hadrosaurid ('duckbill') measuring 1.36 m (4 ft 5½ in) long and 81 cm (2 ft 8 in) wide were discovered in Salt Lake City, Utah, USA. Other reports from Colorado and Utah refer to footprints 95–100 cm (3 ft 1 in–3 ft 4 in) wide. Footprints attributed to the largest *brachiosaurids* may have had hind feet as much as 100 cm (3 ft 4 in) wide.

## Classification
### Earliest dinosaur
The most primitive dinosaur, *Eoraptor lunensis* ('dawn stealer'), was named from a skeleton found in the Andes in Argentina and dated as 228 million years old. It was 1 m (3 ft 3 in) long and is classified as a theropod, a group of meat-eating dinosaurs.

### Most confusing dinosaur
The Therizinosaurids (formerly called Segosaurus) had bird-like hips, a toothless beak at the front of the snout and four functional toes on their feet.

### Longest name
*Micropachycephalosaurus* ('small thick-headed lizard') has 23 letters.

## Size
### Largest herbivorous dinosaurs
The largest land animals were the Sauropod dinosaurs, long-necked, long-tailed, four-legged plant-eaters of the Jurassic and Cretaceous periods, 208–65 million years ago. The largest measured 40 m (131 ft) and weighed up to 100 tonnes.

### Largest carnivorous dinosaur
The skeleton of the largest predatory dinosaur, *Giganotosaurus*, was discovered in Neuquen, Argentina, in 1995. It was over 12 m (40 ft) long and weighed 8 tonnes.

### Heaviest dinosaurs
The heaviest dinosaurs are probably the titanosaurid *Antarctosaurus giganteus* ('Giant Antarctic lizard') from Argentina and India, at

40–80 tonnes; the brachiosaurid *Brachiosaurus* ('arm lizard', from its long front legs) *altithorax* (45–55 tonnes); and the diplodocids *Seismosaurus halli* ('earthquake lizard') and *Supersaurus vivianae* (both over 50 tonnes, and estimated by some as weighing nearer 100 tonnes). A titanosaurid from Argentina, *Argentinocaurus*, was estimated in 1994 to have weighed up to 100 tonnes, based on its vast vertebrae.

### Smallest dinosaur
*Compsognathus* ('pretty jaw') of southern Germany and south-east France, was the size of a chicken. It was 60 cm (23 in) from the snout to the tip of the tail, and weighed 3 kg (6 lb 8 oz).

### Tallest dinosaur
The tallest and largest dinosaur species known from a complete skeleton is *Brachiosaurus brancai* from the Tendaguru site in Tanzania, from the Late Jurassic period (150–144 million years ago). It measured 22.2 m (72 ft 9½ in) in length, 6 m (19 ft 8 in) high at the shoulder and with a raised head height of 14 m (46 ft). It may have been 30–40 tonnes.

### Longest dinosaur
Footprints suggest that the brachiosaurid *Breviparopus* ('long dinosaur') may have attained a length of 48 m (157 ft). In 1994 a diplodocid from

The largest and most numerous dinosaur tracks found in Britain were discovered at Keats Quarry, Worth Maltravers, Dorset, in Sept 1996. They were made by a group of around a dozen Sauropods weighing around 30 tonnes during the Lower Cretaceous period 140 million years ago.

### Dinosaur with most teeth
*Pelecanimimus* was an ornithomimid ('bird like dinosaur'). It had over 220 very sharp teeth.

# LARGEST EGG 12 M LONG

## Largest dinosaur claws

The therizinosaurids ('scythe lizards') of the Late Cretaceous period from the Nemegt Basin, Mongolia, had the largest claws of the dinosaurs. *Therizinosaurus cheloniformis* measured up to 91 cm (3 ft) along the outer curve (compared with 20.3 cm or 8 in for *Tyrannosaurus rex*). They had a feeble skull, lacked teeth and probably lived on termites.

## Widest dinosaur

Anklosaurs could be as much as 2.5 m (8 ft 2 in) wide. They were the most heavily armoured of the dinosaurs and were protected by bony plates, studs and spikes which went all the way down their backs and heads to their eyelids. These dinosaurs were distinguished by having a 'club' at the end of their tails.

## Speed and intelligence
### Fastest dinosaur

Trackways can be used to estimate dinosaur speeds, and one from the Late Jurassic period in the Morrison formation in Texas, USA, discovered in 1981, indicated that a carnivorous dinosaur had been moving at a speed of 40 km/h (25 mph). Some ornithomimids were even faster, and the large-brained 100-kg (220-lb) *Dromiceiomimus* ('emu mimic lizard') of the Late Cretaceous period from Alberta, Canada, could outsprint an ostrich, which has a top speed of 60 km/h (37 mph). Peculiar features of the group are very large eyes and a toothless, beaked mouth.

IN EXCESS OF 60 KM/H

100%

This suggests that they were one of the few groups of theropods that had abandoned a predatory lifestyle, possibly developing into herbivores, much like the modern-day ostrich.

In Jan 1983 a claw-bone measuring 30 cm (11⁸/₁₀ in) long was found by amateur fossil collector William Walker near Dorking, Surrey, UK. The claw was identified as possibly belonging to a spinosaur, which was estimated to measure more than 9 m (29 ft 6 in) in overall length. Its estimated weight was 2 tonnes. It could also be distinguished from the other theropods as it had 128 teeth instead of the usual 64. This unique specimen was later named after Walker—*Baryonyx walkeri* ('heavy claw').

## Largest dinosaur skull

The long-frilled herbivore *Torosaurus* ('piercing lizard'), a caratopsid which measured about 7.6 m (25 ft) in total length and weighed up to 8 tonnes, had a skull (including its fringe) of up to 3 m (9 ft 10 in) long, weighing up to 2 tonnes. It was found in a band stretching from Montana to Texas in the USA.

## Largest dinosaur eggs

The largest known dinosaur eggs belonged to the *Hypselosaurus priscus* ('high ridge lizard'), a 12-m (40-ft) long titanosaurid that lived around 80 million years ago. Examples of *Hypselosaurus priscus* eggs found in the Durance valley, Aix-en-Provence, France, in Oct 1961 would have been 30 cm (1 ft) long if they had been uncrushed, and would have had a diameter of 25.5 cm (10 in), and a capacity of 3.3 litres (5.8 pt).

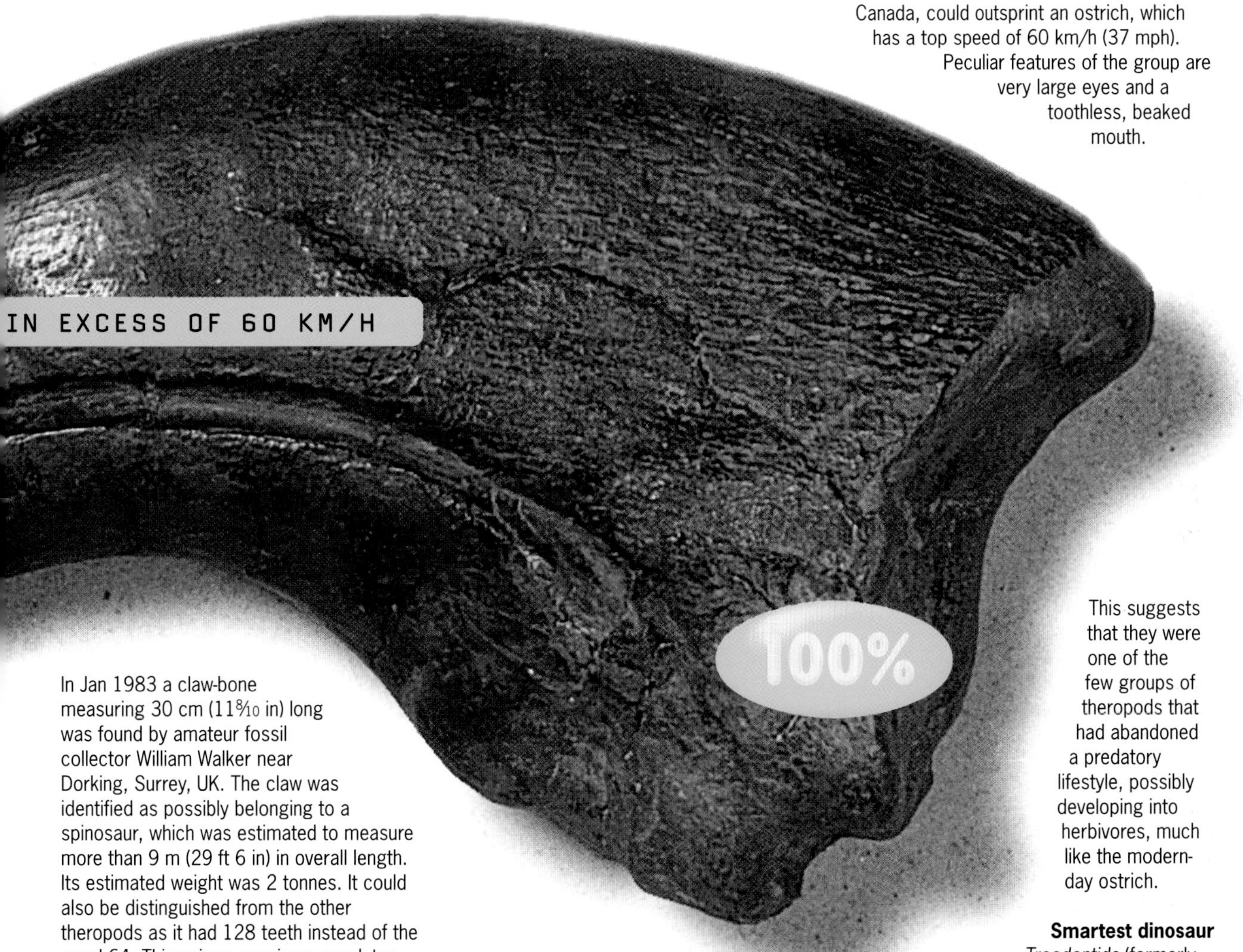

**Left**
A fossil of a claw-bone belonging to the *Baryonyx walkeri* ('heavy claw'), a spinosaur measuring more than 9 m (29 ft 6 in), weighing 2 tonnes and with a height of 3–4 m (9–13 ft). It is the most important dinosaur fossil found in Europe this century.

## Smartest dinosaur

*Troodontids* (formerly saurornithoidids) had the largest brain-to-body size ratio of all non-avian dinosaurs, making them the most intelligent dinosaurs—on a par with the cleverest birds.

## Most brainless dinosaur

*Stegosaurus* ('plated lizard'), from Colorado, Oklahoma, Utah and Wyoming, USA, lived around 150 million years ago, was up to 9 m (30 ft) long but had a walnut-sized brain of 70 g (2½ oz). This represents 0.002 of 1% of its computed bodyweight of 3.3 tonnes.

# Reptiles

## Snakes

### Longest snake
The record length is 10 m (32 ft 9½ in) for a reticulated python (*Python reticulatus*) shot in Celebes, Indonesia, in 1912.

### Shortest snake
The world's shortest snake is the thread snake (*Leptotyphlops bilineata*), found only in Martinique, Barbados and St Lucia in the Caribbean. The longest known specimen measured 108 mm (4¼ in). The Brahminy blind snake (*Ramphotyphlops braminus*) is also less than 108 mm (4¼ in) long.

The smallest native British snake is the smooth snake (*Coronella austriaca*), which averages up to 60 cm (1 ft 11 in) in length.

### Heaviest snake
The average length of the anaconda (*Eunectes murinus*) found in tropical South America and Trinidad is 5.5–6.1 m (18–20 ft). A female which was shot in Brazil *c.* 1960 was not weighed, but as it was 8.45 m (27 ft 9 in) long with a girth of 111 cm (3 ft 8 in), it is estimated that it must have been nearly 227 kg (500 lb).

### Fastest snake
The black mamba (*Dendroaspis polylepis*) of eastern Africa is capable of achieving top speeds of 16–19 km/h (10–12 mph) in short bursts over level ground.

### Oldest snake
A common boa (*Boa constrictor constrictor*) named 'Popeye' lived for 40 years 3 months and 14 days. He died at Philadelphia Zoo, Pennsylvania, USA, on 15 April 1977.

### Only parthenogenic snakes
The only snake which reproduces without needing to be fertilized is the Brahminy snake, which is found in a variety of tropical environments.

## Crocodiles

### Largest crocodilian
The estuarine or saltwater crocodile (*Crocodylus porosus*), found in Asia and the Pacific, is the largest reptile. At Bhitarkanika Wildlife Sanctuary, Orissa, India, there are four specimens more than 6 m (19 ft 8 in) long. The largest is over 7 m (23 ft) long.

### Smallest crocodilian
The maximum length of a dwarf caiman (*Paleosuchus palpebrosus*) of northern South America is 1.5 m (4ft 11 in) for male specimens and 1.2 m (4 ft) for females.

### Oldest crocodilian
The greatest authenticated age for an American alligator (*Alligator mississippiensis*) is 66 years. It arrived at Adelaide Zoo, South Australia, on 5 June 1914 as a two-year-old, and died on 26 Sept 1978.

## Lizards

### Largest lizard
Komodo dragon (*Varanus komodoensis*) males, found in Indonesia average 2.25 m (7 ft 5 in) in length and weigh about 59 kg (130 lb). The largest to be accurately measured was given to a US zoologist in 1928 by the Sultan of Bima. When it was displayed in the zoo at St Louis, Missouri, USA, in 1937 it was 3.10 m (10 ft 2 in) long and weighed 166 kg (365 lb).

### Longest lizard
The slender Salvadori or Papuan monitor (*Varanus salvadorii*) of Papua New Guinea has been reliably measured at up to 4.75 m (15 ft 7 in) in length, but nearly 70% of its total length is taken up by the tail.

### Smallest lizard
*Sphaerodactylus parthenopion*, a tiny gecko indigenous to the island of Virgin Gorda, British Virgin Islands, is known only from 15 specimens, including some pregnant females found between 10 and 16 Aug 1964. The three largest females measured 18 mm (⁷⁄₁₀ in) from snout to vent, with a tail of approximately the same length.

### Fastest lizard
The highest recorded speed by a reptile on land is 34.9 km/h (21.7 mph), by a spiny-tailed iguana (*Ctenosaura*) from Costa Rica,

in a series of experiments by Professor Raymond Huey from the University of Washington, USA, and colleagues at the University of California, Berkeley, USA.

### Oldest lizard
A male slow worm (*Anguis fragilis*) that was kept in the Zoological Museum in Copenhagen, Denmark, from 1892 until 1946 lived for more than 54 years.

## Tortoises and Turtles

### Largest turtle
The leatherback turtle (*Dermochelys coriacea*), which can weigh up to 450 kg (1,000 lb), averages between 1.8 and 2.1 m (6 and 7 ft) from the tip of the beak to the end of the tail and 2.1 m (7 ft) across the front flippers. A male found dead on the beach at Harlech, Gwynedd, UK, in 1988 was 2.91 m (9 ft 5½ in) in total length over the carapace, 2.77 m (9 ft) across the front flippers and weighed 961.1 kg (2,120 lb).

### Largest tortoise
The largest living specimen is a Galapagos tortoise (*Geochelone elephantopus elephantopus*) named 'Goliath', who has resided at the Life Fellowship Bird Sanctuary in Sessner, Florida, USA, since 1960. It is 135.5 cm (4 ft 5⅝ in) long, 102 cm (3 ft 4½ in) wide and 68.5 cm (2 ft 3 in) high, and weighs 385 kg (849 lb).

### Smallest chelonian (turtle or tortoise)
The stinkpot or common musk turtle (*Sternotherus odoratus*) has an average shell

# OLDEST ALLIGATOR 66 YEARS

length of 7.6 cm (3 in) when fully grown and weighs only 227 g (8 oz).

The smallest marine turtle is the Atlantic ridley (*Lepidochelys kempii*), with a shell length of 50–70 cm (1 ft 8 in–2 ft 4 in) and a maximum weight of 80 kg (176 lb).

### Oldest chelonian
The greatest authentic age recorded for a chelonian is over 152 years for a male Marion's tortoise (*Geochelone sumeirei*), brought from the Seychelles to Mauritius in 1766 by the Chevalier de Fresne, who presented it to the Port Louis army garrison. It was killed accidentally in 1918.

### Fastest chelonian
The highest speed claimed for any reptile in water is 35 km/h (22 mph) by a Pacific leatherback turtle (*Dermochelys coriacea*).

`08:58:12`

### Deepest dive by a chelonian
In May 1987 it was reported by Dr Scott Eckert that a leatherback turtle (*Dermochelys coriacea*) fitted with a pressure-sensitive recording device had reached a depth of 1,200 m (3,973 ft) off the Virgin Islands in the West Indies.

### Longest migration of a sea animal
'Rosita', a loggerhead turtle, turned up 10,459 km (6,500 miles) off the coast of Japan after being tagged and released from Baja California, Mexico, in 1994 following an experiment at the University of Arizona, USA.

## Prehistoric reptiles
### Earliest reptile fossil
The oldest reptile fossil, nicknamed 'Lizzie the Lizard', was found in Scotland, UK, by Stan Wood in March 1988. The 20.3-cm (8-in) long reptile is estimated to be *c.* 340 million years old, 40 million years older than previously discovered reptiles. 'Lizzie' was named *Westlothiana lizziae* in 1991.

### Largest predator
The largest ever land predator may have been an alligator found on the banks of the Amazon in rocks dated at 8 million years old. Estimates from a skull 1.5 m (5 ft) long, complete with 10-cm (4-in) long teeth, indicate a total length of 12 m (40 ft) and a weight of about 18 tonnes, making it larger than the fearsome *Tyrannosaurus rex*. It was identified as a giant example of the species *Purussaurus brasiliensis*, smaller examples of which were first found in 1892.

`08:58:13`

### Longest snake
The longest prehistoric snake was the python-like *Gigantophis garstini*, which inhabited what is now Egypt *c.* 38 million years ago. Parts of a spinal column and a small piece of jaw discovered at Fayum in the Western Desert indicate a length of about 11 m (36 ft). This is 1 m (3 ft 3 in) longer than the longest present-day snake.

### Largest flying creature
The largest ever flying creature was the pterosaur *Quetzalcoatlus northropi*. Its name comes from the Aztec and Toltec god Quetzalcoatl, whose name means 'feathered serpent'. About 70 million years ago it

soared over what is now Texas, Wyoming and New Jersey in the USA, Alberta in Canada, Senegal in Africa and Jordan. Partial remains discovered in Big Bend National Park, Texas, USA, in 1971 indicate that this reptile must have had a wing span of 11–12 m (36–39 ft) and weighed about 86–113 kg (190–250 lb).

### Largest flying creature found in the UK
The fossilized remains of *Ornithodesmus latidens* were found on the Wealden Shales of Atherfield on Isle of Wight. The reptile lived around 120 million years ago. Scientists have estimated its wing span to be approximately 5 m (16 ft 4 in).

**Left**
The black mamba (*Dendroaspis polylepis*) is a slender, agile snake with large scales and long front teeth. Highly aggressive, it can achieve speeds of 16–19 km/h (10–12 mph) in short bursts over level ground and its bite is fatal to humans without antivenin treatment.

# Arachnids

**Right**
A member of the Indian genus *Stegodyphus*, which build the largest continuous area of webs.

**Greatest size difference between sexes**
In some species of the golden orb-web spider (genus *Nephila*), females weigh almost 1,000 times more than their mates. The males are smaller than the females' normal prey so they are not eaten by them.

**Noisiest spider**
The male European buzzing spider (*Anyphaena accentuata*) vibrates his abdomen rapidly against the surface of a leaf, producing a buzzing sound, as part of courtship behaviour. This is audible to the human ear, but cannot be 'heard' by the female spider, who can only detect the sound through vibrations.

The male of the American species *Lycosa gulosa*, or the purring spider, is equally audible. He taps his palps and abdomen on dry leaves to produce a purring sound.

**Only underwater spider**
The European water spider *Argyroneta aquatica*, spends all of its life underwater in

## Spiders

### Largest spider
The world's largest known spider is the goliath bird-eating spider (*Theraphosa leblondi*) of the coastal rainforests of Surinam, Guyana and French Guiana, but isolated specimens have also been reported from Venezuela and Brazil. A male collected by members of the Pablo San Martin Expedition at Rio Cavro, Venezuela, in April 1965 had a record leg-span of 280 mm (11 in)—enough to cover a dinner plate.

The cardinal spider (*Tegenaria gigantea*) has the greatest average leg-span of a British spider. In Sept 1994 Lynda and John Culley of Wantage, Oxon, UK, found a cardinal spider with a leg span of 149 mm (5⅞ in) in their bathroom sink.

The well-known 'daddy longlegs' spider (*Pholcus phalangioides*) rarely exceeds 114 mm (4½ in) in leg-span, but one specimen collected in the United Kingdom measured 15.2 cm (6 in) across.

### Heaviest spider
In Feb 1985 Charles J. Seiderman of New York City, USA, captured a female bird-eating spider near Paramaribo, Surinam, which weighed a record peak 122.2 g (4.3 oz), had a maximum leg-span of 267 mm (10½ in), a total body length of 102 mm (4 in) and 25-mm (1-in) long fangs.

The heaviest spider found in the United Kingdom is the orb weaver (*Araneus quadratus*). On 10 Sept 1979 a female weighing 2.25 g (²⁄₂₅ oz) was collected at Lavington, W Sussex, by J. R. Parker.

### Smallest spider
The smallest known spider is *Patu marplesi* (family Symphytognathidae) of Western Samoa. A male specimen found in moss at *c.* 600 m (2,000 ft) in Madolelei, Upolu, in Jan 1965 measured 0.43 mm (¹⁷⁄₁₀₀₀ in) overall—about the same size as one of the full-stops on this page.

The smallest British spider is the extremely rare money spider (*Glyphesis cottonae*), found only in a swamp near Beaulieu Road Station, Hants, and on Thursley Common, Surrey. Both sexes have a body length of only 1 mm (¹⁄₂₅ in).

### Longest lived spiders
The female tarantula *Aphonopelma* have the longest lifespan and can live up to 30 years.

A female tropical bird-eater (from the *Theraphosidae* family) collected in Mexico in 1935 lived for an estimated 26–28 years.

The British spider which lives the longest is probably the purse web spider (*Atypus affinis*). One of these spiders was kept in a greenhouse for nine years.

ponds, where it lives in a silken 'diving-bell' which it fills with air bubbles collected from the surface.

**Strongest spider**
Californian trap-door spiders (*Bothriocyrtum californicum*), named because they weave a silken 'door' covering the entrance to their underground burrows, have been shown to be able to resist a force 38 times their own weight attempting to open the trap-door

**Most sociable spider**
Several thousand members of both sexes of the South African species *Anelosimus eximus* live together peaceably on light webs that stretch for over a metre (just over 3 ft) across bushes and small trees.

**Most maternal spider**
Females of the common European species *Theridion sisyphium* initially feed their newly-hatched young with liquid from their own mouths. When a few days old the young begin to share their mother's prey. As the young grow older they help to capture food by throwing extra silken strands over the struggling prey. The maternal relationship ends when the young devour their mother after she dies.

**Smallest number of spider eggs**
*Oonops domesticus*, a tiny European pink spider, lays only two eggs.

# OLDEST SPIDER 28 YEARS

**AND EVEN ENTANGLE MAMMALS AS LARGE AS HUMANS**

**Smallest spider's egg**
The eggs of *Oonus domesticus* are only a fraction of 1 mm across.

**Largest number of spider eggs**
Spiders of the genus *Mygalomorphus* may lay up to 3,000 eggs in a single batch.

**Largest spider's egg**
The eggs of spiders of the genus *Mygalomorphus* are the size of a small pea.

## Spiders' webs
### Strongest web
The web made by the American spider *Achaearenea tepidariorum* has been known to trap a small mouse.

The webs built by spiders of the genus *Nephila* can catch small birds and are capable of slowing the passage of large mammals. Some webs have a special 'rubbish line' where the sucked-out remains of small birds have been found.

**Simplest web**
Species of the genus *Miagrammopes*, found in Africa, Australia and North America, have reduced their web to a single strand, about 1 m (just over 3 ft) long, woven between two small branches or twigs. The American bolas spider (genus *Mastophora*) also uses a small single strand to attach itself to a branch and a second much longer strand as a 'fishing-line' to catch passing moths.

The South African bolas spider (*Cladomelea akermani*) has a similar arrangement but rotates the 'fishing' strand continuously for about 15 minutes. If unsuccessful, the spider consumes the sticky globe on the end of the line and replaces it with a new one.

## Scorpions
### Largest scorpion
Males of the species *Heterometrus swannerderdami* of southern India, often grow to more than 180 mm (7 in) from the tips of the pedipalps or 'pincers' to the end

**Smallest scorpion**
The species *Microbothus pusillus*, which is found on the Red Sea coast, measures around 13 mm (½ in) in total length.

**Deepest-living scorpion**
The scorpion species that lives deepest underground is *Alacran tartarus* which has been found in caves more than 800 m (2,625 ft) below the Earth's surface.

**Most sociable scorpion**
Offspring of the species *Pandinus imperator* may remain with the family group even when adult. Families often co-operate with each other in order to capture prey.

**Only British scorpion**
There are no indigenous species of scorpion in the British Isles. However, a colony of the harmless *Euscorpius flavicaudis* normally found in parts of southern Europe has been thriving for over a century in the walls of the old dockyard at Sheerness in Kent.

**TIMES MORE THAN HER MATE, WHO IS MUCH SMALLER THAN HER NORMAL PREY**

**Largest continuous area of webs**
Members of the Indian genus *Stegodyphus* build huge three-dimensional interwoven and overlapping webs that have been known to cover vegetation in a continuous silken mass stretching out for several kilometres.

**Largest web**
The biggest webs that are built are the yellow silk constructions of tropical orb-web spiders of the genus *Nephila*. They can be up to 3 m (nearly 10 ft) in length and have even been found crossing rivers.

of the sting. A specimen found during WWII measured 292 mm (11½ in) long overall.

The tropical emperor, or imperial, scorpion (*Pandinus imperator*) of West Africa also grows to 180 mm (7 in). A male from Sierra Leone measured 229 cm (9 in).The tropical African species *Pandinus giganticus* can be nearly 200 mm (8 in) long.

**Heaviest scorpion**
The large black West African species *Pandinus imperator* can weigh up to 60 g (just over 2 oz).

## Ticks
### Largest ticks
Ticks are small, parasitic arachnids that often live on warm-blooded animals' skin. The largest are members of the suborder *Ixodida* and grow up to 30 mm (1⅖ in) long.

**Smallest tick**
Ticks from the subclass *Acarina* are only 0.08 mm (⅓,₀₀₀ in) in length.

**Left**
The tropical emperor or imperial scorpion (*Pandinus imperator*), the world's largest and heaviest scorpion.

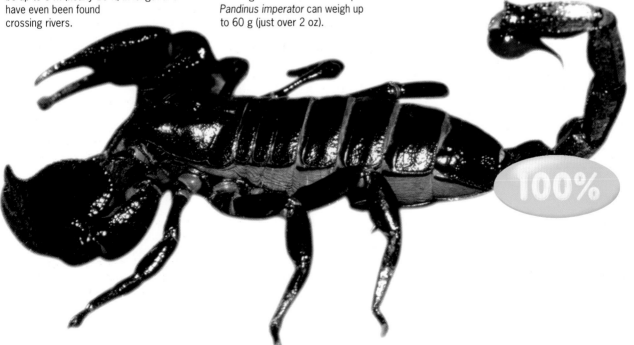

100%

# Winged insects

MALE EMPEROR MOTHS CAN DETECT THE ALCOHOL SCENT OF A VIRGIN FEMALE

**Below right**
The dragonfly, also known as devil's arrow or devil's darning needle, is an extremely agile, fast and predatory animal. It can eat its own weight in food in as little as 30 minutes.

## Largest and smallest

**Largest dragonfly**
*Megaloprepus caeruleata* of Central and South America has been measured at up to 120 mm ($4\frac{3}{4}$ in) in length with a wingspan of up to 191 mm ($7\frac{1}{2}$ in).

**Largest dragonfly in the UK**
*Anax imperator* has a wingspan of up to 106 mm ($4\frac{1}{5}$ in).

**Smallest dragonfly**
*Agriocnemis naia* of Myanmar (Burma) is the world's smallest dragonfly. A specimen in The Natural History Museum, London, UK, had a wingspan of 17.6 mm ($\frac{69}{100}$ in) and a body length of 18 mm ($\frac{71}{100}$ in).

**Smallest dragonfly in the UK**
*Lestes dryas* has a body length of 20–25 mm ($\frac{9}{10}$–1 in).

**Largest butterfly**
The largest known butterfly is the Queen Alexandra's birdwing (*Ornithoptera alexandrae*) of Papua New Guinea. Females may have a wingspan exceeding 280 mm (11 in) and weigh over 25 g ($\frac{9}{10}$ oz).

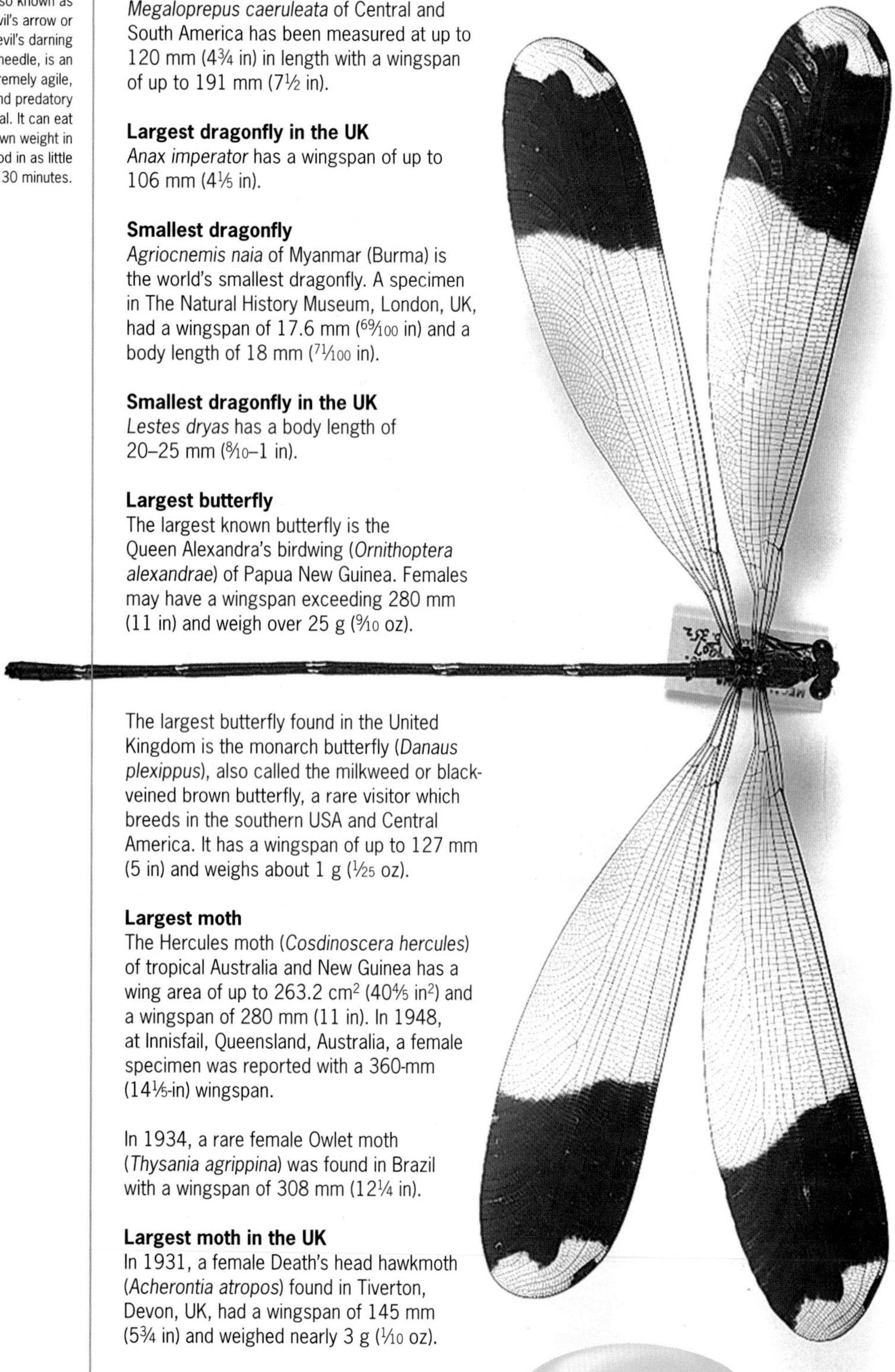

The largest butterfly found in the United Kingdom is the monarch butterfly (*Danaus plexippus*), also called the milkweed or black-veined brown butterfly, a rare visitor which breeds in the southern USA and Central America. It has a wingspan of up to 127 mm (5 in) and weighs about 1 g ($\frac{1}{25}$ oz).

**Largest moth**
The Hercules moth (*Cosdinoscera hercules*) of tropical Australia and New Guinea has a wing area of up to 263.2 $cm^2$ ($40\frac{4}{5}$ $in^2$) and a wingspan of 280 mm (11 in). In 1948, at Innisfail, Queensland, Australia, a female specimen was reported with a 360-mm ($14\frac{1}{5}$-in) wingspan.

In 1934, a rare female Owlet moth (*Thysania agrippina*) was found in Brazil with a wingspan of 308 mm ($12\frac{1}{4}$ in).

**Largest moth in the UK**
In 1931, a female Death's head hawkmoth (*Acherontia atropos*) found in Tiverton, Devon, UK, had a wingspan of 145 mm ($5\frac{3}{4}$ in) and weighed nearly 3 g ($\frac{1}{10}$ oz).

**Smallest butterfly**
The smallest butterfly, *Zizula Hylax*, is found in Africa, Madagascar, Mauritius, Arabia, tropical Asia and Australia. It measures 6 mm ($\frac{1}{4}$ in) across its forewings.

100%

**Smallest butterfly in the UK**
The small blue (*Cupido minimus*) has a wingspan of 19–25 mm ($\frac{3}{4}$–1 in).

**Smallest moth**
The smallest of the 165,000 known species of Lepidoptera is a micro-moth called *Stigmella ridiculosa* found in the Canary Islands. It has a wingspan of 2 mm ($\frac{2}{25}$ in) with a similar body length.

## Flight

**Fastest flying insects**
The North American deer bot-fly (*Cephenemyia pratti*), hawk moths (*Sphingidae*), horseflies (*Tabanus bovinus*) and some tropical butterflies (*Hesperiidae*), can fly at 39 km/h (24 mph), the highest maintainable airspeed of any insect.

The Australian dragonfly *Austrophlebia costalis* is able to fly at 58 km/h (36 mph) for short bursts.

**Fastest insect wing-beat**
A tiny midge of the genus *Forcipomyia* has the fastest wing-beat of any insect under natural conditions, at 62,760 per min. The muscular contraction–expansion cycle necessary for such rapid wing-beats is 0.00045 seconds, the fastest muscle movement ever measured.

**Slowest insect wing-beat**
The wingbeat of the swallowtail butterfly (*Papilio machaon*) is 300 per min.

**Longest migration**
A tagged female monarch or milkweed butterfly (*Danaus plexippus*) released by Donald Davis at Presqu'ile Provincial Park near Brighton, Ontario, Canada, on 6 Sept 1986 was recaptured 3,432 km (2,133 miles) away on a mountain near Angangueo, Mexico, on 15 Jan 1987.

## Lifespan and reproduction

**Shortest lives**
Mayflies of the family Ephemmeroidea may spend two to three years as nymphs at the bottom of lakes and streams and then live for as little as an hour as winged adults.

**Most fertile animal**
With unlimited food and no predators, a single cabbage aphid (*Brevicoryne brassicae*) could give rise in a year to a mass of descendants weighing 822 million

DESERT LOCUSTS ARE ONL

# FASTEST WING-BEAT 62,760 PER MIN

AT A RANGE OF 11 KM

tonnes—more than three times the total weight of the world's human population.

## Most acute sense of smell
The male emperor moth (*Eudia pavonia*) can detect the sex attractant of the virgin female at a range of 11 km (6$\frac{8}{10}$ miles). The female carries less than 0.0001 mg of this scent, which has been identified as one of the higher alcohols ($C_{16}H_{29}OH$). The chemoreceptors on the male moth's antennae are so sensitive that they can detect a single molecule of scent.

## Loudest insect
At 7,400 pulses/min, the tymbal organs of the male cicada (family *Cicadidae*) produce a noise which is detectable more than 400 m ($\frac{1}{4}$ mile) away.

The only British species is the very rare New Forest cicada (*Cicadetta montana*), found in the New Forest area of Hampshire.

## Greediest animal
The larva of the polyphemus moth (*Antheraea polyphemus*) of North America consumes an amount equal to 86,000 times its own birthweight in its first 56 days. In human terms this is equivalent to a 3.17-kg (7-lb) baby taking in 273 tonnes of nourishment.

## Most destructive insect
Desert locusts (*Schistocerca gregaria*) from the dry and semi-arid regions of Africa, the Middle East and western Asia, are the most destructive insects. They are only 4.5–6 cm (1$\frac{4}{5}$–2$\frac{2}{5}$ in) long but can eat their own weight in food every day. Under certain weather conditions vast numbers will breed and gather in swarms that devour almost all vegetation in their path. In a single day, a swarm of 50 million locusts can eat food that would sustain 500 people for a year.

## Only marine fly
Flies have colonized almost every environment on Earth, from mountain tops and sub-Arctic tundra to the Tropics. However there is only one fly which is completely marine—the midge *Pontomyia natans* which lives on and above the surface of the Pacific Ocean.

## Mantle of bees
Jed Shaner was covered by a mantle of an estimated 343,000 bees weighing 36.3 kg (80 lb) at Staunton, Virginia, USA, on 29 June 1991.

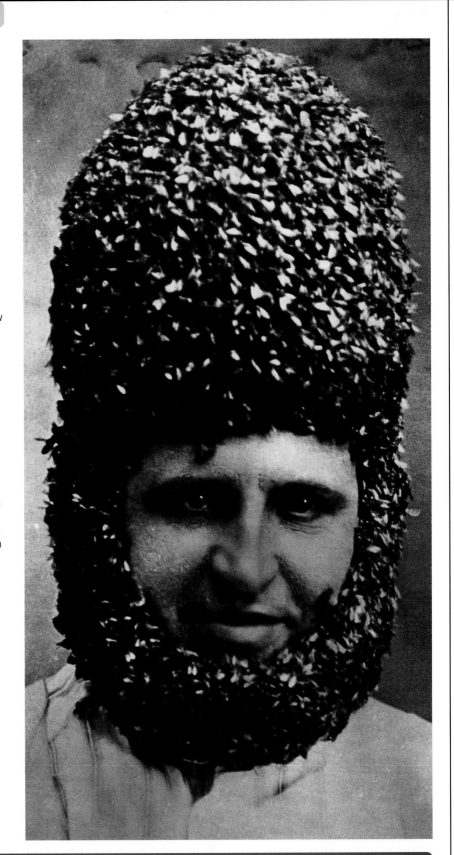

**Left**
Bees rarely sting and to prove this Frank Bornhofer had himself photographed wearing a helmet and chin-strap covered in a mantle of bees in Cincinatti, Ohio, USA, in June 1924. He did not receive a single sting.

4.5–6 CM IN LENGTH, BUT CAN EAT THEIR OWN WEIGHT IN FOOD EVERY DAY

# Creepy crawlies

## Largest and smallest

### Longest
The longest insect is *Pharnacia kirbyi*, a stick insect from Borneo, that reaches 54.6 cm (21½ in) in length including its legs.

### Smallest
The 'feather-winged' beetles of the family *Ptiliidae* (or *Trichopterygidae*) and the battledore-wing fairy flies (parasitic wasps) of the family *Mymaridae* are smaller than some species of *protozoa* (single-celled animals).

### Heaviest
Specimens of male Goliath beetles (family *Scarabaeidea*) of equatorial Africa weighed 70–100 g (2½–3½ oz). They measured 11 cm (4⅓ in) from the tips of the small frontal horns to the end of the abdomen.

A species of stag beetle (*Lucanus cervus*) is the heaviest insect in the UK. The largest recorded specimen was a male 8.74 cm (3⁷⁄₁₆ in) in length (including body and mandibles), which probably weighed over 6 g (⅕ oz) when alive.

On 2 June 1994, 10-year-old Ryan Morris and his friends James Simpson, Scott Cowan and Ross Cowan found a 8.9-cm-long (3½-in) stag beetle near their homes in Sheppey, Kent, UK.

It was later identified as *Odontolabis delessertii*, a species that does not naturally occur in the UK.

### Lightest
The male bloodsucking banded louse (*Enderleinellus zonatus*) and the parasitic wasp (*Caraphractus cinctus*) may each weigh as little as 0.005 mg (equal to 5,670,000 creatures to an oz).

### Strongest
In proportion to their size, the strongest animals in the world are the larger beetles of the family *Scarabaeidae*, which are found mainly in the tropics.

### Longest beetle
Male hercules beetles (*Dynastes hercules*), found in Central and South America and the

Caribbean islands, have been known to reach a length of 19 cm (7½ in), although more than half is taken up by long opposing horns.

### Largest cockroach
A preserved *Megaloblatta longipennis* female, found in Colombia, measured 9.7 cm (3¹³⁄₁₆ in) in length and 4.5 cm (1¾ in) in width.

### Largest earwig
The largest earwig in the world is the St Helena giant earwig (*Labidura herculeana*), which has a total body length (including pincers) of 7.8 cm (3¹⁄₁₀ in). This insect, native to the island of St Helena, is extremely rare, and may even be extinct.

### Largest flea
The world's largest flea is the female *Hystrichopsylla schefferi*, described from a single specimen taken from the nest of a mountain beaver (*Aplodontia rufa*) at Puyallup, Washington, USA, in 1913. It can reach a length of 8 mm (⅓ in).

### Largest grasshopper
An unidentified species of grasshopper from the border of Malaysia and Thailand measured 25.4 cm (10 in) in length and could leap a height of 4.6 m (15 ft).

### Most legs
The millipede *Illacme plenipes*, which is found in California, USA, has 375 pairs of legs (750 in total).

### Largest egg
The 15-cm (6-in) long Malaysian stick insect, *Heteropteryx dilitata*, lays an egg that measures 1.3 cm (½ in) in length.

### Largest termite mound
In proportion to their size, termites build the largest structures of all land-living creatures. Workers put each grain of soil into place, one piece at a time, cementing them together with their saliva. The tallest mounds are built by the African species *Macrotermes bellicosus*. A record-breaking termite mound in Congo (ex-Zaïre) was 12.8 m (42 ft) high, equivalent to 2,000 termite workers laid end to end. In comparison, the Sears building in Chicago, 443 m (1,454 ft) high, is the equivalent to the length of 250 people.

# MOST LEGS 375 PAIRS

HAT OF A SPACE ROCKET

## Speed and activity

### Fastest moving on land
The world's fastest insects on land are certain large tropical cockroaches of the family *Dictyoptera*. In 1991 a record speed of 5.4 km/h (3.4 mph), or 50 body lengths per second, was achieved by a *Periplaneta americana* specimen. This is equivalent to a human sprinter reaching speeds of up to 330 km/h (205 mph).

### Strangest defence
The bombardier beetle (genus *Brachinus*) stores two relatively benign chemicals in a special chamber in its abdomen. When it feels threatened, they are released into a second chamber and mix with an enzyme, resulting in a violent chemical reaction which causes great heat (up to 100°C or 212°F) to be released from the anus. This gas can be turned on and off 500 times a second.

### Best jumper
The cat flea (*Cteneocephalides felis*) is believed to be the best insect jumper, and is known to have reached a height of 34 cm (13⅓ in) in a single jump, which requires an acceleration over 20 times that of a space rocket. In a 1910 experiment, a common flea (*Pulex irritans*) made a long jump of 33 cm (13 in) and a high jump of 19.7 cm (7¾ in).

### Highest g force endured by an insect
The click beetle (*Athous haemorrhoidalis*) averages 400 g when 'jack-knifing' into the air to escape predators. One beetle, measuring 1.2 cm (½ in) in length and weighing 40 mg (just under ¹⁄₇,₀₀₀ oz), which jumped to a height of 30 cm (11¾ in), was calculated to have endured a peak brain deceleration of 2,300 g by the end of the movement.

### Most dangerous
The oriental rat flea (*Xenopsylla cheopsis*) is the carrier of the bubonic plague, and is believed to be responsible for the majority of the world's most catastrophic pandemics.

### Longest lives
The longest-lived insects are the splendour beetles (family *Buprestidea*). On 27 May 1983, a specimen of *Buprestis aurulenta* appeared from the staircase timber in the home of Mr W. Euston of Prittlewell, Southend-on-Sea, Essex, UK, after having been in a larval state for at least 47 years.

AFTER BEING A LARVA FOR AT LEAST 47 YEARS

**Above**
A stick insect specimen from the Natural History Museum in London, UK, has a body length of 32.8 cm (12⁹⁄₁₀ in) and a total length, including the legs, of 54.6 cm (21½ in).

**Left**
Coloured scanning electron micrograph of the male bloodsucking banded louse, the lightest insect.

# Dangerous killers

## Snakes

### Most venomous snake

The sea snake species *Hydrophis belcheri*, which is found around Ashmore Reef in the Timor Sea off north-west Australia has a myotoxic venom many times more toxic than the venom of any land snake.

The common beaked sea snake (*Enhydrina schistosa*) is probably equally as venomous as *Hydrophis belcheri* but is more dangerous as it is much more common, more widely distributed and more aggressive.

The most venomous land snake is the small-scaled or fierce snake (*Oxyuranus microlepidotus*), found mainly in the Diamantina River and Cooper's Creek drainage basins in Channel County, Queensland, and western NSW, Australia. One specimen yielded enough venom to kill 250,000 mice, but no human fatalities have ever been reported.

### Longest venomous snake

The king cobra (*Ophiophagus hannah*), also called the hamadryad, averages 3.65–4.5 m (12–15 ft) in length and is found in South-east Asia and India.

### Snakebites

In Sri Lanka an average of 800 people are killed annually by snakes.

The saw-scaled or carpet viper (*Echis carinatus*), found from West Africa to India, bites and kills more people than any other.

## Spiders and scorpions

### Most venomous spider

The Brazilian wandering spiders of the genus *Phoneutria*, particularly the Brazilian huntsman *P. fera*, have the most active neurotoxic venom. They often hide in clothing, and bite furiously when disturbed. An antivenin is now available.

### Most venomous scorpion

The Tunisian fat-tailed scorpion (*Androctomus australis*) is reponsible for 80% of stings and 90% of deaths from scorpion stings in North Africa.

### Most deaths from scorpion stings

In 1946, 1,933 people died from scorpion stings in Mexico. About 1,000 people still die in Mexico from scorpion stings each year.

## Marine predators

### Most ferocious fish

The piranhas of the genera *Serrasalmus* and *Pygocentrus* are the most ferocious freshwater fish. They live in the sluggish waters of the large rivers of South America, and will attack any creature, regardless of size. Over 300 people were killed in 1981 when a boat capsized at Obidos, Brazil.

### Most venomous fish

The stonefish (*Synanceidae*) of the tropical waters of the Indo-Pacific oceans, and in particular *Synanceia horrida*, has the largest venom glands of any known fish. Direct contact with its fin spines can be fatal.

## Reptiles and amphibians

### Most poisonous animal

The brightly-coloured poison-arrow frogs (*Dendrobates* and *Phyllobates*) of South and Central America secrete some of the most deadly biological toxins. The golden poison-arrow frog (*Phyllobates terribilis*) of western Colombia is the most poisonous.

### Most dangerous lizard

The Gila monster (*Heloderma suspectum*) is a large, up to 60 cm (24 in), heavily built, brightly coloured lizard that lives in arid areas of Mexico and the south-western USA. Unusually for a lizard it has a poisonous bite, passing venom down grooves in its teeth.

The Mexican beaded lizard (*Heloderma horridum*), from western coastal Mexico, is slightly larger and darker than the Gila monster. It too has a venomous bite—fatalities from either species are rare.

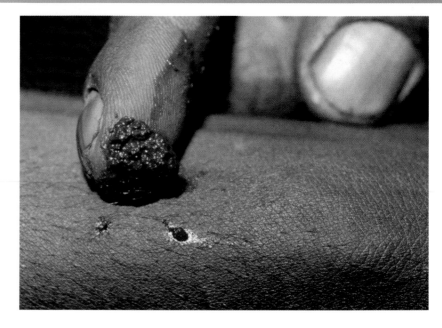

# 800 SNAKEBITE FATALITIES PER YEAR

KILLED AT LEAST 70 PEOPLE OFF THE COAST OF AUSTRALIA THIS CENTURY

The puffer fishes (*Tetraodon*) of the Red Sea and Indo-Pacific region deliver a fatally poisonous toxin called tetrodotoxin, one of the most powerful non-proteinous poisons.

### Most venomous jellyfish
The Australian sea wasp or box jellyfish (*Chironex fleckeri*) is the most venomous cnidarian. Its cardiotoxic venom has killed at least 70 people off the coast of Australia this century, with some victims dying within four minutes. One effective defence, however, is women's hosiery which was once worn by lifesavers in Queensland, Australia, at surfing tournaments.

### Most venomous mollusc
*Hapalochlaena maculosa* and *H. lunulata*, two species of blue-ringed octopus found around the coast of Australia and parts of South-east Asia, carry a neurotoxic venom that can kill in minutes. Just one octopus is believed to carry sufficient venom to cause the paralysis (or even death) of 10 adults. Fortunately, blue-ringed octopuses are not considered aggressive and normally bite only when they are taken out of the water and provoked.

### Most venomous gastropod
Members of the genus *Conus*—cone shells—can inject a fast-acting neurotoxic venom into prey by means of 'harpoons'. The poison can kill a fish instantly and some people have been killed by larger specimens of the species. The geographer cone (*Conus geographus*) is the most dangerous.

**Left**
On 19 Sept 1981, more than 300 people were reportedly killed and eaten by piranhas when an overloaded passenger-cargo boat capsized and sank as it was docking at the port of Obidos, Brazil.

IN QUEENSLAND AND NSW, AUSTRALIA, IS THE MOST VENOMOUS LAND SNAKE

### Most dangerous sea urchin
Toxin from the spines and pedicellaria (small pincer-like organs) of the flower sea urchin (*Toxopneustes pileolus*) causes severe pain, respiratory problems and paralysis.

## Insects
### Most dangerous insect
Malarial parasites of the genus *Plasmodium*, carried by mosquitoes of the genus *Anopheles*, have probably been responsible for 50% of all human deaths since the Stone Age (excluding wars and accidents). Each year in sub-Saharan Africa alone 1.4–2.8 million people die from malaria.

### Most dangerous bee
The Africanized honey bee (*Apis mellifera scutellata*), which is descended from the African sub species, will generally only attack when provoked but is persistent in

pursuit. Its venom is no more potent than that of other bees, but the number of stings it inflicts is greater than any other, and can result in death.

## Mammals
### Most dangerous small mammals
The solenodon is an innocuous-looking small rat-like Caribbean mammal. Both species, the Haitian solenodon (*Solenodon paradoxus*) and the very rare Cuban solenodon (*Solenodon cubanus*), are 28 cm (11 in) long. Their saliva is toxic to prey and potentially dangerous to humans.

The most dangerous small mammal to humans is the rat. Both the brown or Norway rat (*Rattus norvegicus*) and the black or ship rat (*Rattus rattus*) are indirectly potential killers. Rats are important transmitters of diseases, and over 20 pathogens are carried

by them. Among them is the bacterium that causes bubonic plague (the 'Black Death'), which is transmitted to humans by the bite of the rat flea. In all, some 25 million people died of the Black Death in Europe between the 14th and 17th century. Rats also carry leptospirosis (Weil's disease), Lassa fever, rat-bit fever and murine typhus, all of which can be fatal.

### Most dangerous big cats
Lions, tigers and other big cats (family Felidae) can become 'man-eaters'. Tigers seem to attack humans more than other cats and the causes of this behaviour have been much discussed. The most likely cause is that humans fall within the natural size range of a tiger's prey and are fairly easy to attack, particularly for old and injured tigers. There are a great many unsubstantiated claims for the man-eating tiger with the most human victims.

# Endangered species

**Right**
The Californian condor vulture is the rarest bird of prey. After a successful captive breeding programme specimens were released into the wild. There are still around 70 birds left in captivity.

## Rarest British mammal
The United Kingdom's rarest mammals are the wallabies (genus *Petrogale*) that escaped from captivity during WWII to form a breeding colony in Staffordshire. In May 1997 it was reported that there might not be any alive.

## Marine life
**Most endangered fish**
The Devil's hole pupfish (*Cyprinodon diabolis*) is restricted to one pool in Nevada, USA. There are thought to be only between 200 and 500 specimens left.

**Rarest seal**
The rarest seal is the Mediterranean monk seal (*Monarchus monarchus*) with a population of between 427 and 557 in 1997.

**Rarest British freshwater fish**
The vendance (*Corregonus albula*) is restricted to two lakes in Cumbria—Derwent Water and Bassenthwaite Lake.

**Right**
The aye-aye is one of the world's rarest primates and is now the subject of a breeding programme at Jersey Zoo, Channel Islands. When it was first discovered by scientists on the island of Madagascar it was thought to be a rodent because it has rodent-like front teeth.

## Mammals
### Most 'sighted' extinct animal
The thylacine, or Tasmanian wolf (*Thylacinus cynocephalus*), became extinct in 1936 when a captive specimen died in Hobart Zoo. However, it has since been the subject of numerous unconfirmed reports not only in Tasmania but also in mainland Australia and Papua New Guinea. It looked like a wolf but had a long, stiff tail and a sandy-coloured coat with dark stripes across its back.

### Most influential rare animal
The distinctive black-and-white giant panda (*Ailuropoda melanoleuca*) has engendered immense international support for the cause of preservation. There are currently about 700 pandas in the wild in China and a small number in zoos.

### Rarest large land mammal
The Javan rhinoceros (*Rhinoceros sondaicus*), a solitary, single-horned species, was once widely distributed in South-east Asia, but there are only 70 known specimens in Java and Vietnam. The decline is mainly due to the illegal hunting of its horns for use in Oriental medicines and the destruction of its habitats. There are none held in captivity.

### Most endangered primate
All of the 21 species of lemur, largely restricted to forested parts of Madagascar, are threatened by the destruction of their habitat. Probably the most endangered

species is the aye-aye (*Daubentonia madagascariensis*), with around only 20 known specimens in the wild.

### Rarest antelope
The Arabian oryx (*Oryx leucoryx*) is the world's rarest antelope. It became extinct in the wild in Saudi Arabia and Oman in 1972 due to hunting, but is being bred in captivity, principally at Marwell Zoo, Hants, UK, for reintroduction into the wild.

### Rarest wild cats
The Iriomote cat (*Felis iriomotensis*) is wholly confined to the island of Iriomote, in the Ryukyu chain, Japan. It numbers no more than 100 specimens, as well as a few in Japanese zoos.

The rarest big cat is the Indian lion (*Panthera leo persica*) with under 200 in the wild, many in Gir Lion National Park, Gujarat, India.

### Most endangered mustelid
North America's black-footed ferret (*Mustela nigripes*) resembles the common ferret but has a black mask across its eyes. It was believed extinct but has been rediscovered.

### Rarest wild ox
The Cambodian wild ox, or kouprey (*Bos sauveli*), was discovered in 1936. Since then this grey or dark-brown species of wild cattle has often been dismissed as extinct but may still live in woodland in South-east Asia.

# JAVAN RHINOS 70 SURVIVORS

## THE GALAPAGOS ISLANDS, IS THE ONLY SURVIVING MEMBER OF THE SPECIES

## Reptiles and amphibians

### World's loneliest creature
The Abingdon Island giant tortoise (*Geochelone elephantopus abingdoni*) is represented by one specimen, 'Lonesome George', an aged male living in the Galapagos Islands, Ecuador. With little hope of finding another specimen, this subspecies of giant tortoise is effectively extinct.

### Rarest amphibian
The population of the Costa Rican golden toad (*Bufo periglenes*) has plummeted in little over a decade. The last recorded sightings (11 specimens) were in 1990.

### Rarest snakes
The Round Island, Mauritius, has the distinction of being home to the two rarest snakes—the Round Island burrowing boa (*Bolyeria multicarinata*), which may already be extinct, and the Round Island keel-scaled boa (*Casarea dussumieri*), which is maintained in Jersey Zoo, Channel Islands.

### Rarest bird of prey
Only a few Californian condors (*Gymnogyps californianus*), which were bred in captivity and released in 1992, exist in the wild.

### Rarest British bird
Four species—the scarlet, or common rosefinch (*Carpodacus erythrinus*), the serin (*Serinus serinus*), the little gull (*Larus minutus*) and the black winged stilt (*Himantopus himantopus*)—are known from one breeding pair per year in the United Kingdom during the 1990s.

## Insects

### Most endangered butterfly
There are several contenders for the most endangered butterfly species including the Queen's Alexandra's birdwing of Papua New Guinea, which has the distinction of being the largest butterfly in the world. The species' survival has not been helped by the attentions of collectors.

A number of species of beetle in the United Kingdom can be considered the rarest: the spangled water beetle (*Graphoderus zonatus*), found in a pond in north Hampshire; the moccas beetle (*Hypebaeus flavipes*), found on a trees at a site in Herefordshire; the darkling beetle (*Omophilus rufitarsis*), confined to a beach in Dorset; the soldier beetle (*Malthodes brevicollis*), which lives on the red rot of ancient oaks at a site in Herefordshire; and two species of click beetle (*Ampedus nigerrimus/ruficeps*), which live in the red rot of ancient oaks in Windsor Forest and Windsor Great Park respectively.

**ONLY ABOUT 10 SPECIMENS ARE KNOWN TO REMAIN**

### Rarest giant lizard
The Komodo dragon (*Varanus komodoensis*), is a gigantic species of monitor lizard that lives on the Indonesian island of Komodo. There are now fewer than 200 specimens, making it the world's rarest monitor lizard.

### Rarest British amphibian
The Pool frog (*Rana lessonae*) was introduced to the United Kingdom from continental Europe, but is now considered a native species. There is one site in the United Kingdom where the frog is indigenous, but no specimen has been seen since 1994.

## Birds

### Most endangered birds
Spix's macaw (*Cyanopsitta spixii*) is currently known only from a single wild specimen but there are about 30 in captivity.

The Kauai o-o (*Moho bracattus*), a Hawaiian songbird, was rediscovered in 1960 and is believed to number no more than two pairs.

There are less than 20 known (mainly captive) Japanese crested ibis (*Nipponia nippon*), all believed to be too old to breed.

The New Zealand kakapo, or owl parrot (*Strigops habroptilus*) has been hunted almost to extinction. This flightless bird does not flee from predators and there are only 10 known specimens left.

### Rarest insect
The giant earwig of St Helena (*Labidura herculeana*) was last recorded in 1965 though entomologists still look for it.

### Rarest insects in the UK
The Laura's wall snail (*Lauria semproni*) is only found on a short stretch of limestone wall in Gloucestershire.

Two species of spider are equally rare: *Agroeca lusatica*, known only in one sand dune in Kent; and *Carorita limnaea*, found in a mire in Staffordshire.

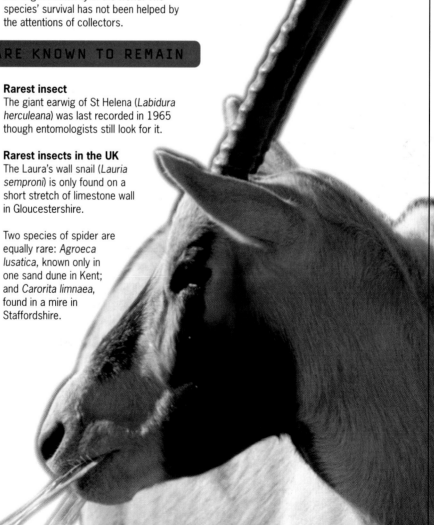

**Left**
With its long, graceful horns the Arabian oryx, the world's rarest antelope, may well be the source of the unicorn legend.

# Animal discoveries

**Right**
The horns of the kting voar or holy goat. The animal is still a mystery to science, although the local population in the parts of Vietnam where it is to be found describe it as a brown cow-like creature.

Irian Jaya (western New Guinea), Indonesia. It is 1.2 m (4 ft) long and weighs 15 kg (33 lb).

## Most recently discovered monkeys
The Maues marmoset (*Callithrix mausei*) was first described in Brazil in 1992, while the Satere marmoset (*Callithrix saterei*) was described in 1996, also in Brazil.

## Britain's newest mammal
In 1997, British scientists formally described a new species of pipistrelle bat which had not previously been distinguished from the common pipistrelle (*Pipistrellus pipistrellus*).

## Newest land-living fish
A small red worm-like species of the trichomycterid catfish, called the *Phreatobius walkeri*, was found in the mid-1980s in Brazil. This species lives a fully terrestrial existence among leaf litter on river banks and when placed in water will swiftly jump back out again.

*CEPHALODISCUS GRAPTOLITOIDES*, DISCOVERED IN 1993, WAS KNOWN ONLY

**Right**
The black and white Mbaiso tree kangaroo, recently discovered by scientists in Irian Jaya, Indonesia, is unique among tree kangaroos in that it spends much of its time on the ground.

## Land animals
### Greatest concentration of new animals
The greatest concentration of animals that are new to science is in Indochina. In the 1990s, 10 new species of large land mammals were discovered, or rediscovered, in Vietnam, Laos and Cambodia. These include the Vu Quang ox (*Pseudoryx nghetinhensis*), the holy goat or kting voar (*Pseudonovibos spiralis*), the giant muntjac (*Megamuntiacus vuquangensis*), the Vietnamese warty pig (*Sus bucculentis*), the Laotian black muntjac, the giant cream loris and the slow-running deer.

### Largest new land mammal
The largest recently discovered land mammal is the Vu Quang ox (*Pseudoryx nghetinhensis*), which is the size of a small buffalo. Discovered in northern Vietnam in 1992, it is the largest new species of land mammal to be discovered since the kouprey (Cambodian wild ox) in 1936.

### Largest species of barking deer
At least a third larger than any other species of barking deer, the giant muntjac (*Megamuntiacus vuquangensis*) was discovered in 1994, in northern Vietnam. It is not only a new species but a new genus.

### Largest new marsupial
The bondegezou, or Mbaiso tree kangaroo (*Dendrolagus mbaiso*), a black and white whistling species of kangaroo, was discovered in 1994 by Dr Tim Flannery in

# NEWEST PHYLUM DISCOVERED 1995

## WHERE 10 SPECIES OF LAND MAMMALS HAVE BEEN DISCOVERED IN THE 1990s

**Most sensational comeback**
The colonial marine invertebrate (*Cephalodiscus graptolitoides*) formally described in 1993, is believed to be a living species of graptolite, a group of invertebrates hitherto known only from fossils and believed to have been extinct for 300 million years.

**Most recently discovered ecosystem**
The Movile Cave mini-ecosystem of Romania, completely sealed off from sunlight, has revealed at least 47 new species of invertebrate since its discovery in late 1986. The new species all exhibit troglomorphy, which is a reduction or loss of eyes and pigmentation and an enlargement of 'antennae' to cope with life in a world devoid of sunlight. The ancestors of some of these species—spiders, water scorpions, leeches and microbes—probably became isolated from their surface dwelling relatives five million years ago.

## FROM FOSSILS AND BELIEVED TO HAVE BEEN EXTINCT FOR 300 MILLION YEARS

**World's most mysterious new mammal**
The holy goat or kting voar (*Pseudonovibos spiralis*), which was scientifically named in 1994, is still only known to scientists by its distinctive horns. Although there had been reports of the animal by local hunters in southern Vietnam and neighbouring Cambodia, there are still no official sightings of it, either living or dead.

## Marine animals
**Most recently discovered whale**
Bahamonde's beaked whale (*Mesoplodon bahamondi*) was first described in 1996 when a skull was washed up on the beach at Robinson Crusoe Island, Chile. This hitherto unknown species of whale is estimated to be as large as a full-grown elephant in total body size.

**First vampire fish**
A tiny parasitic fish, previously unknown to science, was documented by Dr Wilson Coasta in Brazil in 1994. The creature lives entirely upon blood which is drained from the gills of larger fish.

**First social crustaceans**
*Synalpheus regalis*, a species of shrimp which was discovered on the barrier reef off the Central American state of Belize in 1996, is the only known social crustacean with a breeding queen and sterile workers, just like ants, bees and other social insects.

**Most recently discovered new phylum**
*Cycliophora*, formally named and described in Dec 1995, is a new phylum, a major division of animal life. It was recognized in order to accommodate a dramatically new species of tiny multicellular invertebrate called *Symbion pandora*, which lives on the lips of North Sea lobsters.

## Birds
**Newest genus of bird**
The graveteiro (*Acrobatornis fonsecai*), a pink-legged ovenbird-related species from Brazil, was first sighted by scientists in Nov 1994.

**Most elusive new bird**
The Nechisar nightjar (*Caprimulgus solala*) is still only known from a single wing, which was found in 1990 after it was squashed by a truck on a dirt road in the middle of Ethiopia's Nechisar National Park. The bird was recognized as a new species in 1995.

## Extinction and ecosystems
**Most unexpected recent discovery**
Gilbert's potoroo (*Potorous tridactylus gilberti*), a type of Australian rat kangaroo which was believed to have been extinct since 1869, was rediscovered by scientists in Western Australia in 1994. In May 1997 there were known to be over a dozen individuals.

**Sport**

# Olympics

## Olympic Games
### Earliest Games
The earliest celebration of the ancient Olympic Games of which there is a certain record is that of July 776 BC, when Coroibos, a cook from Elis, won the foot race, though their origin dates from perhaps as early as c. 1370 BC. The ancient Games were terminated by an order issued in AD 393 by the Roman Emperor Theodosius I.

The Olympic Games of the modern era were inaugurated at the instigation of Pierre de Fredi, Baron de Coubertin, in Athens, Greece, on 6 April 1896.

### Most regular competitors
Five countries have always been represented at the 24 Summer Games (1896–1996): Australia, France, Greece, Great Britain and Switzerland.

Estimates of the number of spectators who watched the marathon race through the streets of Tokyo, Japan, on 21 Oct 1964 ranged from 500,000 to 1,500,000.

The total attendance at the Los Angeles Olympics, USA, in 1984 was given as 5,797,923.

### Largest Olympic Torch relay
The longest torch journey within one country was for the XV Olympic Winter Games, which were held in Canada in 1988. The torch was first taken from Greece to St John's, Newfoundland, Canada, on 17 Nov 1987. From there it was transported to Calgary, Canada, where it arrived on 13 Feb 1988 after travelling a total distance of 18,060 km (11,222 miles).

The record at one celebration is eight, by gymnast Aleksandr Nikolayevich Dityatin (USSR) in 1980.

### Most consecutive wins
The only Olympians to win four consecutive individual titles in the same event are Alfred Adolph Oerter (USA), in the discus between 1956 and 1968 and Frederick Carleton 'Carl' Lewis (USA), in the long jump between 1984 and 1996.

Raymond Clarence Ewry (USA) won both the standing long jump and the standing high jump at four games in succession, in 1900, 1904, 1906 (Intercalated Games) and 1908.

Paul Bert Elvstrøm (Denmark) won four successive gold medals at monotype yachting events, in the

500-m gold in 1984, and 1,000-m gold and 500-m silver in 1988.

## Competitors
### Youngest and oldest gold medallist
The youngest ever winner was a French boy (whose name was possibly Marcel Depaillé) who coxed the Netherlands pair in 1900. He was between seven and 10 years old.

The youngest ever female champion was Kim Yoon-mi (South Korea), aged 13 years 85 days, in the 1994 women's 3,000-m short-track speedskating relay event.

Oscar Swahn was in the winning Running Deer shooting team in 1912, aged 64 years 258 days. He was also the oldest medallist, with a silver, at 72 years 280 days in 1920.

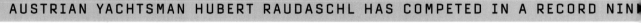

However, in 1956 Switzerland only contested the Equestrian events, which were held in Stockholm, Sweden, and did not attend the rest of the Games in Melbourne. Only France, Great Britain and Switzerland have taken part in all the Winter celebrations (1924–94).

### Most participants
The greatest number of competitors at a Summer Games celebration is a registered 10,744 (7,060 men, 3,684 women), who represented all 197 National Olympic Committees, at Atlanta, USA, in 1996.

The greatest number of people participating at the Winter Games was 1,737 (1,216 men, 521 women), representing 67 countries, at Lillehammer, Norway, in 1994.

### Largest crowd
The 1952 ski-jumping competition at the Holmenkøllen, Oslo, Norway, was watched by 104,102 people.

## Medals
### Most gold medals
The most individual gold medals won by a male competitor in the modern Games is 10, by Raymond Ewry (USA).

The women's record is seven, by Vera Caslavska-Odlozil (Czechoslovakia).

### Gold medals by British competitors
The most gold medals won by a British competitor is four, by: Paul Radmilovic in water polo in 1908, 1912 and 1920 and 4 x 200 m freestyle relay in 1908; swimmer Henry Taylor in 1906 and 1908 and rower Steven Geoffrey Redgrave in coxed fours in 1984 and in coxless pairs in 1988, 1992 and 1996.

### Most medals
Gymnast Larisa Semyonovna Latynina (USSR) won a record 18 medals.

The men's record for the most medals is 15, by gymnast Nikolay Yefimovich Andrianov of the USSR.

Firefly class in 1948 and in the Finn class in 1952, 1956 and 1960.

### Most gold medals at one Games
Swimmer Mark Spitz (USA) won seven gold medals at one Games at Munich, Germany, in 1972.

The most won in individual events at one celebration is five, by speed skater, Eric Arthur Heiden (USA) at Lake Placid, New York, USA, in 1980.

### Summer and Winter golds
The only man to win a gold medal in both the Summer and Winter Games is Edward Patrick Francis Eagan (USA) who won the 1920 light-heavyweight boxing title and was a member of the winning four-man bob in 1932.

Christa Luding (GDR) became the first woman to ever win a medal at both the Summer and Winter Games when she won a silver in the cycling sprint event in 1988. She had previously won medals for speed skating,

The youngest British Olympic competitor was Magdalena Colledge, who was 11 years 73 days when she skated in the 1932 Games.

The oldest British Olympic competitor was Hilda Johnstone, who was 70 years 5 days when she took part in the equestrian dressage in the 1972 Games in Munich, Germany.

### Longest Olympic careers
The longest span of an Olympic competitor is 40 years, by: Dr Ivan Joseph Martin Osiier (Denmark) in fencing from 1908 to 1948; Magnus Andreas Thulstrup Clasen Konow (Norway) in yachting from 1908 to 1948; Paul Elvstrøm (Denmark) in yachting from 1948 to 1988; and Durward Randolph Knowles (Great Britain 1948, then Bahamas) in yachting from 1948 to 1988.

The longest span by a female competitor is 28 years, by Anne Jessica Ransehousen (USA) in

## 30TH THE SUMMER AND WINTER GAMES

**SUMMER GAMES (1896–1996)**
USA 2,015:
833 gold, 634 silver, 548 bronze
Soviet Union (Includes CIS, or Unified
team, in 1992) 1,234:
485 gold, 395 silver, 354 bronze
Great Britain 635:
177 gold, 233 silver, 225 bronze
France 562:
176 gold, 181 silver, 205 bronze
Germany (1896–1964 and 1992–94)
516:
151 gold, 181 silver, 184 bronze
Sweden 459:
134 gold, 152 silver, 173 bronze
Italy 444:
166 gold, 136 silver, 142 bronze
Hungary 425:
142 gold, 128 silver, 155 bronze
German Democratic Republic
(1968–88) 410:
153 gold, 130 silver, 127 bronze

**WINTER GAMES (1924–94)**
Soviet Union (includes CIS, or Unified
team, in 1992) 217:
87 gold, 63 silver, 67 bronze
Norway 214:
73 gold, 77 silver, 64 bronze
USA 146:
53 gold, 56 silver, 37 bronze
Austria 128:
36 gold, 48 silver, 44 bronze
Finland 123:
36 gold, 45 silver, 42 bronze
German Democratic Republic
(1968–88) 110:
39 gold, 36 silver, 35 bronze
Sweden 99:
39 gold, 26 silver, 34 bronze
Germany
(1896–1964 and 1992–94) 87:
34 gold, 29 silver, 24 bronze
Switzerland 85:
27 gold, 29 silver, 29 bronze

**Far Left**
Christa Luding is the
first woman to have
won a medal in both
the Winter and Summer
Olympic Games. She
won medals for speed
skating in 1984 and
1988 before going
on to win a silver in
the cycling sprint
event in 1988.

**Right**
The British javelin
thrower Tessa
Sanderson was 40
when she appeared
at her record sixth
Olympic Games in
Atlanta, Georgia,
USA, in 1996.

## OLYMPIC GAMES FROM 1964 TO 1996

dressage from 1960 to 1988 and
Christilot Hanson-Boylen (Canada),
dressage from 1964 to 1992.

Fencer Kerstin Palm of Sweden
competed in a women's record of
seven celebrations, between
1964 and 1988.

The longest span for any British
competitor is 32 years, by Enoch
Jenkins who competed in clay pigeon
shooting in 1920, 1924 and 1952.

The longest span by a female British
competitor is 20 years, by: Dorothy
Jennifer Beatrice Tyler who high-jumped
between 1936 and 1956; and Tessa
Sanderson who competed in the
javelin from 1976 to 1996.

British competitor Divina Mary
Galicia competed in alpine skiing
from 1964 to 1972, and took part
in speed skiing in 1992 (at the time
a demonstration sport), completing
a span of 28 years.

**Most Games competed**
Yachtsman Hubert Raudaschl (Austria)
competed in nine Games between
1964 and 1996. He also went to
Rome in 1960, but did not compete.

The record for Games appearances by
a British competitor is six, by: swimmer
and water polo player Paul Radmilovic,
between 1906 and 1928; fencer Bill
Hoskyns between 1956 and 1976
and javelin thrower Tessa Sanderson
between 1976 and 1996.

David Broome, the British showjumper,
who competed in 1960, 1964, 1968,
1972 and 1988, was a member of
the British team that travelled to
Barcelona in 1992. He was, however,
not selected to compete.

**Most medals**
The total medals, for leading nations,
for all Olympic events (including those
now discontinued but excluding medals
won in Official Art competitions from
1912 to 1948) are as follows:

Australia 294:
87 gold, 85 silver, 122 bronze
Finland 292:
99 gold, 80 silver, 113 bronze
Japan 280:
93 gold, 89 silver, 98 bronze
Romania 239:
63 gold, 77 silver, 99 bronze
Poland 227:
50 gold, 67 silver, 110 bronze
Canada 217:
49 gold, 77 silver, 91 bronze
Federal Republic of Germany
(1968–88) 200:
56 gold, 64 silver, 80 bronze
Netherlands 187:
49 gold, 57 silver, 81 bronze
Bulgaria 182:
43 gold, 76 silver, 63 bronze
Switzerland 174:
46 gold, 68 silver, 60 bronze
China 164:
52 gold, 63 silver, 49 bronze
Denmark 156:
39 gold, 60 silver, 57 bronze
Czechoslovakia (until 1994) 149:
49 gold, 50 silver, 50 bronze
Belgium 136:
37 gold, 50 silver, 49 bronze

Italy 67:
25 gold, 21 silver, 21 bronze
Canada 64:
19 gold, 20 silver, 25 bronze
France 53:
16 gold, 16 silver, 21 bronze
Netherlands 50:
14 gold, 19 silver, 17 bronze
Federal Republic of Germany
(1968–88) 39:
11 gold, 15 silver, 13 bronze
Czechoslovakia (includes Bohemia) 26:
2 gold, 8 silver, 16 bronze
Russia (includes Tsarist Russia) 24:
12 gold, 8 silver, 4 bronze
Great Britain 23:
7 gold, 4 silver, 12 bronze
Japan 19:
3 gold, 8 silver, 8 bronze
Korea 10:
6 gold, 2 silver, 2 bronze
Liechtenstein 9:
2 gold, 2 silver, 5 bronze
Hungary 6:
0 gold, 2 silver, 4 bronze
China 6:
0 gold, 4 silver, 2 bronze
Poland 4:
1 gold, 1 silver, 2 bronze

# Athletics

**Right**
Ed Moses (USA)
won a record
122 consecutive
competitions at 400-m
hurdles between 1977
and 1987. Eventually
he lost to Danny Lee
Harris at Madrid, Spain,
on 4 June 1987.

MERLENE OTTEY (JAMAICA) HAS WON THREE GOLD, FOUR SILVER AND SI

## World Championships
### Most gold medals
Carl Lewis won a record eight gold medals, between 1984 and 1992.

The most gold medals won by a woman is four, by Jackie Joyner-Kersee (USA); the long jump in 1987 and 1991 and the heptathlon in 1987 and 1993.

### Most medals
Carl Lewis has won a record 10 medals: a record eight gold in 100 m, long jump and 4 x 100-m relay in 1983; in 100 m, long jump and 4 x 100-m relay in 1987; in 100 m and 4 x 100-m relay in 1991; plus silver at long jump in 1991 and bronze at 200 m in 1993.

The most medals by a women is 13, by Merlene Ottey (Jamaica), three gold, four silver and six bronze, 1983–95.

### Most participants
The greatest number of participants at a world championships is 11,475

(9,328 men, 2,147 women) for the 1993 World Veterans' Athletic Championships at Miyazaki, Japan.

### World Indoor Games
The most individual titles is four, by: Stefka Kostadinova (Bulgaria) for the high jump in 1985, 1987, 1989 and 1993; Mikhail Shchennikov (Russia) for the 5,000-m walk in 1987, 1989, 1991 and 1993; and Sergey Bubka (Ukraine) for the pole vault in 1985, 1987, 1991 and 1995.

## World records
### Fastest speed
An analysis of the times taken by Ben Johnson (Canada) and Carl Lewis (USA) to cover each successive 10 m in the 1988 Olympic Games 100-m final in Seoul on 24 Sept 1988 shows that both reached a peak speed (at 40–50 m and 80–90 m respectively) of 0.83 seconds for 10 m, i.e. 43.37 km/h (26.95 mph). Johnson won the race in a time of 9.79 seconds but he was later disqualified.

In the 1988 women's 110-m final Florence Griffith-Joyner (USA) was timed at 0.91 seconds for each 10 m from 60 m to 90 m—a speed equivalent to 39.56 km/h (24.58 mph).

### Highest jump above own head
Franklin Jacobs (USA) cleared 59 cm (23¼ in) above his head when he jumped 2.32 m (7 ft 7¼ in) at New York, USA, on 27 Jan 1978.

Yolanda Henry (USA) cleared 32 cm (12¾ in) above her head when she jumped 2 m (6 ft 6¾ in) at Seville, Spain, on 30 May 1990.

### Oldest world record breakers
Gerhard Wiedner (West Germany) was 41 years 71 days when he set a world record of 2 hr 30 min 38.6 sec for the 20-mile walk at Hamburg, Germany, on 25 May 1974.

### Youngest world record breakers
On 9 March 1986, Wang Yan (China) set a record for the women's 5,000-m

walk of 21 min 33.8 sec at the age of 14 years 334 days at Jian, China.

Thomas Ray (GB) was 17 years 198 days old when he pole-vaulted 3.42 m (11 ft 2¾ in) on 19 Sept 1879.

### Most records in a day
Jesse Owens (USA) set six world records in 45 minutes at Ann Arbor, Michigan, USA, on 25 May 1935 with a 9.4-sec 100 yd at 3:15 p.m., an 8.13-m (26-ft 8¼-in) long jump at 3:25 p.m., a 20.3-sec 220 yd (now also taken as a 200-m record) at 3:45 p.m. and a 22.6-sec 220-yd low hurdles (also taken as a 200-m record) at 4 p.m.

### Longest winning sequence
Iolanda Balas (Romania) won a record 150 consecutive competitions at high jump from 1956 to 1967.

The longest winning sequence for a track event is 122, at the 400-m hurdles by Edwin Moses (USA) between 1977 and 1987.

# OLDEST CHAMPION 42 YEARS 26 DAYS

## Olympic Games
### Most Olympic golds
The most Olympic gold medals ever won by one athlete is 10, by Raymond Clarence Ewry (USA) in the standing high, long and triple jumps in 1900, 1904, 1906 and 1908. This is also an absolute Olympic record.

The most gold medals won by a woman is four, by Francina 'Fanny' Elsje Blankers-Koen (Netherlands), for the 100-m, 200-m, 80-m hurdles and 4 x 100-m relay in 1948; Elizabeth 'Betty' Cuthbert (Australia) for the 100 m, 200 m and 4 x 100-m relay in 1956 and the 400 m in 1964; Bärbel Wöckel (GDR) for the 200 m and 4 x 100-m relay in 1976 and 1980; and Evelyn Ashford (USA), for the 100 m and 4 x 100-m relay in 1984, 1988 and 1992.

won by a woman with seven—three gold, one silver and three bronze in the 1948, 1952 and 1956 Games. A recently discovered photo-finish of the 1948 200-m event indicates that she finished third, not fourth, thus unofficially increasing her medal total to eight.

Merlene Ottey (Jamaica) has won seven Olympic medals—two silver and five bronze between 1980 and 1996.

Irena Szewinska (Poland) is the only woman athlete to win a medal in four successive Games. She won three gold, two silver and two bronze in 1964, 1968, 1972 and 1976.

### Most British medals
The most medals won by a British athlete is four, by Guy Montagu Butler

in 1900 in the 60-m, 110-m hurdles, 200-m hurdles and long jump.

### Oldest Olympic champions
The oldest athlete to win an Olympic title was Irish-born Patrick Joseph 'Babe' McDonald (USA) who was aged 42 years 26 days when he won the 25.4-kg (56-lb) weight throw at Antwerp, Belgium, on 21 Aug 1920.

The oldest female champion was Lia Manoliu (Romania) who was 36 years 176 days when she won the discus at Mexico City, Mexico, on 18 Oct 1968.

### Youngest Olympic champions
The youngest gold medallist, Barbara Pearl Jones (USA), was 15 years 123 days when she was a member of the winning 4 x 100-m relay team, at Helsinki, Finland, on 27 July 1952.

Geoffrey Lewis Capes at shot, six indoor and seven out.

The record for the most WAAA outdoor titles won by one athlete is 14, by Suzanne Allday with seven each at shot and discus from 1952 to 1962. She also won two WAAA indoor shot titles.

### Most international appearances
The greatest number of full Great Britain international appearances is 76 (outdoors and indoors), by Judy Oakes from 1976 to 1996.

The shot-putter Geoff Capes holds the men's record with 67 appearances, from 1969 to 1980. The pole vault and decathlete Mike Bull appeared at 66 full internationals or 69 including the European Indoor Games, before these were official internationals.

43.37 km/h

## BRONZE, A RECORD OF 13 MEDALS

### Most British gold medals
The most gold medals won by a British athlete (excluding tug of war and walking) is two, by: Charles Bennett for the 1,500-m and 5,000-m team in 1900; Alfred Edward Tysoe for the 800-m and 5,000-m team in 1900; John Thomas Rimmer for the 4,000-m steeplechase and 5,000-m team in 1900; Albert George Hill for the 800 m and 1,500 m in 1920; Douglas Gordon Arthur Lowe for the 800 m in 1924 and 1928; Sebastian Newbold Coe for the 1,500 m in 1980 and 1984 and Francis Morgan 'Daley' Thompson for the decathlon in 1980 and 1984. Thompson was also the decathlon world champion in 1983.

### Most Olympic medals
The most medals ever won is 12 (nine gold and three silver), by Paavo Nurmi (Finland) in the Games of 1920, 1924 and 1928.

Shirley Barbara de la Hunty (Australia) holds the record for the most medals

with gold for the 4 x 400-m relay and silver for 400 m in 1920 and bronze for each of these events in 1924, and by Sebastian Coe, with gold in the 1,500 m in 1980 and 1984 and silver medals at 800 m in 1980 and 1984.

The record for British women is three, by: Dorothy Hyman with a silver (100 m, 1960) and two bronze (200 m, 1960 and 4 x 100-m relay, 1964), Mary Denise Rand, with a gold (long jump), a silver (pentathlon) and a bronze (4 x 100-m relay), all in 1964 and Kathryn Cook, bronze at 4 x 100-m relay 1980 and 1984, and at 400 m in 1984.

### Most wins at one Games
The most gold medals at one celebration is five, by Paavo Johannes Nurmi (Finland) in 1924 for the 1,500 m, 5,000 m, 10,000-m cross-country, the 3,000-m team and the cross-country team.

The most wins at individual events is four, by Alvin Christian Kraenzlein (USA)

The youngest male champion was Robert Bruce Mathias (USA) who was aged 17 years 263 days when he won the decathlon at the London Games in the UK on 5–6 Aug 1948.

### British Championships
### Most national titles
The record for the most national senior titles won by one athlete is 37, by Judith Miriam Oakes at the shot: 14 WAAA or AAA outdoor, 14 indoor (WAAA/AAA), and nine UK titles from 1977 to 1996.

The men's record for senior AAA titles won by one athlete (excluding those in tug of war events) is 14 individual and one relay title by Emmanuel McDonald Bailey (Trinidad), between 1946 and 1953.

The most national titles won outdoors in a single event is 13 by Denis Horgan (Ireland) in the shot put between 1893 and 1912.

The most senior AAA titles won is 13 by: Michael Anthony Bull at pole vault, eight indoor and five out, and by

### Most outdoor appearances
The most outdoor appearances is 61, by hammer thrower Andrew Howard Payne (South Africa, then GB) from 1960 to 1974.

### British competitors
### Oldest British internationals
Boyd Millen was 60 years 233 days old when he took part in the Roubaix 28-hour walking race against France on 14–15 Sept 1996.

The oldest British woman, Ann Sayer, competed in the 200-km walk at Bazencourt, France, on 2–3 April 1994, aged 57 years 169 days. She also represented England in a walking match at Roubaix, France, on 16–17 Sept 1995, aged 58 years 335 days.

### Youngest British international
The youngest man was high jumper Ross Hepburn (b. 14 Oct 1961) v. the USSR on 26 Aug 1977, aged 15 years 316 days, and the youngest woman was Janis Walsh (now Cue) (b. 28 March 1960) v. Belgium (indoor) at 60 m and 4 x 200-m relay on 15 Feb 1975, aged 14 years 324 days.

# Athletics: world records

**Right**
Jan Zelezny of the Czech Republic holds the javelin record of 98.48 m (323.1 ft) which he achieved in 1996 in Jena, Germany.

**Far right**
In Sept 1996, Daniel Komen of Kenya broke the 3,000-m record which had previously been held by the Algerian Noureddine Morceli.

**1 hour:** 21,101 m
Arturo Barrios (Mexico, now USA)
La Flèche, France, 30 March 1991
**110-m hurdles:** 12.91
Colin Ray Jackson (GB)
Stuttgart, Germany, 20 Aug 1993
**400-m hurdles:** 46.78
Kevin Curtis Young (USA)
Barcelona, Spain, 6 Aug 1992
**3,000-m steeplechase:** 7:59.18
Moses Kiptanui (Kenya)
Zürich, Switzerland, 16 Aug 1995
**4 x 100-m:** 37.40
USA (Michael Marsh, Leroy Burrell, Dennis A Mitchell, Frederick Carleton 'Carl' Lewis) Barcelona, Spain, 8 Aug 1992
and: USA (John A Drummond Jr, Andre Cason, Dennis A Mitchell, Leroy Burrell) Stuttgart, Germany, 21 Aug 1993
**4 x 200-m:** 1:18.68
Santa Monica Track Club, USA

**FIELD EVENTS**
**High jump:** 2.45 m (8 ft ½ in)
Javier Sotomayor (Cuba)
Salamanca, Spain, 27 July 1993
**Pole vault (high alt.):** 6.14 m (20 ft 1¾ in)
Sergey Nazarovich Bubka (Ukraine)
Sestriere, Italy, 31 July 1994
**Pole vault (low alt.):** 6.13 m (20 ft 1¼ in)
Sergey Bubka (Ukraine)
Tokyo, Japan, 19 Sept 1992.
**Long jump:** 8.95 m (29 ft 4½ in)
Michael Anthony 'Mike' Powell (USA)
Tokyo, Japan, 30 Aug 1991
**Triple jump:** 18.29 m (60 ft ¼ in)
Jonathan David Edwards (GB)
Gothenburg, Sweden, 7 Aug 1995
**Shot:** 23.12 m (75 ft 10¼ in)
Eric Randolph 'Randy' Barnes (USA)
Los Angeles, USA, 20 May 1990
**Discus:** 74.08 m (243 ft)

World outdoor records are scheduled by the International Amateur Athletics Federation (IAAF). Fully automatic electric timing is mandatory for events up to 400 m.

## MEN

### RUNNING
**100 m:** 9.84*
Donovan Bailey (Canada)
Atlanta, Georgia, USA, 27 July 1996
**200 m:** 19.32
Michael Duane Johnson (USA)
Atlanta, Georgia, USA, 1 Aug 1996
**400 m:** 43.29
Harry Lee 'Butch' Reynolds Jr (USA)
Zürich, Switzerland, 17 Aug 1988
**800 m:** 1:41.73
Sebastian Coe (GB)
Florence, Italy, 10 June 1981
**1,000 m:** 2:12.18
Sebastian Coe (GB)
Oslo, Norway, 11 July 1981
**1,500 m:** 3:27.37
Noureddine Morceli (Algeria)
Nice, France, 12 July 1995

**1 mile:** 3:44.39
Noureddine Morceli (Algeria)
Rieti, Italy, 5 Sept 1993
**2,000 m:** 4:47.88
Noureddine Morceli (Algeria)
Paris, France, 3 July 1995
**3,000 m:** 7:20.67
Daniel Komen (Kenya)
Rieti, Italy, 1 Sept 1996
**5,000 m:** 12:44.39
Haile Gebrselassie (Ethiopia)
Zürich, Switzerland, 16 Aug 1995
**10,000 m:** 26:38.08
Salah Hissou (Morocco)
Brussels, Belgium, 23 Aug 1996
**20,000 m:** 56:55.6
Arturo Barrios (Mexico, now USA)
La Flèche, France, 30 March 1991
**25,000 m:** 1:13:55.8
Toshihiko Seko (Japan)
Christchurch, New Zealand, 22 March 1981
**30,000 m:** 1:29:18.8
Toshihiko Seko (Japan)
Christchurch, New Zealand, 22 March 1981

(Michael Marsh, Leroy Burrell, Floyd Wayne Heard, Carl Lewis)
Walnut, California, USA, 17 April 1994
**4 x 400-m:** 2:54.29
USA (Andrew Valmon, Quincy Watts, Butch Reynolds, Michael Johnson)
Stuttgart, Germany, 21 Aug 1993
**4 x 800-m:** 7:03.89
Great Britain (Peter Elliott, Garry Peter Cook, Stephen Cram, Sebastian Coe)
Crystal Palace, London, UK, 30 Aug 1982
**4 x 1,500-m:** 14:38.8
West Germany (Thomas Wessinghage, Harald Hudak, Michael Lederer, Karl Fleschen) Cologne, Germany, 17 Aug 1977

* Ben Johnson of Canada ran a time of 9.78 seconds in this event at the Olympic Games in Seoul, South Korea, in 1988. However, he was disqualified after testing positive for drugs. He later admitted to having used steroids for years, invalidating his 9.83 seconds at Rome, Italy, in 1987.

Jürgen Schult (GDR)
Neubrandenburg, Germany, 6 June 1986
**Hammer:** 86.74 m (284 ft 7 in)
Yuriy Georgiyevich Sedykh (USSR, now Russia) Stuttgart, Germany, 30 Aug 1986
**Javelin:** 98.48 m (323 ft 1 in)
Jan Zelezny (Czech Republic)
Jena, Germany, 25 May 1996
**Decathlon:** 8,891 points
Dan Dion O'Brien (USA)
Talence, France, 4–5 Sept 1992:
100-m: 10.43
Long jump: 8.08 m (26 ft 6¼ in)
Shot: 16.69 m (54 ft 9¼ in)
High jump: 2.07 m (6 ft 9½ in)
400 m: 48.51
110-m hurdles: 13.98
Discus: 48.56 m (159 ft 4 in)
Pole vault: 5.00 m (16 ft 4¼ in)
Javelin: 62.58 m (205 ft 4 in)
1,500 m: 4:42.10

# FASTEST 200 M 19.32 SECS

## SECONDS AT ATLANTA, USA, IN 1996

### WOMEN

#### RUNNING

**100 m:** 10.49
Delorez Florence Griffith Joyner (USA)
Indianapolis, Indiana, USA,
16 July 1988
**200 m:** 21.34
Delorez Florence Griffith Joyner (USA)
Seoul, South Korea, 29 Sept 1988
**400 m:** 47.60
Marita Koch (GDR)
Canberra, Australia, 6 Oct 1985
**800 m:** 1:53.28
Jarmila Kratochvílová (Czechoslovakia)
Munich, Germany, 26 July 1983
**1,000 m:** 2:28.98
Svetlana Masterkova (Russia)
Brussels, Belgium, 23 Aug 1996
**1,500 m:** 3:50.46
Qu Yunxia (China)
Beijing, China, 11 Sept 1993

**1 mile:** 4:12.56
Svetlana Masterkova (Russia)
Zürich, Switzerland, 14 Aug 1996
**2,000 m:** 5:25.36
Sonia O'Sullivan (Ireland)
Edinburgh, UK, 8 July 1994
**3,000 m:** 8:06.11
Wang Junxia (China)
Beijing, China, 13 Sept 1993
**5,000 m:** 14:36.45
Fernanda Ribeiro (Portugal)
Hechtel, Belgium, 22 July 1995
**10,000 m:** 29:31.78
Wang Junxia (China)
Beijing, China, 8 Sept 1993
**20,000 m:** 1:06:48.8
Isumi Maki (Japan)
Amagasaki, Japan, 20 Sept 1993
**25,000 m:** 1:29:29.2
Karolina Szabo (Hungary)
Budapest, Hungary, 23 April 1988
**30,000 m:** 1:47:05.6
Karolina Szabo (Hungary)
Budapest, Hungary, 23 April 1988
**1 hour:** 18,084 m
Silvana Cruciata (Italy)
Rome, Italy, 4 May 1981
**100-m hurdles:** 12.21
Yordanka Donkova (Bulgaria)
Stara Zagora, Bulgaria, 20 Aug 1988
**400-m hurdles:** 52.61
Kim Batten (USA)
Gothenburg, Sweden, 11 Aug 1995
**4 x 100-m:** 41.37
GDR (Silke Gladisch, Sabine Rieger,
Ingrid Auerswald, Marlies Göhr)
Canberra, Australia, 6 Oct 1985
**4 x 200-m:** 1:28.15
GDR (Marlies Göhr, Romy Müller,
Bärbel Wöckel, Marita Koch)
Jena, Germany,
9 Aug 1980

**4 x 400-m:** 3:15.17
USSR (Tatyana Ledovskaya, Olga
Nazarova, Maria Pinigina, Olga
Bryzgina)
Seoul, South Korea, 1 Oct 1988
**4 x 800-m:** 7:50.17
USSR (Nadezhda Olizarenko, Lyubov
Gurina, Lyudmila Borisova, Irina
Podyalovskaya) Moscow, USSR,
5 Aug 1984

#### FIELD EVENTS

**High jump:** 2.09 m (6 ft 10¼ in)
Stefka Kostadinova (Bulgaria)
Rome, Italy, 30 Aug 1987
**Pole vault:** 4.55 m (14 ft 11 in)
Emma George (Australia)
Melbourne, Australia, 20 Feb 1997
**Long jump:** 7.52 m (24 ft 8¼ in)
Galina Chistyakova (USSR)
Leningrad, USSR, 11 June 1988
**Triple jump:** 15.50 m (50 ft 10¼ in)
Inessa Kravets (Ukraine)
Gothenburg, Sweden, 10 Aug 1995
**Shot:** 22.63 m (74 ft 3 in)
Natalya Venedictovna Lisovskaya
(USSR)
Moscow, USSR, 7 June 1987
**Discus:** 76.80 m (252 ft)
Gabriele Reinsch (GDR)
Neubrandenburg, Germany,
9 July 1988

**Hammer:** 69.58 m (228 ft 3 in)
Mihaela Melinte (Romania)
Bucharest, Romania,
11 March 1997
**Javelin:** 80.00 m (262 ft 5 in)
Petra Felke (GDR)
Potsdam, Germany, 9 Sept 1988
**Heptathlon:** 7,291 points
Jacqueline Joyner-Kersee (USA)
Seoul, South Korea, 23–24 Sept 1988:
100-m hurdles: 12.69
High jump: 1.86 m (6 ft 1¼ in)
Shot: 15.8 m (51 ft 10 in)
200 m: 22.56
Long jump: 7.27 m (23 ft 10¼ in)
Javelin: 45.66 m (149 ft 10 in)
800 m: 2:08.51

**Left**
Svetlana Masterkova
of Russia holds two
running world records.
On 14 Aug 1996, she
ran the mile in 4 min
12.56 sec in Zürich,
Switzerland, and nine
days later she set
a new world record
of 2 min 28.98 sec
for the 1,000 m in
Brussels, Belgium.

# Indoor and British athletics

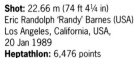

RECORD DISTANCE FOR THE TRIPLE JUMP OF 17.83 M WAS ACHIEVED BY ALLIACER

## MEN'S INDOOR RECORDS
### RUNNING
**50 m (high altitude):** 5.56*
Donovan Bailey (Canada)
Reno, Nevada, USA, 9 Feb 1996
**50 m (low altitude):** 5.61
Manfred Kokot (GDR)
Berlin, Germany, 4 Feb 1973
and James Sanford (USA)
San Diego, California, USA,
20 Feb 1981
**60 m:** 6.41*
Andre Cason (USA)
Madrid, Spain, 14 Feb 1992
**200 m:** 19.92
Frank Fredericks (Namibia)
Liévin, France, 18 Feb 1996
**400 m:** 44.63
Michael Johnson (USA)
Atlanta, Georgia, USA, 4 March 1995
**800 m:** 1:42.67
Wilson Kipketer (Denmark)

**Shot:** 22.66 m (74 ft 4¼ in)
Eric Randolph 'Randy' Barnes (USA)
Los Angeles, California, USA,
20 Jan 1989
**Heptathlon:** 6,476 points
Dan Dion O'Brien (USA),
Toronto, Canada, 13–14 March 1993:
60 m: 6.67
long jump: 7.84 m (25 ft 8½ in)
shot: 16.02 m (52 ft 6½ in)
high jump: 2.13 m (6 ft 11¾ in)
60-m hurdles: 7.85
pole vault: 5.20 m (17 ft ¾ in)
1,000 m: 2:57.96

## WOMEN'S INDOOR RECORDS
### RUNNING
**50 m:** 5.96
Irina Privalova (Russia)
Madrid, Spain, 9 Feb 1995
**60 m:** 6.92
Irina Privalova (Russia)

**50-m hurdles:** 6.58
Cornelia Oschkenat (GDR)
Berlin, Germany, 20 Feb 1988
**60-m hurdles:** 7.69*
Lyudmila Narozhilenko (Russia)
Chelyabinsk, Russia, 4 Feb 1993
**4 x 200 m:** 1:32.55
S. C. Eintracht Hamm, West Germany
(Helga Arendt, Silke-Beate Knoll,
Mechthild Kluth, Gisela Kinzel)
Dortmund, Germany, 19 Feb 1988
**4 x 400-m:** 3:26.84
Russia (Tatyana Chebykina, Olga
Goncharenko, Olga Kotlyarova,
Tatyana Alekseyeva)
Paris, France, 9 March 1997
**3,000-m walk:** 11:44.00
Alina Ivanova (Ukraine)
Moscow, Russia, 7 Feb 1992

### FIELD EVENTS
**High jump:** 2.07 m (6 ft 9½ in)

Paris, France, 9 March 1997
**1,000 m:** 2:15.26
Noureddine Morceli (Algeria)
Birmingham, W Midlands, UK,
22 Feb 1992
**1,500 m:** 3:31.18
Hicham El Gerrouj (Morocco)
Stuttgart, Germany, 2 Feb 1997
**1 mile:** 3:48.45
Hicham El Gerrouj (Morocco)
Ghent, Belgium, 12 Feb 1997
**3,000 m:** 7:30.72
Haile Gebrselassie (Ethiopia)
Stuttgart, Germany, 4 Feb 1996
**5,000 m:** 12:59.04
Haile Gebrselassie (Ethiopia)
Stockholm, Sweden, 20 Feb 1997
**50-m hurdles:** 6.25
Mark McKoy (Canada)
Kobe, Japan, 5 March 1986
**60-m hurdles:** 7.30
Colin Jackson (GB)
Sindelfingen, Germany, 6 March 1994
**4 x 200-m:** 1:22.11
United Kingdom (Linford Christie,
Darren Braithwaite, Ade Mafe,
John Regis) Glasgow, UK
3 March 1991
**4 x 400-m:** 3:03.05
Germany (Rico Lieder, Jens Carlowitz,

Karsten Just, Thomas Schönlebe)
Seville, Spain
10 March 1991
**5,000-m walk:** 18:07.08
Mikhail Shchennikov (Russia)
Moscow, Russia, 14 Feb 1995

*Ben Johnson (Canada) set a world
record for 50 m of 5.55 seconds at
Ottawa, Canada, on 31 Jan 1987 and a
60-m world record of 6.41 seconds at
Indianapolis, USA, on 7 March 1987,
but these were invalidated when he
admitted to having taken drugs
following his disqualification after the
100-m final at the 1988 Olympics.

### FIELD EVENTS
**High jump:** 2.43 m (7 ft 11½ in)
Javier Sotomayor (Cuba)
Budapest, Hungary, 4 March 1989
**Pole vault:** 6.15 m (20 ft 2¼ in)
Sergey Nazarovich Bubka (Ukraine)
Donetsk, Ukraine, 21 Feb 1993
**Long jump:** 8.79 m (28 ft 10¼ in)
Frederick Carleton 'Carl' Lewis (USA)
New York, USA, 27 Jan 1984
**Triple jump:** 17.83 m (58 ft 6 in)
Alliacer Urrutia (Cuba)
Sindelfingen, Germany, 1 March 1997

Madrid, Spain, 11 Feb 1993
and 9 Feb 1995
**200 m:** 21.87
Merlene Ottey (Jamaica)
Liévin, France, 13 Feb 1993
**400 m:** 49.59
Jarmila Kratochvílová (Czechoslovakia)
Milan, Italy, 7 March 1982
**800 m:** 1:56.40
Christine Wachtel (GDR)
Vienna, Austria, 13 Feb 1988
**1,000 m:** 2:31.23
Maria Lurdes Mutola (Mozambique)
Stockholm, Sweden, 25 Feb 1996
**1,500 m:** 4:00.27
Doina Melinte (Romania)
East Rutherford, New Jersey, USA
9 Feb 1990
**1 mile:** 4:17.14
Doina Melinte (Romania)
East Rutherford, New Jersey, USA,
9 Feb 1990
**3,000 m:** 8:33.82
Elly van Hulst (Netherlands)
Budapest, Hungary, 4 March 1989
**5,000 m:** 15:03.17
Elizabeth McColgan (GB)
Birmingham, W Midlands, UK,
22 Feb 1992

Heike Henkel (Germany)
Karlsruhe, Germany, 9 Feb 1992
**Pole vault:** 4.40 m (14 ft 5 in)
Emma George (Australia)
Melbourne, Australia, 10 Dec 1996
Stacy Dragila (USA)
Paris, France, 9 March 1997
**Long jump:** 7.37 m (24 ft 2¼ in)
Heike Drechsler (GDR)
Vienna, Austria, 13 Feb 1988
**Triple jump:** 15.03 m (49 ft 3½ in)
Iolanda Chen (Russia)
Barcelona, Spain, 11 March 1995
**Shot:** 22.50 m (73 ft 10 in)
Helena Fibingerová (Czechoslovakia)
Jablonec, Czechoslovakia,
19 Feb 1977
**Pentathlon:** 4,991 points
Irina Belova (Russia),
Berlin, Germany, 14–15 Feb 1992:
60-m hurdles: 8.22
high jump: 1.93 m (6 ft 3¾ in)
shot: 13.25 m (50 ft 5½ in)
long jump: 6.67 m (21 ft 10½ in)
800 m: 2:10.26

* Narozhilenko recorded 7.63 sec at
Seville, Spain, on 4 Nov 1993, but was
disqualified on a positive drugs test.

# 5,000 M IN 12:59.04

## URRUTIA OF CUBA ON 1 MARCH 1997

### MEN'S BRITISH RECORDS
**RUNNING**
**100 m:** 9.87
Linford Christie
Stuttgart, Germany, 15 Aug 1993
**200 m (high altitude):** 19.87
John Paul Lyndon Regis
Sestriere, Italy, 31 July 1994
**200 m (low altitude):** 19.94
John Regis
Stuttgart, Germany, 20 Aug 1993
**400 m:** 44.37
Roger Anthony Black
Lausanne, Switzerland
3 July 1996
**800 m:** 1:41.73
Sebastian Newbold Coe
Florence, Italy, 10 June 1981
**1,000 m:** 2:12.18
Sebastian Coe
Oslo, Norway, 11 July 1981
**1,500 m:** 3:29.67
Stephen Cram
Nice, France, 16 July 1985
**1 mile:** 3:46.32
Stephen Cram
Oslo, Norway, 27 July 1985
**2,000 m:** 4:51.39
Stephen Cram
Budapest, Hungary, 4 Aug 1985
**3,000 m:** 7:32.79
David Robert Moorcroft
Crystal Palace, London, UK,
17 July 1982
**5,000 m:** 13:00.41
David Moorcroft
Oslo, Norway, 7 July 1982
**10,000 m:** 27:23.06
Eamonn Thomas Martin
Oslo, Norway, 2 July 1988
**20,000 m:** 57:28.7
Carl Edward Thackery
La Flèche, France, 31 March 1990
**25,000 m:** 1:15:22.6
Ronald Hill
Bolton, Manchester, UK, 21 July 1965
**30,000 m:** 1:31:30.4
James Noel Carroll Alder
Crystal Palace, London, UK,
5 Sept 1970
**1 hour:** 20,855 m
Carl Thackery
La Flèche, France, 31 March 1990
**110-m hurdles:** 12.91
Colin Ray Jackson
Stuttgart, Germany, 20 Aug 1993
**400-m hurdles:** 47.82
Kriss Kezie Uche Chukwu Duru Akabusi
Barcelona, Spain, 6 Aug 1992
**3,000-m steeplechase:** 8:07.96
Mark Robert Rowland
Seoul, South Korea, 30 Sept 1988
**4 x 100-m:** 37.77
National team (Colin Jackson, Anthony
Alexander Jarrett, John Regis, Linford
Christie)
Stuttgart, Germany, 22 Aug 1993
**4 x 200-m:** 1:21.29
National team (Marcus Adam, Adeoye
Mafe, Linford Christie, John Regis)
Birmingham, UK, 23 June 1989

**4 x 400-m:** 2:56.60
National team (Iwan Thomas, Jamie
Baulch, Mark Richardson, Roger Black)
Atlanta, Georgia, USA, 3 Aug 1996
**4 x 800-m:** 7:03.89
National team (Peter Elliott, Garry Peter
Cook, Stephen Cram, Sebastian Coe)
Crystal Palace, London, UK,
30 Aug 1982
**4 x 1,500-m:** 14:56.8
National team (Alan David Mottershead,
Geoffrey Michael Cooper, Stephen John
Emson, Roy Wood)
Bourges, France, 24 June 1979

### FIELD EVENTS
**High jump:** 2.37 m (7 ft 9¼ in)
Stephen James Smith
Seoul, South Korea, 20 Sept 1992
and Stuttgart, Germany, 22 Aug 1993
**High jump (indoors):** 2.38 m
(7 ft 9¾ in)
Stephen James Smith
Wuppertal, Germany, 4 Feb 1994
**Pole vault:** 5.71 m (18 ft 8¾ in)
Nick Buckfield
Birmingham, W Midlands, UK
16 June 1996
**Long jump:** 8.23 m (27 ft)
Lynn Davies
Berne, Switzerland, 30 June 1968
**Triple jump:** 18.29 m (60 ft ¼ in)
Jonathan David Edwards
Gothenburg, Sweden, 7 Aug 1995
**Shot:** 21.68 m (71 ft 1½ in)
Geoffrey Lewis Capes
Cwmbran, Torfaen, UK, 18 May 1980
**Discus:** 64.32* m (211 ft)
William Raymond Tancred
Woodford, London, UK, 10 Aug 1974
**Hammer:** 77.54 m (254 ft 5 in)
Martin Girvan
Wolverhampton, W Midlands, UK,
12 May 1984
**Javelin:** 91.46 m (300 ft 1 in)
Stephen James Backley
Auckland, New Zealand, 25 Jan 1992
**Decathlon:** 8,847 points
'Daley' Thompson
Los Angeles, USA, 8–9 Aug 1984:
100 m: 10.44
Long jump: 8.01 m (26 ft 3½ in)
Shot: 15.72 m (51 ft 7 in)
High jump: 2.03 m (6 ft 8 in)
400 m: 46.97
110-m hurdles: 14.33
Discus: 46.56 m (152 ft 9 in)
Pole vault: 5.00 m (16 ft 4¾ in)
Javelin: 65.24 m (214 ft)
1,500 m: 4:35.00

*William Tancred threw 64.94 m
(213 ft 1 in) at Loughborough, Leics,
UK, on 21 July 1974 and Richard
Charles Slaney threw 65.16 m
(213 ft 9 in) at Eugene, Oregon,
USA, on 1 July 1985, but these
records were not ratified.

### WOMEN'S BRITISH RECORDS
**RUNNING**
**100 m:** 11.10
Kathryn Jane Smallwood (later Cook)
Rome, Italy, 5 Sept 1981
**200 m:** 22.10
Kathryn Cook
Los Angeles, California, USA,
9 Aug 1984
**400 m:** 49.43
Kathryn Cook
Los Angeles, California, USA,
6 Aug 1984
**800 m:** 1:57.42
Kirsty Margaret McDermott
Belfast, UK, 24 June 1985
**1,000 m:** 2:32.55
Kelly Holmes
Sheffield, S Yorkshire, 15 June 1997
**1,500 m:** 3:59.96
Zola Budd
Brussels, Belgium, 30 Aug 1985

**1 mile:** 4:17.57
Zola Budd
Zürich, Switzerland, 21 Aug 1985
**2,000 m:** 5:26.93
Yvonne Carol Grace Murray
Edinburgh, UK, 8 July 1994
**3,000 m:** 8:28.83
Zola Budd
Rome, Italy, 7 Sept 1985
**5,000 m:** 14:46.76
Paula Radcliffe
Cologne, Germany
16 Aug 1996
**10,000 m:** 30:57.07
Elizabeth McColgan
Hengelo, Netherlands,
25 June 1991
**100-m hurdles:** 12.80
Angela Thorp
Atlanta, Georgia, USA
31 July 1996
**400-m hurdles:** 52.74
Sally Gunnell
Stuttgart, Germany, 19 Aug 1993
**4 x 100-m:** 42.43
Regina Hunte, Kathryn Smallwood,
Beverley Goddard, Sonia Lannaman

Moscow, USSR, 1 Aug 1980
**4 x 200-m:** 1:31.57
Donna-Marie Hartley, Verona Elder,
Sharon Colyear, Sonia Lannaman
Crystal Palace, London, UK, 20 Aug 1977
**4 x 400-m:** 3:22.01
National team (Phyllis Smith, Lorraine I.
Hanson, Linda Keough, Sally Gunnell)
Tokyo, Japan, 1 Sept 1991
**4 x 800-m:** 8:19.9
National team (Ann Margaret Williams,
Paula Tracy Fryer, Yvonne Murray,
Diane Delores Edwards)
Sheffield, S Yorkshire, UK, 5 June 1992

### FIELD EVENTS
**High jump:** 1.95 m (6 ft 4¾ in)
Diana Clare Elliot
Oslo, Norway, 26 June 1982
**Pole vault:** 4.03 m (13 ft 2½ in)
Janine Whitlock
Leeds, W Yorkshire, 15 June 1997

**Long jump:** 6.90 m (22 ft 7¾ in)
Beverly Kinch
Helsinki, Finland, 14 Aug 1983
**Triple jump:** 14.78 m (48 ft 5 ¾ in)
Ashia Hansen
Sheffield, S Yorkshire, UK, 25 Aug 1996
**Shot:** 19.36 m (63 ft 6¼ in)
Judith Miriam Oakes
Gateshead, UK, 14 Aug 1988
**Hammer:** 64.90 m (212 ft 11 in)
Lorraine Anne Shaw
Bedford, UK, 10 June 1995
**Discus:** 67.48 m (221 ft 5 in)
Margaret Elizabeth Ritchie
Walnut, California, USA, 26 April 1981
**Javelin:** 77.44 m (254 ft 1 in)
Fatima Whitbread
Stuttgart, Germany, 28 Aug 1986
**Heptathlon:** 6,645 points
Denise Lewis
Götzis, Austria, 25–26 May 1996:
100-m hurdles: 13.18
High jump: 1.84 m (6 ft ¼ in)
Shot: 14.36 m (47 ft 1¼ in)
200 m: 24.06
Long jump: 6.60 m (21 ft 7¾ in)
Javelin: 47.86 m (157 ft)
800 m: 2:16.84

**Below left**
On 25 June 1991,
Liz McColgan set the
British record for
the 10,000 m in a
time of 30:57.07 at
Hengelo, Netherlands.

## WILSON KIPKETER RAN A RECORD 1:42.67 IN THE 800 M IN 1997

# Running and walking

## Marathon

### Oldest

The Boston marathon, the oldest major marathon, was first held on 19 April 1897, when it was run over 39 km (24 miles 1,232 yd).

### Fastest

It should be noted that courses may vary in severity. The following are the best times recorded, on all courses whose distance has been verified.

The men's world record is 2 hr 6 min 50 sec, by Belayneh Dinsamo (Ethiopia) at Rotterdam, Netherlands, on 17 April 1988.

The women's world record is 2 hr 21 min 6 sec, by Ingrid Kristiansen (Norway) at London on 21 April 1985.

The British men's record is 2 hr 7 min 13 sec, by Stephen Henry Jones at Chicago, Illinois, USA, on 20 Oct 1985.

The British women's record is 2 hr 25 min 56 sec, by Véronique Marot at London, UK, on 23 April 1989.

### Most competitors

A record 38,706 runners finished the centennial Boston race on 15 April 1996.

### Most run by an individual

Horst Preisler (Germany) has run 631 marathons of 42 km 195 m (26 miles 385 yd) or longer from 1974 to 29 May 1996.

Henri Girault (France) has run 330 races at 100 km (62 miles) from 1979 to June 1996 and completed a run on every continent except Antarctica.

John A. Kelley (USA) finished the Boston Marathon 61 times from 1928 to 1992. He won in 1933 and 1945.

### Oldest finishers

The oldest man to run a marathon was Dimitrion Yordanidis (Greece), aged 98, in Athens, Greece on 10 Oct 1976, finishing in 7 hr 33 min.

Thelma Pitt-Turner (New Zealand) set the women's record in Aug 1985, completing the Hastings Marathon in New Zealand in 7 hr 58 min, aged 82.

### Half marathon

The world best time on a properly measured course is 59 min 47 sec, by Moses Tanui (Kenya) at Milan, Italy, on 3 April 1993.

The best British time is 60 min 59 sec, by Steve Jones from Newcastle to South Shields, Tyne & Wear, UK, on 8 June 1986.

Paul Evans ran a half marathon in 60 min 9 sec at Marrakech, Morocco, on 15 Jan 1995, and Ingrid Kristiansen

(Norway) ran 66 min 40 sec at Sandnes, Norway on 5 April 1987, but there is uncertainty about the distance of both courses.

Liz McColgan (GB) ran a half marathon in 67 min 11 sec at Tokyo, Japan, on 26 Jan 1992, but the course was 33 m downhill—a little more than the allowable 1 in 1,000 drop. She also ran a British best of 68 min 42 sec at Dundee, UK, on 11 Oct 1992.

## Long distance running

### Longest running race

The 1929 trans-continental race from New York City to Los Angeles, California, USA, covered 5,898 km (3,665 miles). The Finnish-born Johnny Salo won in 1929 in 79 days. His elapsed time of 525 hr 57 min 20 sec (averaging 11.21 km/h or 6.97 mph) left him only 2 min 47 sec ahead of Englishman Pietro 'Peter' Gavuzzi.

The longest annual race is the New York 1,300 Mile race, held at Ward Island Park, New York, USA. Georg Jermolajevs (Latvia) completed the race in the fastest time of 16 days 14 hr 28 min 19 sec, in Sept 1995.

### Longest runs

Robert Sweetgall (USA) ran 17,071 km (10,608 miles) around the edge of the USA, starting and finishing his circuit in Washington DC, from 9 Oct 1982 to 15 July 1983.

In 1983 Ron Grant (Australia) ran around Australia, covering 13,383 km (8,316 miles) in 217 days 3 hr 45 min.

Max Telford (NZ) ran 8,224 km (5,110 miles) from Anchorage, Alaska, USA, to Halifax, Nova Scotia, Canada, in 106 days 18 hr 45 min from 25 July to 9 Nov 1977.

Al Howie (GB) ran across Canada, from St Johns to Victoria, covering 7,295.5 km (4,533.2 miles), in 72 days 10 hr 23 min, in Sept 1991.

### Greatest mileage

Douglas Alistair Gordon Pirie (GB), who set five world records in the 1950s, estimated that he had run a total distance of 347,600 km (216,000 miles) in 40 years to 1981.

Dr Ron Hill, the 1969 European and 1970 Commonwealth marathon champion, has trained every day since 20 Dec 1964. His training log book shows a total of 211,765 km (131,585 miles) from 3 Sept 1956 to 20 May 1996. He has finished 115 marathons, all sub 2:52 (except his last) and has raced in 57 countries.

### Mass relay records

The 160.9-km (100-mile) record by 100 runners is 7 hr 53 min 52.1 sec

by Baltimore Road Runners Club, Towson, Maryland, USA, in May 1981.

The women's best is 9 hr 49 min 8 sec by the Houston Area Road Runners Association, Texas, USA, in Aug 1996.

The 100 x 100 m record is 19 min 14.19 sec by a team from Antwerp at Merksem, Belgium, on 23 Sept 1989.

The longest relay was 17,391 km (10,806 miles). It was run on Highway No. 1 in Australia by 23 runners of the Melbourne Fire Brigade, in 50 days 43 min from 6 Aug to 25 Sept 1991.

The greatest distance covered in 24 hours by a team of 10 is 487.343 km (302 miles 495 yd) by Puma Tyneside RC at Monkton Stadium, Jarrow, UK, on 10–11 Sept 1994.

## Cross-country running

### World Championships

The greatest ever margin of victory is 56 seconds or 356 m (390 yd) by John 'Jack' Thomas Holden (England) at Ayr Racecourse, S Ayrshire, Scotland, UK, on 24 March 1934.

### Most team wins

The record for most team victories is held by England with 45 for men, 11 for junior men and seven for women.

The USA and USSR each has a record eight women's team victories.

### Most individual wins

The greatest number of men's individual victories is five, by John Ngugi (Kenya), from 1986 to 1989 and in 1992.

The women's race has been won five times by Doris Brown-Heritage (USA), from 1967 to 1971; and by Grete Waitz (Norway), from 1978 to 1981 and in 1983.

## Most appearances

Marcel van de Wattyne (Belgium) ran in 20 races, from 1946 to 1965.

The women's record is 16 by Jean Lochhead (Wales), from 1967 to 1979, in 1981 and from 1983 to 1984.

### English Championship

The most individual titles is four by Percy Stenning (Thames Hare and Hounds) in 1877–80 and Alfred Shrubb (South London Harriers) in 1901–04.

The most successful club in the team race has been Birchfield Harriers from Birmingham with 28 wins and one tie between 1880 and 1988.

The most individual wins in the English women's championships is six by Lillian Styles, 1928–30, 1933–34 and 1937.

The most successful team in the women's championship is Birchfield Harriers with 13 titles.

### Largest field

The largest recorded field in any cross-country race was 11,763 starters (10,810 finished) in the 30-km (18-mile 1,125-yd) Lidingöloppet,near Stockholm, Sweden, on 3 Oct 1982.

## Orienteering

### Most titles

The men's world relay has been won a record seven times by Norway, in 1970, 1978, 1981, 1983, 1985, 1987 and 1989.

Sweden have won the women's relay a record 10 times in 1966, 1970, 1974, 1976, 1981, 1983, 1985, 1989, 1991 and 1993.

The record for the greatest number of women's titles in orienteering is three, by Annichen Kringstad (Sweden), in 1981, 1983 and 1985.

**Right**
Moses Tanui of Kenya winning the 100th Boston marathon (USA), the world's longest-lasting major marathon. Tanui holds the record for the fastest time for a half marathon, at 59 min 47 sec, at Milan, Italy, in 1993.

# OLDEST MARATHON RUNNER 98 YEARS

## 10 HOURS 23 MIN

The greatest number of men's titles won by one person is two, by Åge Hadler (Norway), in 1966 and 1972; Egil Johansen (Norway), in 1976 and 1978; Øyvin Thon (Norway), in 1979 and 1981; and Jorgen Martensson (Sweden) in 1991 and 1995.

Carol McNeill won the women's British title six times, in 1967, 1969, and from 1972 to 1976.

Geoffrey Peck won the men's individual British title a record five times, in 1971, 1973, 1976, 1977 and 1979.

Terry Dooris of Southern Navigators has competed in all 31 British individual championships from 1967 to 1997.

### Most competitors
The most competitors at an event in one day is 38,000 for the Ruf des Herbstes at Sibiu, Romania, in 1982.

The largest event is the five-day Swedish O-Ringen at Småland, which attracted 120,000 in July 1983.

### Walking
#### Most Olympic medals
The only walker to win three gold medals has been Ugo Frigerio (Italy) with the 3,000 m in 1920, and 10,000 m in 1920 and 1924.

Ugo Frigerio also holds the record for most medals with four (he won the bronze medal at 50,000 m in 1932). He shares this with Vladimir Stepanovich Golubnichiy (USSR), who won gold medals for the 20 km in 1960 and 1968, the silver in 1972 and the bronze in 1964.

The record for gold medals by a British walker is two, by George Larner for the 3,500 m and the 10 miles in 1908.

The greatest number of medals won by a British walker is three, by Ernest James, who finished second three times—twice when Larner won the gold and in 1912 for the 10,000 m.

### Most titles
Four-time Olympian, Ronald Owen Laird of the New York AC, won a total of 65 US national titles from 1958 to 1976, plus four Canadian Championships.

The greatest number of British national titles won by a British walker is 27 by Vincent Paul Nihill from 1963 to 1975.

### 24 hours
The greatest distance walked in 24 hours is 228.930 km (142 miles 440 yd) by Jesse Castenda (USA) at

Albuquerque, New Mexico, USA, on 18–19 Sept 1976.

The best by a woman is 211.25 km (131.27 miles) by Annie van der Meer-Timmermann (Netherlands) at Rouen, France, on 10–11 May 1986.

### ULTRA LONG-DISTANCE (TRACK)

**MEN**
**50 km:** 2:48:06
Jeff Norman (GB)
Timperley, Manchester, UK,
7 June 1980
**50 miles:** 4:51:49
Don Ritchie (GB)
Hendon, London, UK, 12 March 1983
**100 km:** 6:10:20
Don Ritchie (GB)
Crystal Palace, London, UK,
28 Oct 1978
**100 miles:** 11:30:51
Don Ritchie (GB)
Crystal Palace, London, UK,
15 Oct 1977
**200 km:** 15:11:10*
Yiannis Kouros (Greece)
Montauban, France,
15–16 March 1985
**200 miles:** 27:48:35
Yiannis Kouros (Greece)
Montauban, France,
15–16 March 1985
**500 km:** 60:23:00
Yiannis Kouros (Greece)
Colac, Australia, 26–29 Nov 1984
**500 miles:** 105:42:09
Yiannis Kouros (Greece)
Colac, Australia, 26–30 Nov 1984
**1,000 km:** 136:17:00
Yiannis Kouros (Greece)
Colac, Australia, 26 Nov–1 Dec 1984
**24 hours** 295.030 km
Yiannis Kouros (Australia)
Canberra, Australia, 1–2 March 1997
**48 hours:** 473.496 km
Yiannis Kouros (Australia)
Surgères, France, 3–5 May 1996
**Six days:** 1,022.068 km
Yiannis Kouros (Greece)
New York, USA, 2–8 July 1984
**Six days (indoors):** 1,030 km
Jean-Gilles Bossiquet (France)
La Rochelle, France, 16–23 Nov 1992
**WOMEN**
**50 km:** 3:18:52
Carolyn Hunter-Rowe (GB)
Barry, Vale of Glamorgan, UK,
3 March 1996
**50 miles:** 6:07:58
Linda Meadows (Australia)
Burwood, Australia, 18 June 1994
**100 km:** 7:50:09
Ann Trason (USA)
Hayward, California, USA,
3–4 Aug 1991
**100 miles:** 14:29:44
Ann Trason (USA)
Santa Rosa, California, USA,
18–19 March 1989

**200 km:** 19:28:48*
Eleanor Adams (GB)
Melbourne, Australia, 19–20 Aug 1989
**200 miles:** 39:09:03
Hilary Walker (GB)
Blackpool, Lancashire, UK,
5–6 Nov 1988
**500 km:** 77:53:46
Eleanor Adams (GB)
Colac, Australia, 13–15 Nov 1989
**500 miles:** 130:59:58
Sandra Barwick (New Zealand)
Campbelltown, Australia,
18–23 Nov 1990
**One hour:** 18.084 km
Silvana Cruciata (Italy)
Rome, Italy, 4 May 1981
**24 hours:** 240.169 km
Eleanor Adams (GB)
Melbourne, Australia, 19–20 Aug 1989
**48 hours:** 366.512 km
Hilary Walker (GB)

Blackpool, Lancashire, UK,
5–7 Nov 1988
**Six days:** 883.631 km
Sandra Barwick (New Zealand)
Campbelltown, Australia,
18–24 Nov 1990
*No stopped time known.

### TRACK-WALKING WORLD
The International Amateur Athletic Federation (IAAF) recognizes men's records at 20 km, 30 km, 50 km and two hours. The body also recognises women's records at 5 km and 10 km.

**MEN**
**10 km:** 38:02.60
Jozef Pribilinec (Czechoslovakia)
Banská Bystrica, Czechoslovakia,
30 Aug 1985
**20 km:** 1:17:25.6
Bernardo Segura (Mexico)
Fana, Norway, 7 May 1994
**30 km:** 2:01:44.1
Maurizio Damilano (Italy)
Cuneo, Italy, 4 Oct 1992

**50 km:** 3:40:57.9
Thierry Toutain (France)
Héricourt, France, 29 Sept 1996
**One hour:** 15,577 m
Bernardo Segura (Mexico)
Fana, Norway, 7 May 1994
**Two hours:** 29,572 m
Maurizio Damilano (Italy)
Cuneo, Italy, 4 Oct 1992

**WOMEN**
**3 km:** 11:48.24
Ileana Salvador (Italy)
Padua, Italy, 19 Aug 1993
**5 km:** 20:07.52 (unratified)
Beate Anders (GDR)
Rostock, Germany, 23 June 1990
**5 km:** 20:13.26
Kerry Saxby-Junna (Australia)
Hobart, Australia, 25 Feb 1996
**10 km:** 41:56.23
Nadezhda Ryashkina (USSR)

Seattle, Washington, USA,
24 July 1990

### WALKING
It should be noted that severity of road race courses and the accuracy of their measurement may vary. This sometimes makes comparisons of times unreliable.

**MEN**
**30 km:** 2:02:41
Andrey Perlov (USSR)
Sochi, USSR, 19 Feb 1989
**50 km:** 3:37:41
Andrey Perlov (USSR)
Leningrad, USSR, 5 Aug 1989
**WOMEN**
**10 km:** 41:04
Yelena Nikolayeva (Russia)
Sochi, Russia, 20 April 1996
**20 km:** 1:27:30
Liu Hongyu (China)
Beijing, China, 1 May 1995
**50 km:** 4:41:57
Kora Boufflert (France)
Ay-Champagne, France, 17 Sept 1995

**Below left**
Ingrid Kristiansen of Norway runs past the Tower of London, UK, in 1985 on her way to breaking the women's record for a marathon. She finished in a time of 2 hr 21 min 6 sec.

# Gymnastics and stamina

## Gymnastics
### World Championships
The most women's titles won in the World Championships (including Olympic Games) is 12 individual wins and six team wins by Larisa Semyonovna Latynina of the USSR, between 1954 and 1964.

The USSR won the team title on 21 occasions (11 world and 10 Olympics).

The highest number of individual men's gymnastics titles is 13, by Vitaliy Scherbo (Belarus) from 1992 to 1995; he also won a team gold in 1992. Boris Anfiyanovich Shakhlin (USSR) won 10 individual titles from 1954 to 1964 but also had three team wins.

The USSR won the team title a record 13 times (eight World Championships, five Olympics) from 1952 to 1992.

Aurelia Dobre (Romania) won the women's overall world title when she was 14 years 352 days at Rotterdam, Netherlands, on 23 Oct 1987.

Daniela Silivas (Romania) revealed in 1990 that she was born on 9 May 1971, a year later than previously claimed, so that she was 14 years 185 days when she won the gold medal for balance beam on 10 Nov 1985.

The youngest male world champion was Dmitriy Bilozerchev (USSR) at 16 years 315 days at Budapest, Hungary, on 28 Oct 1983.

### Olympics
The men's team title has been won a record five times by both Japan (1960, 1964, 1968, 1972 and 1976) and the USSR (1952, 1956, 1980, 1988 and 1992). The USSR won the women's title 10 times (1952–80, 1988 and 1992). The successes in 1992 were by the Unified team from the republics of the former USSR.

The most men's individual gold medals is six by: Boris Shakhlin (USSR), one in 1956, four (two shared) in 1960 and one in 1964; and Nikolay Yefimovich Andrianov (USSR), one in 1972, four in 1976 and one in 1980.

Vera Caslavska-Odlozil representing Czechoslovakia won seven women's individual gold medals, three in 1964 and four (one shared) in 1968.

Larisa Latynina (USSR) won nine gold medals (six individual and three in winning teams) from 1956–64 and also five silver and four bronze, making 18 medals in all—an Olympic record.

The most medals won by a male gymnast is 15 (seven gold, five silver and three bronze) by Nikolay Andrianov (USSR) between 1972–80.

Aleksandr Nikolayevich Dityatin (USSR) is the only man to win a medal in all eight categories in the same Games, with three gold, four silver and one bronze at Moscow in 1980.

### Perfect scores
Hans Eugster (Switzerland) achieved a perfect score of 10.00 in the compulsory parallel bars at the 1950 World Championships.

Nadia Comaneci (Romania) was the first to get a perfect score (10.00) in the Olympics, and scored 10.00 seven times at Montreal, Canada, in 1976.

### Youngest international
Pasakevi 'Voula' Kouna was 9 years 299 days at the start of the Balkan Games at Serres, Greece, on 1 Oct 1981, when she represented Greece.

### British Championships
Arthur John Whitford won the British Gymnastic Championship a record 10 times, in 1928–36 and 1939. He was also in four winning teams. Wray 'Nik' Stuart equalled the record of nine successive wins, 1956–64.

The women's record for championships is eight, by Mary Patricia Hirst (1947, 1949–50 and 1952–56).

Jackie Brady uniquely won all the apparatus titles and the overall title in the same year, 1993.

Sharon Taylor won the most overall titles in Modern Rhythmic Gymnastics, with five successive wins, 1977–81.

### World Cup
Two World Cup overall titles have been won by three men: Nikolay Andrianov (USSR), Aleksandr Dityatin (USSR) and Li Ning (China), and one woman: Maria Yevgenyevna Filatova (USSR).

### Rhythmic Sportive Gymnastics
The most overall individual world titles in rhythmic gymnastics is three, by Maria Gigova (Bulgaria), in 1969, 1971 and 1973 and Maria Petrova (Bulgaria), in 1993, 1994 and 1995.

Bulgaria has a record nine team titles: 1969, 1971, 1981, 1983, 1985, 1987, 1989, 1993 and 1995. In 1987 Bianka Panova (Bulgaria) won all four apparatus gold medals with maximum scores, and won a team gold.

At the 1988 Olympic Games Marina Lobach (USSR) won the rhythmic gymnastic title with perfect scores in all six disciplines.

### Somersaults
Ashrita Furman performed 8,341 forward rolls in a time of 10 hr 30 min

covering a distance of 19.67 km (12 miles 390 yards) from Lexington to Charleston, Massachusetts, USA, on 30 April 1986.

Furman also completed a mile of forward rolls in a record time of 26 min 25 sec at The Mall, Washington DC, USA, in Nov 1995.

Vitaliy Scherbo (Belarus) backwards somersaulted 50 m (54 yd) in 10.22 seconds at Makuhar Messe Event Hall, Chiba, Japan, on 31 Aug 1995.

### Trampolining
#### Most titles
The most World Championship titles ever won is nine, by Judy Wills (USA), a record five individual 1964–68, two pairs 1966–67 and two tumbling 1965–66.

The men's record is five, by Aleksandr Moskalenko (Russia), three individual 1990–94 and two pairs 1992–94.

Brett Austine (Australia) won three individual titles on the double mini trampoline between 1982–86.

A record nine British titles have been won by Sue Challis (1980–82, 1984–85, 1987, 1990, 1992–93).

Stewart Matthews has won five men's trampolining titles (1976–80).

### Youngest British international
Andrea Holmes competed at 12 years 131 days in the World Championships at Montana, USA, on 13 May 1982.

## Modern pentathlon
### Most titles
András Balczó (Hungary) won a record number of world titles, six individual and seven team. He won the world individual title in 1963, 1965–67 and 1969 and the Olympic title in 1972. His seven team titles (1960–70) comprised five world and two Olympic.

The USSR has won a record 14 world and four Olympic team titles.

Hungary has won a record four Olympic team titles in the modern pentathlon and 10 world titles.

Poland has won a record seven women's world team titles: 1985, 1988–92, 1995.

Great Britain has won three world titles, 1981–83, and three World Cups, 1978–80.

Eva Fjellerup (Denmark) has won the women's individual pentathlon title three times, 1990–91, 1993.

### Olympics
The greatest number of gold medals won is three, by András Balczó a

# 8,794 ONE-ARM PRESS-UPS IN 5 HOURS

member of the winning Hungarian team in 1960 and 1968, and the 1972 individual champion.

Lars Hall (Sweden) has uniquely won two individual championships (1952 and 1956).

Pavel Serafimovich Lednyev (USSR) has won a record seven medals (two team gold, one team silver, one individual silver, three individual bronze), 1968–80.

The best British individual placing is by Jeremy Robert 'Jim' Fox, fourth in 1972, and Richard Lawson Phelps, fourth in 1984.

The best British result is the team gold medal in 1976 by Jim Fox, Adrian Philip Parker and Daniel Nightingale.

The most women's titles is two: Anfissa Restzova of Russia, (7.5 km 1992, 4 x 7.5 km in 1994); and Myriam Bédard of Canada, (7.5 km, 15 km in 1994).

**World Championships**
Frank Ullrich (GDR) has won a record six individual world titles, four at 10 km, 1978–81, and two at 20 km, 1982–83.

Aleksandr Tikhonov was in 10 winning Soviet relay teams, from 1968 to 1980, and won four individual titles.

The Biathlon World Cup was won four times by Frank Ullrich, 1978 and 1980–82; and Franz Peter Rötsch (GDR), 1984–85 and 1987–88.

The most individual women's titles is three, by Anne-Elinor Elvebakk

The most wins in the men's race is six, by Dave Scott (USA), 1980, 1982–84 and 1986–87 and Mark Allen (USA), 1989–93, 1995.

The fastest time recorded over the Ironman distances is 7 hr 57 min 2 sec, by Lothar Leider (Germany) at Roth, Germany, on 14 July 1996.

The women's record over the Ironman distances is 8 hr 55 min, by Paula Newby-Fraser at Roth, Germany, in July 1992.

Julian Jenkinson (UK) recorded 8 hr 15 min 21 sec over the Ironman distances at Juma, Germany in 1995.

Paula Newby-Fraser has a record four women's wins, 1989–92.

The men's race record of 5 hr 46 min 10 sec was set by Mark Allen in 1986.

The women's race record of 6 hr 27 min 6 sec was set by Erin Baker (New Zealand) in 1988 .

**Speed and stamina**
**Press-ups—1 year**
1,500,230, by Paddy Doyle, from Oct 1988 to Oct 1989.

**Press-ups (push-ups)—24 hours**
46,001, by Charles Servizio in Fontana, California, USA, on 24–25 April 1993.

**Below**
Mark Allen has won the 'World Championship' held annually in Nice a record 10 times. He also holds the race record, completing the course's gruelling 3,200-km swim, 120-km cycle and 32-km run in 5 hr 46 min.

## PENTATHLON GOLD MEDALS, TWO AS A TEAM MEMBER AND ONE INDIVIDUALLY

Probably the greatest margin of victory was by William Oscar Guernsey Grut (Sweden) in the 1948 Games, when he won three events and was placed fifth and eighth in the other two.

Richard Phelps has achieved eleven British titles, 1979, 1981–84, 1986, 1988, 1990–91, 1993 and 1995.

Wendy Norman, has won a record seven British women's titles, 1978–80, 1982, 1986–88.

### Biathlon
**Olympics**
Two men's Olympic individual titles have been won by Magnar Solberg (Norway), in 1968 and 1972, and Frank-Peter Rötsch (GDR) at both 10 km and 20 km in 1988.

Aleksandr Ivanovich Tikhonov (USSR) won four relay gold medals, from 1968 to 1980 and also won a silver in 1968 in the 20 km.

(Norway), in the 10 km in 1988, and the 7.5 km from 1989 to 1990.

Kaya Parve (USSR) has won six titles, two individual and four relay, from 1984 to 1986, and in 1988.

### Triathlon
**Hawaii ironman**
Distances for each of the phases can vary, but for the best established event, the Hawaii Ironman (instituted 1978), competitors first swim 3.8 km (2.4 miles), then cycle 180 km (112 miles), and finally run a full marathon of 42.195 km (26 miles 385 yards).

The record times for the Hawaii Ironman are: (men) 8 hr 4 min 8 sec, by Luc van Lierde (Belgium) in 1996; (women) 8 hr 55 min 28 sec by Paula Newby-Fraser (Zimbabwe) in 1992.

The most wins in the women's race is eight, by Paula Newby-Fraser, 1986, 1988–89, 1991–94 and 1996.

**World Championships**
The internationally recognized distances for the world championship are a 1,500-m swim, a 40-km cycle ride and a 10-km run.

The annual race has been won three times by Simon Lessing (UK), 1992, 1995 and 1996.

The most wins in the women's event is two by Michelle Jones (Australia), 1992–93, and Karen Smyers (USA), 1990 and 1995.

**'World Championship' in Nice**
A 'World Championship' race has been held annually in Nice, France since 1982; the distances are 3,200 m (swim), 120 km (cycle) and 32 km (run). The swimming distance was increased to 4,000 m in 1988.

Mark Allen (USA) has won the race 10 times, from 1982 to 1986, and from 1989 to 1993.

**Press-ups (one arm)—5 hours**
8,794, by Paddy Doyle in Birmingham, W Midlands, UK, on 12 Feb 1996.

**Press-ups (finger tip)—5 hours**
8,200, by Terry Cole in Walthamstow, Greater London, UK, on 11 May 1996.

**Press-ups (1 finger)—consecutive**
124, by Paul Lynch at the Hippodrome, Leicester Square, London, UK, in 1992.

**Squat thrusts—1 hour**
3,552, by Paul Wai Man Chung at the Yee Gin Kung Fu of Chung Sze Health (HK) Association, Kowloon, Hong Kong, on 21 Aug 1992.

**Burpees—1 hour**
1,840, by Paddy Doyle in Polesworth, Birmingham, UK, in Feb 1994.

**Double leg circles (pommel horse)**
97, by Tyler Farstad in Surrey, British Columbia, Canada, on 27 Nov 1993.

# Football

**Below far right**
Paul Gascoigne celebrates Glasgow Rangers' victory in the Scottish League Championship. Rangers have won the Scottish league a record 47 times.

**Below right**
Lothar Matthäus lifts the World Cup after Germany won the final in 1990. He played in a record 21 games in the World Cup finals tournament between 1982 and 1994.

## The World Cup
### Most team wins
Brazil has won the World Cup four times; 1958, 1962, 1970 and 1994.

### Most team appearances
Brazil are the only team to have taken part in all 15 finals tournaments. France and the USA are the only two nations to have entered all World Cup competitions.

### Most goals in a game
The record for the most goals in one game was set in a qualifying match on 2 June 1997 when Iran beat the Maldives 17–0.

The highest score during the final stages was achieved by Hungary in a 10–1 win over El Salvador at Elche, Spain, on 15 June 1982.

Pelé (Brazil) is the only player to have been with three World Cup-winning teams, in 1958, 1962 and 1970.

### Youngest and oldest players
The youngest ever to play in a finals match is Norman Whiteside, who played for Northern Ireland v. Yugoslavia aged 17 years 41 days on 17 June 1982.

The oldest is Albert Roger Milla for Cameroon v. Russia on 28 June 1994, aged 42 years 39 days.

### Most individual goals
Oleg Salenko scored five goals in Russia's 6–1 win v. Cameroon at Palo Alto, California, USA, on 28 June 1994.

The most goals in a tournament is 13, by Just Fontaine (France) in 1958.

the lack of nets and the consequent waste of retrieval time. Seven further goals were disallowed for offside.

The highest margin ever recorded in a full international match is 17, when England beat Australia 17–0 at Sydney, NSW, Australia, on 30 June 1951, though this match is not listed by England as a full international; and when Iran beat the Maldives 17–0 at Damascus, Syria, on 2 June 1997 in a World Cup qualifying match.

The highest score between English clubs in any major competition is 26, when Preston North End beat Hyde 26–0 in an FA Cup tie at Deepdale, Lancs, on 15 Oct 1887.

The highest score by one side in a Football League (First Division) match

## League Championships
### Most national championships
The record number of successive national league championships is 10, by Dinamo Berlin, from 1979 to 1988.

CSKA, Sofia (Bulgaria), holds a European post-war record of 26 league titles, including two under the name CFKA Sredets (re-named CSKA).

### English
The most League Championships (First Division) is 18, by Liverpool (1901, 1906, 1922–3, 1947, 1964, 1966, 1973, 1976–7, 1979–80, 1982–4, 1986, 1988 and 1990).

The record number of wins in a season is 33 from 42 matches, by Doncaster Rovers in Third Division (North) in 1946/7.

The highest match aggregate in the finals tournament is 12, when Austria beat Switzerland 7–5, at Lausanne, Switzerland, on 26 June 1954.

### Most goals in a tournament
The greatest number in a single finals tournament is 27 (five games) by Hungary in 1954.

Brazil have scored the most overall—159 in 73 matches.

### Most individual appearances
Antonio Carbajal is the only player to have appeared in five World Cup finals tournaments, as goalkeeper for Mexico in 11 games in 1950, 1954, 1958, 1962 and 1966.

The most games in finals tournaments is 21, by: Uwe Seeler for West Germany, 1958–70; Wladyslaw Zmuda for Poland, 1974–86; Diego Armando Maradona for Argentina, 1982–94; and Lothar Matthäus for Germany, 1982–94.

Fontaine, Jaïrzinho (Brazil) and Alcide Ghiggia (Uruguay) are the only players to have scored in every match in a final series. Jaïrzinho scored seven in six games in 1970 and Ghiggia scored four in four games in 1950.

Gerd Müller scored 10 goals in 1970 and four in 1974 for the record aggregate of 14 goals.

The most goals scored in a final is three, by Geoffrey Hurst for England v. West Germany on 30 July 1966.

Three players have scored in two finals: Vava (real name Edevaldo Izito Neto) (Brazil) in 1958 and 1962, Pelé in 1958 and 1970; and Paul Breitner (West Germany) in 1974 and 1982.

### First-class team records
#### Highest scores
The highest score in a first-class match was Arbroath's 36–0 Scottish Cup win over Bon Accord on 5 Sept 1885. The score would have been higher but for

is 12, by: West Bromwich Albion, who beat Darwen 12–0 on 4 April 1892; Nottingham Forest, who beat Leicester Fosse 12–0 at Nottingham on 21 April 1909; and Aston Villa, who beat Accrington 12–2 on 12 March 1892.

The highest aggregate in League Football was 17 goals, in Tranmere Rovers' 13–4 win over Oldham Athletic on 26 Dec 1935.

The record margin in a League match was 13, in Newcastle United's 13–0 defeat of Newport County on 5 Oct 1946 and in Stockport County's 13–0 defeat of Halifax Town on 6 Jan 1934.

### Most goals in a season
In a professional league, the most goals by a British team is 142 in 34 matches, by Raith Rovers (Scottish Second Division) in 1937/8.

The English League record is 134 in 46 matches by Peterborough United (Fourth Division) in 1960/61.

The First Division record is 31 wins from 42 matches, by Tottenham Hotspur in 1960/1.

In 1893/4 Liverpool won 22 and drew six in 28 Second Division games. They also won the promotion match.

The most points in a season under the current system is 102 from 46 matches, by Swindon in the Fourth Division in 1985/6. Under the new system the First Division record is Liverpool's 98 in 1978/9.

The only FA Cup and League Championship 'doubles' are those of Preston North End in 1889, Aston Villa in 1897, Tottenham Hotspur in 1961, Arsenal in 1971, Liverpool in 1986 and Manchester United in 1994 and 1996.

### Scottish
Glasgow Rangers have won the Scottish League Championship 47 times between 1891 and 1997. Their 76 points in the 1920/1 Scottish First

# HIGHEST WORLD CUP SCORE 10-1

Division (from a possible 84) is a record for any division. A better percentage was achieved by Rangers in 1898/9 when they gained the maximum of 36 by winning all their 18 matches.

## Cup competitions
### FA Cup
The most wins is nine, by Manchester United in 1909, 1948, 1963, 1977, 1983, 1985, 1990, 1994 and 1996.

The most goals in a final was in Blackburn Rovers' 6-1 defeat of Sheffield Wednesday in 1890 and Blackpool's 4-3 defeat of Bolton Wanderers in 1953.

The biggest margin of victory was in Bury's 6-0 defeat of Derby County in 1903.

### Youngest FA Cup players
The youngest player in an FA Cup final was James Prinsep for Clapham Rovers v. Old Etonians on 29 March 1879, aged 17 years 245 days.

The youngest goal-scorer in an FA Cup final was Norman Whiteside for Manchester United v. Brighton, at 18 years 19 days on 26 May 1983.

The youngest FA Cup player, Andrew Awford, was 15 years 88 days when he played for Worcester City on 10 Oct 1987.

### Most medals
The most FA Cup-winners' medals is five, by: James Henry Forrest in 1884-86, 1890-91; the Hon. Sir Arthur Fitzgerald Kinnaird in 1873, 1877-78, 1879, 1882; and Charles Harold Reynolds in 1872-73 and 1876-78.

The most Scottish Cup-winners' medals won is eight, by Charles Campbell (Queen's Park), 1874-76, 1880-82, 1884 and 1886.

### Scottish FA Cup
The greatest number of wins is 30, by Celtic in 1892, 1899, 1900, 1904, 1907-8, 1911-12, 1914, 1923, 1925, 1927, 1931, 1933, 1937, 1951, 1954, 1965, 1967, 1969, 1971-72, 1974-75, 1977, 1980, 1985, 1988-89 and 1995.

### Scottish League Cup
The most wins is 20, by Glasgow Rangers between 1947 and 1996.

### Football League Cup
The most wins is five, by Liverpool from 1981 to 1984 and in 1995 and by Aston Villa in 1961, 1975, 1977, 1994 and 1996.

## Spectators
### Greatest crowds
The greatest recorded crowd at a football match was 199,854 for the Brazil v. Uruguay World Cup match in the Maracanã Municipal Stadium, Rio de Janeiro, Brazil, on 16 July 1950.

The record attendance for a European Cup match is 136,505, at the semi-final between Glasgow Celtic and Leeds United at Hampden Park, Glasgow, on 15 April 1970.

The record paid attendance in the United Kingdom is 149,547, at the Scotland v. England international at Hampden Park, Glasgow on 17 April 1937. This total was probably exceeded at the FA Cup final between Bolton Wanderers and West Ham United at Wembley Stadium on 28 April 1923, when the crowd spilled onto the pitch and the start was delayed 40 minutes. The counted admissions were 126,047 but there were an estimated 160,000 spectators.

### Smallest crowd
The smallest crowd at a full home international was 2,315, at a game between Wales and Northern Ireland on 27 May 1982 at the Racecourse Ground, Wrexham, UK.

The smallest paying attendance at a Football League fixture was for the Stockport County v. Leicester City match at Old Trafford, Manchester, UK, on 7 May 1921. Stockport's own ground was under suspension and the 'crowd' numbered 13 but an estimated 2,000 gained free admission.

Due to disciplinary action by the European Football Union, there were no paying spectators when West Ham beat Castilla (Spain) 5-1 in the European Cup Winners' Cup at Upton Park, London, UK, on 1 Oct 1980, or when Aston Villa beat Besiktas (Turkey) 3-1 in the European Cup at Villa Park, Birmingham, UK, on 15 Sept 1982.

## FOOTBALL COMPETITIONS
### MOST WINS
#### National
Olympic Games (1896) (unofficial until 1908):
3 Great Britain; 1900, 1908, 1912
3 Hungary; 1952, 1964, 1968

S. American Championships (1910) (Copa America since 1975):
15 Argentina; 1910, 1921, 1925, 1927, 1929, 1937, 1941, 1945-47, 1955, 1957, 1959, 1991, 1993

Asian Cup (1956):
3 Iran, 1968, 1972, 1976
3 Saudi Arabia 1984, 1988, 1996

African Cup of Nations (1957):
4 Ghana, 1963, 1965, 1978, 1982

European Championships (1958):
3 West Germany/Germany, 1972, 1980, 1996

#### Club level
World Club Championship (1960) (between the winners of the European Cup and the Copa Libertadores):
3 Peñarol (Uruguay), 1961, 1966, 1982
3 Nacional (Uruguay), 1971, 1980, 1988
3 Milan (Italy), 1969, 1989, 1990

#### Europe
UEFA Cup (1955): 3 Barcelona (Spain), 1958, 1960, 1966

European Cup (1956):
6 Real Madrid; 1956-60, 1966

Cup Winners Cup (1960):
4 Barcelona; 1979, 1982, 1989, 1997

#### South America
Copa Libertadores (1960):
7 Independiente (Argentina); 1964-65, 1972-75, 1984

#### Africa
Cup of Champion Clubs (1964):
4 Zamalek (Egypt); 1984, 1986, 1993, 1996

Cup Winners Cup (1975):
4 Al Alhy Cairo (Eygpt); 1984-86, 1993

### HIGHEST SCORE (SINGLE GAME)
#### National level
Olympic Games (1896) (unofficial until 1908): 17-1 Denmark v.

France 'A', 1908
S. American Championships (1910) (Copa America since 1975):
12-0 Argentina v. Ecuador, 1942

Asian Cup (1956):
10-1 China v. Brunei, 1976
10-0 Oman v. Sri Lanka, 1996

African Cup of Nations (1957):
9-1 Ghana v. Niger, 1969

European Championships (1958):
12-1 Spain v. Malta, 1983

#### Club level
World Club Championship (1960) (between winners of the European Cup and the Copa Libertadores):
5-1 Real Madrid (Spain) v. Peñarol, 1960; 5-0 Peñarol v. Benfica (Portugal), 1961

#### Europe
UEFA Cup (1955):
14-0 Ajax (Netherlands) v. Red Boys (Luxembourg), 1984

European Cup (1956):
12-2 Feyenoord (Netherlands) v. KR Reykjavik (Iceland), 1969

Cup Winners Cup (1960):
16-1 Sporting Club Portugal v. Apoel Nicosia (Cyprus), 1963

#### South America
Copa Libertadores (1960):
11-2 Peñarol v. Valencia (Venezuela), 1970

#### Africa
Cup of Champion Clubs (1964):
9-0 Kambe Warriors (Zambia) v. Manjantja Maseru (Lesotho), 1972

Cup Winners Cup (1975):
12-1 SC Pamba (Tanzania) v. Anse Boileau (Seychelles), 1990

### Above left
An aerial view of the 1923 FA Cup final at Wembley Stadium, London, UK. The crowd can be seen spilling on to the pitch before the start of the match. Some estimates put the total crowd at as many as 160,000.

# Footballers

## Goal scoring

### Match
The most goals scored by one player in a first-class match is 16, by Stephan Stanis for Racing Club de Lens v. Aubry-Asturies, in Lens, France, on 13 Dec 1942.

The most goals scored by one player in an international match is 10, by Sofus Nielsen for Denmark in their 17–1 victory over France in the 1908 Olympics, and by Gottfried Fuchs for Germany who beat Russia 16–0 in the 1912 Olympic tournament in Sweden.

### Season
The most goals in a League season is 60 in 39 games, by William Ralph 'Dixie' Dean for Everton (First Division) in 1927/8 and 66 in 38 games, by James Smith for Ayr United (Scottish Second Division) in the same season. With three more in Cup ties and 19 in representative matches, Dean scored 82 in the 1927/8 season.

### Career
Artur Friedenreich (Brazil) scored an undocumented 1,329 goals in a 26-year first-class football career, which ran from 1909 to 1935.

The most goals scored in a specified period is 1,279, by Edson Arantes do Nascimento (Brazil), known as Pelé, in 1,363 games from 7 Sept 1956 to 1 Oct 1977. His best year was 1959 with 126 goals, and his 1,000th was a penalty for his club Santos at the Maracana Stadium, Rio de Janeiro, on 19 Nov 1969 when playing his 909th

Albert E. Mundy for Aldershot in a Fourth Division match against Hartlepool United at Victoria Ground, Hartlepool, Co. Durham, on 25 Oct 1958; by Barrie Jones for Notts County in a Third Division match against Torquay United on 31 March 1962; and by Keith Smith for Crystal Palace in a Second Division match against Derby County at the Baseball Ground, Derby, on 12 Dec 1964.

**Right**
In Nov 1996 Andy Legg achieved the longest throw ever recorded. He threw the ball a total distance of 44.54 m (146 ft 1 in).

## Youngest
The youngest British international was Norman Whiteside, who played for Northern Ireland v. Yugoslavia, aged 17 years 41 days on 17 June 1982.

England's youngest international was James Frederick McLeod Prinsep who played against Scotland at Kennington Oval, London, UK, on 5 April 1879, aged 17 years 252 days.

The youngest Welsh cap was Ryan Giggs who was aged 17 years 321 days when he played against Germany at Nürnberg, Germany, on 16 Oct 1991.

Scotland's youngest cap was John Alexander Lambie, who was 17 years 92 days old when he played against Ireland on 20 March 1886.

first-class match. He later added two more goals in special appearances.

Franz 'Bimbo' Binder scored 1,006 goals in 756 games in Austria and Germany between 1930 and 1950.

The international career record by an English player is 49 goals, by Robert 'Bobby' Charlton from 1958 to 1970.

The most goals scored in British first-class football is 550 (410 in Scottish League matches), by James McGrory of Glasgow Celtic from 1922 to 1938.

The most goals scored in League matches is 434, by George Arthur Rowley for West Bromwich Albion, Fulham, Leicester City and Shrewsbury Town, between 1946 and April 1965. Rowley also scored 32 goals in the FA Cup and one for England 'B'.

### Fastest goals
The fastest Football League goals on record were scored in six seconds by:

### Hat tricks
The fastest confirmed hat trick is in 2½ minutes, by Ephraim 'Jock' Dodds for Blackpool v. Tranmere Rovers on 28 Feb 1942, and by Jimmy Scarth for Gillingham v. Leyton Orient in Third Division (Southern) on 1 Nov 1952.

Tommy Bryce scored for Queen of the South in the 9th, 10th and 11th minute v. Arbroath on 18 Dec 1993.

A hat trick in 1 min 50 sec is claimed for Maglioni of Independiente against Gimnásia y Escrima de la Plata in Argentina on 18 March 1973.

John McIntyre (Blackburn Rovers) scored four goals in five minutes v. Everton at Ewood Park, Blackburn, Lancs, UK, on 16 Sept 1922.

William 'Ginger' Richardson (West Bromwich Albion) scored four goals in five minutes from the kick-off against West Ham United at Upton Park on 7 Nov 1931.

The international record is three goals in 3½ minutes by George William Hall for England against Ireland on 16 Nov 1938 at Old Trafford, Manchester, UK.

### Fastest own goal
Torquay United's Pat Kruse equalled the fastest goal on record when he headed the ball into his own net only six seconds after kick-off against Cambridge United on 3 Jan 1977.

### Longest throw-in record
Andy Legg (Birmingham City) achieved a throw-in of 44.54 m (146 ft 1 in) in Nov 1996.

## International caps

### Oldest
The oldest international was William Henry 'Billy' Meredith (Manchester City and United) who played outside right for Wales against England at Highbury, London, UK, on 15 March 1920 at the age of 45 years 229 days. He played international football for a record span of 26 years, between 1895 and 1920.

The youngest Republic of Ireland cap was James Holmes, who was 17 years 200 days old when he played against Austria in Dublin, Republic of Ireland, on 30 May 1971.

### Most international appearances
The most appearances for a national team is 147, by Majed Abdullah Mohammed for Saudi Arabia from 1978 to 1994.

The British record for the most appearances is 125, by goalkeeper Peter Shilton of England.

### Longest careers
Peter Shilton made 1,390 senior British appearances, including a record 1,006 League appearances, 286 for Leicester City, 110 for Stoke City, 202 for Nottingham Forest, 188 for Southampton, 175 for Derby County, 34 for Plymouth Argyle, one for Bolton Wanderers and 10 for Leyton Orient, one League play-off, 86 FA Cup, 102 League Cup, 125 international, 13

# 1,279 GOALS IN 1,363 GAMES

## ONCE STOPPED A GAME BY SNAPPING THE CROSS BAR

Under-23, four Football League XI and 53 European and other competitions.

Norman Trollope made 770 League appearances for Swindon Town, between 1960 and 1980.

### Goalkeeping
The longest that a goalkeeper has prevented a goal being scored in top-class competition is 1,275 minutes, by Abel Resino of Atlético Madrid to 17 March 1991.

The record in international matches is 1,142 min for Dino Zoff (Italy), between Sept 1972 and June 1974.

The British club record in competitive matches is 1,196 minutes, by Chris Woods for Glasgow Rangers from 26 Nov 1986 to 31 Jan 1987.

Ilinden FC of Yugoslavia, with the collusion of the opposition, Mladost, and the referee, won their final game of the season 134–1. Their rivals for promotion won their match, under similar circumstances, 88–0.

### Highest individual score
Dean Goodliff scored a record 26 individual goals for Deleford Colts in their 33–0 win over Iver Minors in the Slough Boys Soccer Combination Under-14 League at Iver, Bucks, UK, on 22 Dec 1985.

The women's record is 22 goals by Linda Curl of Norwich Ladies in a 40–0 win over Milton Keynes Reserves at Norwich, UK, on 25 Sept 1983.

The most goals in a season by one player in junior professional league

Beazer Homes League Premier Division match on 2 Jan 1989.

The fastest own goal on record was in four seconds, by Richard Nash of Newick v. Burgess Hill Reserves at Newick, E Sussex, UK, on 8 Feb 1992.

### Goalkeeping
Thomas McKenna of Folkestone Invicta under-13s played 1,417 minutes without conceding a goal, from 24 Sept 1995 to 5 May 1996.

### Most and least successful teams
Winlaton West End FC, Tyne & Wear, UK, completed a run of 95 league games without defeat between 1976 and 1980.

Penlake Junior Football Club remained undefeated for 153 games (winning

Glencraig United, Faifley, near Clydebank, W Dunbartonshire, UK, had all 11 team members and two substitutes for their 2–2 draw against Goldenhill Boys' Club on 2 Feb 1975 booked in the dressing room before a ball was kicked. The referee, Mr Tarbet of Bearsden, took exception to the chant which greeted his arrival. It was not his first meeting with Glencraig.

It was reported on 1 June 1993 that in a league match between Sportivo Ameliano and General Caballero in Paraguay, referee William Weiler sent off 20 players. Trouble flared after two Sportivo players were sent off, a 10-minute fight ensued and Weiler then dismissed a further 18 players, including the rest of the Sportivo team. Not surprisingly the match was abandoned.

**Below far left**
Peter Shilton of Leyton Orient being awarded a shield for his 1,000th League game. Leyton Orient went on to win the match 2–0.

## E. MUNDY IN 1958, BARRIE JONES IN 1962 AND BY KEITH SMITH IN 1964

### Heaviest goalkeeper
The English international Willie Henry 'Fatty' Foulke was 1.90 m (6 ft 3 in) tall and weighed 141 kg (22 st 3 lb). His last games were for Bradford City, by which time he was 165 kg (26 st). He once stopped a game by snapping the cross bar.

### Non first-class games
#### Highest team scores
The highest team score was 49–0, by Drayton Grange Colts v. Eldon Sports Reserves in a Daventry and District Sunday League match at Grange Estate, Northants, UK, on 13 Nov 1988. Every member of the side scored at least one goal, including the goalkeeper.

The full-time score in an Under-14 League match between Midas FC and Courage Colts, in Kent, UK, on 11 April 1976, was 59–1 after 70 minutes.

Needing to improve their goal 'difference' to gain promotion in 1979,

football is 96, by Tom Duffy for Ardeer Thistle FC, Strathclyde, UK, in 1960/61.

Paul Anthony Moulden scored 289 goals in 40 games for Bolton Lads Club in Bolton Boys Federation intermediate league and cup matches in 1981/2. An additional 51 goals scored in other tournaments brought his total to 340—the highest season figure for one player in any class of competitive football.

### Fastest goals
Goals scored in three seconds and under after the kick-off have been achieved by a number of players:

Damian Corcoran scored three goals within a minute for 7th Fulwood Cubs v. 4th Fulwood Cubs on 1 Feb 1987.

The shortest time for a semi-professional team to score three goals from the kick-off is 122 seconds, by Burton Albion v. Redditch United in a

152, including 85 in succession) in the Warrington Hilden Friendly League from 1981 until they were beaten in 1986.

The most consecutive losses is 39 league and cup games, by Stockport United FC, of the Stockport Football League, from Sept 1976 to Feb 1978, and by Poole Town of the Beazer Homes League Southern Division in the 1995/6 season.

### Most indisciplined
In the local cup match between Tongham Youth Club, Surrey, and Hawley, Hants, UK, on 3 Nov 1969, the referee booked all 22 players including one who went to hospital, and one of the linesmen. The match, won by Tongham 2–0, was described by a player as 'a good, hard game'.

In a Gancia Cup match at Waltham Abbey, Essex, UK, on 23 Dec 1973, the referee, Michael J. Woodhams, sent off the entire Juventus-Cross team and some club officials.

### Best ball control
On 15–16 July 1994, Ricardinho Neves (Brazil) juggled a regulation soccer ball non-stop for 19 hr 5 min 31 sec with feet, legs and head, without the ball ever touching the ground, at the Los Angeles Convention Center, California, USA.

The record time for ball control by a woman is 7 hr 5 min 25 sec, by Cláudia Martini (Brazil) at Caxias do Sul, Brazil, on 12 July 1996.

The heading record is 8 hr 12 min 25 sec, by Goderdzi Makharadze (Georgia) at the Boris Paichadze National Stadium, Tbilisi, Georgia, on 26 May 1996.

Jan Skorkovsky from Prague, Czechoslovakia (now Czech Republic), managed to keep a football up for 7 hr 18 min 55 sec while he travelled a distance of 42.195 km (26.219 miles) for the Prague City Marathon, Czechoslovakia, on 8 July 1990.

**Above left**
Cláudia Martini seen demonstrating her football skills. She holds the woman's record for soccer ball control.

# American ball sports

## National Football League
### Most NFL titles
The Green Bay Packers won a record 11 NFL titles, 1929–31, 1936, 1939, 1944, 1961–62, 1965–67.

### Most consecutive wins
The record is 18 achieved twice by the Chicago Bears, 1933–34 and 1941–42; the Miami Dolphins, 1972–73; and the San Francisco 49ers, 1988–89.

The most consecutive games without defeat is 25, by Canton in 1921–23.

### Most games played
George Blanda played in a record 340 games in 26 seasons in the NFL (Chicago Bears 1949–58, Baltimore Colts 1950, Houston Oilers 1960–66 and Oakland Raiders 1967–75).

Jim Marshall played 282 consecutive games (Cleveland Browns 1960 and Minnesota Vikings 1961–79).

### Longest run from scrimmage
Tony Dorsett scored on a run of 90.5 m (99 yards) for the Dallas Cowboys v. the Minnesota Vikings on 3 Jan 1983.

### Longest pass completion
A 99-yard pass completion has been achieved on eight occasions and has always resulted in a touchdown. The most recent was a pass from Brett Favre to Robert Brooks of the Green Bay Packers on 11 Sept 1995.

## Super Bowl
### Most team wins
The most wins in a Super Bowl is five by: the San Francisco 49ers, 1982, 1985, 1989–90 and 1995 and the Dallas Cowboys, 1972, 1978, 1993–94 and 1996.

### Most individual wins
The most wins by an individual is five, by Charles Hayley, San Francisco 49ers 1989–90, Dallas Cowboys 1993–94 and 1996.

### Highest Scores
The highest team score and record victory margin was when the San Francisco 49ers beat the Denver Broncos 55–10 at New Orleans, Louisiana on 28 Jan 1990.

The highest aggregate score was in 1995 when the San Francisco 49ers beat the San Diego Chargers 49–26.

### Highest team score
Georgia Tech, Atlanta, Georgia scored 222 points, including a record 32 touchdowns, against Cumberland University, Lebanon, Tennessee (nil) on 7 Oct 1916.

## NATIONAL FOOTBALL LEAGUE RECORDS
### MOST POINTS
**Career 2,002**
George Blanda
(Chicago Bears, Baltimore Colts, Houston Oilers, Oakland Raiders), 1949–75
**Season 176**
Paul Hornung
(Green Bay Packers), 1960
**Game 40**
Ernie Nevers
(Chicago Cardinals v. Chicago Bears), 28 Nov 1929

### MOST TOUCHDOWNS
**Career 165**
Jerry Rice
(San Francisco 49ers), 1985–96
**Season 25**
Emmitt Smith
(Dallas Cowboys), 1995
**Game 6**
Ernie Nevers
(Chicago Cardinals v. Chicago Bears), 28 Nov 1929
William Jones
(Cleveland Browns v. Chicago Bears), 25 Nov 1951
Gale Sayers
(Chicago Bears v. San Francisco 49ers), 12 Dec 1965

### MOST YARDS GAINED RUSHING
**Career 16,726**
Walter Payton
(Chicago Bears), 1975–87
**Season 2,105**
Eric Dickerson
(Los Angeles Rams), 1984
**Game 275**
Walter Payton
(Chicago Bears v. Minnesota Vikings), 20 Nov 1977

### MOST YARDS GAINED RECEIVING
**Career 16,377**
Jerry Rice
(San Francisco 49ers), 1985–96
**Season 1,848**
Jerry Rice
(San Francisco 49ers), 1995
**Game 336**
Willie Anderson
(Los Angeles Rams v. New Orleans Saints), 26 Nov 1989

### MOST NET YARDS GAINED
**Career 21,803**
Walter Payton
(Chicago Bears), 1975–87
**Season 2,535**
Lionel James
(San Diego Chargers), 1985
**Game 404**
Glyn Milburn
(Denver Broncos v. Seattle Seahawks), 10 Dec 1996

### MOST YARDS GAINED PASSING
**Career 51,636**
Dan Marino
(Miami Dolphins), 1983–96
**Season 5,084**
Dan Marino
(Miami Dolphins), 1984
**Game 554**
Norm Van Brocklin
(Los Angeles Rams v. New York Yanks), 28 Sept 1951

### MOST PASSES COMPLETED
**Career 4,134**
Dan Marino
(Miami Dolphins), 1983–96
**Season 404**
Warren Moon
(Houston Oilers), 1991
**Game 45**
Drew Bledsoe
(New England Patriots v. Minnesota Vikings), 13 Nov 1994

### PASS RECEPTIONS
**Career 1,050**
Jerry Rice
(San Francisco 49ers), 1985–96
**Season 123**
Herman Moore
(Detroit Lions), 1995
**Game 18**
Tom Fears
(Los Angeles Rams v. Green Bay Packers), 3 Dec 1950

### FIELD GOALS
**Career 383**
Nick Lowery
(New England Patriots, Kansas City Chiefs, New York Jets), 1978, 1980–96
**Season 37**
John Kasay (Carolina Panthers), 1996
**Game 7**
Jim Bakken
(St Louis Cardinals v. Pittsburgh Steelers),
24 Sept 1967
Rich Karlis
(Minnesota Vikings v. Los Angeles Rams),
5 Nov 1989
Chris Boniol
(Dallas Cowboys v. Green Bay Packers), 18 Nov 1996
**Longest 63 yd**
Tom Dempsey
(New Orleans Saints v. Detroit Lions), 8 Nov 1970

### SUPER BOWL GAME AND CAREER RECORDS
### POINTS
**Game 18**
Roger Craig (San Francisco 49ers), 1985
Jerry Rice (San Francisco 49ers), 1990 and 1995
Ricky Watters (San Francisco 49ers), 1995
**Career 42**
Jerry Rice, 1989–90, 1995

### TOUCHDOWNS
**Game 3**
Roger Craig, 1985
Jerry Rice, 1990 and 1995
Ricky Watters, 1990
**Career 7**
Jerry Rice, 1989–90, 1995

### TOUCHDOWN PASSES
**Game 6**
Steve Young (San Francisco 49ers), 1995
**Career 11**
Joe Montana (San Francisco 49ers), 1982, 1985, 1989–90

### YARDS GAINED PASSING
**Game 357**
Joe Montana, 1989
**Career 1,142**
Joe Montana, 1982, 1985, 1989–90

### YARDS GAINED RECEIVING
**Game 215**
Jerry Rice 1989
**Career 512**
Jerry Rice 1989–90, 1995

### YARDS GAINED RUSHING
**Game 204**
Timmy Smith (Washington Redskins), 1988
**Career 354**
Franco Harris, 1975–76, 1979–80

# LONGEST BASEBALL THROW 135.88 M

**COWBOYS IN 1983**

**PASSES COMPLETED**
**Game 31**
Jim Kelly (Buffalo Bills), 1994
**Career 83**
Joe Montana, 1982, 1985, 1989–90

**PASS RECEPTIONS**
**Game 11**
Dan Ross (Cincinnati Bengals), 1982
Jerry Rice, 1989
**Career 28**
Jerry Rice, 1989–90, 1995

**FIELD GOALS**
**Game 4**
Don Chandler (Green Bay Packers),
1968
Ray Wersching (San Francisco 49ers),
1982
**Career 5**
Ray Wersching, 1982, 1985

**MOST VALUABLE PLAYER AWARD**
**3 times**
Joe Montana, 1982, 1985, 1990

## Baseball World Series
**Most wins**
The most wins is 23, by the New York
Yankees between 1923 and 1996 from
a record 34 series appearances
between 1921 and 1996.

The most National League titles is 19,
by the Dodgers (Brooklyn 1890–1957,
Los Angeles 1958–88).

**Most valuable players**
Only three men have won this award
twice: Sanford 'Sandy' Koufax (Los
Angeles NL 1963, 1965), Robert
'Bob' Gibson (St. Louis NL 1964,
1967) and Reginald Martinez 'Reggie'
Jackson (Oakland AL 1973, New
York AL, 1977).

## Major League
**Most games played**
Peter Edward 'Pete' Rose played in a
record 3,562 games with a record
14,053 at bats for Cincinnati NL
1963–78 and 1984–86, Philadelphia
NL 1979–83, Montreal NL 1984.

**Batting**
Henry Louis 'Hank' Aaron holds the
major league career record with 755
home runs; 733 for the Milwaukee
Braves (1954–65) and Atlanta Braves
(1966–74) in the National League
and 22 for the Milwaukee Brewers
(AL) 1975–76.

The major league record for home
runs in a season is 61, by Roger
Eugene Maris for New York Yankees
in 162 games in 1961. 'Babe' Ruth
hit 60 for the New York Yankees
in 1927.

The most home runs in a major league
game is four, first achieved by Robert
Lincoln 'Bobby' Lowe for Boston v.
Cincinnati on 30 May 1894.

## Pitching
**Longest home run**
The longest home run in a major
league game is 193 m (634 ft) by
Mickey Mantle for the New York
Yankees on 10 Sept 1960.

**Most games won by a pitcher**
Denton True 'Cy' Young had a record
511 wins and a record 749 complete
games from a total of 906 games and
815 starts in his career. He pitched a
record total of 7,357 innings.

The career record for the most games
pitching is 1,070, by James Hoyt
Wilhelm, 1952–72; he has the record
of 143 wins by a relief pitcher.

**Most consecutive hits**
Michael Franklin 'Pinky' Higgins had 12
consecutive hits for Boston (AL)
19–21 June 1938. This was
equalled by Walter 'Moose' Droppo
for Detroit (AL) 14–15 July 1952.

Joe DiMaggio hit in 56 consecutive
games for New York from 15 May–16
July 1941; he was 223 times at bat,
with 91 hits, scoring 16 doubles, 4
triples and 15 home runs.

**Most scoreless innings**
Orel Leonard Hershiser IV pitched a
record 59 consecutive shutout
innings, 30 Aug–28 Sept 1988.

**Perfect game**
The first was achieved by John Lee
Richmond for Worcester against
Cleveland in the NL on 12 June
1880. On 26 May 1959 Harvey
Haddix Jr. for Pittsburgh pitched a
perfect game for 12 innings against
Milwaukee in the National League, but
lost in the 13th.

**Cy Young award for top pitcher**
The most wins is four, by Stephen
Norman Carlton (Philadelphia) 1972,
1977, 1980, 1982 and Greg Maddux
(Chicago, Atlanta) 1992–95.

**Fastest pitcher**
Lynn Nolan Ryan pitched at
162.3 km/h (100.9 mph) for the
California Angels on 20 Aug 1974.

## Throws and base runs
**Longest throw**
Glen Edward Gorbous threw 135.88 m
(445 ft 10 in) on 1 Aug 1957.

**Fastest base runner**
In 1932 Ernest Evar Swanson circled
the bases in 13.3 sec at Columbus,
Ohio, USA, at an average speed of
29.70 km/h (18.45 mph).

## US MAJOR LEAGUE
**BATTING RECORDS**
**Average**
Career average: .366, Tyrus Raymond
'Ty' Cobb (Detroit AL, Philadelphia AL)

1905–28. Season average: .440,
Hugh Duffy (Boston NL) 1894.
**Runs**
Career: 2,245, Tyrus Raymond Cobb
1905–28. Season: 192, William Robert
Hamilton (Philadelphia NL) 1894.
**Home runs**
Career:* 755, Henry 'Hank' Aaron
(Milwaukee NL, Atlanta NL, Milwaukee
AL) 1954–76. Season: 61, Roger
Eugene Maris (New York AL) 1961.
*Japanese League records that are
superior: 868 Sadaharu Oh (Yomiuri)
1959–80.
**Runs batted in**
Career: 2,297, Henry 'Hank' Aaron
1954–76. Season: 190, Lewis Rober
'Hack' Wilson (Chicago NL) 1930.
Game: 12, James LeRoy Bottomley
(St Louis NL) 16 Sept 1924; Mark
Whiten (St Louis NL) 7 Sept 1993.

Innings: 7, Edward Cartwright (St Louis
AL) 23 Sept 1890.
**Base hits**
Career: 4,256, Peter Edward Rose
(Cincinnati NL, Philadelphia NL,
Montreal NL, Cincinnati NL) 1963–86.
Season: 257, George Harold Sisler
(St Louis AL) 1920.
**Total bases**
Career: 6,856, Henry 'Hank' Aaron
1954–76. Season: 457, 'Babe' Ruth
(New York AL) 1921.
**Hits**
Consecutive: 12, Michael Franklin
'Pinky' Higgins (Boston AL) 19–21 June
1938; Walter 'Moose' Dropo (Detroit
AL) 14–15 July 1952.
**Stolen bases**
Career: 1,186 Rickey Henley
Henderson (Oakland AL, New York AL,
Oakland AL, Toronto AL, Oakland AL,
San Diego NL) 1979–96. Season: 130,
Rickey Henderson (Oakland AL) 1982.
**Consecutive games played**
2,358, Calvin Edwin Ripken Jr
(Baltimore AL) 30 May 1982–1997.
**PITCHING RECORDS**
**Games won**
Career: 511, Denton True 'Cy' Young
(Cleveland NL, St Louis NL, Boston AL,

Cleveland AL, Boston NL) 1890–1911.
Season: 60, Charles Gardner Radbourn
(Providence NL) 1884.
**Consecutive games won**
24, Carl Owen Hubbell (New York NL)
1936–37.
**Shutouts**
Career: 113, Walter Perry Johnson
(Washington AL) 1907–27. Season:
16, George Washington Bradley
(St Louis NL) 1876; Grover
Cleveland Alexander (Philadelphia NL)
1916.
**Strikeouts**
Career: 5,714 Lynn Nolan Ryan (New
York NL, California AL, Houston NL,
Texas AL) 1966–93. Season: 383 Lynn
Nolan Ryan (California AL) 1973. Game
(9 innings): 20, Roger Clemens (Boston
AL) v. Seattle 29 April 1986 and v.
Detroit 18 Sept 1996.

**No-hit games**
Career: 7, Lynn Nolan Ryan 1973–91.
**Earned run average**
Season: .90, Ferdinand Schupp (140
inns) (New York NL) 1916; .96, Hubert
'Dutch' Leonard (222 inns) (Boston AL)
1914; 1.12, Robert Gibson (305 inns)
(St Louis NL) 1968.

**WORLD SERIES**
**Most series played: 14**
Lawrence Peter 'Yogi' Berra (New York
AL) 1947–63.
**Most series played by pitcher: 11**
Edward Charles 'Whitey' Ford (New
York AL) 1950–64.
**Most home runs in a game: 3**
'Babe' Ruth (New York AL) 6 Oct 1926
and 9 Oct 1928; and Reginald
Martinez Jackson (New York, AL)
18 Oct 1977.
**Most runs batted in: 6**
Robert C. Richardson (New York AL)
8 Oct 1960.
**Most strikeouts: 17**
Robert Gibson (St Louis NL)
2 Oct 1968.
**Perfect game (9 innings)**
Donald James Larson (New York AL)
8 Oct 1956.

**Below**
The Los Angeles
Dodgers discuss their
strategy against the
Houston Astros during
a 1994 game attended
by over 42,000 fans.
The Dodgers have won
the National League
title a record 19 times.

# Ball sports

**Right**
Hands have to be on the ball as it goes through the hoop in a vertical slam dunk competition. Sean Williams and Michael Wilson of the Harlem Globetrotters jointly hold the record for the highest slam dunk. On 16 Sept 1996, they both successfully dunked a basketball at a rim height of 3.58 m (11 ft 8 in) in Orlando, Florida, USA.

## Basketball: titles and scores
### Most Olympic titles
The USA has won 11 men's Olympic titles, and 63 consecutive matches from 1963 to 1972. Since then, they have won a further 37 matches but sustained a loss to the USSR (in 1988).

The women's title was won three times by the USSR in 1976, 1980 and 1992 (by a team of ex-Soviet states), and by the USA in 1984, 1988 and 1996.

### Most World Championship titles
The USSR has won three men's World Championships (1967, 1974 and 1982) and six women's (1959, 1964, 1967, 1971, 1975 and 1983). Yugoslavia has also won three men's world titles (1970, 1978 and 1990).

### Most European titles
The USSR has won the men's European Championships 14 times, and the women's event a total of 21 times.

Real Madrid, Spain, has won seven European Champions Cups, 1964–65, 1967–68, 1974, 1978 and 1980.

Daugava, Riga, Latvia, has won the women's European title 18 times between 1960 and 1982.

### Highest international score
Iraq scored 251 against Yemen (33) at New Delhi, India, in November 1982.

### Highest British scores
The highest match score is 250, by the Nottingham YMCA Falcons v. Mansfield Pirates at Nottingham in June 1974.

The highest score in a senior National League match is 174–40, by Chiltern Fast Break v. Swindon Rakers in 1990.

### Highest individual scores
Mats Wermelin scored all the points in a 272–0 win in a boys' tournament in Stockholm, Sweden, in 1974.

The record score by a woman is 156 points by Marie Boyd of Central HS, Lonaconing, Maryland, USA, in a 163–3 defeat of Ursaline Academy, Cumbria in 1924.

## NBA
### Most titles
Boston Celtics have won a record 16 NBA titles (1957, 1959–66, 1968–69, 1974, 1976, 1981, 1984, 1986).

### Highest score
The highest aggregate score in an NBA match is 370, when the Detroit Pistons beat the Denver Nuggets 186–184 on 13 Dec 1983. Overtime was played after a 145–145 tie in regulation time.

The highest score in regulation time is 320, when the Golden State Warriors beat Denver 162–158, on 2 Nov 1990.

## Individual scoring
Wilton Norman 'Wilt' Chamberlain set an NBA record of 100 points for the Philadelphia v. New York game at Hershey, Pennsylvania on 2 March 1962. This included a record 36 field goals and 28 free throws (from 32 attempts) and a record 59 points in a half (the second). The free throws game record was equalled by Adrian Dantley for Utah v. Houston at Las Vegas on 5 Jan 1984.

### Most games
Robert Parish has played a record 1,611 NBA regular seasons for the Golden State Warriors (1976–80), Boston Celtics (1980–94), Charlotte Hornets (1994–96) and Chicago Bulls (1996–97).

Kareem Abdul-Jabbar (formerly Ferdinand Lewis Alcindor) played for 57,446 minutes for the Milwaukee Bucks (1969–75) and the Los Angeles Lakers (1975–89). He also played a record 237 play-off games.

The most successive NBA games is 906, by Randy Smith for Buffalo, San Diego, Cleveland and New York from 18 Feb 1972 to 13 March 1983.

The record for complete games in one season is 79, by Wilt Chamberlain for Philadelphia in 1962, when he was on court for a record 3,882 minutes.

### Most points
Kareem Abdul-Jabbar set NBA career records with 38,387 points (average 24.6 points per game), including 15,837 field goals in regular season games, and 5,762 points, including 2,356 field goals in play-off games.

### Highest career average
The highest career average for players that exceeds 10,000 points is 31.7, by Michael Jordan, who gained 26,920 points in 848 games for the Chicago Bulls, 1984–97. Jordan also holds the career scoring average record for play-offs, at 33.6 for 5,307 points in 158 games between 1984 and 1997.

### Winning margin
The record for the greatest winning margin ever in an NBA game is 68 points when the Cleveland Cavaliers beat the Miami Heat, 148–80 on 17 Dec 1991.

### Winning streak
Los Angeles Lakers won a record 33 NBA games in succession from 5 Nov 1971 to 7 Jan 1972.

The most wins in a season is 72, by the Chicago Bulls in the 1995/6 season.

### Youngest and oldest player
The youngest NBA player was Jermaine O'Neal, who made his debut for the

Portland Trail Blazers against the Denver Nuggets on 5 Dec 1996, at the age of 18 years 53 days.

The oldest NBA regular player was Robert Parish, who was 43 years 231 days when he last played for the Chicago Bulls in 1997.

### Tallest NBA player
Gherorghe Muresan of the Washington Bullets is 2.31 m (7 ft 7 in), the tallest player in NBA history. He made his debut in 1994.

## Other records
### Tallest players
Suleiman Ali Nashnush was reputed to be 2.45 m (8 ft ¼ in) when he played for the Libyan team in 1962.

### Shooting speeds
On 11 June 1992 Jeff Liles scored 231 out of 240 attempts in 10 minutes at Southern Nazarene University, Bethany, Oklahoma, USA. He scored 231 (241 attempts) on 16 June.

### Greatest shooting demonstration
On 28 April 1996 Ted St Martin scored a record 5,221 consecutive free throws at Jacksonville, Florida, USA.

Fred Newman scored 20,371 free throws out of 22,049 taken (92.39%) at Caltech, Pasadena, California, USA, in 24 hours from 29 to 30 Sept 1990.

### Vertical dunk
Both Sean Williams and Michael Wilson of the Harlem Globetrotters successfully dunked a basketball at a rim height of 3.58 m (11 ft 8 in) at Disney-MGM Studios, Orlando, Florida, USA, on 16 Sept 1996.

### Longest goal
Christopher Eddy scored a field goal from 27.49 m (90 ft 2¼ in) for Fairview High School v. Iroquois High School at Erie, Pennsylvania, USA, on 25 Feb 1989. The shot, which was made as time expired in overtime, was vital as it won the game for Fairview High School, 51–50.

# FASTEST SNOOKER 147 5 MIN 20 SEC

## Handball
### Olympics
The USSR won five Olympic handball titles: three in the men's competition, 1976, 1988 and 1992 (by the Unified Team of ex-Soviet republics), and the women's 1976 and 1980 titles. South Korea shares the record of two women's titles, 1988 and 1992.

### World Championships
Romania has won four men's indoor titles, in 1961, 1964, 1970 and 1974.

Germany/West Germany won the outdoor title five times between 1938 and 1966 and have won the indoor title twice, in 1938 and 1978.

A record three women's titles have been won by: Romania in 1956, 1960

individual is 543, by Irene van Dyk, (South Africa) in 1995.

## Volleyball
### Most world titles
The USSR won a record six men's titles (1949, 1952, 1960, 1962, 1978 and 1982) and five women's titles (1952, 1956, 1960, 1970 and 1990).

### Most Olympic titles
The USSR has won a record three men's titles (1964, 1968 and 1980) and four women's titles (1968, 1972, 1980 and 1988).

The only player ever to win four medals is Inna Valeryevna Ryskal (USSR), who won silver medals in the Olympic games of 1964 and 1976 and gold medals in 1968 and 1972.

### Youngest champion
Mike Russell, was the youngest player to win a professional title. He was 20 years 49 days when he won at Leura, Queensland, Australia, on 23 July 1989.

### Highest breaks
Tom Reece made an unfinished break of 499,135 in 85 hr 49 min against Joe Chapman in London between 3 June and 6 July 1907. However this was not recognized, as press and public were not continuously present.

The highest certified break made by the anchor cannon is 42,746, by William Cook (England) from 29 May to 7 June 1907.

The official world record under the then baulk-line rule is 1,784, by Joe Davis in

Maureen Baynton won a record eight Women's Amateur Championships between 1954 and 1968, as well as seven at billiards.

### Youngest champions
The youngest man to win the world title is Stephen O'Connor (Ireland), aged 18 years 40 days when he won the World Amateur Snooker Championship, Colombo, Sri Lanka, on 25 Nov 1990.

Stephen Hendry (Scotland) became the youngest World Professional champion, at 21 years 106 days on 29 April 1990.

### Highest breaks
The first to make the 'maximum' break of 147 was E. J. 'Murt' O'Donoghue (NZ) at Griffiths, NSW, Australia on 26 Sept 1934.

**Below left**
South Korea shares the record for the most women's Olympic handball titles, with wins in 1988 and 1992.

20:12:36

20:12:37

KOREA 10

## VOLLEYBALL PLAYER TO HAVE WON FOUR OLYMPIC MEDALS

(both outdoor) and 1962; the GDR in 1971, 1975 and 1978; and the USSR in 1982, 1986 and 1990.

### Highest international score
The USSR beat Afghanistan 86–2 in the 'Friendly Army Tournament' at Miskolc, Hungary, in August 1981.

## Netball
### Most titles
Australia won the World Championships a record seven times: 1963, 1971, 1975, 1979, 1983, 1991 and 1995.

The National Club's Championships have been won seven times by Sudbury Netball Club, in 1968–69, 1970 (shared), 1971, 1973, 1984–85.

### Highest scores
On 9 July 1991, at Sydney, Australia, the Cook Islands beat Vanuatu by a record 120–38.

The record number of goals at one World Championship tournament by an

The men's record is held by Yuriy Mikhailovich Poyarkov (USSR) (gold 1964 and 1968, bronze 1972), and by Katsutoshi Nekoda (Japan) (gold 1972, silver 1968, bronze 1964).

## Billiards
### Most titles
John Roberts Jr (GB) won eight World Championships in 1870 (twice), 1871, 1875 (twice), 1877 and 1885 (twice).

The record for world amateur titles is four, by R. J. P. Marshall (Australia) in 1936, 1938, 1951 and 1962.

Joe Davis won seven British professional titles (1934–39 and 1947), and four world titles (1928–30 and 1932).

Norman Dagley won 15 English Amateur Championships, in 1965–66, 1970–75, and 1978–84.

The record number of English women's championship titles is nine, by Vera Selby from 1970 to 1978.

the UK Championship on 29 May 1936. Walter Albert Lindrum (Australia) made an official break of 4,137 in 2 hr 55 min against Joe Davis on 19–20 Jan 1923, before the baulk-line was in force.

### Fastest century
Walter Lindrum made an unofficial 100 break in 27.5 sec on 10 Oct 1952. His official record is 100 in 46 sec at Sydney, NSW, Australia, in 1941.

## Snooker
### Most world titles
Joe Davis won the World Professional Championship the first 15 times it was contested, 1927–40 and 1946.

The most wins in the Amateur Championship is two, by: Gary Owen (England) in 1963 and 1966; Ray Edmunds (England) 1972 and 1974 and Paul Mifsud (Malta) 1985–86.

Allison Fisher (England) has won seven women's World Championships, 1985–86, 1988–89, 1991–93.

The first officially ratified 147 was by Joe Davis against Willie Smith in London, UK, on 22 Jan 1955.

The youngest to score a competitive maximum was Ronnie O'Sullivan at 15 years 98 days during the English Amateur Championship at Aldershot, Hants, UK, on 13 March 1991.

Stephen Hendry is the only player to have scored three 147s in competition.

Sean Storey scored two 147s on the same day in a tournament at Mexborough, S Yorkshire, UK, on 13 April 1997.

The fastest 147 in a professional tournament is 5 min 20 sec by Ronnie O'Sullivan during the 1997 World Championships at Sheffield, S Yorkshire, UK, on 21 April.

Steve Duggan made a break of 148 in witnessed practice on 27 April 1988 and Tony Drago made a break of 149 in similar circumstances on 1 Feb 1995. Both breaks involved a free ball, which created an 'extra' red.

# Rugby

## Rugby League
### World Cup
Australia have won seven times, in 1957, 1968, 1970, 1977, 1988, 1992 and 1995 and also the International Championship in 1975.

### League Championship
Wigan have won 17 League Championships, in 1909, 1922, 1926, 1934, 1946–47, 1950, 1952, 1960, 1987 and 1990–96.

### League Challenge Cup
Wigan have won the Cup 16 times, in 1924, 1929, 1948, 1951, 1958–59, 1965, 1985 and 1988–95.

### Highest team scores
#### Senior match
The highest aggregate score in a game

involving a senior club is 146 points, when Huddersfield beat Blackpool Gladiators 142–4 at Huddersfield, W Yorkshire, UK, in the first round of the Regal Trophy on 26 Nov 1994.

The highest score in league football is 104–4, by Keighley Cougars v. Highfield on 23 April 1995.

St Helens beat Carlisle 112–0 in the Lancashire Cup on 14 Sept 1986.

### Challenge Cup final
The highest score in a Challenge Cup final is 40–32, by St Helens v. Bradford Bulls, at Wembley, London, UK, on 27 April 1996. The match aggregate of 72 points is also a record.

### International match
Australia beat South Africa 86–6 at Gateshead, Tyne & Wear, UK, on 10 Oct 1995.

Great Britain's highest score is 72, against France (6) in a Test match at

Headingley, Leeds, W Yorks, UK, on 2 April 1993 and against Fiji (4) at Nadi, Fiji, on 5 Oct 1996.

England beat France 73–6 in a European Championship match at Gateshead, UK, on 12 June 1996.

### Most points
During the 1994/5 season, Wigan scored a record 1,735 points in league and cup games, and Highfield conceded a record 1,687 points.

### Highest Individual Scores
#### Most points in a game
George Henry 'Tich' West scored 53 points (10 goals and a record 11 tries) for Hull Kingston Rovers in their 73–5 Challenge Cup defeat of Brookland Rovers on 4 March 1905.

The record points for a League match is 42 (4 tries, 13 goals), by Dean John Marwood in Workington Town's 78–0 win over Highfield on 1 Nov 1992. He repeated this feat in a 94–4 defeat of Leigh on 26 Feb 1995.

#### Most goals in a match
James 'Jim' Sullivan kicked 22 for Wigan against Flimby and Fothergill on 14 Feb 1925.

#### Most points in a season
Benjamin Lewis Jones (Leeds) scored 496 (194 goals, 36 tries) in 1956/7.

#### Most points in a career
Neil Fox scored 6,220 points (2,575 goals including 4 drop goals, 358 tries) in a senior Rugby League career from 10 April 1956 to 19 Aug 1979.

#### Most tries in a season
Albert Aaron Rosenfeld (Huddersfield), an Australian-born wing-threequarter, scored 80 tries in 42 matches in the 1913/14 season.

Brian Bevan (Australia), a wing-threequarter, scored 796 tries in 18 seasons (16 with Warrington, two with Blackpool Borough) from 1945 to 1964. He scored 740 tries for Warrington, 17 for Blackpool and 39 in representative matches.

### Most goals in a season
David Watkins (Salford) scored 221 goals in 47 matches, in 1972/3.

### Most goals in a career
Jim Sullivan (Wigan) kicked 2,867 goals in his career from 1921 to 1946.

### Most consecutive scores
David Watkins (Salford) played and scored in every club game during seasons 1972/3 and 1973/4, contributing 41 tries and 403 goals: a total of 929 points in 92 games.

### Individual international records
Jim Sullivan (Wigan) played the most internationals (60 for Wales and Great Britain, from 1921–1939), and scored the most goals (160) and points (329).

Michael Sullivan played in 51 international games for England and Great Britain and scored a record 45 tries from 1954 to 1963.

The most points scored in a game is 32, by Andrew Johns (Australia) v. Fiji at Newcastle, NSW, Australia, on 12 July 1996 and Bobby Goulding (GB) against Fiji at Nadi, Fiji, on 5 Oct 1996.

### Record kicks and tries
#### Longest kicks
Arthur Atkinson (Castleford) kicked a 68-m (75-yd) penalty from his own 25-yd line in a league game at St Helens, UK, on 26 Oct 1929.

The longest drop goal is 56 m (61 yd) by Joseph Paul 'Joe' Lydon for Wigan against Warrington in a Challenge Cup semi-final at Maine Road, Manchester, UK, on 25 March 1989.

### Fastest try
Lee Jackson scored after nine seconds for Hull against Sheffield Eagles in a Yorkshire Cup semi-final at Don Valley Stadium, Sheffield, S Yorkshire, UK, on 6 Oct 1992.

The fastest try in an international match is 15 seconds by Bobby Fulton for Australia against France at Odsal Stadium, Bradford, W Yorkshire, UK, on 1 Nov 1970.

### Most Challenge Cup finals
The most appearances is 10, by Shaun Edwards for Wigan from 1984 to 1985 and from 1988 to 1995. He was on the winning side nine times.

## Rugby Union
### International Championship
Wales has won a record 22 times outright and tied for first a further 11 times to 1994.

The most Grand Slams (winning all four matches) is 11, by England (1913–14, 1921, 1923–24, 1928, 1957, 1980, 1991–92 and 1995).

### Highest team score
The highest score in an International Championship match was set at Swansea, UK, on 1 Jan 1910, when Wales beat France 49–14 (eight goals, one penalty goal, two tries, to one goal, two penalty goals, one try).

### Season's scoring
Jonathan Mark Webb scored a record 67 points (3 tries, 11 penalty goals, 11 conversions) in the four games of an International Championship series in 1992. England scored a record 141 points in their four games in 1997.

### Individual match records
John 'Jack' Bancroft kicked a record nine goals (eight conversions and one penalty goal) for Wales against France at Swansea, UK, on 1 Jan 1910.

Simon Hodgkinson kicked a record seven penalty goals for England v. Wales at Cardiff, UK, on 19 Jan 1991.

### Highest Team Scores
#### Internationals
The highest score in any full international is when Hong Kong beat Singapore 164–13 in a World Cup qualifying match at Kuala Lumpur, Malaysia, on 27 Oct 1994.

The highest aggregate score for any match between the Four Home Unions is 82, when England beat Wales by 82 points (seven goals, one drop goal and six tries) to nil at Blackheath, London, UK, on 19 Feb 1881.

The highest aggregate score in modern times between top international teams is 93, when New Zealand beat Scotland 62–31 at Dunedin, New Zealand, on 15 June 1996.

### Matches
In Denmark, Comet beat Lindo by 194–0 on 17 Nov 1973.

The highest British score is 177–3, by Norwich against Eccles and Attleborough in a Norfolk Cup match in Dec 1996.

### Season
Neath in South Wales, UK, scored 1,917 points (including a record 345 tries) in 47 games in 1988/9.

# FASTEST TRY NINE SECONDS

**111 FROM 1982-1995**

## Highest Individual Scores
### Internationals
In the World Cup qualifying match between Hong Kong and Singapore at Kuala Lumpur, Malaysia, on 27 Oct 1994, Hong Kong's Ashley Billington scored 50 points (10 tries).

The most points by a British player is 44, by Andrew Gavin Hastings (4 tries, 9 conversions, 2 penalty goals) for Scotland v. Ivory Coast at Rustenberg, South Africa, on 26 May 1995.

The highest individual points score in a match between the major nations is 27, by Rob Andrew (1 try, 2 conversions, 5 penalty goals and a drop goal) for England against South Africa at Pretoria, South Africa, on 4 June 1994.

The most tries in an international match between the major nations is five, by George Campbell Lindsay for Scotland v. Wales on 26 Feb 1887, and by Douglas 'Daniel' Lambert for England v. France on 5 Jan 1907.

Ian Scott Smith (Scotland) scored a record six consecutive international tries in 1925, comprising the last three against France and two weeks later, the first three against Wales.

The most penalty goals kicked in a match is eight by: Mark Andrew Wyatt (Canada) v. Scotland at St John, New Brunswick, Canada, on 25 May 1991; Neil Roger Jenkins (Wales) v. Canada at Cardiff, S Glamorgan, UK, on 10 Nov 1993; Santiago Meson (Argentina) v. Canada at Buenos Aires, Argentina, on 12 March 1995; Gavin Hastings (Scotland) v. Tonga at Pretoria, South Africa, on 30 May 1995; Thierry Lacroix (France) v. Ireland at Durban, South Africa, on 10 June 1995 and Paul Burke (Ireland) v. Italy at Dublin on 4 Jan 1997.

The most points in a career is 911, by Michael Patrick Lynagh in 72 matches for Australia, from 1984 to 1995.

The most tries in one career is 64, by David Campese in 101 internationals for Australia, from 1982 to 1996.

### Season
The first-class season scoring record is 581 points, by Samuel Arthur Doble of Moseley, in 52 matches in 1971/2.

### Career
William Henry 'Dusty' Hare scored 7,337 points in first-class games from 1971 to 1989, comprising 1,800 for Nottingham, 4,427 for Leicester, 240 for England, 88 for the British Isles and 782 in other representative matches.

### Match
Jannie van der Westhuizen scored a record 80 points for Carnarvon in their 88–12 defeat of Williston at North West Cape, South Africa, on 11 March 1972.

### Most tries
Alan John Morley scored 473 tries in senior rugby from 1968 to 1986.

### All-rounder
Canadian international Barrie Burnham scored all possible ways—try, conversion, penalty goal, drop goal, goal from mark—for Meralomas v. Georgians (20–11) at Vancouver, Canada, on 26 Feb 1966.

### Most international appearances
Philippe Sella (France) has played in 111 internationals for France between 1982 and 1995.

The most international appearances by a British player is 91 by Rory Underwood, 85 for England and 6 for the British Isles, from 1984 to 1996.

William James 'Willie John' McBride made a record 17 appearances for the British Isles, as well as 63 for Ireland.

The greatest number of consecutive appearances is 63, by Sean Brian Thomas Fitzpatrick (New Zealand), between 1986 and 1995.

The most consecutive appearances by a British player is 53, by Willie John McBride for Ireland, 1964–75, and by Gareth Owen Edwards who never missed a match throughout his career for Wales, from 1967 to 1978.

### Youngest international
Ninian Jamieson Finlay and Charles Reid were both 17 years 36 days old when they played for Scotland in 1875 and 1881 respectively.

Semi Hekasilau Spec Taupeaafe played in a Test for Tonga against Western Samoa in 1989, aged 16.

## Record kicks and tries
### Longest kicks
The longest recorded successful drop goal is 82 m (90 yd) by Gerald Hamilton 'Gerry' Brand for South Africa v. England at Twickenham, Greater London, UK, on 2 Jan 1932. It was taken 6 m (7 yd) inside the England 'half', 50 m (55 yd) from the posts, and dropped over the dead ball line.

The place kick record is reputed to be 91 m (100 yd) at Richmond Athletic Ground, London, UK, by Douglas Francis Theodore Morkel in an unsuccessful penalty for South Africa against Surrey on 19 Dec 1906. It was not measured until 1932.

Ernie Cooper landed a penalty 74 m (81 yd) from the post with a kick which carried over the dead ball line in the Bridlington School 1st XV match

against an Army XV at Bridlington, E Yorkshire, UK, on 29 Jan 1944.

The record in an international is 64.22 m (70 yd 8½ in), by Paul Huw Thorburn for Wales against Scotland on 1 Feb 1986.

### Fastest tries
The fastest try in an international game was when Herbert Leo 'Bart' Price scored for England v. Wales at Twickenham, UK, on 20 Jan 1923 less than 10 seconds after kick-off.

The fastest try in any game was scored in 8 seconds by Andrew Brown for Widden Old Boys v. Old Ashtonians at Gloucester, UK, on 22 Nov 1990.

## Club Championships
### RFU Club Competition
Bath have a record 10 outright wins in the RFU Club Competition (now Pilkington Cup), in 1984–87, 1989–90, 1992, and 1994–96.

The highest team score (and aggregate) in the final is for Bath's 48–6 win over Gloucester in 1990.

### English Clubs Championship
Bath has been the winner of the English Clubs Championship a record seven times in 1987, 1989, 1991–94 and 1996.

### Swalec Cup
The most wins in the Welsh Rugby Union Challenge Cup, now Swalec Cup (from 1992/3), is nine, by Llanelli, in 1973–76, 1985, 1988 and 1991–93.

The highest team score in the final is 33 by Cardiff against Swansea in 1997. The aggregate, 59, was a also a record.

Llanelli achieved the first league and cup double in Wales in 1993.

### Scottish League
The most wins in the Scottish League Division One is 10, by Hawick between 1973 and 1986.

### Hong Kong Sevens
The record of seven wins in the Hong Kong Sevens is held by Fiji, in 1977–78, 1980, 1984, 1990–92.

**Left**
Jonathan Webb scored a record 67 points (three tries, 11 penalty goals, 11 conversions) for England in the four games of an International Championship series in 1992.

# Hockey and Gaelic games

PAUL LITJENS (NETHERLANDS) HAS SCORED THE MOST GOALS IN INTERNATIONA

**Above**
Pakistan have won the men's World Cup hockey title a record four times, in 1971, 1978, 1982 and 1994. Pakistan were also the first team to beat India in the Olympics when they won 1–0 at Rome in 1960. From 1928 until then India had played 30 games without being defeated.

HIGHEST SCORE BY AN INTERNATIONAL LACROSSE TEAM WAS BY GREAT BRITAIN

## Hockey
### Most Olympic medals
India held the men's Olympic title from the re-introduction of Olympic hockey in 1928 until 1960, when Pakistan beat them 1–0 at Rome. They had their eighth win in 1980.

Of the six Indians who have won three Olympic team gold medals, two have also won a silver medal: Leslie Walter Claudius, in 1948, 1952, 1956 and 1960 (silver), and Udham Singh, in 1952, 1956, 1964 and 1960 (silver).

A women's tournament was added in 1980, and Australia have won twice, in 1988 and 1996.

### World Cup
The record for the most men's wins in the FIH World Cup is four, by Pakistan in 1971, 1978, 1982 and 1994.

The record for the most women's titles is five, by the Netherlands in 1974, 1978, 1983, 1986 and 1990.

### Champions' Trophy
The most men's titles is six, by Australia, from 1983 to 1985, in 1989, 1990 and 1993.

Australia has won the women's title a record three times, in 1991, 1993 and 1995.

### International matches, men's
The highest score in an international was when India defeated the USA 24–1 at Los Angeles, California, USA, in the 1932 Olympic Games.

The most goals in an international in the United Kingdom was England's 16–0 defeat of France at Beckenham, Greater London, on 25 March 1922.

### Most international appearances
Heiner Dopp represented West Germany 286 times between 1975 and 1989, indoors and out.

The most by a player from the United Kingdom is 234, by Jonathan Nicholas

Mark Potter, 106 for England and 128 for Great Britain, from 1983 to 1994.

The most international appearances by an Irish player is 135, by William David Robert McConnell from 1979 to 1993, and Stephen Alexander Martin from 1980 to 1993.

The most indoor caps is 85, by Richard Clarke (England) from 1976 to 1987.

### Greatest scoring feats
The greatest number of goals scored in international hockey is 267 by Paul Litjens (Netherlands) in 177 games.

M. C. Marckx (Bowdon 2nd XI) scored 19 goals against Brooklands 2nd XI (score 23–0) on 31 Dec 1910.

David Ashman scored a record 2,164 goals for Hampshire, Southampton, Southampton Kestrals and Hamble Old Boys—for whom he has scored 2,005 goals, a record for one club—from 1958 to 1996.

### Fastest goal in an international
John French scored 7 sec after the bully-off for England v. West Germany at Nottingham, UK, on 25 April 1971.

### Greatest goalkeeping
Richard James Allen (India) conceded no goals during the 1928 Olympic tournament and only three in 1936.

### International matches, women's
The highest score in an international match was England's defeat of France 23–0 at Merton, Greater London, UK, on 3 Feb 1923.

Alison Ramsay has made a record 257 international appearances, 150 for Scotland and 107 for Great Britain, between 1982 and 1995.

### Women's club hockey
The most goals in a women's club hockey match is 21, by Edna Mary Blakelock during Ross Ladies' defeat of Wyeside, at Ross-on-Wye, Hereford & Worcester, UK, on 24 Jan 1929.

# FASTEST GOAL 7 SEC

## HOCKEY, A RECORD 267 IN 177 GAMES

**Highest attendance**
The highest ever attendance at a hockey match was 65,165 on 11 March 1978 at Wembley, London, UK, when England played the USA.

**Hockey umpire**
Graham Dennis Nash umpired in five successive Olympics, from 1976 to 1992, and retired after the Barcelona Olympics having officiated in a record 144 international matches.

### Lacrosse
**Men's**
The USA has won six of the seven World Championships, in 1967, 1974, 1982, 1986, 1990 and 1994. Canada won the title in 1978 beating the USA 17–16 after extra time—this was the first drawn international match.

Vivien Jones played in 86 internationals (74 for Wales, 9 for the Celts and three for Great Britain) from 1977–94.

Caro Macintosh has played in 56 international matches (52 for Scotland and four for Great Britain).

The highest score by an international team was by Great Britain and Ireland with their 40–0 defeat of Long Island during their 1967 tour of the USA.

### Hurling
**Most hurling titles**
The most All-Ireland Championships by one team is 27, by Cork between 1890 and 1990.

The most successive wins is four, by Cork from 1941 to 1944.

defeated Wexford (five goals, 10 points) by 39 to 25 in the 1970 80-minute final.

The highest recorded individual score was by Nick Rackard (Wexford), who scored seven goals and seven points against Antrim in the 1954 All-Ireland semi-final.

**Lowest score**
The lowest score in an All-Ireland final was when Tipperary (one goal, one point) beat Galway (nil) in the first championship at Birr, in 1887.

**Hurling referee record**
Mick Quinn refereed 5,500 hurling, Gaelic football and camogie games under GAA rules over 50 years, including 6 games in one day. He was still refereeing hurling games aged 80.

is four, by Wexford from 1915–18, and by Kerry twice, from 1929–32 and from 1978–81.

The most finals to have been contested by an individual is 10, including eight wins by the Kerry players Pat Spillane, Paudie O'Shea and Denis Moran, in 1975 and 1976, from 1978–82, and from 1984–86.

The highest team score in a final was the 27–15 victory by Dublin (five goals, 12 points) over Armagh (three goals, six points) on 25 Sept 1977.

The highest individual score in an All-Ireland final is two goals (six points) by Jimmy Keaveney for Dublin v. Armagh in 1977, and Michael Sheehy for Kerry v. Dublin in 1979.

## AND IRELAND WHO DEFEATED LONG ISLAND BY 40 POINTS TO ZERO IN 1967

The English Club Championship has been won the most times by Stockport with 17 wins, 1897–1989.

The highest ever score in an English Club Championship final is Stockport's 33–4 win over London University on 9 May 1987.

Peter Daniel Roden (Mellor) has made a record 42 international representations from 1976 to 1990.

The highest win in an international match is Scotland's 34–3 win over Germany at Manchester, UK, on 25 July 1994.

**Women's**
The first Lacrosse World Cup was held in 1982—this replaced the World Championships.

The USA has won the world title four times: the World Championship in 1974, and the World Cup in 1982, 1989 and 1993.

**Most hurling appearances**
Three players have appeared in the All-Ireland hurling finals 10 times: Christy Ring for Cork and Munster, John Doyle for Tipperary and Frank Cummins for Kilkenny.

Christy Ring and John Doyle share the record for the most All-Ireland medals, with a total of eight each. Ring's appearances on the winning side were 1941–44, 1946 and 1952–54, while Doyle's were 1949–51, 1958, 1961–62 and 1964–65.

Christy Ring played in a record 22 inter-provincial finals, 1942–63, and was on the winning side 18 times.

**Highest hurling scores**
The highest ever score in an All-Ireland final was in 1989, when Tipperary (four goals, 29 points) beat Antrim (three goals, 9 points) by 41 to 18.

The highest ever aggregate score was when Cork 9 (six goals, 21 points)

**Largest crowd**
The largest ever attendance for a final was 84,865 for the All-Ireland final between Cork and Wexford at Croke Park, Dublin, in 1954.

**Longest hit**
The greatest distance for a 'lift and stroke' is 118 m (129 yd) credited to Tom Murphy of Three Castles, Kilkenny, in a 'long puck' contest in 1906.

### Gaelic football
**Largest crowd**
The highest ever recorded crowd was 90,556 at the Down v. Offaly All-Ireland final at Croke Park, Dublin, Republic of Ireland, in 1961.

**All-Ireland Championships**
The greatest number of All-Ireland Championships to have been won by one team is 30, by Kerry between 1903 and 1986.

The greatest number of successive wins in the All-Ireland Championships

The highest ever combined score was 45 points, when Cork beat Galway 26–19 in 1973.

### Shinty
**Most titles**
Newtonmore, Highland, has won the Camanachd Association Challenge Cup 28 times, between 1907 and 1986.

David Ritchie and Hugh Chisholm of Newtonmore, have won a record 12 winners' medals.

In 1984 Kingussie Camanachd Club won all five senior shinty competitions, including the Camanachd Cup final. Newtonmore equalled this in 1985.

**Highest shinty scores**
The highest Scottish Cup final score was in 1909 when Newtonmore beat Furnace 11–3 at Glasgow, Dr Johnnie Cattanach scoring eight hails or goals. In 1938 John Macmillan Mactaggart scored ten hails for Mid-Argyll in a Camanachd Cup match.

# Cricket records

## Test Records
### Test appearances
The most Test matches played is 156, by Allan Robert Border (Australia) from 1979 to 1994.

The English record for most Tests is 118, by Graham Alan Gooch from 1975 to 1995.

The English record for consecutive Tests is 65, by Alan Philip Eric Knott, from 1971 to 1977, and Ian Botham from 1978 to 1984.

### Longest match
The Test between England and South Africa at Durban, South Africa, on 3–14 March 1939 was abandoned after ten days because the ship taking the England team home was due to leave. The total playing time was

The greatest recorded attendance at a cricket match on one day was 90,800 on the second day of the Test between Australia and the West Indies at Melbourne, Australia, on 11 Feb 1961.

The highest attendance for a limited-overs game is an estimated 90,450 at Eden Gardens to see India play South Africa on the latter's return to official international cricket, on 10 Nov 1991.

## Limited-overs Internationals
### World Cup
The West Indies are the only double winners in the World Cup, winning in both 1975 and 1979.

### Team
The highest innings score is 398–5, by Sri Lanka v. Kenya at Kandy, Sri Lanka, on 6 March 1996.

Indies in 238 matches, from 1977 to 1994; included in this total are a record 17 centuries.

The most wickets taken is 291, by Wasim Akram (Pakistan) in 201 matches, from 1985 to 1996.

The most dismissals is 230, by Ian Andrew Healy (Australia) in 168 matches, from 1988 to 1997.

The most catches by a fielder is 127, by Allan Border (Australia).

## English County Championship
The most victories has been by Yorkshire, with 29 outright wins (the last in 1968), and one shared (1949).

The most consecutive title wins is seven, by Surrey from 1952 to 1958.

(India), for Gujarat v. Baroda at Ahmedabad, India, on 10 Jan 1951, aged 11 years 261 days.

### Test
The oldest man to play in a Test match was Wilfred Rhodes, aged 52 years 165 days, for England v. West Indies at Kingston, Jamaica, on 12 April 1930.

W. G. Grace was the oldest ever Test captain, at 50 years 320 days at Nottingham, UK, on 3 June 1899 .

The youngest Test captain was the Nawab of Pataudi (later Mansur Ali Khan), at 21 years 77 days on 23 March 1962 for India v. West Indies at Bridgetown, Barbados.

The youngest Test player was Mushtaq Mohammad, aged 15 years 124 days,

43 hr 16 min and a record Test aggregate of 1,981 runs was scored.

### Most successful Test captain
Clive Hubert Lloyd led the West Indies in 74 Test matches from 22 Nov 1974 to 2 Jan 1985. Of these, 36 were won, 12 lost and 26 were drawn. His team set records for most successive Test wins, 11 in 1984, and most Tests without defeat, 27, between losses to Australia in Dec 1981 and Jan 1985.

### Most extras in a Test match
The West Indies conceded 71 extras (21 byes, 8 leg byes, 4 wides and 38 no-balls) in Pakistan's 1st innings in Guyana, on 3–4 April 1988.

### Most extras in a one-day match
The West Indies conceded 59 extras (8 byes, 10 leg byes, 4 no balls and 37 wides) against Pakistan at Brisbane, Australia, on 7 Jan 1989.

### Largest crowds
The greatest attendance at a match is about 394,000 for the Test between India and England at Eden Gardens, Calcutta, India, on 1–6 Jan 1982.

The highest innings score between Test-playing nations is 363–7, by England v. Pakistan at Trent Bridge, Nottingham, UK, on 20 Aug 1992.

The lowest completed innings total is 43, by Pakistan v. the West Indies at Newlands, Cape Town, South Africa, on 25 Feb 1993.

The largest victory margin is 232 runs, by Australia v. Sri Lanka (323–2 to 91), at Adelaide, Australia, on 28 Jan 1985.

### Individual
The best score is 194, by Saeed Anwar for Pakistan v. India at Madras, India, on 21 May 1997.

The best bowling analysis is 7 for 37, by Aqib Javed for Pakistan v. India at Sharjah, UAE, on 25 Oct 1991.

### Career
The most matches played in one career is 273, by Allan Border of Australia, from 1979 to 1994.

The most runs scored is 8,648, by Desmond Leo Haynes of the West

The most appearances in County Championship matches is 762, by Wilfred Rhodes for Yorkshire between 1898 and 1930.

The most consecutive appearances in County Championship matches is 423, by Kenneth George Suttle of Sussex between 1954 and 1969.

James Graham 'Jimmy' Binks played in all 412 County Championship matches for Yorkshire between his début in 1955 and his retirement in 1969.

## Oldest and youngest
### First-class
The oldest player in first-class cricket was the Governor of Bombay, Raja Maharaj Singh (India), who was 72 years 192 days when he batted on the opening day of the match played on 25–27 Nov 1950 at Bombay, India for his XI against the Commonwealth XI.

The youngest first-class player is reputed to be Esmail Ahmed Baporia

for Pakistan v. West Indies at Lahore, Pakistan, on 26 March 1959.

## Wicket-keeping
### Most dismissals in an innings
The most dismissals is nine, by Tahir Rashid (eight catches and a stumping) for Habib Bank v. Pakistan Automobile Corporation at Gujranwala, Pakistan, on 29 Nov 1992; and Wayne Robert James (seven catches, two stumpings) for Matabeleland v. Mashonaland Country Districts at Bulawayo, Zimbabwe, on 19 April 1996.

Three players have taken eight catches in an innings: Arthur Theodore Wallace 'Wally' Grout for Queensland v. Western Australia at Brisbane, Australia, on 15 Feb 1960; David Edward East for Essex v. Somerset at Taunton, UK, on 27 July 1985; Stephen Andrew Marsh for Kent v. Middlesex on 31 May and 1 June 1991.

The most stumpings in an innings is six, by Henry 'Hugo' Yarnold for

# NINE DISMISSALS IN ONE INNINGS

WON, 12 LOST AND 26 WERE DRAWN

Worcestershire v. Scotland at Broughty Ferry, Dundee, UK, on 2 July 1951.

**Most dismissals in a match**
The most dismissals is 13, by Wayne James (11 catches, two stumpings) for Matabeleland v. Mashonaland Country Districts at Bulawayo, Zimbabwe, on 19–21 April 1996.

The most catches in a match is 11, by: Arnold Long, for Surrey v. Sussex at Hove, UK, on 18 and 21 July 1964; Rodney Marsh for Western Australia v. Victoria at Perth, Australia, on 15–17 Nov 1975; David Bairstow for Yorkshire v. Derbyshire at Scarborough, UK, on 8–10 Sept 1982; Warren Hegg for Lancashire v. Derbyshire at Chesterfield, UK, on 9–11 Aug 1989; Alec Stewart for Surrey v. Leicestershire at Leicester, UK, on 19–22 Aug 1989; and Timothy Neilsen for South Australia v. Western Australia at Perth, Australia, on 15–18 March 1991.

The most stumpings in a match is nine, by Frederick Huish for Kent v. Surrey at The Oval, London, UK, on 21–23 Aug 1911.

**Most dismissals in a Test innings**
The most dismissals in an innings is seven (all caught), by Wasim Bari for Pakistan v. New Zealand at Auckland, New Zealand, on 23 Feb 1979; Bob Taylor for England v. India at Bombay, India, on 15 Feb 1980; Ian David Stockley Smith for New Zealand v. Sri Lanka at Hamilton, New Zealand, on 23–24 Feb 1991.

**Most dismissals in a Test match**
The most dismissals in a match is 11, all caught, by Robert Charles 'Jack' Russell for England v. South Africa at Johannesburg, South Africa, on 30 Nov–3 Dec 1995.

**Most dismissals in a Test series**
The most dismissals in a Test series is 28, by Rodney Marsh (all caught) for Australia v. England in five matches in 1982/3.

**Most English first-class dismissals**
The most dismissals in an English first-class season is 128, by Leslie Ames (79 caught, 49 stumped) for Kent and England in 1929.

**Most first-class dismissals**
Robert William Taylor made 1,649 dismissals for Derbyshire and England from 1960 to 1988.

**Most individual Test dismissals**
Rodney Marsh made a record 355 dismissals in Test matches for Australia from 1970 to 1984.

**Most individual first-class catches**
Robert Taylor made 1,473 catches for Derbyshire and England, 1960–88.

**Most individual Test catches**
Rodney Marsh made 343 catches for Australia, from 1970 to 1984.

**Most catches in one season**
James Graham Binks achieved 96 catches for Yorkshire in 1960.

**Most first-class stumpings**
Leslie Ames made 418 stumpings for Kent and England from 1926 to 1951.

**Most individual Test stumpings**
William Oldfield made 52 stumpings for Australia from 1920 to 1937.

**Most stumpings in a season**
Leslie Ames achieved 64 stumpings for Kent in 1932.

**Most stumpings in a match**
The most stumpings is nine, by Percy William Sherwell for South Africa v. Australia in five matches in 1910/11.

## Fielding
**Most catches in an innings**
The record is seven, by: Michael Stewart for Surrey v. Northamptonshire at Northampton, UK, on 7 June 1957; Anthony Brown for Gloucestershire v. Nottinghamshire at Trent Bridge, Nottinghamshire, UK, on 26 July 1966.

**Most catches in a match**
Walter Hammond held 10 catches (four in the first innings, six in the second) for Gloucestershire v. Surrey at Cheltenham, UK, on 16–17 Aug 1928.

**The most catches in a Test match**
The most catches in a Test match is seven, by: Greg Chappell for Australia v. England at Perth, Australia, on 13–17 Dec 1974; Yajurvindra Singh for India v. England at Bangalore, India, on 28 Jan–2 Feb 1977; and Hashan Prasantha Tillekeratne for Sri Lanka v. New Zealand at Colombo, Sri Lanka, on 7–9 Dec 1992.

**Most catches in a test series**
Jack Gregory made 15 catches for Australia v. England in 1920/21.

**Most catches in an English season**
Walter Hammond made 78 catches for Gloucestershire and England in 1928.

**Most first-class catches**
Frank Edward Woolley made 1,018 catches for Kent and England between 1906 and 1938.

**Most Test catches**
Allan Border made 156 catches for Australia between 1978 and 1994.

## ENGLISH ONE DAY CRICKET
NatWest Trophy (1981) (previously Gillette Cup 1960–80), Sunday League (1969), Benson & Hedges (1972)
**HIGHEST TEAM TOTALS**
**NatWest Trophy**
413–4, Somerset v. Devon, Torquay, 1990
**Sunday League**
375–4, Surrey v. Yorkshire, Scarborough, 1994
**Benson & Hedges**
388–7, Essex v. Scotland, Chelmsford, 1992
**LOWEST TEAM TOTALS**
**NatWest Trophy**
39, Ireland v. Sussex, Hove, 1985
**Sunday League**
23, Middlesex v. Yorkshire, Headingley, 1974
**Benson & Hedges**
50, Hampshire v. Yorkshire, Headingley, 1991
**HIGHEST INDIVIDUAL INNINGS**
**NatWest Trophy**
206, Alvin Isaac Kallicharran, Warwickshire v. Oxon, Edgbaston, 1984
**Sunday League**
176, Graham Alan Gooch, Essex v. Glamorgan, Southend, 1983
**Benson & Hedges**
198 not out, Graham Gooch, Essex v. Sussex, Hove, 1982
**BEST BOWLING**
**NatWest Trophy**
8–21, Michael Anthony Holding, Derbyshire v. Sussex, Hove, 1988
**Sunday League**
8–26, Keith David Boyce, Essex v. Lancashire, Old Trafford, 1971
(Alan Ward took 4 wickets in 4 balls, Derbyshire v. Sussex, Derby, 1970)
**Benson & Hedges**
7–12, Wayne Wendell Daniel, Middlesex v. Minor Counties (East), Ipswich, 1978
(Shaun Maclean Pollock took 4 wickets in 4 balls, Warwickshire v. Leicestershire, Edgbaston, 1996)
**WICKET-KEEPING: MOST DISMISSALS**
**NatWest Trophy**
7, Alec James Stewart, Surrey v. Glamorgan, Swansea, 1994
**Sunday League**
7, Robert William Taylor, Derbyshire v. Lancashire, Old Trafford, 1975
**Benson & Hedges**
8, Derek John Somerset Taylor, Somerset v. Combined Universities, Taunton, 1982
**BATTING CAREER**
**NatWest Trophy**
2,547 runs, Graham Gooch, Essex 1973–96
**Sunday League**
8,545 runs, Graham Gooch, Essex 1973–96
**Benson & Hedges**
5,106 runs, Graham Gooch, Essex 1973–96

**Left**
South African bowler Shaun Pollock took a record four wickets in four balls for Warwickshire against Leicestershire in 1996.

**BOWLING CAREER**
**NatWest Trophy**
81 wickets, Geoffrey Graham Arnold, Surrey, Sussex 1963–80
**Sunday League**
386 wickets, John Kenneth Lever, Essex 1969–89
**Benson & Hedges**
149 wickets, John Lever, Essex 1972–89
**WICKET-KEEPING CAREER**
**NatWest Trophy**
66 dismissals, Bob Taylor, Derbyshire 1963–84
**Sunday League**
257 dismissals, David Bairstow, Yorkshire 1970–90
**Benson & Hedges**
122 dismissals, David Bairstow, Yorkshire 1972–90
**MOST WINS**
**NatWest Trophy**
6 Lancs 1970–72, 1975, 1990, 1996
**Sunday League**
4 Kent 1972–3, 1976, 1995
**Benson & Hedges**
4 Lancs 1984, 1990, 1995–6

AWAB OF PATAUDI AT 21 YEARS 77 DAYS, IN MARCH 1962 FOR INDIA

# Batting and bowling

**Right**
Andrew Symonds batting for Gloucestershire against Somerset in the English Sunday League in 1995. Symonds hit a record 16 sixes in an innings against Glamorgan on 24–25 Aug 1995.

**Far Right**
Kapil Dev bowling for India against England in the 4th Test in Calcutta, India, in 1982. From 1978 to 1994 he took 434 wickets in 131 matches.

## Team batting
### Highest innings
Victoria scored 1,107 in 10 hr 30 min v. New South Wales in an Australian Sheffield Shield match at Melbourne, Australia, on 27–28 Dec 1926.

The highest Test innings is by England who scored 903 runs for seven wickets declared in 15 hr 17 min, v. Australia at The Oval, London, UK, on 20, 22 and 23 Aug 1938.

### Lowest innings
The traditional first-class record is 12, by Oxford University (who batted a man short) v. the Marylebone Cricket Club (MCC) at Cowley Marsh, Oxford, on 24 May 1877, and by Northamptonshire v. Gloucestershire at Gloucester on 11 June 1907. However, 'The Bs' scored 6 in their second innings against England at Lord's, London, UK, in June 1810.

The lowest Test innings is 26, by New Zealand v. England at Auckland, New Zealand, on 28 March 1955.

The lowest aggregate for two innings is 34 (16 and 18), by Border v. Natal in

the South African Currie Cup at East London on 19 and 21 Dec 1959.

Leicestershire totalled only 23 (15 and 8) against Nottinghamshire (61) at Leicester, UK, on 25 Aug 1800.

## Individual batting
### Highest innings
Brian Charles Lara scored 501 not out in 7 hr 54 min for Warwickshire v. Durham at Edgbaston, UK, on 3 and 6 June 1994. His innings included the most runs in a day (390 on 6 June) and the most runs from strokes worth four or more (308, 62 fours and 10 sixes).

The highest Test innings score is 375 in 12 hr 48 min, by Brian Lara for West Indies v. England at Recreation Ground, St John's, Antigua, on 16–18 April 1994.

The English Test record is 364, by Sir Leonard Hutton v. Australia at The Oval, UK, on 20, 22 and 23 Aug 1938.

### Most runs in a Test series
Sir Donald Bradman scored 974 runs for Australia v. England in five tests in 1930.

Sir Clyde Leopold Walcott scored five centuries for West Indies v. Australia in five tests in 1954/5.

Walter Reginald Hammond had an average of 563.00 for England v. New Zealand in two innings 1932/3.

### First-class and Test career
The most runs in first-class cricket is 61,237 (average 50.65), by Sir John Berry 'Jack' Hobbs of Surrey and England, between 1905 and 1934.

The most runs in Test cricket is 11,174 (average 50.56), by Allan Border (Australia) from 1978 to 1994.

The most centuries in first-class cricket is 197, by Sir Jack Hobbs between 1905 and 1934.

The most centuries in Test cricket is 34, by Sunil Gavaskar of India between 1971 and 1987.

The highest average in first-class cricket is 95.14, by Sir Donald Bradman for NSW, South Australia, and Australia between 1927 and 1949.

The highest average in Test cricket is 99.94, by Sir Donald Bradman for Australia between 1928 and 1948.

### Most runs off an over
The first batsman to score 36 runs off a six-ball over was Sir Garfield St Aubrun Sobers, off Malcolm Andrew Nash, for Nottinghamshire against Glamorgan at Swansea on 31 Aug 1968.

In a Shell Trophy match for Wellington v. Canterbury at Christchurch, New Zealand, on 20 Feb 1990, Robert Howard Vance, who was deliberately trying to give away runs, bowled an over containing 17 no-balls and conceded 77 runs.

### Most runs off a ball
The most runs off a single ball is 10, by Samuel Hill Wood off Cuthbert James Burnup for Derbyshire v. MCC at Lord's, London, UK, on 26 May 1900.

### Most sixes in an innings
Andrew Symonds hit 16 sixes in an innings of 254 not out for Gloucestershire v. Glamorgan at Abergavenny, Monmouthshire, UK, on 24–25 Aug 1995. He added a further four in his second innings of 76 on 26 August, for a record match total of 20.

The most sixes in a Test match is 12, by Wasim Akram in his 257 not out for Pakistan v. Zimbabwe at Sheikhupura, Pakistan, on 18–20 Oct 1996.

The most sixes in a limited-overs international match is 11, by Sanath Teran Jayasuriya in his 134 for Sri Lanka v. Pakistan at Singapore on 2 April 1996, and by Shahid Afridi in a total of 102 for Pakistan v. Sri Lanka at Nairobi, Kenya, on 4 Oct 1996.

### Multiple centuries
The only batsman to have scored a triple hundred and a hundred in the same match is Graham Alan Gooch, for England v. India at Lord's, London, UK, in 1990. He scored 333 in the first innings and 123 in the second for a record Test aggregate of 456 runs.

The only batsman to score double hundreds in both innings is Arthur Edward Fagg, who made 244 and 202 not out for Kent v. Essex at Colchester, Essex, UK, from 13–15 July 1938.

### Fastest scoring
'Jim' Smith scored 50 in 11 minutes for Middlesex v. Gloucestershire at Bristol, UK, on 16 June 1938.

Clive Clay Inman scored 50 runs off a record 13 balls in 8 minutes in his innings of 57 not out for Leicestershire v. Nottinghamshire at Trent Bridge, Nottingham, UK, on 20 Aug 1965.

### Fastest centuries
The fastest century against genuine bowling took 35 minutes off 40–46 balls by Percy Fender, in his 113 not out for Surrey v. Northamptonshire at Northampton, UK, on 26 Aug 1920.

Glen Chapple hit a century in about 21 minutes off 27 balls for Lancashire v. Glamorgan at Old Trafford, Manchester, UK, on 19 July 1993.

The fastest Test hundred is 70 minutes, by Jack Morrison Gregory off 67 balls for Australia v. South Africa at Johannesburg, South Africa, in Nov 1921.

The fastest century in terms of balls received is 56, by Viv Richards for the West Indies v. England at St John's, Antigua, on 15 April 1986. His final score was 110 not out in 81 minutes.

The fastest international limited-overs century was off 37 balls, by Shahid Afridi for Pakistan v. Sri Lanka at Nairobi, Kenya, on 4 Oct 1996.

The fastest limited-overs century was scored by Graham Rose off 36 balls for Somerset v. Devon at Torquay, UK, on 27 June 1990.

### Fastest 200
The fastest 200 ever scored was by Ravi Shastri in a record 113 minutes off 123 balls for Bombay v. Baroda at Bombay, India, on 10 Jan 1985.

# 200 RUNS IN 113 MINUTES

AND SHAHID AFRIDI, BOTH IN 1996

**Fastest 300**
Denis Compton scored 300 in 181 minutes for the MCC v. North-Eastern Transvaal at Benoni, South Africa, on 3–4 Dec 1948.

**Slowest scoring**
The longest time a batsman has ever taken to score his first run is 1 hr 37 min by Thomas Godfrey Evans, before he scored 10 not out for England v. Australia at Adelaide, Australia, on 5–6 Feb 1947.

**Highest partnership**
The highest partnership is 577, by Vijay Hazare, 288, and Gulzar Mahomed, 319, for Baroda v. Holkar at Baroda, India, on 8–10 March 1947.

The highest partnership in a Test is 467, by Martin David Crowe (299) and Andrew Howard Jones (186) for New Zealand v. Sri Lanka at Wellington, New Zealand, on 3–4 Feb 1991.

## Bowling
**Most wickets in an innings**
Alfred Percy 'Tich' Freeman, who played for Kent, UK, between 1929 and 1931, is the only bowler who has ever taken all 10 wickets in an innings on three occasions.

The fewest runs scored off a bowler taking all 10 wickets is 10, off Hedley Verity for Yorkshire v. Nottinghamshire at Leeds, UK, on 12 July 1932.

**Most wickets in a match**
James Charles 'Jim' Laker took 19 wickets for 90 runs (9–37 and

**Most wickets in Test cricket**
Kapil Dev Nikhanj took 434 wickets for India in 131 tests between 1978 and 1994.

**Lowest average in Test cricket**
George Alfred Lohmann had an average of 10.75 for England in 18 Tests, between 1886 and 1896.

**Most consecutive wickets**
No bowler in first-class cricket has yet achieved five wickets with five consecutive balls.

Charles Warrington Leonard Parker of Gloucestershire struck the stumps with five successive balls in his own benefit match against Yorkshire at Bristol, UK, on 10 Aug 1922. However, the second was called as a no-ball.

The only man to have taken four wickets with consecutive balls more than once is Robert James Crisp, for Western Province v. Griqualand West at Johannesburg, South Africa, on 24 Dec 1931 and against Natal at Durban, South Africa, on 3 March 1934.

Patrick Ian Pocock took a record five wickets in six balls, six in nine balls and seven in eleven balls for Surrey v. Sussex at Eastbourne, E Sussex, UK, on 15 Aug 1972.

In his own benefit match at Lord's, London, UK, on 22 May 1907, Albert Edwin Trott of Middlesex took four Somerset wickets with four consecutive balls and then later in the same innings achieved a 'hat trick'.

West Indies v. England, 7 for 49 and 2 for 179, at Edgbaston, Birmingham, UK, on 29 May–4 June 1957. In the second innings he bowled a world record 588 balls (98 overs).

**Most expensive bowling**
The most runs conceded by a bowler in a match is 428, by Cottari Nayudu for Holkar v. Bombay at Bombay, India, on 4–9 March 1945.

The most runs hit off one bowler in an innings is 362, off Arthur Mailey of New South Wales by Victoria at Melbourne, Australia, on 24–28 Dec 1926.

The most runs conceded in a Test innings is 298, by Leslie O'Brien 'Chuck' Fleetwood-Smith for Australia v. England at The Oval, London, UK, on 20–23 Aug 1938.

innings in the same Test, with 108 and 8–34 for England v. Pakistan at Lord's, London, UK on 15–19 June 1978.

Ian Botham scored a century (114) and took more than 10 wickets (6–58 and 7–48) in a Test match, for England v. India in the Golden Jubilee Test at Bombay, India, on 15–19 Feb 1980.

This record achievement was emulated by Imran Khan Niazi with 117, 6 for 98 and 5 for 82 for Pakistan v. India at Faisalabad, Pakistan, on 3–8 Jan 1983.

**The English 'double'**
The 'double' of 1,000 runs and 100 wickets in the same season was performed on a record-breaking 16 occasions by Wilfred Rhodes between 1903 and 1926.

**Below**
In 1947, Denis Compton scored a total of 3,816 runs and 18 centuries for Middlesex and England, both of which are English cricket records. He also holds the record for scoring the fastest 300, in 181 minutes.

SCORE A CENTURY AND TAKE EIGHT WICKETS IN A TEST MATCH INNINGS

10–53) for England v. Australia at Old Trafford, Manchester, UK, from 27 to 31 July 1956.

**Most wickets in a Test series**
Sydney Francis Barnes took 49 wickets for England v. South Africa in four test matches in 1913/14.

**Lowest average in a Test series**
George Alfred Lohmann had an average 5.80 (35 wkts) for England v. South Africa in three test matches in 1895/6.

**Most wickets in an English season**
Alfred Percy 'Tich' Freeman took 304 wickets for Kent and England in 1928.

**Lowest average in a season**
Alfred Shaw had a bowling average of 8.54 for Nottinghamshire and England in 1880.

**Most wickets in first-class cricket**
Wilfred Rhodes took 4,187 wickets for Yorkshire and England between 1898 and 1930.

**Most consecutive maidens**
Hugh Joseph Tayfield bowled 16 consecutive eight-ball maiden overs (137 balls without conceding a run) for South Africa v. England at Durban, South Africa, on 25–26 Jan 1957.

The greatest number of consecutive six-ball maiden overs bowled is 21, by Rameshchandra Gangaram 'Bapu' Nadkarni for India v. England at Madras, India, on 12 Jan 1964.

Alfred Shaw of Nottinghamshire bowled 23 consecutive 4-ball maiden overs for North v. South at Trent Bridge, Nottingham, UK, on 17 July 1876.

**Most balls**
The most balls bowled in a match is 917, by Cottari Subbanna Nayudu, with figures of 6 for 153 and 5 for 275, for Holkar v. Bombay at Bombay, India, on 4–9 March 1945.

The most balls bowled in a Test match is 774, by Sonny Ramadhin for the

**Fastest**
The highest electronically measured speed for a ball bowled is 160.45 km/h (99.7 mph), by Jeffrey Thomson of Australia v. West Indies in Dec 1975.

## All-Rounders
**Test career**
The best all-round record is by Kapil Dev (India) who scored 5,248 runs (average 31.05), took 434 wickets (average 29.64) and held 64 catches in 131 matches, from 1978 to 1994.

Ian Botham (England) scored 5,200 runs (average 33.54), took 383 wickets (average 28.40) and 120 catches in 102 matches, 1977–92.

**Test series**
George Giffen scored 475 runs and took 34 wickets for Australia v. England in five Tests in 1894/5.

**Test match and innings**
Ian Botham is the only player to score a century and take eight wickets in an

The most consecutive seasons in which a player has performed the 'double' is 11 (1903–13), by George Hirst, of Yorkshire and England.

Hirst is also the only player to score 2,000 runs (2,385) and take 200 wickets (208) in the same season (1906).

**Début century and first ball wicket**
Frederick Stocks of Nottinghamshire scored a century on his first-class début against Kent at Trent Bridge, UK, on 13 May 1946, and took a wicket with his first ball in first-class cricket, against Lancashire at Old Trafford, Manchester, UK, on 26 June 1946.

Kimberley John Hughes also scored a century on his first-class début for Western Australia v. New South Wales at Perth, Australia, on 7 Nov 1975 and took a wicket with his first ball in first-class cricket for the Australians against Guyana at Georgetown, Guyana, on 28 March 1978.

# Tennis

**Below right**
Rod Laver holds up the men's singles Wimbledon trophy in 1969. In 1971 he became the first tennis player to win more than $1,000,000 (£410,000) in prize money.

## Grand Slam
### Men's titles
In 1935, Frederick John Perry (GB) became the first player to win all four major championship singles titles (Wimbledon, US, Australian and French Open championships).

The first man to hold all four championships simultaneously was John Donald Budge (USA) in 1938. (Including Wimbledon and US in 1937, he won six successive major titles).

The first man to achieve the grand slam twice was Rodney George Laver (Australia), in 1962 and again in 1969.

### Women's titles
Four women have achieved a grand slam, the first three winning six successive grand slam tournaments:

1969 and 1970 when this was held as well as the US Open.

The men's record is 12, by Roy Stanley Emerson (Australia) (six Australian, two French, two USA, two Wimbledon), from 1961 to 1967.

The most grand slam tournament wins by a doubles partnership is 20 (five Wimbledon, three French, 12 US), by Althea Louise Brough (USA) and Margaret Evelyn Du Pont (USA), from 1942 to 1957; and by Martina Navrátilová and Pam Shriver, (seven Australian, five Wimbledon, four French, four USA), from 1981 to 1989.

## Wimbledon
### Most titles
The most Wimbledon titles is 20, by Billie Jean King (USA) who won six

1953–56; Kenneth Norman Fletcher (Australia) in 1963, 1965, 1966 and 1968; and Owen Keir Davidson (Australia) in 1967, 1971, 1973 and 1974.

The women's record for mixed doubles is seven, by Elizabeth Ryan (USA) from 1919 to 1932.

### Youngest champions
The youngest champion is Martina Hingis (Switzerland) who was 15 years 282 days old when she won the women's doubles in 1996.

Charlotte 'Lottie' Dod was 15 years 285 days old when she won the singles in 1887.

The youngest men's winner was Boris Becker (West Germany) who won the

## US Championships
### Most wins
Margaret Evelyn Du Pont won a record 25 titles between 1941 and 1960: a record 13 women's doubles (12 with Althea Louise Brough), nine mixed doubles and three singles.

The record for most men's titles is 16, by William Tatem Tilden, which included seven men's singles, from 1920 to 1925 and in 1929.

Tilden's record of seven singles is shared with Richard Dudley Sears, from 1881 to 1887, and by William A. Larned, from 1901 to 1902, and from 1907 to 1911.

The record for women's singles is seven, by Molla Mallory (USA) (1915–16, 1918, 1920–22, 1926),

**Above far right**
Billie-Jean King (USA) receiving the Wimbledon trophy for women's singles after she had defeated Maria Bueno on 2 July 1968. She turned professional in 1968 and in 1971 was the first woman athlete to make more than $100,000 (£40,000) in one season.

Maureen Catherine Connolly (USA), in 1953; Margaret Jean Court (Australia) in 1970; and Martina Navrátilová (USA) in 1983–84. The fourth was Stefanie Maria 'Steffi' Graf (West Germany) in 1988, when she also won the women's singles Olympic gold medal.

### Doubles titles
Pamela Howard Shriver (USA) won a record eight successive grand slam tournament women's doubles titles with Navrátilová and 109 successive matches in all events from April 1983 to July 1985.

The first doubles pair to win the grand slam were the Australians Frank Allan Sedgeman and Kenneth Bruce McGregor in 1951.

### Most singles championships
The most singles titles won in grand slam tournaments is 24, by Margaret Court (11 Australian, 5 USA, 5 French, 3 Wimbledon), between 1960 and 1973. She also won the US Amateur in

singles, ten women's doubles and four mixed doubles from 1961 to 1979.

Elizabeth Montague Ryan (USA) won a record 19 doubles titles (12 women's and seven mixed) from 1914 to 1934.

The most men's titles at Wimbledon is 13, by Hugh Laurence Doherty (GB), with five singles titles between 1902 and 1906 and a record eight doubles from 1897 to 1901, and from 1903 to 1905, partnered by his brother Reginald Frank.

Martina Navrátilová won the women's singles a record nine times: 1978–79, 1982–87 and 1990.

The most men's singles wins since the Challenge Round was abolished in 1922 is five (consecutive), by Björn Rune Borg (Sweden) from 1976 to 1980.

The men's record for mixed doubles is four, by: Elias Victor Seixas (USA) in

men's 1985 singles title at the age of 17 years 227 days.

The youngest ever match winner was Jennifer Capriati (USA), at 14 years 89 days on 26 June 1990.

### Oldest champions
Margaret Evelyn Du Pont was 44 years 125 days old when she won the mixed doubles in 1962 with Neale Fraser (Australia).

The oldest singles champion was Arthur 'Wentworth' Gore (GB) at the age of 41 years 182 days in 1909.

### Most appearances
Arthur Gore (GB) made a record 36 appearances at Wimbledon between 1888 and 1927.

Jean Borotra (France) made 35 appearances in the men's singles, between 1922 and 1964. He then played in the Veterans' Doubles in 1977, when he was 78 years old.

and Helen Newington Moody (USA) (1923–25, 1927–29, 1931).

### Youngest and oldest
Vincent Richards (USA) was just 15 years 139 days old when he won the men's doubles US Championship title with Bill Tilden in 1918.

The youngest ever singles champion is Tracy Ann Austin (USA) who was 16 years 271 days old when she won the women's singles in 1979.

The youngest ever men's US champion is Pete Sampras (USA), who was 19 years 28 days old when he won the title in 1990.

The oldest champion was Margaret Du Pont who won the mixed doubles when she was 42 years 166 days old in 1960.

The oldest singles champion was William Larned who was 38 years 242 days old in 1911.

# LONGEST SINGLES GAME 37 DEUCES

## WAS 15 YEARS 282 DAYS OLD WHEN SHE WON THE LADIES DOUBLES IN 1996

### French Championships
**Most wins**
Margaret Court won a record 13 titles (five singles, four women's doubles and four mixed doubles) between 1962 and 1973.

The most men's titles is nine, by Henri Cochet (France) (four singles, three men's doubles and two mixed doubles) from 1926 to 1930.

The singles record is seven, by Chris Evert (USA) (1974–75, 1979–80, 1983, 1985–86).

Björn Borg won a record six men's singles (1974–75, 1978–81).

**Youngest and oldest**
Andrea Jaeger and Jimmy Arias (USA) were aged 15 years 339 days and 16

A record six men's singles were won by Roy Stanley Emerson (Australia) in 1961 and from 1963 to 1967.

Thelma Long (Australia) won 12 women's doubles and four mixed doubles for a total of 16 doubles titles.

Adrian Quist (Australia) won 10 consecutive men's doubles from 1936 to 1950 (the last eight with John Bromwich) and three men's singles.

### Grand Prix Masters
**ATP Tour Championship**
Five titles have been won by Ivan Lendl (USA), in 1982, 1983, 1986 (two) (Jan and Dec) and 1987. He appeared in nine successive finals, 1980–88.

James Scott 'Jimmy' Connors (USA) is the only player to have qualified for 14

Bill Tilden (USA) played in a record 28 finals, winning 21 (17 out of 22 singles and four out of six doubles). He was in seven winning sides from 1920 to 1926.

Nicola Pietrangeli (Italy) played a record 163 rubbers (66 ties) between 1954 and 1972, winning 120. He played 109 singles (winning 78) and 54 doubles (winning 42).

The most wins by a Briton is 45 from 52 rubbers by Fred Perry, including 34 of 38 singles, from 1931 to 1936.

### Wightman Cup
The annual women's match was won 51 times by the USA.

Christine Marie Evert (USA) won all 26 of her singles matches between 1971

### Individual records
**Longest span as national champion**
Keith Gledhill won the US National Boys' Doubles Championship with Sidney Wood in Aug 1926. He won the US National 75 and Over Men's Doubles Championship at Goleta, California, USA, 61 years later.

Dorothy May Bundy-Cheney (USA) won 180 US titles at various age groups from 1941 to 1988.

**Fastest tennis service**
On 25 May 1997, Mark Philippoussis (Australia) served at 229 km/h (142.3 mph) at Düsseldorf, Germany.

The women's best is 196 km/h (121.8 mph) by Brenda Schultz-McCarthy (Netherlands) at the Australian Championships in 1996.

**Below far left**
Slovak-born Martina Hingis (Switzerland) playing in the Australian Open in Melbourne in 1997. She went on to win the title and became the youngest ever winner, aged just 16 years 117 days. Later in the same year she won the Wimbledon singles title, the youngest winner this century.

## AND MICHAEL CHANG IN THE US CHAMPIONSHIPS SEMI-FINAL IN SEPT 1992

years 296 days respectively when they won the mixed doubles in 1981.

The youngest singles winner is Monica Seles (Yugoslavia, now USA), at 16 years 169 days in 1990.

Michael Chang (USA) is the youngest ever men's winner, aged 17 years 109 days in 1989.

Elizabeth Ryan (USA) won the 1934 women's doubles with Simone Mathieu (France), aged 42 years 88 days.

The oldest singles champion is Andrés Gimeno (Spain) in 1972, aged 34 years 301 days.

### Australian Championships
**Most wins**
The player to have won the most titles is Margaret Jean Court, who won a record 21 titles, the women's singles 11 times (1960–66, 1969–71 and 1973) as well as eight women's doubles and two mixed doubles.

consecutive years, from 1972 to 1985. He chose not to play in 1975, 1976 and 1985, and won in 1977. He qualified again in 1987 and 1988, but did not play in 1988.

Seven doubles titles were won by John Patrick McEnroe and Peter Fleming (both USA), from 1978 to 1984.

### Virginia Slims Championship
Martina Navrátilová has a record six singles wins, between 1978 and 1986.

Navrátilová has nine doubles wins, one with Billie Jean King in 1980, and eight with Pam Shriver from 1981 to 1991.

### International Team
**Davis Cup**
The most wins in the Davis Cup is 31 by the USA between 1900 and 1995.

The most appearances for Cup winners is eight by Roy Emerson (Australia), from 1959 to 1962 and from 1964 to 1967.

and 1985. Including doubles, she achieved a record 34 wins from 38 rubbers played.

At 13 years 168 days, Jennifer Capriati became the youngest ever Wightman Cup player when she beat Clare Wood (GB) 6–0, 6–0 at Williamsburg, Virginia, USA, on 14 Sept 1989.

### Federation Cup
The most wins in the Federation Cup (Fed Cup from 1995), the women's international team championship, is 15 by the USA between 1963 and 1996.

Chris Evert won 40 out of 42 singles matches from 1977 to 1989.

### Olympic Games
A record four gold medals, as well as a silver and a bronze, were won by Max Decugis (France) from 1900 to 1920.

Kitty McKane (GB) won a record five medals (one gold, two silver, two bronze) in 1920 and 1924.

### Longest match in a grand slam
The semi-final of the US Championships on 12–13 Sept 1992 between Stefan Edberg (Sweden) and Michael Chang (USA) lasted 5 hr 26 min.

### Longest games
The longest known singles game lasted 31 minutes and consisted of 37 deuces (80 points) between Anthony Fawcett (Rhodesia) and Keith Glass (GB) in the first round of the Surrey Championships, UK, in 1975.

Noëlle van Lottum and Sandra Begijn played a game for 52 minutes in the semi-finals of the Dutch Indoor Championships on 12 Feb 1984.

### Longest tiebreak
A tiebreak for the fourth set of a first round men's doubles at Wimbledon in 1985 went to 26–24. Jan Gunnarsson (Sweden) and Michael Mortensen (Denmark) defeated John Frawley (Australia) and Victor Pecci (Paraguay) 6–3, 6–4, 3–6, 7–6.

**Above left**
Mark Philippoussis (Australia) has the world's fastest serve. In 1997, one of his services was timed at 229 km/h (142.3 mph) at Düsseldorf, Germany.

# Racket sports

## Badminton
### World Championships
A record five titles have been won by Park Joo-bong (South Korea): men's doubles in 1985 and 1991 and mixed doubles in 1985, 1989 and 1991.

Three Chinese players have each won two individual world titles: Yang Yang won the men's singles in 1987 and 1989; Li Lingwei won the women's singles in 1983 and 1989; and Han Aiping won the women's singles in 1985 and 1987.

Indonesia has achieved the most wins at the men's World Team Badminton Championships for the Thomas Cup, winning a record 10 times: in 1958, 1961, 1964, 1970, 1973, 1976, 1979, 1984, 1994 and 1996.

### Longest game
In the World Championship men's singles final at Glasgow, UK, on 1 June 1997, Peter Rasmussen (Denmark) beat Sun Jun (China) 16–17, 18–13, 15–10, in a match that lasted 2 hr 4 min.

### Highest speed
In tests at Warwickshire Racquets and Health Club, UK, on 5 Nov 1996, Simon Archer (GB) hit a shuttlecock at a record 260 km/h (162 mph).

## Squash rackets
### World Championships
Jansher Khan (Pakistan) has won eight World Open titles, in 1987, 1989 and 1990, and from 1992 to 1996.

Jahangir Khan (Pakistan) won six World Open titles, from 1981 to 1985 and in

Hashim Khan (Pakistan) won seven times, from 1950 to 1955 and in 1957. He also won the Vintage title six times from 1978 to 1983.

Heather McKay (Australia) has won the British Open women's title 16 times from 1961 to 1977. She won the World Open in 1976 and 1979.

### Amateur Championship
The most wins in the Amateur Championship is six, by Abdelfattah Amr Bey (Egypt), who won in 1931, 1932 and 1933 and from 1935 to 1937. Norman Francis Borrett of England won from 1946 to 1950.

### Longest unbeaten sequences
Heather McKay remained unbeaten from 1962 to 1980.

The women's record is 119, by Rebecca O'Callaghan for Ireland.

### Highest speed
In tests at Wimbledon Squash and Badminton Club, UK, in Jan 1988, Roy Buckland hit a squash ball by an overhead service at a measured speed of 232.7 km/h (144.6 mph) over the distance to the front wall—equivalent to an initial speed at the racket of 242.6 km/h (150.8 mph).

### Largest crowd and tournament
On 30 Oct 1987, the finals of the ICI World Team Championships at the Royal Albert Hall, London, UK, had a record attendance of 3,526.

The InterCity National Squash Challenge was contested by 9,588

The most wins at the women's World Team Badminton Championships for the Uber Cup is five, by Japan in 1966, 1969, 1972, 1978 and 1981 and by China in 1984, 1986, 1988, 1990 and 1992.

### All-England Championships
Rudy Hartono Kurniawan of Indonesia has won a record of eight men's singles titles from 1968 to 1974 and in 1976.

The greatest number of titles won (including doubles) is 21, by George Alan Thomas between 1903 and 1928.

The most championship titles won by a woman is 17, by Muriel Lucas from 1899 to 1910 and by Judith Margaret 'Judy' Hashman (USA) including a record 10 singles, in 1954, 1957, 1958, 1960, 1961, 1962, 1963, 1964, 1966, and 1967.

### Shortest game
Ra Kyung-min (South Korea) beat Julia Mann (England) 11–2, 11–1 in six minutes during the 1996 Uber Cup at Hong Kong on 19 May 1996.

1988, and the International Squash Rackets Federation world individual title in 1979, 1983 and 1985.

Geoffrey B. Hunt (Australia) won four World Open titles in 1976, 1977, 1979 and 1980 and three World Amateur titles in 1967, 1969 and 1971.

The most women's World Open titles is four, by Susan Devoy (New Zealand), in 1985, 1987, 1990 and 1992.

The most men's world team titles is six, by Australia in 1967, 1969, 1971, 1973, 1989 and 1991 and Pakistan in 1977, 1981, 1983, 1985, 1987 and 1993.

The women's titles have been won four times, by England in 1985, 1987, 1989 and 1990 (Great Britain won in 1979) and Australia in 1981, 1983, 1992 and 1994.

### Open Championship
The Open Championship is held annually in the United Kingdom. Jahangir Khan has won it most often, a total of 10 times, from 1982 to 1991.

Jahangir Khan remained unbeaten for over 500 games until Ross Norman (New Zealand) ended his winning streak in the World Open final on 11 Nov 1986.

### Longest championship match
The longest competitive match lasted a record 2 hr 45 min when Jahangir Khan beat Gamal Awad (Egypt) 9–10, 9–5, 9–7, 9–2, in the final of the Patrick International Festival at Chichester, W Sussex, UK, on 30 March 1983. The first game of the match lasted a record 1 hr 11 min.

### Shortest championship match
Philip Kenyon (England) beat Salah Nadi (Egypt) in just 6 min 37 sec (9–0, 9–0, 9–0) in the British Open at Lamb's Squash Club, London, UK, on 9 April 1992.

### Most international appearances
The men's record is 122, by David Gotto for Ireland.

players in 1988 which is a knock-out tournament record.

## Table tennis
### Most titles
G. Viktor Barna (Hungary, then GB) won a record five world singles titles, in 1930 and from 1932 to 1935, and eight men's doubles from 1929 to 1935 and in 1939. With two more at mixed doubles and seven team, Viktor Barna had a total of 22 world titles.

Angelica Rozeanu (Romania) won a record six women's singles, from 1950 to 1955.

Mária Mednyánszky (Hungary) won seven women's doubles, in 1928 and from 1930 to 1935, and a record 18 world titles.

The most men's team titles (Swaythling Cup) is 12, by Hungary from 1927 to 1931, from 1933 to 1935 and in 1938, 1949, 1952 and 1979, and

# LONGEST SQUASH MATCH 2 HR 45 MIN

## ON 5 NOV 1996

China in 1961, 1963, 1965, 1971, 1975, 1977, 1981, 1983, 1985, 1987, 1995 and 1997.

The women's record (Marcel Corbillon Cup) is 12, by China in 1965, eight successive 1975–89 (biennially), and in 1993, 1995 and 1997.

### English Open
Richard Bergmann (Austria, then GB) won a record six singles, in 1939, 1940, 1948, 1950, 1952 and 1954 and Viktor Barna won seven men's doubles, in 1931, 1933, 1934, 1935, 1938, 1939 and 1949.

The women's singles record is six, by Maria Alexandru (Romania) in 1963, 1964, 1970, 1971, 1972 and 1974 and Diane Rowe who won 12 women's doubles titles, from 1950 to 1956, in 1960 and from 1962 to 1965.

Viktor Barna won 20 titles in all, and Diane Rowe 17.

### English Closed
The most titles won in the English Closed is 27, by Desmond Hugh Douglas, with a record 11 men's singles, in 1976, from 1979 to 1987 and in 1990, plus 12 men's doubles and four mixed doubles titles.

A record seven women's singles were won by Jill Patricia Hammersley, in 1973, 1974, 1975, 1976, 1978, 1979 and 1981.

### Youngest international
Joy Foster was aged eight when she represented Jamaica in the West Indies Championships at Port of Spain, Trinidad, in Aug 1958.

### Youngest English international
The youngest to play for England was Katy Parker, aged 12 years 144 days, at Manchester, UK, on 30 April 1997.

### Counter hitting
The record number of hits in 60 seconds is 173, by Jackie Bellinger and Lisa Lomas at the Northgate Sports Centre, Ipswich, Suffolk, UK, on 7 Feb 1993.

Holding a bat in each hand, S. Ramesh Babu (India) completed a record 5,000 consecutive volleys over the net in 41 min 27 sec at Jawaharal Nehru Stadium, Swargate, India, on 14 April 1995.

### Racketball
#### World Championships
The USA has won all seven team titles, in 1981, 1984, 1986 (tie with Canada), 1988, 1990, 1992 and 1994.

The most men's singles won is two, by Egan Inoue (USA) in 1986 and 1990.

The most women's singles titles won is two, by Cindy Baxter (USA) in 1981 and 1986, Heather Stupp (Canada) in 1988 and 1990, and Michelle Gould (USA) in 1992 and 1994.

### British National Championships
Six titles have been won in the women's event by Elizabeth 'Bett' Dryhurst, from 1985 to 1988 (1988 shared), in 1989 and 1991.

The men's record is three, by Nathan Dugan in 1993, 1994 and 1995.

## Rackets
### World Championships
Of the 22 world champions since 1820, the longest reign is by Geoffrey Willoughby Thomas Atkins who gained the title by beating the professional James Dear in 1954, and held it until retiring, after defending it four times, in April 1972.

### Most Amateur titles
The most titles won by an individual is nine, by Edgar Maximilian Baerlein between 1903 and 1923 and William Robin Boone between 1976 and 1993.

The most shares in amateur doubles titles is 12, by William Boone between 1975 and 1996.

The most doubles world titles by one pair is 10, by David Sumner Milford and John Ross Thompson between 1948 and 1959.

## Real tennis
### Earliest titles
The first recorded world tennis champion was Clergé (France) c.1740.

Jacques Edmond Barre (France) held the title for a record 33 years, from 1829 to 1862.

Pierre Etchebaster (France) holds the record for the greatest number of successful defences of the title—eight between 1928 and 1952.

The Women's World Championships has been won a record four times by Penny Lumley (GB) in 1989, 1991, 1995 and 1997.

### British Amateur Championship
The Amateur Championship of the British Isles has been won a record 16 times by Howard Rea Angus between 1966 and 1980 and in 1982.

Howard Angus also won eight Amateur Doubles Championships with David

Warburg, from 1967 to 1970, in 1972, 1973, 1974 and 1976.

### Oldest court
The oldest of the surviving active courts in the United Kingdom is at Falkland Palace, Fife, built in 1539.

## Fives
### Eton Fives
One pair, Brian Matthews and John Reynolds, won the amateur championship (Kinnaird Cup) a record 10 times, from 1981 to 1990.

### Rugby Fives
Wayne Enstone has won the most National singles titles, with 22 from 1973 to 1978 and 1980 to 1995.

The record for the National Doubles Championship is 10, by David Hebden and Ian Fuller, from 1980 to 1985 and from 1987 to 1990. Wayne Enstone has won the title 13 times with three different partners.

### Pelota Vasca (Jaï Alaï)
#### World Championships
Pelota Vasca is played in a walled court, or *cancha*, with two, four, or six players. The Federación Internacional de Pelota Vasca stage the World Championships every four years.

The most successful pair were Roberto Elias (Argentina) and Juan Labat (Argentina), who won the Trinquete Share a record four times, in 1952, 1958, 1962 and 1966.

Juan Labat won a record seven world titles in all, between 1952 and 1966.

Riccardo Bizzozero (Argentina) also won seven world titles in various Trinquete and Frontón Corto events, from 1970 to 1982.

The most wins in the long court game Cesta Punta is three, by José Hamuy (Mexico), with two different partners, in 1958, 1962 and 1966.

# Golf

## British Open

### Any round
The record is 63 strokes, by: Mark Stephen Hayes (USA) at Turnberry, S Ayrshire, on 7 July 1977; Isao Aoki (Japan) at Muirfield, E Lothian, on 19 July 1980; Gregory John Norman (Australia) at Turnberry on 18 July 1986; Paul Broadhurst (GB) at St Andrews, Fife, on 21 July 1990; Joseph Martin 'Jodie' Mudd (USA) at Royal Birkdale, Lancs, on 21 July 1991; Nicholas Alexander 'Nick' Faldo (GB) on 16 July and William Payne Stewart (USA) on 18 July, both at Royal St George's, Sandwich, Kent, in 1993.

### First 36 holes
Nick Faldo completed the first 36 holes at Muirfield in 130 strokes (66, 64) on 16 and 17 July 1992. He added a third round of 69 to equal the 54-hole record of 199 which he had set at St Andrews, Fife, in 1990 (67, 65, 67).

### Total aggregate
The record aggregate is 267 (66, 68, 69, 64) by Greg Norman (Australia) at Royal St George's, from 15 to 18 July 1993.

## US Open

### Any round
The record for any round is 63, by: Johnny Miller at the Oakmont Country Club course, Pennsylvania, on 17 June 1973; Jack Nicklaus and Tom Weiskopf (USA) both at Baltusrol Country Club, Springfield, New Jersey, on 12 June 1980.

### First 36 holes
The record is 134, by Jack Nicklaus (63, 71) at Baltusrol, on 12 and 13 June 1980; Chen Tze-Chung (Taiwan) (65, 69) at Oakland Hills, Birmingham, Michigan, in 1985; and Lee Janzen (USA) (67, 67) at Baltusrol, on 17 and 18 June 1993.

### Total aggregate
The record is 272, by Jack Nicklaus (63, 71, 70, 68) at Baltusrol, from 12 to 15 June 1980; and by Lee Janzen (67, 67, 69, 69) at Baltusrol, from 17 to 20 June 1993.

## US Masters

### Any round
The lowest score for any round is 63, by Nicholas Raymond Leige Price (Zimbabwe) in 1986 and Greg Norman (Australia) in 1996.

### First 36 holes
The record for the first 36 holes is 131 (65, 66) by Raymond Loran Floyd in 1976.

### Total aggregate
The record for the total aggregate in the US Masters is 270 by Eldrick 'Tiger' Woods (70, 66, 65, 69) in 1997.

## US PGA

### Any round
The record is 63, by: Bruce Crampton (Australia) at Firestone, Akron, Ohio, in 1975; Raymond Floyd (USA) at Southern Hills, Tulsa, Oklahoma, in 1982; Gary Player (South Africa) at Shoal Creek, Birmingham, Alabama, in 1984; Vijay Singh (Fiji) at Inverness Club, Toledo, Ohio, in 1993; Michael Bradley (USA) and Brad Faxon (USA) both at Riviera Pacific Palisades, California, in 1995.

### Total aggregate
The record is 267, by Steve Elkington (Australia) (68, 67, 68, 64) and Colin Montgomerie (GB) (68, 67, 67, 65) at Riviera GC, Pacific Palisades, in 1995.

## Youngest and oldest winners

### Youngest Open winner
Tom Morris Jr was aged 17 years 249 days when he won at Prestwick, S Ayrshire, UK, in 1868.

### Oldest Open winners
'Old Tom' Morris was aged 46 years 99 days when he won at Prestwick, UK, in 1867.

The oldest this century was the 1967 champion, Roberto de Vincenzo, at 44 years 93 days.

The oldest US Open champion was Hale Irwin (USA) at 45 years 15 days on 18 June 1990.

## Team Competitons

### World Cup (formerly Canada Cup)
The World Cup has been won most often by the USA, with 21 victories between 1955 and 1995.

The only men to have been on six winning teams have been Arnold Palmer (1960, 1962–64, 1966–67) and Jack Nicklaus (1963–64, 1966–67, 1971 and 1973).

Jack Nicklaus has taken the individual title a record three times (1963–64, 1971).

The lowest aggregate score for 144 holes is 536 by the USA (Fred Couples and Davis Love III), at Dorado, Puerto Rico, from 10 to 13 Nov 1994. The lowest individual score is 265, by Couples on the same occasion.

### Ryder Cup
The USA has won 23 times, drawn twice and lost six times to 1995.

Arnold Palmer has won the most matches, with 22 won, two halved and eight lost out of a total of 32.

The most contests played in is 10, by Christy O'Connor Sr (Ireland), from 1955 to 1973, and by Nick Faldo (GB) from 1977 to 1995.

### Walker Cup
The USA has won 30 times, Great Britain and Ireland four times (1938, 1971, 1989 and 1995). The match played in 1965 was tied.

Jay Sigel (USA) has won a record 18 matches, with five halved and 10 lost, between 1977 and 1993.

Joseph Boynton Carr (GB and Ireland) played in 10 contests between 1947 and 1967.

### Solheim Cup
The USA has won three times, 1990, 1994 and 1996. Europe won in 1992.

The most wins by a player is nine from 14 matches by Laura Davis (GB/Europe), from 1990 to 1996.

The most by an American is eight from 13 matches by Dottie Pepper, from 1990 to 1996.

### Curtis Cup
The USA has won 20 times to 1994.

Carole Semple Thompson (USA) has won a record 15 matches and played in nine ties between 1974 and 1996.

Mary McKenna (GB) has also played in a record nine ties, 1970–86.

## Individual Records

### Most tournament wins
John Byron Nelson (USA) won a record 18 tournaments in one year, including a record 11 consecutive wins between 8 March and 4 Aug 1945.

Sam Snead won 84 official US PGA tour events between 1936 and 1965.

The ladies' PGA record is 88, by Kathy Whitworth between 1959 and 1991.

The most career victories in European Order of Merit tournaments is 55, by Severiano Ballesteros (Spain) between 1974 and 1995.

### Biggest winning margin
The greatest margin of victory in a major tournament is 21 strokes, by Jerry Pate (USA), who won the Colombian Open with 262 from 10 to 13 Dec 1981.

Charlotte Pitcairn Leitch won the Canadian Ladies' Open Championship in 1921 by the biggest margin for a major title, 17 up and 15 to play.

### Youngest champion
On 29 April 1989, Thuashni Selvaratnam won the 1989 Sri Lankan Ladies Amateur Open Golf Championship aged 12 years 324 days.

### Oldest champion
Maria Teresa 'Isa' Goldschmid won the Italian Women's Championship, aged 50 years 200 days, at Oligata, Rome, Italy, on 2 May 1976.

## Best strokes and drives

### Longest drives
The greatest recorded drive on an ordinary course is one of 471 m (515 yd) by Michael Hoke Austin of Los Angeles, California, USA, in the US National Seniors Open Championship at Las Vegas, Nevada, USA, on 25 Sept 1974. Austin drove the ball to within a yard of the green on the par-4 412-m (450-yd) fifth hole of the Winterwood Course and it rolled 59 m (65 yd) past the flagstick. He was assisted by an estimated 56 km/h (35 mph) tailwind.

### Longest putt
The longest holed putt in a major tournament is 33.5 m (110 ft), by Jack Nicklaus in the 1964 Tournament of Champions, and Nick Price in the 1992 US PGA.

Bob Cook (USA) sank a putt measured at 42.74 m (140 ft 2¾ in) on the 18th at St Andrews, UK, in the International Fourball Pro Am Tournament on 1 Oct 1976.

## Scores

### Lowest 18 holes, men's
At least four players have played a long course (over 6,000 m or 6,561 yd) in a score of 58, most recently Monte Carlo Money (USA) at the par-72, 6,041-m (6,607-yd) Las Vegas Municipal GC, Nevada, USA, on 11 March 1981.

Alfred Edward Smith achieved an 18-hole score of 55 (15 under par 70) on his home course of 3,884 m (4,248 yd), scoring four, two, three, four, two, four, three, four, three (29 out), and two, three, three, three, three, two, five, four, one (26 in), on 1 Jan 1936.

The US PGA Tournament record is 59, by Al Geiberger in the second round of the Danny Thomas Classic, on the 72-par, 6,628-m (7,249-yd) Colonial GC course, Memphis, Tennessee, on 10 June 1977; and by Chip Beck in the third round of the Las Vegas Invitational, on the 72-par, 6,381-m (6,979-ud) Sunrise GC course, Las Vegas, Nevada, on 11 Oct 1991.

### Lowest 18 holes, women's
The lowest score on an 18-hole course (over 5,120 m or 5,600 yd) for a woman is 62 (30+32) by Mary Kathryn Wright (USA) on the Hogan Park Course (par-71, 5,747 m or 6,286 yd) at Midland, Texas, USA, in November 1964; Janice Arnold (NZ) (31+31) at the Coventry Golf Club, W Midlands,

# LONGEST DRIVE 471 M

UK, (5,317 m or 5,815 yd) on 24 Sept 1990; Laura Davies (GB) (32+30) at the Rail Golf Club, Illinois, USA, on 31 Aug 1991; and Hollis Stacy (USA) at Meridian Valley, Washington, USA, on 18 Sept 1994.

### Lowest British score
The lowest score in a professional tournament on a course of more than 5,490 m (6,000 yd) is 60, by: Paul Curry in the second round of the Bell's Scottish Open on the King's course (5,899 m or 6,452 yd), Gleneagles, on 9 July 1992; and Keith MacDonald in the third round of the Barratt Golf Mid Kent Classic at the Mid Kent GC (5,675 m or 6,206 yd) on 6 Aug 1993.

### Lowest 72 holes
The lowest recorded score on a first-class course is 255 (29 under par) by

(68, 66, 67, 66) by Betsy King (USA) in the Mazda LPGA Championship on the par-71 5,735-m (6,272-yd) Bethesda Country Club course, Bethesda, Maryland, USA, on 14–17 May 1992. She won by 11 strokes and was 17 under-par, both of which are LPGA Championship records.

### Holes-in-One
**Longest**
The longest straight hole ever holed in one shot was the 10th (408 m or 447 yd) at Miracle Hills GC, Omaha, Nebraska, USA, by Robert Mitera on 7 Oct 1965. A 80-km/h (50-mph) gust of wind carried his shot over a 265-m (290-yd) drop-off.

The longest 'dog-leg' hole achieved in one stroke is the 453-m (496-yd) 17th by Shaun Lynch at Teign Valley GC,

Dr Joseph Boydstone on the 3rd, 4th and 9th at Bakersfield GC, California, USA, on 10 Oct 1962 and Rev. Harold Snider who aced the 8th, 13th and 14th holes of the par-3 Ironwood course, Arizona, USA, on 9 June 1976.

### Youngest and oldest
Coby Orr of Littleton, Colorado, USA, shot a hole-in-one on the 94-m (103-yd) fifth at the Riverside Golf Course, San Antonio, Texas, USA, in 1975, at the age of five years.

The youngest girl was Kathryn Webb, who was nine years 275 days when she shot a hole-in-one on the 98-m (107-yd) eighth at Forbes GC, NSW, Australia, on 14 May 1972.

The oldest man to have shot a hole-in-one is Otto Bucher (Switzerland) on the

(Sweden) at Prästholmen, Mora, Sweden, on 20 Aug 1992.

### Fastest individual round
The fastest round played when the golf ball comes to rest before each new stroke is 27 min 9 sec by James Carvill at the 18-hole, 5,628-m (6,154 yd) Warrenpoint Golf Course, Co. Down, UK, on 18 June 1987.

### Fastest team round
The Fore Worcester's Children team of golfers completed 18 holes in 9 min 28 sec at the Tatnuck Country Club, Worcester, Massachusetts, USA, on 9 Sept 1996. They scored 70.

### Most holes in 24 hours, on foot
Ian Colston played a record 22 rounds and five holes (401 holes) at the par-73, 5,542 m (6,061 yd) Bendigo

Leonard Peter Tupling (GB) in the Nigerian Open at Ikoyi GC, Lagos, in Feb 1981. The score was made up of 63, 66, 62 and 64, with an average of 63.75 per round.

The lowest 72 holes in a US professional event is 257 (60, 68, 64, 65) by Mike Souchak in the 1955 Texas Open at San Antonio.

The 72-hole record on the European tour is 258 (64, 69, 60, 65), by David Llewellyn in the Biarritz Open from 1 to 3 April 1988, and by Ian Woosnam (Wales) (66, 67, 65, 60) in the Monte Carlo Open from 4 to 7 July 1990.

The lowest 72 holes in an open championship in Europe is 262 (67, 66, 66, 63) by Percy Alliss (GB) in the 1932 Italian Open at San Remo, and by Lu Liang Huan (Taiwan) in the 1971 French Open at Biarritz.

The lowest four-round total in a US LPGA Championship event is 267

Christow, near Exeter, Devon, UK, on 24 July 1995.

The longest hole-in-one by a woman is 359 m (393 yd), by Marie Robie on the first hole of the Furnace Brook GC, Wollaston, Massachusetts, USA, on 4 Sept 1949.

### Consecutive
There are at least 20 known cases of 'aces' being achieved in two consecutive holes, of which the greatest was Norman L. Manley's unique 'double albatross' on the par-4, 301-m (330-yd) seventh and par-4, 265-m (290-yd) eighth holes on the Del Valle Country Club course, Saugus, California, USA, on 2 Sept 1964.

The first woman to record consecutive 'aces' was Sue Prell, on the 13th and 14th holes at Chatswood GC, Sydney, Australia on 29 May 1977.

The closest to achieving three consecutive holes in one were

119-m (130-yd) 12th at La Manga GC, Spain, on 13 Jan 1985, at the age of 99 years 244 days.

The oldest woman was Erna Ross on the 102-m (112-yd) 17th at The Everglades Club, Palm Beach, Florida, USA, on 23 April 1986, at the age of 95 years 257 days.

### Other records
**World one-club record**
Thad Daber (USA) played the 5,520-m (6,037-yd) Lochmore GC, Cary, North Carolina, USA, with a six-iron in 70, to win the 1987 World One-Club Championship.

### Throwing the golf ball
The lowest score for throwing a golf ball round 18 holes (over 5,490 m or 6,000 yd) is 82, by Joe Flynn (USA) at the 5,695-m (6,228-yd) Port Royal course, Bermuda, on 27 March 1975.

The longest throw on record is 120.24 m (394 ft 5 in), by Stefan Uhr

GC, Victoria, Australia, from 27 to 28 Nov 1971.

### Most holes in 24 hours, with carts
David Cavalier played 846 holes at the nine-hole 2,755 m (3,013 yd) Arrowhead Country Club, North Canton, Ohio, USA, from 6 to 7 Aug 1990.

### Most holes played in a week
Steve Hylton played 1,128 holes at the Mason Rudolph GC (5,541 m or 6,060 yd), Clarksville, Tennessee, USA, from 25 to 31 Aug 1980.

Using a buggy for transport, Joe Crowley (USA) completed 1,702 holes at Green Valley Country Club (6,076 m or 6,458 yd), Clermont, Florida, USA, from 23 to 29 June 1996.

### Most balls hit in one hour
The most balls hit in an hour, over 100 yards and into a target area, is 2,146, by Sean Murphy of Vancouver, Canada, at Swifts Practice Range, Carlisle, Cumbria, UK, on 30 June 1995.

# Skiing

**Below right**
Vreni Schneider (Switzerland) is the skier who has won the most World Cup events in one season. She has also won the most Olympic medals in women's Alpine skiing.

**Below far right**
Carole Merle is one of France's most successful skiers, winning the women's World Cup Super Giant Slalom title for a then-unprecedented four successive years running.

## Skiing
### World/Olympic Championships
The World Alpine Championships were inaugurated at Mürren, Switzerland, in 1931. The greatest number of titles won has been by Christl Cranz of Germany, with seven individual (four slalom titles in 1934 and 1937–39, and three downhill in 1935, 1937, and 1939), and five combined (1934–35, 1937–39). She also won a gold for the combined in the 1936 Olympics.

The most titles won by a man is seven, by Anton 'Toni' Sailer (Austria), who won all four in 1956 (giant slalom, slalom, downhill and the non-Olympic Alpine combination) and the downhill, giant slalom and combined in 1958.

The first World Nordic Championships were held at the 1924 Winter Olympics

was not then a separate event, but only a segment of the combined event).

### World Cup
The World Cup was introduced for Alpine events in 1967. Ingemar Stenmark (Sweden) has won the most individual events with 86 (46 giant slalom, 40 slalom from a total of 287 races) from 1974 to 1989. This included a men's record of 13 in one season in 1978/9, of which 10 were part of a record 14 successive giant slalom wins from 18 March 1978 to 21 Jan 1980.

Franz Klammer (Austria) won a record 25 downhill races from 1974 to 1984.

Annemarie Moser of Austria won a women's record 62 individual events from 1970 to 1979. She had 11

### Highest speed
The official world record for a skier (as recognized by the International Ski Federation), is 241.448 km/h (150.028 mph), by Jeffrey Hamilton (USA) at Vars, France on 14 April 1995. The fastest speed ever achieved by a woman is 226.700 km/h (140.864 mph), by Karine Dubouchet (France) at Les Arcs, France, on 20 April 1996.

Nigel Brockton set a British men's speed record of 222.358 km/h (138.167 mph) at Les Arcs, France, in April 1997.

On 21 April 1993, Divina Galica set a British women's record when she achieved a speed of 200.667 km/h (124.689 mph), at Les Arcs, France.

### Races and runs
### Longest races
The world's greatest Nordic ski race is the Vasaloppet, which commemorates an event of 1521 when Gustav Vasa, later King Gustavus Eriksson, fled 85.8 km (53 miles 528 yd) from Mora to Sälen, Sweden. He was overtaken by loyal scouts on skis, who persuaded him to return to Mora to lead a rebellion and become the king of Sweden. The re-enactment of this return journey of 89 km (55 miles 528 yd) is now an annual event.

There were a record 10,934 starters on 6 March 1977 and a record 10,650 finishers on 4 March 1979.

The fastest time is 3 hr 48 min 55 sec, by Bengt Hassis (Sweden) on 2 March 1986.

in Chamonix, France. The greatest number of titles won is 11, by Gunde Svan (Sweden): seven individual (15 km 1989, 30 km 1985 and 1991, 50 km 1985 and 1989, and Olympics, 15 km 1984, 50 km 1988); four relays (4 x 10 km, 1987 and 1989, and Olympics, 1984 and 1988).

The most titles ever won by a woman is 16 by Yelena Välbe (Russia), 10 individual and six relay, 1989–97. Raisa Petrovna Smetanina (USSR) has won the most medals—23 including seven gold, between 1974 and 1992. Ulrich Wehling (GDR) is the only skier to win the same event at three successive Olympics, with the Nordic combined in 1972, 1976 and 1980.

From 1931–32 and 1935–37 Birger Ruud (Norway) won five titles—the most by a jumper. Ruud is the only person to win Olympic events in each of the dissimilar Alpine and Nordic disciplines. In 1936 he won the Ski-jumping and the Alpine downhill (which

consecutive downhill wins from Dec 1972 to Jan 1974. Vreni Schneider (Switzerland) won a record 13 events (and one combined) including all seven slalom events in the 1988/9 season.

The Nations' Cup, awarded on the combined results of the men and women in the World Cup, has been won a record 18 times by Austria: 1969, 1973–80, 1982 and 1990–97.

### Ski-jumping
Andreas Goldberger (Austria) made the longest ski-jump ever recorded in a World Cup event. He achieved 204 m (669 ft) at Harrachov, Czech Republic, on 9 March 1996.

Eva Ganster (Austria) holds the women's record, for 112 m (367 ft) at Bischofshofen, Austria, on 7 Jan 1994.

The longest dry ski-jump is 92 m (302 ft), achieved by Hubert Schwarz (West Germany) at Berchtesgarten, Germany, on 30 June 1981.

Patrick Knaff of France set a record for the fastest speed skiing on one leg of 185.567 km/h (115.306 mph) on 16 April 1988.

William Johnson (USA) holds the record for the highest average speed in the Olympic downhill race, with 104.53 km/h (64.95 mph) at Sarajevo, Yugoslavia (now Bosnia Herzegovina), on 16 Feb 1984.

On 15 March 1993 Armin Assinger (Austria) achieved a speed of 112.4 km/h (69.8 mph) at Sierra Nevada, Spain—the fastest in a World Cup downhill.

### Highest speed-cross-country
The record time for a 50 km speed-cross-country race in a major championship is 1 hr 54 min 46 sec. It was set by Aleksey Prokurorov of Russia at Thunder Bay, Canada, on 19 March 1994. His average speed was measured at 26.14 km/h (16.24 mph).

The Finlandia Ski Race, 75 km (46 miles 1,056 yd) from Hämeenlinna to Lahti, on 26 Feb 1984 had a record 13,226 starters and 12,909 finishers.

The longest downhill race is the Inferno in Switzerland, 15.8 km (9 miles 1,408 yd) from the top of the Schilthorn to Lauterbrunnen. The course record is 13 min 53.40 sec by Urs von Allmen (Switzerland) in 1991.

### Longest run
The longest all-downhill ski run is the Weissfluhjoch-Küblis Parsenn course, near Davos, Switzerland at 12.23 km (7 miles 1,056 yd).

### Cross-country (Nordic)
From 8–9 April 1988 Seppo-Juhani Savolainen covered 415.5 km (258 miles 315 yd) in 24 hours at Saariselkä, Finland.

The women's record is 330 km (205 miles 35 yd) by Sisko Kainulaisen at Jyväskylä, Finland, 23–24 March 1985.

# ONE-LEGGED SPEED 185.567 KM/H

## BY ALEKSEY PROKUROROV (RUSSIA) ON 19 MARCH 1994

Rainer Grossmann, 1991; and (women) Ingrid Hirschhofer, 1993.

### Highest speed
The speed record is 92.07 km/h (57.21 mph) by Klaus Spinka (Austria) at Waldsassen, Germany on 24 Sept 1989. Laurence Beck set a British record of 79.49 km/h (49.39 mph) at Owen, Germany on 8 Sept 1985.

## Snowshoeing
### Fastest
The IASSRF (International Amateur SnowShoe Racing Federation) record for covering 1 mile (1.6 km) is 5 min 56.7 sec, by Nick Akers of Edmonton, Alberta, Canada, on 3 Feb 1991. The 100-m record is 14.07 sec, by Jeremy Badeau at Canaseraga, New York, USA, on 31 May 1991.

## Orienteering
### Most titles
Sweden have won the men's skiing relay title six times, in 1977, 1980, 1982, 1984, 1990 and 1996.

Finland have won the women's skiing relay five times, in 1975, 1977, 1980, 1988 and 1990.

The most individual skiing titles is four by Ragnhild Bratberg (Norway), with victories in the Classic in 1986, 1990, and in the Sprint in 1988 and 1990.

### MOST OLYMPIC TITLES
**Men**
**Alpine – 3**
Anton 'Toni' Sailer (Austria)
*Downhill, slalom, giant slalom* (1956)
Jean-Claude Killy (France)
*Downhill, slalom, giant slalom* (1968)
Alberto Tomba (Italy)
*Slalom, giant slalom* (1988);
*giant slalom* (1992)
**Nordic – 5**
Bjørn Dæhlie (Norway)
*15 km, 50 km, 4 x 10 km* (1992);
*10 km, 15 km* (1994)
**Nordic (jumping) – 4**
Matti Nykänen (Finland)
*70 m hill* (1988); *90 m hill*
(1984, 1988); *team* (1988)
**Women**
**Alpine – 3**
Vreni Schneider (Switzerland)
*Giant slalom, slalom* (1988);
*slalom* (1994)
**Nordic – 6**
Lyubov Yegorova (Russia)
*10 km, 15 km, 4 x 5 km* (1992);
*5 km, 10 km, 4 x 5 km* (1994)

### MOST OLYMPIC MEDALS
**Men (Nordic) – 9**
Sixten Jernberg (Sweden), four gold, three silver and two bronze in Nordic events (1956–64)
**Women (Nordic) – 10**
Raisa Smetanina (USSR/CIS), four gold, five silver and one bronze in Nordic events (1976–92)

### Alpine – 5
In addition to their three gold medals, Alberto Tomba won silver in the 1992 and 1994 *slalom*, and Vreni Schneider won silver in the *combined* and bronze in the *giant slalom* in 1994. Kjetil André Aamodt (Norway) won one gold (*super giant slalom*, 1992), two silver (*downhill, combined*, 1994) and two bronze (*giant slalom*, 1992; *super giant slalom*, 1994).

### MOST WORLD CUP ALPINE TITLES
**Men**
**Overall – 5**
Marc Girardelli (Luxembourg)
1985–86, 1989, 1991, 1993
**Downhill – 5**
Franz Klammer (Austria)
1975–78, 1983
**Slalom – 8**
Ingemar Stenmark (Sweden)
1975–81, 1983
**Giant Slalom – 7**
Ingemar Stenmark (Sweden)
1975–76, 1978–81, 1984
**Super Giant Slalom – 4**
Pirmin Zurbriggen (Switzerland)
1987–90

Two men have won four titles in one year: Jean-Claude Killy (France) won all four possible disciplines (downhill, slalom, giant slalom and overall) in 1967; and Pirmin Zurbriggen (Switzerland) won four of the five possible disciplines (downhill, giant slalom, super giant slalom (added 1986) and overall) in 1987.

**Women**
**Overall – 6**
Annemarie Moser-Pröll (Austria)
1971–75, 1979
**Downhill – 7**
Annemarie Moser-Pröll (Austria)
1971–75, 1978–79
**Slalom – 6**
Vreni Schneider (Switzerland)
1989–90, 1992–95
**Giant Slalom – 5**
Vreni Schneider (Switzerland)
1986–87, 1989, 1991, 1995
**Super Giant Slalom – 4**
Carole Merle (France)
1989–92
Katja Seizinger (Germany)
1993–96

### MOST WORLD CUP NORDIC TITLES
**Men**
**Jumping – 4**
Matti Nykänen (Finland)
1983, 1985–86, 1988
**Cross-Country – 5**
Gunde Svan (Sweden)
1984–86, 1988–89
Bjørn Dæhlie (Norway)
1992–93, 1995–97

**Women**
**Cross-Country – 4**
Yelena Välbe (USSR/CIS/Russia)
1989, 1991–92, 1995

## OF WHEELS' IS 166 KM/H, SET IN 1964

In 48 hours Bjørn Løkken (Norway) covered 513.568 km (319 miles 205 yd) on 11–13 March 1982.

### Freestyle
The first ever World Championships were held at Tignes, France in 1986, with titles awarded in ballet, moguls, aerials and combined. Edgar Grospiron (France) has won a record three titles, moguls 1989 and 1991, and aerials 1995. He has also won an Olympic title in 1992.

Connie Kissling (Switzerland) has won the most overall titles in the World Cup (instituted 1980): 10 from 1983–92.

The men's record is five, by Eric Laboureix (France), from 1986–88 and 1990–91.

### Ski-bob
The ski-bob was the invention of J. C. Stevenson of Hartford, Connecticut, USA in 1891, and patented on 19 April 1892 as a 'bicycle with ski-runners'.

The Fédération Internationale de Skibob was founded on 14 Jan 1961 in Innsbruck, Austria, and the first World Championships were held at Bad Hofgastein, Austria, in 1967.

The highest speed is 166 km/h (103.1 mph), attained by Erich Brenter (Austria) in 1964 at Cervinia, Italy.

Petra Tschach-Wlezcek (Austria) has won the most individual combined titles in the World Championships—four from 1988–91. The most by a man is three by Walter Kronseil (Austria), 1988–90.

### Grass skiing
#### World Championships
Ingrid Hirschhofer (Austria) has won the most titles: 14 from 1979 to 1993.

The most by a man is seven by: Erwin Gansner (Switzerland), 1981–87; and Rainer Grossmann, 1985–93.

The feat of winning all four titles in one year has been achieved by: (men)

# Winter sports

## Bobsledding
### Most titles
The world four-man bob title has been won 20 times by Switzerland (1924, 1936, 1939, 1947, 1954–57, 1971–73, 1975, 1982–83, 1986–90, 1993), including five Olympic victories (1924, 1936, 1956, 1972 and 1988). Switzerland has also won the two-man title 17 times (1935, 1947–50, 1953, 1955, 1977–80, 1982–83, 1987, 1990, 1992 and 1994) including four Olympic successes (1948, 1980, 1992 and 1994).

Eugenio Monti was a member of 11 world championship crews (eight two-man and three four-man) in 1957–68.

The most Olympic gold medals won by an individual is three, by Meinhard Nehmer (GDR) and Bernhard

Germeshausen (GDR) in the 1976 two-man event, and the 1976 and 1980 four-man events.

The most medals won is seven (one gold, five silver, one bronze) by Bogdan Musiol (GDR), 1980 to 1992.

## Tobogganing
### Cresta Run
On 23 Feb 1992 Christian Bertschinger (Switzerland) made a record run of 50.41 sec. He achieved an average speed of 86.56 km/h (53.79 mph).

The most Grand National wins on the Cresta Run is eight, by the 1948 Olympic champion Nino Bibbia (Italy) in 1960–64, 1966, 1968 and 1973; and by Franco Gansser (Switzerland) in 1981, 1983–86, 1988–89 and 1991.

The most ever wins in the Curzon Cup (first instituted 1910) is eight, by Nino Bibbia in 1950, 1957–58, 1960, 1962–64 and 1969.

Prince Constantin von Liechtenstein is the oldest person to have ridden the Cresta Run, on 11 Feb 1997, aged 85.

## Snowboarding
### Most successful snowboarder
Karine Ruby (France) has won two FIS titles—the giant slalom in 1996 and board cross in 1997.

## Lugeing
### Most titles
The most World Championship titles won (including Olympics) is five, by Thomas Köhler (GDR), single-seater 1962, 1964 and 1967, two-seater 1967 and 1968; Hans Rinn (GDR) single-seater 1973 and 1977, two-seater 1976–77 and 1980; Stefan Krausee and Jan Behrendt (both GDR/Germany) two-seater 1989, 1991–93 and 1995. Georg Hackl (GDR/Germany) won four single-seater titles, 1989, 1990, 1992 and 1994.

Margit Schumann (GDR) has won five women's titles, 1973–75, 1976 (Olympic) and 1977. Steffi Walter (GDR) became the first rider to win two Olympic single-seater luge titles, with victories at the women's event in 1984 and 1988.

### Fastest speed
Asle Strand (Norway) recorded the highest photo-timed speed in the Luge, registering 137.4 km/h (85.38 mph), at Tandådalens Linabana, Sälen, Sweden, on 1 May 1982.

## Curling
### Most titles
Canada has won the men's World Championships 24 times; 1959–64, 1966, 1968–72, 1980, 1982–83, 1985–87, 1989–90, 1993–96.

The most Strathcona Cup wins is seven by Canada (1903, 1909, 1912, 1923, 1938, 1957, 1965) against Scotland.

Canada has won the women's World Championships 10 times (1980, 1984–87, 1989, 1993–94, 1996–97).

### Fastest game
On 4 April 1986, eight players from the Burlington Golf and Country Club curled an eight-end game in 47 min 24 sec, with time penalties of 5 min 30 sec, at Burlington, Ontario, Canada. The time was taken from when the first rock crossed the near hogline until the game's last rock came to a stop.

### Largest bonspiel
The largest bonspiel in the world is the Manitoba Curling Association Bonspiel held annually in Winnipeg, Canada. In 1988 there were 1,424 teams of four men, a total of 5,696 players, using 187 sheets of curling ice.

### Longest throw
On 29 Jan 1989, Eddie Kulbacki (Canada) threw a curling stone 175.66 m (576 ft 4 in) at Park Lake, Neepawa, Manitoba, Canada.

### Largest rink
The Big Four Curling Rink, Calgary, Alberta, Canada, could hold 96 teams and 384 players on 24 sheets of ice.

## Championship ice hockey
### World/Olympic titles
The USSR won 22 world titles between 1954 and 1990 (and Russia won in 1993), including the Olympic titles of 1956, 1964 and 1968. They have a record eight Olympic titles: a further five were won in 1972, 1976, 1984, 1988 and 1992 (as the CIS).

The most gold medals won by an individual is three, by Soviet players Vitaliy Semyenovich Davydov, Anatoliy Vasilyevich Firsov, Viktor Grigoryevich Kuzkin and Aleksandr Pavlovich Ragulin in 1964, 1968 and 1972, Vladislav Aleksandrovich Tretyak in 1972, 1976 and 1984, and by Andrey Khomutov in 1984, 1988 and 1992.

### Most team goals
The record for the most goals in a world championship match is 58, when Australia beat New Zealand 58–0 at Perth, Australia, on 15 March 1987.

## National Hockey League
### Stanley Cup
The Montreal Canadiens have won the Stanley Cup 24 times in 1916, 1924, 1930–31, 1944, 1946, 1953, 1956–60, 1965–66, 1968–69, 1971, 1973, 1976–79, 1986, 1993, from a record 32 finals. Joseph Henri Richard played on a record 11 winning teams for the Montreal Canadiens.

Wayne Gretzky (Edmonton, Los Angeles, St Louis and New York Rangers) has scored 382 points in Stanley Cup games and a record 122 goals and 260 assists. Gretzky scored a season's record of 47 points (16 goals and a record 31 assists) in 1985.

10:22:52

The most goals in a season is 19, scored by Reginald Joseph Leach for Philadelphia in 1976 and Jari Kurri (Finland) for Edmonton in 1985.

A record five goals have been scored on 4 occasions in a Cup game—by Maurice Richard in Montreal's 5–1 win over Toronto on 23 March 1944, by Darryl Glen Sittler for Toronto against Philadelphia on 22 April 1976, by Reggie Leach for Philadelphia against Boston on 6 May 1976 and by Mario Lemieux for Pittsburgh against Philadelphia on 25 April 1989.

The record for assists in a game is six, by Mikko Leinonen for New York Rangers v. Philadelphia on 8 April 1982, and Wayne Gretzky for Edmonton v. Los Angeles on 9 April 1987, when his team set a 13-goal Cup record.

The most points scored in a game is eight by Patrik Sundström (three goals and five assists) for New Jersey v. Washington on 22 April 1988, and by Mario Lemieux (five goals and three assists) for Pittsburgh v. Philadelphia on 25 April 1989.

### Most games played
Gordon Howe played in a 1,767 regular season games (and 157 play-off games) over 26 seasons, 1946–71, for the Detroit Red Wings and for the Hartford Whalers, 1979/80. He also played 419 games (and 78 play-off games) for the Houston Aeros and New England Whalers in the World Hockey Association from 1973 to 1979.

### Most goals and points in a season
Wayne Gretzky holds the NHL scoring records for the regular season as well as for play-off games. He has scored 862 goals, 1,843 assists for a record 2,705 points from 1,335 games. He has also scored the most goals in a season, 92 for the Edmonton Oilers,

# LONGEST CURLING THROW 175.66 M

## 2,705 POINTS, FROM 1,335 GAMES

1981/2. He scored a record 215 points, including a record 163 assists in 1985–86. In 1981/2 in all games, adding Stanley Cup play-offs and World Championship games, he scored 238 points (103 goals, 135 assists).

### Most goals in a career
The North American career record for goals is 1,071 by Gordie Howe in 32 seasons, 1946–80. He took 2,204 games to achieve his 1,000th goal, but Robert Marvin 'Bobby' Hull scored his 1,000th in his 1,600th game.

### Most goals in a game
The most points scored in a North American major league game is 10 (three goals, seven assists), by Jim Harrison for Alberta, later Edmonton Oilers, in a WHA match at Edmonton on 30 Jan 1973, and by Darryl Sittler

### Goaltending
Terry Sawchuk (1929–70) played a record 971 games as a goaltender, for Detroit, Boston, Toronto, Los Angeles and New York Rangers, 1950–70. He achieved 435 wins (to 337 losses and 188 ties) and had a record 103 career shutouts.

Jacques Plante, with 434 NHL wins, surpassed Sawchuk's figure by adding 15 wins in his one season in the WHA, for a senior league total of 449 from 868 games.

Bernie Parent achieved a record 47 wins in a season, with 13 losses and 12 ties, for Philadelphia in 1973/4.

Gerry Cheevers of the Boston Bruins went a record 32 successive games without a defeat in 1971–72.

The single team record is 16, by Montreal Canadiens v. Québec Bulldogs (3), at Québec City, Canada, on 3 Nov 1920.

The longest match was 2 hr 56 min 30 sec (playing time) when Detroit Red Wings beat Montreal Maroons 1–0 in the sixth period of overtime at the Forum, Montreal, Canada, on 25 March 1936. Norm Smith, the Red Wings goaltender, turned aside 92 shots for the NHL's longest single shutout.

### Hockey scores
#### Fastest scoring
In minor leagues, Per Olsen scored for Rungsted two seconds after the start of the match against Odense in the Danish First Division at Hørsholm, Denmark, on 14 Jan 1990. Jørgen Palmgren Erichsen achieved three

The Icy Smith Cup, the premier British club competition until 1981, was won by Murrayfield Racers nine times, in 1966, 1969–72, 1975 and 1979–81.

The British Championship has been won a record four times by Durham Wasps, in 1987–88 and 1991–92.

The British League title has been won five times by Durham Wasps, in 1985, 1988–89 and 1991–92.

The 'Grand Slam' of Autumn/Benson & Hedges Cup, British League and British Championships has been won by Dundee Rockets (1983/4), Durham Wasps (1990/1), Cardiff Devils (1992/3), Sheffield Steelers (1995/6).

The highest score and aggregate in a British League match was set when

**Below left**
Snowboarding has become increasingly popular in the 1990s and it is estimated that between four and five million people participate in the sport each year. For the first time snowboarding will be contested at the Olympic Games to be held in Nagano, Japan, in 1998.

10:23:03

10:23:20

## THE OPENING WHISTLE WAS ACHIEVED IN ONLY 5 SEC, BY DOUG SMAIL

(six goals, four assists) for Toronto Maple Leafs v. Boston Bruins in an NHL match at Toronto on 7 Feb 1976.

The most goals in a game is seven, by Joe Malone in Québec's 10–6 win over Toronto St. Patricks at Québec City, Canada, on 31 Jan 1920.

The most assists is seven, by Billy Taylor for Detroit v. Chicago on 16 March 1947 and three times by Wayne Gretzky for Edmonton, v. Washington on 15 Feb 1980, v. Chicago on 11 Dec 1985, and v. Québec on 14 Feb 1986.

### Fastest goal
From the opening whistle, the fastest goal was in 5 seconds by Doug Smail (Winnipeg Jets) v. St Louis Blues at Winnipeg, USA, on 20 Dec 1981, and by Bryan John Trottier (New York Islanders) v. Boston Bruins at Boston, USA, on 22 March 1984. Bill Mosienko (Chicago Black Hawks) scored three goals in 21 sec v. New York Rangers on 23 March 1952.

### Most successful teams
The Detroit Red Wings won a record 62 games in the 1995/6 season.

The Montreal Canadiens scored a record 132 points (60 wins and 12 ties) from 80 games played in 1976/7.

The Boston Bruins won 30 out of 44 times in 1929/30 (68%)—the highest percentage of wins in a season.

The longest undefeated run during a season, 35 games (25 wins and ten ties), was by the Philadelphia Flyers from 14 Oct 1979 to 6 Jan 1980.

The Edmonton Oilers scored the most goals, 446, and the most points, 1,182, in a season in 1983/4.

The highest aggregate score is 21: the Montreal Canadiens beat Toronto St Patrick's, 14–7, at Montreal, Canada, on 10 Jan 1920, and Edmonton Oilers beat Chicago Black Hawks, 12–9, at Chicago, USA, on 11 Dec 1985.

goals in 10 seconds for Frisk v. Holmen in a junior league match in Norway on 17 March 1991. The Vernon Cougars scored five goals in 56 seconds against Salmon Arm Aces at Vernon, BC, Canada on 6 Aug 1982. The Kamloops Knights of Columbus scored seven goals in 2 min 22 sec v. Prince George Vikings on 25 Jan 1980.

The fastest goal in the British League was scored after four seconds by Stephen Johnson for Durham Wasps v. Ayr Bruins at Ayr, South Ayrshire, on 6 Nov 1983.

### Other competitions
#### British competitions
The English (later British) League Championship has been won by Streatham (later Redskins) a record five times, in 1935, 1950, 1953, 1960 and 1982.

Murrayfield Racers have won the Northern League seven times, in 1970–72, 1976, 1979–80 and 1985.

Medway Bears beat Richmond Raiders 48–1 at Gillingham in a Second Division fixture on 1 Dec 1985. Kevin MacNaught scored a record 25 points from seven goals and 18 assists.

#### Individual scoring records
The most individual goals scored in a senior game is 18, by Rick Smith in a 27–2 win for Chelmsford Chieftains against Sheffield Sabres.

Steve Moria achieved the highest number of assists, 13, for Fife Flyers at Cleveland on 28 March 1987. Rick Fera set British season's records of 165 goals and 318 points for Murrayfield Racers in 1986/7.

Tim Salmon (Canada) achieved a season's record 183 assists in 47 games for Ayr Bruins in 1985/6.

The highest points for the Heineken League is 2,136 (875 goals, 1,281 assists) by Tony Hand in 449 games at the end of the 1994/5 season.

# Skating

## Ice skating
### Figure skating

The most Olympic gold medals is three, by Gillis Grafström (Sweden) in 1920, 1924 and 1928; Sonja Henie (Norway) in 1928, 1932 and 1936; and Irina Konstantinovna Rodnina (USSR) in 1972, 1976 and 1980.

The most men's individual world figure skating titles is 10, by Ulrich Salchow (Sweden) in 1901–05 and 1907–11.

The women's record is also 10 individual titles, by Sonja Henie (Norway) between 1927 and 1936.

Irina Rodnina (USSR) won 10 pairs titles, four with Aleksey Nikolayevich Ulanov, 1969–72, and six with her husband Aleksandr Gennadyevich Zaitsev, 1973–78.

The most ice dance titles won is six, by Lyudmila Alekseyevna Pakhomova (1946–86) and her husband Aleksandr Georgiyevich Gorshkov (USSR), 1970–74 and 1976. They also won the first Olympic ice dance title in 1976.

The most individual British men's titles won is 11, by Jack Ferguson Page in 1922–31 and 1933, and the most individual British women's titles won is six, by Magdalena Cecilia Colledge in 1935–36, 1937 (two), 1938 and 1946, and by Joanne Conway, 1985–91.

The most pairs titles won by an ice dance couple is seven by Jayne Torvill and Christopher Colin Dean (GB), 1978–83 and 1994.

Karl Schäfer (Austria) and Sonja Henie (Norway) achieved double 'Grand Slams', both in the years 1932 and 1936. This feat was repeated by Katarina Witt (GDR) in 1984 and 1988.

The only British skaters to win the 'Grand Slam' of World, Olympic and European titles in the same year are John Curry in 1976 and the ice dancers Jayne Torvill and Christopher Dean in 1984.

### Youngest champion
Tara Lipinski (USA) became the youngest winner of a world title when she won the individual title on 22 March 1997, aged 14 years 286 days.

### Highest marks
The highest tally of maximum six marks awarded in an international championship is 29, to Jayne Torvill and Christopher Dean in the World Ice Dance Championships at Ottawa, Canada, on 22–24 March 1984 (seven in the compulsory dances, a perfect set of nine for presentation in the set

pattern dance and 13 in the free dance, including another perfect set from all nine judges for artistic presentation). They were also awarded a perfect set of nine sixes for artistic presentation in the free dance at the 1983 World Championships in Helsinki,

Finland, and at the 1984 Winter Olympic Games in Sarajevo, Bosnia (then Yugoslavia).

The most six marks by a soloist is seven, by Donald George Jackson (Canada) in

the World Men's Championship at Prague, Czech Republic (then Czechoslovakia), in 1962; and by Midori Ito (Japan) in the World Women's Championships at Paris, France, 1989.

### Distance
Robin Cousins (UK) set a distance record of 5.81 m (19 ft 1 in) in an axel jump and 5.48 m (18 ft) with a back flip at Richmond Ice Rink, Greater London, UK, on 16 Nov 1983.

### Most mid-air rotations
Kurt Browning (Canada) was the first to achieve a quadruple jump in competition—a toe loop—in the World Championships at Budapest, Hungary, on 25 March 1988. The first woman to do so was Surya Bonaly (France) in the World Championships at Munich, Germany, on 16 March 1991.

### Speed skating
The most Olympic gold medals won is six (two in 1960, four in 1964), by Lidiya Pavlovna Skoblikova (USSR).

The men's record for Olympic golds is five, by Clas Thunberg (Finland), in 1924 and 1928, and Eric Arthur Heiden (USA), both at the Olympics at Lake Placid, New York, USA, in 1980.

The most Olympic medals is eight, by Karin Kania (GDR) (three gold, four silver and a bronze), 1980–88.

The men's world record is seven, by Clas Thunberg (five gold, one silver and one bronze), and Ivar Ballangrud (Norway) (four gold, two silver and a bronze), 1928–36.

The greatest number of world overall titles won by any skater is five, by Oscar Mathisen (Norway), 1908–09 and 1912–14, and by Clas Thunberg, 1923, 1925, 1928–29 and 1931.

The most titles won in the women's events is five, by Karin Kania (GDR) in 1982, 1984, 1986–88. Kania also won a record six overall titles at the World Sprint Championships 1980–81, 1983–84, 1986–87.

A record six men's sprint overall titles have been won by Igor Zhelezovskiy (USSR/Belarus), 1985–86, 1989 and 1991–93.

Rintje Ritsma achieved a record score of 156.201 points at Hamar, Norway, on 7–9 Jan 1994 for the world title.

Emese Hunyady (Austria) achieved a record low women's score of 164.658 points at Calgary, Canada, on 26–27 March 1994.

### World Short-track Championships
The most successful skater in the World Short-track Championships has been Sylvia Daigle (Canada), women's overall champion in 1979, 1983 and 1989–90.

The first British skater to ever win the short-track world title was Wilfred John O'Reilly at Sydney, Australia, on 24 March 1991.

### Longest race
The 'Elfstedentocht' ('Tour of the Eleven Towns'), which originated in the 17th century, was held in the Netherlands from 1909–63, in 1985, 1986, and 1997, covering 200 km (124 miles 483 yd). When the weather will not allow the race to take place in the Netherlands, other venues are chosen. The record time for 200 km is: men, 5:40:37, by Dries van Wijhe (Netherlands); and women, 5:48:8, by Alida Pasveer (Netherlands), both at Lake Weissen, Austria, on 11 Feb 1989.

Jan-Roelof Kruithof (Netherlands) has won the race nine times, 1974, 1976–77, 1979–84.

### 24 hours
Martinus Kuiper (Netherlands) skated 546.65 km (339 miles 1,183 yd) in 24 hours in Alkmaar, Netherlands, on 12–13 Dec 1988.

### Barrel jumping on ice skates
The official distance record for jumping over 18 barrels is 8.97 m (29 ft 5 in), by Yvon Jolin at Terrebonne, Québec, Canada, on 25 Jan 1981.

The women's world record over 13 barrels is 6.84 m (22 ft 5¼ in), by Marie-Josée Houle at Lasalle, Québec, Canada, on 1 March 1987.

### Roller skating
#### Most titles
Alberta Vianello (Italy) has won 18 world speed titles, eight track and 10 road competitions (1953–65); at distances from 500 m to 10,000 m.

# LONGEST SWIM IN 24 HOURS 101.9 KM

EVERN RIVER BORE

### Underwater swimming

Paul Cryne (GB) and Samir Sawan al Awami of Qatar swam 78.92 km (49 miles 68 yd) in a 24-hr period from Doha to Umm Said (both Qatar) and back, from 21 to 22 Feb 1985. The men, who were using sub-aqua equipment, were swimming underwater for 95.5% of the time.

The relay team record is 151.987 km (94 miles 773 yd), by six swimmers in a pool at Olomouc, Czechoslovakia, from 17–18 Oct 1987.

## Diving

### Most Olympic medals

The most medals won by a diver is five, by Klaus Dibiasi (Italy) with three gold, two silver between 1964 and 1976; and by Gregory Efthimios Louganis

springboard event and 710.91 for the highboard at the 1984 Olympic Games.

The first diver awarded a perfect score of 10.0 by all seven judges was Michael Holman Finneran, for a backward 1½ somersault, 2½ twist, from the 10-m board, in the 1972 US Olympic Trials, in Chicago, Illinois, USA.

Greg Louganis was awarded 10.0 by all seven judges for his highboard inward 1½ somersault in the pike position at the World Championships in Guayaquil, Ecuador, in 1984.

## Water polo

### Most Olympic titles

Hungary has the most Olympic tournament wins with six; in 1932, 1936, 1952, 1956, 1964 and 1976.

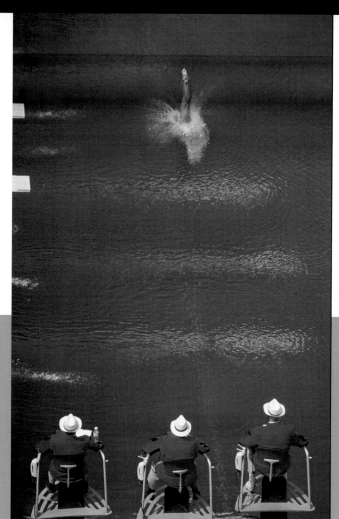

**Below far left**
Hungary has won the Olympic water polo title a record six times in 1932, 1936, 1952, 1956, 1964 and 1972.

**Left**
The most successful diver in the history of the sport is the American Greg Louganis. He won a record five Olympic medals, including both highboard and springboard golds at two Olympic Games, in 1984 and 1988.

EVEN JUDGES FOR A HIGHBOARD INWARD 1¹/₂ SOMERSAULT IN THE PIKE POSITION

(USA), with four golds and one silver in 1976, 1984 and 1988.

Klaus Dibiasi is the only diver to have ever won the same event at three successive Games (highboard in 1968, 1972 and 1976).

Two divers have won the highboard and springboard doubles at two games: Patricia Joan McCormick (USA) in 1952 and 1956 and Greg Louganis (USA) in 1984 and 1988.

### Most world titles

Greg Louganis (USA) won a record five world titles (highboard in 1978, and both highboard and springboard in 1982 and 1986), and four Olympic gold medals in 1984 and 1988. Three golds in one event have been won by Philip Boggs (USA) (springboard in 1973, 1975 and 1978).

### Highest scores

Greg Louganis achieved record scores of 754.41 points for the 11-dive

The record for the most gold medals is three, by George Wilkinson (GB) in 1900, 1908 and 1912; by Paulo 'Paul' Radmilovic (GB), and Charles Sidney Smith (GB) in 1908, 1912 and 1920 (the former also won a gold medal for the 4 x 200-m freestyle swimming in 1908); and by Deszö Gyarmati (Hungary) and György Kárpáti (Hungary) in 1952, 1956 and 1964.

### Most world titles

The USSR (1975 and 1982), Yugoslavia (1986 and 1991), and Italy (1978 and 1994) have all won the World Championships twice.

### Most goals

The most scored by an individual in an international is 13, by Debbie Handley during Australia's 16–10 defeat of Canada at the World Championship in Guayaquil, Ecuador, in 1982.

### Most international appearances

The greatest number of international appearances is 412, by Aleksey

Stepanovich Barkalov (USSR) between 1965 and 1980.

The most international appearances by a British player is 126, by Martyn Thomas, of Cheltenham, Glos, UK, between 1964 and 1978.

## Surfing

### Most World Amateur titles

The record for the most Amateur Championship titles is three, by Michael Novakov (Australia), who won the Kneeboard event in 1982, 1984 and 1986.

### Most World Professional titles

Mark Richards (Australia) has won the men's World Professional surfing title five times in 1975 and from 1979 to 1982.

The most women's titles won is four, by Frieda Zamba (USA), from 1984 to 1986 and in 1988, and Wendy Botha (Australia, formerly South Africa), in 1987, 1989, 1991 and 1992.

### Highest waves ridden

Waimea Bay in Hawaii reputedly provides the most consistently high waves, often reaching the rideable limit of 9–11 m (30–35 ft).

The highest wave ever ridden was the tsunami of 'perhaps 50 ft', which struck Minole, Hawaii, on 3 April 1868. An Hawaiian named Holua rode the wave to save his life.

### Longest sea wave ride

About four to six times each year rideable surfing waves break in Matanchen Bay near San Blas, Nayarit, Mexico, making rides of c. 1,700 m (5,700 ft) long possible.

### Longest ride

The longest recorded rides on a river bore have been set on the Severn bore, UK. The official British Surfing Association world record for riding a surfboard is 9.1 km (5.7 miles) by David Lawson from Windmill Hill to Maisemore Weir on 29 Aug 1996.

# Swimming records

## Olympic Games

### Most men's medals

Mark Spitz (USA) won nine gold medals: 100-m and 200-m freestyle 1972; 100-m and 200-m butterfly 1972; 4 x 100-m freestyle 1968 and 1972; 4 x 200-m freestyle 1968 and 1972; 4 x 100-m medley 1972. All but the 1968 4 x 200-m freestyle were also new world records.

He also won a silver (100-m butterfly) and a bronze (100-m freestyle) in 1968, making a record 11 medals.

Spitz's record seven medals at one Games in 1972 was equalled by Matt Biondi (USA) who took five gold, one silver and one bronze in 1988. Biondi also shares Spitz's record total of 11 medals, as he won a gold in 1984, and two golds and a silver in 1992.

### Most women's medals

Kristin Otto (GDR) won a record six medals at Seoul in 1988: 100-m freestyle, backstroke and butterfly, 50-m freestyle, 4 x 100-m freestyle and 4 x 100-m medley.

### Most individual wins

Only two swimmers have won the same event on three occasions, Dawn Fraser (Australia), 100-m freestyle, 1956, 1960 and 1964 and Krisztina Egerszegi (Hungary), 200-m backstroke, 1988, 1992 and 1996.

The most medals won by a woman is eight by: Dawn Fraser, four golds and four silvers 1956–64; Kornelia Ender (GDR), four golds and four silvers 1972–76; and Shirley Babashoff (USA) two golds and six silvers 1972–76.

### Most individual gold medals

The most individual gold medals won is five by Krisztina Egerszegi (Hungary) with 100-m backstroke in 1992, 200-m backstroke in 1988, 1992 and 1996 and 400-m medley in 1992.

The most by a man is four, by Charles Daniels (USA) in the 100-m freestyle in 1906 and 1908, 220-yd freestyle in 1904, 440-yd freestyle in 1904; Roland Matthes (GDR) in the 100-m and 200-m backstroke in 1968 and 1972; Mark Spitz and Tamás Daryni (Hungary) in the 200-m and 400-m medley in 1988 and 1992; Aleksandr Popov (Russia) in the 50-m and 100-m freestyle in 1992 and 1996.

### Fastest swimmer

In a 25-yd pool, Tom Jager (USA) achieved an average speed of 8.64 km/h (5.37 mph) for 50 yards in 19.05 sec at Nashville, Tennessee, USA, on 23 March 1990.

The fastest women's speed is 7.34 km/h (4.56 mph) by Le Jingyi (China) in her 50-m world record.

### Most world records

The most men's world records is 32, held by Arne Borg of Sweden, from 1921–29.

The most women's world records is 42, by Ragnhild Hveger (Denmark), 1936–42.

For currently recognized events (only metric distances in 50-m pools), the most men's world records is 26, by Mark Spitz (USA), 1967–72, and the women's is 23, by Kornelia Ender (GDR), 1973–76.

The most world records set in a single pool is 86 in the North Sydney pool, Australia, between 1955 and 1978.

### Most world titles

Michael Gross (West Germany) won 13 World Championship medals, five gold, five silver and three bronze, 1982–90.

The most medals won by a woman is 10, by Kornelia Ender with eight gold and two silver in 1973 and 1975.

The most gold medals by a man is six by James Paul Montgomery (USA) in 1973 and 1975.

The most medals won at a single championship is seven, by Matthew Nicholas Biondi (USA) in 1986.

### SHORT-COURSE WORLD RECORDS
(set in 25-m pools)

### MEN

#### Freestyle

**50 m:** 21.50 Aleksandr Popov (Russia) Desenzano, Italy, 13 March 1994
**100 m:** 46.74 Aleksandr Popov (Russia) Gelsenkirchen, Germany, 19 March 1994
**200 m:** 1:43.64 Giorgio Lamberti (Italy) Bonn, Germany, 11 Feb 1990
**400 m:** 3:40.46 Danyon Loader (New Zealand) Sheffield, S Yorkshire, UK, 11 Feb 1995
**800 m:** 7:34.90 Kieren Perkins (Australia) Sydney, Australia, 25 July 1993
**1,500 m:** 14:26.52 Kieren Perkins (Australia) Auckland, New Zealand, 15 July 1993
**4 x 50-m:** 1:27.62 Sweden Stavanger, Norway, 2 Dec 1994
**4 x 100-m:** 3:12.11 Brazil Palma de Mallorca, Spain, 5 Dec 1993
**4 x 200-m:** 7:02.74 Australia, Gothenburg, Sweden, 18 April 1997

#### Backstroke

**50 m:** 24.25 Chris Renaud (Canada) St Catharine's, Canada, 1 March 1997
**100 m:** 51.43 Jeff Rouse (USA) Sheffield, S Yorkshire, UK, 12 April 1993
**200 m:** 1:52.51 Martin López-Zubero (Spain) Gainesville, Florida, USA, 11 April 1991

#### Breaststroke

**50 m:** 26.97 Mark Warnecke (Germany) Paris, France, 8 Feb 1997
**100 m:** 59.02 Frédéric Deburghgraeve (Belgium) Bastogne, Belgium, 17 Feb 1996
**200 m:** 2:07.66 Ryan Mitchell (Australia) Melbourne, Australia, 21 Dec 1996

#### Butterfly

**50 m:** 23.35 Denis Pankratov (Russia) Paris, France, 8 Feb 1997
**100 m:** 51.78 Denis Pankratov (Russia) Paris, France, 9 Feb 1997
**200 m:** 1:52.64 Denis Pankratov (Russia) Gelsenkirchen, Germany, 1 Feb 1997
*1:52.34 Denis Pankratov (Russia) Paris, France, 3 Feb 1996
* Not ratified.

#### Medley

**100 m:** 53.10 Jani Sievinen (Finland) Malmö, Sweden, 30 Jan 1996
**200 m:** 1:54.65 Jani Sievinen (Finland) Kuopio, Finland, 21 Jan 1994
**400 m:** 4:05.41 Marcel Wouda (Netherlands) Paris, France, 9 Feb 1997
**4 x 50-m:** 1:36.69 Auburn Aquatics Auburn, New York, USA, 9 April 1996
**4 x 100-m:** 3:30.66 Australia Gothenburg, Sweden, 17 April 1997

### WOMEN

#### Freestyle

**50 m:** 24.23 Le Jingyi (China) Palma de Mallorca, Spain, 3 Dec 1993
**100 m:** 53.01 Le Jingyi (China) Palma de Mallorca, Spain, 2 Dec 1993
**200 m:** 1:54.17 Claudia Poll (Costa Rica) Gothenburg, Sweden, 17 April, 1997
**400 m:** 4:00.03 Claudia Poll (Costa Rica) Gothenburg, Sweden, 19 April, 1997
**800 m:** 8:15.34 Astrid Strauss (GDR) Bonn, Germany, 6 Feb 1987

**1,500 m:** 15:43.31 Petra Schneider (GDR) Gainesville, Florida, USA, 10 Jan 1982
**4 x 50-m:** 1:40.63 Germany Espoo, Finland, 22 Nov 1992
**4 x 100-m:** 3:34.55 China Gothenburg, Sweden, 19 April 1997
**4 x 200-m:** 7:51.92 China Gothenburg, Sweden, 17 April 1997

#### Backstroke

**50 m:** 27.64 Bai Xiuyu (China) Desenzano, Italy, 12 March 1994
**100 m:** 58.50 Angel Martino (USA) Palma de Mallorca, Spain, 3 Dec 1993
**200 m:** 2:06.09 He Cihong (China) Palma de Mallorca, Spain, 5 Dec 1993

#### Breaststroke

**50 m:** 30.77 Han Xue (China) Gelsenkirchen, Germany, 2 Feb 1997

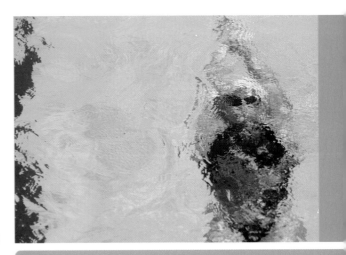

DENIS PANKRATOV BROKE TWO WORLD

**100 m:** 1:05.70 Samantha Riley (Australia) Rio de Janeiro, Brazil, 2 Dec 1995
**200 m:** 2:20.85 Samantha Riley (Australia) Rio de Janeiro, Brazil, 1 Dec 1995

#### Butterfly

**50 m:** 26.55 Misty Hyman (USA) Gothenburg, Sweden, 19 April 1997
**100 m:** 57.79 Jenny Thompson (USA) Gothenburg, Sweden, 19 April 1997
**200 m:** 2:05.65 Mary Terstegge Meagher (USA) Gainesville, Florida, USA, 2 Jan 1981

#### Medley

**100 m:** 1:01.03 Louise Karlsson (Sweden) Espoo, Finland, 22 Nov 1992
**200 m:** 2:07.79 Allison Wagner (USA) Palma de Mallorca, Spain, 5 Dec 1993
**400 m:** 4:29.00 Dai Gouhong (China) Palma de Mallorca, Spain, 5 Dec 1993
**4 x 50-m:** 1:52.44 Germany Espoo, Finland, 21 Nov 1992
**4 x 100-m:** 3:57.73 China Palma de Mallorca, Spain, 5 Dec 1993

# FASTEST AVERAGE SPEED 8.64 KM/H

**WORLD RECORDS**
(set in 50-m pools)

**MEN**
**Freestyle**
**50 m:** 21.81 Tom Jager (USA) Nashville, Tennessee, USA, 24 March 1990
**100 m:** 48.21 Aleksandr Popov (Russia) Monte Carlo, Monaco, 18 June 1994
**200 m:** 1:46.69 Giorgio Lamberti (Italy) Bonn, Germany, 15 Aug 1989
**400 m:** 3:43.80 Kieren Perkins (Australia) Rome, Italy, 9 Sept 1994
**800 m:** 7:46.00 Kieren Perkins (Australia) Victoria, Canada, 24 Aug 1994
**1,500 m:** 14:41.66 Kieren Perkins (Australia) Victoria, Canada, 24 Aug 1994

**4 x 100-m:** 3:34.84 USA Atlanta, GA, USA, 26 July 1996

**WOMEN**
**Freestyle**
**50 m:** 24.51 Le Jingyi (China) Rome, Italy, 11 Sept 1994
**100 m:** 54.01 Le Jingyi (China) Rome, Italy, 5 Sept 1994
**200 m:** 1:56.78 Franziska van Almsick (Germany) Rome, Italy, 6 Sept 1994
**400 m:** 4:03.85 Janet Evans (USA) Seoul, South Korea, 22 Sept 1988
**800 m:** 8:16.22 Janet Evans (USA) Tokyo, Japan, 20 Aug 1989
**1,500 m:** 15:52.10 Janet Evans (USA) Orlando, Florida, USA, 26 March 1988
**4 x 100-m:** 3:37.91 China Rome, Italy, 7 Sept 1994
**4 x 200-m:** 7:55.47 GDR Strasbourg, France, 18 Aug 1987

**BRITISH NATIONAL RECORDS**

**MEN**
**Freestyle**
**50 m:** 22.43 Mark Foster Sheffield, S Yorkshire, UK, 24 May 1992
**100 m:** 50.04 Nicholas Shackwell Sheffield, S Yorkshire, UK, 11 May 1997
**200 m:** 1:48.84 Paul Palmer Sheffield, S Yorkshire, UK, 3 Aug 1993
**400 m:** 3:48.14 Paul Palmer Sheffield, S Yorkshire, UK, 6 Aug 1993
**800 m:** 7:59.48 Graeme Smith Sheffield, S Yorkshire, UK, 22 March 1996
**1,500 m:** 15:03.43 Graeme Smith Sheffield, S Yorkshire, UK,

**4 x 100-m:** 3:41.66 GB Sheffield, S Yorkshire, UK, 8 Aug 1993

**WOMEN**
**Freestyle**
**50 m:** 26.01 Caroline Woodcock Bonn, Germany, 20 Aug 1989
**100 m:** 55.79 Karen Pickering Rome, Italy, 5 Sept 1994
**200 m:** 1:59.74 June Croft Brisbane, Australia, 4 Oct 1982
**400 m:** 4:07.68 Sarah Hardcastle Edinburgh, UK, 27 July 1986
**800 m:** 8:24.77 Sarah Hardcastle Edinburgh, UK, 29 July 1986
**1,500 m:** 16:39.46 Sarah Hardcastle Edinburgh, UK, 31 March 1994
**4 x 100-m:** 3:45.52 GB Rome, Italy, 7 Sept 1994
**4 x 200-m:** 8:09.62 England Victoria, Canada, 20 Aug 1994

**Below far left**
Although competitive swimming can be traced back to the 18th century, the world governing body FINA was not established until 1908.

**Below centre**
Irish swimmer Michelle Smith won three gold medals at the 1996 Olympics, Atlanta, USA.

**Below right**
Aleksandr Popov (second from right) set a new 100-m freestyle record of 48.21 sec at Monte Carlo, Monaco on 18 June 1994.

## RECORDS ON CONSECUTIVE DAYS FOR 50-M AND 100-M BUTTERFLY, 8-9 FEB 1997

**4 x 100-m:** 3:15.11 USA Atlanta, Georgia, USA, 12 Aug 1995
**4 x 200-m:** 7:11.95 CIS Barcelona, Spain, 27 July 1992
**Breaststroke**
**100 m:** 1:00.60 Frédéric Deburghgraeve (Belgium) Atlanta, GA, USA, 20 July 1996
**200 m:** 2:10.16 Michael Barrowman (USA) Barcelona, Spain, 29 July 1992
**Butterfly**
**100 m:** 52.27 Denis Pankratov (Russia) Atlanta, GA, USA, 24 July 1996
**200 m:** 1:55.22 Denis Pankratov (Russia) Paris, France, 14 June 1995
**Backstroke**
**100 m:** 53.86 Jeff Rouse (USA) (relay leg) Barcelona, Spain, 31 July 1992
**200 m:** 1:56.57 Martin López-Zubero (Spain) Tuscaloosa, Alabama, USA, 23 Nov 1991
**Medley**
**200 m:** 1:58.16 Jani Sievinen (Finland) Rome, Italy, 11 Sept 1994
**400 m:** 4:12.30 Tom Dolan (USA) Rome, Italy, 6 Sept 1994

**Breaststroke**
**100 m:** 1:07.02 Penelope 'Penny' Heyns (South Africa) Atlanta, GA, USA, 21 July 1996
**200 m:** 2:24.76 Rebecca Brown (Australia) Brisbane, Australia, 16 March 1994
**Butterfly**
**100 m:** 57.93 Mary Meagher (USA) Brown Deer, Wisconsin, USA, 16 Aug 1981
**200 m:** 2:05.96 Mary Meagher (USA) Brown Deer, Wisconsin, USA, 13 Aug 1981
**Backstroke**
**100 m:** 1:00.16 He Cihong (China) Rome, Italy, 11 Sept 1994
**200 m:** 2:06.62 Krisztina Egerszegi (Hungary) Athens, Greece, 25 Aug 1991
**Medley**
**200 m:** 2:11.57 Lu Bin (China) Hiroshima, Japan, 7 Oct 1994
**400 m:** 4:36.10 Petra Schneider (GDR) Guayaquil, Ecuador, 1 Aug 1982
**4 x 100-m:** 4:01.67 China Rome, Italy, 11 Sept 1994

22 March 1996
**4 x 100-m:** 3:21.34 GB Atlanta, GA, USA, 23 July 1996
**4 x 200-m:** 7:18.74 GB Atlanta, GA, USA, 21 July 1996
**Breaststroke**
**100 m:** 1:01.33 Nicholas Gillingham Sheffield, S Yorkshire, UK, 21 May 1992
**200 m:** 2:11.29 Nicholas Gillingham Barcelona, Spain, 29 July 1992
**Butterfly**
**100 m:** 53.30 Andrew Jameson Seoul, South Korea, 21 Sept 1988
**200 m:** 1:58.16 James Hickman Atlanta, GA, USA, 22 July 1996
**Backstroke**
**100 m:** 55.00 Martin Harris, Sheffield, S Yorkshire, UK, 22 April 1995
**200 m:** 1:59.52 Adam Ruckwood Sheffield, S Yorkshire, UK, 23 April 1995
**Medley**
**200 m:** 2:03.20 Neil Cochran Orlando, Florida, USA, 25 March 1988
**400 m:** 4:24.20 John Davey, Crystal Palace, London, UK, 1 Aug 1987

**Breaststroke**
**100 m:** 1:10.39 Susannah 'Suki' Brownsdon Strasbourg, France, 21 Aug 1987
**200 m:** 2:30.63 Marie Hardiman Crystal Palace, London, UK, 31 July 1994
**Butterfly**
**100 m:** 1:01.33 Madeleine Scarborough, Auckland, New Zealand, 28 Jan 1990
**200 m:** 2:11.97 Samantha Paula Purvis Los Angeles, California, USA, 4 Aug 1984
**Backstroke**
**100 m:** 1:03.27 Katharine Osher Victoria, Canada, 21 Aug 1994
**200 m:** 2:13.91 Joanne Deakins Barcelona, Spain, 31 July 1992
**Medley**
**200 m:** 2:16.41 Susan Rolph Sheffield, S Yorkshire, UK, 23 March 1996
**400 m:** 4:46.83 Sharron Davies Moscow, USSR, 26 July 1980
**4 x 100-m:** 4:11.88 England Auckland, New Zealand, 29 Jan 1990

# Yachts and powerboats

## Yachting

### Olympic titles

The first sportsman to win individual gold medals in four successive Olympic Games was Paul B. Elvstrøm (Denmark) in the Firefly class in 1948 and the Finn class in 1952, 1956 and 1960. He also won eight other world titles in a total of six classes.

The least penalty points by the winner of any class is three points (five wins, one disqualified and one second in seven starts), by *Superdocious* of the Flying Dutchman class sailed by Lt Rodney Stuart Pattisson, RN, and Iain Somerled Macdonald-Smith, at Acapulco Bay, Mexico, in Oct 1968.

The only British yachtsman to win in two Olympic regattas is Rodney

A record 19 nations competed in 1975, 1977 and 1979.

Great Britain holds the record for the most wins, with nine.

### Ocean racing

The first modern ocean race (in moderate or small sailing yachts, rather than professionally manned sailing ships) covered 1,166 km (630 nautical miles) from Brooklyn, New York, USA, to Bermuda in June 1906. Organized by Thomas Fleming Day, editor of the magazine *The Rudder*, the race is still held in even numbered years, from Newport, Rhode Island, USA, to Bermuda.

The sloop *Nirvana*, owned by Marvin Green (USA), holds the record for both

### Oldest round-the-world race

The oldest regular sailing race around the world is the quadrennial Whitbread Round the World race, originally organized by the Royal Naval Sailing Association in Aug 1973. It starts in England and the course is varied from race to race. The distance for 1993–94 was 59,239 km (32,000 nautical miles) beginning and finishing in Southampton, UK, with stops and re-starts at Punta del Este, Uruguay; Fremantle, Australia; Auckland, New Zealand; Punta del Este, Uruguay and Fort Lauderdale, Florida, USA.

### America's Cup

There have been 29 challenges since 8 Aug 1870, and the USA has won on every occasion except 1983 (to Australia) and 1995 (to New Zealand).

*Reliance*, designed by Nathanael Herreshoff, with an overall length of 43.89 m (144 ft), a record sail area of 1,501 m$^2$ (16,160 ft$^2$) and a rig 53.3 m (175 ft) high.

### Yacht and dinghy classes

The oldest racing class still sailing is the Water Wag class of Dublin, formed in 1887. The design of the boat has remained the same since 1900.

The oldest classes in Britain, both established in 1898, and both still racing in the same boat design, are the Seabird Half Rater, a centreboard sailing dinghy of Abersoch and other north-western ports, and the Yorkshire One-design keel boat. The latter races from the Royal Yorkshire Yacht Club at Bridlington, E Yorkshire, UK.

Pattisson in 1968 and in 1972 with *Superdoso*, crewed by Christopher Davies at Kiel, Germany. Pattisson also gained a silver medal in 1976 with Julian Brooke Houghton.

### Oldest surviving race

The oldest yacht race in the world that is still regularly run is the Chicago to Mackinac race which takes place on Lakes Michigan and Huron in the USA. First sailed in 1898, it was held next in 1904, and then annually until the present day, except between 1917 and 1920.

The record for the course, which covers a distance of 616 km or 333 nautical miles, is 1 day 1 hr 50 min, at an average speed of 12.89 knots (23.84 km/h), by the sloop *Pied Piper*, owned by Dick Jennings (USA) in 1987.

### Admiral's Cup

The Admiral's Cup has the most participating nations of all the ocean racing team series, with each nation allowed three boats. The race is organized by the Royal Ocean Racing Club.

the Newport, Rhode Island to Bermuda race and the Fastnet race, the premier American and British ocean races.

The record for the Bermuda race, which covers 1,176 km (635 nautical miles), is 2 days 14 hr 29 min, in 1982. *Nirvana* had an average speed of 10.16 knots (18.81 km/h).

The record for the Fastnet race, which covers 1,120 km (605 nautical miles), is 2 days 12 hr 41 min in 1985. *Nirvana* managed an average speed of 9.97 knots (18.45 km/h).

### Longest race

The world's longest sailing race is the Vendée Globe Challenge, first raced from Les Sables d'Olonne, France, on 26 Nov 1989. The distance circumnavigated without stopping was 22,500 nautical miles (41,652 km). The race is for 50–60-ft (15–18-m) boats sailed single-handed.

The course record time is 105 days 20 hr 31 min, by Christophe Auguin (France) in the sloop *Geodis*. It finished at Les Sables on 17 March 1997.

In individual races sailed, American boats have won 81 races and foreign challengers have won 13.

Dennis Conner (USA) has been in more races as a member of the afterguard than any other, with six appearances since 1974, when he was starting helmsman with Ted Hood as skipper. He was winning skipper/helmsman in 1980, 1987 and 1989 and losing skipper in 1983 and 1995.

Charlie Barr (USA), who defended in 1899, 1901 and 1903, and Harold S. Vanderbilt (USA) in 1930, 1934 and 1937, each steered the successful winner three times in succession.

The closest finish in a race for the cup was on 4 Oct 1901, when *Shamrock II* (GB) finished two seconds ahead of the American *Columbia*.

The largest yacht to have competed in the America's Cup was the 1903 defender, the gaff-rigged cutter

The first international class for racing dinghies was the 14-foot International. The principal trophy in the United Kingdom for this class is the Prince of Wales Cup which has been contested annually since 1927, except from 1940 to 1945. Stewart Morris has a record 12 wins from 1932–65.

### Highest speeds

The highest speed reached under sail on water by any craft over a 500-m (1,640-ft) timed run is 46.52 knots (86.21km/h) by trifoiler *Yellow Pages Endeavour*, piloted by Simon McKeon and Tim Daddo, both of Australia, at Sandy Point near Melbourne, Australia, on 26 Oct 1993.

The British record is 42.16 knots (78.13 km/h), by David White at West Kirby, Merseyside, UK, in Oct 1991.

The British record for women is 37.21 knots (68.95 km/h) by Samantha Metcalfe at Fuerteventura, Canary Islands, on 27 July 1995.

# RECORD SAIL AREA 1,501 M²

## FOR SAILING 41,652 KM WITHOUT STOPPING IS 105 DAYS 20 HR 31 MIN

**Most competitors**
The most boats to enter a race was 2,072 in the Round Zeeland (Denmark) race on 21 June 1984, over a course of 235 nautical miles (435 km).

The most to start in a British race was 1,781 keeled yachts and multihulls on 17 June 1989 from Cowes in the Annual Round-the-Island Race. The fastest time in this event was 3 hr 55 min 28 sec, by the trimaran *Paragon*, sailed by its owner Michael Whipp on 31 May 1986.

The largest trans-oceanic race was the ARC (Atlantic Rally for Cruisers), when 204 boats out of 209 starters from 24 nations completed the race, run from Las Palmas, Gran Canaria, Canary Islands, to Barbados in 1989.

Bielak (France) at Saintes Maries de-la-Mer Canal, Camargue, France, on 24 April 1993.

The women's world speed record for any craft is by windsurfer Babethe Coquelle (France), who achieved 40.38 knots (74.83 km/h) at Tarifa, Spain, on 7 July 1995.

**Longest sailboard**
The world's longest 'snake' of boardsails was made by 70 windsurfers in tandem at the 'Sailboard Show '89' event at Narrabeen Lakes, Manly, Australia, on 21 Oct 1989.

The world's longest sail board is 50.2 m (165 ft). It was constructed at Fredrikstad, Norway, and first sailed on 28 June 1986.

**Far left**
The annual Cowes to Torquay race covers 320.4 km (199 miles). In 1989 a record 1,781 keeled yachts and multihulls started the race.

**Left**
Since its invention in 1970, windsurfing has become a popular amateur pastime and a highly competitive professional sport. Stephan van den Berg (Netherlands) won the first Olympic windsurfing gold medal when the sport was introduced to the 1984 Olympic Games.

## SINGLE RACE WAS 2,072 IN THE ROUND ZEELAND RACE ON 21 JUNE 1984

**Oldest yacht club**
The world's oldest club is the Royal Cork Yacht Club which claims descent from the Cork Harbour Water Club, established in Ireland in 1720.

The oldest active British club is the Starcross Yacht Club at Powderham Point, Devon. It held its first regatta in 1772.

The oldest existing club to have been formed as a yacht club is the Royal Yacht Squadron, Cowes, Isle of Wight, which was instituted as 'The Yacht Club' at a meeting at the Thatched House Tavern, St James's Street, London, UK, on 1 June 1815.

### Windsurfing
**Most titles**
Stephan van den Berg (Netherlands), has won five world titles, 1979–83.

**Speed records**
The fastest speed for a windsurfer is 45.34 knots (84.02 km/h) by Thierry

### Powerboat Racing
**APBA Gold Cup**
The American Power Boat Association (APBA) was formed in 1903 and held its first Gold Cup on the Hudson River, New York, USA, in 1904.

The most wins is 10, by Chip Hanauer (USA), 1982–88, 1992–93 and 1995.

The highest average speed for the APBA race is 240.050 km/h (149.160 mph) by Chip Hanauer, piloting *Miss Budweiser* in 1995.

**Cowes to Torquay race**
This British race was first instituted in 1961. From 1968 it included the return journey, making a distance of 320.4 km (199 miles).

The most wins is four by Renato della Valle (Italy), from 1982 to 1985.

The highest average speed is 148 km/h (92 mph) by Sergio Mion (Italy), piloting *SM-Racer* in 1993.

**Longest races**
The world's longest offshore race was the Port Richborough, London–Monte Carlo Marathon Offshore International Event. The race extended over 4,742 km (2,947 miles) in 14 stages from 10 to 25 June 1972.

The race was won by *H.T.S.* (GB), driven by Mike Bellamy, Eddie Chater and Jim Brooker in 71 hr 35 min 56 sec, at an average speed of 66.24 km/h (41.15 mph).

**Longest circuit race**
The longest circuit race is the 24-hour race held annually since 1962 on the River Seine at Rouen, France.

**Transatlantic crossing**
The fastest ever transatlantic crossing was from Ambrose Light Tower, New Jersey/New York, USA, to Bishop Rock Light, Isles of Scilly, Cornwall, UK, on 24–27 July 1989. *Gentry Eagle*, skippered by Tom Gentry (USA), took 2 days 14 hr 7 min 47 sec.

### Ice and sand yachting
**Highest speeds**
The highest officially recorded speed is 230 km/h (143 mph), by John D. Buckstaff in a Class A stern-steerer on Lake Winnebago, Wisconsin, USA, in 1938. Such a speed is possible in a wind of 115 km/h (72 mph).

The official world record for a sand yacht is 107 km/h (66.48 mph), by Christian-Yves Nau (France) in *Mobil* at Le Touquet, France, on 22 March 1981, when the wind speed reached 120 km/h (75 mph).

On 15 April 1976, Nord Embroden (USA) in *Midnight at the Oasis* attained a speed of 142.26 km/h (88.4 mph) at Superior Dry Lake, California, USA.

**Largest yacht**
*Icicle*, built in 1869 for Commodore John E. Roosevelt for racing on the Hudson River, New York, USA, was 21 m (68 ft 11 in) long and carried 99 m² (1,070 ft²) of canvas.

# Canoeing and rowing

**Below right**
Ethan Ayer (USA) is the tallest man to row in the Boat Race, at 2.05 m (6 ft 8¾ in). In 1997 he rowed for Cambridge giving them victory for the fifth successive year.

## Rowing
### Earliest rowing race
The earliest established sculling race is the Doggett's Coat and Badge, which was first rowed on 1 Aug 1716 from London Bridge to Chelsea, London, UK, as a race for apprentices.

### Olympics & World Championships
Four gold medals have been won by Steven Redgrave (GB), in the coxed fours in 1984, and the coxless pairs in 1988, 1992 and 1996.

The most gold medals won by a woman is three: by Canadian pair Kathleen Heddle and Marnie McBean, coxless pairs in 1992, eights in 1992 and double sculls in 1996.

The most gold medals won at World Championships and Olympic Games is

### Boat Race
The first University Boat Race was won by Oxford. It was from Hambledon Lock to Henley Bridge on 10 June 1829. Outrigged eights were first introduced to the race in 1846.

In the 143 races up to 1997, Cambridge has won 74 times, and Oxford 68 times. There has been one dead heat on 24 March 1877.

The race record time for the 6.779-km (4-mile 374-yd) Putney to Mortlake course is 16 min 45 sec, by Oxford on 18 March 1984. This is the equivalent to an average speed of 24.28 km/h (15.09 mph).

The smallest winning margin in the race was by a canvas when Oxford won in 1952 and 1980.

entry limit of 420 crews (3,780 competitors). The record for the Mortlake-Putney course (the reverse of the Boat Race) is 16 min 37 sec by the ARA National Squad in 1987.

### Longest race
The longest annual rowing race is the annual Tour du Lac Léman, Geneva, Switzerland, which is for coxed fours (the five-man crew taking turns as cox) over 160 km (99 miles).

The record winning time is 12 hr 22 min 29 sec, by RG Red Bull Bonn, Germany, on 2 Oct 1994.

The longest open rowing race is across the Irish Sea from Arklow, Co Wicklow, Ireland to Aberystwyth, Ceredigion, UK—a distance of 137 km (85 miles).

### Highest team speed
The world record for 2,000 m (2,187 yd) on non-tidal water is 5 min 23.90 sec (a speed of 22.22 km/h or 13.80 mph) by the Dutch National Team (eight) at Duisburg, Germany, on 19 May 1996.

The women's fastest time is 5 min 58.50 sec, by the Romanian team at Duisburg, Germany, on 18 May 1996.

### Highest single scull speed
The single sculls record is 6 min 37.03 sec (a speed of 18.13 km/h or 11.26 mph), by Juri Jaanson (Estonia) at Lucerne, Switzerland, on 9 July 1995.

On 17 July 1994 at Lucerne, Silken Laumann (Canada) set a women's record of 7 min 17.09 sec.

10 by Steven Redgrave who, in addition to his four Olympic successes, won world titles at coxed pairs in 1986, and coxless pairs in 1987, 1991, 1993, 1994 and 1995.

Francesco Esposito (Italy) won a record nine titles at lightweight events: coxless pairs 1980–84, 1988 and 1994, and coxless fours in 1990 and 1992.

At women's events Yelena Tereshina (USSR) has won a record seven golds, all eights, 1978–79, 1981–83 and 1985–86.

The most wins at single sculls is five by: Peter-Michael Kolbe (West Germany) in 1975, 1978, 1981, 1983 and 1986; Pertti Karppinen in 1979 and 1985, plus three Olympic wins in 1976, 1980 and 1984; Thomas Lange (GDR/Germany) in 1987, 1989 and 1991, plus two Olympic wins in 1988 and 1992.

The most women's wins at single sculls is five, by Christine Hahn (GDR), who won from 1974–75, 1977–78 and took the Olympic title in 1976.

The greatest margin (apart from sinking) was Cambridge's win by 20 lengths in 1900.

Boris Rankov rowed in a record six winning boats, for Oxford, 1978–83.

Susan Brown was the first woman to take part and coxed the winning Oxford boats in 1981 and 1982.

Daniel Topolski coached Oxford to a record 10 successive victories, from 1976 to 1985.

The tallest man to row in the race was Ethan Ayer at 2.05 m (6 ft 8¾ in), for Cambridge in 1996 and 1997.

The heaviest was Christopher Heathcote, the Oxford No. 6, who weighed 110 kg (243 lb) in 1990.

The youngest rowing 'blue' ever was Matthew John Brittin at 18 years 208 days, for Cambridge in 1986.

### Head of the River
Instituted in 1926, the Head is a processional race for eights. It has an

### Henley Royal Regatta
The annual regatta at Henley-on-Thames, Oxon, UK was started on 26 March 1839. The most wins in the Diamond Challenge Sculls is six by Guy Nickalls (GB), 1888–91, 1893–94 and by Stuart Alexander Mackenzie (Australia and GB), 1957–62.

The record time is 7 min 23 sec, by Vaclav Chalupa (Czechoslovakia) on 2 July 1989.

The record for the Grand Challenge Cup is 5 min 58 sec by Hansa Dortmund, West Germany, on 2 July 1989.

The most wins in the Silver Goblets and Nickalls Challenge Cup is seven by Steven Redgrave (GB) 1986–87 (with Andrew Holmes), 1989 (with Simon Berrisford), 1991 and 1993–95 (with Matthew Pinsent).

The record time in the Silver Goblets Cup is 6 min 56 sec by Redgrave and Pinsent on 1 July 1995.

### Distance (24 hours)
The greatest distance rowed in 24 hours (upstream and downstream) is 227.33 km (141 miles 450 yd), by six members of Dittons Skiff & Punting Club on the River Thames between Hampton Court and Teddington, Greater London, UK, 3–4 June 1994.

### Cross-Channel
A team from the Dittons Skiff & Punting Club rowed across the English Channel in a record 2 hr 42 min 20 sec on 30 May 1996.

The individual record is by Arne Lindström (Norway) who sculled across in 3 hr 35 min on 14 July 1994.

### River Thames (UK)
Five members of the Lower Thames Rowing Club, Gravesend, rowed the navigable length of the Thames, 299.14 km (185 miles 1,543 yd), from Lechlade Bridge, Glos, to Southend Pier, Essex, UK, in 38 hr 43 min 20 sec from 8–9 May 1993.

# HIGHEST KAYAK SPEED 23.05 KM/H

The fastest time from Folly Bridge, Oxford, to Westminster Bridge, London, (180 km or 112 miles) is 14 hr 25 min 15 sec by an eight from Kingston Rowing Club on 1 Feb 1986.

## Thames solo sculling
Peter Goodchild sculled down the 299.14-km (185-mile 1,550-yd) Thames from Lechlade to Gravesend, 60 hr 23 min, 15–17 Dec 1996.

## International Dragon Boat Races
Instituted in 1975 and held annually in Hong Kong, the race is over a 640-m (700-yd) course. Teams have 28 members—26 rowers, one steersman and one drummer.

The fastest time ever achieved is 2 min 27.45 sec, by the Chinese Shun De team on 30 June 1985.

The most men's world titles is 13, by Gert Fredriksson, from 1948 to 1960, Rüdiger Helm (GDR), from 1976 to 1983, and Ivan Patzaichin (Romania), from 1968 to 1984.

The most individual titles by a British canoeist is five by Richard Fox at K1 slalom in 1981, 1983, 1985, 1989 and 1993. He also won five gold medals at K1 team, 1981–93.

## Highest speed
The German four-man kayak Olympic champions in 1992 at Barcelona, Spain, covered 1,000 m in 2 min 52.17 sec in a heat on 4 August. This represents an average speed of 20.90 km/h (12.98 mph).

The Hungarian four won the 200-m title at the 1995 World Championships in a

eastern USA via Chicago, New Orleans, Miami, New York and the Great Lakes from 22 Sept 1930 to 15 Aug 1931. They covered a record longest distance of 9,820 km (6,102 miles).

## North Sea
On 17–18 May 1989, Kevin Danforth and Franco Ferrero completed the Felixstowe to Zeebrugge route in 27 hr 10 min in a double sea kayak. The open crossing, which was over 177 km (110 miles), was self-contained and unsupported.

## River Rhine
The 'Rhine Challenge', as organized by the International Long River Canoeists Club, begins from an official marker-post in Chur, Switzerland, and ends at Willemstad, Netherlands, a distance of approximately 1,130 km (702 miles).

1,530 yd) along the Florida coast, USA, from 26 to 27 June 1986.

## Eskimo rolls (1,000)
Ray Hudspith completed 1,000 eskimo rolls in 34 min 43 sec, at the Elswick Pool, Newcastle upon Tyne, UK, on 20 March 1987.

## Eskimo rolls (100)
Ray Hudspith did 100 rolls in 3 min 7.25 sec, at Killingworth Leisure Centre, Tyne and Wear, UK, in 1991.

The women's record for 100 eskimo rolls is 3 min 47.54 sec by Helen Barnes at Crystal Palace, Greater London, UK, on 18 Feb 1995.

## Most eskimo rolls
Randy Fine (USA) completed a record 1,796 continuous eskimo rolls at

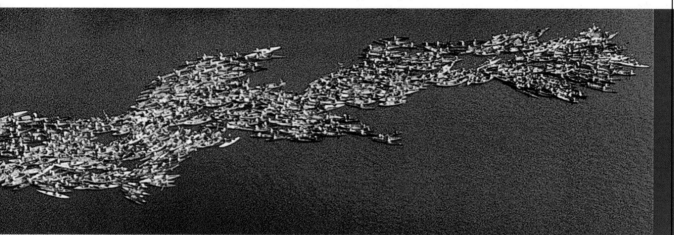

**HOURS IS 227.33 KM BY SIX MEMBERS OF DITTONS SKIFF & PUNTING CLUB**

The best time for a British team was 2 min 36.40 sec, by the Kingston Royals crew on 3 June 1990.

## Canoeing
### Most Olympic titles
Gert Fredriksson (Sweden) won a record six Olympic gold medals, from 1948 to 1960. He added a silver and a bronze, totalling a record eight medals.

The most Olympic titles by a woman is five by Birgit Schmidt (GDR), from 1980 to 1996. She has also won three silver medals for a record-equalling total of eight medals.

### Most Olympic golds at one Games
The most Olympic gold medals at one Games is three by Vladimir Parfenovich (USSR) in 1980, and by Ian Ferguson (New Zealand) in 1984.

### Most world titles
A record 25 titles, including Olympic medals, have been won by Birgit Schmidt, from 1979 to 1996.

time of 31.227 sec, at an average speed of 23.05 km/h (14.32 mph).

### Longest race
The 1967 Canadian Government Centennial Voyageur Canoe Pageant and Race from Rocky Mountain House, Alberta, to Montreal, Québec, was 5,283 km (3,283 miles) long. Canoes representing the 10 Canadian provinces and territories took part.

The race, which took from 24 May to 4 Sept, was won by the Province of Manitoba canoe *Radisson*.

### Longest journey
Father and son Dana and Donald Starkell paddled a record 19,603 km (12,181 miles) from Winnipeg, Manitoba, Canada, to Belem, Brazil, from 1 June 1980 to 1 May 1982, carrying their canoe when required.

Without ever carrying their canoe, or having aid of any kind, Richard H. Grant and Ernest Lassy circumnavigated the

### Fastest solo 'Rhine Challenge'
The fastest time, solo and supported, for the 'Rhine Challenge' is 7 days 13 hr 56 min by Roel Kimpe (Netherlands), 22–29 May 1993.

The fastest ever woman, solo and supported, is Tracy Allen (GB) who completed the 'Rhine Challenge' in a time of 12 days 15 hr 10 min, between 17–29 May 1993.

### Distance (24 hours)
Zdzislaw Szubski (Poland) paddled 252.9 km (157 miles 255 yd) in a Jaguar K1 canoe on the River Vistula from Wlocklawek to Gdansk, Poland, on 11–12 Sept 1987.

Marinda Hartzenberg (South Africa) paddled, without benefit of current, 220.69 km (137 miles 229 yd) on Loch Logan, Bloemfontein, South Africa, on 31 Dec 1990–1 Jan 1991.

Randy Fine (USA) paddled a total distance of 194.1 km (120 miles

Biscayne Bay, Florida, USA, on 8 June 1991.

### 'Hand' rolls (1,000)
Colin Hill achieved 1,000 'hand' rolls in a record time of 31 min 55.62 sec at Consett, Co. Durham, UK, on 12 March 1987.

### 'Hand' rolls (100)
Colin Hill also achieved 100 'hand' rolls in 2 min 39.2 sec, at Crystal Palace, London, UK, on 22 Feb 1987.

### Most 'hand' rolls
Colin Hill completed a record 3,700 continuous 'hand' rolls at Durham City Swimming Baths, Co. Durham, UK, on 1 May 1989.

### Largest canoe raft
A raft of 648 kayaks and canoes, organized by the United States Canoe Association, was held together by hands only, while free floating for 30 seconds, on the Rock River, Byron, Illinois, USA, on 17 Aug 1996.

# Weightlifting

LAMAR GANT WAS THE FIRST MAN TO DEADLIFT FIVE TIMES HIS WEIGHT

## Weightlifting
### Most titles
The weightlifter with the most world title wins, including Olympic Games, is Naim Suleymanoğlü of Turkey (previously known as Neum Shalamanov and Naim Suleimanov of Bulgaria), with 10, 1985–86, 1988–89, 1991–96.

total (285 kg) at 16 years 62 days at Allentown, New Jersey, USA, on 26 March 1983.

### Oldest world record holder
Norbert Schemansky (USA) snatched 164.2 kg (362 lb) in the unlimited heavyweight class, when aged 37 years 333 days, at Detroit, Michigan, USA, on 28 April 1962.

Suleymanoğlü, who lifted 150 kg (330½ lb) at Cardiff, S Glamorgan, UK, on 27 April 1988.

The first woman to clean and jerk more than twice her own bodyweight was Cheng Jinling (China), who lifted 90 kg (198 lb) in the 44 kg class of the World Championships at Jakarta, Indonesia, in 1988.

### Women's World Championships
The most gold medals won in a championship is 13 by Li Hongyun (China), in the 60/64 kg class, between 1992 and 1996.

at 60 kg (1976–79) and 67.5 kg (1980–89). He also won four world titles, at 60 kg (1976–77, 1979), 67.5 kg (1985) and a record 10 European titles, at 60 kg (1978–79), and 67.5 kg (1981, 1983–89).

### Most successful woman powerlifter
Cathy Millen (New Zealand) currently holds 11 world records in three bodyweight categories, as well as 16 British Commonwealth and 20 New Zealand records in five categories. She has also won five World Championships and her 1994 total (682.5 kg or 1,505 lb) is the highest lifted by a woman.

### Powerlifting feats
Lamar Gant (USA) was the first man to deadlift five times his own bodyweight, lifting 299.5 kg (661 lb) in 1985.

Cammie Lynn Lusko (USA) became the first woman to lift more than her own bodyweight with one arm, with a 59.5 kg (131 lb) lift at Milwaukee, Wisconsin, USA, on 21 May 1983.

### Timed lifts
A 24-hour deadlifting record of 3,041,450 kg (6,705,241 lb) was set by a team of 10 at the Forum Health Club, Birmingham, UK, on 30 and 31 March 1996.

The world record for the individual 24-hour deadlift is 450,095 kg (992,288 lb). It was set by Chris Lawton at Barnsdale Country Club, Rutland, UK, between 5–6 April 1997.

The 24-hour record for the bench press is 4,322,150 kg (9,528,700 lb). It was set by a nine-man team at HMP Wayland, Griston, Norfolk, UK, on 19–20 April 1997.

A 10-man team from the St Albans Weightlifting Club and Ware Boys Club, Hertfordshire, UK, set a squat record of 2,168,625 kg (4,780,994 lb) from 20 to 21 July 1986.

### Timed lifts
An individual 12-hour bench press record of 815,448 kg (1,797,724 lb) was set by Glen Tenove (USA) at Irvine, California, USA on 17 Dec 1994.

## Strandpulling
### Strandpulling feats
The greatest ratified poundage to date for strandpulling is a super heavyweight right-arm push of 369.5 kg (815 lb) by Malcolm Bartlett of Oldham, Greater Manchester, UK.

The record for the back press anyhow is 319 kg (703 lb) by Andy Michealas, at Oldham, Lancs, UK, in 1996.

### Most successful British lifters
The only British lifter to ever win an Olympic title was Launceston Elliot in the open one-handed lift champion in 1986.

Louis Martin won four world and European mid-heavyweight titles (1959, 1962–63, and 1965). He also won an Olympic silver medal (1964) an Olympic bronze (1960) and three Commonwealth gold medals (1962, 1966, 1970).

## Powerlifting
### Most titles
Hideaki Inaba (Japan) has won 17 titles at 52 kg (1974–83, 1985–91).

The most titles ever won by a women is six, achieved by Beverley Francis of Australia at 75 kg (1980 and 1982) and 82.5 kg (1981 and 1983–85); and also by Sisi Dolman of the Netherlands at 52 kg (1985–86 and 1988–91).

The most world titles to have ever been won by a British lifter is seven, from Ron Collins at 75 kg in 1972 and 1974 and 82 kg in 1975, 1976, 1977 and 1979.

### Most Olympic medals
Naim Suleymanoğlü won a record three Olympic golds, at 60 kg in 1988 and 1992 and at 64 kg in 1996.

Norbert Schemansky (USA) won a record four Olympic medals: gold, middle-heavyweight in 1952; silver, heavyweight in 1948; bronze, heavyweight 1960 and 1964.

### Youngest world record holder
Naim Suleymanoğlü set 56-kg world records for clean and jerk (160 kg) and

### Heaviest lift to bodyweight
The first man to clean and jerk more than three times his own bodyweight was Stefan Topurov (Bulgaria), who lifted 180 kg (396¾ lb) in Moscow, USSR, on 24 Oct 1983.

The first man to snatch two-and-a-half times his own bodyweight was Naim

Edward John Pengelly won a record 14 consecutive British national titles,

CATHY MILLEN OF NEW ZEALAND HAS 11 POWERLIFTING WORLD RECORDS

# 12-HOUR BENCH PRESS 815,448 KG

## WORLD WEIGHTLIFTING RECORDS
From 1 Jan 1993, the International Weightlifting Federation (IWF) introduced modified weight categories, making the existing records redundant. This is the current list.

### Bodyweight 54 kg (119 lb)
Snatch: 132.5 kg (292 lb) by Halil Mutlu (Turkey)
Atlanta, USA, 20 July 1996
Jerk: 160 kg (352¾ lb) by Halil Mutlu (Turkey)
Istanbul, Turkey, 18 Nov 1994
Total: 290 kg (639¼ lb) by Halil Mutlu (Turkey)
Istanbul, Turkey, 18 Nov 1994

### Bodyweight 59 kg (130 lb)
Snatch: 140 kg (308½ lb) by Hafiz Suleymanoğlü (Turkey) Warsaw, Poland, 3 May 1995
Jerk: 170 kg (374¼ lb) by Nikolai Pershalov (Bulgaria) Warsaw, Poland, 3 May 1995
Total: 307.5 kg (677¾ lb) by Tang Ningsheng (China) Atlanta, USA, 21 July 1996

### Bodyweight 64 kg (141 lb)
Snatch: 150 kg (330½ lb) by Wang Guohua (China)
Pusan, South Korea, 12 May 1997
Jerk: 187.5 kg (413¼ lb) by Valerios Leonidis (Greece)
Atlanta, USA, 22 July 1996
Total: 335 kg (738½ lb) by Naim Suleymanoğlü (Turkey)
Atlanta, USA, 22 July 1996

### Bodyweight 70 kg (154¼ lb)
Snatch: 162.5 kg (358¼ lb) by Zhan Xugang (China)
Atlanta, USA, 23 July 1996
Jerk: 195 kg (429¾ lb) by Zhan Xugang (China)
Atlanta, USA, 23 July 1996
Total: 357.5 kg (788 lb) by Zhan Xugang (China)
Atlanta, USA, 23 July 1996

### Bodyweight 76 kg (167½ lb)
Snatch: 170 kg (374¾ lb) by Ruslan Savchenko (Ukraine) Melbourne, Australia, 16 Nov 1993
Jerk: 208 kg (458½ lb) by Pablo Lara (Cuba)
Szekszárd, Hungary, 20 April 1996
Total: 372.5 kg (821 lb) by Pablo Lara (Cuba)
Szekszárd, Hungary, 20 April 1996

### Bodyweight 83 kg (183 lb)
Snatch: 180 kg (396¾ lb), by Pyrros Dimas (Greece)
Atlanta, USA, 26 July 1996
Jerk: 213.5 kg (470½ lb) by Marc Huster (Germany)
Atlanta, USA, 26 July 1996
Total: 392.5 kg (865¼ lb) by Pyrros Dimas (Greece)
Atlanta, USA, 26 July 1996

### Bodyweight 91 kg (200½ lb)
Snatch: 187.5 kg (413½ lb) by Aleksey Petrov (Russia) Atlanta, USA, 27 July 1996
Jerk: 228.5 kg (503¾ lb) by Akakide Kakhiasvilis (Greece) Warsaw, Poland, 6 May 1995
Total: 412.5 kg (909¼ lb) by Aleksey Petrov (Russia) Sokolov, Czech Republic, 7 May 1994

### Bodyweight 99 kg (218¼ lb)
Snatch: 192.5 kg (424¼ lb) by Sergey Syrtsov (Russia)
Istanbul, Turkey, 25 Nov 1994
Jerk: 235 kg (518 lb) by Akakide Kakhiasvilis (Greece)
Atlanta, USA, 28 July 1996
Total: 420 kg (925¾ lb) by Akakide Kakhiasvilis (Greece)
Atlanta, USA, 28 July 1996

### Bodyweight 108 kg (238 lb)
Snatch: 200 kg (440¾ lb) by Timur Taimazov (Ukraine)
Istanbul, Turkey, 26 Nov 1994

Jerk: 236 kg (520¼ lb) by Timur Taimazov (Ukraine)
Atlanta, USA, 29 July 1996
Total: 435 kg (959 lb) by Timur Taimazov (Ukraine)
Istanbul, Turkey, 26 Nov 1994

### Bodyweight over 108 kg (238 lb)
Snatch: 205 kg (451¾ lb) by Aleksandr Kurlovich (Belarus) Istanbul, Turkey, 27 Nov 1994
Jerk: 260 kg (573 lb) by Andrey Chemerkin (Russia)
Atlanta, USA, 30 July 1996
Total: 457.5 kg (1,008½ lb) by Aleksandr Kurlovich (Belarus) Istanbul, Turkey, 27 Nov 1994

## WOMEN'S WEIGHTLIFTING RECORDS

### Bodyweight 46 kg (101¼ lb)
Snatch: 81.5 kg (179½ lb) by Jiang Yinsu (China)
Pusan, South Korea, 11 March 1997
Jerk: 105 kg (231½ lb) by Guang Hong (China)
Yachiyo, Japan, 4 April 1996
Total: 185 kg (407¾ lb) by Guang Hong (China)
Yachiyo, Japan, 4 April 1996

### Bodyweight 50 kg (110¼ lb)
Snatch: 88 kg (194 lb) by Jiang Baoyu (China)
Pusan, South Korea, 3 July 1995
Jerk: 110.5 kg (243½ lb) by Liu Xiuhia (China)
Hiroshima, Japan, 3 Oct 1994
Total: 197.5 kg (435¼ lb) by Liu Xiuhia (China)
Hiroshima, Japan, 3 Oct 1994

### Bodyweight 54 kg (119 lb)
Snatch: 92.5 kg (204 lb) by Zhang Juhua (China)
Hiroshima, Japan, 3 Oct 1994
Jerk: 113.5 kg (250 lb) by Zhang Xixiang (China)
Yachiyo, Japan, 5 April 1996
Total: 202.5 kg (446¼ lb) by Zhang Juhua (China)
Hiroshima, Japan, 3 Oct 1994

### Bodyweight 59 kg (130 lb)
Snatch: 99 kg (218¼ lb) by Chen Xiaomin (China)
Warsaw, Poland, 6 May 1996
Jerk: 124 kg (273¼ lb) by Xiu Xiongying (China)
Warsaw, Poland, 6 May 1996
Total: 220 kg (485 lb) by Chen Xiaomin (China)
Hiroshima, Japan, 4 Oct 1994

### Bodyweight 64 kg (141 lb)
Snatch: 106 kg (233½ lb) by Li Hongyun (China)
Warsaw, Poland, 7 May 1996
Jerk: 130 kg (286½ lb) by Li Hongyun (China)
Istanbul, Turkey, 22 Nov 1994
Total: 235 kg (518lb) by Li Hongyun (China)
Istanbul, Turkey, 22 Nov 1994

### Bodyweight 70 kg (154¼ lb)
Snatch: 102.5 kg (226 lb) by Tang Weifang (China)
Hiroshima, Japan, 4 Oct 1994
Jerk: 129 kg (284¼ lb) by Tang Weifang (China)
Guangzhou, China, 22 Nov 1995
Total: 230 kg (507 lb) by Tang Weifang (China)
Hiroshima, Japan, 4 Oct 1994

### Bodyweight 76 kg (167¼ lb)
Snatch: 106 kg (233½ lb) by Dai Yanan (China)
Warsaw, Poland, 10 May 1996
Jerk: 140 kg (308½ lb) by Zhang Guimei (China)
Shilong, China, 18 Dec 1993
Total: 235 kg (518 lb) by Zhang Guimei (China)
Shilong, China, 18 Dec 1993

### Bodyweight 83 kg (183 lb)
Snatch: 110 kg (242½ lb) by Wei Xiangying (China)

Warsaw, Poland, 11 May 1996
Jerk: 135.5 kg (298¾ lb) by Song Zhaomei
Pusan, South Korea 16 May 1997
Total: 242.5 kg (534¹/ lb) by Wei Xiangying
(China) Warsaw, Poland, 11 May 1996

### Bodyweight over 83 kg (183 lb)
Snatch: 108.5 kg (239 lb) by Wang Yanmei (China)
Warsaw, Poland, 12 May 1996
Jerk: 155 kg (341½ lb) by Li Yajuan (China)
Melbourne, Australia, 20 Nov 1993
Total: 260 kg (573 lb) by Li Yajuan (China)
Melbourne, Australia, 20 Nov 1993

## WORLD POWERLIFTING RECORDS
(All weights in kilograms)

### 52 kg
Squat: 271.5, Andrzej Stanaszek (Poland), 1996
Bench press: 177.5, Andrzej Stanaszek, 1994
Deadlift: 256, E. S. Bhaskaran (India), 1993
Total: 592.5, Andrzej Stanaszek (Poland), 1996
### 56 kg
Squat: 287.5, Magnus Karlsson (Sweden), 1996
Bench press:187.5, Magnus Karlsson, 1996
Deadlift: 289.5, Lamar Gant (USA), 1982
Total: 625, Lamar Gant, 1982
### 60 kg
Squat: 295.5, Magnus Karlsson, 1994
Bench press: 180.5, Magnus Karlsson, 1993
Deadlift: 310, Lamar Gant, 1988
Total: 707.5, Joe Bradley (USA), 1982
### 67.5 kg
Squat: 300, Jessie Jackson (USA), 1987
Bench press: 200, Kristoffer Hulecki (Sweden), 1985
Deadlift: 316, Daniel Austin (USA), 1991
Total: 765, Aleksy Sivokon (Kazakhstan), 1995
### 75 kg
Squat: 328, Ausby Alexander (USA), 1989
Bench press: 217.5, James Rouse (USA), 1980
Deadlift: 337.5, Daniel Austin, 1994
Total: 850, Rick Gaugler (USA), 1982
### 82.5 kg
Squat: 379.5, Mike Bridges (USA), 1982
Bench press: 240, Mike Bridges, 1981
Deadlift: 357.5, Veli Kumpuniemi (Finland), 1980
Total: 952.5, Mike Bridges, 1982
### 90 kg
Squat: 375, Fred Hatfield (USA), 1980
Bench press: 255, Mike MacDonald (USA), 1980
Deadlift: 372.5, Walter Thomas (USA), 1982
Total: 937.5, Mike Bridges, 1980
### 100 kg
Squat: 423, Ed Coan (USA), 1994
Bench press: 261.5, Mike MacDonald, 1977
Deadlift: 390, Ed Coan, 1993
Total: 1,035, Ed Coan, 1994
### 110 kg
Squat: 415, Kirk Karwoski (USA), 1994
Bench press: 270, Jeffrey Magruder (USA), 1982
Deadlift: 395, John Kuc (USA), 1980
Total: 1,000, John Kuc, 1980
### 125 kg
Squat: 455, Kirk Karwoski, 1995
Bench press: 278.5, Tom Hardman (USA), 1982
Deadlift: 387.5, Lars Norén (Sweden), 1987
Total: 1,045, Kirk Karwoski, 1995
### 125+ kg
Squat: 447.5, Shane Hamman (USA), 1994
Bench press: 310, Antony Clark (USA), 1994
Deadlift: 406, Lars Norén, 1988
Total: 1,100, Bill Kazmaier (USA), 1981

# Boxing

## Fight duration
### Longest fights
The longest recorded fight with gloves was between Andy Bowen (1867–94) and Jack Burke in New Orleans, Louisiana, USA, on 6–7 April 1893. It lasted 110 rounds, 7 hr 19 min (9:15 p.m.–4:34 a.m.) and was declared a no contest (later changed to a draw). Bowen later won a 85-round bout on 31 May 1893.

The longest bare-knuckle fight was 6 hr 15 min, between James Kelly and Jack Smith at Fiery Creek, Dalesford, Victoria, Australia, on 3 Dec 1855.

The greatest number of boxing rounds was 276 in 4 hr 30 min, when Jack Jones beat Patsy Tunney in Cheshire, UK, in 1825.

Dave Charnley knocked out David 'Darkie' Hughes after 40 seconds (including the count) in a lightweight championship defence in Nottingham, UK, on 20 Nov 1961.

Eugene Brown, on his professional debut, knocked out Ian Bockes of Hull in Leicester, UK, on 13 March 1989. The fight was officially stopped after 10 seconds of the first round. Bockes got up after a count of six, but the referee stopped the contest.

## Heavyweight champions
### Longest reign
Joe Louis (USA) was the undefeated heavyweight champion for 11 years 252 days, from 22 June 1937 until he announced his retirement on 1 March 1949. During his reign he made a record 25 defences.

### Shortest reign
Tony Tucker (USA) was IBF champion for 64 days, 30 May–2 Aug 1987.

### Most recaptures
Two boxers have regained the heavyweight championship twice; Muhammad Ali first won the

(269 lb). He had the longest recorded reach at 217 cm (85½ in) and an expanded chest of 137 cm (54 in).

### Lightest heavyweight champion
Robert James 'Bob' Fitzsimmons, from Helston, Cornwall, UK, weighed 75 kg (165 lb), when he won the heavyweight title by knocking out James J. Corbett at Carson City, Nevada, USA, on 17 March 1897.

### Youngest champion
Mike Tyson (USA) was 20 years 144 days when he beat Trevor Berbick (USA) to win the WBC version at Las Vegas, Nevada, USA, on 22 Nov 1986. He added the WBA title when he beat James 'Bonecrusher' Smith on 7 March 1987 at 20 years 249 days. He became universal champion on

## Shortest fights
There is a distinction between the quickest knock-out and the shortest fight. A knock-out in 10.5 seconds (including a 10 sec count) occurred on 23 Sept 1946, when Al Couture struck Ralph Walton while the latter was still in his corner at Lewiston, Maine, USA. If the time was accurate Couture must have been half-way across the ring from his own corner at the opening bell.

The shortest fight on record appears to be one in a Golden Gloves tournament at Minneapolis, Minnesota, USA, on 4 Nov 1947, when Mike Collins floored Pat Brownson with the first punch and the contest was stopped, without a count, four seconds after the bell.

The shortest world title fight was 20 seconds, when Gerald McClellan (USA) beat Jay Bell in a WBC middleweight bout at Puerto Rico on 7 Aug 1993.

The shortest ever heavyweight world title fight was between James J. Jeffries and Jack Finnegan in Detroit, USA, on 6 April 1900. It was won by Jeffries in 55 seconds.

## Most fights won
### Most fights without defeat
Edward Henry Greb (USA) (1894–1926) was unbeaten in 178 consecutive bouts, but these included 117 'no decision', of which five were unofficial losses, in 1916–23.

Packey McFarland (USA) had 97 undefeated fights (5 draws) from 1905 to 1915.

Pedro Carrasco (Spain) won 83 consecutive fights from 22 April 1964 to 3 Sept 1970, drew once, and had a further nine wins before his loss to Armando Ramos in a WBC lightweight contest on 18 Feb 1972.

### Most knock-outs
The most finishes classed as 'knock-outs' in a career is 145 (129 in professional bouts) by Archie Moore (USA) from 1936 to 1963.

The record for consecutive 'knock-outs' is 44 by Lamar Clark (USA) from 1958 to 11 Jan 1960. He knocked out six opponents in one night at Bingham, Utah, USA, on 1 Dec 1958.

title on 25 Feb 1964, defeating Sonny Liston. He was stripped of the title by the world boxing authorities on 28 April 1967 but defeated George Foreman on 30 Oct 1974. He won the WBA title from Leon Spinks on 15 Sept 1978.

Evander Holyfield won the title in October 1990, defeating James Douglas, regained the WBA and IBF versions when he beat Riddick Bowe in November 1993 and regained the WBA version again, on 9 Nov 1996 when he beat Mike Tyson.

### Undefeated career
Rocky Marciano (USA) is the only world champion at any weight to have won every fight of his entire completed professional career, from 17 March 1947–21 Sept 1955; 43 of his 49 fights were decided by knock-outs or stoppages.

### Heaviest champion
Primo Carnera (Italy), the 'Ambling Alp', who won the title from Jack Sharkey in New York City, USA, on 29 June 1933, weighed 118 kg (260 lb) for this fight, but his peak weight was 122 kg.

2 Aug 1987 when he defeated Tony Tucker (USA) for the IBF title.

### Oldest champion
George Foreman (USA) was 45 years 287 days when he knocked out Michael Moorer (USA) at Las Vegas, Nevada, USA, on 5 Nov 1994. He defended the IBF version on 22 April 1995.

## World Champions
### Longest reign
The heavyweight duration record set by Joe Louis of 11 years 252 days stands for all divisions.

### Shortest reign
Tony Canzoneri (USA) was world light-welterweight champion for 33 days, from 21 May to 23 June 1933.

### Youngest champion
Wilfred Benitez of Puerto Rico, became the youngest world champion aged 17 years 176 days when he won the WBA light welterweight title in San Juan, Puerto Rico, on 6 March 1976.

# LONGEST FIGHT 7 HR 19 MIN

### Oldest champion
Archie Moore was recognized as a light heavyweight champion from 17 Dec 1952–10 Feb 1962 when his title was removed. He was then believed to be between 45 and 48.

### Longest career
Bob Fitzsimmons' career lasted from 1883 to 1914. He fought his last world title bout on 20 Dec 1905 at the age of 42 years 208 days.

Jack Johnson (USA) also had a career of over 31 years, from 1897–1928.

### Longest world title fight
The longest world title fight (under Queensberry Rules) was between the lightweights Joe Gans, USA, and Oscar Matthew 'Battling' Nelson, the 'Durable

titles. However, despite the fact that the WBC sanctioned the fight, it is contrary to their rules to contest two divisions in one fight. Consequently, although Leonard won the match, he was forced by the WBC to relinquish one of his titles.

### Three titles at different weights
Henry 'Homicide Hank' Armstrong (USA) held three world titles at different weights simultaneously: featherweight, lightweight and welterweight from Aug–Dec 1938.

Barney Ross (USA) may have held the lightweight, junior-welterweight and welterweight, simultaneously, from 28 May–17 Sept 1934. However there is some dispute as to when he relinquished his lightweight title.

### Greatest weight difference
Primo Carnera (Italy), weighing in at 122 kg (269 lb), fought Tommy Loughran (USA), at 83 kg (183 lb), for the world heavyweight title in Miami, Florida, USA, on 1 March 1934. The weight difference between the two fighters of 39 kg (86 lb) was a new world record. Carnera went on to win the fight on points.

### Tallest boxers
The tallest boxer to fight professionally was Gogea Mitu of Romania in 1935. Mitu was 2.23 m (7 ft 4 in) tall and weighed 148 kg (326 lb).

John Rankin, who won a fight in New Orleans, Louisiana, USA, in Nov 1967, was also reputed to have been 2.23 m (7 ft 4 in) tall.

### Oldest gold medallist
Richard Gunn (GB) won the Olympic featherweight gold on 27 Oct 1908 in London, aged 37 years 254 days.

### Most World Championship titles
A record number of five world titles have been won by Félix Savon (Cuba); heavyweight in 1986, 1989, 1991, and 91 kg in 1993 and 1995.

### British titles
#### Most British titles
The most defences of a British heavyweight title is 14 by Billy Wells (1889–1967) from 1911–19.

#### Lonsdale Belts
A Lonsdale Belt is awarded to a boxer who wins three British title fights in one weight division.

### Bottom left
Thomas Hearns was the first boxer to have won WBA world titles at four weight categories: welterweight, super welterweight, light heavyweight and middleweight.

### Bottom right
Heavyweight Henry William Cooper is the only British boxer to have won three Lonsdale Belts (for winning three British title fights in one weight division).

## HELD THREE WORLD TITLES AT DIFFERENT WEIGHTS AT THE SAME TIME

Dane', at Goldfield, Nevada, USA, on 3 Sept 1906. The fight was stopped in the 42nd round when Gans was declared the winner on a foul.

### Most titles at different weights
The first boxer to have won world titles at four weight categories was Thomas Hearns, WBA welterweight in 1980, WBC super welterweight in 1982, WBC light-heavyweight in 1987 and WBC middleweight in 1987. He added a fifth weight division when he won the super middleweight title recognized by the World Boxing Organization (WBO) on 4 Nov 1988, and he won the WBA light heavyweight title on 3 June 1991.

'Sugar' Ray Leonard (USA) has also claimed world titles in five weight categories. Having previously won the WBC welterweight in 1979 and 1980, WBA junior middleweight in 1981 and WBC middleweight in 1987, he beat Donny Lalonde (Canada) on 7 Nov 1988, for both the WBC light-heavyweight and super middleweight

### Most recaptures
The only boxer to win a world title five times at one weight is 'Sugar' Ray Robinson (USA) who beat Carmen Basilio (USA) in the Chicago Stadium on 25 March 1958, to regain the world middleweight title for the fourth time.

Dennis Andries became the first British boxer to regain a world title twice. He won the WBC light-heavyweight title on 30 April 1986 and then regained it on 22 Feb 1989 after being beaten in 1987. He regained the title for a second time on 28 July 1990.

### Most title bouts
The record number of title bouts in a career is 37 by three-time world welterweight champion Jack Britton (USA) between 1915–22; 18 of these bouts ended in 'no decision'.

The record number of title bouts without 'no decision' contests is 34, including a record 31 wins by Julio César Chávez (Mexico), from 1984 to 1996.

Jim Culley, 'The Tipperary Giant', who was both a boxer and a wrestler in the 1940s is also reputed to have been 2.23 m (7 ft 4 in).

### Most knock-downs in title fights
Vic Toweel (South Africa) knocked down Danny O'Sullivan (UK) 14 times in 10 rounds in their world bantamweight fight at Johannesburg, South Africa, on 2 Dec 1950, before the latter retired.

### Amateur
#### Most Olympic titles
Only two boxers have won three Olympic gold medals. László Papp (Hungary) won the middleweight in 1948 and also the light-middleweight in 1952 and 1956. Teofilo Stevenson (Cuba), won the Olympic heavyweight title in 1972, 1976 and 1980.

### Youngest Olympic champion
Jackie Fields (USA) became the youngest ever Olympic boxing champion when he won the 1924 featherweight title at 16 years 162 days.

The only boxer to have won three Lonsdale Belts outright was heavyweight Henry William Cooper. He retired after losing to Joe Bugner (b. Hungary), having held the heavyweight title from 12 Jan 1959 to 28 May 1969 and from 24 March 1970 to 16 March 1971.

The shortest time ever taken to win a Lonsdale Belt, for three successive championship wins, is 90 days by the light-middleweight Ryan Rhodes, from 14 Dec 1996 to 14 March 1997.

The longest time taken to win a Lonsdale Belt is 8 years 236 days by Kirkland Laing, from 4 April 1979 to 26 Nov 1987.

### Most British amateur titles
The greatest number of Amateur Boxing Association (ABA) titles that have been won by any boxer is eight, by John Lyon at light-flyweight from 1981–1984 and at flyweight from 1986–1989.

# Combat sports

**Below right**
Judo was created in 1882 out of the principles of the ancient Japanese martial art of jujitsu. Yasuhiro Yamashita is now manager of the Japanese men's national team and the senior instructor at his *alma mater*, Tokai University.

## Wrestling
### Most titles and medals
Three Olympic titles have been won by Carl Westergren (Sweden) in 1920, 1924 and 1932; Ivar Johansson (Sweden) in 1932 (two) and 1936; Aleksandr Vasilyevich Medved (USSR) in 1964, 1968 and 1972; and Aleksandr Karelin (Russia) in 1988, 1992 and 1996.

Four Olympic medals were won by Eino Leino (Finland) at freestyle 1920–32; Imre Polyák (Hungary) at Greco-Roman 1952–64; and Bruce Baumgartner (USA) at freestyle 1984–96.

The freestyler Aleksandr Medved (USSR) won a record ten World Championships at three weight categories (1962–64, 1966–72).

The only wrestler to win the same title in nine successive years is Aleksandr Kareline (Russia) in the Greco-Roman under 130-kg class in 1988–96.

### Most British titles
The most British titles won in one weight class is 14, by welterweight Fitzlloyd Walker, 1979–92.

The longest span for British Amateur Wrestling Association titles is 24 years by George Mackenzie between 1909 and 1933. He represented Great Britain in five successive Olympiads, from 1908 to 1928.

### Most wins
In international competition Osamu Watanabe (Japan), the 1964 Olympic freestyle 63 kg champion, was unbeaten and did not concede a score in 189 consecutive matches.

Outside of FILA sanctioned competition, Wade Schalles (USA) won 821 bouts from 1964 to 1984, with 530 of these victories by pin.

### Longest bout
The longest recorded bout was one of 11 hr 40 min when Martin Klein (Estonia representing Russia) beat Alfred Asikáinen (Finland) for the Greco-Roman 75-kg 'A' event silver medal in the 1912 Olympic Games in Stockholm, Sweden.

### Heaviest heavyweight
The heaviest wrestler in Olympic history is Chris Taylor (USA), bronze medallist in the super-heavyweight class in 1972, who stood 1.96 m (6 ft 5 in) tall and weighed over 190 kg (420 lb). FILA introduced an upper weight limit of 130 kg (286 lb) for international competition in 1985.

## Sumo Wrestling
### Most successful wrestlers
*Yokozuna* Sadji Akiyoshi, alias Futabayama, set the all-time record of 69 consecutive wins in sumo wrestling from 1937 to 1939.

*Yokozuna* Koki Naya, alias Taiho ('Great Bird'), won the Emperor's Cup 32 times up to his retirement in 1971.

The *ozeki* Tameemon Torokichi, alias Raiden, won 254 bouts in 21 years from 1789 to 1810 and lost only 10 (a record 96.2% wins).

*Yokozuna* Mitsugu Akimoto, alias Chiyonofuji, won the Kyushu Basho, one of the six annual tournaments, for a record eight successive years from 1981 to 1988.

Akimoto holds the record for the most career wins (1,045) and *Makunouchi* (top division) wins (807).

### Most consecutive bouts
In all six divisions, the greatest number of consecutive bouts is 1,631, by Yukio Shoji, alias Aobajo, 1964–86.

The most bouts in a career is 1,891 by Kenji Hatano, alias Oshio, 1962–88.

### Youngest grand champion
In 1978 Toshimitsu Ogata, alias Kitanoumi, won a record 82 of the 90 bouts that top *rikishi* fight annually. In July 1974, aged 21 years and 2 months, he became the youngest of the 65 men to have attained the rank of *yokozuna* (grand champion).

### First non-Japanese champion
Hawaiian-born Jesse Kuhaulua, alias Takamiyama, was the first non-Japanese to win an official top-division tournament, in July 1972. In Sept 1981 he set a record of 1,231 consecutive top-division bouts.

### Heaviest *yokozuna*
In Jan 1993 Hawaiian-born Chad Rowan, alias Akebono, became the first foreign *rikishi* to be promoted to the top rank of *yokozuna*. He is the tallest (2.4 m or 6 ft 8 in) and heaviest (227 kg or 501 lb) *yokozuna* in sumo history.

### Heaviest *rikishi*
The heaviest ever *rikishi* is Samoan-American Salevaa Fuali Atisanoe, alias Konishiki, of Hawaii, who weighed in at 267 kg (589 lb) at Tokyo's Ryogoku Kokugikan on 3 Jan 1994.

## Judo
### Most world and Olympic titles
Yasuhiro Yamashita won nine consecutive Japanese titles from 1977 to 1985. He has won five world and Olympic titles, the Over 95-kg category in 1979, 1981 and 1983, the Open category in 1981, and the Olympic Open category in 1984. He retired undefeated after 203 successive wins from 1977 to 1985.

Two other men have won four world titles: Shozo Fujii (Japan) (Under 80-kg in 1971, 1973 and 1975, Under 78-kg in 1979); and Naoya Ogawa (Japan) (Open in 1987, 1989 and 1991 and Over 95-kg in 1989).

Four men have won two Olympic gold medals: Wilhelm Ruska (Netherlands), (Over 93-kg and Open in 1972); Peter Seisenbacher (Austria) (86-kg in 1984 and 1988); Hitoshi Saito (Japan) (Over 95-kg in 1984 and 1988); and Waldemar Legien (Poland) (78-kg in 1988 and 86-kg in 1992).

### Women's titles
Ingrid Berghmans (Belgium) has won a record six women's world titles: Open in 1980, 1982, 1984 and 1986 and Under 72-kg in 1984 and 1989. She has also won four silver medals and a bronze. She won the Olympic 72-kg title in 1988, when women's judo was introduced as a demonstration sport.

Karen Briggs is the most successful British player, with four women's world titles, Under 48-kg in 1982, 1984, 1986 and 1989.

### Most British titles
The most British titles won is nine, by David Colin Starbrook: Middleweight (1969–70), Light-heavyweight (1971–75) and the Open division (1970–71).

Karen Briggs has won a women's record seven titles. She won the Open in 1981, 1982, 1986, 1987, 1989, 1990 and 1992.

Adrian Neil Adams has the most successful international record of any British male player. He won two junior (1974 and 1977) and five senior (1979–80, 1983–85) European titles, four World Championship medals (one gold, one silver, two bronze) and two Olympic silver medals. He also won eight British senior titles.

### 10-hour Judo records
Brian Woodward and David Norman completed 33,681 judo throwing techniques in a 10-hour period at the Whybridge Parent's Association Children Club, Rainham, Essex, UK, on 10 April 1994.

## Ju-Jitsu
### World Championships
The World Council of Jiu-Jitsu Organization has staged World Championships biennially since 1984. The Canadian team has been the team winner on each occasion.

## Karate
### World Championships
Great Britain has won a record six world titles at the kumite team event (1975, 1982, 1984, 1986, 1988 and 1990).

### Men's kumite titles
Four men have won two men's individual kumite titles: Pat McKay (GB) (Under 80 kg, 1982 and 1984); Emmanuel Pinda (France) (Open in 1984 and Over 80 kg in 1988); Thierry Masci (France) (Under 70 kg in 1986

# LONGEST PULL 24 MIN 45 SEC

and 1988) and José Manuel Egea (Spain) (Under 80 kg in 1990 and in 1992).

### Women's kumite titles
Guus van Mourik (Netherlands) has won a record four women's kumite titles. She won the Over 60 kg in 1982, 1984, 1986 and 1988.

### Men's kata titles
Tsuguo Sakumoto (Japan) has won a record three individual men's kata titles in 1984, 1986 and 1988.

### Women's kata titles
Three individual women's kata titles have been won by Mie Nakayama (Japan) in 1982, 1984 and 1986 and by Yuki Mimura (Japan) in 1988, 1990 and 1992.

as well as two individual Olympic titles in 1952 and 1956.

Four women foilists have won three world titles: Helene Mayer (Germany) in 1929, 1931 and 1937; Ilona Schacherer-Elek (Hungary) in 1934, 1935 and 1951; Ellen Müller-Preis (Austria) in 1947, 1949 and 1950; and Cornelia Hanisch (West Germany) in 1979, 1981 and 1985.

Ilona Schacherer-Elek also won two individual Olympic titles, in 1936 and 1948.

The longest span for winning an individual world or Olympic title is 20 years. Aladár Gerevich of Hungary won the Olympic sabre title from 1935 to 1955.

The record for medals by a woman is seven (two gold, three silver, two bronze) by Ildikó Sági (Hungary) from 1960 to 1976.

### British fencers
Three British fencers have won individual world titles: Gwen Neligan at foil in 1933; Henry 'Bill' Hoskyns at épée in 1958; and Allan Louis Neville Jay at foil in 1959, when he also won silver in épée.

The only British fencer to win an Olympic gold medal is Gillian Mary Sheen in the 1956 foil.

A record three Olympic medals were won by Edgar Isaac Seligman, who won silver medals in the épée team event in 1906, 1908 and 1912.

They have won 16 titles in all categories from 1975 to 1993.

Sweden have won the 520 kg category three times and the 560 kg at all five women's World Championships between 1986 and 1994.

The Wood Treatment team (formerly called the Bosley Farmers) of Cheshire won 20 consecutive AAA Catchweight Championships (1959–1978), two world titles (1975–76) and 10 European titles at 720 kg.

Hilary Brown has been in every one of the Wood Treatment winning teams.

Trevor Brian Thomas of the British Aircraft Corporation Club is the only holder of three winners' medals in the

**Below left**
Hawaiin-born Chad Rowan, alias Akebono, is the tallest and heaviest *yokozuna* in sumo history, can expect a monthly salary of ¥812,000 (£4,250).

**Below right**
Though sword fighting dates back many centuries, fencing was not established as a sport until the end of the 19th century. Aleksandr Romankov has won the most individual world titles at the foil.

## LONGEST RECORDED DISTANCE FOR A TUG OF WAR CONTEST IS 3,623 M

### Top world exponents
The leading exponents among karateka are a number of 10th dans in Japan. The leading exponents of karateka in the United Kingdom are 8th dans: Tatsuo Suzuki (*Wado-ryu*), Steve Arneil (*Kyokushinkai*), Keinosuke Enoeda and Shiro Asano (both *Shotokan*).

## Fencing
### Most world titles
The different swords used in fencing are the foil, the epée and the sabre. Men's fencing has been part of the Olympic Games since 1896, while women's fencing was introduced in 1924, using the foil only. The 1996 games saw the introduction of epée events for women.

The most individual world titles won is five by Aleksandr Romankov (USSR), at foil in 1974, 1977, 1979, 1982 and 1983.

Christian d'Oriola (France) won four world foil titles, 1947, 1949, 1953–54,

### Most Olympic medals
The most individual Olympic gold medals won is three, by Ramón Fonst (Cuba) in 1900 and 1904 (two), and by Nedo Nadi (Italy) in 1912 and 1920 (two).

Nedo Nadi also won three team gold medals in 1920, making five gold medals at one celebration, the record for fencing. This is also a record for any sport.

Aladár Gerevich (Hungary) won seven golds (one individual and six team medals) from 1932 to 1960—a record Olympic span for 28 years.

Edoardo Mangiarotti (Italy) won a record 13 Olympic medals (six gold, five silver and two bronze) for foil and épée from 1936 to 1960.

The most gold medals by a woman is four (one individual, three team) by Yelena Dmitryevna Novikova (USSR) from 1968 to 1976.

Bill Hoskyns has competed most often for Great Britain with six Olympic appearances from 1956 to 1976.

### Amateur Fencing Association titles
The most titles won at one weapon is 10 at women's foil by Gillian Sheen, 1949, 1951–58, 1960.

The men's records are: foil, seven by John Emyrs Lloyd, 1928, 1930–33, 1937–38; epée, six by Edward Owen 'Teddy' Bourne, 1966, 1972, 1974, 1976–78 and William Ralph Johnson 1968, 1982, 1984–85, 1987, 1990; and sabre, six by Dr Roger F. Tredgold, 1937, 1939, 1947–49, 1955.

## Tug of War
### World Championships
Championships were held annually from 1975 to 1986 and biennially since. The women's event started in 1986.

### Most titles
England has been the most successful team at the World Championships.

European Open club competitions and added a world gold medal in 1988.

### Longest pre-AAA rules pull
The longest recorded pull (pre-AAA rules) is one of 2 hr 41 min when 'H' Company beat 'E' Company of the 2nd Battalion of the Sherwood Foresters (Derbyshire Regiment) at Jubbulpore, India, on 12 Aug 1889.

### Longest pull under AAA rules
The longest recorded pull under AAA rules (in which lying on the ground or entrenching the feet is not permitted) is one of 24 min 45 sec for the first pull between the Republic of Ireland and England during the World Championships (640 kg class) at Malmö, Sweden, on 18 Sept 1988.

### Record distance
The record distance for a tug of war competition is 3,623 m (3,962 yd), between Freedom Square and Independence Square at Lódz, Poland, on 28 May 1994.

# Target sports

## Archery

### Oldest club
The oldest archery body in the British Isles is the Society of Archers in Yorkshire, formed on 14 May 1673, though the Society of Kilwinning Archers, in Scotland, has contested the Pa-pingo Shoot since 1488.

### World Championships
The most World Championship titles won by a man is four, by Hans Deutgen of Sweden from 1947–50.

The most titles ever won by a woman is seven, by Janina Spychajowa-Kurkowska of Poland in 1931–34, 1936, 1939 and 1947.

The USA has won a record 14 men's and 8 women's team titles.

### Olympic Games
Hubert van Innis (Belgium) won six gold and three silver medals at the 1900 and 1920 Olympic Games.

The most successful woman is Kim Soo-nyung (South Korea) who has won three gold medals and one silver medal, between 1988 and 1992.

### British Championships
The most British Championship titles ever won is 12, by Horace Alfred Ford in 1849–59 and 1867.

The most women's titles is 23, by Alice Blanche Legh, in 1881, 1886–92, 1895, 1898–1900, 1902–09, 1913 and 1921–22. She could not win in 1882–85 because her mother was champion, or between 1915–1918, when WWI halted the Championships.

### British records
The British record during a York round (1,296 pts possible maximum) is 1,204 in a single round by Richard Priestman at Rochdale on 6 Oct 1996; and 2,356 in a double round, by Steven Hallard at Lichfield, Staffs, UK, on 13–14 Aug 1994.

The British record in a women's Hereford round (possible maximum 1,296 pts) is 1,208 for a single round, by Pauline Edwards on 30 June 1994; and 2,380 for a double round, by Joanne Franks at the British Target Championships on 8 Sept 1987.

The record for a men's FITA round is 1,323 for a single round, by Steven Hallard on 3 May 1995; and 2,632 for a double round, by Steven Hallard on 29–30 July 1995.

The women's FITA round record is 1,323 for a single round at the 1992 Olympics, Barcelona, Spain, by Alison Williamson; and 2,591 for a double round, also by Alison Williamson at the FITA Star competition (Belgium) on 5 June 1989.

### 24 hour-target archery
The record score over 24 hours by a pair of archers is 76,158, during 70 Portsmouth Rounds (60 arrows per round at 20 yd, at 60-cm FITA targets) by Simon Tarplee and David Hathaway at Evesham, Worcs, UK, on 1 April 1991. Tarplee also set an individual record of 38,500 during this attempt.

### Greatest draw
Gary Sentman, of Oregon, USA, drew a longbow weighing 79.83 kg (176 lb) to the maximum draw on the arrow of 72 cm (28¼ in) at Forksville, Pennsylvania, USA, on 20 Sept 1975.

### WORLD CROSSBOW RECORDS
**MEN**
**50 m Final** Jürgen Baumann (Germany) scored 1,820 points from a possible 1,900 in 1996
**2XIR–900** Jürgen Baumann (Germany) scored 1,725 points from a possible 1,800 in 1996
**1XIR–900** Jürgen Baumann (Germany) scored 871 points from a possible 900 in 1996
**65 m** Stuart Atkins (Australia) scored 279 points from a possible 300 in 1994
**50 m** Jürgen Baumann (Germany) scored 296 points from a possible 300 in 1996
**35 m** Rolfe Pfeiffer (Germany) scored 300 points from a possible 300 in 1993
**Team** Chinese Taipei (Taiwan) scored 8,405 points from a possible 9,000 in 1994

**WOMEN**
**50 m Final** Elke Poth (Germany) scored 1,780 points from a possible 1,900 in 1994
**2XIR–900** Branka Pereglin (Croatia) scored 1,684 points from a possible 1,800 in 1996
**1XIR–900** Branka Pereglin (Croatia) scored 851 points from a possible 900 in 1995
**65 m** Branka Pereglin (Croatia) scored 275 points from a possible 300 in 1995
**50 m** Marja-Liisa Heino (Sweden) scored 288 points from a possible 300 in 1994
**35 m** Sieglinde Wagner (Germany) scored 299 points from a possible 300 in 1993
**Team** Germany scored 8,405 points from a possible 9,000 in 1994

### WORLD ARCHERY RECORDS
**Men—single FITA rounds**
**FITA** Oh Kyo-moon (South Korea) scored 1,368 points from a possible 1,440 in 1995
**90 m** Vladimir Yesheyev (USSR) scored 330 points from a possible 360 in 1990
**70 m** Hiroshi Yamamoto (Japan) scored 344 from a possible 360 in 1990

**50 m** Han Seung-hoon (South Korea) scored 348 points from a possible 360 in 1994
**30 m** Han Seung-hoon (South Korea) scored 360 points from a possible 360 in 1994
**Team** South Korea scored 4,053 points from a possible 4,320 in 1995
**Women—single FITA rounds**
**FITA** Kim Jung-rye (South Korea) scored 1,377 points from a possible 1,440 in 1995
**70 m** Artin Kaynak (Turkey) scored 339 points from a possible 360 in 1996
**60 m** He Ying (China) scored 349 points from a possible 360 in 1995
**50 m** Kim Hyun-ji (South Korea) scored 342 points from a possible 360 in 1996
**30 m** Joanne Edens (GB) scored 357 points from a possible 360 in 1990

**Team** South Korea scored 4,094 points from a possible 4,320 in 1992
**Indoor (18 m)**
**Men**
Magnus Pattersson (Sweden) scored 596 points from a possible 600 in 1995
**Women**
Natalya Valeyeva (Moldova) scored 590 points from a possible 600 in 1995
**Indoor (25 m)**
**Men**
Magnus Pattersson (Sweden) scored 593 points from a possible 600 in 1993
**Women**
Petra Ericsson (Sweden) scored 592 points from a possible 600 in 1991

## Shooting

### Most Olympic medals
Carl Townsend Osburn (USA) won a record 11 medals, in 1912, 1920 and 1924. He won five gold, four silver and two bronze.

Marina Logvinenko (Russia) won the most women's medals (two gold, one silver, two bronze), from 1988–1996.

Gudbrand Gudbrandsönn Skatteboe (Norway) is the only marksman to win three individual gold medals in 1906.

### Bisley
The Queen's (King's) Prize, shot since 1860, has only once been won by a woman, Marjorie Elaine Foster, who scored 280 in July 1930.

Two men have won three times. Arthur George Fulton (GB) in 1912, 1926 and 1931, and Alain Marion (Canada) in 1980, 1983 and 1996.

The highest score out of a possible maximum of 300 for the final of the Queen's Prize is 298 by Alain Marion on 27 July 1996.

The record for the Silver medal is 150 out of a possible 150. This has been achieved 10 times, most recently by Alain Marion, Peter Bromley, John Pugsley and Simon Belither in 1996.

### Small-bore
The British individual small-bore rifle record for 60 shots in the prone position is 597/600, held jointly by Philip Scanlon, Alister Allan, John Booker, William Murray and William Brown.

### Clay pigeon
The record for the most clay pigeon world titles is six, held by Susan Nattrass (Canada) in 1974, 1975, 1977–79 and 1981.

### Bench rest shooting
The smallest group on record at 914 m (1,000 yd) is 10.058 cm (3²⁴⁄₂₅ in) by Frank Weber (USA) with a .308 Baer at Williamsport, Pennsylvania, USA, on 14 Nov 1993.

The smallest group that is on record at 500 m (546 yd) is 3.81 cm (1½ in) by Ross Hicks of Australia who used a rifle of his own design at Canberra, Australia, on 12 March 1994.

# 501 IN NINE DARTS

## 1XIR-900 AND 50 M FINAL CATEGORIES

### INDIVIDUAL WORLD SHOOTING RECORDS

In 1986, the International Shooting Union (UIT) brought in new regulations for major championships and world records. The leading competitors now undertake an additional round with a target subdivided to tenths of a point for rifle and pistol shooting, and an extra 25, 40 or 50 shots for trap and skeet. Harder targets have since been introduced. The table below shows UIT-recognized world records, at the end of 1995, for the 15 Olympic shooting disciplines contested at Atlanta in 1996, giving in brackets the score for the number of shots specified plus the score in the additional round.

### MEN
**Free Rifle 50 m 3 x 40 shots**
1287.9 (1,186+101.9)
Rajmond Debevec (Slovenia)
Munich, Germany, 29 Aug 1992
**Free Rifle 50 m 60 shots prone**
704.8 (600+104.8)
Christian Klees (Germany)
Atlanta, Georgia, USA, 25 July 1996
**Air Rifle 10 m 60 shots**
699.4 (596+103.4)
Rajmond Debevec (Yugoslavia)
Zürich, Switzerland, 7 June 1990
**Free Pistol 50 m 60 shots**
675.3 (580+95.3)
Taniu Kiriakov (Bulgaria)
Hiroshima, Japan, 21 April 995
**Rapid-Fire Pistol 25 m 60 shots**
699.7 (596+107.5)
Ralf Schumann (Germany)
Barcelona, Spain, 8 June 1994
**Air Pistol 10 m 60 shots**
695.1 (593+102.1)
Sergey Pyzhyanov (USSR)
Munich, Germany, 13 Oct 1989
**Running Target 10 m 30/30 shots**
685.6 (585+100.6)
Miroslav Janus (Czechoslovakia)
Seoul, South Korea 2 May 1995
**Skeet 125 targets**
150 (125+25)
Marcello Titarelli (Italy)
Suhl, Germany, 11 June 1996
**Trap 125 targets**
150 (125+25)
Jen Henrik Heinrich (Germany)
Lonanto, Italy, 5 June 1996
Andrea Bellini (Italy)
Suhl, Germany, 11 June 1996
**Double Trap 150 targets**
191 (143+48)
Joshua Lakatos (USA)
Barcelona, Spain, 15 June 1993

### WOMEN
**Standard Rifle
50 m 3 x 20 shots**
689.7 (592+97.7)
Vessela Letcheva (Bulgaria)
Munich, Germany, 15 June 1995
**Air Rifle 10 m 40 shots**
501.5 (398+103.5)
Vessela Letcheva (Bulgaria)
Havana, Cuba, 12 April 1996

**Sport Pistol 25 m 60 shots**
696.2 (594+102.2)
Diana Jorgova (Bulgaria)
Milan, Italy, 31 May 1994
**Air Pistol 10 m 40 shots**
492.7 (392+100.7)
Jasha Sekaric (Yugoslavia)
Nafels, Switzerland, 22 Sept 1996
**Double Trap 120 targets**
149 (113+36)
Deborah Gelisio (Italy)
Nicosia, Cyprus, 19 June 1995

## Darts
### Most titles
Eric Bristow (GB) has won the most World Masters Championships. He has won five times—1977, 1979, 1981 and 1983–84. He has won the World Professional Championship five times—1980–81 and 1984–86, and the World Cup Singles four times—1983, 1985, 1987 and 1989.

Phil Taylor (GB) has also won five World Championships (WDO 1990, 1992, WDC 1994–96).

John Lowe (GB) is the only other man who has won each of the four major darts titles: World Masters (1976 and 1980); World Professional (1979, 1987 and 1993); World Cup Singles (1981); and News of the World (1981).

### World Cup
England has a record eight wins at the World Cup biennial tournament.

England have won the women's biennial World Cup four times.

### Speed records
The fastest time ever taken to complete three games of 301, finishing on doubles, is 1 min 38 sec by Ritchie Gardner on BBC TV's *Record Breakers*, on 12 Sept 1989.

The record time to go round the board clockwise in 'doubles' at arm's length is 9.2 seconds by Dennis Gower at the Millers Arms, Hastings, E Sussex, UK, on 12 Oct 1975. The record for going round in numerical order is 14.5 seconds by Jim Pike at the Craven Club, Newmarket, Suffolk, UK, in March 1944.

The record for this feat at the 2.7 m (9 ft) throwing distance, retrieving own darts, is 2 min 13 sec by Bill Duddy at The Plough, Haringey, London, UK, on 29 Oct 1972.

### Least darts
Scores of 201 in four darts, 301 in six darts, 401 in seven darts and 501 in nine darts, have been achieved on various occasions.

Roy Edwin Blowes (Canada) was the first person to achieve a 501 in nine

darts, 'double-on, double-off', at the Widgeons pub, Calgary, Canada, on 9 March 1987. His scores were: bull, treble 20, treble 17, five treble 20s and a double 20 to finish.

This was equalled by Steve Draper (UK) at the Ex-Serviceman's Club, Wellingborough, Northants, UK, on 10 Nov 1994, with double 20, six treble 20s, treble 17 and bull.

The lowest number of darts thrown for a score of 1,001 is 19, by Cliff Inglis with 160, 180, 140, 180, 121, 180, 40 at the Bromfield Men's Club, Devon, UK, on 11 Nov 1975; and by Jocky Wilson with 140, 140, 180, 180, 180, 131, and bull at The London Pride public house, Bletchley, Bucks, UK, on 23 March 1989.

A score of 2,001 in 52 darts was achieved by Alan Evans at Ferndale, South Wales, UK, on 3 Sept 1976.

Tony Benson reached a score of 3,001 in 73 darts at the Plough Inn, Gorton, Manchester on 12 July 1986.

Linda Batten set a woman's record of 117 darts for a score of 3,001 at the Old Wheatsheaf, Enfield, London, on 2 April 1986.

A total of 100,001 in 3,579 darts was achieved by Chris Gray at The Dolphin, Cromer, Norfolk, on 27 April 1993.

### DARTS SCORING RECORDS
**24-hour
Men
(eight players)**
1,722,249 was scored by the Broken Hill Darts Club team at Broken Hill, NSW, Australia, from 28–29 Sept 1985.
**Women
(eight players)**
744,439 was scored by a team from the Lord Clyde public house, Leyton, London, UK, between 13–14 Oct 1990.

**Individual**
567,145 was scored by Kenny Fellowes at The Prince of Wales, Cashes Green, Glos, UK, on 28–29 Sept 1996.
**Bulls and 25s
(eight players)**
526,750 was scored by a team at the George Inn, Morden, London, UK, on 1–2 July 1994.

**10-hour
Most trebles**
3,056 (from 7,992 darts) was scored by Paul Taylor at the Woodhouse Tavern, Leytonstone, London, UK, on 19 Oct 1985
**Most doubles**
3,265 (from 8,451 darts) achieved by Paul Taylor at the Lord Brooke, Walthamstow, London, UK, on 5 Sept 1987

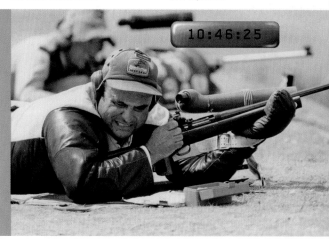

**Highest score
(retrieving own darts)**
465,919 scored by John Archer and Neil Rankin at the Royal Oak, Cossington, Leics, UK, 17 Nov 1990
**Bulls (individual)**
1,321 by Jim Damore (USA) at the Parkside Pub, Chicago, Illinois, USA, on 29 June 1996

**6-hour
Men**
210,172 by Russell Locke at the Hugglescote Working Mens' Club, Coalville, Leics, UK, on 10 Sept 1989
**Women**
99,725 by Karen Knightly at the Lord Clyde, Leyton, London, UK, on 17 March 1991
**Million and One Up
Men (8 players)**
36,583 darts by a team at Buzzy's Pub and Grub, Lynn, Massachusetts, USA, on 19–20 Oct 1991
**Women (8 players)**
70,019 darts by the Delinquents darts team at Top George, Combe Martin, Devon, UK, 11–13 Sept 1987

**Below left**
On 27 July 1996 Alain Marion of Canada achieved a record 298 (out of a possible 300) in the final of the Queen's Prize. He has also won the title a record three times, in 1980, 1983 and 1996.

# Angling

## Angling

### Oldest existing club
The Ellem fishing club was formed by a number of Edinburgh and Berwickshire gentlemen in Scotland in 1829. Its first annual general meeting was held on 29 April 1830.

### Largest single catch
The largest officially ratified fish ever caught on a rod was a man-eating great white shark (*Carcharodon carcharias*) that weighed 1,208.38 kg (2,664 lb) and measured 5.13 m (16 ft 10 in) long. It was caught on a 59-kg (130-lb) test line by Alf Dean at Denial Bay, near Ceduna, South Australia, on 21 April 1959.

A great white shark weighing 1,537 kg (3,388 lb) was caught by Clive Green off Albany, Western Australia, on 26 April 1976. However, the record will remain unratified since whale meat was used as bait.

The biggest ever fish caught on a rod by a British angler is a 620-kg (1,366-lb) great white shark, by Vic Samson at The Pales, South Australia, on 8 April 1989.

In 1978, a great white shark measuring 6.2 m (20 ft 4 in) in length and weighing over 2,268 kg (5,000 lb) was harpooned and landed by fishermen in the harbour of San Miguel, Azores.

### IGFA world records
The International Game Fish Association (IGFA) recognizes world records for a large number of species of game fish, both freshwater and saltwater. Their thousands of categories include all-tackle, various line classes and tippet classes for fly fishing. New records recognized by the IGFA reached an annual peak of 1,074 in 1984.

The heaviest freshwater category recognized is for the sturgeon-record weight of 212.28 kg (468 lb) caught by Joey Pallotta on 9 July 1983 off Benicia, California, USA.

### World Freshwater Championship
The *Confédération Internationale de la Pêche Sportive* (CIPS) championships were inaugurated as European championships in 1953 and recognized as World championships in 1957.

France won the European title in 1956 and a record 13 world titles between 1959 and 1995.

Brian Leadbetter (GB) has won two individual titles, in 1987 and 1991.

### Casting
The longest ever freshwater cast under ICF (International Casting Federation) rules is 175.01 m (574 ft 2 in) by Walter Kummerow (West Germany), for the bait distance double-handed 30-g event held at Lenzerheide, Switzerland, in the 1968 Championships.

Andy Dickison set the British national record of 148.78 m (488 ft 1 in) on the same occasion.

At the currently contested weight of 17.7 g—known as 18-g bait distance—the longest double-handed cast is 139.31 m (457 ft ½ in) by Kevin Carriero (USA) at Toronto, Canada, on 24 July 1984.

16:25:12

The individual title has been won a record three times by Robert Tesse (France), in 1959, 1960 and 1965, and by Bob Nudd (England), in 1990, 1991 and 1994.

The record weight (team) is 34.71 kg (76 lb 8¼ oz) in 3 hours, by West Germany on the River Neckar at Mannheim, Germany, on 21 Sept 1980.

The world record by an individual is 16.99 kg (37 lb 7⅕ oz) by Wolf-Rüdiger Kremkus (West Germany) at Mannheim, Germany, on 20 Sept 1980.

The greatest number of fish ever caught is 652 by Jacques Isenbaert (Belgium) at Dunaújváros, Hungary, on 27 Aug 1967.

### Fly fishing World Championships
World fly fishing championships were inaugurated by the CIPS in 1981.

The most team titles is five by Italy, in 1982, 1984, 1986 and 1992.

The British record for fixed-spool reel is 138.79 m (455 ft 3 in), by Hugh Newton at Peterborough, Cambs, UK, on 21 Sept 1985.

The British record for multiplier reel is 108.97 m (357 ft 6 in), set by James Tomlinson at Torrington, Devon, UK, on 27 April 1985.

The world record for the longest ever fly distance double-handed cast is 97.28 m (319 ft 1 in), by Wolfgang Feige (West Germany) at Toronto, Canada, on 23 July 1984.

Hywel Morgan set a British record for the fly distance double-handed cast with a distance of 91.22 m (299 ft 2 in) at Torrington, Devon, UK, on 27 April 1985.

The British Surfcasting Federation record (150 g or 5¼ oz weight) is 257.32 m (844 ft 3 in), by Neil Mackellow at Peterborough, Cambs, UK, on 1 Sept 1985.

# LONGEST FRESHWATER CAST 175.01 M

**ON 5 JUNE 1995**

## World Angling Records

### Freshwater and Saltwater Fish:

A selection of All-Tackle records ratified by the International Game Fish Association at Nov 1995

**Barracuda, Great:** 38.55 kg (85 lb)
John W. Helfrich
Christmas Island, Kiribati,
11 April 1992

**Bass, Striped:** 35.6 kg (78 lb 8 oz)
Albert R. McReynolds
Atlantic City, New Jersey, USA,
21 Sept 1982

**Catfish, Flathead:** 41.39 kg (91 lb 4 oz)
Mike Rogers
Lake Lewisville, Texas, USA,
28 March 1982

**Cod, Atlantic:** 44.79 kg (98 lb 12 oz)
Alphonse J. Bielevich

**Shark, Hammerhead:** 449.5 kg (991 lb)
Allen Ogle
Sarasota, Florida, USA, 30 May 1982

**Shark, Porbeagle:** 230 kg (507 lb)
Christopher Bennett
Pentland Firth, Caithness, UK,
9 March 1993

**Shark, Thresher:** 363.8 kg (802 lb)
Dianne North
Tutukaka, New Zealand, 8 Feb 1981

**Shark, Great White:** 1,208.38 kg (2,664 lb)
Alfred Dean
Ceduna, South Australia, 21 April 1959

**Sturgeon, White:** 212.28 kg (468 lb)
Joey Pallotta III
Benicia, California, USA, 9 July 1983

**Swordfish:** 536.15 kg (1,182 lb)
L. Marron
Iquique, Chile, 17 May 1953

**Trout, Brook:** 6.57 kg (14 lb 8 oz)

## BRITISH ANGLING RECORDS

### COARSE FISH:

Coarse fish includes all freshwater fish except those from the salmon and trout family. The following records are for a selection of fish that are recognized by the British Record (rod-caught) Fish Committee

**Barbel:** 7.314 kg (16 lb 2 oz)
P. Woodhouse
River Medway, Kent, 1994

**Bleak:** 0.120 kg (4 oz 4 dr)
B. Derrington
River Monnow, Wye Mouth, 1982

**Bream:** 7.512 kg (16 lb 9 oz)
M. McKeown
Southern water, 1991

**Bream, Silver:** 0.425 kg (15 oz)
D. E. Flack
Grime Spring, Lakenheath,
Suffolk, 1988

**Perch:** 2.523 kg (5 lb 9 oz)
J. Shayler
Private water, Kent, 1985

**Pike:** 21.236 kg (46 lb 13 oz)
R. Lewis
Llandefgfedd Reservoir,
Pontypool, Torfaen, 1992

**Roach:** 1.899 kg (4 lb 3 oz)
R. N. Clarke
Dorset Stour, 1990

**Stickleback:** 0.005 kg (3 dr)
M. Drinkwater
River Calder, Brighouse,
W Yorkshire, 1995

**Tench:** 6.548 kg (14 lb 7 oz)
G. Bevan
Southern stillwater, 1993

**Zander (Pikeperch):** 8.448 kg (18 lb 10 oz)
R. Armstrong
River Severn, 1993

**Below left**
A 'double haul' cast—this method can achieve greater distances with single-handed rods. Coarse fishing has become one of Britain's most popular sports—every year 850,000 licences are issued. Combined with other types of fishing, it is estimated that over 2 million people fish in the United Kingdom each year.

16:25:13

16:25:14

## KG AND 6.2 M IN LENGTH WAS HARPOONED BY FISHERMEN IN THE AZORES

Isle of Shoals, New Hampshire, USA,
8 June 1969

**Conger:** 60.44 kg (133 lb 4 oz)
Vic Evans
Berry Head, Devon, UK, 5 June 1995

**Halibut, Pacific:** 208.2 kg (459 lb)
Jack Tragis
Dutch Harbor, Alaska, USA,
11 June 1996

**Mackerel, King:** 40.82 kg (90 lb)
Norton I. Thomton
Key West, Florida, USA, 16 Feb 1976

**Marlin, Black:** 707.61 kg (1,560 lb)
Alfred C. Glassell Jr
Cabo Blanco, Peru, 4 Aug 1953

**Pike, Northern:** 25 kg (55 lb 1 oz)
Lothar Louis
Lake of Grefeern, Germany,
16 Oct 1986

**Sailfish (Pacific):** 100.24 kg (221 lb)
C. W. Stewart
Santa Cruz Island, Ecuador,
12 Feb 1947

**Salmon, Atlantic:** 35.89 kg (79 lb 2 oz)
Henrik Henriksen
Tana River, Norway, 1928

Dr W. J. Cook
Nipigon River, Ontario, Canada,
July 1916

**Trout, Brown:** 18.25 kg (40 lb 4 oz)
Howard L. Collins
Heber Springs, Arkansas, USA,
9 May 1992

**Trout, Lake:** 30.16 kg (66 lb 8 oz)
Rodney Harback
Great Bear Lake, NWT, Canada,
19 July 1991

**Trout, Rainbow:** 19.1 kg (42 lb 2 oz)
David Robert White
Bell Island, Alaska, USA, 22 June 1970

**Tuna, Bluefin:** 679 kg (1,496 lb)
Ken Fraser
Aulds Cove, Nova Scotia, Canada,
26 Oct 1979

**Tuna, Yellowfin:** 176.35 kg (388 lb 12 oz)
Curt Wiesenhutter
San Benedicto Island, Mexico,
1 April 1977

**Wahoo:** 71.89 kg (158 lb 8 oz)
Keith Winter
Loreto, Baja California, Mexico,
10 June 1996

**Carp:** 25.06 kg (55 lb 4 oz)
A. White
Mid Northants water, 1995

**Carp, Grass:** 13.005 kg (28 lb 12 oz 8dr)
S. Dolman
Church Lake, Horton, Berks, 1995

**Catfish (Wells):** 25.968 kg (57 lb 4 oz)
R. Coote
Withy Pool, Beds, 1995

**Chub:** 3.912 kg (8 lb 10 oz)
P. Smith
River Tees, 1994

**Dace:** 0.574 kg (1 lb 4 oz 4 dr)
J. L. Gasson
Little Ouse, Thetford, Norfolk, 1960

**Eel:** 5.046 kg (11 lb 2 oz)
S. Terry
Kingfisher Lake, Ringwood, Hants,
1978

**Gudgeon:** 0.141 kg (5 oz)
D. Hall
River Nadder, Salisbury, Wilts, 1990

**Orfe, Golden:** 3.80 kg (7 lb 7 oz 4 dr)
D. Smith
Horton Pool, 1995

**FRESHWATER GAME FISH:**
The Freshwater game fish category includes members of the salmon and trout family.

**Salmon:**
29.03 kg (64 lb)
Miss G. W. Ballantine
River Tay, Scotland, 1922

**Trout, American Brook:**
2.72 kg (6 lb)
D.Caisley
Fontburn Reservoir
Hants, 1981

**Trout, Brown:**
11.50 kg (25 lb 5 oz 12 dr)
A. Finlay
Loch Awe,
Argyll and Bute, 1996

**Trout, Rainbow:**
16.74 kg (36 lb 14 oz 8 dr)
C. White
Dover Springs Fishery,
Hants, 1995

**Trout, Sea:**
12.85 kg (28 lb 5 oz 4 dr)
J. Forrest
River Test, Hants, 1989

# Horse racing

**Below right**
Lester Piggott rode his first winner at the age of 12 and missed winning his first Derby by less than a length at the age of 16. However, he went on to win the Derby nine times.

**Below far right**
The American trainer Dale Baird has the career record for the most wins, with 7,200, between 1962 and 1996.

## Winning horses
### Best win-loss record
*Kincsem* was unbeaten in 54 races in Europe between 1876 and 1879.

### Longest winning sequence
*Camarero* was unbeaten in 56 races in Puerto Rico from 19 April 1953 to his first defeat on 17 Aug 1955.

### Most career wins
*Chorisbar* won 197 of her 324 races in Puerto Rico, between 1937 and 1947.

### Most wins in a year
*Lenoxbar* won 46 races from 56 starts in 1940 in Puerto Rico.

### Most same race wins
*Doctor Syntax* won the Preston Gold Cup on seven successive occasions, between 1815 and 1821.

### Triple Crown winners
The English Triple Crown (2,000 Guineas, Derby and St Leger) has been won 15 times, most recently by *Nijinsky* in 1970.

The fillies' equivalent (1,000 Guineas, Oaks and St Leger) has been won nine times, most recently by *Oh So Sharp* in 1985.

The American Triple Crown (Kentucky Derby, Preakness Stakes and Belmont Stakes) has been achieved 11 times, most recently by *Affirmed* in 1978.

### World speed records
*Big Racket* reached 69.62 km/h (43.26 mph), in a ¼ mile (402 m) race at Mexico City, Mexico, on 5 Feb 1945. *Onion Roll* achieved the same speed at Thistledown, Cleveland, Ohio, USA, on 27 Sept 1993.

### Oldest winners
The oldest horses to win on the Flat are 18-year-olds *Revenge* at Shrewsbury in 1790, *Marksman* at Ashford, Kent, in 1826 and *Jorrocks* at Bathurst, Australia, in 1851. At the same age *Wild Aster* won three hurdle races in six days in 1919 and *Sonny Somers* two steeplechases in 1980.

## Jockeys
### Most successful
The 1.50-m-tall (4-ft 11-in) tall Billie Lee 'Bill' Shoemaker (USA) rode a record 8,833 winners from 40,350 mounts from 19 March 1949 to 3 Feb 1990.

The most races won by a jockey in a year is 598 from 2,312 rides, by Kent Jason Desormeaux (USA) in 1989.

### Most winners in one day
The most winners ridden in one day is nine, by Chris Wiley Antley (USA) on 31 Oct 1987. They consisted of four in the afternoon at Aqueduct, New York, USA, and five in the evening at The Meadowlands, New Jersey, USA.

### Most winners on one card
The record is eight, by six riders, and most recently (and from fewest rides) by Patrick Alan Day from nine rides at Arlington International, Illinois, USA, on 13 Sept 1989.

### Most wins in one race meeting
Frankie Dettori had wins in all seven races at Ascot, Berks, UK, on 28 Sept 1996.

### Winning streak
The most consecutive wins is 12, by: Sir Gordon Richards with one race at Nottingham on 3 Oct, six out of six at Chepstow on 4 Oct and the first five races the next day at Chepstow in 1933; and Pieter Stroebel at Bulawayo, Southern Rhodesia (now Zimbabwe), from 7 June to 7 July 1958.

## Trainers and owners
### Trainers
The most wins in a year is 496, by Jack Charles Van Berg (USA) in 1976.

The career record is 7,200, by Dale Baird (USA) from 1962 to May 1997.

The only trainer to saddle the first five finishers in a championship race is Michael William Dickinson of Dunkeswick, W Yorkshire, UK, in the Cheltenham Gold Cup on 17 March 1983. He won a record 12 races in one day on 27 Dec 1982.

### Owners
The most lifetime wins by an owner is 4,775, by Marion H. Van Berg in North America in 35 years.

The most wins in a year is 494, by Dan R. Lasater (USA) in 1974.

## British flat racing
### Best win-loss record
*Eclipse* still has the best win-loss record, unbeaten in a career of 18 races from May 1769 to Oct 1770.

### Longest winning sequence
The longest winning sequence is 21 races, by *Meteor* from 1786 to 1788.

### Most races won in a season
The most races won in a season is 23 (from 34 starts), by *Fisherman* in 1856.

### Most career wins
*Catherina* won a career record 79 out of 176 races between 1832 and 1841.

### Most successful sire
The most successful sire was *Stockwell* whose progeny won 1,153 races between 1858 and 1876.

### Biggest winning margin in a Classic
The biggest winning margin in a Classic is 20 lengths, by *Mayonaise* in the 1,000 Guineas on 12 May 1859.

### Most Pattern-race wins
The most prolific British-trained winner of all time is *Brigadier Gerard* with 13 wins in 1971 and 1972.

Since the 1977 introduction of official ratings in the International Classifications, the highest-rated is 141, for *Dancing Brave* in 1986.

### Most successful jockeys
Sir Gordon Richards won 4,870 races from 21,815 mounts from his first mount on 16 Oct 1920 to his last on 10 July 1954. His first win was on 31 March 1921. In 1953, at his 28th and final attempt, he won the Derby, six days after his knighthood. He was champion jockey 26 times between 1925 and 1953 and won a record 269 races (from 835 rides) in 1947.

Lester Keith Piggott won 4,513 races in the United Kingdom between 1948 and 1995, and his global total exceeds 5,300 race wins.

The most wins in a day is seven, by Patrick James John Eddery at Newmarket and Newcastle on 26 June 1992 and Frankie Dettori (on one card) at Ascot on 28 Sept 1996.

The most Classic races won by a jockey is 30, by Lester Piggott from his first on *Never Say Die* in the 1954 Derby to the 2,000 Guineas in 1992 on *Rodrigo de Triano*. He won the Derby nine times, the St Leger eight times, the Oaks six times, the 2,000 Guineas five times and the 1,000 Guineas twice.

### Most successful trainers
Richard Michael Hannon of East Everleigh, Wilts, had 182 wins (from 1,215 starts) in 1993.

The most Classics won by a trainer is 40, by John Scott of Malton, Yorkshire, between 1827 and 1863.

James Croft of Middleham, Yorkshire, trained the first four horses in the St Leger on 16 Sept 1822.

Alexander Taylor of Manton, Wilts, the most financially successful trainer, won a record 12 times between 1907 and 1925.

Henry Richard Amherst Cecil of Newmarket has been champion in races won a record nine times, between 1978 and 1989.

### Most successful owners
The Aga Khan III was leading owner a record 13 times, between 1924 and 1952.

The horses of Sheikh Mohammed bin Rashid al Maktoum of Dubai, won a record 185 races in 1992.

George Fitzroy, 4th Duke of Grafton, won 20 Classics between 1813 and 1831 as did Edward Stanley, 17th Earl of Derby, between 1910 and 1945.

### The Derby
*Shergar* won the Derby by a record 10 lengths in 1981. There have been two dead-heats: in 1828 when *Cadland* beat *The Colonel* in the run-off, and in 1884 between *St Gatien* and *Harvester* (stakes divided).

## Jumping
### Most successful horses
*Sir Ken*, who won the Champion Hurdle in 1952–54, won a record 16 hurdle races in succession, from April 1951 to March 1953.

Three other horses have also won a record three Champion Hurdles; *Hatton's Grace* 1949–51; *Persian War* 1968–70; *See You Then* 1985–87.

The most Cheltenham Gold Cup wins is five, by *Golden Miller*, 1932–36.

**PETER SCUDAMORE**

# RACE SPEED RECORD 69.62 KM/H

## FOR THE MOST WINS AT ONE MEETING

The mare *Dawn Run* is the only horse to win the Champion Hurdle (1984) and Cheltenham Gold Cup (1986).

The greatest number of Horse of the Year awards is four, by *Desert Orchid*, from 1987 to 1990.

**Most successful jockeys**
Peter Scudamore won a career record 1,678 races over jumps, from 7,521 mounts, from 1978 to 1993.

The record for the most wins in a season is 221 (from 663 rides), by Peter Scudamore in 1988/9.

The most wins in a day is six, by two amateurs: Edward Potter Wilson at Crewkerne, Somerset, on 19 March 1878 and Charles James Cunningham at Rugby, Warks, UK, on 29 March 1881.

The record number of successive wins is 10, by: John Alnham Gilbert, in Sept 1959; and Philip Charles Tuck, between 23 Aug and 3 Sept 1986.

The jockey who has won the most championships is Peter Scudamore, with eight (one shared), in 1982 and from 1986 to 1992.

**Grand National**
The only horse to win three times is *Red Rum* in 1973, 1974 and 1977, from a total of five runs. He came second in 1975 and 1976.

*Manifesto* ran a record eight times. He won in 1897 and 1899 and came third three times and fourth once.

## MAJOR BRITISH RACE RECORDS, FLAT
### DERBY
**Record time: 2 min 32.31 sec**
*Lammtarra* in 1995
**Most wins (jockey): 9**
Lester Piggott in 1954, 1957, 1960, 1968, 1970, 1972, 1976, 1977, 1983
**Most wins (trainer): 7**
Robert Robson in 1793, 1802, 1809, 1810, 1815, 1817, 1823
John Porter in 1868, 1882, 1883, 1886, 1890, 1891, 1899
Fred Darling in 1922, 1925, 1926, 1931, 1938, 1940, 1941
**Most wins (owner): 5**
3rd Earl of Egremont in 1782, 1804, 1805, 1807, 1826
HH Aga Khan III in 1930, 1935, 1936, 1948, 1952
### 2,000 GUINEAS
**Record time: 1 min 35.08 sec**
*Mister Baileys* in 1994
**Most wins (jockey): 9**
Jem Robinson in 1825, 1828, 1831, 1833, 1834, 1835, 1836, 1847, 1848

**Most wins (trainer): 7**
John Scott in 1842, 1843, 1849, 1853, 1856, 1860, 1862
**Most wins (owner): 5**
4th Duke of Grafton in 1820, 1821, 1822, 1826, 1827
5th Earl of Jersey in 1831, 1834, 1835, 1836, 1837
### 1,000 GUINEAS
**Record time: 1 min 36.71 sec**
*Las Meninas* in 1994
**Most wins (jockey): 7**
George Fordham in 1859, 1861, 1865, 1868, 1869, 1881, 1883
**Most wins (trainer): 9**
Robert Robson in 1818, 1819, 1820, 1821, 1822, 1823, 1825, 1826, 1827
**Most wins (owner): 8**
4th Duke of Grafton in 1819, 1820, 1821, 1822, 1823, 1825, 1826, 1827
### OAKS
**Record time: 2 min 34.19 sec**
*Intrepidity* in 1993
**Most wins (jockey): 9**
Frank Buckle in 1797, 1798, 1799, 1802, 1803, 1805, 1817, 1818, 1823
**Most wins (trainer): 12**
Robert Robson in 1802, 1804, 1805, 1807, 1808, 1809, 1813, 1815, 1818, 1822, 1823, 1825
**Most wins (owner): 6**
4th Duke of Grafton in 1813, 1815, 1822, 1823, 1828, 1831
### ST LEGER
**Record time: 3 min 1.6 sec**
*Coronach* in 1926 and *Windsor Lad* in 1934
**Most wins (jockey): 9**
Bill Scott in 1821, 1825, 1828, 1829, 1838, 1839, 1840, 1841, 1846
**Most wins (trainer): 16**
John Scott in 1827, 1828, 1829, 1832, 1834, 1838, 1839, 1840, 1841, 1845, 1851, 1853, 1856, 1857, 1859, 1862
**Most wins (owner): 7**
9th Duke of Hamilton in 1786, 1787, 1788, 1792, 1808, 1809, 1814
### KING GEORGE VI AND QUEEN ELIZABETH DIAMOND STAKES
**Record time: 2 min 26.98 sec**
*Grundy* in 1975
**Most wins (jockey): 7**
Lester Piggott in 1965, 1966, 1969, 1970, 1974, 1977, 1984
**Most wins (trainer): 5**
Dick Hern in 1972, 1979, 1980, 1985, 1989
**Most wins (owner): 3**
Sheikh Mohammed 1990, 1993, 1994

## MAJOR BRITISH RACE RECORDS, JUMPING
### GRAND NATIONAL
**Record time: 8 min 47.8 sec**
*Mr Frisk* in 1990
**Most wins (jockey): 5**
George Stevens in 1856, 1863, 1864, 1869, 1870

**Most wins (trainer): 4**
Fred Rimell in 1956, 1961, 1970, 1976
**Most wins (owner): 3**
James Machell in 1873, 1874, 1876
Sir Charles Assheton-Smith in 1893, 1912, 1913
Noel Le Mare in 1973, 1974, 1977
### CHELTENHAM GOLD CUP
**Record time: 6 min 23.4 sec**
*Silver Fame* in 1951
**Most wins (jockey): 4**
Pat Taaffe in 1964, 1965, 1966, 1968
**Most wins (trainer): 5**
Tom Dreaper in 1946, 1964, 1965, 1966, 1968
**Most wins (owner): 7**
Dorothy Paget in 1932, 1933, 1934, 1935, 1936, 1940, 1952
### CHAMPION HURDLE
**Record time: 3 min 48.4 sec**
*Make A Stand* in 1997

**Most wins (jockey): 4**
Tim Molony in 1951, 1952, 1953, 1954
**Most wins (trainer): 5**
Peter Easterby in 1967, 1976, 1977, 1980, 1981
**Most wins (owner): 4**
Dorothy Paget in 1932, 1933, 1940, 1946

## MAJOR INTERNATIONAL RACE RECORDS
### PRIX DE L'ARC DE TRIOMPHE
**Record time: 2 min 26.3 sec**
*Trempolino* in 1987
**Most wins (jockey): 4**
Jacques Doyasbère in 1942, 1944, 1950, 1951
Frédéric Head in 1966, 1972, 1976, 1979
Yves Saint-Martin in 1970, 1974, 1982, 1984
Pat Eddery in 1980, 1985, 1986, 1987
**Most wins (trainer): 4**
Charles Semblat in 1942, 1944, 1946, 1949

Alec Head in 1952, 1959, 1976, 1981
François Mathet in 1950, 1951, 1970, 1982
**Most wins (owner): 6**
Marcel Boussac in 1936, 1937, 1942, 1944, 1946, 1949
### VRC MELBOURNE CUP
**Record time: 3 min 16.3 sec**
*Kingston Rule* in 1990
**Most wins (jockey): 4**
Bobby Lewis in 1902, 1915, 1919, 1927
Harry White in 1974, 1975, 1978, 1979
**Most wins (trainer): 10**
Bart Cummings in 1965, 1966, 1967, 1974, 1975, 1977, 1979, 1990, 1991, 1996
**Most wins (owner): 4**
Etienne de Mestre in 1861, 1862, 1867, 1878

### KENTUCKY DERBY
**Record time: 1 min 59.4 sec**
*Secretariat* in 1973
**Most wins (jockey): 5**
Eddie Arcaro in 1938, 1941, 1945, 1948, 1952
Bill Hartack in 1957, 1960, 1962, 1964, 1969
**Most wins (trainer): 6**
Ben Jones in 1938, 1941, 1944, 1948, 1949, 1952
**Most wins (owner): 8**
Calumet Farm in 1941, 1944, 1948, 1949, 1952, 1957, 1958, 1968
### IRISH DERBY
**Record time: 2 min 25.60 sec**
*St Jovite* in 1992
**Most wins (jockey): 6**
Morny Wing in 1921, 1923, 1930, 1938, 1942, 1946
**Most wins (trainer): 6**
Vincent O'Brien in 1953, 1957, 1970, 1977, 1984, 1985
**Most wins (owner): 5**
HH Aga Khan III in 1925, 1932, 1940, 1948, 1949

**Below left**
*Lord Gyllene* on his way to winning the 1997 Grand National. The race was abandoned on 5 April after terrorist bomb warnings, but it went ahead on 7 April.

# Animal sports

**Below right**
At the Third Royal Equestrian Show held in the Sultanate of Oman in 1995 there were 510 horses, 170 camels and a marching band of 1,000 musicians.

## Equestrian sports
### Olympic show jumping
The most Olympic gold medals to be won by one rider is five, by Hans Günter Winkler (West Germany), four team medals in 1956, 1960, 1964 and 1972 and the individual Grand Prix in 1956. He also won team silver in 1976 and team bronze in 1968 for a record seven medals overall.

Germany has the most wins in the Prix des Nations with seven: 1936, 1956, 1960, 1964, 1972, 1988 (as West Germany) and 1996.

The lowest score obtained by a winner is no faults, by Frantisek Ventura (Czechoslovakia) on *Eliot* in 1928; by Alwin Schockemöhle (West Germany) on *Warwick Rex* in 1976; and by

### World Cup
The World Cup was instituted in 1979. The most wins is three, by Hugo Simon (Austria) in 1979, 1996 and 1997.

### King George V Gold Cup and Queen Elizabeth II Cup
David Broome has won the King George V Gold Cup a record six times, on *Sunsalve* in 1960, on *Mister Softee* in 1966, on *Sportsman* in 1972, on *Philco* in 1977, on *Mr Ross* in 1981 and on *Lannegan* in 1991.

The Queen Elizabeth II Cup has been won five times by Elizabeth Edgar, on *Everest Wallaby* in 1977, on *Forever* in 1979, on *Everest Forever* in 1981 and 1982, and on *Everest Rapier* in 1986.

## Three-Day Eventing
### Olympic and World Championships
Charles Ferdinand Pahud de Mortanges (Netherlands) won a record four Olympic gold medals: team in 1924 and 1928, and individual (riding *Marcroix*) in 1928 and 1932.

Bruce Oram Davidson (USA) is the only rider to have won two individual world titles, on *Irish Cap* in 1974 and *Might Tango* in 1978.

Richard John Hannay Meade is the only British rider to win three Olympic gold medals: team in 1968 and 1972 and individual in 1972.

### Badminton
The Badminton Three-Day Event has been won six times by Lucinda Jane

## World Cup
The only double winners are Christine Stückelberger (Switzerland) on *Gauguin de Lully*, in 1987 and 1988; Monica Theodorescu (Greece) on *Ganimedes Tecrent*, in 1993 and 1994; and Anky van Grunsven (Netherlands) on *Camelion Bonfire*, in 1995 and 1996.

## Equestrian shows
### Largest show of horses and camels
On 30 Dec 1995, at the Third Royal Equestrian Show in the Sultanate of Oman, 510 horses and 170 camels took part.

## Carriage driving
### World Championships
A record three team titles have been won by Great Britain, in 1972, 1974 and 1980; Hungary, in 1976, 1978

Ludger Beerbaum (Germany) on *Classic Touch* in 1992.

Pierre Jonquères d'Oriola (France) is the only rider to have won the individual gold medal twice, in 1952 and 1964.

### World Championships
The men's title has been won twice by Hans Günter Winkler (West Germany) from 1954 to 1955, and by Raimondo d'Inzeo (Italy) in 1956 and 1960.

The women's World Championships were won twice by Jane 'Janou' Tissot (France) on *Rocket*, in 1970 and 1974.

France has won three times, in 1982, 1986 and 1990.

### President's Cup
Great Britain has won the President's Cup a record 14 times, in 1965, 1967, 1970, 1972–74, 1977–79, 1983, 1985–86, 1989 and 1991.

### Nations Cup
David Broome has represented Great Britain 106 times in Nations Cup events, between 1959 and 1994.

*Sunsalve* is the only horse to have won both trophies. This happened in 1957, when ridden by Elisabeth Anderson, and in 1960, ridden by David Broome.

### World jumping records
The official Fédération Equestre Internationale high jump record is 2.47 m (8 ft 1¼ in), by *Huasó*, which was ridden by Capt. Alberto Larraguibel Morales (Chile) at Viña del Mar, Chile, on 5 Feb 1949.

The indoor high-jump record is 2.40 m (7 ft 10¾ in), by *Optibeurs Leonardo*, ridden by Franke Sloothaak (Germany) at Chaudefontaine, Switzerland, on 9 June 1991.

The official record for the long jump over water is 8.40 m (27 ft 6¾ in), by *Something*, ridden by André Ferreira (South Africa) at Johannesburg, South Africa, on 25 April 1975.

### British jump record
The British high-jump record is 2.32 m (7 ft 7¼ in), by *Lastic*, ridden by Nick Skelton at Olympia, London, UK, on 16 Dec 1978.

Green, on *Be Fair* in 1973, on *Wide Awake* in 1976, on *George* in 1977, on *Killaire* in 1979, on *Regal Realm* in 1983 and on *Beagle Bay* in 1984.

### Dressage
#### Olympic and World Championships
Germany (as West Germany from 1968 to 1990) has won a record nine team gold medals, in 1928, 1936, 1964, 1968, 1976, 1984, 1988, 1992 and 1996, and a record seven team wins at the World Championships.

Dr Reiner Klimke (West Germany) has won a record six Olympic golds (team from 1964–88 and individual in 1984). He also holds the record for seven medals overall and is the only rider to win two world titles, on *Mehmed* in 1974 and *Ahlerich* in 1982.

Henri St Cyr (Sweden) won a record two individual Olympic gold medals in 1952 and 1956. This was equalled by Nicole Uphoff (Germany) who won in 1988 and 1992.

and 1984; the Netherlands, in 1982, 1986 and 1988 and Germany in 1992, 1994 and 1996.

Two individual titles have been won by György Bárdos (Hungary), in 1978 and 1980; Tjeerd Velstra (Netherlands), in 1982 and 1986; and Ijsbrand Chardon (Netherlands), in 1988 and 1992.

### British titles
Up until 1994, George Bowman had won a record 17 Horse Teams titles at the National Driving Championships.

## Polo
### Most titles
The British Open Championship for the Cowdray Park Gold Cup has been won five times by Stowell Park, in 1973, 1974, 1976, 1978 and 1980, and by Tramontana, from 1986 to 1989, and in 1991.

### Highest handicap
The highest handicap based on six 7½-min 'chukkas' is ten goals,

# FASTEST GREYHOUND 67.32 KM/H

**Derby 'triple'**
The only greyhounds to win the English, Scottish and Welsh Derby 'triple' are *Trev's Perfection*, owned by Fred Trevillion in 1947, *Mile Bush Pride*, owned by Noel W. Purvis in 1959, and *Patricia's Hope* in 1972.

**Fastest greyhound**
The highest ever timed speed is 366 m (400 yd) in 19.57 sec, or 67.32 km/h (41.83 mph), by *Star Title* on the straightaway track at Wyong, New South Wales, Australia, on 5 March 1994.

The highest speed in the United Kingdom is 63.37 km/h (39.38 mph) by *Ravage Again*, when it ran a course of 250 m (273 yd) in 14.20 sec at Belle Vue, Greater Manchester.

**Pigeon Racing**
**Longest flights**
The official British duration record (flying into the United Kingdom) is 1,887 km (1,173 miles) in 15 days by *C.S.O.*, in the 1976 Palamos Race.

In 1990 it was reported that a pigeon, owned by David Lloyd and George Workman of Nantyffyllon, Bridgend, UK, had completed a flight of 10,860 km (6,750 miles) from its release at Lerwick, Shetland to Shanghai, China.

**Highest speeds**
The highest race speed recorded is 177.14 km/h (110.07 mph) in the East Anglian Federation race from E Croydon, UK, on 8 May 1965. The 1,428 birds were backed by a powerful south-south-west wind.

## ENGLISH GREYHOUND DERBY TWICE, *MICK THE MILLER* AND *PATRICIA'S HOPE*

introduced in the USA in 1891 and in the UK and in Argentina in 1910. A total of 56 players have received 10-goal handicaps. The last (of six) 10-goal handicap players from the United Kingdom was Gerald Matthew Balding, in 1939.

Howard Hipwood's handicap of eight is the highest for a current British player (in 1992 he had a handicap of nine).

Claire J. Tomlinson of Gloucestershire, UK, attained a handicap of five, the highest ever by a woman, in 1986.

A match of two 40-goal teams has been staged on only three occasions, in Argentina, in 1975, in the USA in 1990 and in Australia in 1991.

**Highest score**
The highest ever aggregate number of goals scored in an international match is 30, when Argentina beat the USA 21–9 at Meadowbrook, Long Island, New York, USA, in September 1936.

**Most chukkas**
The greatest number of chukkas that have ever been played on one ground in a day is 43. This was achieved by the Pony Club on the Number 3 Ground at Kirtlington Park, Oxon, UK, on 31 July 1991.

**Greyhound Racing**
**Derby**
Two greyhounds have won the English Greyhound Derby twice: *Mick the Miller* on 25 July 1929 (when owned by Albert H. Williams) and on 28 June 1930 (when owned by Mrs Arundel H. Kempton), and *Patricia's Hope* on 24 June 1972 (when owned by Gordon and Basil Marks and Brian Stanley) and on 23 June 1973 (when owned by G. & B. Marks and J. O'Connor).

**Grand National**
The only greyhound to have won the Grand National three times is *Sherry's Prince* (owned by Mrs Joyce Matthews of Sanderstead, Surrey, UK) from 1970 to 1972.

The fastest automatically timed speed recorded for a full tour-bend race is 62.59 km/h (38.89 mph) by *Glen Miner*. The dog covered a distance of 515 m (563 yd) in a time of 29.62 sec at Hove, E Sussex, UK, on 4 May 1982.

The fastest ever recorded speed over hurdles is 60.58 km/h (37.78 mph) achieved by *Lord Westlands* at Hove, E Sussex, UK.

**Most wins**
The greatest number of career wins is 143, by the American greyhound *JR's Ripper* from 1982 to 1986.

The most consecutive victories is 37, by *JJ Doc Richard*, owned by Jack Boyd, at Mobile, Alabama, USA, up until 29 May 1995.

The most wins in the United Kingdom is 32, including 16 track record times, from 25 Aug 1984 to 9 Dec 1986, by *Ballyregan Bob*.

The highest race speed recorded over more than 1,000 km (621.37 miles) is 133.46 km/h (82.93mph) by a hen in the Central Cumberland Combine race over 1,099.316 km (683 miles 147 yd) from Murray Bridge, South Australia to North Ryde, Sydney, Australia, on 2 Oct 1971.

**Career records**
The greatest competitive distance ever flown is 32,318 km (20,082 miles) by *Nunnies*, a chequer cock owned by Terry Haley of Abbot's Langley, Herts, UK.

**Mass release**
The largest ever simultaneous release of pigeons was at Orleans, France, in Aug 1988, when over 215,000 pigeons were released for a Dutch National race.

The largest British release was at Beachy Head near Eastbourne, E Sussex, UK, on 11 May 1991 when 42,500 birds were released.

# Cycling and motorcycling

**Right**
Tony Rominger of Switzerland racing in the 1996 world road cycling championships in Lugano, Switzerland. He has won the Tour of Spain a record three times.

**Far right**
Jacques Anquetil tries his best to cool off during a Tour de France. He won the race a record five times, between 1957 and 1964.

to 1983, and won 72 individual road TT titles, 14 track pursuit titles and 12 road race titles to 1986. Ian Hallam won a record 25 men's titles between 1969 and 1982.

### Tour de France
The most wins in the Tour de France race is five, by Jacques Anquetil (France), 1957, 1961–64; Eddy Merckx (Belgium), 1969–72 and 1974; Bernard Hinault (France), 1978–79, 1981–82 and 1985; and Miguel Induráin (Spain), 1991–95.

The closest Tour de France race ever was in 1989 when after 3,267 km (2,030 miles) over 23 days (1–23 July) Greg LeMond (USA), who completed the Tour in 87 hr 38 min 35 sec, beat Laurent Fignon (France) in Paris by a margin of only 8 seconds.

The fastest average speed is 42.185 km/h (26.213 mph) by Joey McLoughlin (GB) in the 1986 race (1,714 km or 1,065 miles).

### Six-day races
The most wins in six-day races is 88 out of 233 events by Patrick Sercu (Belgium), from 1964 to 1983.

### Longest one-day race
The longest single-day 'massed start' road race (when the distance varies yearly) is the 551–620 km (342–385 miles) Bordeaux-Paris race, France.

### Cyclo-Cross
**Most titles**
Eric De Vlaeminck (Belgium) won both the Amateur and Open titles in 1966 and six Professional titles between 1968 and 1973.

## Cycling
### Highest speed
The highest speed ever achieved on a bicycle is 268.831 km/h (166.944 mph), by Fred Rompelberg (Netherlands) behind a wind-shield at Bonneville Salt Flats, Utah, USA, on 3 Oct 1995. Considerable help was provided by the slipstreaming effect of the lead vehicle.

The British speed record stands at 158.05 km/h (98.21 mph) over 200 m, by David Le Grys on a closed section of the M42 at Alvechurch, Warks, UK, on 28 Aug 1985.

The 24-hr record behind pace is 1,958.196 km (1,216 miles 1,498 yd), by Michael Secrest at Phoenix International Raceway, Arizona, USA, on 26–27 April 1990.

### Cycling races
**Most Olympic titles**
The most gold medals won is three, by Paul Masson (France) in 1896, Francisco Verri (Italy) in 1906 and Robert Charpentier (France) (1916–66) in 1936. Daniel Morelon (France) won

two in 1968 and a third in 1972; he also won a silver in 1976 and a bronze medal in 1964.

In the 'unofficial' 1904 cycling programme, Marcus Latimer Hurley (USA) won four events.

### World Championships
The most wins at one event is 10, by Koichi Nakano (Japan) for professional sprint from 1977 to 1986.

The greatest number of wins at a men's amateur event is seven, by Daniel Morelon (France), for sprint (1966–67, 1969–71, 1973, 1975); and Leon Meredith (GB) for the 100-km motor-paced race (1904–05, 1907–09, 1911, 1913).

The most women's titles is 10, by Jeannie Longo (France), for pursuit (1986 and 1988–89); road (1985–87, 1989 and 1995) points (1989) and time-trial (1995 and 1996).

### Most British titles
Beryl Burton was 25 times British all-round time trial champion from 1959

The fastest average speed was 39.504 km/h (24.547 mph), by Miguel Induráin (Spain) in 1992.

### Giro d'Italia
The most wins is five, by Alfredo Binda (Italy) in 1925, 1927–29, 1933; Fausto Coppi (Italy) in 1940, 1947, 1949, 1952–53; and Eddy Merckx (Belgium) in 1968, 1970, 1972–74.

### Vuelta a España
The most wins is three, by Tony Rominger (Switzerland), 1992–94.

### Tour of Britain (Open)
Four riders have each won twice: Bill Bradley (GB) (1959–60); Leslie George West (GB) (1965, 1967); Fedor den Hertog (Netherlands) (1969, 1971) and Yuriy Kashurin (USSR) (1979, 1982).

The closest race ever was in 1976 when, after 1,665.67 km (1,035 miles) over 14 days from 30 May to 12 June, Bill Nickson (GB) beat Joe Waugh (GB) by five seconds.

### Fastest Three Peaks
Stephen Poulton cycled from sea level at Caernarfon, Gwynedd, via the peaks of Snowdon, Scafell Pike and Ben Nevis, to sea level Fort William, Highland, UK, in 41 hr 51 min, from 1 to 2 July 1980.

### Fastest Three Peaks in relay
A relay team of John Brown, David Pullen and Richard Teal completed the journey, starting in Fort William, in 36 hours 43 min from 31 Aug to 1 Sept 1996.

### Highest altitude
Canadians Bruce Bell, Philip Whelan and Suzanne MacFadyen cycled at an altitude of 6,960 m (22,834 ft) on the peak of Mt Aconcagua, Argentina, on 25 Jan 1991.

This high altitude cycling record was equalled by Mozart Hastenreiter Catão of Brazil on 11 March 1993 and by Tim Sumner and Jonathon Green on 6 Jan 1994.

# UNICYCLE SPRINT 29.72 KM/H

BEN NEVIS) IN 36 HR 43 MIN IN 1996

## Cycle Speedway
**Most British Championships**
The greatest number of British Senior Team Championships wins is nine, by Poole, Dorset, in 1982, 1984 and from 1987 to 1993.

**Most individual titles**
Derek Garnett took four individual titles, in 1963, 1965, 1968 and 1972.

## Human-powered vehicles
**Fastest land HPV**
The records for human-powered vehicles (HPVs) over a 200-m flying start are: 105.38 km/h (65.48 mph) (single rider) by Fred Markham at Mono Lake, California, USA, on 11 May 1986; 101.26 km/h (62.92 mph) (multiple riders) by Dave Grylls and Leigh Barczewski at the Ontario Speedway, California, on 4 May 1980.

(St John's) course in the Isle of Man on 28 May 1907, and still run in the island on the 'Mountain' circuit.

**Fastest circuits**
The highest average lap speed attained on any closed circuit is 257.958 km/h (160.288 mph) by Yvon du Hamel (Canada) on a modified 903-cc four-cylinder Kawasaki Z1 at the 31-degree banked 4.02-km (2½-mile) Daytona International Speedway, Florida, USA, in March 1973.

The fastest road circuit was the 14.12-km (8-mile 1,355-yd) Francorchamps circuit near Spa, Belgium, which was lapped in 3 min 50.3 sec, at an average speed of 220.721 km/h (137.150 mph), by Barry Stephen Frank Sheene (GB) on a 495-cc 4-cylinder Suzuki. This was

**Longest circuit**
The 60.72-km (37-mile 1285-yd) 'Mountain' circuit on the Isle of Man, over which the principal TT races have been run since 1911 (with minor amendments in 1920), is the longest circuit used for any motorcycle race.

**World Championship titles**
The most titles is 15, by Giacomo Agostini (Italy); seven at 350 cc (from 1968 to 1974); eight at 500 cc (1966 to 1972 and in 1975).

Angel Roldan Nieto (Spain) won a record seven 125 cc titles (1971–72, 1979, 1981–84), and a record six titles at 50 cc, (1969–70, 1972, 1975–77).

Phil Read (GB) won a record four 250 cc titles (1964–65, 1968, 1971).

Redman (Rhodesia). He won the 250 cc and 350 cc events from 1963 to 1965.

The most events won in one year is four (Formula One, Junior, Senior and Production) by Phillip McCallen (Ireland), in 1996.

**Fastest Tourist Trophy speed**
The Isle of Man TT circuit speed record is 198.92 km/h (123.61 mph), by Carl George Fogarty on 12 June 1992.

On the same occasion Steve Hislop set the race speed record, 1 hr 51 min 59.6 sec with an average speed of 195.17 km/h (121.28 mph), to win the 1992 Senior TT on a Norton.

The fastest woman around the 'Mountain' circuit is Sandra Barnett

BY BARRY SHEENE (GB) IN 3 MIN 50.3 SEC, AVERAGING 220.721 KM/H

The one-hour standing start (single rider) record is held by Pat Kinch, riding Kingcycle Bean, averaging a speed of 75.57 km/h (46.96 mph) at Millbrook Proving Ground, Bedford, UK, on 8 Sept 1990.

## Water cycle
The men's 2,000-m record (single rider) is 20.66 km/h (12.84 mph), by Steve Hegg at Long Beach, California, USA, on 20 July 1987.

## Fastest sprint (unicycle)
Peter Rosendahl set a sprint record for 100 m from a standing start of 12.11 sec (29.72 km/h or 18.47 mph) at Las Vegas, Nevada, USA, on 25 March 1994.

## Motorcycle Racing
**Oldest race**
The oldest annually contested motorcycle races in the world are the Auto-Cycle Union Tourist Trophy (TT) series, which were first held on the 25.44-km (15-mile 1,425-yd) 'Peel'

during the Belgian Grand Prix on 3 July 1977, when he set a record time of 38 min 58.5 sec for this 141.20-km (87-mile 1,302-yd) race.

The fastest British circuit was the 4.453-km (2.767-mile) outer circuit at the Brooklands Motor Course, near Weybridge, Surrey, which was open between 1907 and 1939. The lap record was 80 seconds (giving an average speed of 200.37 km/h or 124.51 mph) by Noel Baddow 'Bill' Pope (later Major) (GB) on a Brough Superior powered by a supercharged 996-cc V-twin '8–80' JAP engine developing 110 bhp, in 1939.

The fastest British circuit in current use consists of the public roads at Dundrod, Co. Antrim over which the Ulster Grand Prix is held. In Aug 1990, Steve Hislop (Scotland) set an overall average speed of 195.48 km/h (121.46 mph) for the 'King of the Road' race and in Aug 1994 Jason Griffiths (Wales) set a lap record of 202.94 km/h (126.10 mph).

Rolf Biland (Switzerland) won a record seven world side-car titles, 1978–79, 1981, 1983, 1992–94.

Giacomo Agostini (Italy) won 122 races (68 at 500 cc, 54 at 350 cc) in the World Championship series between 24 April 1965 and 25 Sept 1977, including a record 19 in 1970—a season's total also achieved by Mike Hailwood in 1966.

The most career wins for any one class is 79, by Rolf Biland at side-car.

**Most successful machines**
Japanese Yamaha machines won 45 World Championships between 1964 and 1992.

**Most Tourist Trophy wins**
The record number of victories in the Isle of Man TT races is 22, by William Joseph Dunlop (Ireland), 1977–97.

The first man to win three consecutive TT titles in two events was James A.

(GB), with a speed of 179.86 km/h (111.76 mph) in the 1994 Senior TT.

**Most World Trials Championships**
The record for the most World Trials is six, by Jordi Tarrès (Spain) in 1987, 1989, 1990, 1991, 1993 and 1994.

## Moto-Cross
**Most World Championships**
Joël Robert (Belgium) won six 250-cc Moto-Cross World Championships (1964, 1968–72). Between 25 April 1964 and 18 June 1972 he won a record 50 250-cc Grand Prix.

Eric Geboers (Belgium) is the only rider to have won all three categories of the Moto-Cross World Championships, at 125 cc in 1982 and 1983, 250 cc in 1987 and 500 cc in 1988 and 1990.

**Youngest champion**
The youngest Moto-Cross champion was Dave Strijbos (Netherlands), who won the 125-cc title aged 18 years 296 days on 31 Aug 1986.

# Motor sports

**Below right**
Walter Röhrl driving
his Audi Quattro in
the Monte Carlo Rally.
He has won the rally
a record four times,
in 1980, 1982, 1983
and 1984, each time
in a different car.

**Below far right**
Porsche cars have
won the Le Mans
24-hour race in
France a record
14 times, from
1970 to 1996.

## Motor racing
### Oldest race still run
The oldest race still regularly run is the RAC Tourist Trophy on the Isle of Man, UK, first staged on 14 Sept 1905.

### Fastest circuits
The highest average lap speed ever attained on any closed circuit is 403.878 km/h (250.958 mph) in a trial by Dr Hans Liebold (Germany). He lapped the 12.64 km (7-mile 1,496-yd) high-speed track at Nardo, Italy, in 1 min 52.67 sec in a Mercedes-Benz C111-IV experimental coupé on 5 May 1979. It was powered by a V8 engine with two KKK turbochargers.

### Fastest race
The world's fastest race is the Busch Clash at Daytona, Florida, USA, on a

The most Grand Prix starts is 256 by Ricardo Patrese (Italy), 1977–93.

The greatest number of pole positions is 65, by Ayrton Senna (Brazil) from 161 races (41 wins), 1985–94.

### Oldest and youngest drivers
The youngest world champion was Emerson Fittipaldi (Brazil) who won his first World Championship on 10 Sept 1972, aged 25 years 273 days.

The oldest world champion was Juan-Manuel Fangio who won his last World Championship on 4 Aug 1957 when he was aged 46 years 41 days.

The youngest Grand Prix winner was Bruce Leslie McLaren of New Zealand, who won the United States Grand Prix

Ferrari also holds the record for the most race wins, at 107 by Aug 1996.

The most successes by one team since the Constructor's Championship started in 1958 is 15 of the 16 Grands Prix by McLaren in 1988. Ayrton Senna had eight wins and three seconds, Alain Prost seven wins and seven seconds, and McLaren amassed over three times the points of their nearest rivals, Ferrari.

Excluding the Indianapolis 500 race, which was then included in the World Drivers' Championship, Ferrari won all seven races in 1952 and the first eight (of nine) in 1953.

### Fastest race
The fastest overall average speed for a Grand Prix race is 242.623 km/h

when Alain Prost won in a McLaren at Silverstone on 21 July 1985.

### Most wins by a driver
The most wins by a driver is five, by Jim Clark, from 1962 to 1965 and in 1967, all in Lotus cars.

Jim Clark and Jack Brabham (Australia) won the race on three different circuits: Brands Hatch, Silverstone and Aintree.

### Most wins by a manufacturer
The most wins by a manufacturer is 10 by Ferrari (1951–54, 1956, 1958, 1961, 1976, 1978 and 1990).

## Le Mans
### Greatest distance
The greatest distance ever covered in the 24-hour Grand Prix d'Endurance

4-km (2½-mile) 31-degree banked track over 80.5 km (50 miles). In 1987 Bill Elliott averaged 318.331 km/h (197.802 mph) in a Ford Thunderbird.

Al Unser Jr set the world record for an 805-km (500-mile) race in Aug 1990 when he won the Michigan 500A at an average speed of 305.2 km/h (189.7 mph).

## Grand Prix
### Most successful drivers
The World Drivers' Championship has been won a record five times by Juan-Manuel Fangio (Argentina) in 1951 and 1954–57. He retired in 1958, having won 24 Grand Prix races (two of which were shared) from 51 starts.

Alain Prost (France) holds the records for both the most Grand Prix points in a career, 798.5, and the most Grand Prix victories, 51 from 199 races, between 1980 to 1993.

The most Grand Prix victories in a year is nine by Nigel Mansell (GB) in 1992 and Michael Schumacher (Germany) in 1995.

at Sebring, Florida, USA, on 12 Dec 1959, aged 22 years 104 days.

Troy Ruttman (USA) was 22 years 80 days when he won the Indianapolis 500 on 30 May 1952.

The oldest Grand Prix winner (in pre-World Championship days) was Tazio Giorgio Nuvolari (Italy), who won the Albi Grand Prix at Albi, France, on 14 July 1946, aged 53 years 240 days.

The oldest Grand Prix driver was Louis Alexandre Chiron (Monaco), who finished sixth in the Monaco Grand Prix on 22 May 1955, aged 55 years 292 days.

The youngest driver to qualify for a Grand Prix was Michael Christopher Thackwell (New Zealand) at the Canadian Grand Prix on 28 Sept 1980, at the age of 19 years 182 days.

### Manufacturers
Ferrari of Italy has won a record eight manufacturers' World Championships (1961, 1964, 1975–77, 1979, 1982 and 1983).

(150.759 mph) by Peter Gethin (GB) in a BRM at Monza in the Italian Grand Prix on 5 Sept 1971.

### Qualifying lap record
The qualifying lap record was set by Keke Rosberg (Finland) at 1 min 5.59 sec, with an average speed of 258.802 km/h (160.817 mph), in a Williams-Honda in the British Grand Prix at Silverstone on 20 July 1985.

### Closest finish
Peter Gethin (GB) beat Ronnie Peterson (Sweden) by 0.01 sec in the Italian Grand Prix at Monza on 5 Sept 1971.

Ayrton Senna (Brazil) beat Nigel Mansell (GB) by 0.014 sec in the Spanish Grand Prix at Jerez de la Frontera, Spain, on 13 April 1986.

### British Grand Prix
#### Fastest speed
The fastest race time is 1 hr 18 min 10.436 sec, with an average speed of 235.405 km/h (146.274 mph),

on the old Sarthe circuit at Le Mans, France, is 5,335.302 km (3,315 miles 216 yd) by Dr Helmut Marko (Austria) and Gijs van Lennep (Netherlands) driving a 4,907-cc flat-12 Porsche 917K Group 5 sports car, on 12–13 June 1971.

The record for the greatest distance ever covered for the current circuit is 5,331.998 km (3,313 miles 264 yd) (average speed 222.166 km/h or 138.047 mph) by Jan Lammers (Holland), Johnny Dumfries and Andy Wallace (both GB) in a Jaguar XJR9, on 11–12 June 1988.

The fastest time over the 13.536-km (8-mile 723-yd) lap is 3 min 21.27 sec, at an average speed of 242.093 km/h (150.429 mph) by Alain Ferté (France) in a Jaguar XJR-9 on 10 June 1989.

Hans Stück (West Germany) set the practice lap speed record of 251.664 km/h (156.377 mph), on 14 June 1985.

# HIGHEST TERMINAL VELOCITY 507 KM/H

**Most wins**
Porsche cars have won the race 14 times, in 1970–71, 1976–77, 1979, 1981–87, 1993 and 1996.

Jacques 'Jacky' Ickx of Belgium won six times (1969, 1975–77, 1981–82).

## Indianapolis 500
**Most successful drivers**
Three drivers have four wins: Anthony Joseph 'A. J.' Foyt Jr (USA) in 1961, 1964, 1967 and 1977; Al Unser Sr (USA) in 1970–71, 1978 and 1987; and Rick Ravon Mears (USA) in 1979, 1984, 1988 and 1991.

The record is 2 hr 41 min 18.404 sec (299.307 km/h or 185.981 mph), by Arie Luyendyk (Netherlands) driving a Lola-Chevrolet on 27 May 1990.

Cowan, Colin Malkin and Michael Broad in a Mercedes 280E.

**Safari rally**
The longest annual rally is the Safari Rally (first run in 1953, through Kenya, Tanzania and Uganda, though it is now restricted to Kenya). The 17th Safari held from 8 to 12 April 1971 covered up to 6,234 km (3,874 miles). The rally has been won a record five times by the Kenyan driver Shekhar Mehta in 1973 and 1979–82.

**Paris–Cape Town rally**
The Paris–Cape Town rally in Jan 1992 was scheduled to be raced over about 12,700 km (7,890 miles) from Paris, France, to Cape Town, South Africa, passing through 11 African countries. However, because of civil war, flooding

Arne Hertz (Sweden) was also the co-driver for Stig Blomqvist (Sweden) when he won the RAC Rally in 1971.

**World Championship**
The World Drivers' Championships has been won by Juha Kankkunen (Finland) on a record four occasions, in 1986, 1987, 1991 and 1993.

**Youngest winner**
The youngest ever winner of the World Drivers' Championship is Colin McRae (GB), who was aged 27 years 89 days when he won the 1995 title.

**Most wins**
The greatest number of wins in World Championship races is 21, by Juha Kankkunen (Finland).

(402 m) is 4.445 seconds, by Larry Dixon (USA) at Englishtown, New Jersey, USA, on 19 May 1995.

The highest terminal velocity at the end of a 440-yd (402-m) run is 507 km/h (315.67 mph). This was achieved by Scott Kalitta (USA), at a track in Topeca, Kansas, USA, on 7 July 1996.

**Piston-engined motorcycles**
The lowest elapsed time recorded for a petrol-driven piston-engined motorcycle is 7.386 seconds achieved by David Schultz (USA), at Gainesville, Florida, USA, in March 1996.

The highest terminal velocity that has ever been recorded for a petrol-driven piston-engined motorcycle is 298 km/h

**S 382.216 KM/H, SET BY ARIE LUYENDYK (NETHERLANDS) ON 12 MAY 1996**

The record average speed for four-laps qualifying is 381.392 km/h (236.986 mph), by Arie Luyendyk in a Reynard–Ford–Cosworth on 12 May 1996. This included a one-lap record of 382.216 km/h (237.498 mph).

The unofficial track record is 385.051 km/h (239.260 mph) set by Arie Luyendyk on 9 May 1996.

A. J. Foyt Jr has started in a record 35 races, from 1958 to 1992.

Rick Mears has started from pole position a record six times, 1979, 1982, 1986, 1988–89 and 1991.

## Rallying
**Longest rally**
The world's longest ever rally was the Singapore Airlines London–Sydney Rally over a distance of 31,107 km (19,329 miles) from Covent Garden, London, UK, on 14 Aug 1977 to Sydney Opera House, Australia. It was won on 28 Sept 1977 by Andrew

and environmental concerns, some stages were cancelled or shortened and the rally covered just over 9,500 km (5,900 miles).

**Monte Carlo**
The Monte Carlo Rally has been won a record four times by Sandro Munari (Italy) in 1972, 1975, 1976 and 1977; and Walter Röhrl (West Germany) with his co-driver Christian Geistdorfer in 1980, 1982, 1983 and 1984—each time in a different car.

The smallest car ever to win the Monte Carlo Rally was an 851-cc Saab that was driven by Gunnar Häggbom and Erik Carlsson (Sweden) on 25 Jan 1962 and by Gunnar Palm and Erik Carlsson on 24 Jan 1963.

**RAC Rally**
Hannu Mikkola (Finland) with co-driver Arne Hertz (Sweden) has won a record four times: in a Ford Escort in 1978 and 1979, and an Audi Quattro, in 1981 and 1982.

**Most wins by manufacturer**
Lancia has won a record eleven manufacturers' World Championship titles between 1972 and 1992.

**Most wins (season)**
The most wins in a season is six, by Didier Auriol (France) in 1992.

## Drag Racing
**Piston-engined cars**
The lowest elapsed time recorded for a petrol-driven piston-engined car is 6.948 seconds by Warren Johnson (USA) at Baytown, Texas, USA, on 10 March 1995.

The highest terminal velocity for a petrol-driven piston-engined car is 320 km/h (199.15 mph) by Warren Johnson (USA) at Baytown, Texas, USA, on 10 March 1995

**Piston-engined dragsters**
The lowest elapsed time recorded by a piston-engined dragster from a standing start for 440 yd

(185.15 mph) by John Myers (USA), at the track in Gainesville, Florida, USA, in March 1996.

## Speedway
**World championship**
Wembley, London, UK, hosted the first World Speedway Championship on 10 Sept 1936. The most wins is six, by Ivan Gerald Mauger (New Zealand) in 1968–70, 1972, 1977 and 1979.

The World Pairs Championship (instituted unofficially in 1968, officially in 1970 and renamed the World Team in 1994) has been won nine times by Denmark, 1979, 1985–89 and 1995.

Hans Hollen Nielsen (Denmark) is the most successful driver in world championship competitions with eight Team (formerly Pairs), nine Team and four individual World titles—a record 21.

The greatest number of wins at long track is five, by Simon Wigg (GB), 1985, 1989–90, 1993–94.

# Aerial sports

## Gliding
### Most titles
The highest number of World Individual Championships ever won is four by Ingo Renner (Australia) in 1976 in the Standard class and in 1983, 1985 and 1987 for the Open.

The British National Championship has been won eight times by Ralph Jones. The first woman to win this title was Anne Burns of Farnham, Surrey, UK, on 30 May 1966.

### Women's altitude records
The world record for women's single-seater absolute altitude is 12,637 m (41,460 ft) by Sabrina Jackintell of the USA in an Astir GS on 14 Feb 1979.

The record for the greatest height gain is 10,212 m (33,504 ft) by Yvonne Loader (New Zealand) at Omarama, New Zealand, on 12 Jan 1988.

The British single-seater absolute altitude record is 10,550 m (34,612 ft) by Anne Burns over South Africa on 13 Jan 1961.

Anne Burns also set a British record for a height gain of 9,119 m (29,918 ft).

## Hang gliding
### World Championships
The Great Britain team has won the Hang Gliding World Team Championships the most often—in 1981, 1985, 1989 and 1991).

### World records (men)
The greatest distance achieved in a straight line and greatest declared goal distance is 495 km (307 miles 622 yd), by Larry Tudor (USA) from Rock Springs, Wyoming, USA, on 1 July 1994.

The world record for the greatest height gain is 4,343 m (14,250 ft), made by Larry Tudor at Owens Valley, California, USA, on 4 Aug 1985.

The greatest out and return distance is 310.3 km (192 miles 1,428 yd), by Larry Tudor and Geoffrey Loyns (GB) at Owens Valley, California, USA, on 26 June 1988.

The greatest triangular course distance covered for hang gliding is 205 km (127 miles 704 yd), by Jo Bathmann (Germany) at Schmittenhöhe, Austria, on 17 June 1996.

### World records (women)
The women's distance record is 335.8 km (208 miles 1,056 yd), by Kari Castle (USA) at Owens Valley, on 22 July 1991.

The greatest height gain is 3,970 m (13,025 ft), by Judy Leden (GB) at Kuruman, South Africa, in Dec 1992.

The greatest declared goal distance is 212.50 km (132 miles 70 yd), by Liavan Mallin (Ireland) at Owens Valley, California, USA, on 13 July 1989.

The greatest triangular course distance covered is 114.1 km (70 miles 1,581 yd), by Judy Leden (GB) at Kössen, Austria, on 22 June 1991.

### British distance record
The handglider Geoffrey Loyns completed a national British record distance of 312.864 km (194 miles 712 yd) in Flagstaff, Arizona, USA, on 11 June 1988.

The distance record within the United Kingdom is 244 km (151 miles 1,091 yd), by Gordon Rigg from Lords Seat to Witham Friary, Somerset, on 4 June 1989.

## Microlighting
### World records
The greatest distance covered in a straight line is 1,627.78 km (1,011 miles 792 yd) by Wilhelm Lischak (Austria) from Volsau, Austria, to Brest, France, on 8 June 1988.

The greatest distance in a closed circuit is 2,702.16 km (1,679 miles 70 yd) by Wilhelm Lischak (Austria) at Wels, Austria, on 18 June 1988.

The highest altitude ever reached is 9,720 m (31,890 ft) by Serge Zin (France) at Saint Auban, France, on 18 Sept 1994.

## Paragliding
### Longest flights
The greatest distance flown in a paraglider is 285 km (177 miles 176 yd), by Kat Thurston (GB) from Kuruman, South Africa, on 25 Dec 1995.

The men's record is 283.9 km (176 miles 700 yd) by Alex François Louw (South Africa) also from Kuruman, South Africa on 31 Dec 1992.

The greatest distance within the UK is 175.4 km (108 miles 1,584 yd), from Long Mynd, Shrops to Pulloxhill, Beds, by Steve Ham on 19 May 1994.

### Greatest height gain
The height gain record is 4,526 m (14,849 ft), by Robby Whittal (GB) at Brandvlei, South Africa, on 6 Jan 1993.

The woman's record is 4,325 m (14,190 ft) by Kat Thurston (GB) at Kuruman, South Africa, on 1 Jan 1996.

## Parachuting
### First attempts
Faustus Verancsis is said to have parachuted with a framed canopy in Hungary in 1617.

In 1687 the King of Ayutthaya in Siam (now Thailand) was reported to have

14:22:00

been entertained by an ingenious athlete who parachuted using two large umbrellas.

Louis-Sébastien Lenormand demonstrated a quasi-parachute—a braced conical canopy—from a tower in Montpellier, France, in 1783.

### Longest duration fall
Lt Col. Wm H. Rankin, USMC, took 40 minutes to fall in North Carolina, USA, on 26 July 1956. The slowness of this time was because of thermals.

### Longest delayed drop
The longest delayed drop by a man was 25,820 m (28,233⅓ yd) from a balloon at 31,330 m (102,800 ft), by Capt. Joseph W. Kittinger, at Tularosa, New Mexico, USA, on 16 Aug 1960.

The longest delayed drop made by a woman was a height of 14,800 m (48,556 ft), by Elvira Fomitcheva (USSR) over Odessa, USSR (now Ukraine), on 26 Oct 1977.

### Highest base jump
Nicholas Feteris and Dr Glenn Singleman jumped from a ledge (the 'Great Trango Tower') at 5,880 m (19,300 ft) in the Karakoram, Pakistan, on 26 Aug 1992.

### Mid-air rescue
The first mid-air rescue occurred when Dolly Shepherd brought down Louie May on her single parachute from a balloon at 3,350 m (11,000 ft) over Longton, Staffs, UK, on 9 June 1908.

The lowest rescue occurred when Eddie Turner saved Frank Farnan, who had been injured in a collision after jumping out at 3,950 m (13,000 ft). Turner pulled Farnan's ripcord at 550 m (1,800 ft), less than 10 seconds from impact, over Clewiston, Florida, USA, on 16 Oct 1988.

### Highest escape
Flight Lieutenant J. de Salis (RAF) and Flying Officer P. Lowe (RAF) made the highest ever escape at 17,100 m (56,000 ft), over Monyash, Derby, UK, on 9 April 1958.

### Lowest escape
S/Ldr Terence Spencer (RAF) achieved the lowest ever escape, at a height of 9–12 m (30–40 ft) over Wismar Bay in the Baltic Sea, on 19 April 1945.

### Highest landing
Ten USSR parachutists (four of whom were killed) landed at a record altitude of 7,133 m (23,405 ft) at Lenina Peak, USSR (now the Tajikistan/Kyrgyzstan border), in May 1969.

### Cross-channel (lateral fall)
Sgt. Bob Walters, accompanied by three soldiers and two Royal Marines, parachuted 35.4 km (22 miles) from a height of 7,600 m (25,000 ft), from Dover, Kent, UK, to Sangatte, France, on 31 Aug 1980.

# HANG GLIDING HEIGHT GAIN 4,343 M

**Most parachuting descents**
The most descents made is 22,000, by Don Kellner (USA), at various locations in the USA to May 1996.

The most descents made by a woman is 10,900, by Cheryl Stearns (USA), mainly over the USA up to May 1996.

**Most descents in 24 hours**
Cheryl Stearns (USA) made 352 descents (in accordance with United States Parachute Association rules), over Raeford, North Carolina, USA, from 8–9 Nov 1995.

**Largest canopy stack**
The world record for the most people to form a canopy stack is 46, by an international team at Davis, California, USA. It was held for 37.54 seconds on 12 Oct 1994.

On 23 March 1944, during a WWII bombing raid, Flt-Sgt. Nicholas Stephen Alkemade bailed out of his blazing RAF Lancaster bomber without a parachute at 5,500 m (18,000 ft) over Oberkürchen, Germany, and survived the fall.

**Aerobatics**
**World Championships**
The men's Aerobatics team competition has been won a record six times by the USSR.

Petr Jirmus (Czechoslovakia) is the only man who has become the aerobatics world champion twice, in 1984 and 1986.

Betty Stewart of the USA has won the women's aerobatics competition twice, in 1980 and 1982.

**GLIDING SINGLE-SEATER RECORDS**
**Straight Distance, World**
1,460.8 km (907 miles 1,232 yd)
Hans-Werner Grosse (West Germany)
Lübeck, Germany, to Biarritz, France, 25 April 1972
**Straight Distance, British**
949.70 km (590 miles 176 yd)
Karla Karel
Australia, 20 Jan 1980
**Declared Goal Distance, World**
1,254.26 km (779 miles 634 yd)
Bruce Lindsey Drake, David Napier Speight, Sholto Hamilton Georgeson (New Zealand)
Te Anau to Te Araroa, New Zealand, 14 Jan 1978
**Declared Goal Distance, British**
859.2 km (534 miles)
M. T. Alan Sands
Ridge soaring to Chilhowee, Virginia, USA, 23 April 1986

**SPEED OVER TRIANGULAR COURSE**
**100 km, World**
195.3 km/h (121.35 mph)
Ingo Renner (Australia), Tocumwal, Australia, 14 Dec 1982
**100 km, British**
166.38 km/h (103.38 mph)
Bruce Cooper,
Australia, 4 Jan 1991
**300 km, World**
169.50 km/h (105.32 mph)
Jean-Paul Castel (France), Bitterwasser, Namibia, 15 Nov 1986
**300 km, British**
146.8 km/h (91.2 mph)
Edward Pearson, SW Africa (now Namibia), 30 Nov 1976
**500 km, World**
170.06 km/h (105.67 mph)
Beat Bünzli (Switzerland), Bitterwasser, Namibia, 9 Jan 1988

14:23:15

14:24:06

## IN A MICROLIGHT IS 1,627.78 KM FROM VOLSAU, AUSTRIA TO BREST, FRANCE

**Largest free fall formation**
The biggest ever free-fall formation (not recognised by the FAI) consisted of 297 people, from 26 countries, from 6,500 m (21,300 ft), over Anapa, Russia, on 27 Sept 1996.

The record for the most people to make up an official (recognized by the FAI) free-fall formation is 200. Parachutists from 10 nations held the formation for 6.47 seconds, from 5,030 m (16,500 ft), over Myrtle Beach, South Carolina, USA, on 23 Oct 1992.

100 women, from 20 countries, made a free-fall formation for 5.97 seconds, from a height of 5,200 m (17,000 ft) at the Aéreodrome du Cannet des Maures, France, on 14 Aug 1992.

**Survival from longest fall**
Vesna Vulovic, an air hostess, survived a fall without a parachute from 10,160 m (33,330 ft), when her DC-9 blew up over Srbská Kamenice, Czechoslovakia (now Czech Republic), on 26 Jan 1972.

Lyubov Nemkova (USSR) won a record five medals, coming first in 1986, second in 1982 and 1984 and third in 1976 and 1978.

The oldest ever world champion was Henry Haigh (USA), aged 63 in 1988.

**Inverted flight**
The longest ever inverted flight was 4 hr 38 min 10 sec by Joann Osterud, from Vancouver to Vanderhoof, Canada, on 24 July 1991.

**Loops**
Joann Osterud performed 208 outside loops over North Bend, Oregon, USA, on 13 July 1989.

On 9 Aug 1986, David Childs completed 2,368 inside loops over North Pole, Alaska.

Brian Lecomber completed 180 consecutive inside loops in a Jaguar Extra 230 on 29 July 1988 over Plymouth, Devon, UK.

**Goal and Return, World**
1,646.68 km (1,023 miles 352 yd)
Thomas L. Knauff (USA)
Gliderport to Williamsport, Pennsylvania, USA, 25 April 1983
**Goal and Return, British**
1,127.68 km (700 miles 1,267 yd)
M. T. Alan Sands
Lock Haven, Pennsylvania, to Bluefield, Virginia, USA, May 1985
**Absolute Altitude, World**
14,938 m (49,009 ft)
Robert R. Harris (USA)
California, USA, 17 Feb 1986
**Absolute Altitude, British**
11,500 m (37,729 ft)
H. C. Nicholas Goodhart
California, USA, 12 May 1955
**Height Gain, World**
12,894 m (42,303 ft)
Paul F. Bikle (USA)
Mojave, Lancaster, California, USA, 25 Feb 1961
**Height Gain, British**
10,065 m (33,022 ft)
David Benton
Portmoak, Scotland, UK, 18 April 1980

**500 km, British**
141.3 km/h (87.8 mph)
Bradley James Grant Pearson, South Africa, 28 Dec 1982
**750 km, World**
158.41 km/h (98.43 mph)
Hans-Werner Grosse (W Germany), Alice Springs, Australia, 8 Jan 1985
**750 km, British**
109.8 km/h (68.2mph)
Michael R. Carlton, South Africa, 5 Jan 1975
**1,000 km, World**
169.72 km/h (105.46 mph)
Helmut Fischer (Germany), Hendrik Verwoerd Dam, South Africa, 5 Jan 1995
**1,000 km, British**
112.15 km/h (69.68 mph)
George Lee, Australia, 25 Jan 1989
**1,250 km, World**
133.24 km/h (82.79 mph)
Hans-Werner Grosse (W Germany) Alice Springs, Australia, 9 Dec 1980
**1,250 km, British**
109.01 km/h (67.73 mph)
Robert L. Robertson, USA, 2 May 1986

# Index

# Index

# Acknowledgements

## Acknowledgements

### Founder Editor
Norris McWhirter

### Consultants and contributors
Andrew Adams, John Arblaster, Brian
Bailey, Richard Balkwill, Howard Bass,
Dennis Bird, Richard Braddish, Robert
Brooke, Tony Brown, Prof. Tom Cannon,
Rhonda Carrier, Andy Chipling, Gerry
Cottle, David Crawford, George Else,
Clive Everton, Shelley Flacks, Paulette
Foyle, Tim Furniss, Max Glaskin,
Dr Martin Godfrey, Steven Goldberg, Stan
Greenberg, Liz Hawley, Ron Hildebrant,
Ron Hill, Duncan Hislop, Elizabeth Hussey,
Sir Peter Johnson, Robert Jones, Ove
Karlsson, Jago Lee, Nigel Merrett, Andy
Milroy, Ray Mitchell, John Pimlott, David
Pritchard, John Randall, Chris Rhys, Peter
Rowan, David Rowe, Joshua Rozenberg,
Irvin Saxton, Sandip Shah, Tony Shuker,
Karl Shuker, David Singmaster, Karen
Smith, Martin Stone, Russ Swan, Steve
Trew, Juhani Virola, Phil Walker, John
Watson, Lt. Col. Digby Willoughby, Tony
Wood, Neil Wormald, Hugh Wrampling

### Guinness Publishing Ltd would like to thank the following:
Art Sales Index, BBC, British Tourist
Authority, Christie's, Foreign and
Commonwealth Office, Fortean Times,
Natural History Museum, Nintendo,
Recording Industry Association of
America, Reuters News Service,
Sega, Sony, Sothebys, South Australia
Tourist Commission

### Picture acknowledgements
t=top; c=centre; b=bottom; l=left;
r=right

7t Hulton Deutsch Collection/Corbis
7c Hulton Deutsch Collection/Corbis
7b Guinness PLC
10 Santosh Basak/Gamma/Frank
Spooner Pictures
12 Bettmann/UPI/Corbis
14 Mehau Kulyk/Science Photo Library
15 Rex Features
16 Greg Williams/Rex Features
17b Science Pictures Ltd/Corbis
18/19 Bettmann/UPI/Corbis
22t Rory Blackwell
23t Harold Taylor/Oxford Scientific Films
23b Hulton Getty
24t Richard Hamilton Smith/Corbis
24b Todd Gipstein/Corbis
25 Dale Lyons
26t Richard Hamilton Smith/Corbis
26b Penny Tweedie/Corbis
27 Tecza Sports Club
28t Robert Clifford
28b David J.V. Meenan
29 Rémy Bricka
30l Robert Clifford
30r Robert Clifford
31l Robert Clifford
31r Robert Clifford
32 Amresh Kumar Jha
33t Rupert Parent
33bl Amresh Kumar Jha
33b Rupert Parent
34t Macy's East, Inc. 1996
34/35 Robert Clifford
36t Rob Stratton
36b Ian Sumner/Wessex Water
37 Brian Shuel/Collections
38t/39t Jeff Werner/Incredible Features/
Rex Features
38b Bengt Dorbin/Goteborgs-Tidningen
39b National Pictures
40 Lowell Georgia/Corbis
41 Kobal Collection
42 Arun District Council
42/43 Ali Hassani/Circus Hassani
43 Corbis
44 Zooid Pictures
45t Rex Features
45c John Connor Press Associates
45b Sipa-Press/Rex Features
46 Today/Rex Features
47 Robert Schumann
48 Robert Clifford
49t Martin's Studio

49b Paul Robertson
50 Hulton Deutsch Collection/Corbis
51t The Times/Rex Features
51b Carmontelle
The National Gallery, London/Corbis
54 David Cannon/Allsport
55 Galen Rowell/Corbis
56 Mr. J. McNabb
57 Takamatsu Winter Festival
58 Terry Thessman
59t Joseph Sohm/ChromoSohm Inc/
Corbis
59b Tony Larkin/Rex Features
60t Aerospatiale
60b Lert/Sipa Press/Rex Features
61 Jørgen Jahre Shipping AS
62t Alvey & Towers/Art Forma (Furniture) Ltd
62b W. Janssens
63 Peter Marlow/Magnum Photos
64t Commercial Communications
64b Robert Estall/Corbis
65 Ti-Bao International Co. Ltd
68 Antoine Secco
69t Sun Newspapers
69b Colin Grey
70 Dimitri S. Pistiolas
71 Anne Atkins
72t Institut für Mikrotechnik
72b David Edwards
72/73 David Edwards
73 Oulder Hill Community School
74/75 Robert Clifford
75l Rex Rystedi/Wizards of the Coast
75r Wizards of the Coast
76 1997 Nintendo Co. Ltd
77t Sega Enterprises, Ltd
80 Geoff Somers/Chris Bonnington
Photo Library
81 Popperfoto
82/83 NASA
84 Beken of Cowes
86 Grant family
87t Joseph Sohm/ChromoSohm Inc/
Corbis
88 Agence France Presse/
Bettmann/Corbis
88/89 Bill Stover/Reuters/Popperfoto
89 Yun Suk Bong/Reuter/Popperfoto
90 Sipa Press/Rex Features
91t Popperfoto
91b Denis Cameron/Rex Features
92 Science & Society Picture
93l Francois Robineau/Sipa Press/
Rex Features
93r NASA/Science Photo Library
94 Popperfoto
95 Dave Barr
98 Rex Features
99t Merillon/Gamma/Frank
Spooner Pictures
99b Rex Features
100l Dan Lamont/Corbis
100c David Wells/Corbis
101l Morton Beebe-S.F./Corbis
101c Shelley Gazin/Corbis
101r Adam Woolfitt/Corbis
102 Hulton Getty
103t Sipa Press/Rex Features
103b The National Archives/Corbis
104 Jim Preston/Rex Features
105 Hulton Deutsch Collection/Corbis
106 Adrian Brooks/Rex Features
107 Juan Venegez/Sipa Press/Rex Features
108 Bettmann/UPI/Corbis
109 Mauro Carraro/Rex Features
112 Tim Rooke/Rex Features
113t Rex Features
113b Corbis
114t William Blake/Corbis
114b Corbis
115 Des Jenson/Times/Rex Features
116 Joseph Sohm/Corbis
117t Kevin Schafer/Corbis
117b Library of Congress/Corbis
118 Bettmann/Corbis
119 Kit Kittle/Corbis
120t Brian Fairbanks/The Reporter
120b Robert Clifford
121 Hulton Deutsch Collection/Corbis
122tl Bob Martin/Allsport
122r Allsport
123 Stephen Munday/Allsport
124 The Times/Rex Features
125 Christie's Images
126 Tim Graham
127t Jan Olofsson/Redferns

127b William Gottlieb/Library/Redferns
128 Rex Features
129t De Beers
129b Robert Holmes/Corbis
132 Ray Green/Popperfoto
133t Otto Greule/Allsport
133b Al Bello/Allsport
134t Mega Productions Inc/Rex Features
134b UPI/Bettmann/Corbis
135 Rex Features
136 Readers Digest Association
137 Richard Bickel/Corbis
138 The Purcell Team/Corbis
139 Christine Osborne/Corbis
140 Rex Features
141t Erik Pendzich/Rex Features
141b David Levy
142t P. Souders/Liaison/Gamma/Frank
Spooner Pictures
142b BT Laboratories
143 Psaila/Fig Mag/Gamma/Frank
Spooner Pictures
146t Everett/Corbis
147t Bettmann/UPI/Corbis
147b Warren Cowan & Associates
147b Bettman/UPI/Corbis
148/149 Everett/Corbis
150 Rex Features
151t K. Howard/Frank Spooner Pictures
151 Everett/Corbis
152 Patrick Ward/Corbis
153t J. Minihan/Hulton Getty
153b UPI/Bettmann/Corbis
154t Paul Macapia/Corbis
155 Anthony Medley/SIN
156 Rex Features
157l Massey/Frank Spooner Pictures
157r Kim Tonelli/SIN
158 Bettman/Corbis
159 Wallace & Gromit/Aardman
Animations Ltd 1989
160 Sotheby's Picture Library/
© Succession Picasso/DACS 1997
161 Sotheby's Picture Library/© Estate
of William de Kooning/ARS, NY & DACS,
London 1997
162 Dee Conway
163t Lautterwasser/Sipa Press/
Rex Features
163b Keith Saunders/London String
Quartet Foundation
166 Andree Kaiser/Sipa Press/
Rex Features
167t Adenis/Sipa Press/Rex Features
167b Gilles Saussier/Gamma/Frank
Spooner Pictures
168 Museum of Flight/Corbis
169t R.G. Williamson/Rex Features
169b Morton Beebe S. F. /Corbis
170t Rex Features
170b David Muench/Corbis
171 Nik Wheeler/Corbis
172 Gail Mooney/Corbis
173l Ecoscene/Corbis
174t Macduff Everton/Corbis
174b F. Guenet/Gamma/Frank
Spooner Pictures
175 Angelo Hornak/Corbis
176 Seagaia Group
177t M. Vimenet/Futuroscope
177b M. Vimenet/Futuroscope
178 Eric Weller
179 Rex Features
180t Kevin Fleming/Corbis
180b Jeremy Horner/Corbis
181 Hulton Deutsch Collection/Corbis
182 Paolo Ragazzinil/Corbis
183 David Levenson/Colorific!
184t Jose Nicholas/Sipa Press/
Rex Features
184b Andrew Wong/Popperfoto
185 Rex Features
186 Karen Wilks
187t Henrik T. Kaiser/Rex Features
187b Robert Dowling/Corbis
190t John Morris/Fortean Picture Library
190b Peregrine Mendoza/Fortean
Picture Library
191 Rene Dahinden/Fortean
Picture Library
192 Geophysical Laboratory/Carnegie
Institution Washington
193l J.M. Keslinger & Associates/General
Magnaplate Corporation
193r Lou Odor/General Magnaplate
Corporation

194t Rex Features
194b Shell Oil Company
195 Kevin Schafer/Corbis
197t Directoraat General Rijkswajerstaat
197b Robert Holmes/Corbis
198l Lori Stiles
198r Vortek
199 James Stoots/Lawrence Livermore
National Laboratory, University
of California
200 Robin Adshead/The Military Picture
Library/Corbis
201 Rex Features
202t Michael McKinnon/Planet Earth
Pictures
202b ASL/Sipa Press/Rex Features
203 Edward Igor/Sipa Press/Rex Features
204 Roger Ressmeyer/Corbis
205 A. Dressler & M Dickinson/NASA
206t Lehtikuva Oy/Rex Features
206b Jonas Lemberg/Reuter/Popperfoto
207t Frank Spooner Pictures
207b Asahi Shinbun/Sipa Press/
Rex Features
210 NASA /GSFC/Science Photo Library
211 Frank Zullo/Science Photo Library
212 Grant Fleming/Rex Features
213t NASA/Corbis
213b Jonathan Blair/Corbis
214 Tom Bean/Corbis
215l Robert Dowling/Corbis
215r Tim Fogg
216t Michael Friedel/Rex Features
216b NASA/Rex Features
217 USGS/Corbis
218 Salaber/Liaison/Frank
Spooner Pictures
219 NASA
220 Warren Faidley/Oxford
Scientific Films
221t Harald Sund/Image Bank
221b Warren Faidley/Oxford
Scientific Films
222 Richard Packwood/Oxford
Scientific Films
223t Richard Packwood/Oxford
Scientific Films
223b Galen Rowell/Corbis
224/225t Sipa Press/Rex Features
225b Reuters/Corbis-Bettmann/Corbis
228 Lowell Georgia/Corbis
229t USDA—Forest Services/Corbis
229b Craig Lowell/Corbis
230 Nils Jorgensen/Rex Features
231t Densey Clyne/Mantis Wild/Oxford
Scientific Films
231r Ronald Toms/Oxford Scientific Films
232 Hulton Getty
233 H Hurley
234 Richard Herrmann/Oxford
Scientific Films
235t Perry Conway/Corbis
235b Perry Conway/Corbis
236 Perry Conway/Corbis
237t Dave G. Houser/Corbis
237b Planet Earth Pictures
238 Mike Slater/Oxford Scientific Films
239 Joseph Schallberger
240 Fidelco Guide Dog Foundation
241 Linda Goldyn/Monophoto
242t Reuter/Popperfoto
242b Helen Smylye
243 Peter Brooker/Rex Features
244/245 Wolfgang Kaehler/Corbis
246 Natalie Fobes/Corbis
247 Zig Lescyznski/Oxford
Scientific Films
248/149 Heather Angel/Biofotos
250 Catherine Pouedras/Science
Photo Library
251 Natural History Museum
252 Doug Perrine/Planet Earth Pictures
253 Brian Kenney/Planet Earth Pictures
254 Oxford Scientific Films
255 Eric Hosking/Corbis
256 The Natural History Museum, London
257 Hulton Deutsch Collection/Corbis
258 Natural History Museum
258/259 Natural History Museum
259 Andrew Syred/Science Photo Library
260t Buddy May/Corbis
260b Jeffrey Rotman/Corbis
261 Wolfgang Kaehler/Corbis
262t Ron Austing/Oxford Scientific Films
262b Nick Barbutt/Planet Earth Pictures
263 George Lepp/Corbis

264t Matthew Lee/Agence
France Press
264b Nature Focus
265t David Hulse/WWF Photolibrary
265b Paul Sterry/Nature
Photographers Ltd
268/269l Allsport
269r NBC/Tony Duffy/Allsport
270 Allsport
271l Tony Duffy/Allsport
271r Dave Cannon/Allsport
272l Gray Mortimore/Allsport
272/273 Allsport
274l Phil Cole/Allsport
274r Gary Mortimore/Allsport
275 Allsport
276 Matthew Stockman/Allsport
277 Simon Bruty/Allsport
278/279 Gary Newkirk/Allsport
280l Vladimir Sichob/Sipa Sport/
Rex Features
280r Allsport
281 Allsport
282l Mike Egerton/Empics
283l M.Prior/Allsport
283c/r Hubert Fotografias
284 Mathew Stockman/Allsport
285 Joseph Sohm/ChromoSohm Inc/
Corbis
286 Mike Cooper/Allsport
287 Dave Joiner/Popperfoto
288 Allsport
289 Russell Cheyne/Allsport
290 Chris Cole/Allsport
291l Mike Hewitt/Allsport
291r Power/Crowley/Allsport
292l Jow Mann/Allsport
292r Shaun Botterill/Allsport
293 Clive Mason/Allsport
294l Ben Radford/Allsport
294r Adrian Murell/Allsport
295 Hulton Deutsch Collection/Allsport
296l Allsport
296r Hulton Deutsch Collection/Allsport
297l Oliver Brunskill/Allsport
297r Gary M. Prior/Allsport
298 Peter Richardson
299 Hulton Getty
301 Craig Jones/Allsport
302l Chris Cole/Allsport
302r Simon Bruty/Allsport
303 Shaun Botterill/Allsport
304l Mike Hewitt/Allsport
304/305 Adam Woolfitt/Corbis
305 Adam Woolfitt/Corbis
306 Richard Hamilton Smith/Corbis
307l Chris Cole/Allsport
307r Franck Faugere/Rex Features
308 Hulton Getty
309l Al Bello/Allsport
309r Richard Martin/Vandystadt/Allsport
310 Simon Bruty/Allsport
311l Al Bello/Allsport
311 Simon Bruty/Allsport
312 McDonough/Allsport
312/313 Beken of Cowes
314 Graham Chadwick/Allsport
314/315 Jim Mack/United States
Canoe Association
316 Simon Bruty/Allsport
317 Gary M. Prior/Allsport
318 Bettmann/UPI/Corbis
319l Mike Powell/Allsport
319r Rex Features
320 John Gichigi/Allsport
321l Ben Margot/Sipa Press/
Rex Features
321r Karina Hoskyns
322 Hicks Photographic Service
324l Keith Winter
324/325 Ben Radford/Allsport
326l Allsport
326r D. Wayne Pensinger/Allsport
328 Royal Equestrian Show, Oman
329l Kit Houghton/Corbis
329r Express Newspapers
330l Anton Want/Allsport
330r Agence Daimas/Sipa Press/
Rex Features
331l Pascal Rondeau/Allsport
331r Howard Boylan/Allsport
332l Gamma/Frank Spooner Pictures
332r Mike Cooper/Allsport
333l Pascal Rondeau/Allsport
333r Darrell Ingham/Allsport
334/335 Jonathan Blair/Corbis

# Getting into the book

Maybe you have a particular skill or interest, or are the possessor of an extraordinary collection that you think would be a world-beater. By looking through the pages of this book you may find that someone is already the champion in the category you are considering and you now have a target to aim at. If the challenge you want to attempt isn't listed, contact us to see if we can accept your idea as a new category. If you are unsure what you want to do to become a record-holder, dip into *The Guinness Book of Records* and prepare to be amazed by what other people have achieved, but remember that behind even the most wacky idea there is a purpose, often a charitable one.

Every week we receive many suggestions for new record categories, but only a minority are accepted into the record book. What we are looking for in a new category is a challenge that is interesting, requires skill, is safe, and is likely to attract subsequent challenges from other people. However, the acceptance of a new category or a new record does not mean that we undertake to print it in *The Guinness Book of Records*. With many thousands of records on our database the book is a summary of the subjects and categories that we believe are of the most interest to our readers.

Whatever record you decide to attempt it is important to contact us as early as possible. For most Human Achievement categories we have specific guidelines to ensure that you are attempting a record under exactly the same conditions as previous contestants. Only in this way can we compare achievements. If your idea is accepted as a new category we may have to draw up new guidelines with the assistance of experts. So, please allow us and yourselves plenty of time for preparation.

Each and every record claim must be accompanied by detailed documentation. Two independent witness statements are the minimum requirement. Your witnesses should be persons of some standing in the local community, for example a doctor, police officer, councillor or an official of some professional or sporting body. They should not be relatives. The witnesses should not only be able to confirm that they have seen the successful progress and completion of the record attempt, but also that the guidelines have been adhered to. *The Guinness Book of Records* is unable to supply personnel to invigilate attempts but reserves the right to do so.

Many record attempts also require a log book or similar documentation. The requirements are specified in the guidelines. Photographic evidence is usually required—a video of the attempt is even better proof. Newspaper cuttings, usually local, are additional evidence. It is a good idea to get your local newspaper interested in the record attempt and persuade a reporter to be present. Finally, check with us shortly before your attempt to make sure that the record has not recently been broken.

All record attempts are undertaken at the sole risk of the claimant. The publishers cannot be held responsible for any (potential) liability howsoever arising out of any such an attempt, whether to the claimant or any third party.

**If you wish to contact *The Guinness Book of Records* ring 0891 517 607\* or ++44 891 517 607 if calling from overseas. Alternatively, you can e-mail us at webmaster@guinnessworlds.com, fax us on 0171 891 4504 (++44 171 891 4504 if dialling from overseas), or write to us at Guinness Publishing Ltd, 338 Euston Rd, London, NW1 3BD, UK.**

\*Calls cost no more than 50p per minute.

LARGEST WAIST 3.02 M    MOST BABIES IN SIN

DAYS    SHEEP TO SUIT 1 HR 34 MIN 33.42

PEDAL BOATING RECORD 7,500 KM   BOOMERANG

FOOT 71 HR 40 MIN    LONGEST 'WHEELIE' 331

PLATES SPUN SIMULTANEOUSLY   OLDEST BRI

LONGEST LOAF 9,200 M   LONGEST FREIGHT TRA

TALLEST TOWER 553.34 M   MODEL RAILWAY E

69 DAYS 19 MIN UNDERWATER   357 PEOPLE IN

0-60 MPH IN 3.07 SEC   AROUND THE WORLD I

30 SEC   2,700 SUICIDES PER DAY   OLDEST PR

ODDS 3,072,887 TO 1    MOST EXPENSIVE SH

LONGEST APPLAUSE 1HR 20 MIN   SHORTEST P

MIN   TALLEST OFFICE BLOCK 451.9 M   OLDEST

1,788 ROOMS, 257 LAVATORIES   CINEMA SCR

ROOMS   LONGEST HERBACEOUS BORDER 152

STEEPEST STREET 1 IN 1.266   1 G GOLD D

LARGEST TELESCOPE MIRROR 10 M   HOTTEST

8,000 M   HEAVIEST HAILSTONE 1 KG   FASTES

112.47 M   LONGEST BEAN 121.9 CM   FASTE

MAMMAL 0.1-0.16 KM/H   371 EGGS IN 364 DAY

KM/H   LONGEST FROG JUMP 10.3 M   LARGEST

OLDEST SPIDER 28 YEARS   FASTEST WINGBEAT

SNAKEBITE FATALATIES PER YEAR   1,500 METR

HOURS   LONGEST BASEBALL THROW 135.88 M

CONSECUTIVE VOLLEYS   LONGEST DRIVE 471 M

FIGHT 7 HR 19 MIN   FASTEST GREYHOUND 67.3